ACHI 2023

The Sixteenth International Conference on Advances in Computer-Human Interactions

April 24th – 28th, 2023

Venice, Italy

ACHI 2023 Editors

Susanne Stigberg, Østfold University College, Halden, Norway

Joakim Karlsen, Østfold University College, Halden, Norway

Prima Oky Dicky Ardiansyah, Faculty of Software and Information Science, Iwate Prefecture University, Japan

Printed from e-media with permission by:

Curran Associates, Inc.
57 Morehouse Lane
Red Hook, NY 12571

proceedings.com

Some format issues inherent in the e-media version may also appear in this print version.

Printed with permission by Curran Associates, Inc. (2024)

International Academy, Research, and Industry Association (IARIA)
412 Derby Way
Wilmington, DE 19810

Phone: (408) 893-6407
Fax: (408) 527-6351

petre@iaria.org

Additional copies of this publication are available from:

Curran Associates, Inc.
57 Morehouse Lane
Red Hook, NY 12571 USA
Phone: 845-758-0400
Fax: 845-758-2633
Email: curran@proceedings.com
Web: www.proceedings.com

Table of Contents

ACHI 2023

Forward

The Sixteenth edition of The International Conference on Advances in Computer-Human Interactions (ACHI 2023) conference was held in Venice, Italy, April 24 - 28, 2023.

The conference on Advances in Computer-Human Interaction, ACHI 2023, was a result of a paradigm shift in the most recent achievements and future trends in human interactions with increasingly complex systems. Adaptive and knowledge-based user interfaces, universal accessibility, human-robot interaction, agent-driven human computer interaction, and sharable mobile devices are a few of these trends. ACHI 2023 brought also a suite of specific domain applications, such as gaming, social, medicine, education and engineering.

The event was very competitive in its selection process and very well perceived by the international scientific and industrial communities. As such, it is attracting excellent contributions and active participation from all over the world. We were very pleased to receive a large amount of top quality contributions.

The accepted papers covered a wide range of human-computer interaction related topics such as graphical user interfaces, input methods, training, recognition, and applications.
We believe that the ACHI 2023 contributions offered a large panel of solutions to key problems in all areas of human-computer interaction.

We take here the opportunity to warmly thank all the members of the ACHI 2023 technical program committee as well as the numerous reviewers. The creation of such a broad and high quality conference program would not have been possible without their involvement. We also kindly thank all the authors that dedicated much of their time and efforts to contribute to the ACHI 2023. We truly believe that thanks to all these efforts, the final conference program consists of top quality contributions.

This event could also not have been a reality without the support of many individuals, organizations and sponsors. In addition, we also gratefully thank the members of the ACHI 2023 organizing committee for their help in handling the logistics and for their work that is making this professional meeting a success.

We hope the ACHI 2023 was a successful international forum for the exchange of ideas and results between academia and industry and to promote further progress in the human-computer interaction field. We also hope that Venice provided a pleasant environment during the conference and everyone saved some time for exploring this beautiful city

ACHI 2023 Chairs

ACHI Steering Committee
Flaminia Luccio, University Ca' Foscari of Venice, Italy
Marie Sjölinder, RISE, Sweden
Lasse Berntzen, University of South-Eastern Norway, Norway
Weizhi Meng, Technical University of Denmark, Denmark

ACHI 2023 Publicity Chair

Laura Garcia, Universitat Politècnica de València (UPV), Spain
Javier Rocher Morant, Universitat Politecnica de Valencia, Spain

ACHI 2023

COMMITTEE

ACHI Steering Committee

Flaminia Luccio, University Ca' Foscari of Venice, Italy
Marie Sjölinder, RISE, Sweden
Lasse Berntzen, University of South-Eastern Norway, Norway
Weizhi Meng, Technical University of Denmark, Denmark

ACHI 2023 Publicity Chairs

Javier Rocher Morant, Universitat Politecnica de Valencia, Spain
Laura Garcia, Universitat Politecnica de Valencia, Spain

ACHI 2023 Technical Program Committee

Mark Abdollahian, Claremont Graduate University, USA
Mostafa Alani, Tuskegee University, USA
Marran Aldossari, University of North Carolina at Charlotte, USA
Obead Alhadreti, Umm Al-Qura University, Al-Qunfudah, Saudi Arabia
Asam Almohamed, University of Kerbala, Iraq
Mehdi Ammi, Univ. Paris 8, France
Prima Oky Dicky Ardiansyah, Iwate Prefectural University, Japan
Charles Averill, University of Texas at Dallas, USA
Snježana Babić, Polytechnic of Rijeka, Croatia
Matthias Baldauf, OST - Eastern Switzerland University of Applied Sciences, Switzerland
Catalin-Mihai Barbu, University of Duisburg-Essen, Germany
Yacine Bellik, IUT d'Orsay | Université Paris-Saclay, France
Lasse Berntzen, University of South-Eastern Norway, Norway
Ganesh D. Bhutkar, Vishwakarma Institute of Technology (VIT), Pune, India
Cezary Biele, National Information Processing Institute, Poland
Christos J. Bouras, University of Patras, Greece
Christian Bourret, UPEM - Université Paris-Est Marne-la-Vallée, France
James Braman, The Community College of Baltimore County, USA
Justin Brooks, University of Maryland Baltimore County / D-Prime LLC, USA
Pradeep Buddharaju, University of Houston - Clear Lake, USA
Idoko John Bush, Near East University, Cyprus
Minghao Cai, University of Alberta, Canada
Lindsey D. Cameron, Wharton School | University of Pennsylvania, USA
Klaudia Carcani, Østfold University College, Norway
Alicia Carrion-Plaza, Sheffield Hallam University, UK
Stefano Caselli, Institute of Digital Games | University of Malta, Malta
Meghan Chandarana, NASA Ames Research Center, USA
Chen Chen, University of California San Diego, USA
Mathieu Chollet, University of Glasgow, UK
Bhavya Chopra, Indraprastha Institute of Information Technology, Delhi, India

Lara Jessica da Silva Pontes, University of Debrecen, Hungary
Andre Constantino da Silva, Federal Institute of São Paulo - IFSP, Brazil
Verena Distler, University of Luxembourg, Luxembourg
Vesna G. Djokic, Institute of Language Logic & Computation (ILLC) | University of Amsterdam, Netherlands
Krzysztof Dobosz, Silesian University of Technology - Institute of Informatics, Poland
Margaret Drouhard, University of Washington, USA
Robert Ek, Luleå University of Technology, Sweden
Ahmed Elkaseer, Karlsruhe Institute of Technology, Germany
Pardis Emami-Naeini, Carnegie Mellon University, USA
Marina Everri, University College Dublin, Ireland
Ben Falchuk, Peraton Labs, USA
Matthias Fassl, CISPA Helmholtz Center for Information Security, Germany
Stefano Federici, University of Perugia, Italy
Kenneth Feinstein, Sunway University, Malaysia
Emma Frid, IRCAM / KTH Royal Institute of Technology, Sweden
Peter Fröhlich, AIT - Austrian Institute of Technology, Austria
Jicheng Fu, University of Central Oklahoma, USA
Somchart Fugkeaw, Mahidol University - Nakhonpathom, Thailand
Pablo Gallego, Independent Researcher, Spain
Nermen Ghoniem, Jabra / Hello Ada, Denmark
Dagmawi Lemma Gobena, Addis Ababa University, Ethiopia
Benedikt Gollan, Research Studios Austria FG mbH, Austria
Denis Gracanin, Virginia Tech, USA
Andrina Granic, University of Split, Croatia
Lea Gröber, CISPA Helmholtz Center for Information Security, Saarbrücken, Germany
Celmar Guimarães da Silva, University of Campinas, Brazil
Ibrahim A. Hameed, Norwegian University of Science and Technology (NTNU), Norway
Ragnhild Halvorsrud, SINTEF Digital, Norway
Richard Harper, Lancaster University, UK
Liang He, Paul G. Allen School of Computer Science & Engineering | University of Washington, USA
Lars Erik Holmquist, Northumbria University | School of Design, UK
Gerhard Hube, University of Applied Sciences in Würzburg, Germany
Haikun Huang, University of Massachusetts, Boston, USA
Yue Huang, University of British Columbia, Canada
Maria Hwang, Fashion Institute of Technology (FIT), New York City, USA
Gökhan İnce, Istanbul Technical University, Turkey
Francisco Iniesto, Institute of Educational Technology - The Open University, UK
Jamshed Iqbal, University of Hull, UK
Angel Jaramillo-Alcázar, Universidad de Las Américas, Ecuador
Sofia Kaloterakis, Utrecht University, Netherland
Yasushi Kambayashi, Nippon Institute of Technology, Japan
Ahmed Kamel, Concordia College, USA
Suzanne Kieffer, Université catholique de Louvain, Belgium
Jeongyeon Kim, KAIST, South Korea
Si Jung "SJ" Kim, University of Nevada, Las Vegas (UNLV), USA
Elisa Klose, Universität Kassel, Germany
Susanne Koch Stigberg, Østfold University College, Norway

Josef Krems, Chemnitz University of Technology, Germany
Wen-Hsing Lai, National Kaohsiung University of Science and Technology, Taiwan
Monica Landoni, Università della Svizzera italiana, Switzerland
Chien-Sing Lee, Sunway University, Malaysia
Maria Teresa Llano Rodriguez, Monash University, Melbourne, Australia
Tsai-Yen Li, National Chengchi University, Taiwan
Wenjuan Li, The Hong Kong Polytechnic University, Hong Kong
Xiaomeng Li, Centre for Accident Research and Road Safety-Queensland (CARRS-Q) | Queensland University of Technology (QUT), Australia
Fotis Liarokapis, Cyprus University of Technology, Cyprus
Richen Liu, Nanjing Normal University, China
Sunny Xun Liu, Stanford University, USA
Jun-Li Lu, University of Tsukuba, Japan
Zhicong Lu, University of Toronto, Canada
Flaminia Luccio, Universita' Ca' Foscari Venezia, Italy
Sergio Luján-Mora, University of Alicante, Spain
Yan Luximon, The Hong Kong Polytechnic University, Hong Kong
Damian Lyons, Fordham University, USA
Galina Madjaroff, University of Maryland Baltimore County, USA
Sebastian Maneth, University of Bremen, Germany
Guido Maiello, Justus Liebig University Giessen, Germany
Sanna Malinen, University of Turku, Finland
Matthew Louis Mauriello, University of Delaware, USA
Laura Maye, School of Computer Science and Information Technology - University College Cork, Ireland
Horia Mărgărit, Stanford University, USA
Weizhi Meng, Technical University of Denmark, Denmark
Xiaojun Meng, Noah's Ark Lab | Huawei Technologies, Shenzhen, China
Daniel R. Mestre, CNRS Institute of Movement Sciences - Mediterranean Virtual Reality Center, Marseilles, France
Mariofanna Milanova, University of Arkansas at Little Rock, USA
Harald Milchrahm, Institute for Software technology - Technical University Graz, Austria
Leslie Miller, Iowa State University - Ames, USA
Alexander Mirnig, Center for Human-Computer Interaction | University of Salzburg, Austria
Arturo Moquillaza, Pontificia Universidad Católica del Perú, Peru
Nicholas H. Müller, University of Applied Sciences Würzburg-Schweinfurt, Germany
Sachith Muthukumarana, Auckland Bioengineering Institute | The University of Auckland, New Zealand
Yoko Nishihara, College of Information Science and Engineering - Ritsumeikan University, Japan
Rikke Toft Nørgård, Aarhus University, Denmark
Yoshimasa Ohmoto, Shizuoka University, Japan
Deepak Ranjan Padhi, IDC School of Design - IIT Bombay, India
Aditeya Pandey, Northeastern University, Boston, USA
Athina Papadopoulou, Massachusetts Institute of Technology (MIT), USA
Evangelos Papadopoulos, National Technical University of Athens, Greece
Vida Pashaei, University of Arizona, USA
Freddy Alberto Paz Espinoza, Pontificia Universidad Católica del Perú, Peru
Gerald Penn, University of Toronto, Canada
Jorge Henrique Piazentin Ono, New York University - Tandon School of Engineering, USA
Ana C. Pires, Universidade de Lisboa, Portugal

Jorge Luis Pérez Medina, Universidad de Las Américas, Ecuador
Brian Pickering, IT Innovation Centre - University of Southampton, UK
Thomas M. Prinz, Friedrich Schiller University Jena, Germany
Annu Sible Prabhakar, University of Cincinnati, USA
Mike Preuss, Leiden University, Netherlands
Namrata Primlani, Northumbria University, UK
Marina Puyuelo Cazorla, Universitat Politècnica de València, Spain
Yuanyuan (Heather) Qian, Carleton University in Ottawa, Canada
Claudia Quaresma, Universidade NOVA de Lisboa, Portugal
Mariusz Rawski, Warsaw University of Technology, Poland
Radiah Rivu, Bundeswehr University Munich, Germany
Carsten Röcker, inIT - Institute Industrial IT / TH OWL University of Applied Sciences and Arts, Germany
Joni Salminen, Qatar Computing Research Institute, Qatar
Sandra Sanchez-Gordon, Escuela Politécnica Nacional, Ecuador
Antonio-José Sánchez-Salmerón, Instituto de Automática e Informática Industrial - Universidad Politécnica de Valencia, Spain
Paulus Insap Santosa, Universitas Gadjah Mada - Yogyakarta, Indonezia
Markus Santoso, University of Florida, USA
Diana Saplacan, University of Oslo, Norway
Hélène Sauzéon, Centre Inria Bordeaux, France
Trenton Schulz, Norwegian Computing Center, Norway
Kamran Sedig, Western University, Ontario, Canada
Sylvain Senecal, HEC Montreal, Canada
Fereshteh Shahmiri, Georgia Tech, USA
Yuhki Shiraishi, Tsukuba University of Technology, Japan
Marie Sjölinder, RISE, Sweden
Zdzisław Sroczyński, Silesian University of Technology, Gliwice, Poland
Ben Steichen, California State Polytechnic University, Pomona, USA
Han Su, RA - MIT, USA
Federico Tajariol, University Bourgogne Franche-Comté, France
Sheng Tan, Trinity University, Texas, USA
Cagri Tanriover, Intel Corporation (Intel Labs), USA
Ranjeet Tayi, User Experience - Informatica, San Francisco, USA
Masashi Toda, Kumamoto University, Japan
Milka Trajkova, Indiana University, Indianapolis, USA
David Unbehaun, University of Siegen, Germany
Teija Vainio, School of Arts, Design and Architecture - Aalto University, Finland
Simona Vasilache, University of Tsukuba, Japan
KatiaVega, University of California, Davis, USA
Nishant Vishwamitra, University at Buffalo, USA
Konstantinos Votis, Information Technologies Institute | Centre for Research and Technology Hellas, Greece
Lin Wang, U.S. Census Bureau, USA
Gloria Washington, Howard University, USA
Zhanwei Wu, Shanghai Jiao Tong University, China
Shuping Xiong, KAIST, South Korea
Tong Xue, Beijing Film Academy, China

Rui Yang, Xi'an Jiaotong-Liverpool University, China
Ye Zhu, Cleveland State Unviersity, USA

Copyright Information

Reflections on Participatory Design Practices in Public Sector IT Project Management

Klaudia Çarçani
Faculty of Computer Science, Engineering and Economics
Østfold University College
1757 Halden, Norway
e-mail: klaudia.carcani@hiof.no

Selda Gorovelli
Deapartment of MBA and Business Management
Rome Business School
Rome, Italy
e-mail: sgorovelli@eservicios.indra.es

Abstract— **Participatory Design (PD) is the field that stands by the principles of democratic design practices and user involvement in the design of technologies meant for them. PD is often critiqued as not finding its place in project management in private or public institutions, where technological innovation is constrained by time, costs, organizational rules, and, most important, outcomes. Conducting a critical reflective analysis guided by PD principles, we study in this paper if PD principles are present in Information Technology (IT) project management process in the public sector and provide some guidelines on how PD can contribute further to the process. Findings are presented as open discussion points that require further investigation and application in practice.**

Keywords- Participatory Design; IT project management; public sector.

I. INTRODUCTION

Participatory Design (PD) is the field that stands by the principles of democratic design practices and user involvement in the design of technologies meant for them. PD emerged in the context of workers requiring more rights in decision-making about technologies in the workplace and developed into other contexts where marginalized user groups were given a voice and say in technology development [1]. Despite the noble aim, PD is often critiqued as not finding its place in private or public business settings, where technological innovation is constrained by time, costs, organizational rules, regulations, and, most importantly, outcomes.

Both private and public sectors need to keep competitive advantage and growth by fostering innovation and sustainable development [2]. To do so, innovation and product development in the Information Technology (IT) world is driven by establishing projects. "Projects" are defined as temporary structures that aim to deliver outcomes within specific timelines, budget, quality, risk, and benefits [3]. Moreover, due to the compartmentalization of knowledge where specific companies/institutions/organizations specialize in offering specific services and products, achieving the project outcomes has shifted from exclusive internal development (R&D) to cooperation with external partners [4]. Hence, making IT sourcing projects a common business practice.

While PD principles seem to align with multidisciplinary project management practices, the explorative nature of PD and the challenge that it adds to timelines seem to limit its usage.

In the public sector, project management practices are common. However, these practices are subject to constraints dictated by rules and regulations. Additionally, there is a strong call in the public sector for citizens' involvement in every instance to represent their views better and increase the accountability for services delivered.

Hence, in this paper, we question to what extent PD principles are applied in IT project management process in the public sector. We studied two cases in two different countries. Data was collected through official public document analysis, interviews, and minutes of meeting notes.

Based on the data collected, we conducted a critical reflective analysis to what extent and how the principle of PD was present in the two-project studied. Based on these theoretically grounded reflections, in the findings, we present remarks for embracing PD in the public sector. These remarks should be further investigated in future research.

Section 2 will initially present a theoretical background for our work, followed by the method we used for data collection and analysis in Section 3. Further, we present the results of our reflective analysis in Section IV and finally discuss the findings in relation to the theory in Section 5. We contribute to the body of knowledge for public sector IT project management and to PD and the discourse for its application outside of academia.

II. THEORY

In this section, we present the theoretical ground for this paper. We start by presenting PD, its principles, and what characterizes it as a research field. Then, we present the theories on public sector IT project management by starting with what project management is, what characterizes project management in the public sector and some of the latest discourses in public sector IT project management regarding participatory practices.

A. *Participatory Design*

PD is the field of research and evolving practice of design that propagates the relevance of users' involvement in the design of technologies meant for them [1]. It has a transformative agenda in building systems for and with people [5]. PD stands by the principle of democratic participation and is concerned with the politics of design and users' participation in the design processes [6]. PD practitioners believe in the relevance of situational knowledge and the promotion of mutual learning as the only way to design adequate solutions that address real needs [7]. Mutual learning is a practice-driven concept representing sharing of values and knowledge in PD activities. Capturing situated knowledge and achieving mutual learning is conducted through choosing and applying the right techniques and tools that engage people in telling, making, and enacting [8].

"Participatory design project is set up, so the users are enabled to take an active part in the activities and decisions through which new IT is designed and built." [9]. A PD perspective poses challenges in new projects, such as developing a complex technological solution and opening it for additional learning during design and after. Based on the concept of seeing-moving-seeing from Schon, Bratteteig and Wagner [10] defined participation as involving relevant stakeholders in choice creation, selecting among them, concretizing choices, and evaluating the choices. The design decisions should be reflected in the design result. Bratteteig and Wagner [11], in their discussion, argue that the design result can be the artifact developed that influences the context for which it was designed by contributing to changing existing power structures. Another PD result is to give users a voice – and a say, so they can assume power over their situation by participating in major design decisions that are visible in the artifact. Moreover, it is important to understand if the designed artifact presupposes (or suggests) changes of power structures in the use situation as a prerequisite or as an effect of using the artifact.

Finally, reflecting on projects without being able to promote concrete change but sharing participants' insights and experiences is a key aspect of research and may, over time, contribute to the changes PD argues for.

Hertzum and Simonsen [12] discuss PD application in organizational settings and propose an effects-driven IT development to pursue and reinforce PD when applied in commercial IT projects. This approach has three steps: specify effects, iterative prototyping, and pilot implementation. Whittle [13], with a similar approach, studies 6 PD projects in terms of outcomes and concludes that PD is much more focused on processing and would benefit if managing the process focuses on defining outcomes and keeping track of their deliveries. They also suggest that an Agile approach can contribute to PD to make the process leaner. Additionally, they state that while software development researchers have looked into PD to integrate its principles [14], scarce efforts (e.g., [15]) have been the other way around to reflect on agile PD practices. Ferrario, et al. [16] describe a project management framework for software engineering for "social good" where elements of agile and iterative development are integrated with actions research and PD principles. The process has four phases: prepare, design, build, and sustain, which move incrementally and promote partnerships and mutual learning among all relevant stakeholders by applying PD creative problem-solving techniques and delivering working prototypes that can be moved further to product development.

B. *Project Management and the Public Sector*

Project Management (PM) emerged in the mid-20th century, and since then, it has become a prevalent way to manage business activities. Project Management Institute (PMI) defines a "project" as "a temporary endeavor undertaken to create a unique result" [3]. A result could be a product, service, document, capability, deliverable, or outcome. Project types vary in terms of their level of complexity, technology uncertainty, pace, and novelty [17]. In technology-driven organizations, project types can be categorized based on the types of organizational change described by Orlikowski and Hofman [18]: planned or anticipated, emergent, and opportunity-based. The emergent and opportunity-based ones are defined as innovation projects [19].

Distinctive methodologies have been developed for conducting a project from the start till delivery (such as PMI, PRINCE 2, PM2, AMP, SCRUM etc.). These methodologies variate in focus, and while some can be descriptive (PMI), others are more prescriptive (PRINCE 2) [20]. The study of Ghosh, et al. [21] shows that, in general, projects involve initiation, planning, execution (in distinct stages and iterations and by aligning with software design and development phases), controlling, and closing.

User requirements and business justification drive the project. The stages of project management can be distinguished by the phases of product delivery involving design, building, and testing [21]. Each of the techniques has its strengths and drawbacks. For example, PRINCE 2 has strength in framing the process but does not elaborate on the involvement of human resources and suitable techniques for project leadership and procurement issues. All methodologies propagate the necessity to tailor the project management based on the project needs, and in practice, the different project management approaches are merged. However, in each project, the following elements should be managed (PRINCE 2 ref): Time – When will the project be finished? Cost – Projects need to give a return on investment, and costs need to be controlled. Quality – Are products passing their quality checks, and will users be able to use the project product as expected when delivered? Scope – Is the scope clear to all stakeholders? Benefits – Expected benefits must be known, agreed and measurable. Risk – All projects have risk, so risk needs to be managed so the project has a better chance of succeeding.

While the project management approach is commonly encountered in the private sector, citizens' demand for better public services and accountability for using taxpayers' funds incentivized the public sector organizations to apply this approach [22]. Moreover, with the digitalization of public services being a big part of governmental budgets, public organizations find many IT projects over budget, behind schedule, and producing fewer benefits than expected [22].

Project management practices in the public sector are influenced by the necessity for accountability, legally regulated conduct, resource management, and the political motivation to deliver results within specific time limits [23]. Accountability is exercised toward a broad range of stakeholders, such as elected officials, various members of the government management structure, employees, citizens, special interest groups, and the media [23].

The field of collaborative public innovation recognizes the necessity of collaboration among multi-actors and -institutions. Each stakeholder contributes knowledge, imagination, creativity, resources, transformative capacities, and political authority [24].

Citizens' involvement varies in regard to different conceptions of democracy and a certain mode of governance [25]-[29] such as: a) Traditional Public Administration (TPA) that position citizens as clients and relies on experts' perspectives to decide the agendas for the public sector services, b) New Public Management (NPM) that regards citizens as customers who can influence the public services by choosing to use them or opting out from them [23], and c) New Public Governance (NPG) where citizens are given a more active role as co-producer [24]-[25] and co-creators [26]. However, achieving such cooperation with citizens is challenging because the public administration mistrusts citizens' expertise and their motives [30]. Additionally, for citizens, it is time demanding. It usually attracts resourceful citizens, thus, lacking the perspective of the rest of the population.

Agger and Lund [25] use the concept of co-innovation as an umbrella term for the involvement of citizens in public innovation in all stages as co-initiators, co-designers, and co-implementers. In each phase, citizens can, as public consumers, engage more directly in producing new public services, thereby becoming the locus of value creation.

Marketization has also influenced public sector IT service provision. Marketization refers to a broad span of arrangements where private sector organizations contract with public sector bodies to deliver a welfare service in exchange for public funds [31]. Marketization can be applied by contracting out public services to private companies or by promoting free choice reforms where citizens are given the right to choose between public and private providers of welfare services [32].

Contracting in the public sector follows regulations on how to manage procurement to incentivize competitive advantage for all interested private companies. However, the procurement processes are usually rigid and, instead of promoting innovation, impede it. Lean Agile procurement applies principles and practices from design thinking and agile software development to propose changes to procurement and the contracting process between public and private to promote partnerships that can promote innovation [33].

III. Method

We collected data from two public IT project management cases, one in Albania and one in Norway. The cases were selected strategically to address different public sector IT project management practices representing a developing and developed country with established democracies and a free market.

For Albania, we applied document analysis to map the process of IT project management in the municipalities. With that knowledge, we interviewed an expert in auditing such projects. The selected project was inspired by observing the changes in IT infrastructure in the municipality area and the aim of such infrastructure change to contribute to citizens' well-being.

For Norway, the case selected was a project where the first author had been involved from the initiation phase as part of the project group. The project took a stand in applying a PD approach and involved the interaction of many stakeholders at different stages to deliver a public IT project within healthcare. The data collected consisted of documents, emails, and minutes of meeting notes from the whole process.

Data analysis was done in three phases. Initially, we applied content analysis [34] with apriori codes from the project management phases presented in the literature: initiation, planning, execution, closing, and controlling. The result of this analysis is presented in section IV with the presentation of the cases.

To assess the degree to which the PD approach was applied, in each case, we conducted a reflective practice analysis [35]. Reflective practice is "learning through and from experience towards gaining new insights of self and practice" [4]. Dewey [5] was among the first to identify reflection as a specialized form of thinking ignited by doubt, hesitation, or perplexity related to a directly experienced situation. In design, reflective practices have been commonly applied [36] and contribute to advancing knowledge. Initially, we reflected on how and to what degree the two main PD elements described in the literature were present in each case: a) participation – seen both in terms of mutual learning and power balance concerns and b) the PD design result. Then, we conducted a second round of reflections by looking across cases.

IV. Findings

In this section, we initially present the findings regarding the project management lifecycle for both cases by describing in rich details what activities entailed in each case. Then we present our findings regarding the application of PD in public sector IT project management as critical reflections that end in proposed remarks on how to apply PD in such context.

A. *Case Vignettes*

Below we present the findings from our two case studies. Findings are organized based on the project management phases described in the Section 2.

a) Safety Cameras (SC)

As municipalities make up a large part of the public sector and have standardized and regulated processes they need to follow, we decided to study the project management process for municipalities in Albania. Specifically, we present the case of a project to install cameras around the city to guarantee citizens' safety and increase the chances for accountability in case of misconduct. We found that the municipality outsources most IT products or services projects. The project unfolded as below:

Initiation phase – The Municipality has established practices to engage with citizens and identify prevailing needs in the community. This is done through reports or meetings. Different departments are responsible for different social aspects within their area of expertise. In this way, the municipality's experts in citizens' safety mapped the need to have a way to increase control in all the urban areas through the installation of safety cameras. This project brief and other project briefs were submitted to the Budget Committee. The projects are usually discussed in different working groups and prioritized by applying various criteria such as urgency, necessity, budget availability, and in compliance with the long-term plan that the municipality has. A budget proposal is presented to the municipal council. After due review and further discussion, the final budget for the year is approved. SC followed the same process. A budget estimation was approved to be applied in 4 months.

Planning phase – A project work group was established, involving the citizen safety department as the project executive, a functional safety specialist representing the citizens' view, and a technical safety specialist representing the technical requirements. Together with the project manager, they started drafting the requirements. A procurement officer was appointed and joined the project group to help prepare the solicitation package - define sourcing strategy, evaluation criteria, and communication methods. Moreover, the project group worked on an initial plan and timelines for delivery. The budget estimation was revised once they knew more about the requirements for the cameras, both functionally and technically. The documents produced involved: Request for Proposal (RfP), product or service specifications, contract conditions, and bid evaluation criteria.

The municipality bids are, by law, to be published on an official sourcing site for public institutions if they surpass a certain fund limit. The safety camera project was established and published there.

When the bidding was open, the procurement specialist received requests for more information from different potential suppliers. The answer was made available to everyone, and it was treated carefully not to allow disclosure of the company information without their consent. On the bid deadline, all offers received via mail were opened in a common meeting with everyone from the project group. Each project member assigned previously to the bid to be part of the evaluation committee was provided with the documents from each company. The evaluators had several meetings to discuss and endorse a winning company. The mayor made the final decision with the approval of the municipal council. The winner was announced on the municipality website. It was only after the contract signing that the project group would meet the supplier and, together with their plan for the implementation.

Implementation – The project started with a design phase where the supplier, in cooperation with the technical and functional experts in the project group, defined the best strategy to deploy the cameras around the city to fulfill the safety need. Different scenarios were discussed during the design. Additionally, the project group discussed the monitoring room and how that will be managed. Once the design was agreed upon, the installation phase started. This lasted for 4 months. Training was provided for the IT experts operating and maintaining the cameras.

Monitoring and control – Many controlling entities were involved in the previously described phases. The project manager must report to the business owner (the citizens' safety department), the mayor, and municipal council. Other controlling and directing entities are the budget committee and the procurement officer. Regarding implementation, the project group controlled the deliveries from the supplier and reported to the adequate board entities regularly.

b) Patient Healthcare Record (PHR)

The aim of this project from the start was to investigate technological possibilities that would support patients in need of rehabilitation after Acquired Brain Injuries (ABI) to take control and get empowered in their rehabilitation process. A rehabilitation hospital offering specialized services to such patients in Norway initiated the project. They engaged with an academic institution to cover the needs and design exploration phase.

Initiation Phase – The common initiative resulted in a PhD researcher funded by the academic institution who worked at the hospital to investigate the need for a collaborative tool between patients and healthcare practitioners to empower the patients throughout their rehabilitation process.

The hospital and the academic institution shared an interest in participative methods and encouraging users (in this case, patients, and healthcare practitioners) to have their say in the design process, being service design of technology design. Two PD workshops with patients and two with healthcare practitioners were organized to investigate needs. Additionally, the PhD researcher spends circa 6 months conducting ethnographic studies and mapping existing practices at the hospital. The knowledge collected was then applied to organize two design workshops for patients and two design workshops for healthcare practitioners to reflect on existing practices and envision future solutions to help patient empowerment. As the design ideas highlighted the necessity to cooperate closely between patients and healthcare practitioners, two power-balanced PD workshops were organized with patients and healthcare practitioners to envision the future solution and practices.

Planning phase – The research and design (R&D) results were applied to ideate a project and apply for external funds to develop a technological solution to support the needs defined during the research phase.

Innovation Norway (IN) is an institution jointly funded by the government and municipalities' budget. IN aims to incentivize business development that is profitable for the business and that contributes to society's needs to boost regional development. Public institutions can apply for funds for projects that can help them address a need and cooperate with the private sector to purchase the solution and academic institutions to contribute to research. Innovation Norge granted the project funds to the rehabilitation hospital to develop the technological solution envisioned.

A project manager was assigned. A project group and project board were established. In the project group, representatives from the hospital (patient representatives, management representatives, IT experts that know the existing technologies), the researcher from the academic institution, and a representative from the funding institution were included. The project board involved all the relevant stakeholders that would contribute to decision-making (each group was represented).

The following project management process was recommended to follow. It included the following phases: Describing Needs; Market Dialogue; Bid; Development, and Implementation, as shown below:

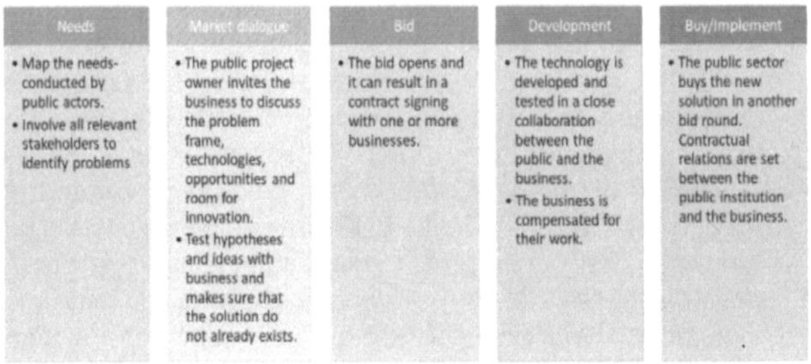

Figure 1: Process followed in PHR.

The initial planning phase activity was to describe the needs. The project group worked jointly on the document. Once consolidated, the document was forwarded for approval to the project board. Once the project board accepted, a date for a market dialogue was published on the Norwegian official public procurement site. The market dialogue aimed to show the business the project's aim and the problem to be solved. The business could discuss with the hospital their current technologies and the extent to which they match their needs. The market dialogue agenda included a presentation of the project and an invitation for each potential supplier to two group workshops to discuss the project and the innovation possibilities the supplier could offer.

The participants from the market dialogue were: The hospital (clinical and technical knowledge representatives), patients (patient representatives), the project manager, the procurement specialist, and the technology regulators in healthcare in Norway, which provide the platform on which this new solution should work.

After the market dialogue, the needs were revised, and the final functional and non-functional requirements were described to be further published as an RfP on the public procurement site 'Doffin'. A date for a Bid Conference was assigned prior to publishing the bid. The conference addressed potential suppliers' questions regarding the bid and the documentation they needed to provide.

Once the bid period was closed, the project group evaluated them in many discussion rounds and provided recommendations to the board to make the final decision.

Implementation phase – The implementation phase started with a kick-off meeting between the project group and the selected supplier. Both parties discussed a plan for the implementation that would follow these stages: design, development, testing, further refinement, and final delivery. The first designs were delivered in March 2023, and the project is still ongoing. Thus, for the project closure, we do not yet have information.

Monitoring and Control – The project was monitored and controlled by several mechanisms. In the initiation phase, the agreed PD approach was a control mechanism for the planned activities. Instead, in the following phases, the project management framework was used for monitoring and control. Moreover, the project manager continuously reported to the board for specific and routine decisions. Another control mechanism is the official procurement site that safeguards a fair procurement process. During implementation, the project team oversees the supplier's work and reports progress to the project board. Codes of conduct that regulate the relationship between patients and healthcare practitioners are considered during the testing phase.

B. PD in public sector IT project management

Here we will present the findings on how PD elements have been applied in the two projects we studied. We conclude the analysis with guidelines on how to increase the presence of PD in public-sector IT project management.

a) Enhance user participation in the planning and implementation phase through PD methods

In both cases, we found that some degree of participation was exercised in each phase of the projects. In the SC project, citizens were involved through established networks of engagement with citizens to evaluate ongoing needs. Similarly, patients' and healthcare practitioners' voices were represented in the identification and articulation of the needs to request external funds for the PHR project. The citizens' and users' representatives remained participants in the project and were involved in discussions with technology experts and possible suppliers.

In the SC project, a technical expert was assigned to work on the project together with the citizens' representative(s). In the PHR project, the market dialogue brought the user needs to the business to discuss possible solutions.

In both cases, the bidding process involved regulated information exchange with the bidders regarding asking questions and providing responses. In the PHR project, such exchange happened during the bidding conference. In each case, the procurement regulating authorities framed how participation was implemented.

The implementation phase in the SC project involved the encounters between the technical experts and the supplier selected. Instead, in the PHR project, the supplier engaged again with end users in the prototype's evaluation and feedback-gathering phase. The way the implementation is organized depends on the final product and how the supplier organizes the work. Due to contractual binding, they are obliged to report back to the project group. It is up to the project group to organize how citizens or end users should be involved in the implementation phase. This was the case with the PHR project, where the experience of the project manager in PD approaches and the interest in participative practices led to public display evaluation not only for the board and higher management but also for end users.

Based on the above findings, we conclude that: The discourse on participation and relevant stakeholders' involvement should also be promoted during the planning and initiation phase. Tools and techniques from PD practices can be applied to promote co-design. Moreover, new PD techniques for project management in public sector digitalization initiatives should be explored.

b) Promote Mutual Learning with Suppliers in Market Dialogue PD workshops

Hearing the voice of users/citizens seems to be a well-established practice in organizing project management work at the municipality. At the hospital, the same approach is present. However, our analysis shows that while policymakers and design experts learn from citizens, the learning is not mutual. Citizens are not involved in later stages where they can learn about design alternatives and possible technologies and eventually make their own decisions. Moreover, each actor in the planning phase represents a specific area of expertise. They engage with each other to draft the high-level requirement document presented in the bid. While some mutual learning happens in those instances, they are detached from the real setting where the knowledge of alternatives stands, the suppliers.

In the PHR project, such a gap in mutual learning is filled by market dialogue. This allows the end users' representatives to sit with the possible suppliers to discuss: What is a viable solution with existing resources? What would the supplier be willing to do to engage in innovative solutions if the requirements are not covered fully by what is provided today? The market dialogue approach is open and does not infringe on any rule imposed by procurement regulation. It also allows the possibility of having an objective, quantifiable evaluation process later, while still providing a true participative venue for mutual learning and creating alternative visions.

During the implementation process in the SC case, no more mutual learning is happening. This has a negative impact because citizens are not consulted on the design and implementation of the solution in practice. Thus, the supplier applies what they consider best and might lose sight of what the citizens need. Meanwhile, citizens not knowing how their needs were addressed and the benefits and risks that the technology brings can experience an unethical impact in the long run. Instead, in the PHR project, the design phase involved the discussion of the designs directly with the end users and higher management by using high-fidelity prototypes. While the project is ongoing, it is relevant that the evaluation of the prototype does not focus only on the look and feel and functionalities provided but is used to capture more in-depth and inherited issues of technology that should be cleared with the users, such as accountability, integrity, and accessibility of data.

Based on the above findings, we conclude that: The market dialog provides the opportunity in sourcing IT projects to have both user and technology representatives to share knowledge and values, engage in co-design moves, and produce design alternatives. PD techniques and tools should be applied in the market dialogue. We will define this as market co-creation techniques and suggest using generative tools [4] that the suppliers can provide.

c) Making "Power" a central theme to consider in each phase

We found that the power dynamics discourse is the most underestimated PD principle in both projects. For the SC project, the discussion of power is inexistent. The municipality considers the elected representatives as guardians of democratic decisions that favor the majority that has elected them. In the PHR project, the discussion on power is deeply considered in the initiation phase. The final result addresses the power imbalance between patients and healthcare practitioners with the aim of patient empowerment. However, the power balancing has been more tacit during the process, counting on representatives having equal power during the project management process.

Project management relies upon established organizational hierarchies and agreed-on processes to deliver on time and within budget. These hierarchies can create power imbalances if all actors' involvement are not treated equally.

Based on the above findings, we conclude that: The power discourse should be part of IT project management. It should become a central theme that is reflected upon in every phase and activity where different stakeholders engage. The discussion on power should be balanced with the necessity to follow the regulations that define the frame for some project management activities. That is why engagement with the possible suppliers during the market dialogue and not after the official bid is published provides a practice that adheres to PD principles and follows project management regulations.

d) Control and monitor the delivery of "PD results"

In the municipality project, the design result addresses an issue that the citizens brought forward, and it is not in principle related to the empowerment of a marginalized user group. While the focus is on the result, the discussion on the solution's impact on marginalized user groups and how to make the solution suitable and understandable for every citizen category remains obsolete. Instead, in the PHR project, the design result is ideated based on PD principles. The project impacts empowering patients and giving them more control in their rehabilitation. The involvement of the PD expert as a project advisor contributes to highlighting all relevant stakeholders and involving them in the design process. The process adopted by IN also promotes PD project management. Moreover, in the project, power dynamics are actively considered and addressed, so the solution represents the views of everyone and creates the opportunity to have emerging new practices.

Based on the above findings, we conclude that: The design result represents the user need in IT project management. However, that is not sufficient. Broadening the scope of the design result toward a "PD design result" can contribute to delivering more citizens' friendly solutions and guarantee an ethical and responsible process and delivery. New methods should emerge in PD literature to become part of IT project management control and monitoring.

V. Discussion And Conclusion

PD is a field that stands by a bold commitment toward bringing voice to marginalized user groups and promoting equality and power balance in design [1]. PD can be applied to any context and strives to find methods, tools and techniques that promote engaged participation in projects from idea and vision to delivery [3]. Conversely, project management is driven by timelines, budgets, quality requirements, risks, benefits, and outcomes. Whittle [9] discusses six projects and states that PD researchers have not engaged with agile approaches and vice versa. This is true because compromising power balance for fast results is not a choice for PD, and compromising timelines for achieving the true power balance among stakeholders is not feasible in the face of resource limitations, existing organizational structures, and defined regulations that halt the project from delivering what is expected. These elements are even more present in public-sector IT project management [20].

However, we found that in the public sector IT project management, PD practices are present. The degree to which participation is considered varies from the SC to the PHR project because PHR was initiated by embracing the PD approach, and it takes place in Norway, where PD emerged and the discussions on equality and power balance are strongly positioned in the public discourse [22]. While in the SC example, citizens are considered consumers of public services and are involved only in the co-initiation of the project, in the PHR project, they are treated more as co-producers and contribute to co-design [24]-[26]. In a similar position are the private sector companies that contribute to the marketization of services [29] who also become just clients in the SC project and co-producers in co-design and co-implementation in the PHR project. We acknowledge that historical, cultural, and political differences between the two countries influence how the project management process is established.

We argue that as agility has become a central theme in project management, participation and power dynamics should also be used as central concepts to revise the project management processes and profit from the benefits that a PD approach enables. Initiatives like lean-agile procurement and practices like the market dialogue(e.g., [30]) are adapting the design thinking approach to the project management world [10]-[12], but adding to this approach PD principles and PD techniques and tools can contribute to delivering projects that matter and are accepted by all end users. Moreover, it can contribute to projects that focus on the design of software used for cooperation [2].

PD initiatives like the effect-driven PD [8][34] have raised the concern that PD should be driven by delivering benefits and contributing to achieving the desired effects. While the effect-driven PD provides a good framework as a high-level approach, the issue remains in finding techniques and tools that can be applied within the project management process and not burden the timelines and budgets of the project.

The market dialogue is an example of a practice of mutual learning and if PD techniques and tools are applied to promote dialogue and engage in co-creation activities, the project will not only deliver but also drive innovation.

However, in both fields, additional questions and remarks should still be explored, such as: who should organize the participatory activities, how to balance between existing hierarchical structures and the necessity to cooperate, how to make PD techniques and tools more efficient and delivery driven, and what tools and techniques are adequate for each phase of project management? What does participation mean in project management? To what extent is power balancing possible?

Answering these questions requires PD and project management researchers to reflect on them in future research by exploring new practices or adapting the existing knowledge to co-flourish and contribute better to society.

References

[1] T. Robertson and J. Simonsen, "Participatory Design: an introduction," in *Routledge international handbook of participatory design*: Routledge, 2012, pp. 21-38.

[2] S. Salomo, K. Talke, and N. Strecker, "Innovation field orientation and its effect on innovativeness and firm performance," *Journal of product innovation management,* vol. 25, no. 6, pp. 560-576, 2008.

[3] A. Guide, "Project management body of knowledge (pmbok® guide)," in *Project Management Institute*, 2001, vol. 11, pp. 7-8.

[4] E. Enkel, O. Gassmann, and H. Chesbrough, "Open R&D and open innovation: exploring the phenomenon," *R&d Management,* vol. 39, no. 4, pp. 311-316, 2009.

[5] T. Bratteteig, *Design for, med og av brukere: å inkludere brukere i design av informasjonssystemer.* Universitetsforlaget, 2021.

[6] F. Kensing and J. Blomberg, "Participatory design: Issues and concerns," *Computer supported cooperative work,* vol. 7, no. 3-4, pp. 167-185, 1998.

[7] F. Kensing and J. Greenbaum, "Heritage: Having a say," in *Routledge international handbook of participatory design*: Routledge, 2012, pp. 41-56.

[8] E. Brandt, T. Binder, and E. B.-N. Sanders, "Tools and techniques: Ways to engage telling, making and enacting," in *Routledge international handbook of participatory design*: Routledge, 2012, pp. 145-181.

[9] T. Bratteteig, K. Bødker, Y. Dittrich, P. H. Mogensen, and J. Simonsen, "Organising principles and general guidelines for Participatory Design Projects," *Routledge international handbook of participatory design,* pp. 117-144, 2013.

[10] T. Bratteteig and I. Wagner, "Unpacking the notion of participation in participatory design," *Computer Supported Cooperative Work (CSCW),* vol. 25, pp. 425-475, 2016.

[11] T. Bratteteig and I. Wagner, "What is a participatory design result?," in *Proceedings of the 14th Participatory Design Conference: Full papers-Volume 1*, 2016, pp. 141-150.

[12] M. Hertzum and J. Simonsen, "Effects-driven IT development: an instrument for supporting sustained participatory design," in *Proceedings of the 11th Biennial Participatory Design Conference*, 2010, pp. 61-70.

[13] J. Whittle, "How much participation is enough? a comparison of six participatory design projects in terms of outcomes," presented at the Proceedings of the 13th Participatory Design Conference: Research Papers - Volume 1, Windhoek, Namibia, 2014. pp. 121-130. [Online]. Available: https://doi.org/10.1145/2661435.2661445.

[14] K. Kautz, "Investigating the design process: participatory design in agile software development," *Information Technology & People,* vol. 24, no. 3, pp. 217-235, 2011.

[15] A. Tedjasaputra and E. R. Sari, "Pair Writing: Towards Agile Participatory Design," 2005: HCII. pp. 1-5.

[16] M. A. Ferrario, W. Simm, P. Newman, S. Forshaw, and J. Whittle, "Software engineering for 'social good': integrating action research, participatory design, and agile development," presented at the Companion Proceedings of the 36th International Conference on Software Engineering, Hyderabad, India, 2014. pp. 520-523. [Online]. Available: https://doi.org/10.1145/2591062.2591121.

[17] D. Dvir, A. Sadeh, and A. Malach-Pines, "Projects and project managers: The relationship between project managers' personality, project types, and project success," *Project Management Journal,* vol. 37, no. 5, pp. 36-48, 2006.

[18] W. J. Orlikowski and J. D. Hofman, "An improvisational model for change management: The case of groupware technologies," *MIT Sloan Management Review,* 1997.

[19] C. Midler, C. P. Killen, and A. Kock, "Project and innovation management: Bridging contemporary trends in theory and practice," vol. 47, ed: SAGE Publications Sage CA: Los Angeles, CA, 2016, pp. 3-7.

[20] S. Matos and E. Lopes, "Prince2 or PMBOK–a question of choice," *Procedia Technology,* vol. 9, pp. 787-794, 2013.

[21] S. Ghosh, D. Forrest, T. DiNetta, B. Wolfe, and D. C. Lambert, "Enhance PMBOK® by comparing it with P2M, ICB, PRINCE2, APM and Scrum project management standards," *PM World Today,* vol. 14, no. 1, pp. 1-77, 2012.

[22] W. Cats-Baril and R. Thompson, "Managing information technology projects in the public sector," *Public administration review,* pp. 559-566, 1995.

[23] K. M. Rosacker and R. E. Rosacker, "Information technology project management within public sector organizations," *Journal of Enterprise Information Management,* 2010.

[24] J. Torfing, "Collaborative innovation in the public sector," in *Handbook of innovation in public services*: Edward Elgar Publishing, 2013, pp. 301-316.

[25] A. Agger and D. H. Lund, "Collaborative Innovation in the Public Sector–new perspectives on the role of citizens?," *Scandinavian Journal of Public Administration,* vol. 21, no. 3, pp. 17-38, 2017.

[26] J. Clarke and J. Newman, "Elusive publics: Knowledge, power and public service reform," in *Changing Teacher Professionalism*: Routledge, 2009, pp. 63-73.

[27] D. Osborne, "Reinventing government," *Public productivity & management Review,* pp. 349-356, 1993.

[28] J. Alford, *Engaging public sector clients: From service-delivery to co-production.* Springer, 2009.

[29] S. P. Osborne, Z. Radnor, and K. Strokosch, "Co-Production and the Co-Creation of Value in Public Services: A suitable case for treatment?," *Public Management Review,* vol. 18, no. 5, pp. 639-653, 2016/05/27 2016, doi: 10.1080/14719037.2015.1111927.

[30] B. E. P. Thapa, B. Niehaves, C. E. Seidel, and R. Plattfaut, "Citizen involvement in public sector innovation: Government and citizen perspectives," *Information Polity,* vol. 20, pp. 3-17, 2015, doi: 10.3233/IP-150351.

[31] T. L. Brown and M. Potoski, "Transaction costs and institutional explanations for government service production decisions," *Journal of Public Administration research and theory,* vol. 13, no. 4, pp. 441-468, 2003.

[32] O. H. Petersen and U. Hjelmar, "Marketization of welfare services in Scandinavia: A review of Swedish and Danish experiences," *Scandinavian Journal of Public Administration,* vol. 17, no. 4, pp. 3-20, 2014.

[33] B. Nicoletti, *Agile Procurement: Volume I: Adding Value with Lean Processes.* Springer, 2017.

[34] C. Erlingsson and P. Brysiewicz, "A hands-on guide to doing content analysis," *African journal of emergency medicine,* vol. 7, no. 3, pp. 93-99, 2017.

[35] J. Dewey, *How we think: A restatement of the relation of reflective thinking to the educative process.* DC Heath, 1933.

[36] D. A. Schön, *Educating the reflective practitioner.* Jossey-Bass San Francisco, 1987.

Making Technology Matter for Processes of Co-Creation and Innovation in Cross-Sectorial Collaborations

Fahd Bin Malek Newaz, Joakim Karlsen
Department of Computer Science and Communication
Østfold University College
Halden, Norway
{fahd.b.newaz, joakim.karlsen}@hiof.no

Jo Herstad
Department of Informatics
University of Oslo
Oslo, Norway
johe@uio.no

Abstract—**This article discusses the use of different representations of technology to expose, inform and engage participants taking part in co-creation activities. In our project, the participants co-create an activity to support the learning of cultural heritage. We build our research on the "design choices framework", which provides a convenient structure for co-creation projects, but does not address the role of technology in such projects. We discuss the benefits of adding a technology choice addressing how to enhance co-creation processes and improve the utility of the framework. By representing technology through, e.g., images, demos, and prototypes, appropriately in different stages of our co-creation project, we see a clear, positive impact.**

Keywords-co-creation; design; design choices; innovation; cross-sectorial collaboration; technology.

I. INTRODUCTION

To address increasingly complex societal challenges, it is imperative to collaborate across organizations and different sectors and conceptualize innovative approaches to tackle them. Involving multiple stakeholders working toward a shared goal, however, creates difficulty in balancing their interests [1]. Taking inspiration from the field of Participatory Design (PD), we look to create a shared understanding through representational tools focusing on ICT solutions, and by this, facilitate for co-creation. Many projects implement co-creation as a process, agenda or tool [2]–[4] to support design and innovation. Lee et al. [4], attempt to provide some structure to the co-creation process through their 'design choices' framework. While this framework is mostly based on technology design projects, there is little focus on the representation of technology and its impact on the co-creation process, which is becoming increasingly relevant [5]. Bjögvinnson et al. [6] discuss the importance of representations to introduce new technologies and make it more accessible for a broader range of stakeholders. In our project, we focus on finding ways to represent technology in co-creation processes and seek to strengthen Lee et al.'s [4] ´design choices´ framework. The technology aspect was fundamental for our design process, having a strong impact on the co-creation experience, and in turn, the project results.

The research has implications for organizations looking to incorporate technology into their co-creation process, and for designers seeking to facilitate stakeholder engagement and drive innovation. The guiding question that is addressed in this paper is: in what ways can the representation of a diverse range of technology be used and be of value in co-creation processes?

We attempt to answer this question from our work in the pARTiciPED project. The overarching goal of the project is to explore a way for teachers in Norwegian schools (current and upcoming), to collaborate with external partners from various cultural institutions, and co-create innovative ways of teaching, resulting in a more engaging, enjoyable, and integrated (in terms of the overall school curriculum) learning experience for secondary school students. The external partners could be artists, musicians, actors, or in our case, museum educators. We, the designers, have facilitated the co-creation process through a series of workshops following the principles of PD, such as 'having a say' and 'mutual learning' [7], and incorporated the representation of technology through various tools, such as interactive prototypes, design cards, images and demonstrations.

In the following, we present the Design Choices Framework developed by Lee et al. [4]. Then we describe our project in relation to the framework, focusing on the impact of the technology choices we made, followed by a discussion on how the framework could benefit from an additional design choice related to how technology should be represented. In conclusion, we present the potential societal impacts of the improved co-creation processes.

II. DESIGN CHOICES FRAMEWORK FOR CO-CREATION

Lee et al. [4] present their design choices framework to build an understanding of what kinds of dimensions a co-creation project consists of, and which attributes and alternatives are relevant when planning and conducting such a project. The framework consists of ten design choices: *1) Openness of the brief*, describing the mode of inquiry with which the project approaches the goals of co-creation, *2) Purpose of Change,* elaborating on what and why certain changes are necessary to be achieved through the co-creation project, *3) Scope of Design* which is often closely related to the purpose of change, but rather than focusing the long term impact of the project, looks at what specifically will be designed during the co-creation process, *4) Diversity in Knowledge,* bringing together stakeholders from different fields of expertise with comprehensive knowledge of the product, service, or process they are developing, *5) Differences in Interests,* requires careful planning to incorporate stakeholders' interests, manage the complexity of their relationships, and potential conflicts, *6) Distribution of Power,* as power dynamics may be influenced by the stakeholders' knowledge, interests, roles and backgrounds but also between designers leading the co-creation activities and those participating; designers need to be aware of their role as facilitators, and decide how active or neutral they will be in the process, *7) Types of Co-creation Activities,* refers to the different events throughout the project, or stages within a single co-creation event that may include techniques such as future workshops, or generative tools to share, disseminate and create knowledge *8) Setting for Co-creation,* making sure that the location and materials used can greatly impact the success of a co-creation, *9) Outputs of the Project* can refer to what is created by participants during the co-creation activities, but can also be in the form of consolidated reports and proposals by researchers or designers, both of which can range from ideas for concrete changes and their visualizations (e.g., improvement ideas, touch points, customer journey maps) to new service concepts (e.g., scenarios, videos, service blueprints, and process models) to future strategies (e.g., a set of experience goals and future roadmaps), *10) Outcomes of the Project* refer to changes achieved on a larger scale, such as changes in mindset, processes, and culture, which have a direct impact on the target population. These design choices are further grouped into four categories where they can be related to the following: *Project Preconditions* (design choices 1-3), *Participants* (design choices 4-6), *Co-creation Events* (design choices 7-8), and *Project Results* (design choices 9-10).

III. Methods

The design process for the project was iterative, as presented in the timeline in Figure 1. We used both participatory prototyping, design cards and probes in our workshops [8]. Brandt et al. [9] present 'the making of things as a means of design participation', which is what we did. A variety of methods, such as observation and interviews, were used to gather data during the co-creation activities. Observation as a research method enables the study of a phenomenon in 'naturally occurring settings' [10][11]. In other words, for our research, we gain knowledge about how different participants experience the collaborative design process by directly observing their interactions in real-life situations and retrospectively through audio recordings, notes, and photographs. Interviews enable the capture of people's point of view, with reflections and rationalizations. In this study, we undertook semi-structured interviews with some of the participants [12]. By analysing the data gathered, with a plan, act, reflect approach [13], we were able to unpack several aspects of the co-creation process, relevant to strengthening the design choices framework.

Throughout the duration of the project, we conducted a total of nine workshops. Four of these workshops were with 4th-year pre-service teachers, which we call student workshops. Five smaller workshops were conducted with the project group, including museum educators and teachers. We call these group workshops. All of these workshops took place over a period of nine months, starting from when we held our first workshop on the 10th of June 2021, until our final workshop on the 4th of March 2022. This timeline is presented in Figure 1. The group workshops consisted of 8 participants, 3 females and 5 males. These participants represented the Østfold Museums (1), the department of education at the Østfold University College (1), secondary school teachers (2) in Viken county, pre-service teachers (1), and designers (3). The main participants for the student workshops were 51 pre-service teachers who were currently in their 4th year of the teaching studies. All participants of the project provided written consent to participate in the project and all its relevant activities. The participants were informed about how the data would be collected, analysed, and stored, as well as who would have access to the data. The data collection was reported to the Norwegian Agency for Shared Services in Education and Research, a public administrative body under the Ministry of Education and Research.

We will now use the design choices framework to present and give a rich description of the project, before moving further to our findings related to how representational tools made technology matter in our workshops.

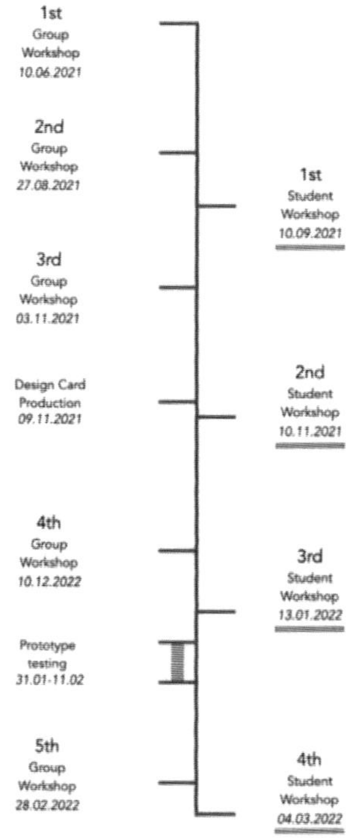

Figure 1. Project Timeline

A. *Design Choices Related to Project Preconditions*

1) *Openness of the Brief*

The goal of the pARTiciPED project is to improve cross sectorial collaborations in schools and more specifically how the school sector and cultural sector collaborate in The Cultural Schoolbag' (TCS), a program set up to provide cultural experiences to Norwegian school children. As the scope was open-ended (focusing on cross sectorial collaborations), the process was also exploratory, enabling us, the design researchers, to create and experiment different types of co-creation methods. There was an additional component to the brief, which was to explore how to create a mixed reality learning experience fitting TCS. Thus, to focus on XR technology throughout the co-creation process, was central.

2) Purpose of Change

In accordance with the open-ended brief, the project team focused on supporting the collaboration between museums and schools, fostering innovation and new ways of thinking through access and exposure to technology. Being exposed to and having participated in co-creation activities, we expected the project members to have a more positive attitude toward collaboration with each other and a better understanding of each other's expertise, needs and priorities. This would in turn serve our purpose of improving the current TCS program.

3) Purpose Scope of Design

As the main purpose of change was to enhance collaboration between multiple organizations, leading to a better TCS program, the scope of design would be on two different levels. One would be to develop co-creation tools and techniques to support cross-sectorial collaboration. The other would be to design digital concepts with complementary teaching curriculum that provided high school students with a more interactive and engaging experience of cultural heritage as part of a TCS activity.

B. Design Choices Related to Participants

1) Diversity in Knowledge

The group participating in the activities represented a high diversity of knowledge: the museum staff had extensive knowledge of cultural heritage including history and artefacts, and the how to disseminate that knowledge; the teachers could bring in their experiences in the field related to the school and teaching processes; the pre-service teachers would also bring in a certain amount of knowledge about teaching, based on their education and previous practical experiences; lastly, the design researchers brought their expertise in design—on the co-creation process and tools applied.

2) Differences in Interests

The design researchers needed to design the process in a way that would support the different interests of the participating stakeholders. The teachers wanted to contribute their expertise in making the experience being designed relevant to the students, the schools and for achieving the learning objectives set out by the government. The teacher-educator's main interest was to provide a relevant learning experience for her students, the pre-service teachers. The pre-service teachers had the primary objective of completing their course in the best way possible. The museum educators were keen to attract the students and make the interested in cultural heritage. The design researchers wanted to develop and experiment new types of co-creation methods.

To accommodate for the negotiation of these interests, we employed various kinds of visual objects and facilitation techniques, for example, mind maps, simulation, scenarios, and idea generation with design cards.

3) Distribution of Power

As the design researchers were the ones at the helm of the project, there was an inherent imbalance of power biased toward the designers, especially since we were choosing the methods to be used. Additionally, the young pre-service teachers who were participating in our workshops, looked up to the more senior teachers, and the museum staff, as authoritative figures. While some authority was needed to conduct the project and its activities, the designers carefully maintained their role as facilitators.

Through participatory design techniques [9], we enabled the project members, and the pre-service teachers participating in our workshops, to contribute with knowledge, ideas, and opinions in different forms. We paid special attention to the power imbalance when designing co-creation activities to engage the participants, regardless of knowledge backgrounds. For example, we introduced various technologies and let the participants try them out to create a common understanding of the possibilities the technologies could provide.

We focused on creating possibilities for teachers and museum staff to share their knowledge and present their ideas. Rather than making creative inputs ourselves, we helped the pre-service teachers perform the co-creation tasks, for instance with the design card game. In the co-creation workshops, the pre-service teachers were asked to reflect on the theme and current challenges from the viewpoint of teachers, to then work on a relatively new concept for a future curriculum, based on the content that was discussed, and the technology that was presented.

C. Design Choices Related to Co-creation Events

1) Types of Co-creation Activities

Our choice of co-creation activities for the project were selected based on the purpose of change and the scope of design. We also considered the knowledge, interest, and power distributions among the participants. The project included a series of workshops leading up to the trial and testing of a prototype learning experience in the field. We conducted two large scale workshops in addition to several smaller workshops within the project team. In the following section, we will focus on the two large workshops.

The first large workshop involved the project members and a class of 51 pre-service teachers, designed to create a shared understanding between the stakeholders. The museum representative set the scene by introducing the theme of Moss town's industrial history. The teacher educators then introduced the current curriculum and teaching goals set for Norwegian secondary schools. In this workshop, we led 3 activities. We first presented current and emerging technologies that are, or could be, used by museums to provide cultural heritage education. Then, we conducted an online 'digital literacy' survey. Lastly, we created a technology probe in the form of a webapp that allows the user to create video, image, or text content and geolocate it on a map. The students used this to create content presenting different parts of the university campus. Through these activities, we were able to learn about how comfortable the pre-service teacher participants were with different forms of technology. At the same time, the participants were exposed to new technology and were given the opportunity to become aware of their possibilities. This was crucial to us, to plan the way forward and reflect on which technologies the pre-service teachers were comfortable with using.

The second large workshop was focused on ideating concepts for a TCS learning experience, and for this, we created a design game using a bespoke deck of design cards. The concepts developed in the workshop were later used to inform the development of a working prototype and tested in the field with secondary school students in the county. All pre-service teachers were allocated practical training / internships for 4 weeks, at various schools. During this period, they would dedicate two classes to run the TCS activity. They had some time beforehand to use the tool themselves and implement it as part of the lessons. We observed six classes across four schools, from the 31st of January to the 11th of February 2022. In some cases, we were able to follow up with interviewing the pre-service teachers conducting the activities, immediately after the class.

2) *Setting for Co-creation*

To encourage the participants to be motivated and productive, we paid careful attention to the physical setting, materials, and atmosphere of the workshops. The pre-service teachers commonly sit in rows, listening to lectures from their professors, so for the indoor part of our workshops, we arranged the tables into groups, where four to six participants could sit around each table. By this, the participants were able to interact with each other much more easily and be active in the creative process. This proved to be particularly useful when doing the design game, as the physical setting not only allowed for better interaction within the group, but also made it easier to arrange the cards on the table, and to draw/sketch their proposals. One activity required the participants to spend time around the campus, to build a virtual museum with one of the technologies that was presented to them. Not only did this provide very valuable results as to how the technology was perceived, but it also created a much more enjoyable experience for the participants, which was apparent from the creative content they created during the activity, and from feedback in the surveys given at the end of the workshop.

D. *Design* Choices Related to Project Results

1) *Outputs of the Project*

Over the course of the workshops, there were several artefacts that were created, and data was collected in various formats including audio recordings, observation notes, and photographs. After the first workshop, we had questionnaire responses regarding technology literacy, and mind maps that the participants had created of the cultural heritage themes related to the selected case for our project (industrial history of the city of Moss). The participants also created a virtual museum/digital campus guide containing content created by the participants, using a purpose-built web-application enabling the creation and publishing of geo-tagged media content. The results and data from this first workshop were analysed, and subsequently informed the design of the second workshop, for which we, the designers also produced a customized deck of design cards. The design cards were also based on a combination of the results from the workshop, and a follow-up workshop conducted within the project team. The design cards themselves, can also be considered as an output of the project.

At the end of the second workshop, each group produced complete concepts for a TCS activity. These were documented and visualized on an A3 sheet of paper and presented to the entire group. Based on these concepts created by the groups, a member of the design team built a web-based tool, that would enable the pre-service teachers to carry out their planned teaching activities. The third workshop, which we had to do digitally, resulted in concrete teaching plans created by the participants, which could then be implemented in the secondary schools that were participating in the project.

Following this third workshop, the design team built a new and improved web-based application with which the pre-service teachers implemented their planned teaching activities. The design team was also able to collect data by visiting the schools, observing the activities, taking notes, and through follow-up interviews with the pre-service teachers.

TABLE I. OVERVIEW OF TECHNOLOGY REPRESENTATION AND CO-CREATION ACTIVITIES

Tools	*Event*	*Goals*	*Participants*
Oral presentation	Group workshop 2	Scoping, Introduction	Pre-service teachers Museum staff
	Student workshop 1	Introduction	
Surveys	Student workshop 1	Understanding participants' familiarity with technology	Pre-service teachers
Images	Group workshop 2	Scoping, Introduction	Pre-service teachers Museum staff
	Student workshop 1	Introduction	
Design Cards	Student workshop 2	Idea generation Concept development	Pre-service teachers
Demonstration	Student workshop 1	Increasing familiarity	Pre-service teachers Museum staff
	Student workshop 3	Increasing familiarity Concept Development	
Interactive prototype	Student workshop 1	Increasing familiarity	Pre-service teachers
	Student workshop 3	Hands-on experience Idea generation	
	Field testing	Identifying pros and cons	

2) *Outcomes of the Project*

In addition to the tangible outputs of the project, there were additional outcomes from each activity as their goals were achieved. This is shown in 0These could also be a basis for change in the way the museums, the teachers, and those in charge of the TCS program collaborate and design future teaching experiences. Regarding technology, there was increased awareness of, and familiarity towards, technology among all participants and an increased willingness to incorporate technology to improve and reform existing processes.

IV. RESULTS

It was clear that the different technology representations had a positive impact on the activities, and consequently on the results. In our first three workshops (two group workshops, one student workshop), we were working to build a shared understanding of each other's expertise, and interests.

A. *Group workshop 1*

Already from the first workshop, we highlighted the technological possibilities. Except for the designers, the members of the workshop initially had little to no concern for the technological aspects of designing a XR learning experience. It was only towards the end of this first introductory workshop that we briefly introduced the possibilities of using Augmented Reality (AR), Virtual Reality (VR) and projection mapping technology to create a learning experience. We proposed the use of these interactive technologies to digitally co-create historical artefacts and sites. Subsequently, the other group members reacted positively, and hinted at the fact that "this could be an interesting way to present cultural heritage to the students". They provided no further input or elaboration, however, which leads us to believe that they had not really thought about how technology could be used to increase engagement and curiosity among the target secondary school students before now.

B. *Group workshop 2*

In the second workshop, which took place at the Moss Town and Industry Museum (Moss, Norway), we again briefly discussed the technological possibilities verbally. Here the goal was to learn about Moss and its history, as well as plan how we would conduct the first workshop with the pre-service teachers. We would also have to decide how to present the technology for the participants at the upcoming workshop, and thus we, the designers would again present several technologies that could be relevant. Interestingly, building on the discussions from the previous workshop, both the museum representative, and one of the teachers discussed how certain technologies could be relevant. The museum representative suggested to create a 'digital assembly line' which would, through VR, allow the students to experience what it was like to work on the assembly line of a factory. A second suggestion from the teacher educator was to use AR technology, so the students could walk around their own towns and place 3D models of historical buildings and artefacts there.

C. *Student workshop 1*

In the third workshop, now involving pre-service teachers, technology was represented in many forms: oral presentation, images, interactive prototype and surveys. Through the different representations of technology, we tried to make the participants familiar with some relevant technologies while at the same time get a better understanding of how familiar the participants already were. In this workshop, we led three technology related activities. We first presented current and emerging technologies could be used by museums to teach about cultural heritage. This was done through an oral presentation, supplemented by images and video of relevant examples. We then conducted an online 'digital literacy' survey. The survey included general questions about the participants' use and familiarity with technology, and specific questions regarding technologies such as VR and AR. Responses from the survey showed a varied level of familiarity with the presented technologies.

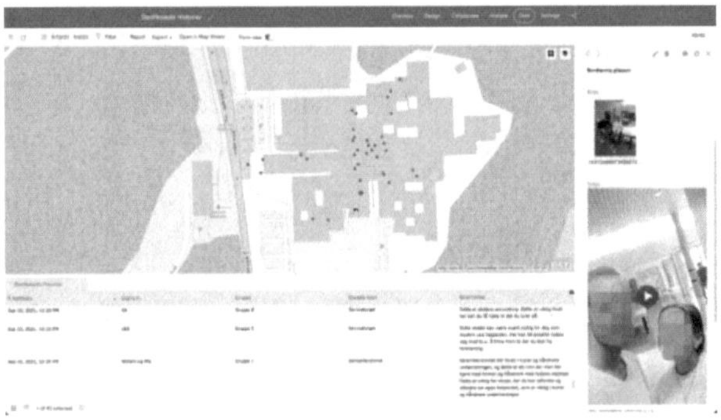

Figure 2. Virtual museum application

We also developed an interactive prototype in the form of a web-based application, that allowed them to create video, image, or text content and automatically incorporate its geographic location from the participants' device. The students essentially created a 'virtual museum', presenting different parts of the university campus, and describing its significance (see Figure 2.

There was a clear positive transformation in the participants' attitudes from when the technologies were presented orally, to when they themselves got to try out the technology. They were much more engaged and seemed to care much more about the entire process. This was apparent when several students exclaimed that initially they "did not quite see how the presented technologies could be relevant in the context of teaching cultural heritage to secondary school students". On the other hand, after the 'virtual museum' activity, most students expressed that "this could be very relevant in the given context". There were many more participants engaging in discussions after the activity, and this was also evident in the subsequent survey responses. They were also excited to share the content they had created in the application and so, due to popular demand, we presented many of their videos in front of the entire group, which also turned out to be quite entertaining.

This understanding was crucial for us designers, to plan the way forward. How could we further incorporate technological aspects in our future co-design activities, while considering the participants' familiarity with those technologies?

D. *Student workshop 2*

In this workshop, building on our previous activities, we needed a way to represent technology that would facilitate brainstorming and creativity. We chose to organize a design game using a bespoke set of design cards. Technology was one of the key categories in the deck. We were able to identify four relevant categories that needed to be addressed when creating a TCS activity. These were the following: things, requirements, actions, and technology. We identified nine 'things' that were relevant to Moss town's industrial history, thirteen 'requirements' from a pedagogical point of view, ten 'technologies' that could be used and twelve 'actions' that could be encouraged. Each card had a title, colour code indicating the category, and a relevant image in the background that provided a visual cue to the title.

Figure 3. Student Workshop 2 – Design Cards

We facilitated the design game to let participants design their ideal concepts (see Figure 3. Using the different categories of cards, the pre-service teachers were able to sketch three concepts. In a second round, participants were asked to identify and select the good parts from all three concepts and design a final concept that would be presented to the class. Technology became the cornerstone of all the concepts that were presented. 9 of the 11 groups in the workshop included some form of technology as a central part of their proposals, with most incorporating several technologies as evident in Figure 4. The example to the left proposed using AR to recreate important historical figures. The example to the right proposes the use of maps and simulation games to get acquainted with the cultural heritage and history, and then create content about some historic event that can be projected Figure 4.

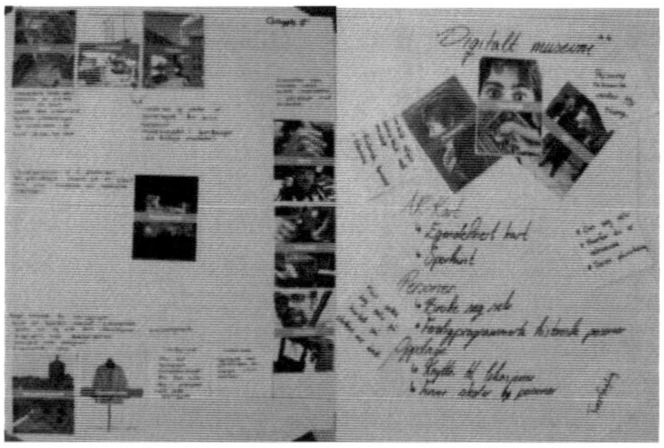

Figure 4. Workshop 2 concept examples, incorporating AR, projection mapping, maps, and simlation games as technological components

E. Student Workshop 3

This workshop was conducted online due to COVID-19 restrictions. We created a demo toolkit in the form of an AR app. This was both a demonstration of the technology, but also allowed the participants to try it out. The goal of this workshop was to conceptualise and plan a larger activity for secondary school students based on the available technology. Participants were to incorporate this demo app into a concreate TCS activity. The app was created using Facebook's Spark AR. The pre-service teachers created a lesson plan including how they would introduce the information about Moss town's industrial history, how they would introduce the toolkit, and how they would incorporate the activities using the toolkit into the learning activity. Again, the app was central to the teaching plans they all made.

F. Field testing

The goal of this activity was to evaluate the outcomes of the previous workshops in the real world, and so, we needed to provide a working technological artefact that could be given to the secondary school students to use. Based on the results of workshop 3, we built a more complete version of the AR tool in the form of a web-based application. The application allowed the students to take pictures of themselves, use filters to apply historical clothing (e.g., uniforms) to the pictures, and place that composite image onto a historical background. The complete image was then used as the basis for more discussions in the class. The secondary school students enjoyed using the application, uploading pictures, putting on filters, and writing stories about what they had made (Figure 5.

Figure 5. Testing web app in secondary schools

As the students were introduced to the web-application, there was increased discussion and dialog between the students and the teachers, as well as among the students. Some students used their mobile phones while some used tablet devices provided by the school. Some groups were also allowed to go out of the classroom to create their content. They were being physically active, running around, posing for the pictures, and applying a variety of filters and background images. Subsequently they discussed what backstory they had conceived to create their final images. One group, for example, placed their own images in front of a group of factory workers, and used that as a basis to discuss the poor working conditions at the time, how the workers would look after each other, and how they later formed unions. Some groups incorporated our application into a larger workflow consisting of other tools they had on their computers. For example, after having generated an image using our tool, some groups further placed that image into a PowerPoint presentation, added more text, recorded audio to narrate their story, and finally combined all of this to present to the class. How the students were able to make this tool their own, and use it creatively in combination with other tools, was a clear signal of how introducing new technology, can lead to solutions and concepts that might not have been conceived otherwise.

G. *Student Workshop 4*

Following the field testing, we had a final workshop with the pre-service teachers. The goal of this workshop was to reflect on the entire co-creation process, the outputs, and the final application in schools. We did not introduce any new technology, nor did we have any specific part of the workshop dedicated to technology. By now, technology had been applied to the problem, informed the concepts that were developed, and constrained the activities that were carried out in the field. However, the participants were given a final chance to design a teaching activity based on their experiences from the field. Surprisingly, almost all groups had very similar concepts, which resembled the activities they had just conducted in the field and proposed minor improvements to how the technology should be used.

H. *Summary*

From the first to the final workshop, we used several forms of representation to present and involve technology. Initially, when the brief was relatively open, we presented different technologies in a more general way through simple representations such as images, through surveys and orally. This allowed us to gain an understanding of the participants' familiarity with different technologies (and technology in general), spark curiosity among the workshop participants, and allowed them to imagine new possibilities involving the use of technologies. We also presented a simple working prototype (virtual museum application), which allowed the participants to become more familiar with AR, and thus become more comfortable the application. Participants started to discuss how the technology could be relevant to the larger problem we were trying to address.

To facilitate idea and concept generation, we incorporated technology in the form of design cards. This allowed the participants to be part of a creative process combining their budding teaching expertise with their newfound knowledge of different technologies, resulting in innovative and realizable concepts. As the concepts became more certain, and context-specific, we could then create high-fidelity technology probes to be used in the real world, and incorporated into larger, more complete teaching/learning activities. As these activities were conducted in secondary schools all over the region, we could also reflect on the pros and cons of those activities, and how they could be improved.

In the final student workshop, following a period of field testing, we also noticed that after having used the high-fidelity probes, it was difficult for the participants to think creatively, as their thinking was very constrained by familiarity with the application they had used. It thus became clear that how the technology is represented matters greatly for what outcomes are achieved in the co-creation process. Low-fidelity, general representations of technology provided the opportunity for creativity and innovation, while high-fidelity representations were more useful for critique and improvements. This leads us to discussing why technology and its representation is also an important design choice.

V. DISCUSSION

What was apparent from all the activities in the different stages of the project was that including an appropriate representation of technology in the right stage of the co-creation process, directly impacted the results of each activity as well as the entire process. We observed three major effects of including a technological aspect throughout our co-design activities.

First and foremost, there was a clear increase in engagement when the workshop participants were introduced to novel technologies and their capabilities. The discussions became more active, more questions were asked, and more suggestions were offered.

Secondly, by being able to interact with, and try out the technology themselves, initially on a smaller scale, the participants gained a level of mastery they could use as a resource later in the process.

Finally, having gotten a good understanding of the technological possibilities, the participants were able to suggest realistic and innovative concepts that incorporated the technology in relevant and beneficial ways.

Judging from the positive impact of technology in the co-creation process, we believe 'representation of technology' should be an additional design choice that needs to be considered when planning co-creation projects. We see that identifying technological possibilities can help with several aspects of Lee et al's [4] design choices framework.

- To help define the *scope of design* as the choice of technology will both limit, and guide it;
- balance the *distribution of power* by familiarizing all participants with the technology;
- enhance *activities* and *settings for co-creation* by providing supportive tools for co-creating with technology;
- help generate *outputs of the project,* as technology is both the means and goals in many co-creation projects; and finally,
- contribute to a new mindset among the participants that is more aware and positive to technology, a first step towards becoming lasting *outcomes of the project* activities.

It must be noted, however, that the choice of technology and its representation must be appropriate to the stage of co-creation, and in accordance to how familiar the project participants are with the technology. One of the challenges in any co-creation or indeed in all co-anything processes is mutual learning [13] and mutual understanding. A shared or common understanding of possibilities, limitations and challenges is the goal with any co-anything processes. At the same time there must be room for respect and wonder about what unique understanding and engagement there is from the different stakeholders.

One approach to make representations of diverse range of technologies is to invoke the concept of familiarity. We are familiar with the tools, technologies, and environment we live in. By focusing on familiarity, we build on people's and user's pre-existing involvement, understanding and relationship of the "everyday" world, such as naive physics (up, down), our own bodies and the surrounding place, or things we use in everyday life. The familiarity concept is introduced by Turner [13] to HCI and inspired by other concepts such as the use of metaphors, analogies, similarities and resemblances. The familiar is often what we are comfortable and safe with. What we are unfamiliar with, are often things that we do not engage with, have no skill or understanding of and are foreign to. To move from something that is unfamiliar and making it familiar is what we often do when learning something "new", and hence the concept is used in pedagogies [14].

One way to operationalize the concept of familiarity in the context of representing technologies and tools is to investigate the three underlying human phenomena of: Understanding of, engagement with and relationship in. In what way do you understand this tool in use? In what way are you engaged or involved with it? And what kind of relationship do you have with this technology or tool in your everyday life? This may be strong indicators of degrees of familiarity with tools and technologies. And learning about the familiarity of tools and technologies among the various stakeholders might then be applied and used when representing technologies and tools in co-design processes that make sense and that engage the participants.

Through such engaging co-design processes, the relevant stakeholders can become active participants contributing to a variety of different design goals, such as: design for experiencing, design for emotion, design for interacting, design for sustainability, design for serving, or design for transforming [3]. Familiarity with technology can first and foremost be a resource, which can be a building block for effective co-creation, as we have discussed in reference to the design choices framework [4]. Through its understanding, designers can suggest the right representations of technology, at the right stages of the co-creation process, with the right participants. Additionally, as the co-creation process progresses, exposure, interaction, and engagement with different representations of technology can help build this familiarity even further, leading to even more insightful participation, better design choices and more innovative and relevant outcomes of co-creation.

VI. Conclusion

Technology matters, as does the practice of co-creation, especially when addressing the increasingly complex challenges of today's society. We have found that using different representations of technology can significantly enhance co-creation processes and improve the utility of existing frameworks, such as the design choices framework. By representing technology through images, demos, and prototypes, we have seen a clear and positive impact on participant engagement and collaboration. We believe that further exploration and experimentation in the use of technology in co-creation projects can help to create more inclusive and equitable design processes.

Acknowledgment

Thanks to all the wonderful participants in schools, museums, and universities!

References

[1] S. B. Page, M. M. Stone, J. M. Bryson, and B. C. Crosby, "Public Value Creation by Cross-Sector Collaborations: a Framework and Challenges of Assessment: Public Value Creation by Cross-Sector Collaborations," *Public Admin*, vol. 93, no. 3, pp. 715–732, Sep. 2015, doi: 10.1111/padm.12161.

[2] K. Halskov and P. Dalsgård, "Inspiration card workshops," in *Proceedings of the 6th ACM conference on Designing Interactive systems - DIS '06*, University Park, PA, USA, 2006, p. 2. doi: 10.1145/1142405.1142409.

[3] E. B.-N. Sanders and P. J. Stappers, "Co-creation and the new landscapes of design," *CoDesign*, vol. 4, no. 1, pp. 5–18, Mar. 2008, doi: 10.1080/15710880701875068.

[4] J. Lee, M. Jaatinen, A. Salmi, T. Mattelmäki, R. Smeds, and M. Holopainen, "Design choices framework for co-creation projects," International Journal of Design [Online], vol. 12, no. 2, 2018.

[5] V. Lember, "The Increasing Role of Digital Technologies in Co-Production and Co-Creation," in *Co-Production and Co-Creation*, 1st ed.New York: Routledge, 2018, pp. 115–127.

[6] E. Bjögvinsson, P. Ehn, and P.-A. Hillgren, "Design Things and Design Thinking: Contemporary Participatory Design Challenges," *Design Issues*, vol. 28, no. 3, pp. 101–116, Jul. 2012, doi: 10.1162/DESI_a_00165.

[7] K. Bødker, F. Kensing, and J. Simonsen, "Participatory Design in Information Systems Development".T. Binder, Computer Professionals for Social Responsibility, and Association for Computing Machinery, Eds., *Proceedings of the Participation Design Conference: Malmö, Sweden, 23 - 25 June, 2002*. Palo Alto, Calif: Computer Professionals for Social Responsibility, 2002.

[8] E. Brandt and J. Messeter, "Facilitating collaboration through design games," in *Proceedings of the eighth conference on Participatory design: Artful integration: interweaving media, materials and practices - Volume 1*, New York, NY, USA, Jul. 2004, pp. 121–131. doi: 10.1145/1011870.1011885.

[9] "Eva Brandt. 2006. Designing exploratory design games: a framework for participation in Participatory Design? In Proceedings of the ninth conference on Participatory design: Expanding boundaries in design - Volume 1 (PDC '06). Association for Computing Machinery, New York, NY, USA, 57–66. DOI:https://doi.org/10.1145/1147261.1147271".

[10] M. Crang and I. Cook, *Doing ethnographies*. Los Angeles: SAGE, 2007.

[11] J. Lazar, J. H. Feng, and H. Hochheiser, *Research methods in human-computer interaction*, Second edition. Cambridge, MA: Elsevier, Morgan Kaufmann Publishers, 2017.

[12] P. Checkland and S. Holwell, "Action Research," in Information Systems Action Research, N. Kock, Ed., in Integrated Series in Information Systems, vol. 13. Boston, MA: Springer US, 2007, pp. 3–17. doi: 10.1007/978-0-387-36060-7_1.

[13] P. Turner, "Being-with: A study of familiarity," *Interacting with Computers*, vol. 20, no. 4–5, pp. 447–454, Sep. 2008, doi: 10.1016/j.intcom.2008.04.002.

[14] R. Parker-Rees, "Liking to be liked: imitation, familiarity and pedagogy in the first years of life," *Early Years*, vol. 27, no. 1, pp. 3–17, Mar. 2007, doi: 10.1080/09575140601135072.

Participatory Design Fictions: Supporting Ethical Awareness in the Digitalisation of Smart Cities' Critical Infrastructure

Joakim Karlsen, Klaudia Carcani, Susanne Koch Stigberg
Department of Computer Science and Communication,
Faculty of Computer Science, Engineering and Economics
Østfold University College
1757 Halden, Norway
{joakim.karlsen, klaudia.carcani, susanne.k.stigberg}@hiof.no

Abstract—**This paper investigates participatory design fictions as a method to involve citizens in the digitalisation of smart city critical infrastructures. By this we contribute to the topic raised by the call for papers to ACHI-COCREATE, to investigate how to make processes of digitalisation accessible to everyone. Based on the observations in one workshop organized for this purpose in a project aiming to install digital water meters in a mid-sized Norwegian city, we find that that participatory design fictions show promise in supporting citizen participation and the discussion of ethical considerations of making cities smarter with the help of Information and Communications Technologies (ICT). We find that it is important to prepare design fictions that heed the basics of storytelling as applied in journalism, to make the story both relevant and provoking. Further, we find that if city officials with professional knowledge of the project at hand participates, more rules of engagement and prepping is needed to make sure that they leave enough room for speculation. Even though the citizens participating in the workshop had little knowledge of digital water meters beforehand, the design fictions enabled them to quickly identify ethical concerns with how the data from these could potentially be misused.**

Keywords- design fiction; smart cities; participatory design.

I. INTRODUCTION

In the last decades, the development of Information and Communications Technology (ICT) is changing our cities. Machine learning, the Internet of Things (IoT), Artificial Intelligence (AI) are promising to make our cities smarter [1]. From a technology perspective, 'a smart city is considered a city with a high presence of ICT applied to critical infrastructure components and services' [2]. The digitalisation of critical infrastructures is opening opportunities for better services for the community and its citizens, but at the same time raises concerns regarding an increased possibility for monitoring and observing citizens' behaviours. Involving people in discussing issues concerning them is a core democratic value, which should also be at the centre of smart city projects. Citizens do not have a clear picture of the opportunities, challenges, and consequences of introducing smart city technologies. While some benefits are predicted from the start, others take shape in use. It would be in both citizens and local authorities benefit to find ways to discuss how smart city technologies can improve the quality of living and at the same time negotiate how risks of such infrastructures should be mitigated.

Participatory Design (PD) is a field of research which investigates how users' can be involved in the design of technologies meant for them [3]. PD has promoted citizens' genuine participation in the discussion, design, and envisioning of new ICT solutions and services. By involving citizens and giving them a voice, local authorities can make environments and technologies more useful and useable. To this end, Ruiz presents a participatory governance model aiming to establish a sustainable development path for the design and implementation of public services delivered through IoT in smart cities [4]. Bratteteig and Wagner discuss how citizens have been involved in design activities for urban planning [5]. There is a lack of studies, however, regarding citizens' involvement in discussing possible upgrades in critical infrastructures to achieve smarter cities. Thus, in this paper, we present a study of using a PD approach, utilizing design fictions, to enable citizens in the discussion of digitalizing of critical infrastructure – more specifically, the water supply system. By this, we contribute to the topic raised by the call for papers to ACHI-COCREATE, to investigate how to make processes of digitalisation accessible to everyone.

In the following, we initially present the theoretical grounds for this work. Then, we describe the case and present our findings concerning citizens participation in the workshop. After a discussion of these findings, we conclude by offering some valuable insights on the use of participatory design fictions to reinforce smart city initiatives that strive to digitally transform critical infrastructures in a responsible and empathetic manner.

II. THEORY

To ground the work theoretically, we initially need to clarify how we conceptualize Critical Infrastructure (CI). CI is a common term used at the political level to refer to lifeline systems, which greatly influence public welfare and economic prosperity [6]. CI's include energy, telecommunication and ICT networks, water, food and agriculture, healthcare and public health, financial systems, civil administration, public, legal order and safety, national monuments and icons, commercial facilities, critical manufacturing, and the defence industry base [7].

Decision making in governing CI's has been the domain of policy makers and within governmental settings [8]. We argue that citizens should be involved in the discussion of evolving CI's and by this raise ethical considerations and awareness in the population [9]. In rich and democratic countries, the legal right of access to government information based on openness and accountability has been established decades ago, but sometimes such rights are eclipsed in favour of competing government interests [10]. The involvement of citizens in the development of CIs has been mostly explored in relation to the concept of smart cities. Smart cities have been defined as cities that promote the digitalisation of CIs to improve citizens quality of life. According to Albino et al. [1], the main themes that has been addressed when citizens has been involved in the design of CIs for smart cities is management of common resources [8], environmental awareness and sustainability [11], safety and privacy [11]–[13].

A. Participatory Design

PD is an approach that provides a framework for technology development with a focus on securing participation from all involved parties in all parts of the process [12]. PD stands by a set of principles that define the field [13]. A core principle is to secure democratic practices by equalizing power and to give everyone a voice. Another one is to foster mutual learning in building new knowledge and values by finding ways of working that emphasize engagement, expressiveness, negotiation, and problem solving. An aim in this is to support the co-creation of alternative visions or future scenarios involving the technologies and services addressed. To enable mutual learning and envisioning alternatives, adequate tools and techniques are needed. PD can be described as a family of design practices that come with a variety of toolboxes. Tools and techniques are commonly adapted, combined and extended and should be appropriated to the design [14]. In the case of involvement of citizens in developing CI's, the principle of mutual learning and building alternative visions becomes particularly challenging. Thus, we investigate how participatory design fiction could enable citizens to actively participate in the process.

B. Participatory Design Fiction

In PD, scenario based techniques are commonly used. Brandt et al. [14] discuss the role that scenario-based design has in enabling envisioning future alternatives as well as in reflection and learning [15]. Using storytelling and critical design as resources, design fiction is a design practice that aims to explore and critique possible futures [14] by creating speculative and often provocative scenarios told using designed objects. It is a way of facilitating and promoting debates as explained by the futurist Scott Smith: '... design fiction as a communication and social object creates interactions and dialogues around futures that were missing before. It helps make it real enough for people that you can have a meaningful conversation with' [15]. Design fiction has been used in PD for enabling participants engagement when it comes to cases of complex technologies [16], [17] or vulnerable user groups [18], [19]. Design fiction is built on fictional stories that represent the creation and construction of possible future worlds, in relation to the actual world [20] and they present possible worlds that have specific accessibility criteria [21].

Muller and Liao [16] have categorised four types of design fiction that can be employed in PD to envision future AI technologies.

- Fictions as probes to elicit user needs by asking questions to users regarding values they perceive in the story or experience.
- Fictions as theatre where users are encouraged to change the story to critique and change a proposed user experience.
- Fictions as participatory constructions where users are encouraged to write the stories themselves by introducing a narrative transformation.
- Fictions as group co-creations where the users are encouraged as a group to engage in hands on activities that contribute to co-creation of stories.

In the following, we explore design fictions that combine elements of all four of these categories, attesting to the dynamic, malleable, and playful properties of the method. The emphasis in our case will be design fictions as a door opener to democratic, open, and emergent discussions of digitalizing CIs in smart city projects.

III. Method

In the following, we will describe how we have collected and analysed data from a workshop organized to shed light on how participatory design fictions can be used to involve citizens in the development of CIs. The workshop was part of a larger project aiming to install water meters with real-time data sensors in every household in a mid-sized city in Norway, to monitor, regulate and tax water consumption (the smart water project). The outcomes of the increased visibility of water consumption on the level of individual households may be positive or negative for citizens, but until this study, they had not been involved in the discussion. The aim of our research was to give the citizens a voice and a chance to be heard, regarding the further digitalisation of the city's water system. The local authorities were interested in understanding the citizens' perspectives on the potential opportunities and threats presented by the installation of such water meters and welcomed the research initiative. They valued the opportunity to go beyond traditional methods like surveys and focus groups, to enable genuine, comprehensive, and accountable citizen involvement in the project.

The workshop brought together citizens and key stakeholders from the city administration who had expertise in the smart water project. Design fictions were created to raise the three key themes related to smart city development, as presented in the literature: safety, sustainability, and privacy. The workshop was organised by a team consisting of a representative from the city, an expert in the field of water infrastructure and digitalisation and three PD experts (the authors of this paper). To ensure broad citizen participation in the workshop, the city issued an open call on their website promising a compensation of 500 NOK for participating in the workshop. The call was designed to reach a diverse cross-section of the population, and citizens were asked to provide information on their age, gender, education level, and area of residence. This helped us select a group that represented the city's population and ensured that multiple perspectives were included in the workshop. In total, 19 citizens responded to the call. Based on the inclusion criteria and a first come first served approach, we selected 12 participants who met the desired demographic characteristics.

The workshop lasted for 1,5 hours and the participants were divided into three groups. Each group was seated at a round table together with a representative from the city with expert knowledge related to the smart water project (see in Figure 4). Participants were equipped with printed materials and one of the PD experts moderated the workshop by guiding the groups through the design fiction scenarios. We collected audio recordings from each table and all the material outputs made. While city experts and citizens participated in the workshop, representing different perspectives in the project, the PD experts took the role of PD facilitators, preparing and moderating the workshop.

To analyse the data collected during the workshop, we conducted an inductive thematic analysis of the audio recordings and the created outputs individually. Afterwards, we discussed and compared our coding of the data related to each category. We identified recurring themes and patterns in the data to gain a deeper understanding of the perspectives and experiences of the workshop participants. We developed thematic maps [22] for each category and discrepancies in the coding were discussed and resolved. To ensure anonymity, the groups' voice recordings were assigned pseudonyms, as detailed in Table 1.

TABLE I. PARTICIPANT PSEUDONYMS USED FOR CODING

Group One	Group Two	Group Three
Roger (expert)	Hans (expert)	Camilla (expert)
Per	Odd	Lise
Leif	Anne	Gunhild
Trine	Kari	Ahmed

A. *Design Fiction in practice*

In the workshop, participants explored three main themes, as suggested by Albino et al. [1], in our case, related to the introduction of digital water meters:

- *Security:* The data generated from digital water meters can help citizens to increase the safety of their households by controlling water leaks and misuse.
- *Sustainability:* Water is a shared and scarce resource raising the dilemma of balancing individual water needs with the need of the whole community served by the water system.
- *Privacy:* Water meters can monitor and record detailed data of citizens' water usage. The usage of IoT systems in homes has been discussed closely to security and privacy issues [23]– [25].

The overall aim of the workshop was to raise citizen's awareness of and engagement with these themes by bespoke design fictions. In the following, we present each fiction with accompanying questions and tasks.

1) Security

This design fiction proposes how monitoring water consumption can provide security for values and property in the city. We tell a story about how a citizen suddenly receives a SMS from the city stating that there probably is a water leak at in their home (shown in Figure 1). The participants get a copy of the SMS and must decide how this should be handled.

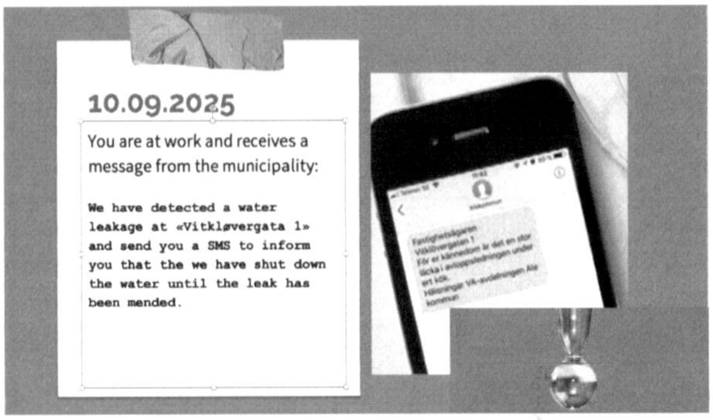

Figure 1. Security design fiction scenario

Questions based on the scenario:

- What should happen if digital water meters detect a water leak?
- Should there be a service so residents can request that the water be turned off?
- How do residents and the city agree that the problem has been solved?
- Complete the sentence: If the digital water meter detects a possible water leakage…

2) Managing scarce resources

This design fiction raises how sustainable water consumption needs to be governed by the city in a situation with severe water shortage during an unusually hot summer (see Figure 2). The participants are issued a "watering fine" by the city and a paper copy of the local regulations. Their challenge is to revise the regulations by removing, modifying, or adding new rules, giving them an opportunity to share their thoughts on sustainability and incorporate them into applicable regulations.

Questions based on the scenario:

- What does it mean to waste water?
- How can digital water meters reduce water use?
- How should the administrative regulations be adapted when new water meters are introduced?

3) Privacy

This design fiction presents a scenario where detailed data from the digital water meters might be misused by the city. A household has been put in a COVID-19 quarantine but due to low water consumption, the city contacts the household by phone to check that the quarantine is being properly observed.

Figure 2. Sustainability design fiction scenario

The participants receive a bill with a detailed overview of the household's water consumption, broken down into days. They are tasked with discussing how this information may possibly be used / misused as illustrated in Figure 3. They can then delete, change, or add to the bill based on what they come up with.

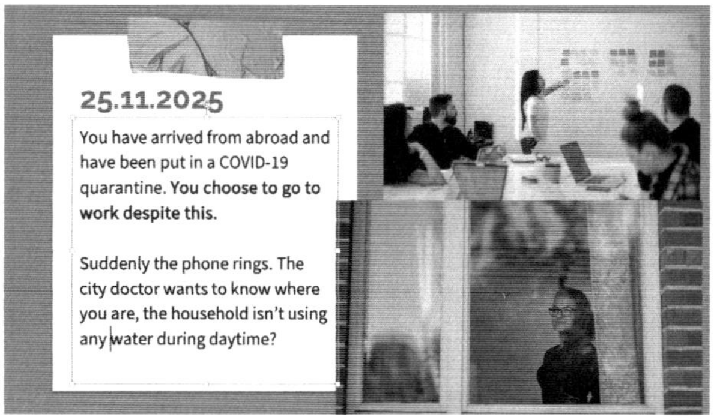

Figure 3. Privacy design fiction scenario

Questions based on the scenario:

- How do you want your data to be handled and stored?
- Who should have access to your data?
- What information are you interested in?
- How may your data be used or misused?

IV. RESULTS

The analysis of the sayings and doings of each group participating in the workshop, will inform the further development of participatory design fictions as a method with the potential to secure citizen involvement in the development of critical smart city infrastructures. Further, the analysis reveals insights into how this format gave the citizens support in identifying and discussing ethical concerns with future upgrades of CI's. In the following, we will relate our findings according to how the provided design fictions secured participation and supported the discussion of ethical concerns. To be able to assess the degree of citizen participation we have looked closer at how the groups: came up with ideas, agreed on which ideas where worth promoting, and whether and how they came up with alternative visions regarding the use of digital water meters that diverged from the ones proposed by the scenarios.

Figure 4. Groups discussing scenarios for sustainable water usage

A. Group One

The group came up with few ideas and the expert contributed with most of the answers to the questions worked on. Two of the citizens, Per and Leif, offered some reflections, often on related but somewhat off topics that they were interested in (still concerning water usage). But every time they started discussing the scenarios from their viewpoints, they were broken off by the expert. The repeated breakdowns of the group dialogue led to a lack of engagement from Per and Leif after a while. Trine kept mostly quiet, but engaged a few times, mostly to ask questions. When the time came to prepare the summaries and agreeing on what to promote to the plenary session, the expert reiterated his initial answers and asked whether all agreed, answered by silence or small acknowledgments from the group. To come up with alternative visions regarding the use of digital water in the future, the citizens explored some initial ideas, but were quickly interrupted by the expert. The expert went so far as to undermine scenario three from the outset, saying that it was unrealistic due to current GDPR regulations. He changed his mind after the initial reaction, and tried to initiate and support further discussion, but then the group had lost interest and started looking at their watches.

The group was not able to speculate alternative futures but was able to articulate ethical concerns during the workshop related to all three scenarios. Per and Leif seemed to be acutely aware of questions concerning privacy and wanted full control of the detailed data from the water meters. They wanted to be in the loop when leakage was discovered, receiving a private message (from the meter) and to then to get hold of a plumber themselves. Scenario three was therefore rejected by Per and Leif outright due to their privacy concerns. Trine, however, thought the detailed data capture was ok (as represented by the bill), and was less concerned by how the data could be misused. She asked the expert whether she was allowed to take this position. The most engaged discussion was about scenario two, when they considered how water should be governed in times of scarcity. They couldn't quite decide whether water should be turned off remotely by the city for households overusing water. They seemed to like the idea that overuse was punished fairly, but also indicated some discomfort with the surveillance needed to enforce this.

B. Group Two

All group members contributed to answering the questions given in the three scenarios and came up with ideas during the workshop. In general, the group was quick to address and discuss the questions asked for each scenario – leading to the expert taking initiative to leave the scenario and interview the group about water meters in general. When it came to agreeing, it was clear that the expert made the final decisions on what could be considered good answers to the questions, recognizable in how he summarized the group's discussions in the plenary sessions. He presented the ideas he had come up with earlier in the discussions – seemingly to reach the other two groups with his reflections and insights. With one exception though, when it came to the idea that house owners should be given a more elaborate consent form or contract when installing water meters – for instance to give the city the rights to turn off the water when detecting a leakage or to give the local health provider access when needed. This suggestion is also an example of how they came up with alternative visions of future use of the water meters, than the ones proposed by the scenarios. Another example is how Anne didn't want to install the new water meter because of fear of radiation (she didn't have an electricity meter either). She gained little understanding from the group, and when suggesting this in the plenary session, the expert in group one explained the concern away. In general, the group didn't speculate too much and kept close to the realities offered by the expert (being the project leader for the smart water project).

As in group one the design fictions raised ethical considerations in the discussions among the group members. Anne was very clear that any unauthorized use of data from the water meters was misuse:

> If the head doctor in city had called me and said, where are you? You are not using water! Then I would be extremely pissed! That's surveillance, that must become illegal. #Anne

The rest of the group agreed. She also brought up several times that any data use should be made explicit in a written agreement between the city and the house owner. Further, how the relevant rules and regulations should be made accessible and understandable to all citizens. When it came to using water meters to monitor and restrict water use in times of scarcity, Anne and Kari were open to this use, and didn't really discuss the privacy dilemma raised by this.

C. Group Three

When it came to coming up with ideas in the group, the expert provided the other participants with information related to the project, that she saw as important to know to be able to discuss the questions. She invited the other participants to share their opinions and ideas, something all the participants did. They listened to each other's ideas and agreed on a common definition of what it meant to waste water: "If someone wouldn't use the water if they had to pay for it, then they are wasting water". Even if the expert talked the most, the group reached agreement on what the answers to the questions should be. The citizens all participated equally, focusing on different aspects of the scenarios. Gunhild highlighted aspects related to costs. Lise focused on how she would like to get more support in the process and Ahmed saw a possibility for a fairer solution. The expert did a good job to summarize and present the groups opinions and ideas in the plenary sessions, not only her own. The group came up with several alternative down-to-earth visions of future use of the water meters. They thought that it was ok to use water for gardening, but that one should pay for the water. They wished for more support from the city resolving problems with e.g., water leakages. They suggested a support line and someone that can come home and discuss different solutions with them.

The group discussed several ethical concerns raised by each of the three scenarios presented. During the water leakage scenario, Gunhild emphasized the importance of identifying the party responsible for fixing the leakage, exemplified by a previous dispute between the municipality and a homeowner. The group agreed that digital water meters should be made mandatory to ensure a fair use for all citizens. However, they recognized the need for clear regulations outlining ownership and servicing of the devices, as well as how data collected from them could be utilized in a transparent way by the municipality and other stakeholders. In addition, they advocated for diverse communication channels between citizens and the municipality such as email, website, mobile app and telephone to enable accessibility for all.

D. All groups

1) Securing participation

a) Coming up with ideas

How the groups generated and promoted ideas differed between them and we see the expert's role understanding as an important factor to explain this. The expert in group three actively invited participants to come up with ideas. In contrast, the expert in group one decided which ideas were feasible and which were not. In general, most of the participants engaged in the discussions and were able to formulate opinions on the themes brought up by the design fictions. There were two participants, however, one in group one and one in group two, who mostly listened and did not speak much.

b) Agreeing

The experts understanding of his / her own role in the discussions to a large degree influenced the power dynamics in the group. The expert in group three summed up the group's findings covering all contributions. This contrasted with how both Roger and Hans summed up their group's discussion relating their own understanding of the topics at hand.

c) Coming up with alternative visions

All three groups came up with concrete suggestions for each design fiction scenario. The solutions were modest and not as radical as we might have hoped. Participants highlighted that they needed more guidance to understand the changes implied by upgrading the water infrastructure. Further, they suggested that they should be able to choose alternative services both for monitoring water and communication between them and the city. Finally, participants highlighted that is important to be transparent who owns and services the digital water meters and how their data is used by the city and possibly other stakeholders.

2) Raising ethical concerns.

The overarching ethical concern brought up in the discussions in all three groups, was how data from the new digital water meters trigger privacy concerns. It seems that all group members, including the experts, were acutely aware of privacy regulations (i.e., GDPR) and didn't want to question these in general. When the groups discussed questions of security and sustainability, however, dilemmas pitting privacy regulations against conceived utility surfaced. The groups were willing to give consent to use data to take care of their properties and health on a case-by-case basis. Further, they considered loosening privacy concerns and lessening the need for informed consent to stop wasteful use of water in times of acute shortages.

V. DISCUSSION

The point of using Design Fictions as method when involving citizens in the project of installing digital water meters was to 1) make digital water meters and the infrastructure they are part of visible, relevant and provoking to the participants, 2) to encourage critical reflections and discussions where all stakeholders could take part and have their voices heard, 3) to envision alternate futures by working out how current policies and regulation should be updated to accommodate "smart" use of the opportunities the digital water meters embody and of course to mitigate negative consequences and lastly 4) to shed light on how participatory design fiction could raise ethical concerns among citizens experiencing them. We will now discuss whether the participatory design fiction method worked as expected and what we learned from applying the method for these purposes?

First, we see how our application of the method made the digital water meters and the infrastructure they are part of visible, relevant, and somewhat provoking to the participants. It created a common ground for discussing the possible consequences of a not yet implemented smart city technology. The stories and materials provided seemed to both initiate and to some degree sustain discussions in all three groups. All three scenarios were taken up in discussions and when the groups had come to an end point on an issue, they came back to the task by looking at the provided materials. A possible takeaway from this is that it is important to use time on developing the scenarios beforehand, so they communicate well. We believe it is crucial for designers, wanting to use this method to heed the basics of storytelling as applied in journalism, to make the stories both relevant and provoking.

Second, while the scenarios encouraged critical reflections and discussions where most of the participants took part, they didn't provide enough support for equalizing power relations between citizens and experts in the workshop. In two of the three groups the citizens suggestions were to a large degree corrected or ignored by the expert in the group. Based on this finding, we believe the method should be updated with more rules when it comes to turn taking and more specific instructions for how the contributions should captured and summarized for each scenario. The many breakdowns in the budding speculative discussions between the citizens could have been avoided with clearer rules of engagement.

Third, the proposed visions of alternative futures in the workshop were rather down to earth and close to what will most likely be implemented in the future. We believe this to be a direct consequence of how the experts performed their role in the workshop. All three were quick to provide facts from the project when the citizens started speculating. A possible takeaway from this is that we should have prepared the experts beforehand, to give them a better understanding of their role in the workshop. We should have asked them to play with the scenario a while longer, before providing the facts (with its many constraints), for the sake of provoking more lively discussions. One example is how they could have suggested the opportunities to regulate water consumption from installing smart water meters, that can't be realized due to privacy regulation.

Lastly, we found that participatory design fictions as applied in the smart water workshop, created a space for citizens to reflect and discuss their ethical concerns and have most likely raised their awareness of these issues further. Participatory Design (PD) has from the start taken an ethical stance, facilitating for such spaces [26], creating regular venues to discuss values [27]. Adding design fictions to the toolbox of PD gives PD practitioners more opportunities to make ethical dilemmas with future smart city technologies relevant and available to citizens. The best evidence from the workshop was how scenarios implying misuse of data from smart water meters, immediately triggered discussions of privacy concerns with the new capabilities offered by the proposed technology.

VI. CONCLUSION AND FUTURE WORK

In this paper, we have explored participatory design fictions as a method to involve citizens in processes of digitalizing critical infrastructures. Based on a workshop to engage citizens in upgrading the water system with digital smart water meters in a mid-sized city in Norway, we find the method promising. It enabled the citizens to discuss multiple aspects of the suggested upgrade, concerning security, sustainability and privacy. We find that we need to strengthen the method further, however, by adding some more rules of engagement and by prepping participating experts beforehand. The main challenge is to move the discussions beyond the easily observable facts and political correctness and towards addressing alternative and maybe thought-provoking visions of the future.

Acknowledgment

We would like to thank everyone who helped organize and who participated in the workshop. A special thanks to Jens Petter Berget who helped us in facilitating the activity.

References

[1] V. Albino, U. Berardi, and R. M. Dangelico, "Smart Cities: Definitions, Dimensions, Performance, and Initiatives", Journal of Urban Technology, vol. 22, no. 1, pp. 3–21, Jan. 2015, doi: 10.1080/10630732.2014.942092.

[2] D. Washburn et al., "Helping CIOs understand smart city initiatives", Growth, vol. 17, no. 2, pp. 1–17, 2009.

[3] T. Bratteteig, K. Bødker, Y. Dittrich, P. H. Mogensen, and J. Simonsen, "Methods: Organising principles and general guidelines for Participatory Design projects", in Routledge International Handbook of Participatory Design, J. Simonsen and T. Robertson, Eds. London, UNITED KINGDOM: Taylor & Francis Group, 2012, pp. 117–145. Accessed: Sep. 27, 2021.

[4] E. Ruiz Ben, "Methodologies for a Participatory Design of IoT to Deliver Sustainable Public Services in Smart Cities", in Beyond Smart and Connected Governments: Sensors and the Internet of Things in the Public Sector, J. R. Gil-Garcia, T. A. Pardo, and M. Gasco-Hernandez, Eds. Cham: Springer International Publishing, 2020, pp. 49–68. doi: 10.1007/978-3-030-37464-8_3.

[5] T. Bratteteig and I. Wagner, Disentangling Participation: Power and Decision-making in Participatory Design. Cham: Springer International Publishing, 2014. doi: 10.1007/978-3-319-06163-4.

[6] M. O'Rourke, "Protecting Our Critical Infrastructure", Risk Management, vol. 64, no. 10, pp. 3–4, 2017.

[7] C. Alcaraz and S. Zeadally, "Critical infrastructure protection: Requirements and challenges for the 21st century", International Journal of Critical Infrastructure Protection, vol. 8, pp. 53–66, Jan. 2015, doi: 10.1016/j.ijcip.2014.12.002.

[8] J. Moteff, C. Copeland, and J. Fischer, "Critical infrastructures: What makes an infrastructure critical?", Library of Congress Washington DC Congressional Research Service, 2003.

[9] J. Betts and S. Sezer, "Ethics and privacy in national security and critical infrastructure protection", in 2014 IEEE International Symposium on Ethics in Science, Technology and Engineering, May 2014, pp. 1–7. doi: 10.1109/ETHICS.2014.6893417.

[10] K. Uhl, "The Freedom of Information Act Post-9/11: Balancing the Public's Right to Know, Critical Infrastructure Protection, and Homeland Security", American University Law Review, vol. 53, no. 1, pp. 261-311, Jan. 2003

[11] T. Bányai, P. Tamás, B. Illés, Ž. Stankevičiūtė, and Á. Bányai, "Optimization of Municipal Waste Collection Routing: Impact of Industry 4.0 Technologies on Environmental Awareness and Sustainability", International Journal of Environmental Research and Public Health, vol. 16, no. 4, 634 , Jan. 2019, doi: 10.3390/ijerph16040634.

[12] T. Robertson and J. Simonsen, "Challenges and Opportunities in Contemporary Participatory Design", Design Issues, vol. 28, no. 3, pp. 3–9, Jul. 2012, doi: 10.1162/DESI_a_00157.

[13] F. Kensing and J. Greenbaum, "Heritage: Having a say", in Routledge international handbook of participatory design, Routledge, 2013, pp. 21–36.

[14] E. Brandt, T. Binder, and E. B.-N. Sanders, Tools and techniques. Routledge Handbooks Online, 2012.

[15] J. M. Carroll, "Scenarios and design cognition", in Proceedings IEEE Joint International Conference on Requirements Engineering, Sep. 2002, pp. 3–5. doi: 10.1109/ICRE.2002.1048498.

[16] M. Muller and Q. V. Liao, "Exploring AI Ethics and Values through Participatory Design Fictions", Human Computer Interaction Consortium, 2017.

[17] S. Prost, E. Mattheiss, and M. Tscheligi, "From Awareness to Empowerment: Using Design Fiction to Explore Paths towards a Sustainable Energy Future", in Proceedings of the 18th ACM Conference on Computer Supported Cooperative Work & Social Computing, New York, NY, USA, Feb. 2015, pp. 1649–1658. doi: 10.1145/2675133.2675281.

[18] L. V. Nägele, M. Ryöppy, and D. Wilde, "PDFi: participatory design fiction with vulnerable users", in Proceedings of the 10th Nordic Conference on Human-Computer Interaction, New York, NY, USA, Sep. 2018, pp. 819–831. doi: 10.1145/3240167.3240272.

[19] L. Ventä-Olkkonen et al., "Nowhere to Now-here: Empowering Children to Reimagine Bully Prevention at Schools Using Critical Design Fiction: Exploring the Potential of Participatory, Empowering Design Fiction in Collaboration with Children", in Designing Interactive Systems Conference 2021, New York, NY, USA, Jun. 2021, pp. 734–748. doi: 10.1145/3461778.3462044.

[20] S. Grand and M. Wiedmer, "Design Fiction: A Method Toolbox for Design Research in a Complex World", DRS Biennial Conference Series, Jul. 2010

[21] T. Markussen and E. Knutz, "The poetics of design fiction", in Proceedings of the 6th International Conference on Designing Pleasurable Products and Interfaces, New York, NY, USA, Sep. 2013, pp. 231–240. doi: 10.1145/2513506.2513531.

[22] V. Braun and V. Clarke, Thematic analysis. American Psychological Association, 2012.

[23] D. Kozlov, J. Veijalainen, and Y. Ali, "Security and privacy threats in IoT architectures.", in BODYNETS, 2012, pp. 256–262.

[24] W. Zhou, Y. Jia, A. Peng, Y. Zhang, and P. Liu, "The Effect of IoT New Features on Security and Privacy: New Threats, Existing Solutions, and Challenges Yet to Be Solved", IEEE Internet of Things Journal, vol. 6, no. 2, pp. 1606–1616, Apr. 2019, doi: 10.1109/JIOT.2018.2847733.

[25] J. S. Kumar and D. R. Patel, "A survey on internet of things: Security and privacy issues", International Journal of Computer Applications, vol. 90, no. 11, pp. 20-26, 2014.

[26] B. Carsten Stahl, "Participatory design as ethical practice – concepts, reality and conditions", Journal of Information, Communication and Ethics in Society, vol. 12, no. 1, pp. 10–13, Jan. 2014, doi: 10.1108/JICES-11-2013-0044.

[27] M. van der Velden, "Re-thinking participatory design: what can we learn from fairphone", University of Oslo, 2014.

Unveiling the Potential of Digital Fabrication in Arts & Crafts Education: A Future Workshop Approach for Technology-Enhanced Teaching

1st Susanne Stigberg
Department of Computer Science and Communication
Østfold University College, Norway
Halden, Norway
susannks@hiof.no

2nd Nils-Christian Walthinsen Rabben
Department of Computer Science and Communication
Østfold University College, Norway
Halden, Norway
nils.c.rabben@hiof.no

***Abstract*—This research paper explores the potential of Digital Fabrication (DF) to incorporate digital competences in arts and crafts (A&C) education. With the growing emphasis on digital literacy in K-12 curricula, we aim to investigate what opportunities and challenges DF can bring to A&C education. To achieve this, we conducted a Future Workshop with seven A&C teachers from two different primary schools. Through the Future Workshop approach, we were able to engage teachers in a participatory design process that enabled them to explore the potential of DF in A&C education. Teachers shared their perspectives, identified challenges, and brainstormed future solutions. The findings reveal that teachers see clear opportunities of DF to introduce topics related to STEAM (Science, Technology, Engineering, the Arts and Mathematics Education), sustainability and product design in A&C education, but there are also challenges that need to be addressed, such as lack of equipment, knowledge, or time constraints.**

***Keywords-** future workshop, teacher training, digital fabrication, arts and crafts education*

I. Introduction

The translation of digital designs into physical objects is known as Digital Fabrication (DF), involving tools like 3D printers, embroidery machines, laser cutters, and vinyl cutters. DF technologies have become affordable and accessible at Makerspaces and FabLabs around the world. They enable individuals to create professional-looking items quickly and at a relatively low cost. According to Blickstein [1], DF and making can have a significant impact on education by introducing powerful ideas, literacies, and expressive tools to children. There have been recent efforts to incorporate programming and digital technologies into A&C curricula [2], with teachers utilizing DF to teach programming, making, and design thinking to students [3]. The potential applications of DF in A&C education are numerous, including accessibility, versatility, collaboration, customization, automation, and innovation. DF provides a distinct approach to model-making, allowing students to experiment with new materials and techniques while facilitating alternative forms of collaboration among students. Song et al. [4] found that DF activities can inspire teachers to explore alternative approaches to A&C, utilizing technology to push the boundaries of traditional crafting techniques. Previous research has explored DF in A&C mainly as part of STEAM projects and with the aim to introduce computing to diverse student groups using robotics, e-textiles and 3D as most common DF themes [5]. However, in K-12 A&C education, the uptake of DF technologies is lagging. A national education report from 2009, which analysis the use of digital tools in Norwegian schools, [6] found that A&C teachers incorporate low levels of technology in their K-12 practice. This corresponds with relevant research on challenges incorporating technology into arts education [4], [7]. In this paper, we are interested in how A&C teachers reflect on DF and its potential in K-12 A&C education, as a first step in creating a local professional development project. In Section 2, we review technology use in A&C education, before discussing the future workshop approach in Section 3. We present our method in Section 4 and our findings in Section 5. We conclude the paper with future work in Section 6.

II. Technology in Arts and Crafts Education

While digital tools have been introduced in education in general, there has been minimal use of technology in arts education compared to other subjects. Song et al. [4] found the reluctance of arts education to embrace technological advancements is not a new phenomenon. Art is considered a media-specific subject, and the interaction between material and process is integral to student learning [8], [9]. Technologies used in this domain have been limited to ICT, image and video editing, and graphic design, which are predominantly virtual and two-dimensional e.g., [10]–[12]. Ettinger [8] has documented the use of digital tools in arts education for information gathering, particularly using the internet. In 2019, policymakers in Norway emphasized the importance of digital literacy by introducing explicit changes in all subjects, including A&C education. The changes in the K-12 curricula include a clear description of digital literacy as core elements. For A&C education in grades 5-7, the changes included:

- Using digital tools to plan and present processes and products (Core element: Art and Design Processes)
- Implementing programming to create interactive and visual expressions (Core element: Visual Communication)
- Learning how to safely and sustainably use electrical crafting devices with specific materials (Core element: Handcrafting)

TABLE I
EMERGING THEMES IN THE CRITIQUE PHASE

Economy	Lacking equipment Difficult to finance purchase Cost of raw materials Lacking dedicated rooms for DF
Knowledge	No experience with DF No experience with the equipment How to evaluate pupils' work How to make good tasks Need new work routines
Structure	Big classes, need extra teachers Need to learn together, in a community Need cross-disciplinary cooperation, can't teach all basic skills in A&C
Time	Need time to learn new skills Time is limited

For A&C education in grades 7-10, the changes included:

- Exploring the use of technology with materials when constructing products (Core element: Handcrafting)
- Exploring how new technologies can enhance creative processes when creating products (Core element: Art and Design Processes)
- Learning how to create interactive illustrations using hand drawing, 3D modeling, and other digital tools (Core element: Visual Communication)

III. Future Workshop in Teacher Training

A future workshop is a participatory and collaborative approach to generate ideas and solutions for a desirable future through critique, fantasy, and implementation phases [13]. The origins of future workshops (FW) can be traced back to the 1950s, when Austrian futurist Robert Jungk organized meetings for a citizen group to address common problems. The aim was to create ideas for a desirable future and critique the establishment through collective decision making and group synergy effects. Three main sources inspired Jungk's approach, as described in [14]: the socialist principles of participative, democratic, and critical citizen decision making for the initial critique phase, Alex Osborne's brainstorming method for the following fantasy phase, and methods based on group synergy effects and individual intuition for the concluding implementation phase. FW has been utilized in teacher training. Forsler [15] introduces teacher students to FW to visualize media infrastructures in teaching spaces. Dirckinck et al. [16] use FW to involve teachers in the design and implementation of digital learning platforms. The bottom-up approach of FW aligns with our research aim, which is to learn about teachers' concerns integrating DF in A&C education; as well as teachers alternative visions of an ideal future using DF in A&C education; ending up with a set of concrete action for us to support teachers in the process.

IV. Method

In the following, we will describe how we have implemented the FW and collected and analysed data from the workshop. The workshop took place on a Thursday from 4:00-6:00 pm in a meeting room at the university, with two DF experts (authors of this paper) and seven teachers from two local secondary schools (four women and three men). An email invitation was sent to A&C teachers from local schools. We invited all interested teachers. They had minimal or no experience with DF. One DF expert facilitated the workshop, while the other gave a short presentation on DF and supported the facilitator during the activities. The workshop began with some food and coffee to help participants get to know each other and warm up for the workshop. The workshop was structured as follows:

- Introduction to DF: 10-15 minutes
- Problem phase: 30 minutes
- Critique phase: 30 minutes
- Implementation phase: 30 minutes
- Summary and planning for the upcoming workshop.

In the *critique phase*, we prompted participants to brainstorm and identify hindrances or problems that could prevent them from using DF in their teaching. Each participant was asked to write down at least three issues individually, while they could talk to each other for about 10 minutes. Next, we sorted and grouped the raised concerns to identify common themes among participants. Finally, we concluded the critique phase with a brief discussion where participants elaborated further on the emerging themes.

In the *fantasy phase*, participants engaged in activities similar to those in the critique phase, where they individually wrote down ideas before we grouped and discussed them. Instead of identifying problems, participants imagined an ideal, utopian situation where they could envision the full potential of DF without any limitations. This included imagining that all identified problems from the previous phase were solved and there were no restrictions. The aim was to gain insight into how teachers envision using DF in their teaching.

During the *implementation phase*, the ideas and limitations, that were identified in the earlier stages, were evaluated against each other to determine their feasibility in the current situation [14]. The teachers reviewed the previous themes and prioritized them, discussing the necessary requirements for implementing each idea, leading to a prioritized action plan for future workshops in the project.

To collect data, we videotaped the workshop and conducted a thematic analysis of the data for each phase. We then engaged in a discussion where we compared and consolidated our coding to identify common themes. Thematic maps [17] were created for each phase, and any discrepancies in the coding were addressed and resolved through further discussion.

V. Findings

During the critique phase, teachers have identified several challenges to using DF in their teaching, which we have

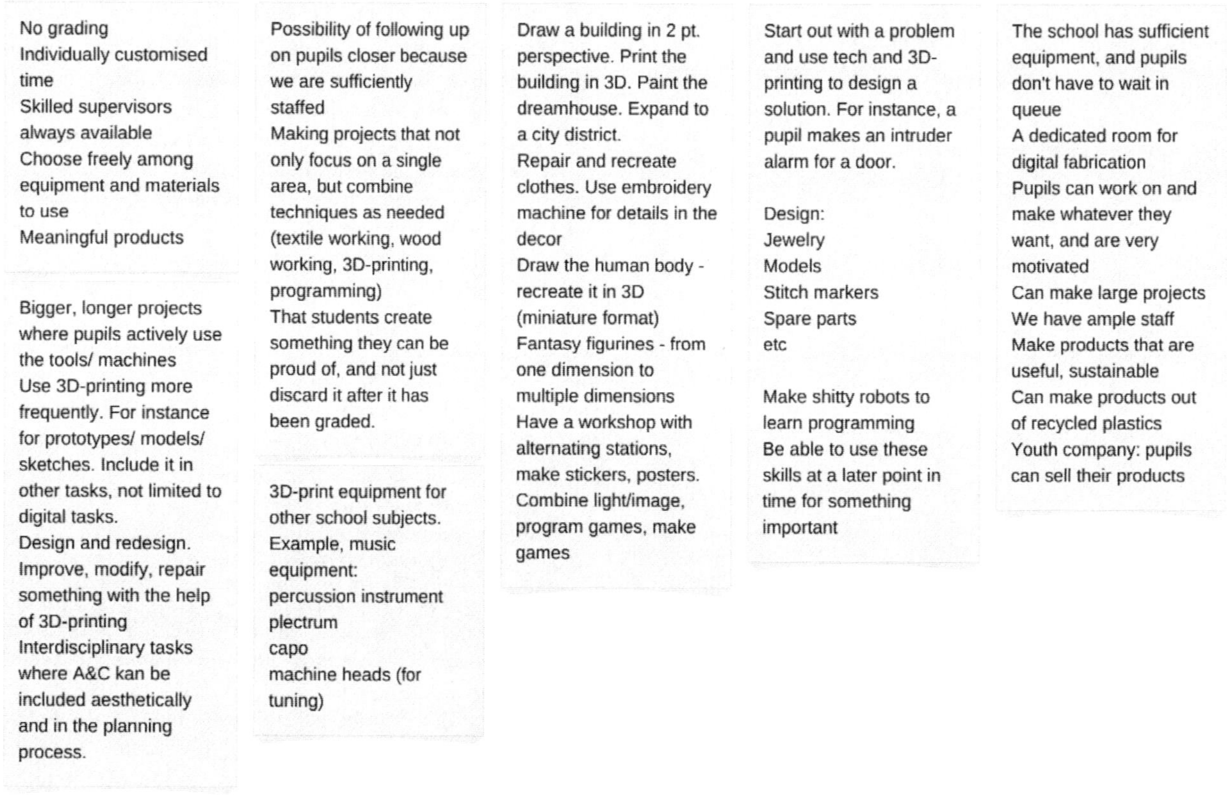

Figure 1. Postit notes from the fantasy phase, translated

grouped into four categories as outlined in Table I. *Economic challenges* are one of the main concerns, such as the lack of access to DF equipment, the cost of materials, and the absence of dedicated spaces for DF activities, such as a makerspace. Teachers find it difficult to ask for money to buy DF tools due to budget constraints and purchase restrictions in schools. However, in one school, the *lack of knowledge* is the most immediate challenge using DF, despite having three 3D printers. The person responsible for buying the printers has left, resulting in the printers being neglected, since no one in the school knows how to use, maintain, or repair them. In addition, teachers also feel that they lack pedagogical knowledge, such as how to create engaging DF tasks and assess student work. Due to *time constraints* and large class sizes, they feel unable to learn new skills on their own. They mention a need to establish a more *structured* way of support such as a community of practice in DF. They also recognize that DF should be incorporated into various subjects to spread the responsibility of teaching DF skills.

We categorized several opportunities for incorporating DF in A&C education, ideated by the teachers during the fantasy phase. One such opportunity is the potential for interdisciplinary projects that utilize a variety of technologies and techniques to create meaningful products. This aligns with the concept of STEAM, as well as the principles of design thinking and making, as discussed in existing literature [1], [18]. The teachers believe that the inclusion of DF in A&C will motivate students to create products they are proud of and that are meaningful to them. Additionally, they see opportunities for DF to be used in redesign, repair, and recycling projects as more sustainable practices. An overview of all generated ideas is depicted in Figure 1. Surprisingly, none of the teachers related their DF fantasies to the core elements of the A&C curricula.

In the implementation phase, the teachers identified two activities that address their lack of knowledge. Firstly, they requested 3D printing training to equip themselves with a better understanding of the technology, which they felt would help them evaluate how to incorporate it into their teaching. Secondly, they expressed a need for more inspiration and teaching examples, which they dubbed an "idea bank". The teachers considered these activities feasible to implement since they did not require input from other stakeholders.

VI. Future Work

In conclusion, the Future Workshop proved to be an effective method for exploring teachers' perspectives on DF for A&C education. Teachers gave positive feedback regarding both receiving information about possibilities in DF and the opportunity to express and share their thoughts on introducing technology in A&C education. The insights gained from the workshop will guide further interventions. To address the challenges raised by the teachers in the critique phase, we have identified several key steps that need to be taken. Firstly, we should establish DF technology workshops to provide teachers with the necessary knowledge and skills to incorporate DF into their teaching. Secondly, we could create a platform for DF ideas and resources based on existing sources such as Thingiverse and Printables. Additionally, we aim to build a community of practice in DF to foster collaboration and support among teachers and DF experts. Finally, we need to communicate with school owners to secure financial and structural resources for our undertaking. By taking these steps, we hope to effectively address the challenges highlighted by the teachers and successfully integrate DF into A&C education. The emergent themes in the fantasy phase inspire our work to develop interdisciplinary STEAM projects that incorporate diverse DF technologies.

REFERENCES

[1] P. Blikstein, "Digital fabrication and 'making'in education: The democratization of invention," *FabLabs: Of machines, makers and inventors*, vol. 4, no. 1, pp. 1–21, 2013.

[2] S. Hoebeke, I. Strand, and P. Haakonsen, "Programming as a New Creative Material in Art and Design Education," *Techne serien - Forskning i slöjdpedagogik och slöjdvetenskap*, vol. 28, no. 2, pp. 233–240, Aug. 2021.

[3] Anders Dahlbom, "Eva breaks the traditions with craftsmanship and programming (Swedish text)," Jan. 2023. [Online]. Available: https://skolvarlden.se/artiklar/eva-bryter-traditionerna-med-slojd-och-programmering

[4] M. J. Song, "The application of digital fabrication technologies to the art and design curriculum in a teacher preparation program: a case study," *International Journal of Technology and Design Education*, vol. 30, no. 4, pp. 687–707, Sep. 2020. [Online]. Available: https://doi.org/10.1007/s10798-019-09524-6

[5] S. Stigberg, D. Blauhut, and F. F. Said, "Digital Fabrication in Arts and Crafts Education: A critical review," in *25th International Conference on Human-Computer Interaction*, Copenhagen, Denmark, 2023, p. in print.

[6] L. Vavik, S. Andersland, T. E. Arnesen, T. Arnesen, M. Espeland, I. Flatøy, I. Grønsdal, P. Fadnes, S. Kjetil, and G. A. Tuset, "School subjects survey 2009: Education, school subjects and technology (Norwegian text)," *Høgskolen Stord/Haugesund*, vol. Vol. 2010/1, 2010.

[7] K. Sømoe, "Arts and crafts – subject or interdisciplinary wrong? (Norwegian)," *FormAkademisk*, vol. 6, no. 3, pp. 1–15, 2013.

[8] L. F. Ettinger, "Art Education and Computing: Building a Perspective," *Studies in Art Education*, vol. 30, no. 1, pp. 53–62, Oct. 1988. [Online]. Available: https://www.tandfonline.com/doi/abs/10.1080/00393541.1988.11650702

[9] A. Marner and H. Örtegren, "Digitala medier i bildämnet : möten och spänningar." Institutionen för estetiska ämnen. Nätverket för ämnesdidaktik, 2013, pp. 28–49. [Online]. Available: http://urn.kb.se/resolve?urn=urn:nbn:se:umu:diva-71269

[10] R. Guillard-Patton and M. Buffington, "Keeping up with our students: The evolution of technology and standards in art education," *Arts Education Policy Review*, vol. 117, pp. 1–9, May 2016.

[11] E. M. Delacruz, "Art Education Aims in the Age of New Media: *Moving Toward Global Civil Society*," *Art Education*, vol. 62, no. 5, pp. 13–18, Sep. 2009. [Online]. Available: https://www.tandfonline.com/doi/full/10.1080/00043125.2009.11519032

[12] G. Hubbard and D. Greh, "Integrating computing into art education: A progress report," *Art education*, vol. 44, no. 3, pp. 18–24, 1991, publisher: Taylor & Francis.

[13] N. Müllert and R. Jungk, "Future Workshops: How to create desirable futures," *London, United Kingdom: Institute for Social Inventions*, 1987.

[14] R. V. V. Vidal, "The future workshop: Democratic problem solving," *Economic analysis working papers*, vol. 5, no. 4, p. 21, 2006, publisher: Citeseer.

[15] I. Forsler, "Imaginary classrooms : Exploring new directions in visual art education through future workshops in teacher training," *IMAG*, vol. 11, pp. 24–29, 2021, publisher: InSEA Publications. [Online]. Available: http://urn.kb.se/resolve?urn=urn:nbn:se:sh:diva-46144

[16] L. Dirckinck-Holmfeld, B. J. Ipsen, A. L. Tamborg, J. Dreyøe, B. B. Allsopp, and M. Misfeldt, "Modes of Teacher Participation in the Digitalization of School," *Designs for Learning*, vol. 11, no. 1, pp. 63–71, 2019, publisher: Stockholm University Press ERIC Number: EJ1235543. [Online]. Available: https://eric.ed.gov/?id=EJ1235543

[17] V. Braun and V. Clarke, "Thematic analysis," in *APA handbook of research methods in psychology, Vol 2: Research designs: Quantitative, qualitative, neuropsychological, and biological*, ser. APA handbooks in psychology®. Washington, DC, US: American Psychological Association, 2012, pp. 57–71.

[18] I. S. Milara, K. Pitkänen, A. Niva, M. Iwata, J. Laru, and J. Riekki, "The STEAM Path: Building a Community of Practice for Local Schools around STEAM and Digital Fabrication," in *Proceedings of the FabLearn Europe 2019 Conference*, ser. FabLearn Europe '19. New York, NY, USA: Association for Computing Machinery, 2019, pp. 1–3.

Exploring Medical Practitioners Abilities to Use Visual Programming to Code Scenarios for Virtual Simulations

Bjørn Arild Lunde, Joakim Karlsen
Department of Computer Science and Communication
Østfold University College
Halden, Norway
bjorn.a.lunde@hiof.no, joakim.karlsen@hiof.no

Abstract— **Virtual simulations provide a safe environment to practice medical skills and has become more common in the health sector. To maintain and update virtual simulations with state-of-the-art medical procedures require expert knowledge in programming and IT development. Significant resources could be saved if medical educators and students could update the virtual simulation with new scenarios themselves. Based on a qualitative study of end users solving visual programming tasks, we identify constraints and opportunities in achieving this. The main constraint was their inability to break down scenarios into smaller codable steps. The main opportunity was how their familiarity with some elements in the visual programming language increased their ability to write code.**

Keywords-end-user programming; virtual simulations medical training

I. Introduction

The healthcare sector is actively pursuing the development of technology to support training [1]. Several experiments indicate that serious games and virtual simulations are promising platforms to support practitioners in the field with learning activities [2]–[4]. Due to rapid advancements in health research, activities are not necessarily done in the same way as they were ten years ago. To keep up with these changes, training tools and learning material must be updated to keep the practitioners' skills up to date. In the case that the learning tools are complex entities, such as virtual simulations and serious games, it is not unusual to hire personnel, either internal or external, who can adapt the training tools to reflect new knowledge. Valuable resources can be saved by giving end users the ability to make these changes themselves, using end-user programming tools.

Having the right skillset to write code and update virtual simulations requires an understanding of programming. A motivation for this study is to lower this knowledge barrier by wrapping text-based programming in a graphical interface that is user-friendly for end users without prior knowledge of programming. Visual programming languages that try to achieve this already exist, with block-based and node-based approaches being the most popular. A familiar example of block-based programming is Scratch, which was created specifically for end users without programming experience [5]..

The purpose of this study is to explore whether end-user programming can provide educators and students in the healthcare sector the ability to code a sequence of events for their training scenarios without the help of external personnel. Visual programming can probably give end users this capability, by being adapted to their requirements. The research question is therefore as follows.

What do observation of health personnel challenged to do visual programming to adapt virtual simulations to their training needs, tell about the opportunities and constraints of providing end-user programming tools for this purpose?

The result of the study will be a consideration of what this means for further development of end user-tool in this context.

In Section II, we will summarize previous work on this topic. After this, in Section III, we will describe the methods for data collection and analysis. Then, we will present the results in Section IV. In Section V, the discussion will be presented. Lastly, conclusion and future work will be discussed in section VI.

II. Background

A typical end user will be a domain expert in a field other than computer science, in our case educators and students in the healthcare sector. End users do not possess the knowledge or understanding required to create and maintain software [6]. Giving the end users the opportunity to customize software without the assistance of external resources is the general idea of end-user tools [7]. Fischer claims that end-user tools are necessary to not get stuck in old routines as a result of outdated software [8].

The main challenge when learning how to write code that computers understand, is the different ways humans and machines interpret signs. Tanaka-Ishii [9] illustrates this issue with the following code example:

```
int x = 15
```

In this example, the content (the number 15) is represented by three different signs. The first is quite obviously the number itself, 15. This value is then represented by x, which points to where the value is stored. Finally, we have int, which represents the data type of the value. The challenge for newcomers according to Tanaka-Ishii, is that it can be confusing how these three signs are interpreted. In end-user tools, this problem can partially be eliminated by relying on visual blocks or nodes, direct manipulation and degrees of domain-specificity.

Variants of node-based and block-based visual programming both scrap the traditional textual programming in favor of visual elements. A block-based approach offers blocks that are put together almost like a puzzle where only certain pieces fit together to prevent error in the code [10]. A node-based language will consist of nodes that often have ports for input and output that are connected by threads where the information flows from node to node through these threads [11]. A strength of some block-based programming languages is that it's quite clear which parts fit together, something which minimizes the possibility of making mistakes. This constraint is not as prevalent in a node-based approaches. Since the user decides how nodes are connected, however, a node-based solution can be seen as more flexible. Both approaches to visual programming relies on "direct manipulation" which provides visual elements that end users can point and click on [12]. Three characteristics define direct manipulation:

- Continuous visual representation of objects.
- All actions involve pressing buttons instead of using syntax.
- Operations must be possible to reverse quickly and easily.

Further, a visual programming tool can implement a Domain Specific Language (DSL), using terminology and concepts used by the target group to create the visual programming language [13]. This provides an additional layer of familiarity to the language, easing the learning process by reducing technical terms and jargon.

III. METHOD

To be able to shed light on the opportunities and constraints in providing end-user programming tools to medical educators and students, two digital task sets were created giving the informants tasks of programming a virtual simulation of a simplified scenario using a block-based or node-based DSL. The DSLs were designed specifically for this study. The tasks and supporting information built on each other so the informants could become familiar with the concepts and see different use cases for each node or block without being overwhelmed.

The final task set consisted of 18 pages in total, of which 6 of these were tasks in different forms that the informants had to answer. Each informant only completed one of the task sets, to prevent the results being skewed based on the informant having more experience with the tasks at hand. Initially in the task set, the study and purpose were introduced so the informants could gain an understanding of what they were about to do. The main purpose of programming and the way humans and computers handle information differently was presented in this step. The informants were then introduced to a task requiring using blocks and nodes to handles text prompts to the players. This was done to provide an easy introduction on how to connect these together. In its simplest form, three different block and nodes were introduced through the task sets, but some variations of these appeared as they progressed.

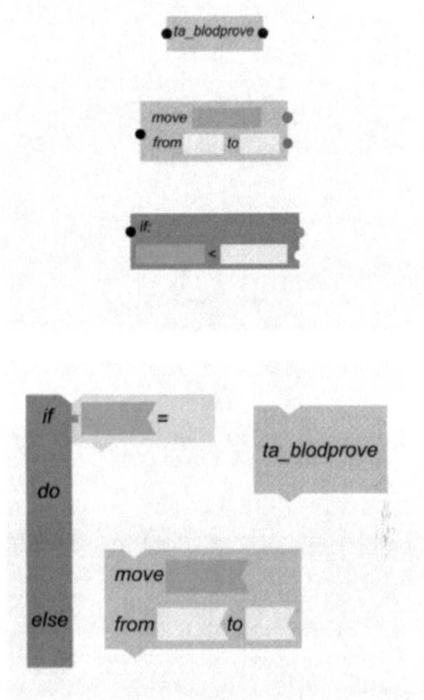

Figure 1. The different nodes (top) and blocks (bottom) in the task sets

Figure 1 illustrates how the different nodes and blocks look. The orange elements handle text prompts, which is displayed to the player going through the scenario. The light blue handle instructions for how the computer should carry out operations such as moving objects, handling time or similar uses. The dark blue represents if / else statements. Inside the nodes and blocks themselves, there are colored fields which have different functionality. The purple fields allow the users to point to objects that exists in the scene they are working on, this includes characters, medicines, devices and more. The green field allow the user to enter manual values such as coordinates, blood levels and more. All of these are introduced and demonstrated both separately and combined with each other through the task set.

The next two tasks were multiple-choice tasks that presented the informants with pre-written code, where the task is to choose the option that the code expresses. These tasks had two intentions: evaluate the understanding of the informants' abilities to read code and to present them with pre-written code so that they could become more familiar with how the blocks or nodes should be connected. From this point, more components were gradually added to the code while removing the aids more and more. In the fourth task, the informants were presented with code and they had to write the meaning of the code, as illustrated in Figure 2.

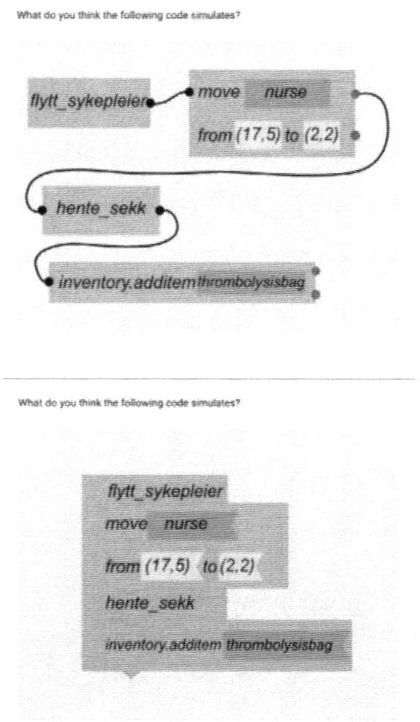

Figure 2. Task 4 in the node-based (top) and block-based (bottom) task set.

The fifth task introduced if / else statements and the informants were presented with a task where they should describe whether they should provide the patients with insulin based on blood sugar values. The informants did not get any alternatives to rely on and were asked to write how they understood the code in their own words.

In the final and heaviest task, the informants were asked to draw code themselves to simulate a sequence of events as given in the medical scenario illustrated in Figure 3. The task was solvable by using the tools they had learned previously.

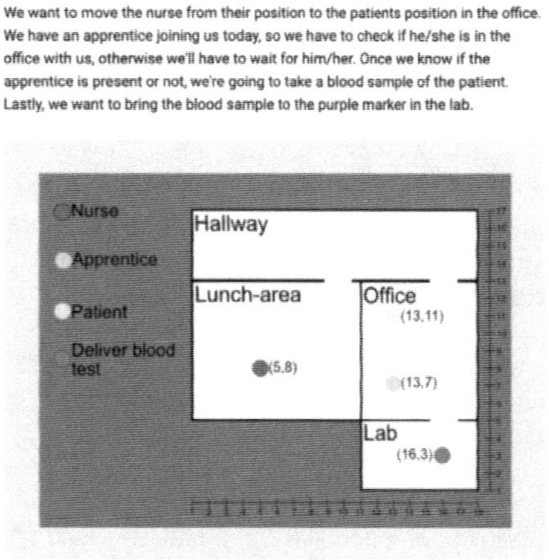

Figure 3. Task 6 in both task sets

A. *Data collection and analysis*

The medical students and educators recruited to the study, were affiliated with a small university college in Norway, having a state-of-the-art simulation center used to educate health personnel. The data was collected both digitally and physically to secure participation from both students and staff at the university. The digital data collection lasted from May 15th to September 15th, 2021. There was a total of 9 informants completing the digital task sets, both male and female nursing students and medical educators ranging from 20-35 years of age. Out of these 9 informants, 5 completed the node-based task set while 4 completed the block-based task set. The physical data collection was completed in weeks 43 and 44 in 2021. There was a total of 5 informants completing the task set, all of them being female medical educators ranging from 35-60 years of age. Out of these 5 informants, 2 completed the node-based task set while 3 completed the block-based task set. All the informants are listed in Table I with the associated task set they completed as well as which data collection they participated in.

TABLE I. INFORMANTS

Participant	Task set	Data Collection
#1-1	Node-based	Digital
#1-2	Node-based	Digital
#1-3	Node-based	Digital
#1-4	Node-based	Digital
#1-5	Node-based	Digital
#2-1	Block-based	Digital
#2-2	Block-based	Digital
#2-3	Block-based	Digital
#2-4	Block-based	Digital
#3-1	Node-based	Physical
#3-2	Node-based	Physical
#4-1	Block-based	Physical
#4-2	Block-based	Physical
#4-3	Block-based	Physical

As the digital collection had to be anonymous in line with the approved application submitted to the Norwegian Center for Research Data (NSD), recruitment had to happen through group pages on social media and neutral third parties reaching out to informants. The subsequent data analysis followed the model proposed by Creswell & Creswell [14], which consists of five steps; 1) sort and prepare data for analysis, 2) create a general understanding of the data, collect and sort thoughts and feelings from the informants, 3) code and categorize data, 4) describe factors such as places, people and sequences of events in the data, 5) consider different perspectives and quotes, and compare them to each other, present data in a narrative giving expected findings, surprising findings and unusual or conceptual findings.

IV. RESULTS

The multiple-choice tasks, tasks 2 and 3, in both task sets were answered correctly by all informants, both in the digital and physical sessions. These were not the most complex tasks, but provided an indication that the programming languages were both readable and understandable. In the physical sessions, a few informants were on the wrong track on task 3 before they ended up with the right answer. The correct answer to task 3 is option "C", but there were two informants who quickly chose alternative "B". These two options are quite similar, where option "C" suggests the code simulates moving the bed from one position to another, while option "B" suggests moving the patient. As soon as the context was removed and they didn't have a visual representation to support them, the informants quickly seemed uncertain. This issue is illustrated in the response from participant #4-1.

> So I'm going to move the bed? Then it is alternative number 2 (B). Move patient from position 10.4 to bed at position... But it is... Yes... or wait.... #4-1

> Author: Why do you think that?

> No, now I'm thinking... I want to... We will move the patient... move... moving the bed is impossible because it's nothing there. There is no code. But we are going from 10.4 to 7.8. Then it must be: Move bed from position 10.4 and to the bed at position 7.8? But it may still be that... This one was a bit more difficult. This is to check if it is easy to use or not, I must think about that. #4-1

> Author: What if you start at the top and work your way down?

> Okay. I'm going to move the bed. From 10.4 to 7.8. Then it must be alternative "C"? #4-1

From task 4 no alternatives were offered, and they had to write their answers without support. This resulted in a major drop in the quality of the results. The correct sequence of events simulates a nurse that moves from where he / she is to where the thrombolysis bag is and retrieves it. The informants took freedom in the way this was interpreted, evident in the following examples from informants #1-2 and #2-1.

> The nurse should go from for example the patient room to the rinsing room and pick up thrombolysis bag #1-2

> Nurse picks up thrombolysis bag #2-1

On the same task there were some misunderstandings regarding how the code worked. In the example below, informant #2-2 interprets the code as the interface itself, and that the blocks are buttons to press.

> If you press the orange block, we will move the nurse from position 17.5 to 2.2. Then press the lower orange block, and bring along the bag on your way. #2-2

Something that is pervasive in these examples is that it is troublesome for the informants to distinguish what is information to the player from the information to the computer. Another observation based on the block-based responses is that it was challenging for the informants to understand which order to read the code.

In the fifth task, that dealt with if / else statements, the general understanding seemed good. The informants all understood that a condition decide the outcome. There were some differences in the way informants read the "greater than" or "lesser than" symbols, however, as seen in the examples below.

> If BS is over 17mmol/l, you should be given insulin, if below, do not give insulin. #1-1

> If the blood sugar value is less than 17mmol/l then give insulin. If not, then do nothing. #2-1

In one of the physical sessions, informant #4-2 seemed to misunderstand the concept of "greater than" and "lesser than" and thought that if the value was anything else than what was being checked, 17mmol/l in this case, that the else condition would be triggered.

> It simulates a blood sugar measurement, that a nurse should manage blood sugar. And if the value is 17mmol/l you should give insulin, if not, then do nothing. #4-2

In task 6, which is the last and most complex task, more effort was required, and the quality of the answers varied accordingly. Overall, Figure 4 illustrates what could be expected. Informant #1-1 took advantage of a variety of nodes with mostly correct use of color codes and proper connections.

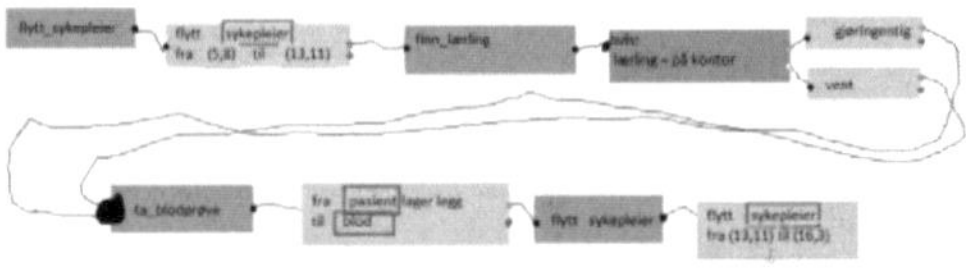

Figure 4. Response from participant #1-1 on task 6

One of the strengths of block-based programming is that you can only connect blocks if they fit together. This seemed to be forgotten or ignored in several of the responses, and the informants took freedoms that would not be possible. The blocks are in some cases stacked on top of each other without regards to these rules as displayed in Figure 5.

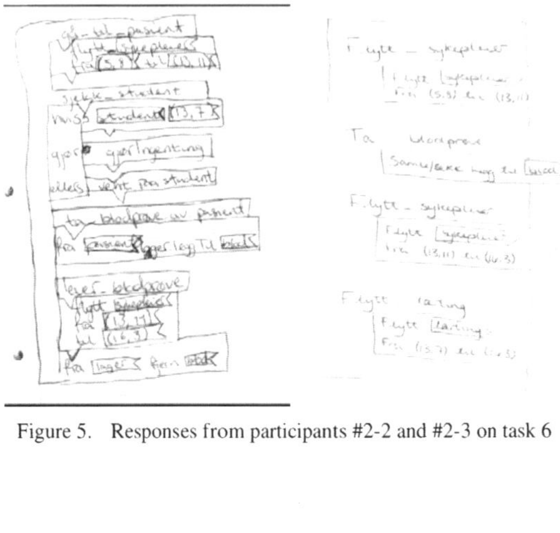

Figure 5. Responses from participants #2-2 and #2-3 on task 6

With multiple hand-drawn responses on task 6 from the digital sessions, it was more appropriate to conduct a discussion with the informants in the physical sessions. This way, the informants could put words to their thought process when solving the tasks. The following quotes from informant #3-1 seem to indicate a pretty good overall understanding.

> I think the first one is perhaps an orange one, considering the task is to move the nurse from one place to another. Behind the orange node there is more code, and that is the purple for the nurse who is going from the office to the lunch area. #3-1

As in all examples presented in the task set, the informant starts with an orange node to prompt the user with information. When asked to check if the apprentice was present, using an if / else statement were quickly suggested. This was also the intended way to solve this part of the problem.

> We need to check if the apprentice is in, then we use that if and else node again, so you do it if he is there, otherwise, we do nothing. I think I get that one correctly. #3-1

While not completely sure on how to connect the orange nodes for the text prompts, the informant was aware of their existence. This was also the only case where breaking down the scenario into tasks was addressed.

> Only I might be a little unsure of how many activities and these orange nodes I should put between the actions. I split up the scenario into tasks, so I thought the first thing about moving the nurse is a task. #3-1

In the responses to the block-based task set in the physical sessions, there were a few more challenges as seen in the response from participant #4-2 below. In the same way as the digital task set, several code components such as text prompts are forgotten. In addition to this, color codes are not commented on at all.

> To me it looks like we are just passing by and going from one place to another, and then I look to see if someone is there. But how the interaction takes place, how to ensure that the nurse brings the apprentice and how they take the blood test, I do not know. #4-2

An interesting observation is the way the informant attacked the problem. Instead of dividing the scenario into smaller parts like in the previous response on the node-based task set, she tried to solve the entire scenario at once.

> I move the nurse to the office, and then I check if the apprentice is there, then I should be able to move on? So, I take a blood test of the patient? #4-2

As soon as all the supporting materials were removed, the informants quickly felt overwhelmed and somewhat insecure about the order to do things. As seen in the quotes above, the informants solving the node-based task set included the concepts of the language itself in explaining how they were trying to solve the problem at hand. The informants solving the block-based task set did this to a lesser degree.

A. *Recurring themes*

While not required to complete the tasks, the informants had the opportunity to display information to the players using the orange nodes or blocks. This, however, seemed to be ignored for the most part. An interesting observation in this regard occurred in one of the physical interviews conducted for the node-based task set, where one of the informants tried to improve the pre-written code by posting questions to the players using the orange nodes.

Several of the informants in the physical sessions had previous experience with real-life simulations at the college in which they as educators observe students and provide them with instructions using a communication system. In these simulations, the students go through different scenarios, and in one of the interviews on the node-based task set, comparisons were drawn between the programming task and these physical simulations. The informant explained that the actions and the way they gave instructions to the students were quite similar, and that the flow of the code running from node to node was kind of the same as reading the instructions in the simulations.

Another comparison occurring in the responses from the informants solving the node-based task set, was that it was reasonably easy to follow the flow of the code as it looked somewhat similar to flow charts. No such comparisons to previous experiences were mentioned in any of the responses for the block-based task set.

While comparing the responses from the last tasks in both digital task sets, it is immediately apparent that the answers in the node-based task set follow the rules as intended when compared to the block-based responses. The nodes are to a greater extent connected properly, and there is more active use of color codes and text prompts to the players, although this is in several cases forgotten here as well.

V. DISCUSSION

Based on the analysis of how the informants solved the task sets, we identify one major constraint and one major opportunity for creating end user programming tools in this case.

The main constraint revolves around the inability to break down scenarios into smaller steps. Instead of looking at the individual steps in the scenarios and which elements were needed to represent them, some looked at the problem as a whole, and tried to code multiple or all the parts of the scenario at the same time. The ability to adapt complex problems to lesser, solvable problems through reduction, algorithmic thinking or other means are referred to in the literature as computational thinking [15]. Increasing the end user's familiarity with this kind of problem-solving may decrease the significance of this constraint over time. In addition to this, the informants wanted to express themselves more freely than the languages allowed them to, and several wrote code that would be syntactically impossible (for a machine to understand).

The main opportunity was the familiarity end users have for certain visual tools and procedures. Even though flow charts were not on the agenda to be explored in the study, it turned out to be a form of visualization healthcare professionals recognize and understand. Further, to rely on elements from their practice, or to make the language domain specific, seemed to work well. The if / else task supported this, as they were already familiar with how the measurement of blood sugar impacts what action should be taken. Based on this knowledge they understood that based on a condition, being the blood sugar values in this case, one of the listed actions should be taken.

We conclude that combining domain specificity in the language, using familiar visual elements such as flow charts and adopting the concepts of direct manipulation, are the three main aspects that could help health educators and students in coding sequences of events in virtual training scenarios.

VI. CONCLUSION AND FUTURE WORK

After investigating different approaches to visual programming, enough data has been collected to answer our research question. The data indicates that the idea of letting medical educators and nursing students manipulate and maintain their own training tools using visual programming is one worth pursuing. As discussed earlier in Section V, there are however several prerequisites and aspects of both the languages themselves and the interfaces to them that needs to be further experimented with to make tools like these accessible to the end users.

The next step will be to develop a new and more in-depth visual programming interface using node-based programming, direct manipulation and incorporating elements from flow charts, as a baseline. While this study indicates that medical educators and students can express a sequence of events in scenarios using code, this is only a step on the way towards developing a fully working end-user tool to create, maintain and adapt virtual simulations for health care education. A telling example of the complexity involved, is the need to code meaningful interactions with the students taking part in the simulation, a challenge touched upon in this study by exploring the use of visual elements to express this (orange nodes or blocks). The ultimate goal of future work is to support further development of virtual simulations for training purposes in healthcare education, by giving the end users the means to make these without the help of trained IT professionals.

REFERENCES

[1] N. Sharifzadeh *et al.*, "Health Education Serious Games Targeting Health Care Providers, Patients, and Public Health Users: Scoping Review," *JMIR Serious Games*, vol. 8, pp. 1-16, Mar. 2020, doi: 10.2196/13459.

[2] C. Foronda, B. MacWilliams, and E. McArthur, "Interprofessional communication in healthcare: An integrative review," *Nurse Educ. Pract.*, vol. 19, pp. 36–40, Jul. 2016, doi: 10.1016/j.nepr.2016.04.005.

[3] D. King *et al.*, "Virtual health education: Scaling practice to transform student learning," *Nurse Educ. Today*, vol. 71, pp. 7–9, Dec. 2018, doi: 10.1016/j.nedt.2018.08.002.

[4] W. Westera, "How people learn while playing serious games: A computational modelling approach," *J. Comput. Sci.*, vol. 18, pp. 32–45, Jan. 2017, doi: 10.1016/j.jocs.2016.12.002.

[5] M. Resnick *et al.*, "Scratch: programming for all," *Commun. ACM*, vol. 52, no. 11, pp. 60–67, Nov. 2009, doi: 10.1145/1592761.1592779.

[6] M. F. Costabile, P. Mussio, L. Parasiliti Provenza, and A. Piccinno, "End users as unwitting software developers," in *Proceedings of the 4th international workshop on End-user software engineering - WEUSE '08*, Leipzig, Germany, 2008, pp. 6–10. doi: 10.1145/1370847.1370849.

[7] Z. Menestrina and A. De Angeli, "End-User Development for Serious Games," in *New Perspectives in End-User Development*, F. Paternò and V. Wulf, Eds. Cham: Springer International Publishing, 2017, pp. 359–383. doi: 10.1007/978-3-319-60291-2_14.

[8] G. Fischer, "End-User Development and Meta-design: Foundations for Cultures of Participation," in *End-User Development*, vol. 5435, V. Pipek, M. B. Rosson, B. de Ruyter, and V. Wulf, Eds. Berlin, Heidelberg: Springer Berlin Heidelberg, 2009, pp. 3–14. doi: 10.1007/978-3-642-00427-8_1.

[9] K. Tanaka-Ishii, *Semiotics of Programming*. Cambridge University Press, 2010.

[10] D. Weintrop and U. Wilensky, "Comparing Block-Based and Text-Based Programming in High School Computer Science Classrooms," *ACM Trans. Comput. Educ.*, vol. 18, no. 1, p. 3:1-3:25, Oct. 2017, doi: 10.1145/3089799.

[11] D. Mason and K. Dave, "Block-based versus flow-based programming for naive programmers," in *2017 IEEE Blocks and Beyond Workshop (B B)*, Oct. 2017, pp. 25–28. doi: 10.1109/BLOCKS.2017.8120405.

[12] B. Shneiderman, "Direct manipulation for comprehensible, predictable and controllable user interfaces," in *Proceedings of the 2nd international conference on Intelligent user interfaces*, New York, NY, USA, Jan. 1997, pp. 33–39. doi: 10.1145/238218.238281.

[13] J. Sprinkle and G. Karsai, "A domain-specific visual language for domain model evolution," *J. Vis. Lang. Comput.*, vol. 15, no. 3, pp. 291–307, Jun. 2004, doi: 10.1016/j.jvlc.2004.01.006.

[14] J. W. Creswell and J. D. Creswell, *Research design : qualitative, quantitative & mixed methods approaches*, 5th edition. Los Angeles, California: Sage, 2018.

[15] J. M. Wing, "Computational thinking," *Commun. ACM*, vol. 49, no. 3, pp. 33–35, 2006.

Finding Common Ground: Design Cards Supporting Mutual Learning in Co-design

Tina Helene Bunæs, Michelle Husebye, Joakim Karlsen
Department of Computer Science and Communication,
Faculty of Computer Science, Engineering and Economics
Østfold University College
1757 Halden, Norway
tina.h.bunas@hiof.no , michelle.husebye@hiof.no, joakim.karlsen@hiof.no

Abstract—**This article explores how design cards can support mutual learning between researchers in design and non-designers in the fuzzy front end of a design process. We present a case where we created and used bespoke design cards in a co-design workshop with educators and students at a medical training center in Norway. The goal of the co-design process was to design a mixed reality training solution for simulating medical procedures. Findings suggest that the cards enabled non-designers to have a say in the design process, facilitated for mutual learning across disciplines, and broke down barriers for collaboration. The cards enabled active participation and empowered the medical educators to take a first step from consumers to designers of information and communication technology (ICT) solutions. The paper contributes to the growing body of literature on design cards, co-design and participatory design, and we discuss the potential of design cards as boundary objects that can facilitate co-realization of ICT solutions across professional boundaries.**

Keywords-design cards; co-design; participatory design; design games; mutual learning.

I. INTRODUCTION

Co-design has become an important approach in the design of ICT solutions in the past decades, and the methods and tools that can be used in the design process has grown exponentially [1]. In this strand of design, collective creativity between designers and people not trained in design practices is a core activity [2]. Designers, developers, end-users, and stakeholders come together in the various phases of a design process.

To secure active participation, Participatory Design (PD) is another design approach where users are invited in as partners equal to designers and developers throughout the different phases of design [3]. Bratteteig and Wagner [4] explain that the power to decide the scope and the shape of a technical solution needs to be shared with those who will use it. Principles like having a say, decision-making, mutual learning, and co-realization lie at the very core of PD. Having a say enables users to influence the design process by having their voices heard in the design decisions being made [5]. With mutual learning, the people involved in a design process should learn from each other's expertise, work context and practice. Bratteteig, Bødker, Dittrich, Mogensen and Simonsen [5] also explain that involvement, or co-realization, is important. Here, visualizing possible solutions is a priority as it may be difficult for different users to imagine design possibilities. While involving users as active participants in a project can lead to more conclusive design outcomes, there are several issues that can arise when researchers, designers and users collaborate. Co-design requires creative initiative from the entire collaborative team, and a lack of design expertise can make the users feel like they can't contribute meaningfully to a design process [6]. One explanation is a lack of familiarity with design processes and the terminology used by expert designers. If the users are to successfully be part of a design team they must be given the right tools. These tools must allow them to express themselves without having to adopt specialized design languages. To ensure constructive and meaningful collaboration, researchers and designers have created various methods, tools and techniques that can be brought into the design process [7]. These are used to provide inspiration to the team and to facilitate collaborative activities. They are especially valuable in early design phases where the object of design is still unknown and the design problems are still being explored.

One such tool is design cards. Design cards are used for fostering creativity in design processes, and have been designed for a variety of different purposes, contexts and domains [8][9]. Described as tools for generating ideas and new design concepts, design cards are reportedly used in domains like education, gaming, in exploring social issues and design of new ICT solutions [10]–[12]. Design cards can support design dialogues and discussions, and can structure the design process by making the process visible and less abstract [9]. Physical, tangible cards are easy to use and manipulate and can act as a common reference between participants.

The aim of the study is to investigate collaboration and creative thinking between researchers in design and non-designers in the early phases of a design process. Together with educators at a medical training center in Norway, we explore the design of a mixed reality training simulator. By mixed reality, we mean combining the physical environment with virtual elements to create immersive experiences. The center wants to implement virtual simulations that enable students and medical practitioners to train on procedures that are hard to simulate with the equipment already available at the center. To facilitate for active participation and meaningful design dialogues, the researchers created the MixED design cards and used them in a co-design workshop with participants from the medical center. The MixED card set contains 46 bespoke cards divided into five categories tailored to the specific context of medical practice and virtual simulations supporting that practice. The goal of using these cards in a co-design workshop was to investigate how the cards could 1) enable non-designers to contribute meaningfully to a design process, and 2) facilitate for collaboration and mutual understanding of the design problem. Based on this, we ask:

RQ: why do a deck of bespoke design cards support researchers in design and non-designers in finding common ground?

The paper is structured as follows: Section II provides an overview of design cards as a tool for co-creativity. In Section III, we explore important principles in co-design and PD. Section IV shed light on the theoretical concept of boundary objects. In Section V, we describe the methods used in this study, and Section VI gives a detailed account of the co-design workshop. Findings from the study are summarized in Section VII. In Section VIII, we discuss what our findings mean for the design community. Lastly, Section IX will summarize and conclude the study with future works.

II. DESIGN CARDS SUPPORTING CO-CREATIVITY

Researchers have created various tools and techniques to successfully bring future users into the design process, including probes, mock-ups, prototypes, design games and toolkits [1][7][13][14]. Design games are promising approaches that can structure design activities [14]. Toolkits have been created for PD activities and are considered appropriate for engaging and inspiring non-designers [1]. In the front end of design, toolkits and design games are used to facilitate collaborative activities and support non-designers in expressing ideas about how they want to live, work and play. In reviewing analogue ideation tools, Peters, Loke and Ahmadpour [13] found that card-based tools, like card decks and card games, have become popular in collaborative ideation with future users. Design cards are accessible, analogue and tangible. They are instantly recognizable and can therefore serve as shared references between groups of diverse people [15]. Previous studies illustrate how design cards have been used in many contexts and domains, including exertion game design [16], tangible designs [17], and for playful experiences [18]. By presenting keywords, pictures and questions the cards facilitate for creativity by acting as a source of inspiration [17][19]. Cards with these types of cues (keywords, pictures, and questions) can lead to a more tangible and applicable transformation of theory [17][20]. Through these cues, design cards can provoke new contextual perspectives that extend beyond personal experiences [19]. Additionally, their tangibility can support integration with objects such as notes and sketches [21]. According to Bornoe, Bruun and Stage [8], design cards can be used to 'rephrase abstract frameworks into something more operational' [ibid, p. 2]. Design cards can help identify design opportunities prior to designing the product or service in the early phase of design and can either be general or tailored to specific contexts and use cases.

As an endeavor to classify design cards, several reviews of design cards have been made [9][13][22]. Reviewing 18 design cards, Wölfel and Merritt [9] divide the cards into three categories constituted by purpose and scope: general (used for open-ended inspiration), Participatory Design (used to facilitate collaboration) and context specific or agenda driven. Of the 18 decks, six of them were used in PD, but with varying degree of customization and rules of use. A newer classification was made by Roy and Warren [22]. In analyzing 155 design cards they propose six main (but overlapping) categories: 1) creative thinking and problem solving, 2) domain-specific design, 3) human-centered design, 4) systematic design methods and procedures, 5) team building and collaborative work, and 6) future thinking. The latter three is proportionally smaller than the first three. After a validation of the classification, only four decks were presented in the category 'team building and collaborative work', including the Group Works, Totem cards, SILK, and Bootleg Method Cards. Further, they explain that within participation and collaboration, three subcategories were found: 1) direct end-user participation (15,5%), 2) help designers identify user's abilities, needs, and wants (11,6%), and 3) facilitate collaboration between professionals and experts (34,8%).

In our search, we have found that design cards are used for co-realization and visualizing future design possibilities. According to Myers, Piccolo and Collins [10], design cards can also democratize knowledge, support collaborative design, and can enable more engaging design experiences and results. They do, however, report limited studies presenting methodologies for collaborative design cards. Studies exploring why design cards can facilitate for collaboration in early design phases of ICT solutions are scarce, especially regarding mutual learning and collaboration across professional boundaries.

III. SECURING PARTICIPATION AND CREATIVE INITIATIVE

Over the last decades, commercial businesses and design and research communities have recognized the importance of the user's needs [6]. User-centric design approaches have been applied in design processes to involve future users in the design of, e.g., ICT solutions. Two strands of user-oriented approaches that involve users in a larger degree is co-design and PD.

In co-design, future users are given room to inform, ideate and conceptualize design solutions, bringing their domain expertise into the design process. Here, researchers, designers and non-designers come together, letting collective creativity influences the design process. These collaborative endeavors are increasingly undertaken early in a design process, in what Sanders and Stappers [6] refer to as the 'fuzzy' front end of design due to the '[...] ambiguity and chaotic nature that characterise it' (ibid, page 4). As illustrate in Figure 1, the design outcome is here often unknown and can be informed and explored alongside future users.

PD evolved as a design approach in Scandinavia in the 70's, and centered around joint-decision making in the workplace empowering resource weak stakeholders (usually local trade unions) [6][23].

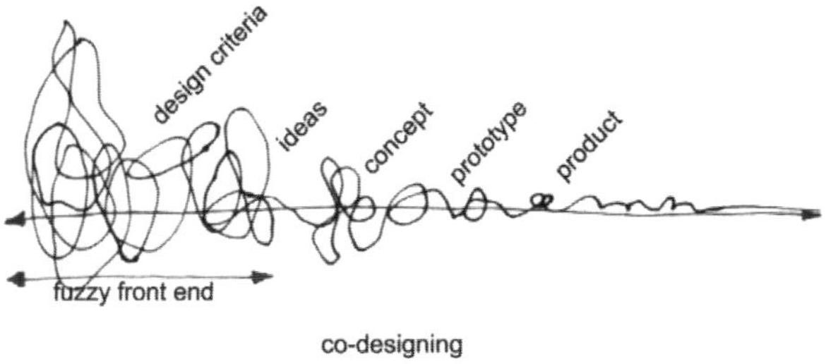

Figure 1. Sanders and Stappers [6] illustrating the co-desing process.

Researchers engaged in PD want to ensure that future users are given more influence and initiative in the design and are seen as 'partner' in the process. The motivation for choosing PD as a design approach varies from being a political position, where users have the right to influence a design solution, to a more pragmatic view where allowing users to inform and participate in the creation of design makes it easier to create suitable design outcomes [3]. Over the decades, the research community has elevated several core principles important for a successful PD process. At the heart of PD lies a premise that those affected by a design solution should 'have a say' in the design process [5][23]. This has consequences for how the process is organized and which methods and tools are made available to the user partaking in the process. Design is about decision-making, and the choices we make during a PD process are shared with future users [4]. PD opens up for collaborative decision-making which Bratteteig and Wagner [4] explain are the exercise of shared power. This shared power, alongside a shared and mutual understanding, regulate the decision-making process. Mutual learning is another guiding principle in PD. Here, mutual respect between two collaborative partners is achieved by letting them learn about each other's mindsets and work practices [5]. Researchers and designers need to learn about the domain and activities of the participants and non-designers in the project, and vice versa. The partners need to build trust and share knowledge across fields of practice. Through mutual learning and interdisciplinary knowledge sharing, the collaborative team can generate ideas and visions about new design solutions and practices. Another principle in PD is co-realization. Here, prototypes, tool and techniques play an important role in visualizing possible design solutions [5]. Tangle artifacts are used to help the team make appropriate decisions.

Bringing together stakeholders with potentially diverging perspectives can challenge participation [7]. The research communities engaged in co-design and PD have shed light on various challenges and issues that can arise in settings of collaborative decision-making [3]. Sanders and Stappers [6] present several issues regarding co-design and society's reluctance to adopt the approach. Firstly, co-design principles are in direct opposition of the power structures in many business communities; hierarchies and control are cornerstones in many manufacturing companies and asking them to give up this control have been met with reluctance. Secondly, in adopting co-design perspectives one must believe that all people are creative. Many people find it difficult to think of themselves as creative and are therefore reluctant to take a more active role as a co-designer in a design project. A successful co-design process requires creative initiative from the entire team and the participants must fully commit to the role.

Securing participation and creative initiative through design artifacts that can support future users in visualizing possible design solutions is therefore important. Enabling future users to communicate and discuss design problems and outcomes through, e.g., mock-ups and prototypes has been important from the very beginning of PD. These design tools lessen the need for users to adopt the specialized and technical language of designers [3].

IV. THEORETICAL CONCEPT

Due to divergent perspectives among stakeholders, maintaining coherence across different practices can be difficult. In studying these differences, Star and Greisemer [24] propose the concept of boundary objects as a key for enabling cross-disciplinary collaboration. Boundary objects are objects or artifacts that serve as a means of communication and translation between interdisciplinary groups. They describe boundary objects as

> ...objects which are both plastic enough to adapt to local needs and the constraints of the several parties employing them, yet robust enough to maintain a common identity across site (ibid, p. 8).

Boundary objects can be both abstract or concrete and can have different meaning depending on the social world observing or using them. Their structure should, however, be common enough to be recognized by multiple worlds. They are external *representations* of reality which simplifies an issue so that it more easily can be communicated [25]. In their work on boundary objects, Morris et al., [26], referring to the work of Zeitlyn [27], shed light on a three-way relationship between 1) what is being represented (reality), 2) the representation itself (the boundary object) and 3) the intentions of the maker of the object and the audience. While boundary objects are created with a specific intention, they take on a separate identity once produced. A person's interpretation of a boundary object reflects their perception of reality, and the maker of the object can not predict how the object will be used and interpretated by a user.

Dalsgaard, Halskov and Basballe [28] provide an overview of the work on boundary objects done by the research community. Here, they explain how Bertelsen [29] used the concept of boundary objects to explain how design artifacts act as mediators between groups in a design process, and how Bechky [30] introduced the concept of *transformative* boundary objects. With transformative boundary objects, knowledge is shared between professional boundaries and members of one group reaches a new understanding of a problem or topic based on the knowledge shared by the other group, altering and enriching their world view. It expands the understanding of a process or product, and this again enhances the person's understanding of his own work, shedding new light on the world.

Jean et al., [31] explain how serious games (games intended for other purposes than entertainment, e.g., for education and training) can function as a catalyst for *boundary crossing* where stakeholders with different professions, ideologies and perspectives collaborate. Here, boundary objects, in the form of artifacts, people or even institutions, play an important role in bridging the space between actors, and act as a mean to align different perspectives. A balance must, however, be found between rigidity and flexibility so that the object can unite different interests and also encompass the many practices they seek to unite. Morris et al., [26] suggest using structured boundary objects in the form of a board game to facilitate exposing and reconciling trade-offs between stakeholders with different incentives, perspectives and values in local agri-food systems. They explain how games can both organize knowledge and produce comparable visual outputs useful for communication.

V. Research Method

In this Section, we give an overview of the research method, including research activities like project meetings and card-making activities. We describe the methods of data collection and analysis, as well as ethical considerations for the study.

A. Research method

In this study we use qualitative methods when inquiring into how and why design cards facilitated for interdisciplinary co-design of ICTs.

1) Data collection

Data was collected through various activities including formal project meetings, direct observation during physical simulations, an online workshop, and a pilot workshop using a first draft of the design cards. Lastly, a co-design workshop using the MixED design cards was held with medical educators and students.

a) Formal project meetings

Three formal project meetings were held between the 17th of June 2021 and 21st of March 2022 between the researchers and three stakeholders from the medical center. The stakeholders were a senior lecturer and educator (early 60s), a facilitator, student advisor and educator (late 30s), and the third was an associate professor (early 50s). The purpose of the meetings was to establish a shared understanding of the project and the fields of practice as a basis for a project plan developed by the first author. Here, note-taking were used to record ideas and discussions. In the third meeting, held online due to Covid-19, were held with the first and second author and the three representatives from the medical center. Data was collected through written notes and a screen recording which was later transcribed.

b) Observation during physical simulations

Unstructured direct observation was made of two physical simulations at the training center. Simulation #1 was a student-driven simulation held on the 1st of December 2021. This simulation included eight Bachelor students in paramedic, two students in continuing education in emergency nursing and two educators facilitating the simulation. The first author followed the group of students for two hours during three different medical scenarios. Data was recorded through field notes, and from informal conversations with the facilitators and three students. The notes were written into the researcher's field diary. A follow-up, semi-structured formal discussion between the first author and one of the facilitators were also held.

Unstructured direct observation was also performed during simulation #2 on the 10th of March 2022. Here, the first and second author observed a full-scale emergency drill involving educators at the medical center, around 100 paramedic and specialist nurse students, medical workers from a Norwegian hospital, emergency services in the municipality and Red Cross. The researchers followed the drill for two hours, and recorded data in the form of individual note-taking and conversations between the researchers documented in a memo by the first author.

The primary goal of observing these activities was to understand how the physical simulations were conducted and their desired learning outcomes.

c) Card-making activities

The design cards were made in an iterative design process using collaborative brainstorming between the first and second author. The brainstorming was based on several activities including 1) project meetings with the three stakeholders in the project, 2) direct observations of physical simulations, 3) e-mail correspondence were stakeholders expressed what type of scenarios they found suitable for a mixed reality simulation, and 4) informal conversations and discussions with the participants. The first and second author held six design workshops lasting between 1 to 4,5 hours. In total, 19 hours were spent designing the cards. In addition to the information from the activities, the researchers took inspiration from previous research on design cards, like the PLEX-cards and the Ideation Decks [18][32], and a similar study undertaken by the third author in another research context. In total, 46 cards divided into five categories were created. The categories, as illustrated in Table 1, include 1) simulation, 2) medium, 3) interaction, 4) learning outcomes and 5) challenges. As illustrated in Figure 2, the layout of the cards is simple: each card has a written label and an abstract or figurative image meant to spark inspiration and individual interpretation. The images were downloaded from royalty free services like Unsplash. The researchers also created rules for the design cards stipulating how the cards should be used in a workshop. These are further explained in Section VI.

TABLE I. CATEGORIES AND LABELS IN THE MIXED DESIGN CARDS

Category	Cards and labels
Scenario	Traffic accident, drowning accident, fire accident, home nursing, psychiatry, accident site, prison, falling accident, inside the body, overdose, heart attack.
Medium	2D images (slideshow), 2D video, 3D video, 360-video, Augment Reality (AR), Virtual Reality (VR), Mixed Reality (MR).
Interaction	Speech, gesticulating, holding objects, movement, looking, feeling, buttons
Learning outcomes	Empathy, time management, stress management, collaboration, multitasking, communication, physical skills, technical skill, confidence, focus, problem-solving, critical thinking, adaptivity, leadership
Challenges	How to perform this individually? How to perform in a group? How does an instructor fit in? There is too little time. Too small or big space. How does teamwork work? How does a marker fit in?

d) Pilot workshop

The three researchers held a pilot test of the design cards in a workshop with ICT students. The workshop was facilitated by the first and second author, with the third author joining the students in testing the cards. Here, data was collected through note-taking during the workshop and in the follow-up discussion with the students.

a) Co-design workshop with desig cards

A two-hour co-design workshop with five educators and facilitators from the medical training center, three bachelor students and the researchers was held on the 1st of March 2022. Data was collected through audio recordings, pictures, note-taking, follow-up conversations with participants, and

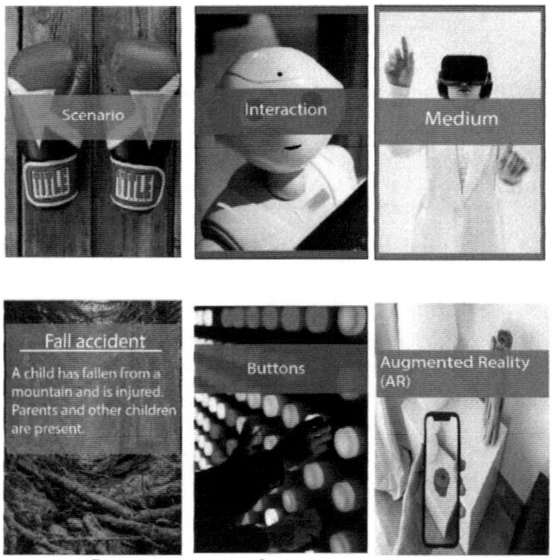

Figure 2. Layout of the design cards.

the design outcomes from each group in the form of Post-it notes and paper sketches. The workshop is further described in Section VI. The primary goal of this activity was to use the design cards as a generative tool to 1) ideate and conceptualize content for a mixed reality training room and 2) to facilitate collaboration between educators, students, and researchers.

2) Data analysis

Data from the observations, project meetings and workshops were analyzed by the first and second author. The first author used data from memos, the research diary and audio and video recordings to categorize important findings that would later be made into the cards.

The second author used thematic analysis when transcribing and analyzing the data. Thematic analysis is a method used for analyzing qualitative data by sorting and coding the data, and create relevant themes across datasets [33]. The process of analysis is illustrated in Table 2 and includes 1) organizing and preparing the data for analysis, transcribing the audio and video recording, 2) coding the datasets, 3) winnowing the data, 4) reviewing categories, 5) generating themes. Themes are data that correlated to each other from multiple sources, like a participant's statements and actions in the workshop. This inductive process ensured the finding of relevant and related information across multiple datasets.

TABLE II. THE PROCESS OF ANALYZING DATA

Steps	Activities	Codes and themes
Preparing data	Transcribing audio and video recordings.	
Code	Color-coding all the data with wider categories.	Codes: working together, explanation, annoyed or angry, creative, impressed, struggling, amused, decisive, personal experience
Winnowing	Winnowing the already color-coded data two times. Narrowing and choosing important finings.	
Reviewing categories	Defining and renaming categories, combining categories,	Positive experience: amused, intrigues/curious, engaged, impressed. Negative experience: confused, having difficulties, annoyed. Collaboration and group dynamic: working together, creativity, decisive. Previous experiences: own experiences, working together, engagement.
Generating themes	Themes emerged for further analyzing the categories	Creative collaboration, own experience, stakeholder experience, technology domain knowledge, health domain knowledge, use of domain-specific terms, understanding the rules [in the workshop], feedback.

B. Research ethics

This study was conducted following institutional guidelines for research ethics from Østfold University College and the Norwegian Center for Research Data (NSD). Data management and consent forms used in the project were approved by NSD (NSD number 788872). Participants partaking in activities where images, video and audio recordings were used for data collection were informed of the purpose of the study and how the data would be used. Participants gave written approval regarding data collection and analysis, permitting information to be used in scientific publications and other dissemination work. To ensure the confidentiality and privacy of the participants, the data collected during the workshops and meetings was stored in a secure location not accessible to the public. Only the three researchers involved in the study has access to the data, and participants were anonymized in the analysis.

Direct observation of the physical simulations took place without informed consent from participants. The purpose of this observation was to gain insight into the everyday life of medical educators, students, and other partitioners. Data collected during these activities are in the form of written notes and memos, and no personal or identifiable data were collected.

VI. USING DESIGN CARDS IN A CO-DESIGN WORKSHOP AT THE MEDICAL TRAINING CENTER

This study aims to explore the design of an immersive and virtual training simulator for the medical training center. The center is currently equipped with manikins, physical simulators, welfare technology, and medical equipment. Personnel at the center want to investigate how a now empty room can function as a virtual training simulator for students and medical practitioners. The goal of the project is to explore how the training simulator can be designed to support learning opportunities by allowing users to practice different sequences of medical events in a safe environment. Together with medical educators and facilitators at the centers, we explore design solutions for this virtual training simulator. The MixED design cards and rules for the co-design workshop were created based on several project meetings between participants and researchers, direct observation of physical simulations, and collaborative brainstorming between the first and second author. The card deck consists of 46 cards divided into five categories. Each card has a written label and an abstract or figurative image meant to spark inspiration and interpretation.

In this two-hour co-design workshop, nine participants were divided into three smaller teams. Two of the teams had two medical educators or facilitators (age mid-30s to early 60s) and one student (in their 20s). In the last group, the third author partook as the third member to get equal groups. The first author facilitated the workshop, beginning with a 15-minute introduction to the design cards and the rules of the co-design activity. The workshop was divided into four phases: individual assignment, group assignment 1, group assignment 2, and presentation of scenarios.

In the individual assignment, each team member selected one random card from each category (except a challenge card which were introduced later). As illustrated in Figure 3, Post-it notes and paper sheets were used to write down ideas about possible medical scenarios in a rapid idea generation activity. This activity lasted five minutes and was repeated three times.

In the second and third phase, the team got together and discussed their ideas, selecting and possible merging the ideas into one scenario. In phase three, we introduced the challenge cards. The participants first picked one challenge-card and repeated the processes three times over the course of 15 minutes. This challenged them to discuss organizational issues with the scenario they were currently working on.

As illustrated in Figure 4, each team presented their scenario in front of the other groups at the end of the workshop, prompting a discussion among the different teams.

Figure 3. Participants discussing and generating ideas with design cards in the workshop.

Figure 4. Participant presenting the scenario.

VII. FINDINGS

The findings are presented in two parts. First, we cover the insights gained from the initial design phase leading up to the creation of the design cards. Here, we identify misunderstandings and design opportunities from the fuzzy front end of the design process. We then present the findings from the co-design workshop using the design cards.

A. *The fuzzy front end*

One of the more evident discoveries from the early design phase was the language barriers that divided the two different practices. We spent a lot of time trying to explain different domain-specific concepts. Concepts that we had already covered in previous meetings were brought up again in the second and third project meeting. One of the participants expressed a lack of understanding and confusions around terminology in the project plan. There were concepts from ICT that medical practitioners found hard to understand, as well as concepts from their practice field that the researchers used incorrectly. The team strived (and failed) to establish the expectations of the collaboration early on. There was no clear consensus on what the researchers expect from the medical practitioners, and vice versa. This was an issue long into the project, where misunderstandings about practices played a large role. We failed to establish a common ground in initial project meetings. The educators at the center alternated between different ICT concepts during this early phase, discussing different technical and physical solutions and requirement. Parallel, the researchers tried to explain that they wanted the practitioners to participate in a co-design process where we explore requirements together through a series of design workshops. Later, in the online project meeting, the participants discussed two different projects that they wanted to simulate. In the first one, they wished to simulate events that are difficult to train on with the equipment they already have (e.g., a fire in a tunnel or a highway car accident) using projector technology. The other project should simulate internal bodily functions, where the student can "stand" inside the body and observe blood levels and explore what happens inside the body, e.g., during an infectious disease. While discussing these two ideas, one participant commented that the important thing was to decide what technology should be installed in the room, and what type of requirements was needed to rig and equip the room, saying:

> ...What kind of projectors should we have, what kind of PC should we have. In other words, all these physical prerequisites, that is what needs to be in place first before you start thinking about different technologies. [...] But in my understanding, the first thing we really have to do is figure out how to rig this room. And I'm missing that in the project plan. #1

The participant explained that they wanted the ICT solution up and running as soon as possible, and wanted the researchers to start investigating possible hardware and software applications that could be bought or developed. One researcher stressed that the technical requirements would be made clearer later in the design process, after we've held collaborative workshops as described in the project plan. The design workshops would clarify what they need this room and the training simulation to be, and then we could decide on which technology would be best suited to support this. As there were disagreements between the participants on what they wanted the room to be, the second author asked them for clarification, where one of the participants answered '[I] don't think we disagree on what we need, but from my perspective it's what we need first'. #1

As the design process progressed, we also found ample opportunities to learn from each other's different experiences and expertise. In the second project meeting, a lot of time were spent cleaning up the terminology to find common ground and a shared understanding. For example, one participant asked what the researchers meant regarding 'Mixed Reality'. Explaining and discussing this, we agreed upon a definition. Likewise, they explained terms like training modules, simulations and simulators, which the researcher had used incorrectly in regard to how these were use in the context of medical practice. Here, they also expressed wanting an adaptable ICT solution that supports continuous creation of training simulations. A platform that could evolve over time so as not to be insufficient in a year or two. During the online workshop, participants partook in brainstorming activities with the researchers regarding the content of the simulator. We already had a list of different scenarios sent in an earlier e-mail correspondence between participants and researchers (e.g., home accidents, drowning accidents, noisy environments). Early in the online meeting, they also expressed wanting state of the art immersive ICT solutions, like Augmented Reality (AR) and Virtual Reality (VR) and reflected on what medium would be best suited for different types of content. After discussing logistics and organizational challenges with these technologies, they further considered more cost-effective solutions, like using standard imagery or 360 video in a CAVE-system. We also discussed interaction types, management of large groups of students, and platform usability.

After clarifying disagreements about ICT requirements and what they wanted from this system, we (to some degree) found a common ground. Participants expressed wanting to focus on projectors with interactive sensors. They wanted to have scenarios that multiple students from different medical fields could use to train on situations that are hard to simulate or teach with the equipment they already have. They also wanted a solution that mixed the physical and the virtual environment. We also agreed upon the need for a user-friendly solution as the students are most likely to operate the simulation themselves.

B. *Using design cards in the co-design workshop*

Using the MixED design cards in the co-design workshop prompted both positive and negative feedback. Most of the participants were not familiar with design workshops using design cards to ideate and generate design solutions. Many expressed confusion early in the workshop and when we introduced the challenge-cards in the third round. It became evident that the concepts had different meanings and connotations based on the background of the participant, which led many participants to ask the facilitator for clarifications. In the audio recordings, one participant that did not understand one of the labels are heard saying 'I don't know the subject. I just have to come up with something' #3-3. Some participants expressed annoyance about improper use of labels. One example being the card suggesting using Mixed Reality as a medium. Here, the designer used the abbreviation MR, which in medical practice in Norway refers to MRI scanning. Another participant said that

> ...what is the difference between [the label] and the practical skills? Yes, [the researchers] does not know the concept here. #3-1

There was confusion about the rules of the card game at the beginning of a new round, e.g., when one participant drew the same card twice. This was not specified in the rule-sheet they were given.

Although there was confusion around the labels and rules at the beginning of a new round, many participants quickly got comfortable using the cards to generate ideas. Many displayed both engagement and enjoyment when creating different scenarios. This is seen during the intended five-minute break, where all groups remained seated, continuing to discuss and create content. Multiple participants expressed that using the cards in an organized co-design workshop provided new perspectives on ICT solutions for simulating medical processes. One participant said that:

> ...this is the kind [of training simulations] that we can actually get to make, isn't it?", another adding that "and what I think is very good now is that this is a very feasible scenario. #1-3

In the follow-up conversation after the workshop were finished, one participant expressed that the workshop was a great learning experience, that the design cards "forced" them to think creatively and to come up with achievable concepts.

> ...[Brainstorming with design cards] makes you think new and differently, and you are influenced by how others think [...] and that's how you come up with new ideas. #4

One participant with extensive experience about learning methodologies explained that the workshop showed them how to "think backwards" regarding the methods they normally would use to achieve specific learning outcomes, and that '[design cards] challenges us to think in a different way, so it was very exciting'. #3

At the end of the workshop the groups presented their ideas for the rest of the participants. They showed excitement for each other's concepts and discussed possibilities and challenges with the scenarios.

VIII. DISCUSSION

In this discussion, we shed light on how the design cards worked in supporting collaboration and finding common ground between the designers and non-designers. We discuss possible explanations for the challenges we faced early in the design process, and why the design cards helped ease the collaboration in the workshop. We also discuss the design cards in regard to the concept of boundary objects. We then discuss the role played by the cards in giving the non-designers a voice and how the cards helped co-realize design solutions across disciplines.

Myers, Piccolo and Collins [10] suggest that design cards can democratize knowledge and support co-design process by enabling more engaging and playful design experiences. We find that this also applies in our study. The layout and design of the cards, alongside the rules in the workshop, provoked new contextual perspectives regarding design problems and possible ICT solutions. This corresponds well with the discussions made by Kwiatkowska, Szóstek and Lamas [19]. The MixED design cards were suitable as a toolkit for promoting collaboration between an interdisciplinary team of researchers in design and non-designers in the fuzzy front end of a design process. As a tangible tool, it helped co-realize and visualizing possible design solutions.

According to Bratteteig, Bødker, Dittrich, Mogensen and Simonsen [5], future users should be given the power to influence the decisions made during a design process. In early projects meetings, the voice the participants had were influenced by their understanding of design and development processes. They are not accustomed to design practices of ICT solutions; the various welfare technologies at the training center are developed by companies specializing in creating and selling medical simulators. The result of this was seen in the early projects meetings; the participants disagreed on what they needed this simulator to be and divided much attention to what technology to buy, how the room should be rigged and how quickly we could get the simulator running. This is discussed by Bratteteig and Wagner [3] as a challenge when dealing with 'wicked' and 'ill-defined' design problems, explain that 'most design processes are open-ended, often exploratory, and highly complex' (ibid, p. 5). It is important to make design decisions that support the ability to remake design choices and closing in on a design solution too early in the process puts unwanted restrictions on the possible design outcome. What is interesting, is that although the participants expressed wanting a solution that where 'open' enough to evolve over time (which were not possible in the welfare technologies they usually bought), they wanted to hasten the design process by jumping straight to buying state of the art ICTs. We understand this contradiction as their unfamiliarity with the practice of design and our role as design researchers (and not developers). Explaining what we wanted to accomplish when inviting them to partake in the project as co-designers, trying to convince them to take a step back from technology specifications and be a part of a design process, was passed over multiple times. This is a common issue with co-design and participatory design. Different practices, unclear roles and diverging perspectives often lead to misunderstandings and tensions within the design team [3].

When introducing the design cards in the workshop we found that many of these tensions and misunderstanding were eased. The educators were given a tool they could use to express design decisions and a voice they didn't know they needed. It allowed them to discuss the problem space and reflect on what ICT solutions were appropriate to implement without being restricted by formal design or development languages. These language barriers are one of the issues when inviting non-designers into a co-design process, and the design cards lessened the need for the users to adopt a specialized design language [3]. As we understand, the workshop broke down their misconceptions about who can design and be creative. As discussed by Sanders and Stappers [6], people find it difficult to believe themselves creative and is therefore reluctant to take an active role in a design team. The cards worked as a tool enabling them to make meaningful decisions about design.

Before introducing the design cards in the workshop, we used the project plan created by the first author as our primary artifact to convey and discuss important aspect of the project and used it to try finding a shared understanding between participants. Looking back, this plan did not adequately help us establish the common ground that was needed to guide the project forward. But in many ways, the workshop did. What, then, was it about the workshop that did that the plan could not?

By taking another glance at the concept of boundary objects, Star and Greisemer [24] explain that these objects need to be plastic enough to adapt to local needs yet 'robust enough to maintain its identity across sites'. Jean et al., [31] further explain how there must be a balance between rigidity and flexibility if these objects are to unite different interests and practices. In the light of this, the project plan that we relied on in the project meetings was not suitable for establishing a shared understanding of the project. It was too rigid and not plastic enough to adapt to our needs. It does, however, seem that we found this balance in the design cards and the rules of the design game. The cards abstracted the specific language from both the medical and the ICT domain. The cards were plastic and flexible enough to adapt to local needs and encompassed the practices they sought to unite. And in combination with the rules and the context of the workshop, they were also rigid enough to unite the different interests in the project.

In their study, Jean et al., [31] also explain how serious game simulations have been 'isolated as a potential boundary object' to bring different stakeholders together. In our experience, however, the boundary object (in their case the simulations and in ours the design cards) should not be seen as an isolated object. It is how the artifact and the context of using the artifact came together that determined whether the artifact could unite the parties in their endeavor to collaborate. We can exemplify this by looking at the last activity in the workshop. Here, the different groups presented their design ideas and concept using a A3 paper sheet and Post-it notes. Using these tangible objects, the groups visualized and communicated possible scenarios and facilitated a discussion between the different groups. According to Morris et al., [26], boundary object can be visual representation of reality, like props, concept maps and mental models, for catalyzing discussions that can lead to a comprehensive exploration of the issues which are understood differently or incompletely by different actors. These can help reach a common level of understanding. However, it was the context of the workshop, the use of design cards and the rules of play, that made this discussion possible and meaningful.

The combination of the design cards and rules in the workshop also enabled the participants to think like designers. The design game expanded the world view of the participants, enriching their understanding of a design process and the terminology used by the different experts, which lies close to the concept of transformative boundary objects introduce by Bechky [30]. We observed that the design game helped the team challenge previous conceptions about each other's practice fields and found common ground regarding possible design solutions. We believe that the design cards in themselves did not give us that shared understanding; they are what Pennington [25] referred to as *representations* of reality, and they exist independently of collaboration and has different meanings for the different people using them. But as a design game, were the cards and the rules of play came together, they facilitated for interpretation and enabled negotiations. This is illustrated in the misunderstandings with the MR-card, where the designer's intent was 'Mixed Reality' and the participant's interpretation was MRI-scanning. If the researchers hadn't been there to clarify, the participant would have created a scenario about using MRI-scanning machines. Which is just as relevant for medical practice, it's just not what the designers had in mind when they created the card.

Facilitating for mutual learning by creating a space where designers can learn from non-designers, and vice versa, is important in a co-design process. As mentioned, we spent a lot of time explaining concepts across disciplines (e.g., cleaning up the project plan). The researchers tried to project the correct medical terminology explained to us by the practitioners onto the cards, but even then we didn't quite get it right; during the workshop, participants express frustration about the labels on the cards – both that they didn't understand ICT terms and that we had used medical terms incorrectly. At the same time, however, the erroneous terminology also triggered the work to create a shared understanding. They felt the need to explain and, in this, shared their expertise with the other stakeholders, something which again helped in the creative process. Seems like this is a positive attribute with design cards – they are "official" representations of problems, terms and technologies triggering critique, opposition, discussions, and the need for clarifications – the groundwork in creating mutual learning and shared understanding across disciplines. How the world is ordered by a deck of cards can be provocation, to one, several or all the stakeholders involved. If handled well, the provocations can be a boon to the co-realization of design solutions.

IX. Conclusion and Future Work

In this study, we found that bespoke design cards structured as a design game can support collaboration and in finding common ground across disciplines. The design game allowed non-designers to discuss the problem space and reflect on appropriate ICT solution without having to adopt a specialized design language. The language barrier between the different practices was an obstacle when trying to move the project forward, but it also allowed mutual learning opportunities between the stakeholders. This mutual learning was not achieved in the early design phase where we relied on a project plan to communicate shared goals and expectations. Introducing design cards in a co-design workshop triggered a more constructive exchange of knowledge across practices. Granted that the design cards are structured by a design game, space is created for the participants to express themselves. The design game acted as a mediator between the participants and researchers, and as a transformative boundary object by extending and transforming the participants understanding of the different practices. The workshop, cards and rules of play were both flexible and rigid enough to encompass and unite the different practices, facilitating a shared understanding of the problem space and project.

For future work, we suggest further analysis on how design games understood as transformative boundary objects, can support interdisciplinarity in design processes. We also suggest introducing design cards earlier in a co-design process and see what this can do for the collaborative process. This may support the collaborative parties to find common ground earlier.

References

[1] E. B.-N. Sanders and P. J. Stappers, "Probes, toolkits and prototypes: three approaches to making in codesigning," *CoDesign*, vol. 10, no. 1, pp. 5–14, Jan. 2014, doi: 10.1080/15710882.2014.888183. Accessed: April 5, 2023.

[2] A. R. Olesen, N. Holdgaard, and A. S. Løvlie, "Co-designing a co-design tool to strengthen ideation in digital experience design at museums," *CoDesign*, vol. 18, no. 2, pp. 227–242, Apr. 2022, doi: 10.1080/15710882.2020.1812668. Accessed: Mar. 2, 2023.

[3] T. Bratteteig and I. Wagner, "Unpacking the Notion of Participation in Participatory Design," *Comput Supported Coop Work*, vol. 25, no. 6, pp. 425–475, Dec. 2016, doi: 10.1007/s10606-016-9259-4. Accessed: April 5, 2023.

[4] T. Bratteteig and I. Wagner, "Disentangling power and decision-making in participatory design," in *Proceedings of the 12th Participatory Design Conference: Research Papers - Volume 1*, Roskilde Denmark: ACM, Aug. 2012, pp. 41–50. doi: 10.1145/2347635.2347642. Accessed: Mar. 2, 2023.

[5] T. Bratteteig, K. Bødker, Y. Dittrich, P. H. Mogensen, and J. Simonsen, "Organising principles and general guidelines for Participatory Design Projects," *Routledge international handbook of participatory design*, pp. 117–144, 2013. Accessed: April 5, 2023

[6] E. B.-N. Sanders and P. J. Stappers, "Co-creation and the new landscapes of design," *CoDesign*, vol. 4, no. 1, pp. 5–18, 2008, doi: 10.1080/15710880701875068. Accessed: Apr. 05, 2023.

[7] E. Brandt, T. Binder, and E. B.-N. Sanders, "Tools and Techniques: Ways to engage telling, making and enacting," in *Routledge international handbook of participatory design*, J. Simonsen and T. Robertson, Eds., London: Routledge, 2013, pp. 145–181.

[8] N. Bornoe, A. Bruun, and J. Stage, "Facilitating redesign with design cards: experiences with novice designers," in *Proceedings of the 28th Australian Conference on Computer-Human Interaction - OzCHI '16*, Launceston, Tasmania, Australia: ACM Press, 2016, pp. 452–461. doi: 10.1145/3010915.3010921. Accessed: Apr. 03, 2023.

[9] C. Wölfel and T. Merritt, "Method Card Design Dimensions: A Survey of Card-Based Design Tools," in *Human-Computer Interaction – INTERACT 2013*, P. Kotzé, G. Marsden, G. Lindgaard, J. Wesson, and M. Winckler, Eds., in Lecture Notes in Computer Science, vol. 8117. Berlin, Heidelberg: Springer Berlin Heidelberg, 2013, pp. 479–486. doi: 10.1007/978-3-642-40483-2_34. Accessed: May 25, 2022.

[10] C. Myers, L. S. G. Piccolo, and T. Collins, "Co-designing cards on social issues for creating educational games," in *Proceedings of the 32nd International BCS Human Computer Interaction Conference*, in HCI '18. Swindon, GBR: BCS Learning & Development Ltd., Jul. 2018, pp. 1–5. doi: 10.14236/ewic/HCI2018.164. Accessed: Aug. 09, 2022.

[11] Y. Deng, A. N. Antle, and C. Neustaedter, "Tango cards: a card-based design tool for informing the design of tangible learning games," in *Proceedings of the 2014 conference on Designing interactive systems*, Vancouver BC Canada: ACM, Jun. 2014, pp. 695–704. doi: 10.1145/2598510.2598601. Accessed: Sept. 07, 2022.

[12] K. Halskov and P. Dalsgård, "Inspiration card workshops," in *Proceedings of the 6th ACM conference on Designing Interactive systems - DIS '06*, University Park, PA, USA: ACM Press, 2006, p. 2. doi: 10.1145/1142405.1142409. Accessed: May 25, 2022.

[13] D. Peters, L. Loke, and N. Ahmadpour, "Toolkits, cards and games – a review of analogue tools for collaborative ideation," *CoDesign*, vol. 17, no. 4, pp. 410–434, Oct. 2021, doi: 10.1080/15710882.2020.1715444. Accessed: Oct. 10, 2022.

[14] E. Brandt and J. Messeter, "Facilitating collaboration through design games," in *Proceedings of the eighth conference on Participatory design Artful integration: interweaving media, materials and practices - PDC 04*, Toronto, Ontario, Canada:

ACM Press, 2004, p. 121. doi: 10.1145/1011870.1011885. Accessed: May 20, 2022.

[15] A. Lucero, P. Dalsgaard, K. Halskov, and J. Buur, "Designing with Cards," in *Collaboration in Creative Design*, P. Markopoulos, J.-B. Martens, J. Malins, K. Coninx, and A. Liapis, Eds., Cham: Springer International Publishing, 2016, pp. 75–95. doi: 10.1007/978-3-319-29155-0_5. Accessed: Sept. 08, 2022.

[16] F. Mueller, M. R. Gibbs, F. Vetere, and D. Edge, "Supporting the creative game design process with exertion cards," in *Proceedings of the SIGCHI Conference on Human Factors in Computing Systems*, Toronto Ontario Canada: ACM, Apr. 2014, pp. 2211–2220. doi: 10.1145/2556288.2557272. Accessed: Apr. 05, 2023.

[17] E. Hornecker, "Creative idea exploration within the structure of a guiding framework: the card brainstorming game," in *Proceedings of the fourth international conference on Tangible, embedded, and embodied interaction*, in TEI '10. New York, NY, USA: Association for Computing Machinery, Jan. 2010, pp. 101–108. doi: 10.1145/1709886.1709905. Accessed: Apr. 05, 2023.

[18] A. Lucero and J. Arrasvuori, "*PLEX Cards*: a source of inspiration when designing for playfulness," in *Proceedings of the 3rd International Conference on Fun and Games - Fun and Games '10*, Leuven, Belgium: ACM Press, 2010, pp. 28–37. doi: 10.1145/1823818.1823821. Accessed: Aug. 26, 2022.

[19] J. Kwiatkowska, A. Szóstek, and D. Lamas, "(Un)structured sources of inspiration: comparing the effects of game-like cards and design cards on creativity in co-design process," in *Proceedings of the 13th Participatory Design Conference on Research Papers - PDC '14*, Windhoek, Namibia: ACM Press, 2014, pp. 31–39. doi: 10.1145/2661435.2661442. Accessed: Apr. 05, 2023.

[20] T. Bekker and A. N. Antle, "Developmentally situated design (DSD): making theoretical knowledge accessible to designers of children's technology," in *Proceedings of the SIGCHI Conference on Human Factors in Computing Systems*, Vancouver BC Canada: ACM, May 2011, pp. 2531–2540. doi: 10.1145/1978942.1979312. Accessed: Apr. 05, 2023.

[21] J. Buur and A. Soendergaard, "Video card game: an augmented environment for user centred design discussions," in *Proceedings of DARE 2000 on Designing augmented reality environments*, Elsinore Denmark: ACM, Apr. 2000, pp. 63–69. doi: 10.1145/354666.354673. Accessed: Apr. 05, 2023.

[22] R. Roy and J. P. Warren, "Card-based design tools: a review and analysis of 155 card decks for designers and designing," *Design Studies*, vol. 63, pp. 125–154, Jul. 2019, doi: 10.1016/j.destud.2019.04.002. Accessed: Sept. 08, 2022.

[23] P. Ehn, "Participation in Design Things," presented at the Participatory Design Conference (PDC), Bloomington, Indiana, USA (2008), ACM Digital Library, 2008, pp. 92–101. Accessed: Mar. 07, 2023. [Online]. Available: http://urn.kb.se/resolve?urn=urn:nbn:se:mau:diva-11060

[24] S. L. Star and J. R. Griesemer, "Institutional Ecology, 'Translations' and Boundary Objects: Amateurs and Professionals in Berkeley's Museum of Vertebrate Zoology, 1907-39," *Social Studies of Science*, vol. 19, no. 3, pp. 387–420, 1989, Accessed: Mar. 07, 2023. [Online]. Available: https://www.jstor.org/stable/285080

[25] D. Pennington, "A conceptual model for knowledge integration in interdisciplinary teams: orchestrating individual learning and group processes," *J Environ Stud Sci*, vol. 6, no. 2, pp. 300–312, Jun. 2016, doi: 10.1007/s13412-015-0354-5. Accessed: Mar. 04, 2023.

[26] J. Morris *et al.*, "Games as boundary objects: charting trade-offs in sustainable livestock transformation," *International Journal of Agricultural Sustainability*, vol. 19, no. 5–6, pp. 525–548, Nov. 2021, doi: 10.1080/14735903.2020.1738769. Accessed: Apr. 01, 2023.

[27] D. Zeitlyn, "Representation/Self-representation: A Tale of Two Portraits; or, Portraits and Social Science Representations," *Visual Anthropology*, vol. 23, no. 5, pp. 398–426, Oct. 2010, doi: 10.1080/08949460903472978. Accessed: Apr. 04, 2023.

[28] P. Dalsgaard, K. Halskov, and D. A. Basballe, "Emergent boundary objects and boundary zones in collaborative design research projects," in *Proceedings of the 2014 conference on Designing interactive systems*, Vancouver BC Canada: ACM, Jun. 2014, pp. 745–754. doi: 10.1145/2598510.2600878. Accessed: Mar. 01, 2023.

[29] O. Bertelsen, "Elements of a Theory of Design Artefacts: a contribution to critical systems development research. PhD Thesis.," *DAIMI Report Series*, no. 531, Art. no. 531, Jan. 1998, doi: 10.7146/dpb.v27i531.7060. Accessed: Mar. 07, 2023.

[30] B. A. Bechky, "Sharing Meaning Across Occupational Communities: The Transformation of Understanding on a Production Floor," *Organization Science*, vol. 14, no. 3, pp. 312–330, Jun. 2003, doi: 10.1287/orsc.14.3.312.15162. Accessed: Mar. 07, 2023.

[31] S. Jean, W. Medema, J. Adamowski, C. Chew, P. Delaney, and A. Wals, "Serious games as a catalyst for boundary crossing, collaboration and knowledge co-creation in a watershed governance context," *Journal of Environmental Management*, vol. 223, pp. 1010–1022, Oct. 2018, doi: 10.1016/j.jenvman.2018.05.021. Accessed: Apr. 04, 2023.

[32] M. Golembewski and M. Selby, "Ideation decks: a card-based design ideation tool," in *Proceedings of the 8th ACM Conference on Designing Interactive Systems - DIS '10*, Aarhus, Denmark: ACM Press, 2010, pp. 89–92. doi: 10.1145/1858171.1858189. Accessed: May 25, 2022.

[33] V. Braun and V. Clarke, "Using thematic analysis in psychology," *Qualitative Research in Psychology*, vol. 3, no. 2, pp. 77–101, Jan. 2006, doi: 10.1191/1478088706qp063oa. Accessed: Apr. 05, 2023.

A Tool for Generating Ambiguous Objects in Two Viewing Directions

Ken Nakaguchi, Koichi Matsuda and Oky Dicky Ardiansyah Prima
Graduate School of Software and Information Science
Iwate Prefectural University
152-52, Sugo, Takizawa, Iwate, Japan
e-mail: g236s003@s.iwate-pu.ac.jp, {matsuda, prima}@iwate-pu.ac.jp

Abstract—**Ambiguous objects provide visual shape information that can be interpreted differently depending on the viewing direction. Generating effective ambiguity objects is difficult and therefore requires easy-to-use computational modelling. In this paper, we propose a Three-Dimensional (3D) modelling tool to generate an object that can be perceived differently from two different viewing directions. The tool uses solid models of cylindrical surfaces parallel to each of the viewing directions. These models are intersected at the central axis and rotated according to the viewing direction, using the intersection as the origin. Finally, by transforming each Two-Dimensional (2D) figure drawn by the user in each viewing direction into a cylindrical surface, a 3D ambiguous object can be generated. These 2D figures can be drawn using mouse click events. The generated ambiguous objects can be fabricated on a 3D printer to demonstrate the usability of the proposed tool. Our experiments show that ambiguous objects consisting of simple and complex shapes were successfully generated.**

Keywords-3D-Illusion; ambiguous object; ambiguous cylinder; 3D modelling; visual perception.

I. INTRODUCTION

An optical illusion is a phenomenon in which our perception of an object differs from its physical reality. This illusion is important in the study of human visual processing. The study of optical illusions began with Two-Dimensional (2D) images but has now been extended to Three-Dimensional (3D) objects. The former are ambiguous figures that represent a single figure but have multiple interpretable meanings, such as Edgar Rubin's "Face-Vase illusion" [1]. These figures are most often represented in binary images, where the white areas are foreground figures and the black areas are the intangible background, or vice versa. The boundaries shared by these areas play an important role in the figure assignment process. The latter are ambiguous objects, the shape of which can appear to be different depending on the direction in which they are viewed. Such objects can be generated in three ways: by making a discontinuous structure appear continuous from certain viewing directions [2], by the use of curved surfaces instead of planes [3], or by the use of angles other than 90 degrees to create a rectangular appearance [4]. Sugihara (2012) classified ambiguous objects into seven generations and showed that all objects are accompanied by illusions [5].

Computer-aided tools are available to assist in the generation of ambiguous figures and objects. The ambiguous figure generation tool finds partial matches by performing shape matching and deformation of the two figures and then stitching them together to produce the resulting image [6]. However, generating ambiguous objects is more complex. The tools used need to be built on a 3D modelling framework, with geometric modifications to the shapes also being performed in 3D [7]. Furthermore, unlike ambiguous figures, the generated ambiguous objects are viewing direction dependent, requiring the viewpoint to be determined prior to modelling.

In this study, we focused on the following two aspects when developing a tool to facilitate generating ambiguous objects. Firstly, the tool is implemented on top of a 3D modelling framework, but the shape of the individual objects is determined by drawing in 2D. Secondly, the shape of the generated ambiguous objects changes adaptively according to the viewing direction. This implementation allows users unfamiliar with 3D modelling to create ambiguous objects.

The rest of this paper is organized as follows. Section II describes related works on ambiguous object generation. Section III describes our proposed tool for generating the ambiguous objects in two viewing directions. Section IV summarizes our results. Finally, Section V concludes our study and discusses future work.

II. RELATED WORKS

The methods used to generate ambiguous figures and objects can be divided into three categories, as described below.

The first method generates ambiguous figures by manipulating the relationship between edges or faces. Shinohara et al. constructed a system that can portray impossible figures realistically using ray tracing [8]. Their system provides predefined basic parts, where the user can interactively manipulate the rendering depth of each surface with respect to the parts. Owada et al. proposed a system for generating ambiguous figures by taking a 3D object as input and interactively editing the edges of its 2D plane from a given viewing direction [9]. These operations can be performed using mouse events. Both systems facilitate the generation of ambiguous figures, but there is no continuity of edges and faces in the resulting 3D objects.

The second is Fukuda's method of generating ambiguous objects in two viewing directions [10]. These works were published in the book "One solid with two shapes" but are difficult to reproduce because the parameters and optimization methods required for their generation were not disclosed.

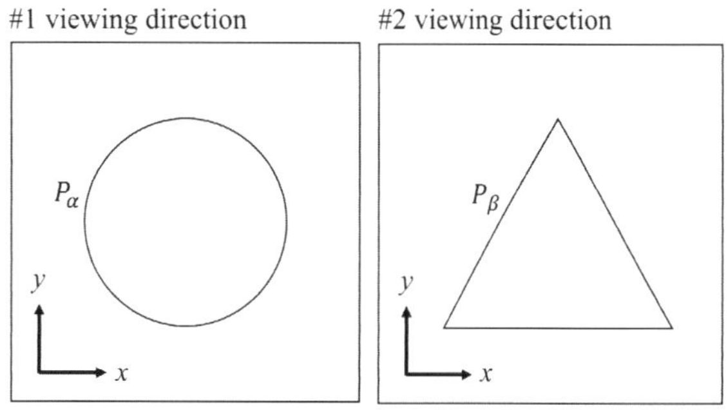

Figure 1. Two 2D figures created to be perceived from two viewing directions.

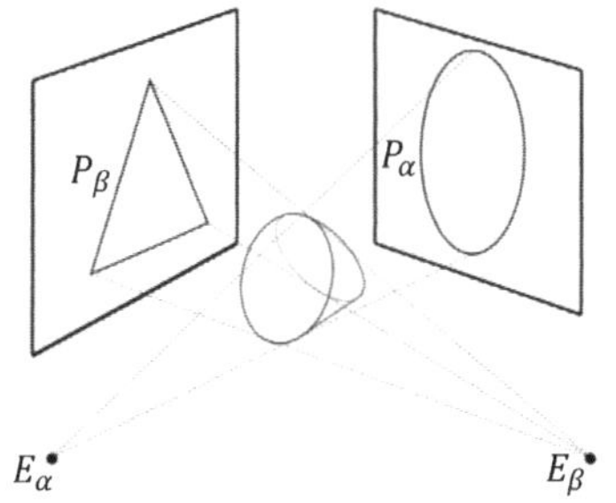

Figure 2. Two 2D figures integrated into a solid 3D object that can be perceived from two viewing directions.

The third is the method of generating ambiguous objects by solving linear equations. Sugihara experimented with generating an ambiguous object using 2D planar shapes such as flowers and stars as input. However, the results showed that the solution of the linear equations could not be obtained depending on the viewing direction and the given input geometry.

Although it does not fit into the above categories, a simple tool for generating ambiguous objects without the need to edit the object's shape has been proposed [11]. This tool generates ambiguous objects by adjusting the position and inclination of several square pillars placed in 3D space. However, due to the requirement of using square pillars, this tool cannot generate objects of arbitrary shape.

All of the above studies focused on modelling the shape of the ambiguous object in its generation but did not consider modelling the shape independent of the viewing direction. The automatic modification of the shape by changing the viewpoint would facilitate the generation of ambiguous objects.

III. Our Proposed Tool

The proposed tool uses an approach that allows the generation of 3D objects seen from each viewing direction, based on 2D figures. The generation of an ambiguous object involves the drawing of 2D figures and the integration of two solid 3D models.

A. *The drawing of 2D figures*

The tool provides two canvases for drawing each figure, where the user can draw a 2D figure by drawing a single stroke on each canvas. Note that the line segments composing each figure are not supposed to self-intersect. Figure 1 shows a circle P_α and a triangle P_β drawn on the canvases, respectively.

The figures on the canvas are stored as polygons. However, their shapes need to be optimized to make them equal in size and to remove unnecessary vertices caused by hand tremors during the drawing process. The proposed tool optimizes the figures drawn by the user through the following pre-processing.

a. *Normalization*

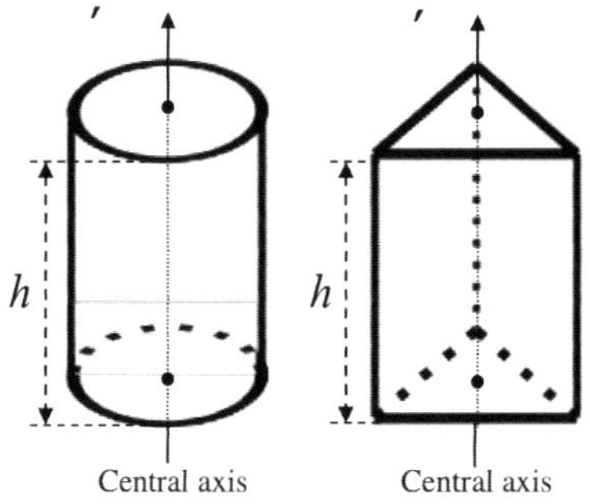

Figure 3. Two cylindrical surfaces for this study.

To make the two figures in an ambiguous object more visible, it is necessary to scale both figures equally. Therefore, the center coordinate

$$C(c_x, c_y) = \left(\frac{1}{n}\sum_{i=1}^{n} P_i^x, \frac{1}{n}\sum_{i=1}^{n} P_i^y\right) \quad (1)$$

of each figure is taken as the origin, and the vertices P_i that makes up the figure is then normalized by

$$P'_i = \frac{w}{\max(P^x, P^y) - \min(P^x, P^y)}\left(P_i^x, P_i^y\right), \quad (2)$$

where w is a user-defined scale of the figure, while P^x and P^y represent the coordinates of the vertices.

b. *Smoothing*

The following smoothing process is applied to each vertex to reduce the distortion of the figure caused by hand tremors during drawing.

$$P''_i = smooth(P'_i) = \frac{1}{3}(P'_{i-1} + P'_i + P'_{i+1}). \quad (3)$$

This process effectively reduces noise in the vertices caused by subtle hand tremors.

c. *Vertices pruning*

To make the density of the vertices that make up the figure uniform, the distance between vertices

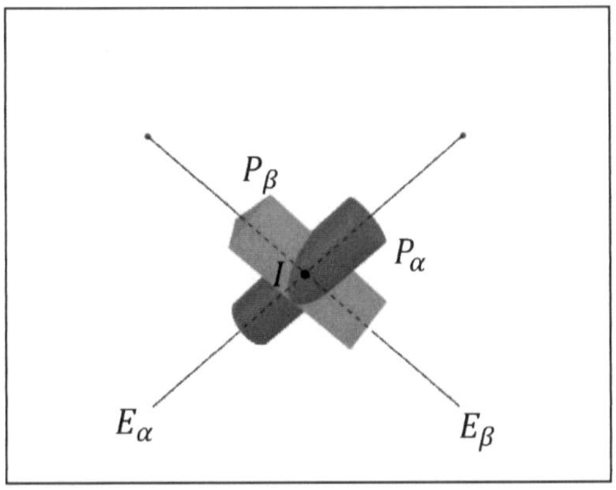

Figure 4. Two cylindrical surfaces A' and B' that intersect with respect to their viewing directions.

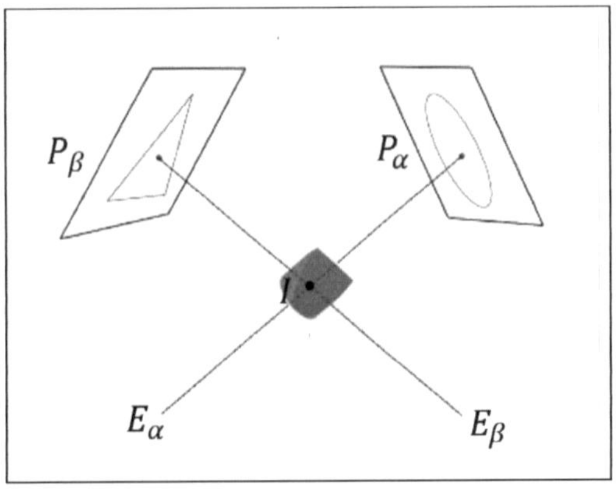

Figure 5. A solid object resulted from the Boolean intersection.

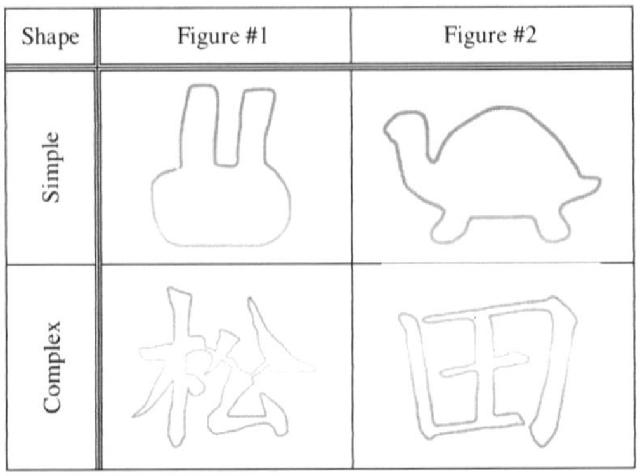

Figure 6. Figures for the construction of a simple and a complex ambiguous object.

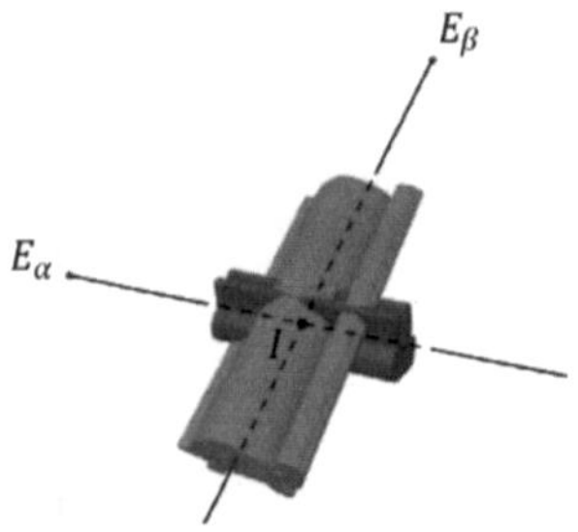

(a) Simple cylindrical surfaces

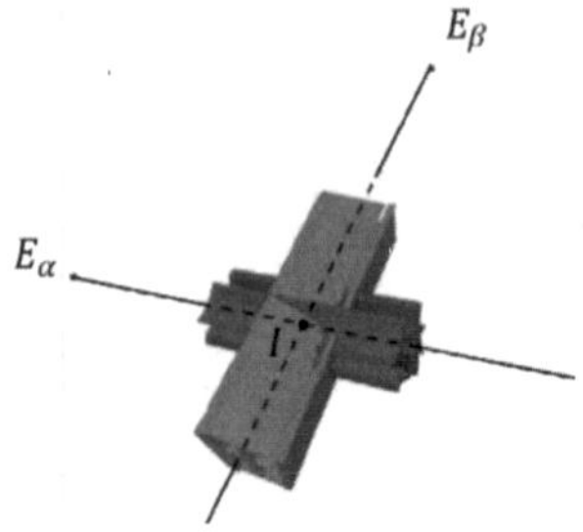

(b) Complex cylindrical surfaces

Figure 7. Cylindrical surfaces used to construct the ambiguous objects.

$$D_i = \sqrt{(P''^x_i - P''^x_{i+1})^2 + \left(P''^y_i - P''^y_{i+1}\right)^2} \tag{4}$$

that are less than a threshold is removed.

B. *The integration of two solid 3D models*

The integration of the two figures, as shown in Figure 1 into a single solid object must be done in a unique way. Figure 2 shows a possible integration in which the shape of P_α and P_β can be perceived from the viewpoint of E_α and E_β, respectively. This integration can be seen as the creation of an ambiguous 3D object representing the two figures. The shape of P_α is represented by an ellipsoid plane, while P_β is by a spherical triangle.

In this study, two cylindrical surfaces are used for the integration of the two figures. The integration takes the following steps.

Step 1: Generate a cylindrical surface for each figure. Figure 3 shows cylindrical surfaces A' and B' for P_α and P_β. The height of the cylindrical surface (h) should be high enough with respect to the viewing direction, as will be described later.

Step 2: Intersect the central axes (dashed lines) of the cylindrical surfaces A' and B', and rotate each cylindrical surface around the intersection point (I) to face the viewing points E_α and E_β, as shown in Figure 4.

Step 3: Perform a Boolean intersection to create a new solid from the intersection of the volumes of A' and B'. Figure 5 shows the resulting ambiguous object and its projected image plane as seen from E_α and E_β, respectively.

IV. Experimental Results

Ambiguous objects consisting of simple and complex shapes were created using the proposed tool. Figure 6 shows

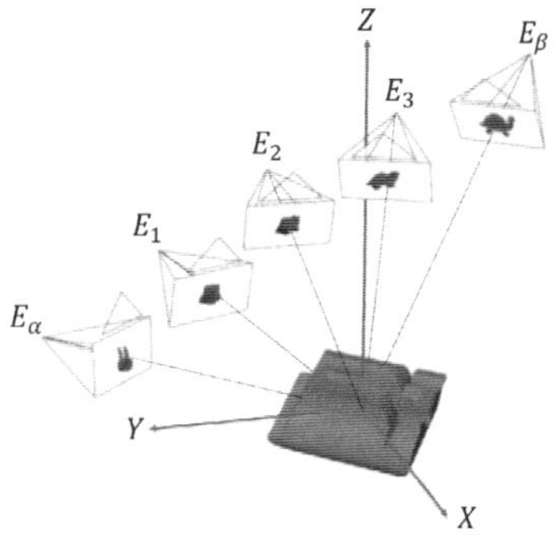

(a) Viewing directions.

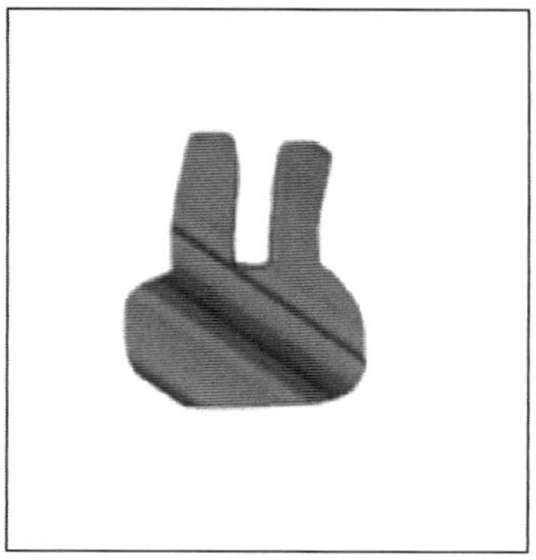

(b) The image plane viewed from E_{α}.

(c) The image plane viewed from E_1.

(d) The image plane viewed from E_2.

(e) The image plane viewed from E_3.

(f) The image plane viewed from E_{β}.

Figure 8. The resulting ambiguous objects constructed by using simple figures.

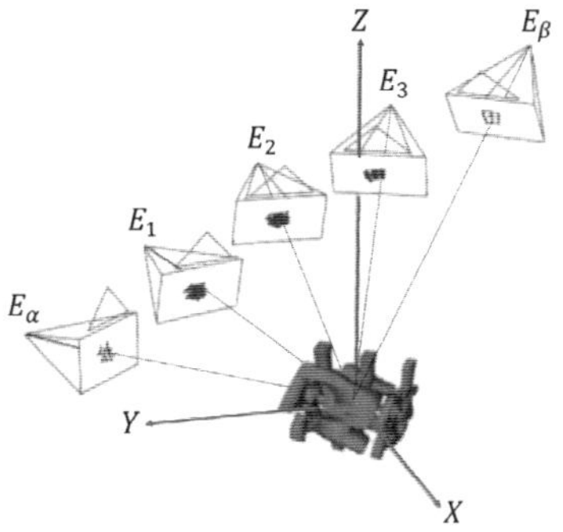

(a) Viewing directions.

(b) The image plane viewed from E_{α}.

(c) The image plane viewed from E_1.

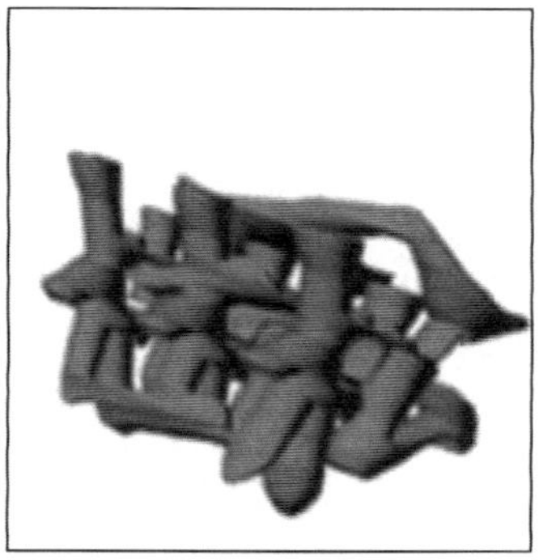

(d) The image plane viewed from E_2.

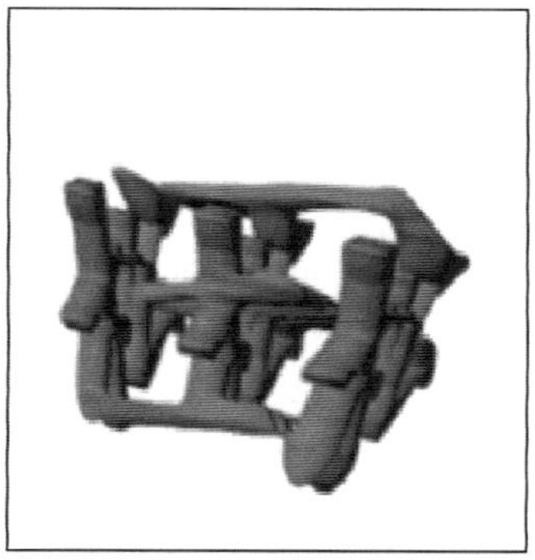

(e) The image plane viewed from E_3.

(f) The image plane viewed from E_{β}.

Figure 9. The resulting ambiguous objects constructed by using complex figures.

the 2D figures used to construct the ambiguous objects. The silhouettes of a turtle and a rabbit were used as simple figures. The figures are drawn almost entirely in outline, with no hollow areas. On the other hand, Japanese kanji characters were used as complex figures but were designed to be drawn with a single stroke.

Cylindrical surfaces associated to the simple and the complex figures were intersected to build ambiguous objects, as shown in Figure 7. Here, w=2.5 was used to rescale each figure to be 1m wide. The pre-processing shows that the cylindrical surfaces that intersect each other can be made to be of the same height. As both cylindrical surfaces are integrated by the Boolean interception, any change in viewing direction can generate a new ambiguous object. Unlike previous studies, the shape of the ambiguous object does not need to be edited each time the viewing direction is changed.

To show the difference between the correct and incorrect viewing directions of the generated ambiguous objects, the appearance of the objects in different viewing directions was captured, as shown in Figures 8 and 9. Let E_α and E_β be the correct viewing points and E_i the arbitrary viewing points (i=1,...,3), the original figures appear in its form when viewed from E_α and E_β.

V. CONCLUSION AND FUTURE WORK

In this paper, we propose a 3D modeling tool for generating ambiguous objects. These objects can be perceived differently from two different viewing directions. Users can easily generate ambiguous objects by simply drawing two 2D figures with this tool. Once the user defines the viewing direction of these figures, the ambiguous object is automatically generated. This approach differs significantly from those proposed in previous studies because the original 2D figures do not need to be modified by changes in viewing direction. Currently, there are several limitations in the proposed tool. First, if the angle between the two viewpoint directions is extremely small, the thickness of the generated ambiguous object becomes extremely thin, making it difficult to fabricate it with a 3D printer. Second, the appearance of the ambiguous object differs from the intended appearance even when it is viewed with only a slight viewpoint misalignment, because there is no tolerance process for viewpoint misalignment. Future work will include performing subjective evaluation experiments to evaluate the robustness of viewing the ambiguous objects generated by our tool.

REFERENCES

[1] E. Rubin, “Figure and Ground,” Readings in Perception, pp. 194–203, 1958.

[2] A. I. Seckel, “Master of Deception,” Sterling Publishing Co., Inc., 2004.

[3] G. Elber, “Modeling (Seemingly) Impossible Models,” Computer and Graphics, vol. 35, no. 3, pp. 632–638, 2011.

[4] K. Sugihara, “Three-Dimensional Realization of Anomalous Pictures: An Application of Picture Interpretation Theory to Toy Design,” Pattern Recognition, vol. 30, no. 7, pp. 1061–1067, 1997.

[5] K. Sugihara, “Evolution of Impossible Objects,” 9th International Conference on Fun with Algorithms, vol. 2, pp. 2:1–2:8, 2012.

[6] Y. -M. Kuo, H. -K. Chu, M. -T. Chi, R. -R. Lee, and T. -Y. Lee, “Generating Ambiguous Figure-Ground Images,” in IEEE Transactions on Visualization and Computer Graphics, vol. 23, no. 5, pp. 1534-1545, 2017.

[7] G. Sera and G. Elber, "Generation of View dependent Models Using Free Form Deformation," The Visual Computer, vol. 23, pp. 219-229, 2007.

[8] Y. Shinohara and Y. Miyashita, "Proposal of a Realistic Representation Method for Impossible Three-Dimensional Objects," Information Processing Society of Japan, HCI 2009-HCI-132, pp. 95-102, 2009.

[9] S. Owada and J. Fujiki, “Interactive Stereopsis of Impossible Objects as Artistic Expression,” Technical Report of the Institute of Image Information and Television Engineers, vol. 32, no. 14, pp. 43-46, 2008.

[10] S. Fukuda, “Shigeo Fukuda's Three-Dimensional Modeling,” Kawade Shobo Shinsha, 1977.

[11] K. Sugihara, “Ambiguous Pillars: a New Class of Impossible Objects,” Computer Aided Drafting, Design and Manufacturing, vol. 25, no. 4, pp. 19-25, 2015.

Toward an Automated Pruning for Apple Trees Based on Computer Vision Techniques

Keming Hu and Oky Dicky Ardiansyah Prima

Graduate School of Software and Information Science, Iwate Prefectural University
152-52 Takizawa, Iwate, 020-0693, Japan
e-mail: g231t015@s.iwate-pu.ac.jp, prima@iwate-pu.ac.jp

***Abstract*—Effective pruning can contribute to the growth of plants. Similarly, pruning apple trees can help them absorb nutrients and grow stronger. However, Japan's apple farming industry is facing many challenges today, such as aging population, talent shortage, and reduced farmland area. Despite many studies attempting to solve the problems of aging population and talent shortage through automated pruning, but as a preliminary step for pruning, the process of identifying apple trees is too complex and difficult to achieve in real-world environments. In this paper, we propose a more straightforward apple trees recognition method based on computer vision to achieve pruning of apple trees in real environments. The method roughly consists of three steps: 1) segmenting apple trees through semantic segmentation, 2) skeletonizing the apple tree by segmentation image, 3) the representation of graph tree is done by applying breadth-first search. We tested 12 models for apple tree segmentation, and the Segfomer model achieved an accuracy of 76.72 and an intersection over union(IoU) of 64.29.**

Keywords-Trees-Pruning; AI, semantic segmentation, thinning tree.

I. Introduction

One of the world's most famous apple-producing regions is in Japan. Due to the high quality and price of Japanese apples, Japan enjoys a high reputation and market share in the international market. However, in recent years, Japan's labor shortage, aging population, and young people's unwillingness to engage in agricultural labor have become one of the bottlenecks restricting the development of Japanese apple orchards. To address these issues, many traditional manual labor practices have been replaced by automation and mechanization. For example, Global Positioning System (GPS) technology is used during the planting stage to achieve automatic navigation, spraying, and fertilization of apple orchards. In the picking stage, apple orchards are also beginning to use automated picking robots. During the pruning stage of apple tree growth, traditional manual pruning is still mostly used. However, manual pruning has some negative effects, including: 1) low efficiency and higher time and labor costs, 2) requiring the operator to have certain skills and experience, otherwise it may affect the growth and yield of apple trees, 3) due to labor shortages, many apple orchards are unable to complete pruning work in a timely and effective manner, 4) manual pruning requires the operator to work on the tree for a long time, which can easily lead to physical fatigue and injury. To address these issues, it is necessary to use robots to replace manual operations.

Pruning refers to the process of removing unwanted branches from apple trees in order to promote better growth. Apple trees grow rapidly, so they require frequent pruning to control their growth and shape in order to obtain better sunlight exposure and nutrition. In addition, apple trees generally bear a lot of apples. If not pruned, too many apples will concentrate on the same branch, leading to excessive apple quantity and density, which can affect the growth and maturity of the apple and make it difficult to harvest.

Generally, the best time for pruning is after the dormant period of the apple tree ends and before new buds' sprout. This can avoid affecting the growth of the fruit tree. The specific timing varies depending on the region and climate conditions, usually between March and April in the spring. When pruning, certain rules should be followed: 1) preserve the main trunk and major lateral branches, and appropriately trim other branches to maintain the tree crown's ventilation, light penetration, and transparency. 2) in the case of a dense tree crown, loosen it appropriately to ensure that each fruit has sufficient sunlight and air. 3) branches should be smaller than the trunk. 4) the lowest branch should be 2 to 3 ft above the ground.

Traditional apple tree pruning is difficult, requires high precision, and has low efficiency. Therefore, the emergence of automated apple tree pruning technology can effectively solve these problems. Automated pruning robots can replace manual pruning of apple trees, which can improve pruning efficiency, ensure pruning precision and quality, and reduce the labor intensity and risks for operators.

In section II of this article, we will introduce some previous research and current problems encountered in apple tree pruning. In section III, we will introduce our proposed method. In section IV, we will evaluate and discuss our results. Finally, we will summarize our paper in section V.

II. Related Works

Karkee et al. [1] attempted to extract branches of apple trees using a depth camera and estimate the length of branches and distance to the next branch to identify the branches that should be pruned. Majeed et al. [2] identified fruit trees and their backgrounds using depth information and extracted branches

(a) Original image (b) Anntotation image

Fig. 1. An example of apple trees for this study.

from image information using semantic segmentation. Zhang et al. [3] demonstrated that accurate branch extraction can be achieved by combining raw depth information with a pseudo-color image obtained by coloring the depth information. While these approaches have shown that the extraction of fruit tree branches using camera sensing is possible, the topology of the extracted branches has not yet been analyzed.

Fumey Damien et al. [4] believed that if the topological structure of fruit tree branches and trunks is known, the relationships between various parts of the tree can be determined, such as the branching of the trunk, the positions of leaves, etc. This allows for pruning while ensuring the growth and yield of the fruit tree. With the topological structure of fruit tree branches and trunks, pruning rules can be more systematic and precise, avoiding inconsistencies in pruning due to subjective factors and differences in experience, thereby improving the efficiency and quality of fruit tree pruning.

```
Input: Masked image (M)
Output: The topological structure of an apple tree
Function findConnection(M):
    process queue ← [root point];
    node link ← [root point];
    while process queue lenght > 0 do
        now point ← process queue.pop(0);
        for each in now point arround(M) do
            node link[now].nextAdd(each);
            process queue.add(each);
        end
    end
    return node link;
```

Fig. 2. Breadth-first search of an apple tree.

III. Materials and Methods

The primary step for successful pruning of apple trees is to obtain the topological structure of the tree, which involves analyzing the intersections of the branches and using these points to determine the topology of the tree. This directed acyclic graph provides information on the distance between nodes, branch lengths, and directions. Obtaining the topological structure of the tree through this method allows for a comprehensive understanding of both the individual branch structure and the overall direction of the tree, thereby ensuring adequate ventilation, light transmission, and pruning effectiveness.

To be able to obtain the topology of the apple tree, here is the method we propose: first, the apple tree is segmented semantically using RGB cameras, and the mask of the tree is obtained. Then, dilation is applied to the mask to connect discontinuous branches. Next, the skeleton of the apple tree is extracted from the dilated mask, and finally, the topological structure of the tree is obtained through a breadth-first search from the root.

A. Semantic Segmentation of Apple Trees

Supervised learning semantic segmentation requires pixel-level annotation of the original images. Due to the complex shape of fruit trees, it is very difficult to label the entire tree, so we chose to annotate by tree branches and trunks, and then integrate them together. We used the labelme [5] annotation tool to annotate the images, as shown in Figure 1, which shows the original dataset images and the annotated images. We use the open-source OpenMMLab [6] framework and initialized the network with the provided pre-trained weights for training. Due to the small size of the dataset, we applied image augmentation techniques, such as random cropping and flipping during training, and used the cosine annealing learning rate update strategy to further stabilize the network training. The network strategy and detailed parameters will be discussed in section IV of this paper.

B. Analysis of Apple Tree Topology

To obtain the topological structure of fruit trees, we aim to refine the mask representing branches that the neural network obtained from semantic segmentation. First, we perform a graphic dilation on the segmented mask to connect any disconnected or disjointed branches, enabling further processing. Next, we perform skeletonization on the dilated image. In computer graphics, skeletonization is the process of converting the edges or curves of a Two-Dimensional (2D), or Three-Dimensional (3D) image or object into its skeleton or centerline. By skeletonizing the fruit tree, this study can extract the object's topological structure, geometric shape, size, and orientation. We refer to the masked image of the skeletonized tree as an array M. The bottom-most point of the array is considered as the root point, and we perform a breadth-first search on all pixels along the paths using the algorithm in Figure 2, while recording the parent-child relationships between nodes, until all nodes have been explored. These

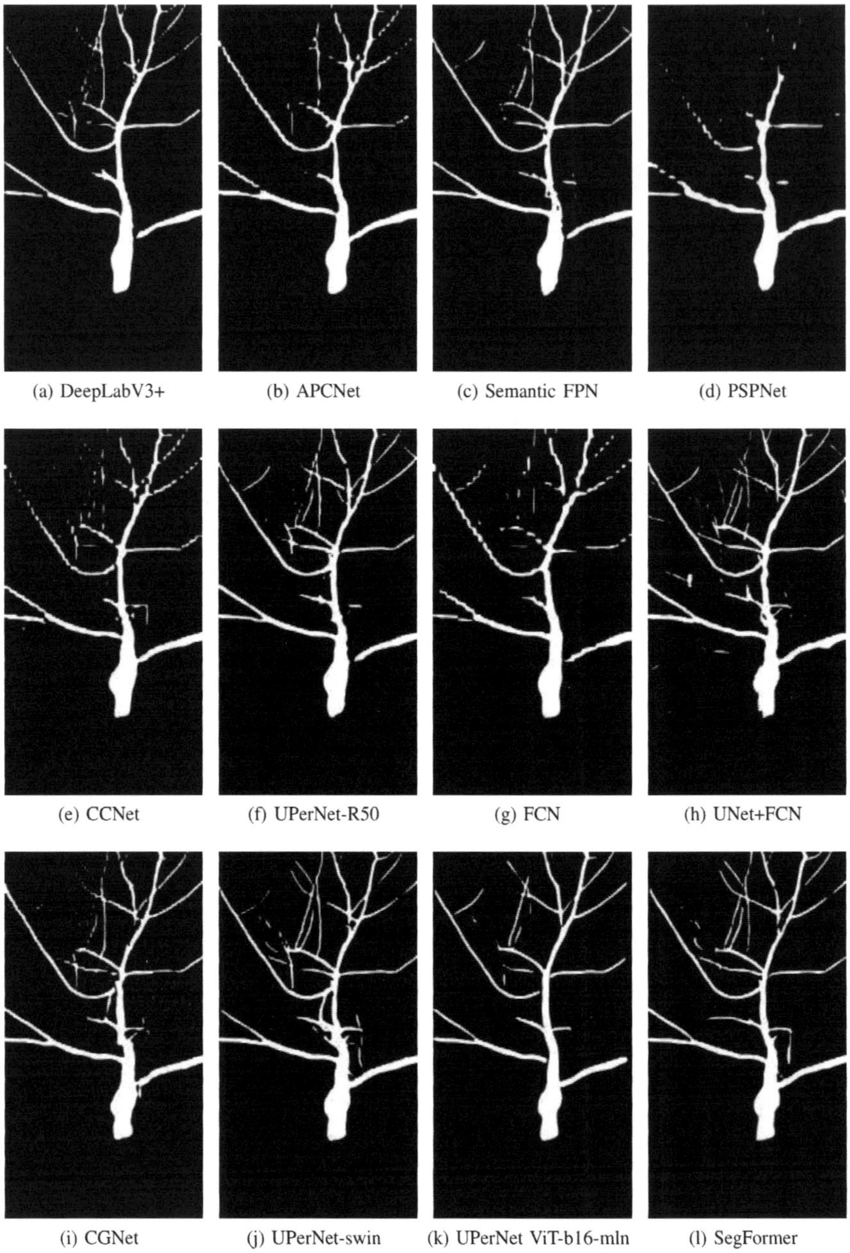

Fig. 3. An example of segmentation results of an apple trees used in this study.

parent-child relationships between nodes can approximate the topological structure of the apple tree, and pruning analysis can be performed based on this structure.

IV. Results and Discussion

Our data was obtained from an apple orchard in Hanamaki City, Iwate Prefecture, Japan. The trees in this orchard do not have a specific spindle-shaped structure and are planted separately, which is advantageous for our research. Figure 1 shows one of the images from our test set, which is part of a dataset that includes 160 images of trees taken from different directions. We used 140 images from five trees as the training set and 20 images from four trees as the test set.

We used OpenMMLab to build 12 semantic segmentation models to attempt to segment branches from apple tree, and completed the training on NVIDIA RTX2080Ti (11G). We evaluated our models using accuracy, IoU, and parameters of those models as shown in Table 1. Traditional models that used Convolution Neural Network (CNN) Resnet [7] as the backbone generally had an IoU of around 55 on the test set, while CNN with Feature Pyramid Networks (FPN) [8] layers could reach 62. Networks that used attention mechanism

TABLE I
THE RESULT OF SEGMENTATION

Name	Backbone	Input Size	Batch Size	Iterations	Acc	IoU
DeepLabV3+ [9]	R50	480x480	6	10000	65.26	54.48
APCNet [10]	R50	512x512	6	10000	67.09	58.39
Semantic+FPN	R50	512x512	16	5000	72.1	62.35
PSPNet [11]	R50	480x480	8	3500	53.29	46.44
CCNet [12]	R50-D8	512x512	6	10000	68.98	59.19
UPerNet [13]	R50	512x512	8	5000	69.99	60.44
FCN [14]	R101	512x512	3	10000	64.48	55.27
UNet [15]+FCN	UNet-S5-D16	64x64	128	1000	73.5	62.29
CGNet [16]	M3N21	680x680	12	10000	74.87	65.13
UPerNet	Swin-S [17]	512x512	8	30000	76.98	64.24
UPerNet	ViT-B [18]+LN+MLN	512x512	4	60000	56.89	43.27
SegFormer [19]	MIT-B5	512x512	4	60000	76.72	64.29

(a) Original (b) Mask (c) Skeleton

Fig. 4. Topological structure result of tree #1.

(a) Original (b) Mask (c) Skeleton

Fig. 5. Topological structure result of tree #2.

(a) Original (b) Mask (c) Skeleton

Fig. 6. Topological structure result of tree #3.

(a) Original (b) Mask (c) Skeleton

Fig. 7. Topological structure result of tree #4.

modules as the backbone achieved higher IoU on the test set and also achieved higher accuracy, but due to the more complex network model with more parameters, the batch size was limited, and more iterations and training time were required.

We tested semantic segmentation on 12 different networks using the image from Figure 1, and the results are shown in Figure 3. The model with ResNet as the backbone for feature extraction generates discontinuous masks for fine branches, while the model incorporating self-attention mechanism can effectively improve this problem. This phenomenon may be due to the fact that CNNs can only sense local structures by scanning images with convolutional kernels, leading to a poor grasp of the overall location and direction of apple trees and branches. By leveraging the attention mechanism in the encoder part of the Transformer, global features can be integrated and facilitate the segmentation of slender branches. Based on the model evaluation results and image testing results, we chose Segformer, which yields higher IoU, relatively coherent tree branches, and more accurate background-foreground segmentation, to explore the topological structure of apple trees.

We used the mask obtained from segmentation by Segformer to perform skeletonization, and the results of breadth-first search from the root of the apple tree on the skeletonized image are shown in Figures 4 to 7. Different colors were used to clearly indicate the different branches connected to each other. Due to the possibility of circular structures caused by too large mask areas in the skeletonized image, we used breadth-first search to break these circular structures and obtained a directed acyclic graph starting from the root node. This directed acyclic graph can represent the topological structure of the apple tree.

Currently, we are developing the automated pruning based on the topological structure of the apple tree by comparing images of the same apple tree before and after pruning. We will present the results in our next paper.

V. CONCLUSION AND FUTURE WORK

In this study, we attempted to explore the topological structure of apple trees by segmenting their branches, skeletonizing them, and conducting exploration. Despite the limited number of training images available for the neural network, we were still able to extract the branches of apple trees from the images. Segformer was found to be the most effective neural network model for segmentation. Future tasks will include the development of apple tree pruning rules in conjunction with the topological structure of the tree. In addition, we will collect more image datasets and modify the hyper-parameters of our neural network to improve the segmentation results to provide a better topological structure of the tree.

REFERENCES

[1] M. Karkee et al., "Identification of pruning branches in tall spindle apple trees for automated pruning," Computers and Electronics in Agriculture, 103, pp. 127–135, 2014.

[2] Y. Majeed et al., "Apple Tree Trunk and Branch Segmentation for Automatic Trellis Training Using Convolutional Neural Network Based Semantic Segmentation," IFAC PapersOnLine, 51-17, pp. 75–80, 2018.

[3] J. Zhang et al., "Branch detection for apple trees trained in fruiting wall architecture using depth features and Regions-Convolutional Neural Network (R-CNN)," Computers and Electronics in Agriculture, 155, pp. 386–393, 2018.

[4] D. Fumey, P. Lauri, Y. Guédon, C. Codin, and E. Costes, "Effects of Pruning on the Apple Tree: from Tree Architecture to Modeling," Proc. IXth IS on Orchard Systems Ed.: T.L. Robinson Acta Hort. 903, ISHS, 2011.

[5] Labelme, https://github.com/wkentaro/labelme [retrieved at April 4, 2023]

[6] OpenMMLab, https://github.com/open-mmlab [retrieved at April 4, 2023]

[7] K. He, X. Zhang, S. Ren, and J. Sun, "Deep Residual Learning for Image Recognition," IEEE Conference on Computer Vision and Pattern Recognition, pp. 770-778, 2016.

[8] A. Kirillov, R. Girshick, K. He, and P. Dollár, "Panoptic Feature Pyramid Networks," 2019 IEEE/CVF Conference on Computer Vision and Pattern Recognition, Long Beach, CA, USA, pp. 6392-6401, 2019.

[9] L. Chen et al., "Encoder-decoder with atrous separable convolution for semantic image segmentation," Proceedings of the European conference on computer vision (ECCV), 2018.

[10] J. He, Z. Deng, L. Zhou, Y. Wang, and Y. Qiao, "Adaptive Pyramid Context Network for Semantic Segmentation," 2019 IEEE/CVF Conference on Computer Vision and Pattern Recognition, Long Beach, CA, USA, pp. 7511-7520, 2019.

[11] H. Zhao, J. Shi, X. Qi, X. Wang, and J. Jia, "Pyramid Scene Parsing Network," IEEE Conference on Computer Vision and Pattern Recognition, Honolulu, HI, USA, pp. 6230-6239, 2017.

[12] Z. Huang et al., "CCnet: Criss-cross attention for semantic segmentation," Proceedings of the IEEE/CVF international conference on computer vision, 2019.

[13] T. Xiao, Y. Liu, B. Zhou, Y. Jiang, and J. Sun, "Unified Perceptual Parsing for Scene Understanding," European Conference on Computer Vision, pp. 418-434, 2018.

[14] J. Long, E. Shelhamer, and T. Darrell, "Fully convolutional networks for semantic segmentation," 2015 IEEE Conference on Computer Vision and Pattern Recognition (CVPR), Boston, MA, USA, pp. 3431-3440, 2015.

[15] O. Ronneberger, P. Fischer, and T. Brox, "U-net: Convo- lutional networks for biomedical image segmentation," Medical Image Computing and Computer-Assisted Intervention–MICCAI 2015, 2015.

[16] T. Wu, S. Tang, R. Zhang, J. Chao, and Y. Zhang, "CGNet: A Light-Weight Context Guided Network for Semantic Segmentation," in IEEE Transactions on Image Processing, 30, pp. 1169-1179, 2020.

[17] Z. Liu et al., "Swin transformer: Hierarchical vision transformer using shifted windows," Proceedings of the IEEE/CVF international conference on computer vision, 2021.

[18] D. Alexey et al., "An image is worth 16x16 words: Transformers for image recognition at scale," ILCR Conference, pp. 1-21, 2021.

[19] E. Xie et al., "SegFormer: Simple and Efficient Design for Semantic Segmentation with Transformers," Neural Information Processing Systems, 2021.

Improvement of the Feeling of Self-Affirmation by Using a Self-Reframing Diary System

Kanayo Ogura, Rie Kimura
Faculty of Software and Information Science
Iwate Prefectural University
Takizawa, Iwate, Japan
e-mail: ogura_k@iwate-pu.ac.jp, g031t305@s.iwate-pu.ac.jp

Abstract—**Self-affirmation is the feeling of being able to affirm one's own value and meaning of existence. It is known that self-affirmation among the Japanese is extremely low compared to that of other countries. Low self-affirmation is a negative influence in various aspects of daily life, and therefore, it is important to increase self-affirmation. We construct a self-reframing diary system that enables users to perform a counseling method called reframing, in which they change the framework in which they look at things and see themselves from a different perspective, in order to enhance their self-affirmation, and examine whether self-reframing can improve self-affirmation. The results of an experiment showed that although self-reframing was not effective in improving self-affirmation for all participants, more than half of them improved their self-affirmation, and in particular, participants who originally had high self-affirmation could expect a further improvement in self-affirmation through self-reframing.**

Keywords; self-affirmation; self-reframing; counseling method; diary system.

I. INTRODUCTION

Recently, a survey on self-esteem conducted by the Cabinet Office [1] showed that the self-affirmation of Japanese people is overwhelmingly lower than that of other countries. The survey covered men and women from seven countries, and the percentage of respondents who answered that they were "satisfied with themselves" was the lowest in Japan. Self-affirmation refers to the feeling of being able to affirm one's own value and meaning of existence. People with a high sense of self-affirmation tend to see things with a positive attitude and are able to honestly accept their own failures. Conversely, people with low self- affirmation often fear failure and find it difficult to take action or to accept praise. Thus, low self-esteem has a negative effect on various aspects of daily life, making it extremely important to improve self-affirmation.

One method of improving self-affirmation is reframing, a technique used in counseling [2]. This is to change the framework in which we look at things and perceive them from a different point of view. For example, a personality that is easily bored can be viewed from a different perspective as being curious. In addition, "surgery with a 10% failure rate" and "surgery with a 90% success rate" both mean the same thing, but the impressions are completely different.

Sano et al. [3] proposed a diary system that uses reframing to reduce self-reflection by having others give positive interpretations to negative content. Self-reflection is the act of focusing on oneself in a state of negative emotion. Repeated self-reflection can lead to negative thoughts and depression. Reducing self-reflection reduces negative views of oneself, which can lead to an increase in self-affirmation. The evaluation results of the proposed system by Sano et al. showed that self-reflection decreased in users of their diary system. This suggests the effectiveness of reframing. However, this study assumed that others who are not the diary writer reframe the diary, but it is not always the case that there are others who reframe diaries in daily life. In addition, if self-affirmation is high, people can overcome negative attitudes and have confidence in themselves, and thus should be able to improve their self-affirmation on their own.

In this study, we developed a diary system that allows self-reframing, and examined whether self-reframing can improve self-affirmation, and whether there is a difference in the improvement of self-affirmation between self-reframing and reframing by others.

The rest of this paper is organized as follows. Section 2 reviews research on improving self-affirmation. Section 3 reports the results of a survey on self-affirmation conducted by the authors among university students. Section 4 describes the diary system developed in this study to enhance self-affirmation. Section 5 describes and discusses the experimental procedures and results of the diary system evaluation described in section 4. Section 6 summarizes this paper and discusses future work.

II. RELATED WORK

This section reviews research on reframing and journaling, which are common methods for increasing self-affirmation. In addition, we introduce an approach to increasing self-affirmation through the act of praise.

A. Research on Reframing

In counseling, reframing is a technique for changing the cognition and meaning-making of the person being counseled (hereafter referred to as the "client"). Yamamoto et al. [4] conducted an experiment in which 48 undergraduate and graduate students were divided into two groups, with those in one group acting as the counselor and those in the other acting as the client, to examine the emotional effects of reframing in a counseling situation. Psychological measures using the Self-Esteem Scale [5] and Emotion Scale [6] were taken before and after the experiment, and the results were analyzed for variance. The results showed that only the client's positive emotions were significantly higher after the experiment, and both the counselor and client's negative emotions were significantly lower after the experiment. This experiment revealed that reframing has an effect of altering the emotional state of the recipient of the reframing, making the recipient more positive.

Sano et al. [3] proposed a diary system for reducing self-reflection and depression. In an experiment to evaluate the system, the experimenter gave positive interpretations to the negative elements written in the diary by the system's users, and verified the effects of the system on self-ruminations and depression of the system users. In the evaluation experiment, 9 participants were classified into 3 personality traits (self-ruminating trait, self-ruminating and self-reflection trait, and self-reflection trait) based on a preliminary questionnaire result about personality traits, and were divided into 3 groups: with intervention, without intervention, and without personality (details are described below.), so that the three personality traits would not overlap. The diary entries consisted of three items: "events," "feelings/behaviors," and "personality." The groups with and without intervention were asked to fill in all items, while the group without personality was asked to fill in two items: events and feelings/behaviors. Comparing the pre-experimental scores on the personality trait scale with the post-experimental scores, the scores of the group with the intervention decreased, while the scores of the other two groups increased. The results showed that the negative attitude was alleviated by providing a positive interpretation. This suggests that the positive interpretations given to the negative content allowed the users to learn new ways of thinking from perspectives they did not have, and helped alleviate their negative thoughts. On the other hand, the mean score of the Self-Introspection Scale increased the most in the group without personality, while there was no increase or decrease in the group with intervention. In Sano et al.'s paper, others need to do the reframing. However, it is not always possible to find others who can reframe. Therefore, our study examines whether it is possible to improve self-affirmation by reframing by oneself.

B. *Research on Journaling*

Journaling is the act of writing down one's feelings and thoughts. Some studies have shown that the incidence of stress-related illnesses varies greatly depending on whether or not a person confides in others about traumatic events experienced in the past [7][8]. Pennebaker et al. [9] checked whether describing past trauma, known as journaling, affects short-term and long-term health status. 46 university students participated in the experiment, journaling for 15 minutes each night for 4 days. The 46 students were divided into three groups: those who wrote about their feelings of the event without mentioning the trauma, those who wrote about the trauma without mentioning their feelings, and those who wrote about both the trauma and their feelings. After each writing session, the participants' heart rate, blood pressure, and physical condition were recorded. To examine the long-term effects on their health, the participants completed questionnaires about their health status and whether or not they visited the hospital during the six months after the end of the experiment. The results of the experiment showed that all experimental participants had a significant decrease in blood pressure after journaling. In addition, the number of hospital visits increased in the group that wrote about their feelings about the event without mentioning the trauma and in the group that wrote about the trauma without discussing their feelings about the trauma. The group that wrote about both the trauma and their feelings reported fewer health problems than the other group. The diary system we are developing has a journal aspect, in which the participants write down daily events, so that daily journaling is conducted, in which they write down their feelings and thoughts.

C. *Research on the act of praise*

Murao et al. [10] focused on the act of giving praise and developed an Social Networking Service to improve self-affirmation through mutual praise within a group. Based on the hypothesis that indirect praise from others is more effective in improving self-affirmation than direct praise, they conducted a two-week experiment using two SNSs, one in which self-praise was not visible (experimental group) and the other in which self-praise was visible (control group), with 11 university students. To test the hypothesis, the degree of improvement in self-affirmation was measured three times before, during, and after the use of the system, using a self-affirmation scale. In our study, we implemented a system that enables self-reframing so that self-affirmation can be increased without other people.

III. Current Survey on Self-affirmation

The target users of the experimental system developed in this study were undergraduate and graduate students at the authors' university. In order to grasp the degree of self-affirmation of the target users, we conducted a survey on the current status of self-affirmation in July 2022. The survey method was to send the URL to a survey form created by Google Forms to all undergraduate and graduate students affiliated with the authors by e-mail. On the survey form, we explained the handling of personal information and collected data at the beginning of the survey, and only those who understood the explanation at the beginning and answered that they could cooperate with the survey were asked to answer the survey questions. The Rosenberg Self Esteem Scale Japanese edition (RSES-J) [11], a measure of self-affirmation, was used for the survey questions. The scale consists of 10 items, which are rated on a 4-point scale, and the total score of all items is used to evaluate the level of self-affirmation.

As a general guideline for judging the level of self-affirmation, a score of 20 or less is considered low, and a score of 30 or more is considered high. The average score for Japanese adults is around 25. 86 responses were obtained for this survey. The results showed that the average score was

23.87. About one out of three participants had low self-affirmation (less than 20 points). From these results, we can conclude that most of the participants in this study did not have high self-affirmation, and that there is room for improving their self-affirmation.

IV. SELF-REFRAMING DIARY SYSTEM

This section provides an overview of our system and describes how it is used.

A. System Overview

The diary system we developed in this study aims to improve self-affirmation. Users of the system can enter events of the day and their feelings at the time, and they can reframe the entries themselves or have them reframed by others. The system is implemented as a web application and can be used from a PC or a smartphone. React.js was used for the front-end development, and Node.js for the back-end development.

B. How to use this system

When logging into the system, each user uses his/her own google account. When logging in for the first time, they were redirected to the new registration screen, where they registered their nickname and reframing method ("your own" or "someone else's").

Figure 1: Diary System's Home Screen.

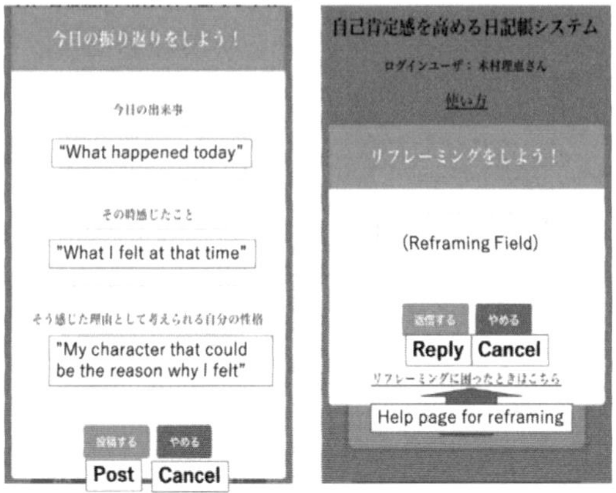

Figure 2: Diary submission page (left) and Reframing page (right).

To post a diary entry, the user clicks the "Post" button on the home screen (Figure 1), and is taken to the diary posting window (Figure 2, left). In this window, three items can be filled in: "What happened today," "What I felt at that time," and "My character that could be the reason why I felt ". If the third item is negative, our system users will reframe the diary when the system is used the next day.

Clicking the "Reply" button at the bottom of the diary allows the user to reframe on the home screen (Figure 1), and the reframing window (Figure 2, right) will appear. Once the reframing is filled in, the user clicks the "Reply" button to complete the reframing.

A help page for reframing (Figure 2, right) is provided in case the user does not know what words to use when reframing, or if the reframing process does not proceed smoothly. This help page includes target words and examples of expressions after reframing (for example, "tenacious" and "single-minded" are examples of expressions for "reluctant to give up") on the reframing window.

V. EXPERIMENT

In this section, we describe the outline of the experiment, the experimental procedure, and the experimental results. Also, we discuss the effect of self-reframing, which is the main point of this study.

A. Outline of experiment

The purpose of the experiment was to confirm whether self-affirmation improves when participants reframe the diary by themselves or by others. Participants kept a diary for two weeks using the diary system described in the previous section and reframed the diary by themselves or with the help of others. The participants were divided into two groups.

Group A: 9 participants reframed the diary entries by themselves.

Group B: Participants reframed the diary entries among themselves (5 pairs of 10 participants).

The reason for pairing up and reframing each other's diaries in group B is to avoid bias in the number of reframing sessions.

B. Experimental procedure

The experimental procedure was as follows.

(1) The participants answered the questions of the RSES-J scale described in Section 3 as a preliminary questionnaire.

(2) As a reframing exercise, participants listed 20 disadvantages and rewrote them as advantages.

(3) Participants started keeping a diary from the first day of the experiment and reframed the previous day's diary from the second day onwards. This process was continued for 14 days.

(4) After the 14 days of the experiment, the participants answered a questionnaire (RSES-J scale questions and questions about the experiment).

C. Results of the experiment

Tables 1 and 2 list the mean and standard deviations of the scores on the self-affirmation scale before and after the Group A and Group B experiments. We also calculated the effect size of the self-affirmation scale scores before and after the Group A (reframing by oneself) experiment and before and after the Group B (reframing by others) experiment. The results showed that the difference between the pre- and post-experiment averages for Group A was small (Glass's Δ=0.26), while the difference between the pre- and post-experiment averages for Group B was almost negligible (Glass's Δ=0.14).

TABLE I. SELF-AFFIRMATION SCALE SCORE MEANS AND STANDARD DEVIATIONS FOR GROUP A (N=9).

	Pre-experiment	Post-experiment
Mean	23.33	25.33
SD	7.20	9.66

TABLE II. SELF-AFFIRMATION SCALE SCORE MEANS AND STANDARD DEVIATIONS FOR GROUP B (N=10).

	Pre-experiment	Post-experiment
Mean	24.40	25.40
SD	6.87	6.81

The participants in Group A and Group B had a mixture of low, average, and high scores on the self-affirmation scale before the experiment. The standard deviations in Tables 1 and 2 indicate that the self-affirmation scores of the participants varied. The self-affirmation scores of all participants before and after the experiment are shown in Figures 3 and 4. The self-affirmation scores are out of 40 points.

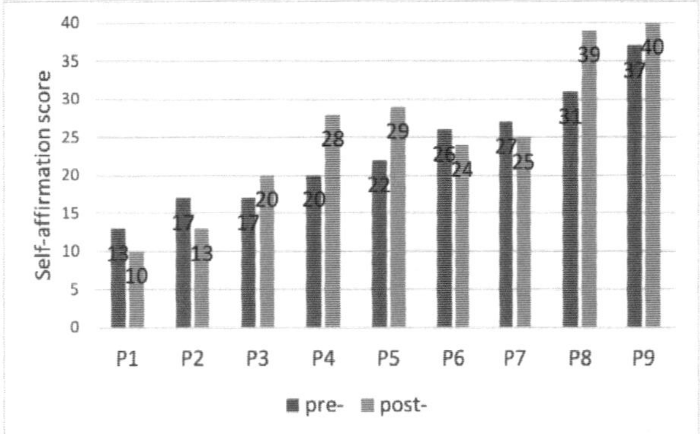

Figure 3: Self-affirmation scale scores of Group A's participants (P1-P9) pre- and post-experiment.

Figure 3 shows that the number of Group A participants whose scores increased before and after the experiment was 5 (the highest score range was 8), while the number of Group A participants whose scores decreased before and after the experiment was 4 (the lowest score range was 4).

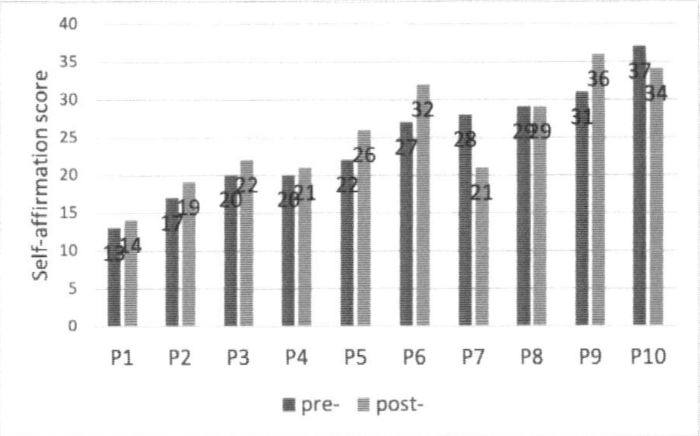

Figure 4: Self-affirmation scale scores of Group B's participants (P1-P10) pre- and post-experiment.

Figure 4 shows that the number of Group B participants whose scores increased before and after the experiment was 7 (the highest score range was 5), while the number of Group B participants whose scores decreased before and after the experiment was 1, and the number of Group B participants whose scores did not change after the experiment was 1.

D. Discussion of the Effects of Self-Reframing

As explained in the previous part, there was no significant difference in the mean scores on the self-affirmation scale before and after the experiment for the participants in Group A, the self-reframing condition. However, examining the pre- and post-experiment changes in the self-affirmation scale scores of the participants in Group A, the self-reframing condition, five of the nine participants in Group A increased their scores and four decreased their scores. In particular, more participants with high self-affirmation scores before the experiment increased their self-affirmation scores after the experiment than those with low self-affirmation scores before the experiment. These results indicate that although it cannot be said that self-reframing is effective in improving self-affirmation for all participants in the experiment, more than half of them improved their self-affirmation, and in particular, those who originally had high self-affirmation could expect further improvement in self-affirmation through self-reframing. Conversely, participants whose self-affirmation was low or average could either improve or decrease their self-affirmation.

We think that one of the reasons why some of the experiment participants' scores on the self-affirmation scale dropped after the experiment is related to their usual habit of keeping a diary. One of the participants said, "I usually do not spend much time in self-reflection, so my self-affirmation dropped when I conducted the reflection exercises during the experiment". From this, we consider it necessary to reconsider the method of self-reframing, including methods other than diaries, as well as other methods of self-reframing.

VI. Conclusion and Future work

In this study, we constructed a self-reframing diary system in which users perform a counseling method called reframing, whereby they change the framework through which they look at things and see themselves from a different perspective, in order to improve their self-affirmation. The results of an experiment indicated that although self-reframing was not effective in improving self-affirmation for all participants, more than half of them improved their self-affirmation, and in particular, those who originally had high self-affirmation could expect further improvement in their self-affirmation through self-reframing. In particular, we concluded that system users with high self-affirmation can expect further improvement in self-affirmation through self-reframing.

In the future, we will reconsider how to implement self-reframing, including methods other than diaries, in order to deal with participants who do not have the habit of keeping diaries and thus become more negative by writing down negative points when they reflect on themselves. We will continue to improve the system so that all of its users can improve their self-affirmation through self-reframing.

References

[1] Cabinet Office, Government of Japan. White Paper on Children and Youth, 2019 edition. [Online]. Available from: https://www8.cao.go.jp/youth/english/whitepaper/2019/pdf/2019.pdf 2022.05.09

[2] T. Nakajima, A Textbook of Self-Affirmation. Textbook of Self-affirmation, SB Creative, 2019. (in Japanese).

[3] F. Sano and M. Sasagawa, "Proposal of a Diary System to Reduce Self-Ruminations by Giving Positive Interpretations to Negative Contents", IPSJ Research Report, Vol. 2022-HCI-197, No. 43, pp. 1-8, 2022. (in Japanese).

[4] M. Yamamoto, "An Experimental Study on the Effects of Reframing on Emotional Effects in Counselors and Clients", Kurume University Psychological Research, No. 7, pp. 29-34, 2008. (in Japanese).

[5] M. Yamamoto, Y. Matsui and Y. Yamanari, "The Structure of Aspects of the Perceived Self", The Japanese Journal of Educational Psychology, Vol. 30, No. 1. pp.64-68, 1982. (in Japanese).

[6] O. Fukushima and Y. Takahashi, "Experimental study on the emotional effects of the assumed letter method Counseling Research", The Japanese journal of counseling science, Vol. 36, No. 3, pp.231-239, 2003. (in Japanese).

[7] J.W. Pennebaker and C.W. Hoover, Inhibition and cognition: Toward an understanding of trauma and disease. In R. J. Davidson, G. E. Schwartz, and D. Shapiro (Eds.), Consciousness and self-regula-tion, Vol. 4, pp. 107-136, 1986.

[8] J.W. Pennebaker and R. C. O'Heeron, Confiding in others and illness rates among spouses of suicide and accidental-death victims, Journal of Abnormal Psychology, 93, pp. 473-476, 1984.

[9] J.W. Pennebaker and S.K. Beall, Confronting a traumatic event: Toward an understanding of inhibition and disease, Journal of Abnormal Psychology, Vol. 95, No. 3, pp.274-281, 1986.

[10] Y. Murao and K. Ogura: "Proposal of SNS focusing on the act of 'praise' to improve self-affirmation," Proc. of Interaction 2021, pp. 372-377, 2021. (in Japanese)

[11] T. Uchida and T . Ueno, "An examination of the reliability and validity of the Rosenberg Self-Esteem Scale: Using the Japanese version translated by Mimura & Griffiths," Annual Report of the Graduate School of Education, Tohoku University, Vol. 58, No. 2, 2010. (in Japanese)

Design of Information-Sharing Media Based on Observation of Reading and Writing Behavior on Message Boards within Large Organizations

Kanayo Ogura
Faculty of Software and Information Science
Iwate Prefectural University
Takizawa, Iwate, Japan
e-mail: ogura_k@iwate-pu.ac.jp

Ryotaro Hoshi
Quick Corporation
Tokyo, Japan
e-mail: hoshi-ryotaro@919.jp

***Abstract*—To provide an unconventional means of information sharing within large organizations such as universities and companies, we set up a whiteboard information-sharing space within our university and observed and analyzed users' writing and reading behavior. As a result, we designed and implemented an electronic bulletin board that clearly segregates topics, provides space for replies, changes the posting display period according to the status of replies, and has a mechanism to make less important information as inconspicuous as possible. From an experiment with our electronic bulletin board, we confirmed that users were able to use the board to continuously post and reply to messages. Our notable achievement is that we have implemented the advantages of the analog world, which were revealed through the observation of reading and posting behavior on the whiteboard, into a system that is the digital world.**

Keywords; information sharing; electronic bulletin board; observational study; user study.

I. INTRODUCTION

There are people around us who have already solved their own problems. Casual conversations with those people often contain useful information. However, because we generally spend most of our time in a small community, such as a laboratory in a university or a department in a company, we do not have many opportunities to share information with people outside of our own community. In fact, a survey [1] on information sharing opportunities at universities shows that opportunities to ask questions and seek advice from friends and seniors are decreasing year by year. The reason for this could be that as students move up through the grades, they spend more time on research activities and spend more time in their laboratories. In other words, as mentioned above, they spend more time in the small community of the laboratory.

To solve this problem, there may be means of information sharing within each organization. For example, Slack can be used for each department [2] and group LINE for each laboratory [3]. However, the information-sharing forums provided by organizations are often used by bosses and supervisors as one-way places for sending out information. Therefore, community members have the impression that the information sharing space is a formal place. This makes it difficult to share information beyond the boundaries of departments and school grade. In addition, communities for information sharing prepared by individuals are often subdivided into close-knit groups over time and cease to function as a community.

To provide an unconventional means of information sharing in large organizations such as universities and companies, we set up an information sharing space using a whiteboard in our university, and we observed and analyzed users' writing and reading behavior. On the basis of the results, we designed and implemented an electronic bulletin board as an information sharing medium, and we discuss its effectiveness and usefulness.

This paper is organized as follows. Section 2 describes related works. Section 3 describes an observational study of the set-up of the whiteboard. Section 4 describes the design policy of the electronic bulletin board based on the results of the study in the previous section. Section 5 describes an observational experiment to verify the effectiveness of the designed electronic bulletin board. Section 6 summarizes this work and discusses future prospects.

II. RELATED WORKS

There have been many studies on information sharing. Nishimoto et al. [4] are known for their research on the promotion of information sharing in large-scale organizations. In their system, a person who has a transponder, a device that automatically sends a signal when it receives a different signal, approaches a large display in a shared space, and a question registered in advance by the person is displayed. This facilitates information sharing with users of the shared space who happen to see the question. The advantage of their system is that it is a system that does not require information providers to register their information with the system in advance, while general knowledge management software requires them to register their information with the system. However, their system has the disadvantage that users with transponders need to stay in the shared space for a long time to actively share information.

Snowdon et al. [5] performed another study on information sharing within a large organization. They propose a recommendation system that semi-automatically displays filtered information on the basis of user comments and feedback for each post. One of the features of their system is that it gives users a more organic impression by randomly arranging the posted information when it is displayed. When they actually operated their system, they found that the contents of the posts were often suited to the characteristics of the organization, but only some users posted, and not a wide range of users contributed.

On the other hand, The Notification Collage [6] is an information sharing system used within small communities.

This system aims to share information not with individuals but with the community as a whole by allowing people in a small community to post their daily discoveries to the system. In this system, posted information is not displayed in a list as in a general chat tool but is arranged randomly as in an analog bulletin board. The Notification Collage can be used from both large displays and personal terminals. However, most of the users post and browse from their personal terminals, so there have been few opportunities to use the large display.

In this study, we propose a message board like that installed in many railroad stations in Japan as a means of sharing information that can be used by anyone without the need for users to stay at that location. We set up a whiteboard in our university that users can freely write on and read information from. On the basis of observing users' writing and browsing behavior on the whiteboard, we design an electronic bulletin board that encourages information sharing among people in the same organization.

III. Observation of Whiteboard Posting and Reading Behavior

As mentioned earlier, to realize information sharing that incorporates the advantages of message boards, we set up a whiteboard in our organization for approximately two months and observed posting and reading behavior. The purpose was to examine the characteristics of information sharing behavior on the whiteboard and the requirements for an electronic bulletin board.

A. Overview of observations

We installed whiteboards in the corridors on the second and third floors of our faculty building in our university (see Figure 1) for about two months. The reason is that these locations are conspicuous to students who are on their way to the student hall building where the cafeteria and store are located and to the common lecture building where many lectures are held. We used the term "bulletin board" except when it was necessary to distinguish between a message board and a bulletin board. The reason is that our use of the term "message board" could have given the impression that it was a place for one-way transmission of information.

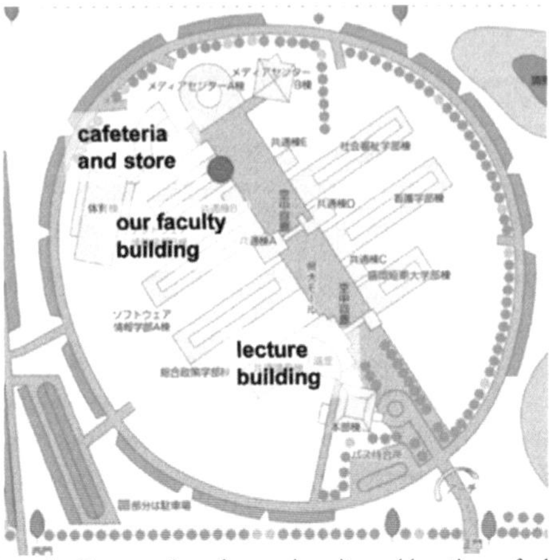

Figure 1. Campus plan of our university and locations of whiteboards [Red circles indicate locations (2nd and 3rd floor)].

We set up a whiteboard with a pen and an eraser (see Figure 2). We posted a sign next to the whiteboard explaining that "this whiteboard is a place for students to write questions and answers about student life" in order to create an environment where interaction among students is likely to occur. When two days had passed since students filled in the whiteboard, or when the board was 80% full, we removed the oldest entries from it.

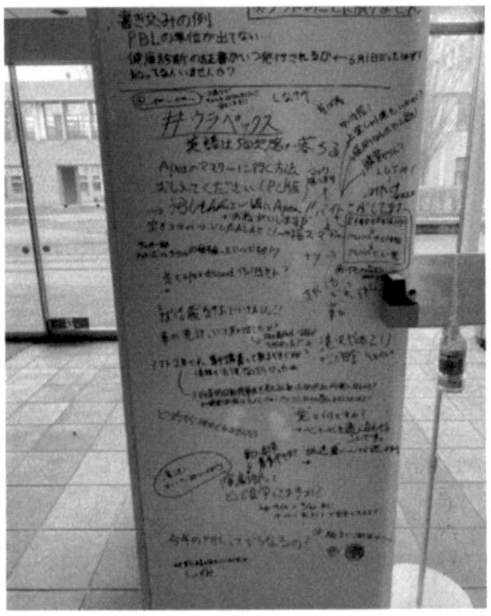

Figure 2. Installed white board.

To collect data to be used to analyze information sharing behavior, we took pictures of the entries on the board every weekday evening. From these pictures, we manually transcribed the contents written on the board, and organized the contents of the writings and their relationships with other writings (related topics, question-answer relationships, etc.). Furthermore, we conducted a questionnaire survey of all students at our university at the end of the observation period. We also posted a notice on the board warning students that their entries were to be used only for academic purposes, and that if they did not agree to the use of their entries, they were not to post on the board.

B. Observation results

In this part, we focus on 3 interesting aspects of posting and reading behavior on the board: the format of the board, the continuity of topics, and the reading and writing by multiple people.

1) Influence of display format

When the whiteboard was first set up, we expected that writing and replies would be more active if there was no fixed area to write on, such as one reserved with a dividing line. Therefore, when the whiteboards were first installed, there was nothing written on them except for an example at the top. To compare the influence of nothing being written on the board and of the board having a fixed writing area, we set up a 2×7 grid on the board about a month and a half after it was set up. To indicate that each grid was prepared for writing about a single topic, we put a "Q" mark in each grid, which means question. A few days later, the "Q"s in the right column were replaced with "A"s by students other than ourselves (see Figure 3).

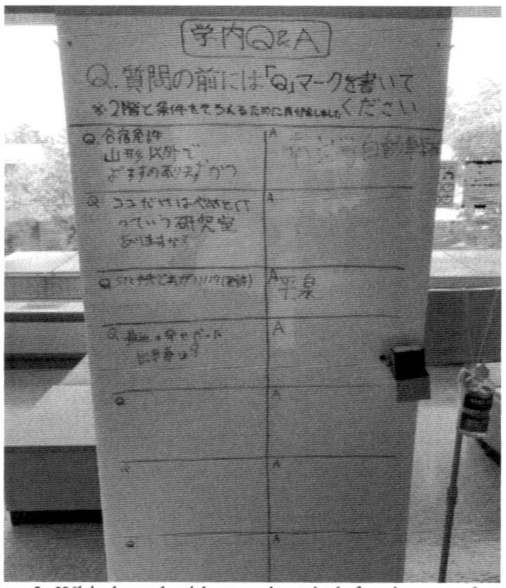

Figure 3. Whiteboard with questions in left column and replies in right column.

As a result, there were 16 entries. Of these, 11 were replies to the "Q" mark. The number of 16 posts on this day was the highest number of posts per day. We assume that the reason is that the topics were clearly delineated and that there was enough writing space for the replies. Therefore, we will design an electronic bulletin board that has a separate area for writing topics and a space for replies.

2) Continuation of topics

As mentioned earlier, we periodically deleted posts. However, when a post received a reply and the topic was continued, the deletion period was extended for two days from the new reply. Since we deleted only on weekdays, there were topics posted for longer than usual because they fell on a Saturday or a Sunday. They continued to receive replies after more than 10 days had passed. Therefore, we will change the deletion period on our electronic bulletin board according to the status of replies to each topic.

3) Writing and reading by two or more people

During the observation period, we frequently observed several people reading the whiteboard, as shown in Figure 4.

Figure 4. Multiple people writing on whiteboard.

In some cases, we observed multiple people filling in the whiteboard (that is, only one person was actually filling in the whiteboard, while the topic was being discussed by multiple people). This is a situation not seen in online communication such as chat rooms or electronic bulletin boards. We believe that it is important to take advantage of the benefits of analog communication, as in this case, to activate information sharing. Therefore, we envision an electronic bulletin board that can be set up in a shared space and be written on and read by multiple people, instead of from individual PCs.

C. Results of questionnaire responses

After the observation period, we conducted a questionnaire survey of all students at our university. The purpose was to gather information that could not be obtained from the observation, such as the attributes of the whiteboard users and their motives for writing on the whiteboards, as well as to gather information on features that should be incorporated into our electronic bulletin board. There were 208 responses. In this paper, we discuss the handling of unimportant information and the presentation of the posting period.

1) Dealing with less important information

In response to the questionnaire question "Have you obtained necessary information or new findings from this whiteboard?", 58.2% of the respondents answered "No." The reasons were "I found it difficult to understand which information was important because there was too much unimportant information (44.8%)," "I felt the quality of the answers was low (22.9%)," and "I found it difficult to understand which information was important because there were many invitations to join club activities (9.5%)." There were also several responses that said, "There was a lot of unimportant information, so I thought I could post any topic I wanted." During the observation of the whiteboard, we left unimportant information and invitations to club activities as they were to facilitate posting. From the results of this survey, we will proactively address less important information on our electronic bulletin board. One approach is to limit the number of replies to only one so that the less important information is less noticeable to the user. Another approach is to demonstrate on the board how long a post will remain to avoid less important information being displayed for a long time.

2) Duration of display of posts

As already explained, during the observation period, we periodically deleted posts. Since we did not indicate the posting period on the board, we received a request in the survey to clarify when posts would be deleted. However, users may be confused if they are directly informed of the time remaining until deletion. Therefore, we would like to add the following new feature to our bulletin board that informs users of how much time has elapsed for their posts by the shade of color of the text.

IV. Design of Electronic Bulletin Board System for Information Sharing

We designed an electronic bulletin board system using a large display based on the results of observations of writing and reading behavior on the whiteboard described above. In this section, we provide an overview of the electronic bulletin board system we designed and explain the features of our system.

A. *Outline of electronic bulletin board system*

As mentioned above, we assume that our electronic bulletin board system will use a large display to allow multiple users to post and view information. We also assume that users can only post to our system from a keyboard connected to the display terminal (Raspberry Pi 4). From our observation that replies are more active when topics are clearly segmented, we will arrange posts and replies so that they are in pairs.

Figure 5. UI of electronic bulletin board (whole).

In addition, to display as many topics as possible on the display, the posts are arranged in a grid (see Figure 5). Also, an area is reserved for writing where no posts exist. The initial design envisioned a 4×4 grid of posting areas, but we decided to increase the font size in a 3×3 grid so that posts can be viewed from a distance. As shown in Figure 5, the UI screen is a single slide, and the screen changes to a slide show every minute. Moreover, if there is no space to post, users can move to another screen using the toggle buttons on the left and right sides of the screen to find a space where no posts have been made and post a message.

Figure 6. Posting area (Upper row: Post, Lower row: Reply to post).

The grid-like posting area is divided into upper and lower rows, with posts displayed in the upper row and replies in the lower row (see Figure 6). If there are multiple replies, replies that have been displayed for less than 12 hours or that have been labeled as "good" by other users are displayed first.

B. *Feature function: Reaction to posts and display time*

Users can react to posts and replies (one per post) by clicking the "good" and "bad" reaction buttons. When a user reacts to a post, he/she can do so from both the post area and the reply area. In the case of replies, the user can react only from the reply area.

We also set a display period of 5 days for each post. If a post receives a "good" reaction, the display time is extended for 12 hours. If there is a reply to a post, the time is extended for 24 hours. If there is a "bad" reaction to a post, the time is reduced to 24 hours. Furthermore, if the number of "bad" reactions to each reply exceeds a threshold value, the reply is not displayed.

TABLE I. TEXT COLOR SHADING CHANGE

Days	Intensity
More than 3 days	1.0
Less than 3 days	0.9
Less than 2 days	0.8
Below 1 day	0.6
Less than 12 hours	0.5
Less than 6 hours	0.4

In addition, to address the opinion in the survey that "it is difficult to know when a post will be deleted," we have incorporated a function to gradually lighten the color of the text as the end of the display period approaches (see Table 1).

V. Experiment

An experiment was conducted for about four months (two months were during the summer vacation) to check the usage of our electronic bulletin board.

Figure 7. Installed electronic bulletin board and its surroundings.

We set up our bulletin board (see Figure 7, the large display is our bulletin board) in front of our university store. We received 70 posts and 134 replies in about 4 months.

A. *Number of posts*

Since summer vacation at our university started soon after the board was installed, the number of posts per day was small. However, after vacation, we found that there were up to 14 posts per day and almost no days without posts. The reason for this is that the electronic bulletin board is located in front of the cafeteria and the store of our university, and the number of students staying in this area has increased since the summer vacation ended and classes started.

B. Number of posts per time of day

In terms of the number of posts and replies by time of day, we found that most posts were made at around 12:00 and 16:00. The reason for this may be that there is a lunch break at 12:00, and many students stop by the store after 16:00 during after-school hours. However, more people stopping by means more people watching. We consider the increase in posts in this situation to be unexpected in light of what is called social embarrassment [7], in which people become less likely to act because they are being watched by others. To investigate why this happened, we conducted field observations and observed that several people were using the board together as mentioned above. This is a situation that does not exist in online interactions.

C. Reply to posts

In the whiteboard observation, replies to posts were concentrated in the first week after posting. However, in this experiment, replies continued for about two weeks to one month. We think that the reason for this is that the duration of the display period was extended due to there being continuous replies.

D. Use of reaction buttons

The number of reactions was 60 good ones and 8 bad ones. At first glance, the reaction button seemed to be utilized, but in reality, it was used only for specific topics and thus not widely used. Therefore, the bad button was often used for meaningless posts, and there were no cases where the posting period was shortened.

VI. CONCLUSION AND FUTURE WORK

In this paper, we designed and implemented an electronic bulletin board for information sharing in a large organization, based on the results of whiteboard observations, and confirmed its usage. From the results of the observations, we used a display format that clearly segregates topics, provides space for replies, changes the posting display period according to the status of replies, and has a feature that makes unimportant information as inconspicuous as possible. In addition, we considered it important for our system design to incorporate the advantages of the analog world, which allows users to post and read together with others in the same space. For this reason, our system is not closed to the Internet, but can be accessed from both the Internet and the analog space through a large display. From an experiment, we confirmed that users are able to continuously post and reply to messages using the electronic bulletin board. Our notable achievement is that we have implemented the analog advantages revealed by our observations into an IT system in the digital world.

On the other hand, it is difficult to say from the results of this experiment that all users were actively using our system. While many users read our electronic bulletin board, we recognize that there are users who cannot post even if they want to because they are afraid of being seen by others.

We plan to further analyze the results of the experiment and add more user-friendly functions in the future. We also intend to improve our system so that users can easily post from their personal mobile devices.

REFERENCES

[1] Japan Association of Private Colleges and Universities. *White Paper on Student Life at Private Colleges and Universities 2018.* [online]. Avairable from : https://www.shidairen.or.jp/topics_details/id=2040 2023.04.06. (in Japanese)

[2] Slack Technology Inc. *Inspiring stories, real Slack customers.* [online]. Available from : https://slack.com/customer-stories 2023.04.06.

[3] J. Chutrtong and W. Chutrtong, "Science Students' Acceptance to use LINE Application in Laboratory Subject," International Journal of Information and Education Technology, vol.10, pp. 227-231, 2020.

[4] K. Nishimoto and K. Matsuda, "Informal Communication Support Media For Encouraging Knowledge-Sharing And Creation In A Community," International Journal of Information Technology & Decision Making (IJITDM), World Scientific Publishing Co. Pte. Ltd., vol. 6, no. 3, pp. 411-426, 2007.

[5] D. Snowdon and A. Grasso, "Diffusing Information In Organizational Settings: Learning From Experience," CHI '02: Proceedings of the SIGCHI Conference on Human Factors in Computing Systems, pp. 331-338, 2002.

[6] S. Greenberg and M. Rounding, "The notification collage: posting information to public and personal displays," CHI '01: Proceedings of the SIGCHI Conference on Human Factors in Computing Systems, pp. 514-521, 2001.

[7] R. Edelmann, "Social Embarrassment: An Analysis of the Process," Journal of Social and Personal Relationships, vol.2, no.2, pp. 195-213, 1985.

How Can Intelligent Persona Features Support Online Advertising Work?

Ilkka Kaate
Department of Marketing
University of Turku
Turku, Finland
iokaat@utu.fi

Joni Salminen
School of Marketing and Communication, Marketing
University of Vaasa
Vaasa, Finland
joni.salminen@uwasa.fi

Soon-gyo Jung
Qatar Computing Research Institute
Doha, Qatar
sjung@hbku.edu.qa

Rami Olkkonen
Department of Marketing
University of Turku
Turku, Finland
rami.olkkonen@utu.fi

Bernard J. Jnasen
Qatar Computing Research Institute
Doha, Qatar
bjansen@hbku.edu.qa

***Abstract*— The concept of "Intelligent Personas" or "AI personas" presented here builds on extant research on data-driven personas and interactive persona systems. With this conceptualization, we particularly focus on outlining a vision for an intelligent end-to-end advertising system that supports human marketers' decision making by deploying data-driven personas throughout the stages of the online advertising process. We start by defining the relevant concepts, continue by discussing intelligent personas for online advertising, and conclude by proposing research directions that need to be addressed in order to realize the value of personas in such a system, as well as discussing its potential value for the digital marketing profession.**

Keywords- Personas; online advertising; optimization

I. INTRODUCTION

Personas are fictitious people representing real customer groups, i.e., different types (e.g., most valuable, most loyal, most responsive – or the least valuable, etc.). Most typically, personas are presented to decision makers as *persona profiles*, i.e., narrative representations of different kinds of users belonging to a particular demographic, behavior, and/or attitude involved in using a product, site, or brand [1]. However, personas can also be accessed via *interactive persona systems* that rely on Web technologies and enable searching, filtering, or even generating personas from raw data [2]. Overall, personas act as surrogate mental models when inputs from actual customers are absent or unavailable for decision makers [1] – essentially, personas provide customer-centric inputs when needed, where needed.

The concept *intelligent persona* (IP) can refer to two aspects: (a) the intelligent features of an interactive persona system, or (b) persona generated through artificial intelligence (AI) technology (this is also called *AI personas* by some authors [3], while yet others refer to *algorithmically-generated personas* [4] or *data-driven personas* [5]). Finally, *persona analytics* refers to either understanding customer or users via systems that combine analytics and personas, or the goal of understanding how stakeholders interact with persona profiles and systems [6].

Overall, the concept of IP builds on extant research on data-driven personas, interactive persona systems, and intelligent system features that leverage state-of-the-art human-computer interaction (HCI) techniques and support marketing functions via the employment of personas [2]. More broadly, the IP concept can aid in outlining a vision for an intelligent end-to-end advertising system that supports human marketers' decision making by deploying data-driven personas throughout the stages of the modern online advertising process. What we mean by this is that the work of online advertisers consists of various tasks, and those tasks can be supported through IP.

In Section 2, we outline a vision for the use of IP in the context of online advertising. In Section 3, we present conclusions and discuss future work on this domain.

II. VISION FOR INTELLIGENT PERSONAS

The value of IP can be particularly salient in the context of *computational advertising* which refers to the use of technology and data to optimize the targeting and delivery of ads [7] (a closely related concept is *intelligent advertising* which refers to the use of features that mimic human intelligence in the advertising process [7]). Hence, the vision of IP in online advertising can be formalized as [personas + computational advertising + intelligent features = ?]. In other words, a scrutiny that considers multiple perspectives: the benefits of personas as empathy-friendly mental modeling instruments, the contributions of computational advertising in terms of algorithms, and user interface (UI) and user experience (UX) aspects brought about by intelligent systems research. If in the equation these are on the numerator side, then *advertiser work tasks* are on the denominator side, resulting in the following formulation: [(personas + computational advertising + intelligent features) / advertiser work tasks = ?]. In other words, we need to consider the benefits or possibilities provided by technology HCI *in regard to* user needs which are reflected in the daily work tasks among advertisers.

What does advertisers' work consist of, then? There are a few prime elements which we discuss. First, we consider *segmentation*. This refers to dividing the total available market into addressable constituents, i.e., segments. Here, we observe that persona is a segment with a name and a face. Hence, segmentation can be done in a persona-assisted manner, yielding personas as outcomes. Once segmentation is done, *targeting* follows; namely, advertisers select which segments to focus on. Here, an IP system can recommend specific personas to target, given an explicit goal such maximize reach, engagement, or sales. After targets are chosen, *ad copywriting* follows. Here, IP can be of use by generating ad headlines, texts, and even imagery personalized to the selected personas. After ad content has been created, advertisers proceed to *campaign set-up*. This means creating the campaigns in the ad platform and configuring the settings. Here, IP can provide a structure; i.e., campaigns can be organized by personas, ensuring that the naming and targeting criteria match the personas [8]. This then yields an advantage in the next stage which is *optimization*; i.e., making decisions based on the results. Namely, once campaigns are running, they start to generate data; if the data is organized by personas, it becomes easier for an algorithm (or a human) to adjust budget allocation given the actual marketing performance of a given persona.

As decision making in online advertising work practice ranges from insights formation to targeting, campaign and ad creation, reporting, and optimization, for each stage, we envision intelligent persona features that support the core tasks associated with the stage. To illustrate, Figure 1a presents AI-generated personas with ad text and image boxes for each persona (highlighted in red) for ad text creation and image selection for a human marketer. In contrast, Figure 1b shows a view where "Tyler" has been expanded for a more detailed view with ad text columns for multiple advertising channels for easier ad creation.

III. CONCLUSION

We have outlined some examples of how IP can be deployed in online advertising. By using algorithms, machine learning, and AI, marketers can create more personalized ad campaigns and more accurately measure the impact of their efforts. This paradigm shift can increase transparency, efficiency, and effectiveness within the industry. While computational advertising is transforming traditional advertising to become more cost-effective and efficient, while allowing marketers to better understand and reach their target audience, personas can accelerate this positive transformation. Nevertheless, much work is needed to capture IP's potential value for the advertising profession, toward the realization of a visionary framework that leverages intelligent personas for more efficient and effective management of online advertising campaigns by human marketers. There is also a need to investigate the dynamics of machines replacing marketing work, and the sharing of labor in situations where intelligent features collaborate with humans towards more optimal advertising performance.

Figure 1. Concept example of intelligent persona features.

REFERENCES

[1] A. Cooper, *The Inmates Are Running the Asylum: Why High Tech Products Drive Us Crazy and How to Restore the Sanity*, 1st ed. Indianapolis, IN: Sams - Pearson Education, 1999.

[2] S.-G. Jung, J. Salminen, and B. J. Jansen, "Giving Faces to Data: Creating Data-Driven Personas from Personified Big Data," in *Proceedings of the 25th International Conference on Intelligent User Interfaces Companion*, in IUI '20. Cagliari, Italy: Association for Computing Machinery, Mar. 2020, pp. 132–133. doi: 10.1145/3379336.3381465.

[3] A. Holzinger, M. Kargl, B. Kipperer, P. Regitnig, M. Plass, and H. Müller, "Personas for Artificial Intelligence (AI) an Open Source Toolbox," *IEEE Access*, vol. 10, pp. 23732–23747, 2022, doi: 10.1109/ACCESS.2022.3154776.

[4] J. Salminen, S.-G. Jung, and B. Jansen, "Intentionally Biasing User Representation?: Investigating the Pros and Cons of Removing Toxic Quotes from Social Media Personas," in *Nordic Human-Computer Interaction Conference*, 2022, pp. 1–13. doi: https://doi.org/10.1145/3546155.3546647.

[5] J. J. McGinn and N. Kotamraju, "Data-driven persona development," in *Proceedings of the SIGCHI Conference on Human Factors in Computing Systems*, Florence, Italy: ACM, 2008, pp. 1521–1524. doi: 10.1145/1357054.1357292.

[6] J. Salminen, S.-G. Jung, and B. Jansen, "Developing Persona Analytics Towards Persona Science," in *27th International Conference on*

Intelligent User Interfaces, in IUI '22. New York, NY, USA: Association for Computing Machinery, Mar. 2022, pp. 323–344. doi: 10.1145/3490099.3511144.

[7] Y. Yang, Y. C. Yang, B. J. Jansen, and M. Lalmas, "Computational Advertising: A Paradigm Shift for Advertising and Marketing?," *IEEE Intell. Syst.*, vol. 32, no. 3, pp. 3–6, May 2017, doi: 10.1109/MIS.2017.58.

[8] J. Salminen, I. Kaate, A. M. S. Kamel, S. Jung, and B. J. Jansen, "How Does Personification Impact Ad Performance and Empathy? An Experiment with Online Advertising," *International Journal of Human–Computer Interaction*, vol. 0, no. 0, pp. 1–15, Aug. 2020, doi: 10.1080/10447318.2020.1809246.

Virtual Reality Environment for Presenting Al-Qatt Al-Asiri Saudi Art

Abeer S. Al-Humaimeedy
Department of Software Engineering
King Saud University
Riyadh, Saudi Arabia
abeer@KSU.EDU.SA

Alhanof S. Alolyan
Department of Software Engineering
King Saud University
Riyadh, Saudi Arabia
437203004@STUDENTS.KSU.EDU.SA

Areej Al-Wabil
College of Engineering
Alfaisal University
Riyadh, Saudi Arabia
Areej@mit.edu

Khalid W. Alzamil
King Abdul-Aziz & his Companions Foundation for Giftedness and Creativity
Riyadh, Saudi Arabia
kwzamil@gmail.com

Ghada AL-Hudhud
Department of Information Technology
Riyadh, Saudi Arabia
galhudhud@ksu.edu.sa

***Abstract*—Virtual museums digitally exhibit art and heritage using virtual reality technology. Such projects are unique in including the past, present, and future. They are teaching the past heritage using modern-day technology to communicate with the future generations. Al-Qatt Al-Asiri is the traditional art of interior wall decoration done by women in the Southern Region of the Kingdom of Saudi Arabia (KSA). In 2017, this art has been inscribed on the UNESCO Representative List of the Intangible Cultural Heritage of Humanity. This paper presents the work conducted towards the development of a virtual museum of Al-Qatt Al-Asiri art, within the framework of the user-centered design and evaluation methodology for virtual environments. The proposed virtual museum simulates the real-world museums found in the Assir region in the South of KSA. Moreover, it adds gaming elements by providing rooms for colouring and storytelling.**

***Index Terms*—Al-Qatt Al-Asiri, virtual reality, virtual museum, Saudi heritage, culture heritage**

I. Introduction

Saudi Arabian arts and heritage are increasingly being recognized in local and global context. The 2030 vision of Saudi Arabia proposed establishing more museums to promote Saudi Arabian arts and heritage [1].

Museums play a key role in promoting the cultural heritage of a country and exhibiting it globally. However, physical museums are restricted by their geographical places, and burden with their enormous budgets. Therefore, the solution of virtual museums was proposed to resolve these issues. Virtual museums are inexpensive and are not geographically restricted. This kind of museum uses the technology of virtual reality to simulate physical objects into a nonphysical computer-based environment [2]. Visitors of these museums use virtual reality devices to interact with their computer-based environment.

In line with the 2030 vision of Saudi Arabia and using the virtual reality technology, we propose in this paper a virtual museum for Al-Qatt Al-Asiri art (which shall be shortened to VMQA for the remainder of this paper). Al-Qatt Al-Asiri is a traditional art of interior wall decoration done by women in the Southern Province of the Kingdom of Saudi Arabia (KSA). In 2017, this art was the first Saudi art to be inscribed on the UNESCO Representative List of the Intangible Cultural Heritage of Humanity [3].

Using virtual environments as exhibition halls for national culture is not new. It was used to explore the Ancient Egyptian heritage [4], to simulate the Italian Drama Theatre from the 19th century [5], and to conduct virtual tours to the famous Louvre Museum in Paris [6]. However, few such museums have been implemented for Saudi heritage like the work proposed in [7] and [8]. To the best of our knowledge, the VMQA project is the first to exhibit Al-Qatt Al-Asiri art in a virtual environment.

VMQA gives a chance for Saudi Arabian art and culture to be exposed to a whole new audience of people to observe, and with the continuation of such products Saudi Arabian art can be taken to a new, international standard, which may give encouragement to the development of new Saudi Arabian artists in the next generation, and will further encourage a surge of tourism to the country to see the historic sights it has to offer, further enhancing and growing Saudi economy.

This paper presents the work conducted to develop a virtual museum of Al-Qatt Al-Asiri art, within the framework of the user-centered design and evaluation methodology for virtual environments. The proposed virtual museum simulates the real-world museums at Assir region at the southern region of KSA. In addition to the exhibition hall for Al-Qatt Al-Asiri art, and for the purpose of enhancing visitors' experience, VMQA provides two rooms for colouring and storytelling. In the colouring room, visitors will be able to colour some of Al-Qatt Al-Asiri's most famous patterns, and in the storytelling room, visitors will engage in a three-dimensional experience which tells the story behind Al-Qatt Al-Asiri art.

Currently, the proposed virtual museum will be a standalone virtual reality software that can be downloaded on PCs which imply with the proposed virtual reality software and hardware specifications. In future work, we will provide a lighter web-

Fig. 1: Al-Qatt Al-Asiri art [9]

based version of the museum to reach even more visitors around the world.

The remainder of this paper is organised as follows: section II introduces Al-Qatt Al-Asiri art, section III explores the related work, section IV explains the design development process and the validation process of VMQA, and section V concludes the paper and suggests future directions for VMQA.

II. BACKGROUND

The focus of this paper is on the development aspects of VMQA. However, in this section, we introduce Al-Qatt Al-Asiri art to justify the importance of dedicating a virtual museum for it. Al-Qatt Al-Asiri is the traditional art of interior wall decoration conducted by local housewives in the Southern region of KSA, see Fig. 1.

It is unknown exactly when Al-Qatt art started. However, field trips to Assir region discover the art at houses aged three years all the way to four hundred years [10]. Moreover, travellers to the Assir region like Cornwallis [11], Tamizier [12], and Philby [13], have documented the existence of this art since 19th century. In 2017, this art was the first Saudi art to be inscribed on the UNESCO Representative List of the Intangible Cultural Heritage of Humanity [3].

To decorate walls of houses in the Assir region, a group of women gather and work under the supervision of an expert female artist [14]. Women express their passion and feelings using patterns and colours. They use brushes made from the hair of goats' tails tied with a wooden stick [14]. Colours are extracted from natural elements - for example, the white colour (called *Gypsum*) is made from many layers of lime taken from surrounding mountains. The green colour is extracted from grass, while blue colour is taken from the *Indigofera Tinctoria* plant (called *Nela*) and colours are restricted to: white, black,

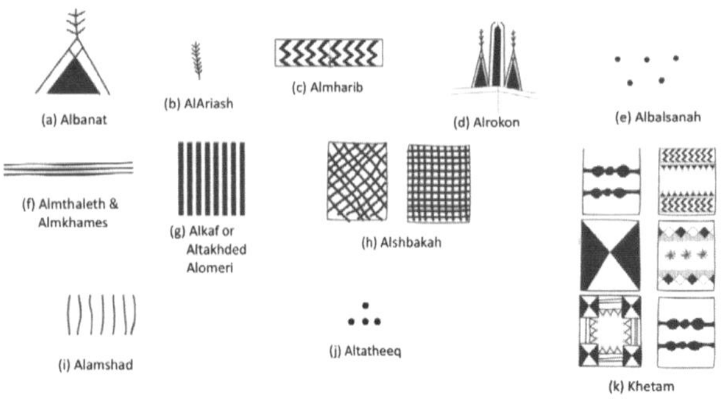

Fig. 2: The symbols of Al-Qatt Al-Asiri art [15]

blue, green, yellow and red. These traditional colours were used until 1970's, and after that, women of Assir started using modern colours [14].

The painting process starts by sketching the pattern outlines with black, then filling them with other colours. The patterns could have many shapes such as *Al-Banat*, *Al-Ariash*, *Al-Mharib*, and *Al-Rokon* - see Fig. 2. Each shape has a specific position in Alqatt patterns. Some of them have meanings - for instance, it is believed that *Al-Banat* symbolizes a female and *Al-Ariash* represents plants.

Al-Qatt art structure is characterized by straight shapes instead of curves. The local citizens of Assir explain that this is inherited from the texture of Arab-Islamic art [14].

III. RELATED WORK

The concept of virtual museums was first introduced by André Malraux [16], and it includes all type of virtual museums. Virtual museums can be a collection of simple two-dimensional images in a website or a complex three-dimensional experience in a virtual environment using sophisticated devices [17].

In the literature, there is a considerable number of virtual museums research. The aspects of designing a virtual museum varies depending on the nature of the virtual museum. Virtual museums could be proposed to allow visitors to live a past experience like the virtual Italian Drama Theatre Museum [5] which reconstructs the Italian drama theatre from the 19th century. Visitors are welcomed by *Meneghino* the virtual guider who accompanies visitors and tells them the story of the theatre. The same concept was used in a more recent project, called *Viking VR* [18]. In this project, the visitors live the virtual experience of being in one of the four Viking encampments designed for this project and are told the story of how the Vikings changed life for people in Britain.

Another type of virtual museums is the one that allows visitors to conduct virtual online tours to real-world museums via internet like the Louvre Museum tour [6]. Recently, Google Arts & Culture has teamed up with the most famous museums around the world to provide virtual tours to them [19].

Virtual tours could be provided inside museum to interact with historical artefacts and learn more about them, as has been implemented at the Archaeological Museum in Milan, to educate visitors about Egyptian funeral objects [4]. In both projects, visitors can interactive with the exhibited objects by zooming and rotating, and they can read a full description about any chosen object. In these projects, the design process concentrates on building the historical artefacts database.

The other type of museums is a mixture of the two previous types, like the *Soviet History* museum [20]. In this museum, they simulate the *Ruijin* city red culture heritage and implant, and also provide the option to search the historical objects of this period of time.

As aforementioned, few virtual museums have been proposed for Saudi heritage and art. The most know endeavours are the virtual tours to Saudi historical places [7] and *Basmoca* [8]. Basmoca is the name of the Saudi artist Basma Alsulaiman's virtual museum for contemporary art [8]. In this museum the artist, Basma, virtually exhibits her collection and allows visitors to interact with the paintings and the art objects. Basmoca also provides a platform for multiple visitors to simultaneously present at the museum to communicate and to discuss art issues.

The other project is the endeavour of the *Saudi Commission for Tourism and National Heritage* (SCTH) to allow the visitors of its website to conduct virtual tours to the most known tourism spots and historical places in KSA [7]. Visitors can see the places in the map and read a short description about them.

In our project (VMQA), we exhibit Al-Qatt Al-Asiri art in a virtual environment. VMQA will be a mixture type museum, where visitors can live the virtual experience by moving around the virtual halls and explore the exhibited artworks of Al-Qatt Al-Asiri. Visitors can also interact with these works of art to learn more about them by clicking the museum guider who will companion visitors during their tours. Additionally, for the sake of enhancing visitors' experience, VMQA provides two rooms for colouring and storytelling. In the colouring room, visitors will be able to colour some of Al-Qatt's most famous patterns and in the storytelling room, visitors will engage in a three-dimensional experience which tells the story behind Al-Qatt art. The designing and validation process for this project will be presented in the next section.

It is essential to present the local artefacts via virtual museums to promote the country local heritage and make it easy access via the internet. VMQA contributes in boosting tourism in Saudi Arabia by providing a virtual environment which allows visitors to explore Al-Qatt Al-Asiri art.

IV. User-Centred Design and Evaluation Process

In this section we present the design and validation processes of VMQA based on the user-centered software development methodology [21] and with insights from the structured development process of virtual environments [22].

We develop the VMQA following the user-centered software development methodology. The framework of this methodology consists of several rounds of systematic user and software requirements (elicitation, documentation, and validation). Each round clarifies the software requirements and refines the prototype functionalities based on the feedbacks of the previous rounds and the input from the software stakeholders who usually include the product owners, and representative end-users.

The framework of the user-centered software development methodology as suggested by Tromp *et al.* [21] consists of five stages: domain analysis, requirements elicitation, requirements analysis, requirements specification and software building. With insights from the structured development process of virtual environments [22], we adopt these stages and structure them following top-down approach to be: problem definition, requirements elicitation, requirements specification, software building, deployment and verification. We further divide the software building stage into five iterations (prototype, reception, tour, storytelling and coloring), each iteration consist of three stages: detailed design, implementation and testing. Therefore, in our project the design and validation process starts by defining the project's problem. Then, the requirements are collected and analyzed before defining the software specification. This is followed by five rounds of detailed design, implementation, and testing. At the end, the final product is deployed and verified.

The details of these stages are presented in the next subsections.

A. Problem Definition and Requirements Elicitation

The problem was clearly defined in previous sections. Requirements for this project were collected by conducting several interviews with artists, specialists, and representative end-users and one co-design workshop (details is at Section IV-D). In addition, a field trip was conducted to *Al-Raqdi Museum* for Al-Qatt Al-Asiri art [9] in the Assir region.

Relying on the collected set of requirements and taking in consideration the virtual museum standards by the *Institute for Cultural and Natural Artistic Heritage*- LEM projects [23], the software context and scope were shaped. In addition, a draft of the museum floorplan was proposed - see Fig. 3.

The proposed museum floorplan consists of five areas:

1) The lobby hall which represents the entrance to the museum - see region 1 in Fig. 3.
2) The garden pathway, which contains a garden that contains the famous plants in the region, in particular the one used for extracting colours - see region 2 in Fig. 3.
3) The main exhibition hall (which represents the hall of the museum that exhibits the collection of Al-Qatt Al-Asiri artworks) - see regions 3 and 4 in Fig. 3. In this hall, visitors will accompany by a 'guide' character, sketched in Fig. 4. This character is responsible for providing help to visitors during their stay at the main exhibition hall.
4) The storytelling room, where the museum narrative (Ms. Fatima) tells story of Al-Qatt art using animation and three-dimensional models - see region 5 in Fig. 3.

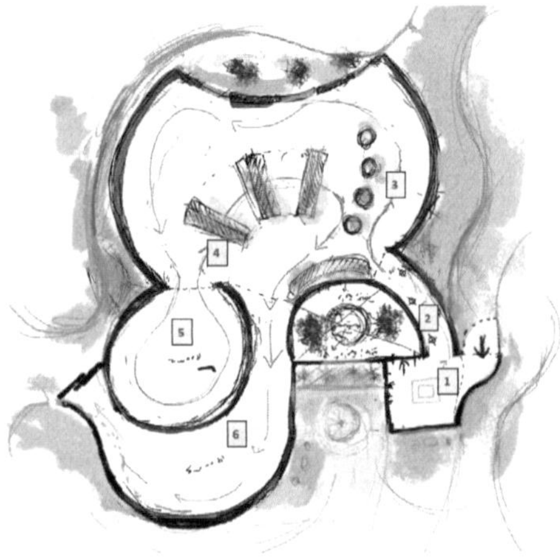

Fig. 3: Floorplan of the VMQA

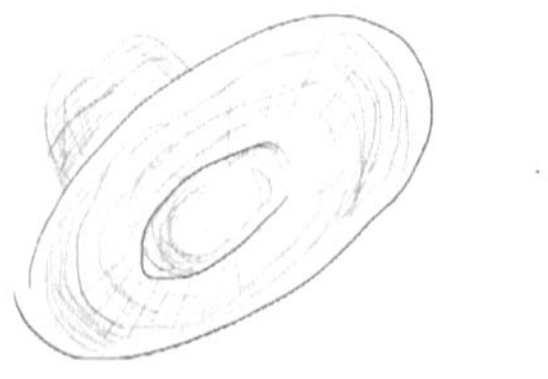

Fig. 4: The design of the museum guide

5) The colouring room, where visitors will be able to colour some of Al-Qatt's most famous patterns - see region 6 in Fig. 3.

Based on the suggested floorplan we also propose five user scenarios for each area as follows:

1) **Scenario 1:** The user (visitor) launches VMQA by clicking on the software icon on the PC desktop. The user wears the virtual reality glass, holds the right controller in their right hand, and holds the left controller in their left hand . They read the pop-up museum instructions message and press any button on the controllers to start their tour at VMQA. The user looks around the lobby hall. If they start moving, the museum sitemap appears on the hall's ground. The user moves to the front, to the right and to the left to explore the lobby hall. The user reaches the garden pathway. The user can stay at the lobby hall or enter the garden pathway where **Scenario 2** starts.
2) **Scenario 2:** The user crosses the lobby hall using the right and left controllers, and stands at the front of the pathway. They see the pathway to the main hall. Using the right and the left controllers, the user can move through the pathway. The pathway has an indoor garden which has famous plants in the region on one side, in particular the ones used for extracting colours. The wall on the other side has descriptions of each of the garden plants. The user looks around the pathway. The user moves to the front, to the right and to the left to explore the garden pathway. The user reaches the main exhibition hall. The user can stay at the garden pathway, return to the lobby hall, or enter the main exhibition hall where **Scenario 3** starts.
3) **Scenario 3:** The user crosses the pathway using the right and left controllers, and stands at the front of the main hall. At this point, the user meets the museum guide. The guide accompanies the user during their stay at the main exhibition hall in order to provide help to then. The user looks around the main hall. The user moves to the front, to the right and to the left to explore the main hall and observes the Al-Qatt artwork. If the user steps near a piece of artwork, the guide will offer to describe it to them. The user also can ask the guide for other types of help, like the museum's instructions. The user can stay at the main exhibition hall, return to the garden pathway, enter the storytelling room where **Scenario 4** starts, or enter the colouring room where **Scenario 5** starts.
4) **Scenario 4:** The user crosses the main exhibition hall using the right and left controllers, and stands in the front of the storytelling room. At this point, the user meets the museum's narrator Ms. Fatima. Ms. Fatima tells the story of Al-Qatt art using animation and three-dimensional models for the user. The user can stay at the storytelling room, or return to the main hall.
5) **Scenario 5:** The user crosses the main exhibition hall using the right and left controllers, and stands in the front of the colouring room. At this point, three different patterns of Al-Qatt art appear and the user can choose one of them to colour. The user can change colours using the colour palette. The user can stay at the storytelling room, or return to the main hall.

During any of these scenarios, the user can immediately exit the museum by clicking on the EXIT button on controllers. A confirmation message appears and the user can press OK using the controller buttons.

B. Requirements Analysis and Specification

In requirements analysis phase we organize, analyze, and validate the collected requirements following the scenario-based approach explained in [22].

First, we designed the form in Fig. 5 which is a scenario-based requirement gathering form inspired by Table 15.2 in [22]. We use this form to group the requirements based on the defined scenarios in Section IV-A, and to ensure that they are complete, clear, linked, and verifiable. To illustrates how this is achieved please see Fig. 6 which presents the requirement form for **Scenario 2**. The requirements in these forms are used to document the final set of the software functional and non-functional requirements. Based on the requirements document, VMQA specification can be defined in terms of software goals, and user tasks. In our project, different techniques such as storyboards, requirements decision tables and interaction models are used to define VMQA software specification.

Scenario x

1. ***Place***: area x (hall\room).

2. ***Function***: What is carried out in this area?

3. ***Goals***: What are the goals of the current function?

3.1 ***Position***: Where is the museum visitor standing at the beginning of this scenario?	3.2 ***Operational***: What are the requirements of this scenario?

4. ***Evaluation***: How should we evaluate that the goals are achieved?

Fig. 5: Requirement gathering form

Scenario 2

1. ***Place***: area 2, the garden pathway of VMQA.

2. ***Function***: Learn about the famous plants in the Assir region.

3. ***Goals***:The visitor shall be able to identify 10-15 plants from Assir region, in particular the ones used for extracting colours for Al-Qatt Al-Asiri art.

3.1 ***Position***:The visitor stands at the front of the pathway, and see through.

3.2 ***Operational***:

- The visitor shall be able to step into the pathway area using controllers.
- The visitor shall be able to move to the front in the pathway area using both controllers.
- The visitor shall be able to move to the left in the pathway area using the left controller.
- The visitor shall be able to move to the right in the pathway area using the right controller.
- The visitor shall be able to move to the back in the pathway area using the left controller twice or the right controller twice.
- The visitor shall be able to look around the pathway with a 360-degree view from where they stand.
- The visitor shall be able to recognize the shape and the colour of the plants in the indoor garden.
- The visitor shall be able to see a picture of each plant in the indoor garden and read a description about it on the wall opposite to the indoor garden.
- The visitor shall be able to exit the pathway area to the lobby hall if they reach the border between the two areas.
- The visitor shall be able to exit the pathway area to the main exhibition hall if they reach the border between the two areas.

4. ***Evaluation***:

- The visitor shall be able to link between the plants in the indoor garden and their descriptions on the opposite wall.
- The visitor shall be able to identify the name, shape, and purpose of each of the 10-15 plants in the indoor garden.
- The visitor shall be able to identify the plants which are used for extracting colours for Al-Qatt Al-Asiri art.
- The visitor shall be able to know which controller to use to move.
- The visitor shall be able to identify the area that they are standing on and all adjacent areas.

Fig. 6: Garden pathway scenario requirements

C. *Software Building*

As mentioned in Section IV, the software building stage is planned to be carried out in 5 iterations. In this section, we show how we build on the output of the previous sections and define the detailed design, implementation, and testing of each iteration of the project as follows:

a) Iteration 1: prototype: To implement the preliminary prototype, we first project the 2D floorplan, presented in Fig. 3, into a 3D floorplan - see Fig. 7a. Secondly, we use the Autodesk AutoCAD software [24] to digitize it - see Fig. 7b. After that, we use the SketchUp Pro software [25] to generate a 3D coloured model of this floorplan - see Fig. 7c. Finally, we use the same software to produce a 3D animated prototype of the museum, and we use the VR plugin within the SketchUp Pro software to enable the VR glass and controllers.

We test the design prototype by conducting a co-design workshop. A number of experts were invited to the workshop to validate the prototype and submit their feedbacks using surveys; the detailed of the workshop well be explained in the next section.

b) Iteration 2: reception: Iteration 2 covers the implementation of scenarios 1 and 2. In these scenarios, it has been mentioned that if visitors start moving at the lobby hall, the museum sitemap appears on the hall's ground. Moreover, it has been mentioned that the pathway has an indoor garden which contains the most famous plants from the region on one side and their picture and descriptions on the other side. Therefore, to implement these scenarios we need to design the sitemap, the plants, and the plants pictures. In addition, the old floorplan design presented in Fig. 3 should be altered to reflect the collected comments during the testing phase of iteration 1.

This is accomplished by using Photoshop software and Wacom painting toolkit [26] to design the museum sitemap and the plants pictures - see Fig. 8, and by using Sketchup to design the plants. To design the plants, we first imported the pants as a block then we modified it to the proposed shape. Fig. 9 shows an example of the designing process of the *Adenium obesum* (desert rose) plant [27].

Fig.10 demonstrates the modification process of the old floorplan design presented in Fig. 3. Fig. 10a presents the new design of the floorplan , Fig. 10b shows the new measurements of the museums internal walls. Fig. 10c shows the 3D coloured model of the new floorplan.

All the designed objects are converted to interactive objects and imported into the Unity software [28] to make them alive objects at the virtual museum environment.

c) Iteration 3: tour: Iteration 3 covers the implementation of scenario 3. In this Scenario, it has been mentioned that visitors first greeted by the museum guide. Visitors move around to explore Al-Qatt artworks on the walls and observe Al-Qatt art pieces at the main hall. If the visitors step near a piece of artwork, a description of this artwork will appears. Therefore, we need to design Al-Qatt artworks and Al-Qatt art pieces. The museum guide was sketched before in Fig. 4

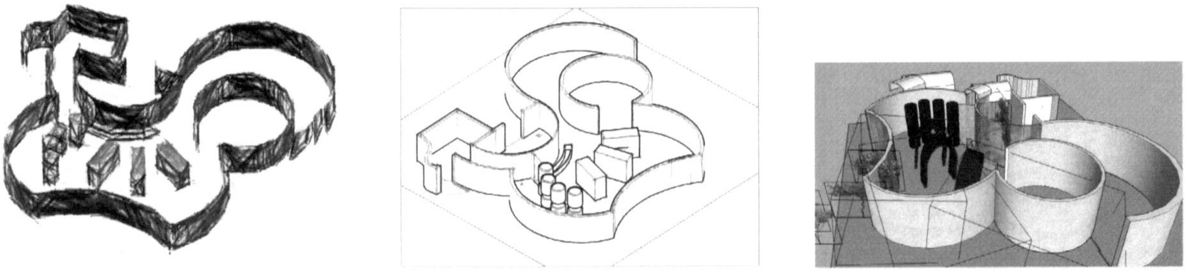

(a) 3-D floorplan sketch (b) 3-D floorplan draw (c) 3-D floorplan model

Fig. 7: Iteration 1: Prototype implementation

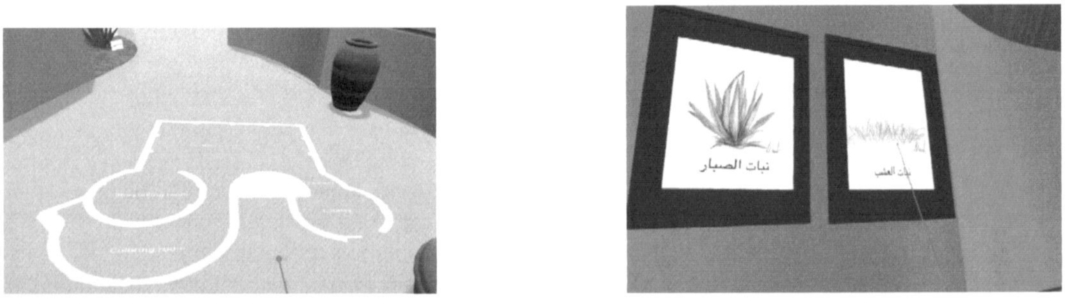

(a) The sitemap appears on the lobby floor (b) The plant pictures appear on the side wall

Fig. 8: sitemap and plant pictures design

(a) The real picture of the *Adenium obesum* (b) Adding flowers to the imported model (c) Adding the *Adenium obesum* stem to the imported model

Fig. 9: The design of the *Adenium obesum*

To draw AL-Qatt artworks on the walls of the main exhibition hall we use Photoshop software and Wacom painting toolkit [26] - see Fig. 11. Each wall represents a house or tribe in Assir [14] region.

Moreover, the main exhibition hall exhibits four pieces from Alraqadi museum [9] -see Figure 12. SketchUp was used to design these pieces.

At the end of the implementation phase of iteration 3, all the designed objects are converted to interactive objects and imported into the Unity software [28] to make them alive objects at the virtual museum environment.

d) Iteration 4: Storytelling: Iteration 4 covers Scenario 4. In this scenario, it has been mentioned that visitors first meets the museum's narrator Ms. Fatima and then Ms. Fatima tells the story of Al-Qatt art using animated pictures.

Ms. Fatima is designed using sketchUp. A sketchUp block was used as a start, then this block was modified to the proposed shape. Fig. 13 shows the steps of designing Ms. Fatima.

The designed items are imported to Unity software [28] to make them interactive objects and add them to the virtual museum environment.

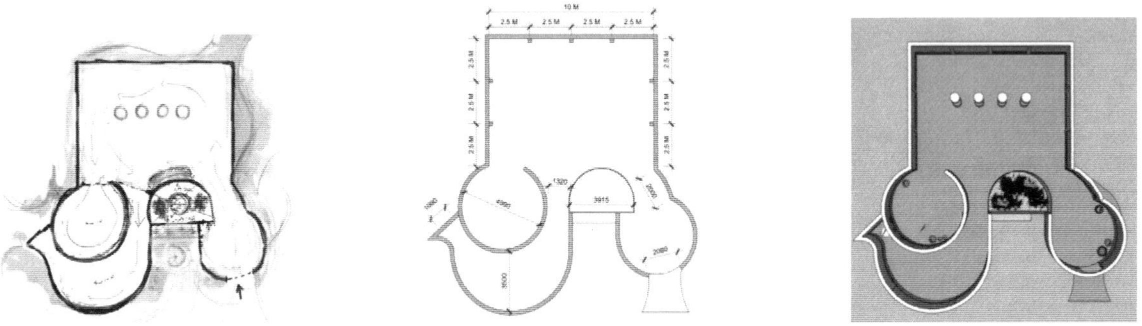

(a) The modified floor plan (b) Measurements of the museum internal walls (c) The new 3-D floorplan model

Fig. 10: The new floorplan

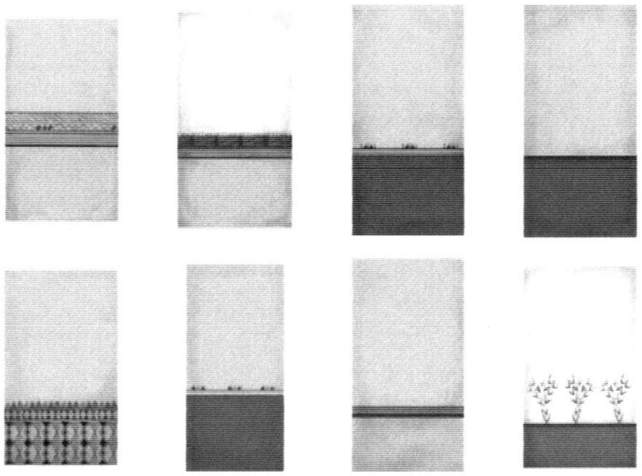

Fig. 11: AL-Qatt artworks

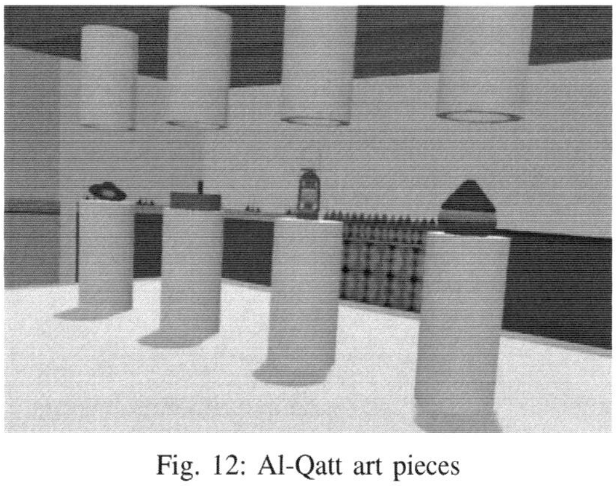

Fig. 12: Al-Qatt art pieces

e) Iteration 5: Colouring: Iteration 5 implements Scenario 5. In this scenario, it has been mentioned that a pattern of Al-Qatt art appears and the visitor can start colouring it. The user can change colours using the colour palette.

The pattern of Al-Qatt art was drawn using Photoshop then it was imported to Unity software to implement the colouring process. Fig. 14 demonstrate the colouring process. First the user chooses the colour - see Fig. 14a, then s/he shouts the colour on the pattern to colour the targeted area - see Fig 14b.

This finishes the implementation phase of iteration 5 which was the last iteration in the project. The next section explains the testing process which was conducted to ensure the correctness of the project implementation.

D. Testing

In this section we present the testing techniques used to verify the correctness of the virtual museum.

To test the design prototype, we conducted a co-design workshop. A number of experts with diverse backgrounds were invited to validate the prototype. We presented our work and collected their feedbacks using surveys, and the discussion during the workshop was also very useful.

The co-design workshop involved subject-matter experts from various domains, including Dr. Salma Al-Zaid, Vice-Dean of Humanities Departments and Assistant Professor in the Department of Art Education, Dr. Abeer Monadher, Vice Chair of Curriculum & Instruction Department at KSU, who is interested in and is a researcher in Al-Qatt Al-Asiri art, Dr. Dafra Al-Shahri, Vice Chair of Archaeology Department at KSU and Princess Rukaya Al Saud, an artist interested in Al-Qatt Al Asiri art.

After studying the notes in the surveys and organizing the reflections from the workshop, two modifications were suggested:

1) To make the lobby hall wider, because the tight design of the lobby hall will restrict the movement of virtual visitors.
2) To change the walls of the main exhibition hall from carved walls to straight walls, because straight walls are more suitable to exhibit Al-Qatt Al-Asiri art patterns.
3) To remove the displaying edges in the main exhibition hall to give a space for visitiors to more around in the hall.

The new floorplan after applying these changes was previously shown in Fig. 10.

(a) The sketchUp block (b) The proposed shape (c) The coloured shape

Fig. 13: The design of Ms. Fatima

(a) Visitor pointed at a colour (b) Visitors shout the colour on the targeted area

Fig. 14: Colouring room

As aforementioned, VMQA was developed in five iterations. After each iteration the outcomes are tested firstly by conducting unit testing to ensure that the implementation is correct, and secondly by conducting usability testing to ensure the practicality and the validity of the design.

After the completion of each iteration we integrate its outcomes with the outcomes of its predecessor and then apply down-top integration testing to ensure that the integrated version is correct.

At the end, we first conduct a system testing to prove that the final software performs as designed, and secondly we carried out a comprehensive usability testing to ensure that the final product meets the user expectation.

In the following we explain briefly each of these testing techniques. Interested reader can refer to [29] for more details.

- *Unit testing* is defined as a type of testing where each main function in the software is tested separately. The result of the unit testing usally presented in table contains the name of the function, the inputs, the excepted output, actual output. If the expected output is the same as the actual output then the unit testing is passed successfully.
- *Integration testing* is defined as a type of testing where software modules are integrated logically and tested as a group. This testing is carried out by testing the functions that only work if the two modules are integrated.
- *System testing* is defined as as a type of testing where a complete, integrated system is tested. The purpose of this test is to evaluate the system's compliance with the specified requirements.
- *Usability testing* is defined as as a type of testing which conducted to evaluating a product by testing it with representative users. Typically, during a test, participants are given realistic scenarios to complete while observed by researchers. This helps to highlight any gaps in the market that can be taken advantage of and illustrate where to focus design effort.

Due to the interactive and entertainment nature of the virtual museum this lies an importance on the results of the comprehensive usability testing. Therefore, we devoted the rest of this section to present the process and the result of the usability testing.

The usability testing was conducted on participants who can use virtual reality toolkits and interested in the art of Al-Qatt and in the rang of 7 – 55 years. 10 participants are observed in every iteration and 40 are observed during the comprehensive usability testing. In each iteration the usability tests were monitored by recording the desktop screen using an outside camera. The visitors feedbacks were collected via paper-based surveys and tasks sheets.

The average time taken by visitors to complete the reception areas (lobby and pathway) is 40 seconds with no system errors observed. The average time taken to complete the reception areas, tour area and storytelling area is around 3 minutes, with also no system errors observed. The average time taken to complete the reception areas, tour area and storytelling area is around 3.5 minutes. The average time inside colouring room is vary depending on visitors preferences of colouring speed and amount.

Finally, validate all functions of the project we held a usability testing at King Saud University campus. The number of participates was 40 and they were faculty, students and staff with different ages and experiences. Participates were monitored by recording the desktop screen using an outside camera. The average time taken by participates to finish the

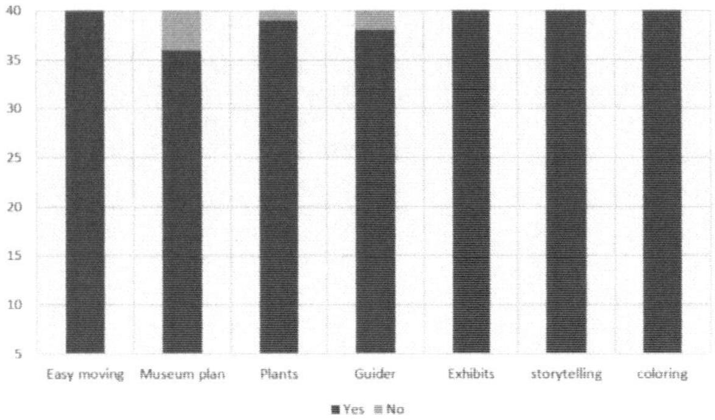

Fig. 15: Participants responses chart

whole museum is 3 minutes, with no system errors observed. The visitors feedbacks were collected via paper-based surveys and tasks sheets. In these surveys, the visitors were been asked questions which cover all the main functions of the museum, and they should answer by YES or NO. Fig. 15 shows the percentage of visitors answers.

Its worth to mention that the comments on the virtual museum tours conducted by the different visitors were in general very positive. However, visitors provided us with some recommendations such as adding background music and drawing arrows on the floor to show museum flow paths.

V. Next Steps and Conclusions

Al-Qatt Al-Asiri is the traditional art of interior wall decoration conducted by women in the Southern region of the Saudi Arabia. This paper presented the work conducted towards the development of a virtual museum of Al-Qatt Al-Asiri art, within the framework of the user-centered design and evaluation methodology for virtual environments. This framework consists of a number of iterations which involve end-users in the software design and evaluation processes. At this stage of the project, we completed the virtual museum of Al-Qatt Al-Asiri art with all its details. The software requirements were collected and the system design was built then the museum was implemented and tested on reasonable number of users.

VMQA is still an ongoing project. The next phase will be to add a second virtual museum for the art of the middle province of Saudi Arabia (Najd) houses. The final aim of the project is to end up with a collection of virtual museums for each province in the Kingdom of Saudi Arabia.

References

[1] S. Government, "Vision2030 report (english version)," https://www.vision2030.gov.sa/media/rc0b5oy1/saudi_vision203.pdf, 2016, accessed on 2019-4-20.

[2] "Virtual reality," in *Oxford Dictionaries*. Lexico.com, 2013, accessed on 2019-4-20. [Online]. Available: https://en.oxforddictionaries.com/definition/virtual_reality

[3] UNISCO, "12.com- decisions," https://ich.unesco.org/doc/src/ITH-17-12.COM-Decisions-EN.docx, 2017, accessed on 2019-4-20.

[4] S. G. Barsanti, G. Caruso, L. Micoli, M. Covarrubias, and G. Guidi, "3d visualization of cultural heritage artefacts with virtual reality devices," *ISPRS - International Archives of the Photogrammetry, Remote Sensing and Spatial Information Sciences*, vol. XL-5/W7, pp. 165–172, 08 2015.

[5] S. Valtolina, S. Franzoni, P. Mazzoleni, and E. Bertino, "Dissemination of cultural heritage content through virtual reality and multimedia techniques: A case study," in *11th International Conference on Multi Media Modeling (MMM 2005), 12-14 January 2005, Melbourne, Australia*, Y. P. Chen, Ed. IEEE Computer Society, 2005, pp. 214–221. [Online]. Available: https://doi.org/10.1109/MMMC.2005.36

[6] "Louvre museum," http://musee.louvre.fr/visite-louvre/index.html?defaultView=rdc.s46.p01&lang=ENG, accessed on 2019-4-20.

[7] "Saudi commission for tourism and national heritage (scth)," https://scth.gov.sa/E-Services/Pages/VirtualToursGuide.aspx, accessed on 2019-4-20.

[8] "Basma alsulaiman's virtual museum," https://www.basmoca.com/virtualgallery, accessed on 2019-4-20.

[9] A. Museum, https://www.instagram.com/alraqdi.museum/, accessed on 2019-4-20.

[10] Ghithan Ali Jrais, *Studies in Recent History of Assir*, 1st ed. Alawaifi Advertising, Jeddah, KSA, 2002, arabic book.

[11] Kinahan Cornwallis, *Asir before World War I : a handbook*. Oleander, New York, 1976.

[12] Maurice Tamisier, *Voyage en Arabie : séjour dans le Hedjaz, campagne d'Assir*. L. Desessart, Paris, 1840, french book.

[13] Harry St. John Bridger Philby, *Arabian Highlands*. New York: Cornell University Press, New York, 1952.

[14] H. Al-Hababi, "The art of women in 'asir (saudi arabia)," *AAS working papers in social anthropology*, vol. 25, pp. 1–8, 01 2012.

[15] ShadaHomes, "Symbols of al-qatt al-asiri art," Al-Qatt Al-Asiri Art Workshop, 2018, conducted in Jeddah, KSA.

[16] Andre Malraux , *Le Musee Imaginaire*. Gallimard Folio Essais, 1996.

[17] S. Styliani, L. Fotis, K. Kostas, and P. Petros, "Virtual museums, a survey and some issues for consideration," *Journal of Cultural Heritage*, vol. 10, no. 4, pp. 520 – 528, 2009. [Online]. Available: http://www.sciencedirect.com/science/article/pii/S1296207409000880

[18] G. Schofield, G. Beale, N. Beale, M. Fell, D. Hadley, J. Hook, D. Murphy, J. Richards, and L. Thresh, "*Viking VR*: Designing a virtual reality experience for a museum," in *Proceedings of the 2018 on Designing Interactive Systems Conference 2018, DIS 2018, Hong Kong, China, June 09-13, 2018*, I. Koskinen, Y. Lim, T. C. Pargman, K. K. N. Chow, and W. Odom, Eds. ACM, 2018, pp. 805–815. [Online]. Available: https://doi.org/10.1145/3196709.3196714

[19] "Google arts & culture virtual tours," https://artsandculture.google.com/partner?hl=en, accessed on 2023-4-14.

[20] C. Donghui, L. Guanfa, Z. Wensheng, L. Qiyuan, B. Shuping, and L. Xiaokang, "Virtual reality technology applied in digitalization of cultural heritage," *Cluster Computing*, pp. 1–12, 2017.

[21] J. G. Tromp, C. V. Le, and T. L. Nguyen, "User-centered design and evaluation methodology for virtual environments," in *Encyclopedia of Computer Graphics and Games.*, N. Lee, Ed. Springer, 2019. [Online]. Available: https://doi.org/10.1007/978-3-319-08234-9_167-1

[22] R. M. Eastgate, J. R. Wilson, and M. D'Cruz, "Structured development of virtual environments," in *Handbook of Virtual Environments - Design, Implementation, and Applications, Second Edition.*, K. S. Hale and K. M. Stanney, Eds. CRC Press, 2014, pp. 353–389. [Online]. Available: https://doi.org/10.1201/b17360-20

[23] A. Nicholls, M. Pereira, and M. Sani, "Report 1 – the virtual museum, the learning museum network project," LEM - The Learning Museum, Tech. Rep. ISBN 978-88-97281-03-0, 2012. [Online]. Available: http://online.ibc.regione.emilia-romagna.it/I/libri/pdf/LEM_report1_theVirtualMuseum.pdf

[24] "Autodesk autocad software," https://www.autodesk.com/products/autocad/overview?term=1-YEAR&tab=subscription, accessed on 2023-4-14.

[25] "Sketchup pro software," https://www.sketchup.com/products/sketchup-pro, accessed on 2023-4-14.

[26] "Wacom painting toolkit," https://www.wacom.com/en-us/discovery/edit/professional-results, accessed on 2023-4-14.

[27] "Wikipedia: Adenium obesum," https://en.wikipedia.org/wiki/Adenium_obesum, accessed on 2023-4-14.

[28] "Unity software," https://unity.com/, accessed on 2023-4-14.

[29] K. Naik and P. Tripathy, *Software Testing and Quality Assurance: Theory and Practice*, 2nd ed. Wiley Publishing, 2018.

Rethinking Usability Heuristics for Modern Biomedical Interfaces

Stefan Röhrl*, Christian Janotte*, Christian Klenk†, Dominik Heim†, Manuel Lengl*, Alice Hein*, Martin Knopp†*, Oliver Hayden† and Klaus Diepold*

*Chair of Data Processing, Technical University of Munich, Arcisstr. 21, 80333 Munich, Germany
†Heinz-Nixdorf Chair of Biomedical Electronics, Technical University of Munich, Einsteinstr. 25, 81675 Munich, Germany

{stefan.roehrl, christian.janotte, christian.klenk, dominik.heim, m.lengl, alice.hein, martin.knopp, oliver.hayden, kldi}@tum.de

Abstract—**High usability is the ultimate goal in user interface development. In order to test this, user studies are often carried out at great expense. An alternative to this is offered by more favorable implementation guidelines and heuristic evaluation that get by with a smaller number of tests. Tools in the area of biomedical research face major challenges here, as they are extremely crucial, the users are highly demanding, and the advent of Artificial Intelligence (AI) requires researchers to take a powerful leap of faith. Since general heuristics are often insufficient for this domain, we introduce new Biomedical Research AI Heuristics and evaluate them among others using a prototype user interface in the domain of blood cell analysis. The comparative study shows our specialized approach competes very well with Nielsen's well-established general heuristics and a recent publication of rules for AI development. Our set finds the most relevant usability issues and can support the review process for the growing number of biomedical systems that will use artificial intelligence technologies in the future.**

Keywords*—*Usability Heuristics; Blood Cell Analysis; Human Assisted Labeling; Quantitative Phase Imaging.

I. INTRODUCTION

One of the current challenges in biomedical research is to interpret the increasing amount of data available from new imaging and analysis techniques. To utilize the new information, more and more Artificial Intelligence (AI) is finding its way into this field. It is being used to facilitate differential diagnostics and to improve the understanding of medical conditions. Here, a new platform technology promises major changes in the field of blood analysis. A microscope working with Quantitative Phase Imaging (QPI) does not require expensive reagents and therefore no time-consuming sample preparation [1][2]. Combining this approach with a microfluidics channel, the optical amplitude and phase information of millions of cells can be recorded within minutes. The simplicity, high statistical power and speed of this approach allow statements about the composition of the blood, morphological changes of the cells and thus the kinetics of diseases [3]–[5]. Nevertheless, the resulting images are rather unknown in the medical domain and reference databases as well as sufficient ground truth data is missing, which hinders the efficient training of machine learning algorithms. To overcome these problems, we have to provide an easy way for researchers to work hand in hand with the machine to explore this new field of hematological analysis based on computer vision and AI.

For successful human-computer interaction, the user interface represents the common language the interdisciplinary researchers and developers have to speak. Misunderstandings can prevent such emerging technologies from being successful, as they cannot rely on the trust and the establishment of the gold standard methods [6]. Here, we would like to introduce and compare new **rule set for heuristic evaluation**, which are specifically designed for the development of AI-infused interfaces in biomedical research. As the target group of biomedical researchers and practitioners stands out for a busy schedule and demand high standards in the aspects of explainability [7], transparency [8] and causality [9], having a set of tailor-made heuristics promises a quicker translation of new technologies to the point of care. While most of the usability heuristics used in the past have been of a rather general nature [10], domain-specific ones have become more prominent in the last decades [11]–[13].

In this work, we propose a new labeling platform for holographic cell images where humans and AI work closely together in (inter-)active learning scenarios. This will facilitate the generation of verified ground truth data and be a valuable representative for this kind of biomedical user interfaces. Our primary interest, however, is to validate the newly developed usability heuristics against the existing ones, and thus to meet the need for guidance in the development process of AI-infused biomedical systems.

In the following, the work is divided into the appropriate sections: Section II motivates the choice of the clinical application and introduces the concepts for comparing heuristic rule frameworks. Then, Section III presents the specially developed web-based prototype of a user interface. The three sets of heuristic rules are introduced in Section IV, followed by their evaluation by experts as well as by user tests in Section V. The results of the study are described and visualized in Section VI. Finally, Section VII discusses the findings and draws conclusions for possible future work.

II. BACKGROUND AND RELATED WORK

Before introducing the prototype, we will investigate the medical relevance of the chosen use case and the methods for evaluating sets of heuristic rules.

A. Medical Relevance of Quantitative Phase Imaging

The process of blood analysis in general is one of the most requested laboratory tests [14] and has been extensively studied in the past, leading to technically advanced solutions.

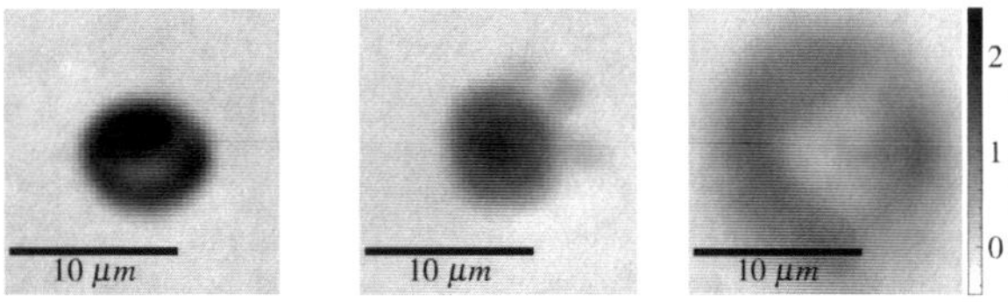

(a) Red Blood Cell (b) Aggregate (c) Defocused Cell

Figure 1. Phase images of different cell classes

As a result, most state-of-the-art instruments work with a blood processing scheme based on marker materials [6]. Although these devices being very precise, they come with several downsides, as they require non-specific and costly labeling as well as time-consuming sample preparation such as *hemolysis* [15]. Using QPI methods combined with machine learning, the exercise translates into a computer vision task, which offers more flexibility. The morphological and internal patterns of blood cells provide insights for oncological [3][16], parasitic infections [17] and other diseases [4]. Also, the aggregation of blood cells can deliver crucial information [5][18].

However, before the images can be automatically interpreted and classified, they must be segmented and labeled by experts. Figure 1 shows representatives of typical cells and structures as they look like under a quantitative phase microscope. Red blood cells (a) are quite simple to detect, whereas aggregates of white blood cells and platelets (b) are more difficult to find due to their complex structure and the associated rarer occurrence. The algorithm as well as the human also have to learn, which objects need to be discarded (c). Note that medical experts are usually only trained on stained thin films and are therefore unfamiliar to this representation [6]. The brightness information directly correlates with the optical phase shift $\Delta\phi$ caused by the cells. Greater detail about the microscope can be found in [2][3].

B. Active Learning for Human Assisted Labeling

Manually labeling large amounts of data such as images is tedious and sometimes even challenging for skilled personnel, as the previous section describes. Therefore, crowd sourcing is not an option. As biomedical experts are expensive and limited in time, the Active Learning (AL) approach seems promising [19]. In AL, an algorithm is trained on a very sparse data set to learn a classification problem. However, instead of leaving the user with the task of correcting a predicted class label when the system is uncertain, the algorithm attempts to minimize the actions that need to be taken [20]. Moreover, AL shows suitable behavior for imbalanced data sets like ours to build a *human-in-the-loop* system [21], as we do in our prototype.

C. Quality Assessment of Usability Heuristics

The developed user interface represents the precedent to put our newly developed heuristics into practice. To make the heuristics more comparable, we need to introduce quality assessment measures as well as standard procedures to obtain these measures. Hartson et al. [22] propose to apply the different evaluation methods to the target system and compare the found usability problems to a baseline of "real" usability problems. In our work, we will determine the baseline by conducting *asymptotic user testing* [22]. As not every usability problem is as crucial as the other, we will further rate each problem then by a *severity score* proposed by Nielsen [23]. Table I shows the weighting of the apparent usability problems in order to compare the heuristics on their ability to prevent major usability issues.

TABLE I. SEVERITY RATINGS FOR USABILITY PROBLEMS [23]

	$s(p)$	**Description**
Rating	0	Violates a heuristic but is not a usability problem
	1	Cosmetic or unimportant usability problem
	2	Minor usability problem
	3	Significant usability problem
	4	Usability catastrophe

Starting from there, Sears [24] defines the **thoroughness** criterion (also known as recall in other disciplines)

$$T = \frac{|E \cap F|}{|E|}, \tag{1}$$

where $|E \cap F|$ denotes the number of problems F found by the heuristics from the baseline set of real usability problems E. Using our mapping of severity scores we can calculate the **weighted thoroughness**

$$T_w = \frac{\sum_i s(f_i)}{\sum_j s(e_j)} \text{ with } f_i \in E \cap F \text{ and } e_j \in E, \tag{2}$$

where $s(p)$ assigns every usability problem its rating according to Table I. Finally, the **validity** criterion [25] (also called precision)

$$V = \frac{|E \cap F|}{|F|} \tag{3}$$

helps us to judge how many of the identified problems F where real and no false alarms.

III. HUMAN ASSISTED LABELING PROTOTYPE

In order to provide an easily accessible and customizable user interface, we developed a web-based prototype for this study, which is divided into different views.

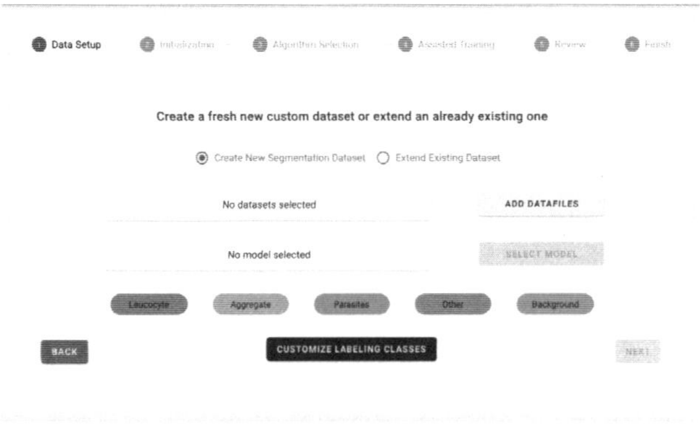

Figure 2. View 1 - Data Setup

The **data setup** view displayed in Figure 2 contains the functionality for setting up the general properties of the project. At the top, there is an option button that allows the user to choose whether to start with an empty data set or expand an existing data set based on a previously trained algorithm. Below, the user finds means to load the respective data containers or models. The lower part of the page displays the currently available classes of cell types. Each of them has its own color scheme and can be customized, added or deleted by clicking the button below them.

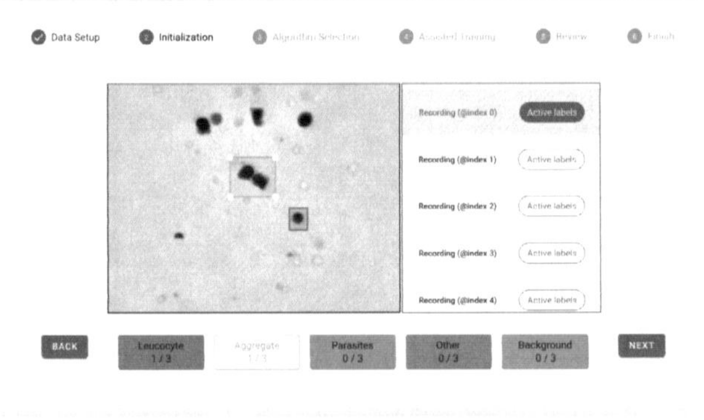

Figure 3. View 2 - Initialization

After having specified the labeling task and the expected classes of cells, clicking the "Next" button opens the **initialization** view (Figure 3). As the name suggests, it is used to provide an initial training set for the later algorithm. A large canvas is the main component of this view, displaying the selected set of cells, but also providing an area for drawing and annotating. In the bottom part of the view, there is a footer that displays the available classes. Clicking on one of them activates the class which is illustrated by highlighting. The user can now click and drag the mouse to draw bounding rectangles around the cells in the image. This combination of location and class is later called a label.

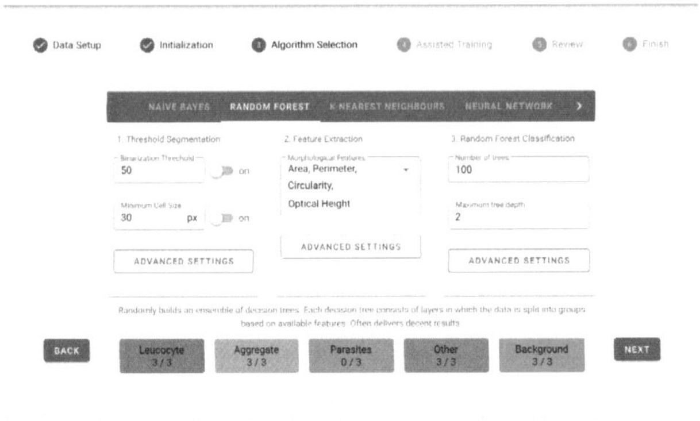

Figure 4. View 3 - Algorithm Selection

In the **algorithm selection** view (Figure 4), users can specify the type of algorithm they want to use to classify cells in the records by selecting the appropriate tab at the top. Currently, users can choose from *Naive Bayes*, *Random Forest*, *k-Nearest-Neighbors* and a small *Neural Network* [26][27]. Depending on the type of classifier, necessary segmentation and feature extraction steps can be customized in the respective tab.

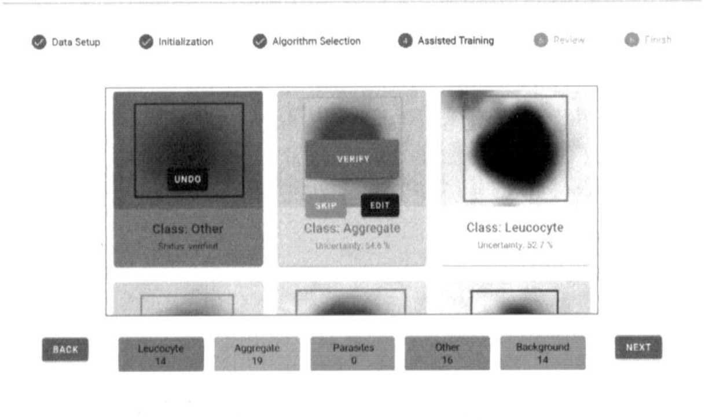

Figure 5. View 4 - Assisted Training

When the algorithm has made its first predictions based on the initial training set the **assisted training** part starts in this reoccurring view (Figure 5). A gallery appears showing the proposed labels that the algorithm found in the data. As suggested by the AL principles from Section II-B, they are ordered by their uncertainty from the highest to the lowest value. Here, users can intervene and verify or correct the algorithm and hence, enlarge the training set without manually scanning the raw data and drawing rectangles. Furthermore, human assistance is only required for difficult objects, reducing the wasted time on already mastered samples. The algorithm can then be periodically retrained on the extended training set and can quickly reach a satisfying performance on the complete data set.

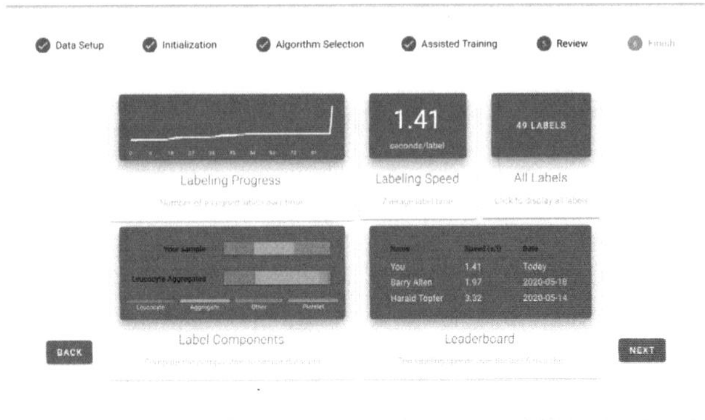

Figure 6. View 5 - Review

Finally, the **review** view (Figure 6) summarizes the labeling progress over time and the current performance. It compares the composition of the data set to other similar data sets and displays the percentages of detected cell classes. As a kind of gamification element, it also shows the labeling speed and ranks it with the performance of other users.

IV. Usability Heuristics

This section gives an overview of the state of the art in usability heuristics and introduces our new set of rules.

A. Nielsen's Heuristics

The general usability heuristics by Nielsen and Molich have been known for decades and are still used today. They are based on some of the most fundamental rules for user interface development. Their strength in finding many usability problems has been demonstrated in the past. Due to their generality, they can be applied to almost any type of system, but they have the disadvantage of not always finding as many usability problems as a set developed specifically for the system's domain. Nevertheless, they are a good starting point and will be a strong competitor and thus valuable for comparing them with our own set of heuristics. For our comparison, we used the rules from Nielsen's most cited publications [10], [28]. Also, minor modifications in wording [29], done in the last years, were considered.

B. Human-AI Interaction Heuristics

With the advent of AI in recent decades, it was only a matter of time before user interface developers began to address the specific requirements of AI-infused interfaces. In collaboration with Microsoft, a group of researchers led by Amershi recently proposed a set of usability guidelines for the development of such systems [30]. Guidelines and heuristics are not technically the same thing, since guidelines are used during the implementation of an interface and heuristics during verification. However, for short lists of guidelines such as this one, they can often be used interchangeably [31]. For our experiments, we converted the guidelines into a set of heuristic rules and provided them with examples for the experts so that this set can be used equivalently for the evaluation. This set of heuristics additionally distinguishes whether a problem occurs **immediately**, while the user is using the tool, or if it appears over a **longer period**. It is to be expected that some of the listed rules of this set will have minor relevance for our labeling interface like Rule 6 that is about mitigating social biases. To be consistent, we will keep the set unaltered.

C. Biomedical Research AI Heuristics

The main idea of this work is not only to compare the proven heuristics by Nielsen and Molich and the recently published AI guidelines interpreted as heuristics. We intend to create our own set of heuristics specifically targeted at biomedical research applications that use AI. The amount of software in this area will increase in the coming years, and it may be beneficial to have custom heuristics at hand for evaluation to save valuable testing time. Table II shows a set of 15 rules grouped in four categories, which constitute our *Biomedical Research AI Heuristics*. They are inspired by several publications in the domain of user interface design, biomedical and AI applications over the last decades. We completed those rules by hints and suggestions from preceding interviews with experts from local institutions working in the field of biomedical research.

Table II. Heuristics for AI in biomedical research

	#	Name	Short Description
Structure	1	Streamline main task	Focus on the main task that a system was created for and make the system easy to learn [32].
	2	Provide full control	Provide global control of important model parameters and the data pipeline [33][34].
	3	Orientation	Always show users where they are, what is currently going on and what they can do next [10].
Interaction	4	Guide attention	Keep the users focused on their task and only alarm them in urgent cases [35][36].
	5	Provide comparisons	Let users compare among similar data or parameters when they need to judge an outcome or make a decision.
	6	Show impact	Users need to see how their actions influence the system and its performance [37].
	7	User over System	Allow users to correct errors of the AI efficiently at all times and even turn off the AI if needed [35].
Presentation	8	Familiar language	Use non-technical language if possible. Pay attention to use correct terminology for medical concepts [38].
	9	Precise language	Avoid ambiguous wording for labels and commands that could trigger confusion [10].
	10	Familiar look	Use ways of presentation for the interface that users know from other tools.
	11	Appeal	Give the users the feeling of using a state-of-the-art and high-quality product.
Explainability	12	Explain data	Foster the interpretability of the data and how it differs from other data sources [39].
	13	Explain processing	There needs to be a high-level explanation for the overall procedure that is performed by the system [9].
	14	Explain reasoning	There has to be an explanation why and how the system derived a certain result or prediction [9].
	15	Strengths / Limitations	Show what the strengths and weaknesses of the system are and what expectations are realistic. [40]

V. Usability Evaluation

Once all the prerequisites are met, the prototype is tested by means of heuristic evaluation and user testing.

A. Heuristic Evaluation

For the evaluation of heuristics, we will compare the three heuristics with different aims and origins presented in the previous section. Their performance will be compared to determine whether general or domain-specific heuristics perform better in the domain of AI-infused interfaces for biomedical research. Most usability researchers like Nielsen classify potential expert evaluators into three different categories: *novices*, *single experts* and *double experts* [41]. Novices are new to usability concepts but often have knowledge in the domain where the user interface will be deployed. In contrast, single experts already have experience in the field of usability engineering but lack knowledge of the designated domain. Double experts are evaluators who are proficient both in usability engineering and the domain. On average, a novice finds only 22% of issues in a system, while single experts manage to find 41% and double experts even around 60% [42]. The experts participating in our review are neither novice evaluators nor have they been conducting such reviews for years. Nevertheless, they have a sound knowledge of usability concepts and have conducted a heuristic evaluation before. In addition, some of them also have a basic understanding of the domain of the system. Each heuristic is applied to our prototype user interface by five different evaluators, a number often recommended for user interface development because of its cost-efficiency [43]. In order to keep focus on the most relevant usability problems, we use the severity rating system introduced in Table I. During the expert review process, each expert will assign a level of potential impact to the usability problems they have discovered. After a final list of aggregated usability problems is compiled for all heuristics, each expert will also assign ratings to the problems found by their peers. In the end, the ratings among the experts will be averaged and rounded.

B. User Testing

In order to compare the different heuristics in this work, we need to gather knowledge about the real usability problems E inherent in our prototype interface. For this, asymptotic user testing [22] is selected as a test procedure. With a conservative detection rate of 19% per user [22][44], the relation between the number of testers and the percentage of discovered usability problems seems to level off at around 20 testers, which is very late. This is shown by the ideal curve in Figure 7b. However, to increase the chances of overlooking as few problems as possible, we decided to conduct a test series with at least this number of testers. Eventually, we found 21 representative users with a biomedical background who were willing to participate. Their demographics are displayed in Figure 7a. The youngest tester was 21 and the oldest 59 years old. What almost all testers had in common was their lack of experience with machine learning. 76.2% said they had no experience at all. This was beneficial to see how they would react to something they had never used before.

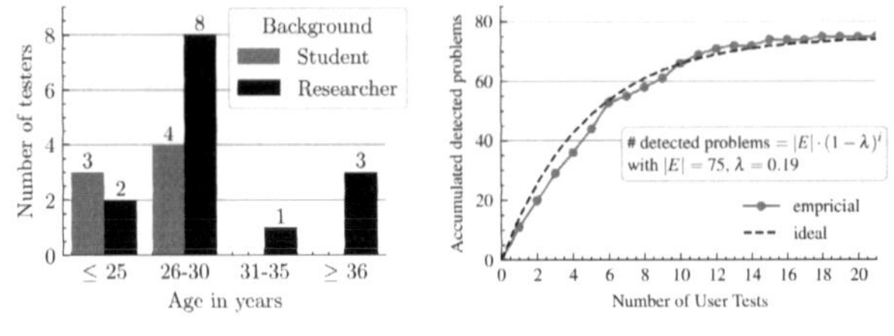

(a) User Demographics (b) Detected problems by users

Figure 7. Composition and performance of the user tests

All users were given two tasks: 1) "In a small sample you are interested in the number of white blood cells, single platelets, and cell aggregates. Extract these components and perform some further evaluation to show them to a co-worker." 2) "Your bigger recording is rich in white blood cell aggregates. You want to detect the same components as before but also keep track of other cells as they might become relevant later. Prepare and store your results for further evaluation." Users were given as much time as they needed to complete the tasks and were encouraged to ask questions and think aloud throughout the test [45]. Meanwhile, the evaluator took informal notes that would later be summarized in a formal test protocol. Testers were also required to complete a short questionnaire after the test.

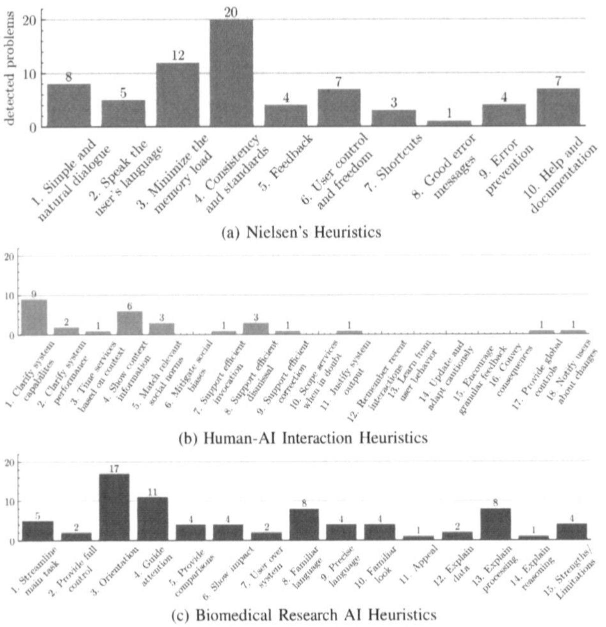

(a) Nielsen's Heuristics

(b) Human-AI Interaction Heuristics

(c) Biomedical Research AI Heuristics

Figure 8. Detected problems by the respective heuristics

VI. Results

This section summarizes findings and compares the results of the different testing strategies by the proposed metrics.

A. Heuristic Evaluation

The first set of rules we applied to our biomedical user interface consisted of **Nielsen's ten general usability heuristics**. They were developed without regard to a specific type of user interface. The review conducted by five evaluators using this rule set identified 60 violations within the system. This number was obtained by comparing and aggregating the results of the individual evaluators. Figure 8a shows the number of usability problems identified by each rule of Nielsen's heuristics. It is important to note that the sum of all bars is greater than the total number of problems identified, since a problem may relate to more than one heuristic. Prominently, Rule 4, which deals with user interface consistency and standards, is responsible for 20 usability problems, which is significantly more than any other rule. The second most problems are related to Rule 3, which focuses on reducing the user's memory load. It is not possible to say whether their numerous occurrence is due to the fact that these rules highlight important aspects of biomedical interfaces very effectively, or whether an unusual high number of violations occurred by chance. The rough list of usability problems merely indicates the presence of these violations. Conclusively, the five evaluators emphasized that they enjoyed working with the set and that it was easy to use. In addition, it is worth noting that each heuristic was applied at least once and no heuristic was omitted.

The second set of rules used in this project were the recently published **guidelines for human-AI interaction**. They were proposed as guidelines that can support the development of interfaces to let human users interact with AI. In our evaluation, the five experts discovered 26 violations and the corresponding usability problems, which is less than half the amount that Nielsen's heuristics helped to find. Figure 8b shows the number of heuristic violations per rule in this set of human-AI heuristics. The distribution of problems looks quite different from that resulting from Nielsen's heuristics. First, there are a number of rules that did not help uncover a usability problem at all. This is mainly due to the fact that these aim for long-term effects which do not apply to the tasks covered in our study. The two heuristics that have received the most attention are Rule 1, which deals with explaining what the system can do, and Rule 4, concerning context and relevancy of the displayed information. What is interesting about this second set of heuristics is the informal feedback from the evaluators. They pointed out that these rules were very difficult to apply to the system. The reason for this could be that they were not developed as heuristics, but as guidelines. As such, they might be too specific and not generally applicable.

The third set of rules we applied to the interface is the one we created specifically for the field of **biomedical research interfaces that use AI**. Here, the five experts reported a list of 55 usability problems. This is slightly less than what they discovered with the general heuristics, but still much more than what the heuristics for human-AI interaction identified. The distribution of usability issues across the different rules within our custom heuristics is shown in Figure 8c. All fifteen rules were found to have at least one violation. The two most frequent heuristics are Rule 3 and Rule 4, which are concerned with providing orientation and guiding the user's attention. The third place is shared by Rule 8 and Rule 13. It is interesting to note that these four heuristics are all aimed at reducing the complexity of AI for the biomedical users or enabling them to better deal with it. Evaluators noted that the set was easy to use and that they felt it covered most usability issues with a large impact on the user experience. This feeling is supported by the fact that it detected the most usability issues with the highest impact among the three heuristic sets, with fourteen violations of the maximum severity level.

B. User Testing

This would lead us to the quality assessment metrics introduced in Section II-C, but before we can apply them we need the baseline of real usability problems E determined by our user tests. With respect to the asymptotic behavior of the usability problem discovery process, we assumed that about 20 testers would be needed to find most of the problems. The test ultimately resulted in the detection of 75 usability problems over the course of 21 user tests. To support the claim that we almost reached an asymptotic upper bound, we plotted the occurrence of problems over tests in Figure 7b, indeed revealing the asymptotic shape of a Poisson process [43].

To obtain the severity ratings of the real usability problems, we sent the complete list of issues to our usability experts and summarized the ratings based on their judgment. Many of the entries in this list are common problems that can occur in any

TABLE III. EXEMPLARY USABILITY PROBLEMS

View	**Description** **Note:** The listed problems all have a maximum severity rating of 4. The numbers indicate the violated heuristic rule or the number of affected users respectively.	Nielsen's	human-AI	biomed-AI	User Test
1	There is no clear indicator that tells the user when the initialization is completed or what happens with empty classes. The "X/3" in the footer is not prominent enough.	5 10		4 6	2
3	The different algorithms are not sufficiently explained and the current explanations are hard to find. Users do not know which algorithm to choose.	1 2		4 6 13 15	1
3	The wording of some parameters and explanations is too technical to understand.			8	2
4	Users do not understand the training process, what they have to do and why multiple iterations with retraining make sense. The initial performance might be disappointing.	3 10	1 2	13	5

type of user interface, such as misleading button descriptions and lack of loading indicators. However, there are also some problems (see Table III) that seem to be rather unique and that can serve as examples of typical problems in environments where users with a biomedical background interact with AI. These were concentrated to uncertainties about the specific workflow of the program and obscure consequences, which certain changes in the settings might have. Only 2 out of 21 users requested major changes before they would use such a system for their daily work. 19% stated that they would use it, but still suggested some minor changes. The majority of 71% of users indicated that they would use the system in the future exactly as it is, after becoming familiar with it.

C. Metric-Based Comparison of Heuristics

Now that we have a baseline, we can relate it to the findings from different heuristics. This results in a list of 104 usability problems, with which we can compute the quality assessment metrics. As listed in Table IV, the three different sets of heuristics did not perform equally well. For almost all metrics, the domain focus of our set of heuristics is noticeable and provides improved results in the criteria **thoroughness** and **validity**. The general heuristics by Nielsen still occupy a stable second place, although it should be noted that all three heuristics were not able to predict usability problems seamlessly. Nevertheless, the high validity of our custom heuristics make them a reliable tool to alert developers of incipient and severe usability issues. We can further compute the thoroughness metric for high severity levels (3 & 4), as these should be addressed early in the development process. Among the highest level of severity (4), our biomedical heuristics account for a thoroughness of

TABLE IV. RESULTS OF THE QUALITY ASSESSMENT METRICS

Metric	Nielsen's	human-AI	biomed-AI
Thoroughness	50.1%	25.3%	**62.7%**
Weighted Thoroughness	54.0%	28.9%	**69.0%**
Average Severity	2.66	**2.84**	2.74
Validity	63.3%	73.1%	**85.5%**

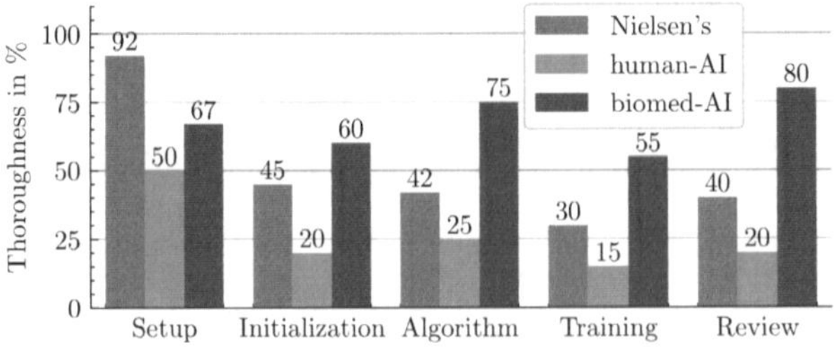

(a) Thoroughness

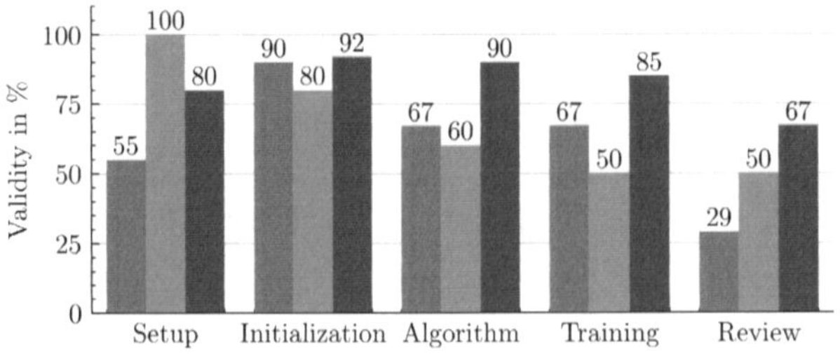

(b) Validity

Figure 9. Quality assessment metrics for the individual views

93.3%. Nielsen's set improves to 73.3% and the human-AI interaction heuristics to 46.7%.

Since not all views of our prototype are equally influenced by AI, we investigate the performance in the individual components of the system. Accordingly, Figure 9a shows the **thoroughness** metric for each set of heuristics. The Nielsen heuristics have the highest thoroughness in the setup view, but as more interaction with the AI is emerging, their performance drops. Surprisingly, the AI emphasized human-AI heuristics score even worse. Our biomedical heuristics have the highest thoroughness in the initialization, algorithm, training and review views, as these require frequent interaction between the users and the machine learning algorithms.

Similarly, we can evaluate the **validity** of the heuristics depending on the view as displayed in Figure 9b. The validity of our biomedical heuristics is always higher as Nielsen's heuristics. This means that Nielsen's heuristics tend to find a lot of irrelevant usability issues in all views. However, the validity for the review view is particularly low, for all three sets.

VII. Discussion and Conclusion

The performance metrics from Section VI-C indicate that there is a noticeable difference in which heuristics we use for an expert evaluation of an AI-infused user interface within the biomedical domain.

Nielsen's well-known heuristics struggle when it comes to finding real usability problems in biomedical interfaces induced with AI. They showed only mediocre thoroughness in these parts of the prototype. However, they found the most genuine usability problems in the parts of the interface that were least affected by machine learning, resulting in a high performance in those views. Unfortunately, this seems to be accompanied by reduced validity. Nielsen's heuristics tend to find more expendable problems than the competing heuristics. All in all, the results suggest that these general heuristics are not always the best choice when it comes to finding usability problems in a specific domain like the one we studied. This is a result that also has been discussed in other publications [46].

The **heuristics for human-AI** interaction did not score particularly well in terms of thoroughness and validity. In addition, the experts in this study indicated that this set was most difficult to use for interface evaluation. This could be due to the fact that this set was originally designed as a guideline and also has large focus on long-term effects that are not relevant here.

The **heuristics for biomedical user-AI** interaction that we developed in this work provided the most compelling results. While their thoroughness was good but not great, their weighted thoroughness and thus their potential to uncover the most important problems in a user interface like our prototype was a positive discovery. This was further emphasized by the set's high thoroughness scores for high severity problems. Moreover, our set performed better than Nielsen's general heuristics, especially in the parts of the interface that focused on user-AI interaction.

When putting the heuristics' evaluation in a larger context, we expected that we could detect at least 70% of the real usability problems as foreseen in literature [11][22][43]. Our experts were not novices, but the best detection rate they could achieve was 62.7% with the biomedical heuristics and even less with the other sets. There is a possibility that this is due to inadequate evaluation of our experts. However, it is more likely that the main reason is that it is simply more difficult to find usability problems in the domain we analyzed. This assertion is supported by studies like [11], pointing out the need for domain-specific heuristics for domains where usability problems are immanently difficult to detect. This was also one of the basic assumptions on which this entire paper is based. As biomedical interfaces seem challenging, an unweighted thoroughness of 62.7% is a satisfactory result.

Finally, we aim to apply our new biomedical heuristics on more user interfaces in this domain. Tools that are used for making diagnoses and more complex reasoning could be of special interest. With a more diverse expert group, we hope to reduce the effort of conducting user tests and help to establish AI based technologies in biomedical research and healthcare.

Acknowledgment

The authors would like to especially honor the contributions C. Janotte for the implementation of the user interface prototype and the execution of the studies. Furthermore, thanks go to D. Heim and C. Klenk for the sample preparation and recording of the measurements. All expert reviewers should also be thanked at this point.

This research was funded by the German Federal Ministry for Education and Research (BMBF) with the funding ID ZN 01 | S17049.

REFERENCES

[1] Y. Park, C. Depeursinge, and G. Popescu, "Quantitative phase imaging in biomedicine," *Nature Photonics*, vol. 12, no. 10, pp. 578–589, 2018.

[2] C. Klenk, D. Heim, M. Ugele, and O. Hayden, "Impact of sample preparation on holographic imaging of leukocytes," *Optical Engineering*, vol. 59, no. 10, p. 102403, 2019.

[3] M. Ugele, M. Weniger, M. Stanzel, M. Bassler, S. W. Krause, O. Friedrich, O. Hayden, and L. Richter, "Label-Free High-Throughput Leukemia Detection by Holographic Microscopy," *Advanced Science*, vol. 5, no. 12, 2018.

[4] T. L. Nguyen, S. Pradeep, R. L. Judson-Torres, J. Reed, M. A. Teitell, and T. A. Zangle, "Quantitative Phase Imaging: Recent Advances and Expanding Potential in Biomedicine," *American Chemical Society Nano*, vol. 16, no. 8, pp. 11 516–11 544, 2022.

[5] M. Nishikawa, H. Kanno, Y. Zhou, T.-H. Xiao, T. Suzuki, Y. Ibayashi, J. Harmon, S. Takizawa, K. Hiramatsu, N. Nitta *et al.*, "Massive image-based single-cell profiling reveals high levels of circulating platelet aggregates in patients with covid-19," *Nature Communications*, vol. 12, no. 1, pp. 1–12, 2021.

[6] J. J. Barcia, "The Giemsa stain: Its History and Applications," *International Journal of Surgical Pathology*, vol. 15, no. 3, pp. 292–296, 2007.

[7] S. Tonekaboni, S. Joshi, M. D. McCradden, and A. Goldenberg, "What clinicians want: contextualizing explainable machine learning for clinical end use," in *Machine Learning for Healthcare Conference*. PMLR, 2019, pp. 359–380.

[8] C. M. Cutillo, K. R. Sharma, L. Foschini, S. Kundu, M. Mackintosh, and K. D. Mandl, "Machine intelligence in healthcare - perspectives on trustworthiness, explainability, usability, and transparency," *Nature Partner Journals Digital Medicine*, vol. 3, no. 1, pp. 1–5, 2020.

[9] A. Holzinger, C. Biemann, C. S. Pattichis, and D. B. Kell, "What do we need to build explainable ai systems for the medical domain?" *arXiv preprint arXiv:1712.09923*, 2017.

[10] J. Nielsen and R. Molich, "Heuristic evaluation of user interfaces," in *Proceedings of the SIGCHI Conference on Human Factors in Computing Systems*, 1990, pp. 249–256.

[11] S. Hermawati and G. Lawson, "Establishing usability heuristics for heuristics evaluation in a specific domain: Is there a consensus?" *Applied Ergonomics*, vol. 56, pp. 34–51, 2016.

[12] A. W. Kushniruk, V. L. Patel, and J. J. Cimino, "Usability testing in medical informatics: cognitive approaches to evaluation of information systems and user interfaces." in *Proceedings of the American Medical Informatics Association Annual Fall Symposium*, 1997, p. 218.

[13] J. Zhang, T. R. Johnson, V. L. Patel, D. L. Paige, and T. Kubose, "Using usability heuristics to evaluate patient safety of medical devices," *Journal of Biomedical Informatics*, vol. 36, no. 1-2, pp. 23–30, 2003.

[14] S. Horton, K. A. Fleming, M. Kuti, L.-M. Looi, S. A. Pai, S. Sayed, and M. L. Wilson, "The Top 25 Laboratory Tests by Volume and Revenue in Five Different Countries," *American Journal of Clinical Pathology*, vol. 151, no. 5, pp. 446–451, 2018.

[15] A. Filby, "Sample preparation for flow cytometry benefits from some lateral thinking," *Cytometry Part A*, vol. 89, no. 12, pp. 1054–1056, 2016.

[16] S. K. Paidi, P. Raj, R. Bordett, C. Zhang, S. H. Karandikar, R. Pandey, and I. Barman, "Raman and quantitative phase imaging allow morpho-molecular recognition of malignancy and stages of B-cell acute lymphoblastic leukemia," *Biosensors and Bioelectronics*, vol. 190, p. 113403, 2021.

[17] M. Ugele, M. Weniger, M. Leidenberger, Y. Huang, M. Bassler, O. Friedrich, B. Kappes, O. Hayden, and L. Richter, "Label-free, high-throughput detection of P. falciparum infection in sphered erythrocytes with digital holographic microscopy," *Lab on a Chip*, vol. 18, pp. 1704–1712, 2018.

[18] M. Finsterbusch, W. C. Schrottmaier, J. B. Kral-Pointner, M. Salzmann, and A. Assinger, "Measuring and interpreting platelet-leukocyte aggregates," *Platelets*, vol. 29, no. 7, pp. 677–685, 2018.

[19] B. Settles, "Active learning literature survey," University of Wisconsin-Madison Department of Computer Sciences, Tech. Rep., 2009.

[20] K. Wang, D. Zhang, Y. Li, R. Zhang, and L. Lin, "Cost-effective active learning for deep image classification," *IEEE Transactions on Circuits and Systems for Video Technology*, vol. 27, no. 12, pp. 2591–2600, 2016.

[21] A. Holzinger, "Interactive machine learning for health informatics: when do we need the human-in-the-loop?" *Brain Informatics*, vol. 3, no. 2, pp. 119–131, 2016.

[22] H. R. Hartson, T. S. Andre, and R. C. Williges, "Criteria for evaluating usability evaluation methods," *International Journal of Human-Computer Interaction*, vol. 13, no. 4, pp. 373–410, 2001.

[23] J. Nielsen, "Severity ratings for usability problems," *Papers and Essays*, vol. 54, pp. 1–2, 1995.

[24] A. Sears, "Heuristic walkthroughs: Finding the problems without the noise," *International Journal of Human–Computer Interaction*, vol. 9, no. 3, pp. 213–234, 1997.

[25] W. D. Gray and M. C. Salzman, "Damaged merchandise? A review of experiments that compare usability evaluation methods," *Human Computer Interaction*, vol. 13, no. 3, pp. 203–261, 1998.

[26] L. Breiman, "Random forests," *Machine learning*, vol. 45, no. 1, pp. 5–32, 2001.

[27] C. M. Bishop, *Pattern Recognition and Machine Learning*. Springer, 2006.

[28] J. Nielsen, "Enhancing the explanatory power of usability heuristics," in *Proceedings of the SIGCHI Conference on Human Factors in Computing Systems*, 1994, pp. 152–158.

[29] ——. (2005) Ten usability heuristics. (accessed 2022.12.17). [Online]. Available: https://www.informaticathomas.nl/heuristicsNielsen.pdf

[30] S. Amershi, D. Weld, M. Vorvoreanu, A. Fourney, B. Nushi, P. Collisson, J. Suh, S. Iqbal, P. N. Bennett, K. Inkpen *et al.*, "Guidelines for human-AI interaction," in *Proceedings of the 2019 CHI Conference on Human Factors in Computing Systems*, 2019, pp. 1–13.

[31] B. Shneiderman, *Designing the user interface: Strategies for effective human-computer interaction*. Addison-Wesley, 1998.

[32] H. Lieberman, "User interface goals, AI opportunities," *AI Magazine*, vol. 30, no. 4, pp. 16–22, 2009.

[33] S. Amershi, M. Cakmak, W. B. Knox, and T. Kulesza, "Power to the people: The role of humans in interactive machine learning," *AI Magazine*, vol. 35, no. 4, pp. 105–120, 2014.

[34] T. G. Gill, "Expert systems usage: Task change and intrinsic motivation," *Management Information Systems Quarterly*, pp. 301–329, 1996.

[35] E. Horvitz, "Principles of mixed-initiative user interfaces," in *Proceedings of the SIGCHI Conference on Human Factors in Computing Systems*, 1999, pp. 159–166.

[36] R. T. Sutton, D. Pincock, D. C. Baumgart, D. C. Sadowski, R. N. Fedorak, and K. I. Kroeker, "An overview of clinical decision support systems: benefits, risks, and strategies for success," *Nature Partner Journals Digital Medicine*, vol. 3, no. 1, pp. 1–10, 2020.

[37] A. D. Jameson, "Understanding and dealing with usability side effects of intelligent processing," *AI Magazine*, vol. 30, no. 4, pp. 23–23, 2009.

[38] C. Rzepka and B. Berger, "User interaction with AI-enabled systems: a systematic review of is research," in *Thirty Ninth International Conference on Information Systems*, vol. 39, 2018, pp. 1–17.

[39] J. De Fauw, J. R. Ledsam, B. Romera-Paredes, S. Nikolov, N. Tomasev, S. Blackwell, H. Askham, X. Glorot, B. O'Donoghue, D. Visentin *et al.*, "Clinically applicable deep learning for diagnosis and referral in retinal disease," *Nature Medicine*, vol. 24, no. 9, pp. 1342–1350, 2018.

[40] High-Level Expert Group on Artificial Intelligence, *Ethics Guidelines for Trustworthy AI*, European Commission, 2019.

[41] J. Nielsen, "Finding usability problems through heuristic evaluation," in *Proceedings of the SIGCHI Conference on Human Factors in Computing Systems*, 1992, pp. 373–380.

[42] J. Noyes and C. Baber, *User-centred design of systems*. Springer Science & Business Media, 1999.

[43] J. Nielsen and T. K. Landauer, "A mathematical model of the finding of usability problems," in *Proceedings of the INTERACT'93 and CHI'93 Conference on Human Factors in Computing Systems*, 1993, pp. 206–213.

[44] J. R. Lewis, "Sample sizes for usability studies: Additional considerations," *Human factors*, vol. 36, no. 2, pp. 368–378, 1994.

[45] M. W. Jaspers, T. Steen, C. Van Den Bos, and M. Geenen, "The think aloud method: a guide to user interface design," *International Journal of Medical Informatics*, vol. 73, no. 11-12, pp. 781–795, 2004.

[46] C. Jimenez, P. Lozada, and P. Rosas, "Usability heuristics: A systematic review," in *2016 IEEE 11th Colombian Computing Conference (CCC)*. IEEE, 2016, pp. 1–8.

An Experimental Study on Providing User Control in E-Commerce Recommendation through Conversational System

Seth Owirodu, Yuchuan Lin, Sheng Tan
Department of Computer Science
Trinity University
San Antonio, Texas, USA
email: {sowirodu, ylin, stan}@trinity.edu

Zhou Tong
Department of Computer Science
Wheaton College
Norton, Massachusetts, USA
email: tong_tony@wheatoncollege.edu

Abstract—**Recommender Systems(RS) are gaining importance across different domains, especially in e-commerce. Existing RS work mainly focuses on improving accuracy while neglecting other concerns associated with commercial RS, such as lack of transparency, little or no user control, and absence of diversity. In this paper, we aim to address those concerns by implementing a conversational system based e-commerce RS using real-world product data. We also conducted a month-long user study with over a hundred participants to investigate how users respond to the conversational system as a control mechanism to mitigate the abovementioned problems. Results show that the majority of the users give positive responses to the conversational system based control mechanism. The post-study questionnaires indicate that better control, transparency, and diversity can be achieved utilizing our system. By considering users' perspectives, this work contributes to a better understanding of how we can utilize the conversational system to mitigate transparency and diversity issues associated with RS.**

Keywords*—*Recommender System; Conversational System; Transparency; User Control; E-commerce.

I. Introduction

In the past decade, the Recommender System (RS) has played an increasingly important role across different domains of the online services such as e-commerce, social media, banking, news, music, and video [1]. The main task of RS is to help the user navigate through an overload of information by providing personalized recommendation to particular users based on explicit or implicit information [2]. For example, recommendations account for about 60% of all video clicks from the home page on Youtube [3], while the recommended items account for around 35% of the total customer purchase on Amazon [4]. Thus, the deployment of RS can not only alleviate the problem of information overload but also make significant contribution to the overall success of the service [5].

In most of these practical applications, RS has been improving over the years by aiming for better recommendation accuracy. However, many researchers have become aware that other than accuracy, existing RS failed to address several other concerns adequately, such as diversity and transparency. For example, RS can create "filter bubbles" that prevent users from accessing more diverse content and lead to potential polarization views [6]. Moreover, RS generally keeps the recommendation process "behind the scenes" which lacks of transparency which allow for very little accountability [7]. Additionally, RS rarely offers users any explicit way to direct or participate in the recommending process [8]. Without providing diversity and transparency, it can greatly diminish user trust and satisfaction which increase the bias of the RS.

Among all the concerns discussed above, the user control has the most direct impact compared to others. This is because by enhancing user control, it is possible to mitigate other problems, including diversity, transparency, and accountability. In particular, by allowing users to participate in the recommendation process, the RS can be more responsive and align with user interests, which leads to better recommendation accuracy [9]. User control also requires RS to be more transparent and accountable through the process [10]. In addition, it increases the diversity of recommendation results by providing user the opportunity to explore beyond default options or known interests [11].

Much researches has been done to implement different mechanisms for increasing user control of the RS [12]. PeerChooser enables the user to increase the weight of the active user represented by nodes in calculating recommendations [13]. TasteWeights allows the user to adjust the weight of different parameters to change their importance in the recommendation process [14]. PARIS achieve user control by utilizing interactive mechanism like drop-down lists and checklists [15]. There is also a large body of work leveraging conversational systems (i.e., chatbots) to help users interact with the RS [16]. Such mechanism allows users to give feedback about the recommendation results through conversational systems [17].

Conversational systems or dialogue systems are designed to serve the user through conversation for various purposes given the context [18]. In recent years, with the significant advancement in natural language processing, deep learning, and cloud computing, conversational systems have already been used in applications across various domains [19]. Compared to other interactive mechanisms, the conversational system has several advantages [20]. First, conversational systems are intuitive and have a much lower learning curve. Second, conversational systems can be easily customized for various purposes without affecting the interface. Those advantages make the conversational system an ideal interactive mechanism to enable user control for RS.

Although there are existing studies for conversational RS,

they mainly focus on how to improve the recommendation results by refining the user preferences [16]. Moreover, since those work mainly aim for recommendation accuracy improvement, they fail to address other concerns for the RS, such as transparency and diversity, especially under the e-commerce setup. In this study, we try to answer the following research question: **how do people view the conversational system as the control mechanism for e-commerce RS, which underlying algorithms do they prefer, does it improve the diversity and transparency of the RS?** We focus on the e-commerce application since it is among the most used domains for both RS and conversational system. Also it is essential to understand user's perspective on how to improve the transparency and diversity of RS utilizing conversational system.

To answer the question, we first build a mockup e-commerce website that leverages real-world customer data and integrates both the recommender and conversational systems. Then, we conduct a month-long user study by allowing participants to freely explore the website and interact with the RS through a conversational system. We customize the RS so users can play around with the underlying recommendation algorithms/parameters and get the updated recommendation results on the fly. We also collect the user feedback to gain insights into the user's perspective on the conversational system as a control mechanism over RS. This study contributes to a better understanding of how the conversational system can be utilized to mitigate the concerns, such as transparency and diversity associated with RS.

The rest of this paper is organized as follows. Section II discusses the related work of E-commerce RS, interactive RS, and conversational system. Section III describes the design details of the system. In Section IV and Section V, we describe the experiment setup and results of the user study. Finally, Section VI and Section VII discussed the limitations and summarize the results of this study.

II. Related Work

A. E-commerce Recommendation Systems

Over the last decade, there has been a growing interest and research effort towards RS for e-commerce websites. This is because RSs have a tremendous impact on both users and e-commerce providers. The products are recommended based on various factors, such as popularity, customer demographics, product rating/comment, and customer's past purchase/browsing history [21]. A RS usually includes three key components: acquire data from customers, compute and rank the recommendation, then present the recommendation results [22].

In general, e-commerce RS can be divided into four categories: content-based filtering, collaborative filtering, hybrid, and social network-based. Content-based filtering RS recommends items similar or closely related to the items the user has purchased previously [23]. The techniques used in content-based filtering approaches include: traditional information retrieval methods (e.g., TF-IDF, LDA) and advanced machine learning methods (e.g., Bayesian, decision tree, ANN) [24]. The major limitation of content-based filtering is overspecialization, limited content analysis due to a lack of keywords [25].

Collaborative filtering RS recommends items based on the items previously preferred or purchased/browsed by other users [23]. In particular, most of the systems can be further sorted into two types: heuristic-based (e.g., KNN, graphy theory, SVM) and model-based (e.g., Bayesian, Clustering, linear-regression) [26]. This approach also has several drawbacks, such as sparsity problem, gray sheep problem, and scalability problem [26].

In order to avoid the shortcomings of above mentioned systems, hybrid RS has emerged to take advantage from the previous two approaches. It is done by combining content-based filtering and collaborative filtering RS together in various ways, such as weighted, switching, mixed, feature combination and cascade [27]. Recently, by leveraging the fast-growing of social network applications, social network-based RS has been proposed to utilize data from other aspects, such as user preferences, social connections to improve recommendation accuracy and overcome major challenges including cold-start problem and sparsity problem [28].

B. Interactive recommendation systems

Since the first introduction of RS in the mid-1990s, the majority of the research efforts have been dedicated to improve the system performance and accuracy [29]. Recently, more and more work has been done to improve the overall quality of RS in other aspects, such as diversity, novelty, context, and serendipity [30]. In particular, RS should also take into consideration of factors including transparency and controllability [31] to further increase the societal value and user trust [32]. Thus, research on human factors by developing interactive RS has gained increasing interest. For the RS, there are three distinctive phases where the user interaction with the system could happen: preparation (preference selection), computation (recommendation computation), presentation (results presentation).

The majority of the existing RS utilize implicit user preferences when generating recommendation results. This means the user has no control over which preference will be used or prioritized compared to others. Since user's preferences are highly complex, contextual, and even contradictory under specific scenarios [33], it is crucial to give the user the freedom to choose and prioritize their preferences in order to improve controllability. For example, the system proposed by Schaffer *et al.* [34] allows user to adjust the weights of different input parameters to change their corresponding importance in the recommendation process.

Much work have been proposed to enable user control over the recommendation computation process by either allowing the user to adjust the algorithm parameters/weights [14] or switch between different types of algorithms [35]. Compare to commonly used one algorithm fit all approach, this type of user control gives users the ability to select different algorithms that can tailor to different scenarios. For example, the content-bases filtering approach has the advantage when there is enough domain knowledge on the feature space while the collaborative filtering approach works better under the scenario where there is no overspecialization on user profile and recommend items. Since the algorithm/parameter change over the recommendation computation process yields a bigger impact on the final results, our study will focus on providing the user interaction with the system during this phase.

The presentation control mechanism allows the user to reorder or present the recommendation results in various ways that better fit a specific user and his/her interest under different scenarios [34]. Specifically, system like TalkExplorer [36] uses a cluster map to visualize relations between recommender agents. MusiCube [37] allow the user to rate more items to refine recommendation directly in the recommendation results. On the other hand, work proposed by Jin *et al.* [38] leverage straightforward post-filtering functionalities to refine recommendation results and achieve cognitive load reduction.

C. Conversational systems

Conversational systems or conversational user interfaces are conversational agents that can interact with different users using natural language [39]. The technology is also known as chatbots which humans could interact with [40]. With the rapid development in the area of artificial intelligence, especially the advancement in natural language processing in the recent years, chatbots are capable of performing many labor-intensive task at a much lower cost and has been widely deployed across a varied range of applications, including intelligent customer service for e-commerce, virtual personal assistance, financial dialogue system, physical healthcare, and pedagogical conversational agent [19].

Based on the specific techniques utilized, typical conversational system can be divided into the six categories: template-based, corpus-based, intent-based, RNN-based, RL-based, and hybrid approaches [19]. Because of the advancement in computational power and deep learning algorithms, more and more research have tried to combine several techniques to improve the performance of the chatbots [18]. For example, it is possible to utilize a ranking algorithm to select the optimal response from candidate responses generated by several chatbots leveraging different techniques [41].

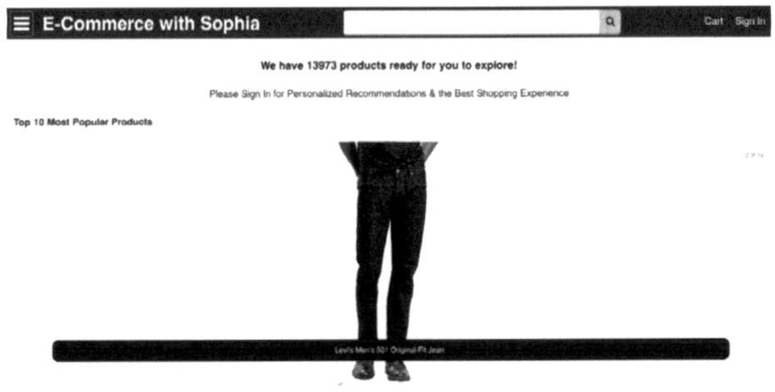

Figure 1. A screenshot of the e-commerce website used for our study.

It is worth noticing that there are existing work attempt to integrate the conversational system with the recommendation system to further improve recommendation performance [17]. It is done by eliciting user preferences and further reduce preference ambiguity through the conversational systems leveraging AI techniques [16]. Although there are many research efforts have been made towards this direction, existing work mainly focuses on how to improve the response from the conversational system or better integration of those two systems [42]. Different from existing work, our study aims to explore the potential of utilizing conversational RS to improve the transparency and controllability of the RS, especially under the e-commerce application scenario.

III. System Design

In this section, we describe the details of how we implemented the system. Specifically, we discuss the data set and frameworks that were chosen as well as how we used them respectively.

A. E-Commerce website and Data set

We implement the e-commerce website using the open-source framework Amazona [43]. The website layout shares high similarities with the popular shopping website Amazon and has been adopted by most e-commerce websites. This way, users can quickly get familiar with the layout and explore the website without much learning curve.

In particular, we made several changes to the website to accommodate our study. First, we change the website from category-based to brand-based. This is because we want the user to focus on the recommendation page without getting overwhelmed by various product category page information. Second, we created two different sections on the home page to display the recommended items based on the underlying recommendation algorithm and randomly selected items which mimic the modern e-commerce website. The website's home page after user login is shown in Figure 1.


```
{
"image": ["https://images-na.ssl-images-
amazon.com/images/I/71eG75FTJJL._SY88.jpg"],
"overall": 5.0,
"vote": "2",
"verified": True,
"reviewTime": "01 1, 2018",
"reviewerID": "AUI6WTTTOQZYS",
"asin": "5120053084",
"style": {
        "Size:": "Large",
        "Color:": "Charcoal"
        },
"reviewerName": "Abbey",
"reviewText": "I now have 4 of the 5 available colors of this
shirt... ",
"summary": "Comfy, flattering, discreet--highly recommended!",
"unixReviewTime": 1514764800
}
```


Figure 2. A sample of the Amazon Review Data

To populate the website, we utilized the Amazon product review data and product metadata of Amazon Review Data (2018) [44] for our implementation. This data set is the updated version of the Amazon Review Data released back in 2014 [45], containing product reviews and metadata from Amazon, including 233.1 million reviews spanning from May 1996 to Oct 2018. The whole dataset has 29 different categories of products in total. A sample of the review data is shown in Figure 2.

In order to reduce excessive information that would distract users, we only picked the Clothing and Shoes sub-dataset category with 32.2 million reviews and 2.6 million products. This is because many of the products from the real-world e-commerce website are from those categories and users are more familiar with the brands from those categories. To reduce the sparsity problem of the review data, we used the 5-core review data, a dense subset extracted from the original product review data where each product has at least five reviews.

B. Recommendation system and Chatbot

For this study, we implemented the recommendation engine using Case Recommender [46], which is an open-source a Python framework of several popular recommendation algorithms for both implicit and explicit feedback. This framework aims to provide a rich set of components that allow us to construct a customized RS based on a set of underlying algorithms and rating prediction.

It is worth noting that this study does not seek to tackle the cold start issue in the recommendation system where the system does not contain prior information about a specific user. To resolve this issue, during the registration process, each user is required to enter basic user information (e.g., age, gender) and select their top favorite brands and products from the list the website provides.

In order to generate the recommended items, our system first computes the estimated ratings for all product candidates with the trained model using the default algorithm or explicitly selected by that user. Next, the product candidates are sorted by their estimated ratings. Next, a list containing the top n products with the highest estimated ratings is sent back as the recommended items. Here, the number of recommended products, the recommendation algorithm, and rating prediction are considered parameters controlled by either the user or default setting. The default number of products being recommended, recommendation algorithm, and rating prediction is 5, most popular, and SVD, respectively.

After comparing various chatbot frameworks implemented, we selected the react-chatbot-kit for building our chatbot [47], a React-based open source chatbot framework. The default chatbot framework contains a message parser, a configuration, and an action provider, which allows us to easily configure the interactive conversational system for our study and integrate it with our implementation of the e-commerce website and underlying RS.

To better handle the user control request for the underlying RS, we first designed and implemented several message parsers that can detect different keywords and determine what kind of responses should be returned to the user. Next, we came up with different keywords related to our user control methods or user control in general. All the control keywords are implemented as buttons so users can easily choose from the conversation without typing. After the user clicks the button, specific actions will be triggered (e.g., switching the algorithm, changing the number of items to be recommended). An example of the chatbot implementation is shown in Figure 3.

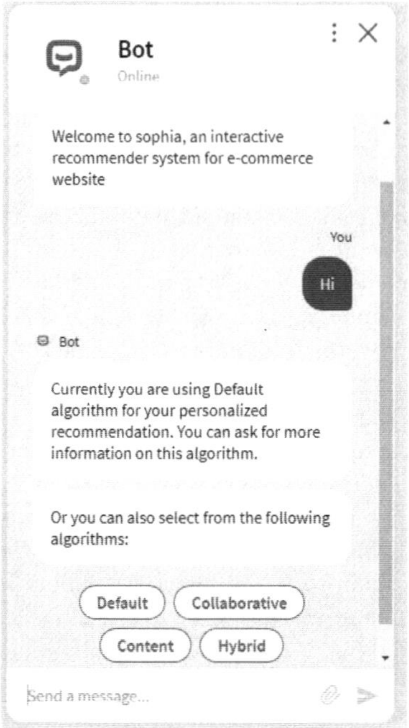

Figure 3. A screenshot of the chatbot used for our study.

IV. Experimental Setup

We studied the user behavior of our system, a conversational system based interactive RS for e-commerce website, where the user can interact with the conversational system to change the underlying algorithms and parameters. The proposed system supports the switching between multiple recommending algorithms, which gives the user the control of the RS and the ability to view the results generated by various algorithms/parameters on the fly. When a user logged into the system, he/she will be assigned the baseline algorithm as his/her initial condition. They will also receive a brief message from the conversational system to inform them about the currently running algorithm and potential options they can switch to.

Our system supports four underlying recommending algorithms. Each algorithm is identified to the user using an abbreviation derived from the original name. Users can interact with the conversational system for further information about each algorithm, such as a simple description of what this algorithm is and how it is being used in the RS. The supported algorithms are as follows:

- The *Baseline* algorithm generates the results by selecting the top reviewed items from randomly selected cate-

gories/brands. This algorithm was called *Default* and was used as "non-personalized" algorithm.
- The *Collaborative* algorithm generates the results utilizing collaborative filtering approach. It searches the similar preference user with the current user to find the similar users. After finding a similar user, it then presents the recommendation for the current user according to the preference of similar ones. The algorithm was called *Collaborative* and was used to improve the user experience for new user of the system.
- The *Content* algorithm generates the results leveraging content-based filtering approach. The item recommended by such an approach often indicates textual information where each item is described with the keyword and its weight. Then the items are recommended based on item characteristics and the user's preference. The algorithm was called *Content* and was used to recommend items similar to what the user has liked or purchased in the past.
- The *Hybrid* algorithm generates the results by taking advantage of both content-based filtering and collaborative filtering approaches. It is done by combing the recommendation results from those two approaches. The algorithm was called *Hybrid* and was used to avoid the disadvantages of content-based filtering and collaborative filtering approaches.

Once in the system, users could change the underlying algorithms and rating prediction parameters by interacting with the website's conversational system. The change will take effect immediately after user specification in the conversational system. After the user types in or selects the desired algorithms or parameters, the system will reload the list of recommended items on the current page (if they are on the item recommendation page) and show the results from the newly selected algorithm/parameter. The user's choice will persist throughout the system and affect all the predictions for item recommendations.

The summary of the experiment data is listed as follows: there are 108 users participated in our study over one month period of time; of all the participants, 45 were female, 52 were male, and the rest declined to reveal that information; the age range is from 21 to 50; 95 of them make the algorithm/parameter at least once. We consider switching from one algorithm/parameter to another as a single change event. There is a total of 1315 change events recorded during the experiment.

We also asked all participants to fill in a questionnaire after the experiment. It is used to assess the participants' experience using the proposed system. The questionnaire uses a five-point Likert scale, ranging from 1 to 5, where 1 represents strong disagreement, and 5 represents strong agreement. There are a total of 98 pieces of feedback collected. The questionnaire statements were as follows:

1) I become familiar with the system very quickly.
2) The information provided by the chatbot was sufficient for me to change the underlying algorithms/parameters.
3) I would like use this system in the future on e-commerce website.
4) I like the item recommendation result generated by the system.
5) I have fun when I am using the system.
6) The recommend results contained a lot of variety when switch to different algorithms/parameters.
7) The system has no real benefit for me.
8) I have to invest a lot of effort to obtain different recommendation results.
9) I feel in control of the recommending process.

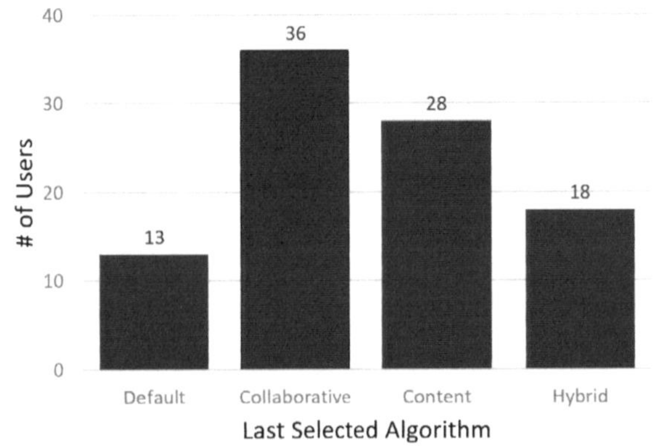

Figure 4. User Preferences of Algorithms

V. RESULTS

In this section, we describe our findings from this study. It contains the results for both algorithm/parameter switching and the questionnaire.

A. User Switch Algorithms

Of the 108 users in our study, 95(87%) changed underlying algorithms at least once, as mentioned before. This means 13 users only use the default algorithm/parameter during the process. These activities likely resulted from users' unawareness of the conversational system on the web page, or the results generated by the default algorithms has already met their expectation. The high percentage of users switching the algorithm/parameter at least once demonstrates that most users utilize the conversational system to adjust underlying algorithms. This also shows the user's willingness to explore RS through conversational system and desire for transparency and user control over RS.

B. User Algorithm Preferences

Here, we study the user preferences of the algorithm. Among the users who tried different algorithms, the collaborative was the most favored algorithm, followed by Hybrid, content, and default algorithms. Figure 4 shows the number of users who switched algorithms at least once and selected one of the algorithms as their final choice (i.e., the algorithm user chose as the active algorithm at the end of the experiment).

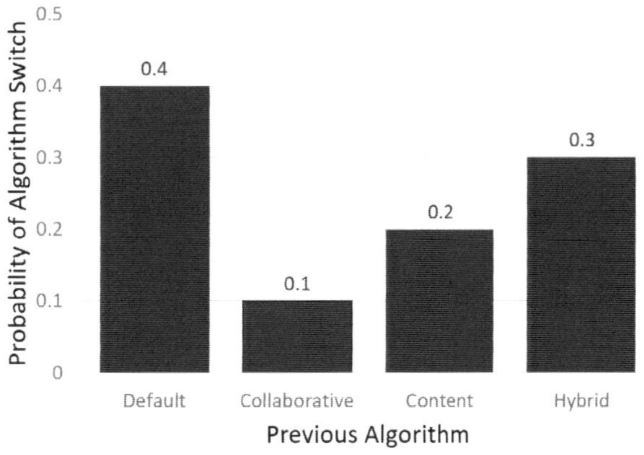

Figure 5. Likelihood to Switch Algorithm

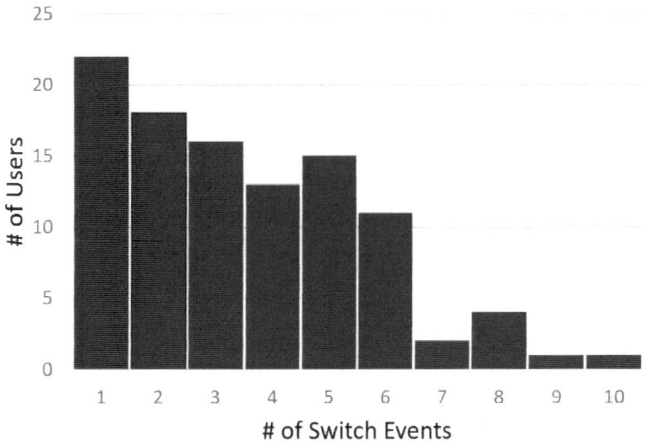

Figure 6. Events Count for User Switch

It is easy to observe that users prefer other algorithms over the default ones. This is because the users knew the default algorithm was non-personalized and could not generate more accurate or personalized results. We can also observe that the user prefers the collaborative filtering-based approach more than the content-based and hybrid approaches. It is likely because the users who switched algorithms at least once are willing to try various options on the parameters. This observation provides insights to support the idea of users' desire for transparency and user control of the recommendation systems.

As we discussed before, most users chose to switch from non-personalized algorithms and try different ones. Figure 5 shows the probability of users in each algorithm who tried a different algorithm afterward. As we can see, users who choose the default algorithm have the highest probability of switching algorithms, followed by hybrid, content, and collaborative. This observation also suggests users' awareness of the non-personalized results generated by the default algorithm. Combining these results with the users' final choice, we can infer that most users are satisfied with the collaborative algorithm. The content algorithm has the next satisfactory rate, followed by the hybrid algorithm.

C. Algorithm Switching Behavior

We also study the user switching behavior by measuring how many times each user switched their algorithms, and the results are shown in Figure 6. The x-axis shows how many switches have been made; the y-axis shows the number of users who made that amount of switches. We only showed the number of switches less than 10 times, which accounts for 97% of the users. The vast majority of the users switched algorithms no more than 6 times. However, there exist users who logged over 95 switches during the experiments. Most users switch just several times. For example, only around 20% of users switched more than 6 times.

The most common pattern for switching was for the user to switch from the default to another algorithm or try the other three algorithms and stop the switching. The median number of switching is 4; after 6 switches, there is a significant drop-off in the number of users. This is because 4 to 6 switches are enough for most users to try other personalized algorithms and decide which one is their favorite. It is worth noticing that most users experiment with the switch early in their use of our system, conduct several switches and then leave the system alone.

D. Questionnaire Results

Figure 7 summarizes user feedback and perception about the system and interaction effectiveness. The feedback of Q1(M=4.00, SD=0.85) and Q8(M=2.45, SD=1.15) show that the proposed system is relatively easy to use and does not require much effort for the user to learn. It is worth noting that among all the users, the younger users (35 years or younger) gave overall higher ratings on Q1 and lower ratings on Q8. On the other hand, the older users (40 years or older) gave overall lower ratings on Q1 and high ratings on Q8. This is likely because e-commerce websites have widely adopted the conversational system, and younger users are already taking advantage of this feature and are familiar with how to interact with it.

The quality of item recommendation Q4(M=3.85, SD=0.92), information variety Q6(M=3.65, SD=1.25), and information sufficiency Q2(M=3.95, SD=0.82) all received positive feedback from the users. This indicates that the proposed system provides an easily understood explanation for the user to explore different algorithms. Meanwhile, it also produces enough transparency and variety on the generated list of recommended items based on different algorithms.

The feedback on Q3(M=4.15, SD=0.74), Q7(M=1.68, SD=0.88), Q9(M=4.08, SD=0.72) show the effectiveness and usefulness of the proposed system. The overall positive feedback of those statements demonstrates that the proposed system increases the user control and transparency of the recommendation system and has the potential to improve the user experience further if adopted by other similar systems. It is worth noticing that the feedback on Q5 (M=4.12, SD=0.63)

Questions	Mean	SD
Q1: I become familiar with the system very quickly.	4.00	0.85
Q2: The information provided by the chatbot was sufficient for me to change the underlying algorithms/parameters.	3.95	0.82
Q3: I would like use this system in the future on e-commerce website.	4.15	0.74
Q4: I like the item recommendation result generated by the system.	3.85	0.92
Q5: I have fun when I am using the system.	4.12	0.63
Q6: The recommend results contained a lot of variety when switch to different algorithms/parameters.	3.65	1.25
Q7: The system has no real benefit for me.	1.68	0.88
Q8: I have to invest a lot of effort to obtain different recommendation results.	2.45	1.15
Q9: I feel in control of the recommending process.	4.08	0.72

Figure 7. Results of Post Study Questionnaire

is also overwhelmingly positive. This is because the conversational system is intuitive and enjoyable to interact with, which can further facilitate the user's control over the RS compared to other interactive mechanisms.

VI. Discussion

The user study and post-study questionnaire show that integrating the conversational system with RS for e-commerce websites is very promising for better user control and transparency. However, there are still several limitations of our study.

First, our study mainly focused on the RS's user control and transparency aspects; we did not thoroughly evaluate other aspects of the RS. For example, we could use RMSE to evaluate the accuracy of the RS. Besides the accuracy, many other metrics can be used to further evaluate an RS in various aspects, including the relevancy metrics like recall and precision.

Second, our RS cannot correctly handle the cold start issue, which means our system performs poorly for users with no information stored in the system. We plan to solve this issue in future research by using additional data sources, such as social network data or choosing the most prominent groups of analogous users [48].

Third, the conversation system could be improved. By only using partial pattern matching, we have not yet fully utilized the power of the conversational system. In the future, we would like to build a more intelligent conversational system by combining NLP and deep learning techniques. So our system can better understand the user's intention and provide a more appropriate response.

Last, due to the limited time, we could not provide additional user control options other than underlying algorithms for the study. For future work, we would like to add other options, such as different rating predictions (e.g., SVD, SVD++, ItemKNN, UserKNN), different hyperparameters, and a different number of recommending items. By providing more user control options, we can gain more insights into the user perspective on our system.

VII. Conclusion

RS plays a vital role across different domains of online services. Despite the fast accuracy improvement over the years, modern RS for e-commerce still fails to address issues, such as lack of transparency and user control. In this paper, we implement an e-commerce RS using real-world product data and integrate a conversational system to enable user control over the recommendation process. We also conduct a user study and questionnaire to gain more insights into the question: how do people view the conversational system as the control mechanism for e-commerce RS. The results show that a majority of the user consider the conversational system an excellent interface to achieve user control and transparency for e-commerce RS. We also find that the collaborative filtering-based algorithm is the most preferred algorithm, while many users agree that our system can improve the diversity and transparency of the RS.

References

[1] R. Burke, A. Felfernig, and M. H. Göker, "Recommender systems: An overview," *Ai Magazine*, vol. 32, no. 3, pp. 13–18, 2011.

[2] J. Bobadilla, F. Ortega, A. Hernando, and A. Gutiérrez, "Recommender systems survey," *Knowledge-based systems*, vol. 46, pp. 109–132, 2013.

[3] J. Davidson *et al.*, "The youtube video recommendation system," in *Proceedings of the fourth ACM conference on Recommender systems*, pp. 293–296, 2010.

[4] I. MacKenzie, C. Meyer, and S. Noble, "How retailers can keep up with consumers," *McKinsey & Company*, vol. 18, no. 1, pp. 1–10, 2013.

[5] D. Jannach and M. Jugovac, "Measuring the business value of recommender systems," *ACM Transactions on Management Information Systems (TMIS)*, vol. 10, no. 4, pp. 1–23, 2019.

[6] U. Chitra and C. Musco, "Analyzing the impact of filter bubbles on social network polarization," in *Proceedings of the 13th International Conference on Web Search and Data Mining*, pp. 115–123, 2020.

[7] S. Garfinkel, J. Matthews, S. S. Shapiro, and J. M. Smith, "Toward algorithmic transparency and accountability," *Communications of the ACM*, vol. 60, no. 9, pp. 5–5, 2017.

[8] J. B. Schafer, "Dynamiclens: A dynamic user-interface for a meta-recommendation system," *Beyond personalization*, pp. 72–76, 2005.

[9] B. P. Knijnenburg, S. Sivakumar, and D. Wilkinson, "Recommender systems for self-actualization," in *Proceedings of the 10th acm conference on recommender systems*, pp. 11–14, 2016.

[10] J. Harambam, D. Bountouridis, M. Makhortykh, and J. Van Hoboken, "Designing for the better by taking users into account: A qualitative evaluation of user control mechanisms in (news) recommender systems," in *Proceedings of the 13th ACM Conference on Recommender Systems*, pp. 69–77, 2019.

[11] N. Helberger, K. Karppinen, and L. D'acunto, "Exposure diversity as a design principle for recommender systems," *Information, Communication & Society*, vol. 21, no. 2, pp. 191–207, 2018.

[12] D. Jannach, S. Naveed, and M. Jugovac, "User control in recommender systems: Overview and interaction challenges," in *International Conference on Electronic Commerce and Web Technologies*, pp. 21–33, Springer, 2016.

[13] J. O'Donovan, B. Smyth, B. Gretarsson, S. Bostandjiev, and T. Höllerer, "Peerchooser: visual interactive recommendation," in *Proceedings of the SIGCHI Conference on Human Factors in Computing Systems*, pp. 1085–1088, 2008.

[14] S. Bostandjiev, J. O'Donovan, and T. Höllerer, "Tasteweights: a visual interactive hybrid recommender system," in *Proceedings of the sixth ACM conference on Recommender systems*, pp. 35–42, 2012.

[15] Y. Jin, K. Seipp, E. Duval, and K. Verbert, "Go with the flow: effects of transparency and user control on targeted advertising using flow charts," in *Proceedings of the international working conference on advanced visual interfaces*, pp. 68–75, 2016.

[16] D. Jannach, A. Manzoor, W. Cai, and L. Chen, "A survey on conversational recommender systems," *ACM Computing Surveys (CSUR)*, vol. 54, no. 5, pp. 1–36, 2021.

[17] Y. Sun and Y. Zhang, "Conversational recommender system," in *The 41st international acm sigir conference on research & development in information retrieval*, pp. 235–244, 2018.
[18] E. Adamopoulou and L. Moussiades, "An overview of chatbot technology," in *IFIP International Conference on Artificial Intelligence Applications and Innovations*, pp. 373–383, Springer, 2020.
[19] B. Luo, R. Y. Lau, C. Li, and Y.-W. Si, "A critical review of state-of-the-art chatbot designs and applications," *Wiley Interdisciplinary Reviews: Data Mining and Knowledge Discovery*, vol. 12, no. 1, p. e1434, 2022.
[20] S. A. Abdul-Kader and J. C. Woods, "Survey on chatbot design techniques in speech conversation systems," *International Journal of Advanced Computer Science and Applications*, vol. 6, no. 7, pp. 72–80, 2015.
[21] J. B. Schafer, J. Konstan, and J. Riedl, "Recommender systems in e-commerce," in *Proceedings of the 1st ACM conference on Electronic commerce*, pp. 158–166, 1999.
[22] K. Wei, J. Huang, and S. Fu, "A survey of e-commerce recommender systems," in *2007 international conference on service systems and service management*, pp. 1–5, IEEE, 2007.
[23] G. Adomavicius and A. Tuzhilin, "Toward the next generation of recommender systems: A survey of the state-of-the-art and possible extensions," *IEEE transactions on knowledge and data engineering*, vol. 17, no. 6, pp. 734–749, 2005.
[24] B. Xu, M. Zhang, Z. Pan, and H. Yang, "Content-based recommendation in e-commerce," in *International Conference on Computational Science and Its Applications*, pp. 946–955, Springer, 2005.
[25] F. Karimova, "A survey of e-commerce recommender systems," *European Scientific Journal*, vol. 12, no. 34, pp. 75–89, 2016.
[26] J. S. Breese, D. Heckerman, and C. Kadie, "Empirical analysis of predictive algorithms for collaborative filtering," *arXiv preprint arXiv:1301.7363*, 2013.
[27] M. Beladev, L. Rokach, and B. Shapira, "Recommender systems for product bundling," *Knowledge-Based Systems*, vol. 111, pp. 193–206, 2016.
[28] T. C.-K. Huang, Y.-L. Chen, and M.-C. Chen, "A novel recommendation model with google similarity," *Decision Support Systems*, vol. 89, pp. 17–27, 2016.
[29] D. H. Park, H. K. Kim, I. Y. Choi, and J. K. Kim, "A literature review and classification of recommender systems research," *Expert systems with applications*, vol. 39, no. 11, pp. 10059–10072, 2012.
[30] P. Pu, L. Chen, and R. Hu, "A user-centric evaluation framework for recommender systems," in *Proceedings of the fifth ACM conference on Recommender systems*, pp. 157–164, 2011.
[31] K. Verbert, D. Parra, P. Brusilovsky, and E. Duval, "Visualizing recommendations to support exploration, transparency and controllability," in *Proceedings of the 2013 international conference on Intelligent user interfaces*, pp. 351–362, 2013.
[32] N. Tintarev and J. Masthoff, "Explaining recommendations: Design and evaluation," in *Recommender systems handbook*, pp. 353–382, Springer, 2015.
[33] U. Lyngs, R. Binns, M. Van Kleek, and N. Shadbolt, "So, tell me what users want, what they really, really want!," in *Extended Abstracts of the 2018 CHI Conference on Human Factors in Computing Systems*, pp. 1–10, 2018.
[34] J. Schaffer, T. Hollerer, and J. O'Donovan, "Hypothetical recommendation: A study of interactive profile manipulation behavior for recommender systems," in *The Twenty-Eighth International Flairs Conference*, pp. 507–512, 2015.
[35] M. D. Ekstrand, D. Kluver, F. M. Harper, and J. A. Konstan, "Letting users choose recommender algorithms: An experimental study," in *Proceedings of the 9th ACM Conference on Recommender Systems*, pp. 11–18, 2015.
[36] D. Parra, P. Brusilovsky, and C. Trattner, "See what you want to see: visual user-driven approach for hybrid recommendation," in *Proceedings of the 19th international conference on Intelligent User Interfaces*, pp. 235–240, 2014.
[37] Y. Saito and T. Itoh, "Musicube: a visual music recommendation system featuring interactive evolutionary computing," in *Proceedings of the 2011 Visual Information Communication-International Symposium*, pp. 1–6, 2011.
[38] Y. Jin, N. Tintarev, and K. Verbert, "Effects of personal characteristics on music recommender systems with different levels of controllability," in *Proceedings of the 12th ACM Conference on Recommender Systems*, pp. 13–21, 2018.
[39] T. L. Smestad, "Personality matters! improving the user experience of chatbot interfaces-personality provides a stable pattern to guide the design and behaviour of conversational agents," Master's thesis, NTNU, 2018.
[40] D. Altinok, "An ontology-based dialogue management system for banking and finance dialogue systems," *arXiv preprint arXiv:1804.04838*, 2018.
[41] Y. Wu *et al.*, "A sequential matching framework for multi-turn response selection in retrieval-based chatbots," *Computational Linguistics*, vol. 45, no. 1, pp. 163–197, 2019.
[42] C. Gao, W. Lei, X. He, M. de Rijke, and T.-S. Chua, "Advances and challenges in conversational recommender systems: A survey," *AI Open*, vol. 2, pp. 100–126, 2021.
[43] "Amazona ecommerce website framework." https://github.com/basir/amazona. Accessed: 2023-03-21.
[44] J. Ni, J. Li, and J. McAuley, "Justifying recommendations using distantly-labeled reviews and fine-grained aspects," in *Proceedings of the 2019 conference on empirical methods in natural language processing and the 9th international joint conference on natural language processing (EMNLP-IJCNLP)*, pp. 188–197, 2019.
[45] R. He and J. McAuley, "Ups and downs: Modeling the visual evolution of fashion trends with one-class collaborative filtering," in *proceedings of the 25th international conference on world wide web*, pp. 507–517, 2016.
[46] "Case recommender - a python framework for recsys." https://github.com/caserec/CaseRecommender. Accessed: 2023-03-21.
[47] "react-chatbot-kit - a react based chatbot development kit." https://github.com/FredrikOseberg/react-chatbot-kit. Accessed: 2023-03-21.
[48] L. H. Son, "Dealing with the new user cold-start problem in recommender systems: A comparative review," *Information Systems*, vol. 58, pp. 87–104, 2016.

A Trial of Prevention of Physical and Social Frailty for Older People via Chatting Bot Installation on Moving Stall

Yoko Nishihara
Col. of Inf. Sci. and Eng.
Ritsumeikan University
Shiga, Japan
email: nisihara@fc.ritsumei.ac.jp

Junjie Shan
Ritsumeikan Global Innovation Research Org.
Ritsumeikan University
Shiga, Japan
email: shan@fc.ritsumei.ac.jp

Yihong Han
Dept. of Inf. Sci. and Eng.
Ritsumeikan University
Shiga, Japan
email: is0387ps@ed.ritsumei.ac.jp

***Abstract*—This research uses information science approach for preventing the physical and social frailty of older people living in an aging community with a low birthrate. In this study, we hypothesize that older peoples' physical activity and sociable communication will increase if they have more interactions with others and the outside environment. We believe that by raising their interest in the surrounding daily activities could help improve their interaction with the outside society. This study is conducted in Yogo Town in Shiga Prefecture, Japan as an area of an aging community with a low birthrate. Yogo Town provides a moving stall for older people to assist them in purchasing daily necessities. We install a chatting bot in the moving stall to attract older people to visit it. If older people visit the moving stall more, their physical frailty could be prevented through these increased physical activities. If older people could interact and communicate more with others through the enjoyment of conversations and games with the chatting bot, their social frailty also has the chance to improve. This paper describes the issues discussed in this study, introduces a developed chatting bot, and reports on plans for future experiments.**

Keywords-frailty prevention; physical and social frailty; chatting-bot; elderly care

I. Introduction

Japan is facing an aging society with a low birthrate. People request to prevent older people's frailty [1]. Frailty is a condition in which the mind and body weaken due to aging. There are three types of frailty; (1) physical frailty, (2) social frailty, and (3) cognitive frailty. To reduce the progression of frailty, older people need to raise motivation of frailty prevention through exercises [2]. However, it is difficult for them to maintain awareness continuously because they have physical constraints and low communication with their neighbor, especially for those older people who live away from urban areas. It is desirable to increase the amount of physical activity and sociable communication. In this paper, we use an approach of information science to try to increase the intention of older people's physical activity and sociable communication to help them prevent frailty indirectly.

A. Targeted Field

This study is conducted in Yogo Town in Shiga Prefecture in Japan as an area of an aging community with a low birthrate. The percentage of residents aged 65 years and older is 43.1%, and the rate of them aged 80 years and more senior is 18.5% (as of December 1st, 2021). In the last few years, the problem of frailty has become more severe due to Covid-19 infection control. The area is facing an urgent need to understand the current situation regarding the physical and mental health of older people and to take measures to address this issue.

Yogo Town provides a moving stall for older people to assist them in purchasing daily necessities. Though the residents in the town use automobiles every day, the older people have returned their driving licenses due to their low physical and cognitive ability. Therefore, the moving stall is indispensable for their lives. The moving stall carries foods and daily necessities in the back and goes to community meeting spaces and doorsteps of individuals. The older people can conduct a walking exercise on their way to the moving stall and back. They can also conduct conversations with others around the moving stall. A saleslady actively talks to the older people coming to the moving stall. She also takes a role in providing daily attention and care for the community.

B. Our Approach for Frailty Prevention

We hypothesize that physical activity and sociable communication will increase if older people have more interactions with others and the outside environment. We believe that by raising their interest in the surrounding daily activities could help improve their interaction with the outside society. To achieve the above, we install a chatting bot in the moving stall. Chatting bots have been used in counseling [3], coaching [4], and conversations with people [5]. However, there is few case of chatting bot used for prevention the physical and social frailty. The chatting bot has functions of conversation and playing a game. We hope that older people could be interested in the chatting bot. If they visit the chatting bot, their physical activity will increase, which prevents their physical frailty. If they enjoy conversations with a chatting bot, their sociable communication will also increase, which prevents their social frailty. This study is approved by The Ritsumeikan University Ethics Review Committee for Medical and Health Research Involving Human Subjects.

II. Proposed Method

This section describes an interaction pattern and a developed chatting bot.

A. Interaction Pattern between Chatting-bot and Older People

Figure 1 illustrates the interaction pattern between our chatting bot and older people. The chatting bot changes its

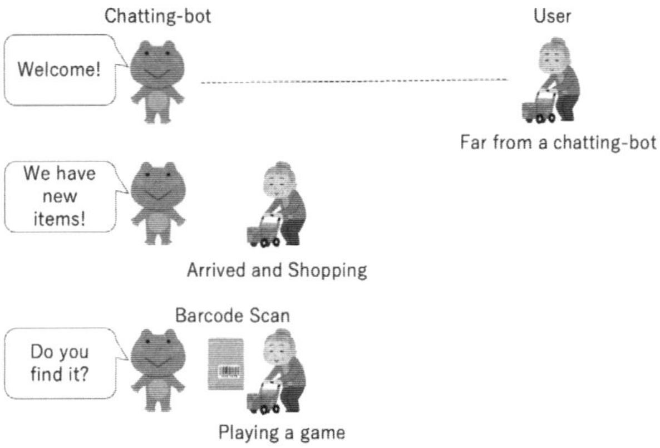

Figure 1. Interaction pattern between our chatting bot and older people.

behavior according to the distance from older people to attract them closer to the chatting bot. If the older person is far from the chatting bot, he says a greeting to draw their attention. If they approach the chatting bot, he will announce new items and invites them to play a game with him. If the person is close to the chatting bot, he welcomes to enjoy the game.

B. Developed Chatting-bot

Figure 2 shows the appearance and construction of the chatting bot. The chatting bot mainly has two functional components: (a) human and object detection by a camera and (b) a speech function using a pair of speakers.

C. Human and Object Detection

For human and object detection, the chatting bot uses a camera to capture real-time frames. YOLO is used for human and object detection. For human detection, the chatting bot will first detect whether a person is in the frame. If a human is found, the chatting bot will estimate the distance from the human to determine whether the older person is far from or close to him. The estimation result is used for the interaction pattern's selection.

In object detection, the chatting bot recognizes the barcode of items to judge whether they are newly listed. A list file is prepared to store the information of the barcode and a the item's name. If a recognized barcode is included in the list, the item is judged as a listed new good. If not, the item will be judged as a former product. The judgment result will be used for speech response selection.

D. Speech according to Detection Result

The chatting bot gives speech responsens depending on the human and object detection result. There are two situations of human detection results; older people are far from the chatting bot or close to it. If the older people are far from the chatting bot, the chatting bot gives speeches designed to attract their attention. For example, "Hello, please come here," and "Welcome to our shop" are given with a synthesized voice. In contrast, if they are close to the chatting bot, the chatting

Figure 2. Inside of a moving stall (left). Foods and daily necessities are sold. Developed chatting bot as a stuffed frog (right).

bot gives speeches to prompt new items and invites playing a game. For example, "New goods are coming" and "Please find it" would be given with a synthesized voice.

There are two results of the selected items' detection: a newly listed product or a former product. If the selected good is a new one, the chatting bot gives a speech "That is correct. The good is a new one called (good's name)." Conversely, if the selected good is not a new one, the chatting bot gives a speech "That is not correct. Please find it again."

III. Conclusion and Future Work

This paper proposes an installation of a chatting bot on a moving stall to prevent the physical and social frailty of older people living in an aging community with a low birthrate. The chatting bot attempts to interact and make conversations with older people. If older people are interested in the chatting bot, the chance of physical exercises and sociable communication will increase, which prevents physical and social frailty.

We ask the residents in Yogo Town (Shiga, Japan) to join the experiments with the chatting bot. We will survey the effect of the installation of the chatting bot for the prevention of frailty.

Acknowledgment

This research is supported by staffs of Yogo area in Japan. We show our best appreciate. This research is partly supported by Ritsumeikan Global Innovation Research Organization and JSPS KAKENHI (22K03041).

References

[1] X. Li, Y. Zhang, Y. Tian, Q.Cheng, Y. Gao, and M. Gao, Research Progress on the Intelligent Health Management of the Cognitive Frailty of the Elderly. In Proceedings of the 2nd International Symposium on Artificial Intelligence for Medicine Sciences, pp.53-57, 2021.

[2] Z. Sáenz-de-Urturi and O. C. Santos, User Modelling in Exergames for Frail Older Adults. In Adjunct Publication of the 26th Conference on User Modeling, Adaptation and Personalization, pp.83-86, 2018.

[3] N. Suresh, N. Mukabe, V. Hashiyana, A. Limbo, and A. Hauwanga, Career Counseling Chatbot on Facebook Messenger using AI. In Proceedings of the International Conference on Data Science, Machine Learning and Artificial Intelligence, pp.65-73, 2022.

[4] J. Casas, E. Mugellini, and O. A. Khaled, Food Diary Coaching Chatbot. In Proceedings of the 2018 ACM International Joint Conference and 2018 International Symposium on Pervasive and Ubiquitous Computing and Wearable Computers, pp.1676-1680, 2018.

[5] M. E. Kamali, L. Angelini, D. Lalanne, O. A. Khaled, and E. Mugellini, Multimodal Conversational Agent for Older Adults' Behavioral Change. In Companion Publication of the 2020 International Conference on Multimodal Interaction, pp.270-274, 2021.

A Study on Circular-coil Characteristics for Displaying Non-contact Tactile Sensation based on Magnetic Field.

Hyung-Sik Kim
Department of Mechatronics Engineering
School of ICT Convergence Engineering, College of Science & Technology, Konkuk University
Chungju, Republic of Korea
email: hskim98@kku.ac.kr

Kyu-Beom Kim, Ji-Su Kim, Soon-Cheol Chung*
Department of Biomedical Engineering
School of ICT Convergence Engineering, College of Science & Technology, Konkuk University
Chungju, Republic of Korea
email: rlarbqja0507@kku.ac.kr; roseee517@kku.ac.kr; scchung@kku.ac.kr*

Abstract—**In this study, characteristics of coil, which is an actuator of magnetic field-based non-contact tactile presentation technology, were simulated. To induce a sense of touch using a magnetic field without wearing any devices on hand, a high-power power supply device, a power semiconductor switch, and a coil for generating a magnetic field are required. Because of the high power used, the power supply and coil require a separate heat sink device. Therefore, a simulation study was conducted on the characteristics of coils in order not to use a heat dissipation device. Simulations were conducted for the strength and field pattern of the magnetic field for each experimental frequency, the density of the magnetic field, and the generated heat for the circular coil. From the results, the magnetic field density and distribution were the same at all frequencies. In the analysis of the change in magnetic field density according to the frequency, the difference in the density of the magnetic field calculated at 5 Hz and 250 Hz was only about 2.03%. In the case of heat analysis, the time required to recover to the ambient temperature of 25 °C is less than 10 seconds in the case of 5 Hz condition, but the time required to return to the ambient temperature is more than 3.6 minutes at 250 Hz. Through this study, it was confirmed that a circular coil with a diameter of about 28 cm made of copper can operate for a long time without a cooling system under natural convection conditions.**

Keywords-Non-conctact tactile stimulator; Circular-coil; Magnetic field strength; Density; Heat, Heat-sink.

I. Introduction

As IT technology develops, research for interaction between devices and humans is also being actively conducted [1]. These studies stimulate sight and hearing among the human senses and exchange information through the process of perception and cognition. Recently, studies to present tactile sensation for more realistic interaction are also being conducted. Until now, most of the devices for presenting the tactile sensation are of a contact type and mainly induce a sense of vibration [2]. An actuator to generate a sense of vibration mainly uses a motor. This is because it is easy to control the magnitude of vibration and the frequency of vibration using electric signals, and it is possible to manufacture in a small size and is inexpensive. However, in the tactile presentation method, the tactile sensation can be evoked only when the person and the device must maintain a contact state. In addition, even if the contact state is maintained, the shape of the tactile sensation caused by changing the area, size, and time of contact is not consistent. Therefore, a technique for presenting a sense of touch in a non-contact method is also being studied. Representatively, a method using focused-ultrasound and a method using compressed-air are being tried [3]. However, these methods always have additional noise, have a short stimulus presentation distance, and complicate the configuration of the control system.

Recently, a method using a pulsed laser has also been introduced. This method has the advantage of a very long stimulus presentation distance, but the price of the laser system for tactile presentation is very expensive and requires a delicate setup using optics. Since the above three methods transmit energy for inducing a tactile sensation to the skin through space, it is impossible to transmit the tactile sensation when there is an object between the actuation source and the skin. Recently, a method using magnetic field induction has been developed [4]. Since this method uses an electromagnetic field, it has the advantage of presenting a sense of touch even when an arbitrary object exists.

However, high power is required to generate a magnetic field. In addition, since high heat is generated in a coil that generates a magnetic field, an additional device for heat dissipation is required when a continuous tactile sensation is generated. The cooling system also has the disadvantage that it is generally large and requires separate operating power. Therefore, in this study, a study on the characteristics to minimize heat generation of the coil, which is an actuator for presenting a magnetic field-based tactile sensation, was conducted through simulation analysis.

II. Materials and Methods

A. Setting up the Simulation Environment for the Stimulation Coil

The analysis of the coil was performed through theoretical analysis and simulation of the magnetic field distribution. ANSYS (ANSYS Inc., USA) was used for computer simulation. Analysis of magnetic field strength, pattern, and thermal analysis according to the amplitude and frequency of voltage input to the coil, and magnetic field and thermal analysis were performed under the pulse voltage input condition of 950 Volts. A coil is a wire wound in a circular shape. Since the strength H of the magnetic field by the entire electric wire is the sum of the length of the minute current and the minute magnetic field, it can be expressed as a line integral as shown in Equation (1) below.

$$H = \int dH = \frac{I}{4\pi}\int \frac{dl\sin\theta}{r^2} \quad [\frac{AT}{m}] \tag{1}$$

The voltage applied to the coil analysis was 950 Volts, the time was 130 μs, and the frequencies were 5, 10, 50, 100, 200, and 250 Hz. The voltage used is converted into current (I) by the specific resistance of copper. The intensity of the magnetic field is adjusted by the magnitude of the current, and through this, the intensity of the tactile sensation can be controlled. Also, the number of turns of the coil is proportional to the intensity of the tactile sensation, but because the size increases, voltage, which is electrically easy to control, was used. The flow of simulation using ANSYS is shown in Figure 1.

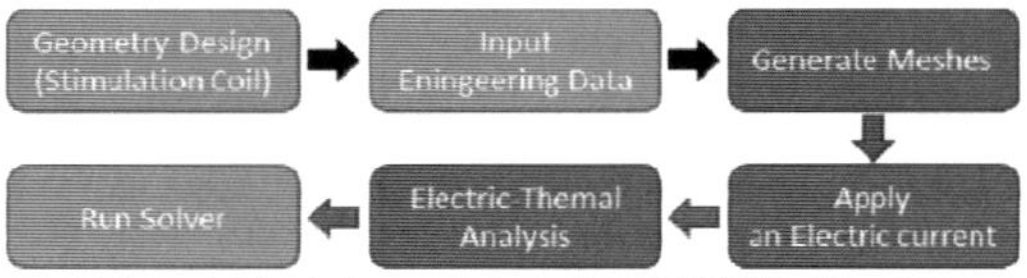

Figure 1. Simulation procedure using ANSYS Workbench.

B. *Coil geometry*

The geometric shape of the coil was modeled as shown in Figure 2, the material was copper, and the number of turns was set to 28 according to the environment in which the coil would be applied. The physical properties of the copper were specific resistance 1.69×10^{-2} [Ω/m], wire length 3.8 [m], specific heat 0.0924 [Cal/g × °C], and weight 800 [gram].

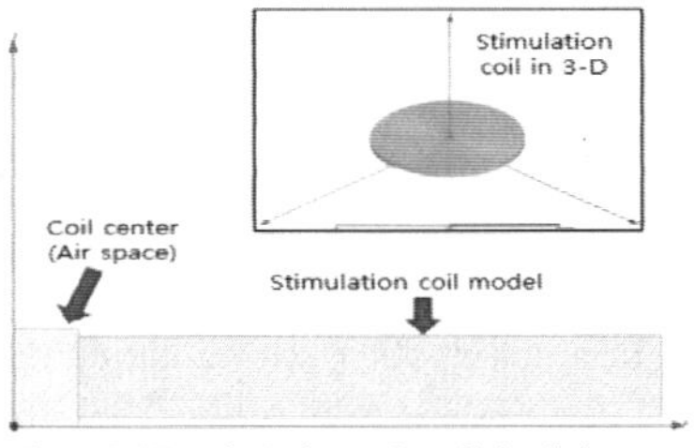

Figure 2. 2D and 3D shapes for coil simulation.

III. RESULTS

In the analysis of the change in magnetic field density according to the frequency, the difference in the density of the magnetic field calculated at a point 5 cm perpendicular to the plane of the coil was approximately 2.03 % at 5 Hz and 250 Hz, and the change was small (Figure 3(a)). When power is applied to the wire, heat is generated by the resistance component of the wire. The maximum temperature varied with frequency in the coil used. In the case of 250 Hz, the maximum temperature was 57.2 °C, and in the case of 5 Hz, the temperature rise was small at 24.2 °C. As heat generation increases, the size of resistance decreases, so more energy must be discharged to generate a magnetic field of the same size. Therefore, since the efficiency is reduced, this must be considered when manufacturing the coil. In addition, at each maximum temperature, heatsink by natural convection fell to the initial temperature within 3.6 minutes (Figure 3(b)). Since the pattern of the magnetic field according to the frequency is constant and the heat rise is not large, it means that the formation of the magnetic field for magnetic stimulation is constant even if the coil used is changed in the set frequency range (Figure 3(c) and (d).

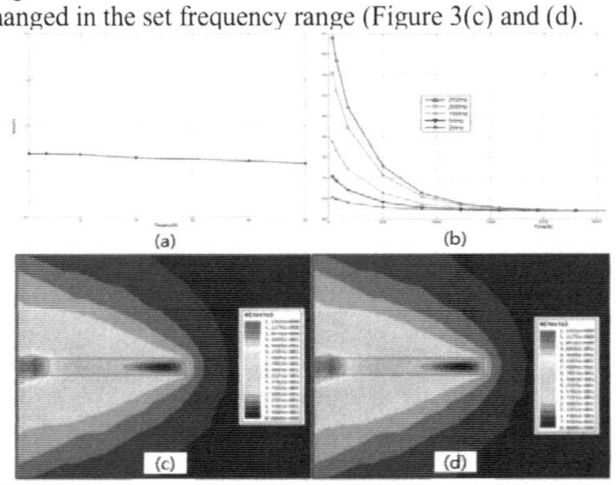

Figure 3. Simulation results for circular-coil. (a) Magnetic field density, (b) Heat dissipation profile, (c) Magnetic field map for 5 Hz and (d) 250 Hz.

IV. CONCLUSION

In this paper, the change in magnetic field pattern and temperature according to the application of pulsed power to the magnetic field generating coil was confirmed. The change in the density and field pattern of the magnetic field was small according to the frequency in the range of 5 to 250 Hz. In the case of temperature, the maximum rose about 33.1°C. It was confirmed that the coil of the proposed shape had a small difference between low frequency and high frequency, so that it was possible to induce a tactile sensation with constant strength and strength even when used for a long time. A large coil is used to induce a tactile sensation in the bare hand, but it is composed with an encloser made of wood or plastic, so it can be used for the purpose of inducing a tactile sensation with an invisible actuator.

ACKNOWLEDGMENT

This work was supported by a Mid-career Researcher Program Grant through the National Research Foundation of Korea (NRF), funded by the Ministry of Education (MOE) (No. NRF-2021R1A2C2009136).

REFERENCES

[1] A. Iftene and D. Trandabăț, "Enhancing the Attractiveness of Learning through Augmented Reality," Procedia. Comput. Sci. vol. 126, pp. 166-175, 2018, https://doi.org/10.1016/j.procs.2018.07.220.

[2] T. Rose, C. S. Nam, and K. B. Chen, "Immersion of virtual reality for rehabilitation – Review," Appl. Ergon. vol. 69, pp. 153-161, 2018, https://doi.org/10.1016/j.apergo.2018.01.009.

[3] T. Hoshi, M. Takahashi, T. Iwamoto, and H. Shinoda, "Noncontact Tactile Display Based on Radiation Pressure of Airborne Ultrasound," IEEE Trans. Haptics. vol. 3, pp. 155-165, 2010, https://doi.org/10.1109/TOH.2010.4.

[4] H. S. Kim, et al., "Development of tactile actuator with non-contact and trans-object characteristics using time-varying magnetic field," Actuators, vol. 10, pp. 1-11, 2021, https://doi.org/10.3390/act10060106.

Marcus: A Chatbot for Depression Screening Based on the PHQ-9 Assessment

Evaluating accuracy and effectivess in college students based on gender and age during the pandemic

Patrick Toulme
AWS Artificial Intelligence
Amazon
Arlington, Virginia, USA
ptoulme@amazon.com

Jude Nanaw
Department of Computer Science
University of Virginia
Charlottesville VA, USA
jn7tez@virginia.edu

Panagiotis Apostolellis
Department of Computer Science
University of Virginia
Charlottesville VA, USA
panaga@virginia.edu

Abstract—**College students are a population particularly susceptible to anxiety and depression, with financial struggles and social stigmatization creating a barrier to seeking psychological support. The recent pandemic has exacerbated these issues, with lockdowns and remote instruction creating extra stress factors and making access to consultation services even harder. Online depression screening tools have tried to address such problems and the development of chatbots for the detection and even therapeutic use of anxiety symptoms has been on the rise. This work reports findings from testing Marcus, a depression screening chatbot based on a popular depression assessment tool, the Patient Health Questionnaire (PHQ-9). Our results indicate that Marcus was comparable to the online version of PHQ-9 in detecting depression based on produced scores, using a within-subjects experimental design with predominantly college students in the USA. Nonetheless, the chatbot was not found to be the most effective method based on comparing participant preferences and initiation rates. Implications of our findings for the development of similar computer-based screening tools are discussed, as well as recommendations for future work in this area.**

Keywords-chatbot design; medical application; computer-based depression screening; user study.

I. INTRODUCTION

Among the various mental health issues faced by millions of individuals worldwide, depression is considered one of the most prevalent with over 280 million people of all ages globally affected by the disorder, being especially prevalent among 15-29-year-olds [1]. Continuous struggle with depression has proven to have personal adverse effects on individuals and has been linked to issues such as low socioeconomic status [2] , family functioning [3], and diminished social support [3]. Among the population age composition, university students are a particular group with exceptionally high depression rates [4]. Despite the detrimental impact of incessant depression including an increased risk of suicide by a factor of 20 among depressed populations compared to non-depressed populations, [5], a significant portion of these individuals do not seek treatment. Studies have found that the most common reasons for not seeking treatment among university students include the stigma associated with mental health issues [6], as well as feeling a lack of perceived need [7] and insufficient mental health education [8]. Moreover, the lack of easy access to depression treatment poses another barrier for university students. Economic barriers are a major cause for not seeking screening or treatment, as associations exist between low socioeconomic status and depression rates [9]. With depression being incredibly widespread, all aspects of treatment are in high demand and a public need, including both therapeutic interventions as well as screening and assessment needs.

To counteract the significant barrier of stigmatization and financial ability, which is especially prominent for university students, online depression screening tools and chatbots have been suggested as a viable solution [10]. The development of such chatbots removes the need for interpersonal communication in this preliminary step of the treatment process, making screening more accessible. The PHQ-9 is the most viable depression screening tool in the industry of primary care and uses a four-point scale to reveal the tendency to depression ranging from minimal to severe depression [11]. With the advancement of artificial intelligence and Natural Language Processing (NLP), there have been various developments of mental health chatbots that focus on anxiety screening using the PHQ-9 [12]–[14], as well as the therapeutic treatment and reduction of depression-like symptoms [15][16].

Additionally, the COVID-19 pandemic drove a fundamental change within the healthcare delivery system due to unprecedented challenges such as social distancing guidelines and stay-at-home orders [17]. In large part, the pandemic accelerated the rise of telehealth, where all healthcare services, including screening, were provided remotely–and oftentimes via virtual agents. Moreover, the pandemic saw the increased development of chatbots that screened for COVID-19, which delivered consistent and accurate results while also providing sustained service at a low operating cost [18]. These systems exemplified the potential of telehealth and chatbots in terms of overcoming obstacles, such as costs and physical barriers that prevent individuals from receiving care.

Inspired by the increased demands caused by the pandemic for easy access to anxiety screening explicitly for college students, we developed Marcus, a chatbot for depression screening, In the current study, we briefly describe our mobile-based chatbot and report results from a study with university students in the United States. We hypothesized that our virtual screening tool will be equally effective in detecting depression as the traditional online PHQ-9. Findings and design implications for similar computer-based screening tools are discussed in light of prior research.

Section II presents a review of related work including background on the PHQ-9, as well as existing virtual agents utilized for depression screening and therapeutic methods.

Section III includes the driving research questions and details regarding the design of the chatbot. Section IV presents the research methods in regards to participants and the data collection process. Section V describes our results including the various statistical analysis used and graphical representations of major findings. Section VI discusses our main findings in light of prior research and acknowledges study limitations. Section V summarizes our research work and presents directions for future research based on our findings.

II. Background

This research builds on past work related to chatbots and virtual agents designed to screen for depression or act as a therapeutic agent to reduce depression-like symptoms.

A. Diagnostic Evaluations: Framework and Administration

The original PHQ-9 is viewed as a dual-purpose instrument, which provides not only provisional depression diagnoses, but also grade depressive symptom severity [19]. Over the years, the nine-item scale has been validated as a depression screening tool in the primary care industry and remains widely utilized [20]. The assessment itself features a straightforward scoring methodology, where each question is rated by the patient with a frequency from 0 to 3 – with 0 indicating "not at all" and 3 indicating "nearly every day". A summation of the scores is performed to provide a final score from 0 to 27, with a higher score representing a greater level of severity.

A study conducted with university students in Iran examined the validity and reliability of the PHQ-9 alongside other assessments [20]. Students completed the self-administered version of the PHQ-9, as well as psychiatrist interviews to determine depression level – with the tool ultimately demonstrating a satisfactory internal consistency. Another study conducted in Kosovo measured depression during the COVID-19 outbreak with an online version of the PHQ-9 administered through Google Forms [21]. Results exhibited a higher-than-average percentage of participants with moderate to severe symptoms. Additionally, a pilot evaluation investigated links between depression references on social media (Facebook) by undergraduate students and depression on a clinical scale using an online version of the PHQ-9 [22]. Over 70% of eligible profile owners participated in the online PHQ-9 survey, indicating a successful administration. Results of the study demonstrated a positive association between the two, with participants who scored higher into a depression category on the PHQ-9, being more likely to display depression symptom references on Facebook.

Prior work has also investigated the effect of gender on depression diagnosis, both in the general population and specifically college students [23]. Research has indicated that when compared to males, females account for a larger proportion of patients with depression [24]. Moreover, studies have shown that the gender differences regarding depression rates are more significant at younger ages than when at an adult age [25]. In addition to the gender depression variance being linked by hormonal differences, studies on the respective clinical aspects have pointed to socialization differences also being a factor in depression rates [26].

B. Computer-Based Methods for Depression Screening

The PHQ-9 has seen adaptations into chatbot versions of the assessment in recent years. The virtual agent implementation aims to bring various benefits to the forefront, including the ability to screen for depressive symptoms remotely on a large scale and at a low cost [13]. The study utilized a chatbot named "Tess", which inquired about the nine PHQ-9 criteria posed on the questionnaire, seeking to discover relationships between demographic variables and PHQ-9 scores by administering the assessment to adults and older adults. The chatbot demonstrated strong reliability in both results and completion rate. While results indicated a correlation between demographic characteristics and PHQ-9 score, the associated effect of this was deemed as weak. As the study primarily recruited adults and older adults (above the age of 65), this posed the limitation of a lack of focus on a population that is more susceptible to depression or depression-like symptoms, such as university students. Moreover, the study only administers the PHQ-9 through the Tess chatbot and not through another means (i.e., online survey or paper format) for validation purposes, thus posing another limitation.

Another study conducted in Spain delivered the development of "Perla," a conversational agent that performed a depression screening interview based on the PHQ-9 [12]. The review found that the chatbot was preferred by internet users more than the form-based questionnaire, and the results were consistent enough to deem the chatbot as a valid alternative to traditional self-report methods. Opportunities for expanding on the study include further research into user preferences, such as having a conversational agent with human face and name characteristics to provide further appeal. Moreover, another work identified employees and those in the workplace as a group with specifically high potential for exposure to mental health problems [14]. The study featured the development of a fully automated chatbot "Viki," which evaluated workers for risks of suffering from depression, anxiety, stress, and burnout. Results found that the conversation and gamification style of the chatbot delivered potential for greater engagement and effectiveness.

Additional studies considered groups with higher possible exposure to depression by screening via a chatbot. During the COVID-19 pandemic, frontline workers were especially impacted, and new tools were necessary to identify individuals that were in need of treatment, especially among those who feared stigma around mental health [27]. The study considered a text interface as well as a conversational speech chatbot based on the PHQ-9 for evaluation, with feasibility based on the Technology Acceptance Model [28]. Results of the study demonstrated that most participants found the chatbot to be acceptable, with perceived usefulness and prior depression-like symptoms being the two most significant factors in predicting the inclination of participants to use the chatbot [27].

C. Therapeutic Chatbots to Reduce Depression-Like Symptoms

In addition to screening chatbots based on the adaptation of the PHQ-9 assessment, strides have also been made into the development of chatbots that act as therapeutic agents. With the purpose of improving mental health via the reduction of depression-like symptoms, therapeutic virtual agents utilize the PHQ-9 as a measurement tool both at baseline and post-treatment stages [29]. A study conducted with university students administered the PHQ-9 – in addition to other questionnaires as measures of separate clinical variables – at baseline and every 4 weeks throughout the 16-week period [29]. During the period, students were randomly assigned to receive either therapy from the chatbot or minimal level bibliotherapy. Results demonstrated that the chatbot-delivered intervention was significantly more efficacious than bibliotherapy, with PHQ-9 scores being reduced further with the virtual agent. In another study, various precursors to depression and other mental health disorders were identified [30]. Through the development of a virtual agent named "Elomia," the study delivered therapy to university students who indicated some level or susceptibility to depression. Results revealed that users of Elomia described a reduction in anxiety and depression symptoms – in addition to 70% of users who noted returning to the chatbot in moments of stress or other related symptoms.

Moreover, additional works have placed an emphasis on groups who have the potential to be more susceptible to mental health issues. In one study, chatbot-based treatment was provided to a post-partum population [16]. Participants either received treatment via chatbot or through traditional means with the PHQ-9 and General Anxiety Disorder (GAD-7) among other assessments, were administered to establish a baseline. While scores did not differ significantly between the varying treatment groups, a large proportion of women (74%) indicated use of the chatbot – demonstrating a greater willingness to interact with the virtual agent. Research conducted in India identified the student population of ages 15-25 as sufferers of mental health issues for a variety of reasons including method of education and the high expectations from family and friends [10]. The study additionally noted the lack of willingness of those affected by depression or precursors of depression (e.g., other emotional issues, social anxiety) to voice their circumstances. Therefore, the development of "Care-Bot"—a therapeutic virtual agent—aimed at providing similar support as that of a counselor or therapist. While the chatbot was not deemed a viable solution as a substitute for a psychologist, the tool did serve as a provider of conversation allowing users to speak out their problems.

Technologies such as DialogFlow and backend applications like NodeJS and Firebase are prevalent in the development of PHQ-9 based screening and therapeutic chatbots [31]. However, we identified a gap in how such technologies can be harnessed to fulfill their significant potential for an explicitly sensitive group to depression, college students, especially during the high-stress environment of the recent pandemic.

III. MARCUS: CHATBOT FOR DEPRESSION SCREENING

This section presents our research questions and the design of Marcus, the chatbot, for testing those questions.

A. Research Questions

Considering there is no published research on the use of chatbots, including their accuracy and effectiveness, explicitly for college students in the U.S., we decided to develop a mobile-based chatbot as a testbed for responding to the following two research questions:

1) Is Marcus an accurate depression screening method as compared to a more conventional online tool, especially for college students? What is the effect of gender, if any?

2) Is Marcus perceived as an effective tool for depression screening by U.S. university students, taking into account interactions with the chabot and selft-reported measures?

Our hypothesis for the first question is based on prior research, especially since we followed the work by [12], and is that the chatbot will be as accurate in detecting depression as the online PHQ-9. We had no specific direction for our hypothesis regarding the effect of gender because no prior work investigated an effect of gender on chatbot vs traditional screening accuracy. As for the second question, we assumed Marcus would be perceived positively by most participants as reported by prior work using screening [12] and therapeutic chatbots [10] [30].

B. Marcus Chatbot Design

When designing Marcus, we faced two important design decisions: the visual representation of the chatbot and the format of user input. Considering we were addressing a younger audience of college students we opted for simulating a more realistic representation of the chatbot, using a young male image that aligns with the name Marcus, to trigger a higher affinity with the chatbot [32]. As for user input, we started with pre-defined multiple-choice options resembling the four levels of the original PHQ-9 about the frequency of experienced depression symptoms. However, this type of input was not deemed natural enough, as we wanted to simulate the chatting that our young population is used to in their everyday digitally enabled interactions. A brief and informal pilot study with undergraduate students at the university using an earlier implementation of Marcus confirmed this assumption. Therefore, we chose to use free-text input and employ NLP to categorize the text input into one of the PHQ-9 levels, despite understanding the challenges involved in this approach in terms of classification accuracy [33].

Based on the decision above, Marcus was developed using a BERT machine learning model and a variety of APIs and platforms. BERT stands for Bidirectional Encoder Representations from Transformers and was developed in 2018 by researchers at Google Artificial Intelligence as a large service-based model for NLP [34]. BERT models are trained for a variety of language tasks, such as sentiment analysis, which Marcus uses to analyze the user's response for positive or negative sentiment. The backend of Marcus is using Google DialogFlow [35], which handles the NLP through a system of intents, entities, and phrase training. A BERT machine learning model is then generated based on the developer-provided training data to handle all inference requests by the user. Intents are the question-response pairs that are expected in the conversation flow, and entities are groups of words detected within the conversation with an integer value assigned. These entities are what the BERT model uses when scoring the users' responses after an inference call is made.

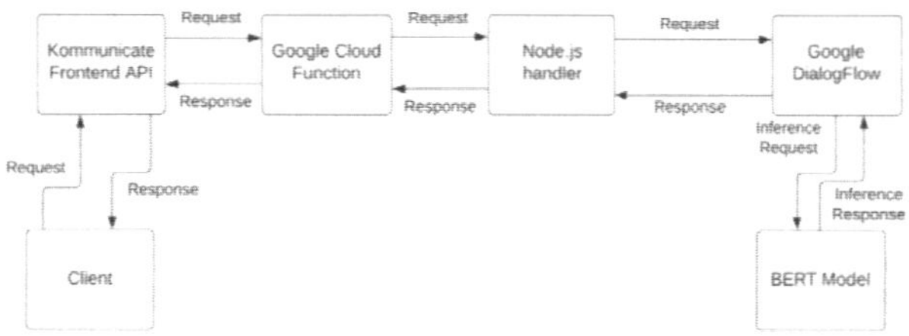

Figure 1. Schematic representation of technologies used for Marcus.

The BERT model performs sentiment analysis on the user's input and assigns a numeric score (i.e., 0-3 from the original PHQ-9 four-item scale) to the user's phrase based on the entities matched in the training data provided.

The technical workflow of Marcus (Figure 1) involves routing the user's natural language through Google DialogFlow fulfillment with each intent linked to a different scripted method in the fulfillment code base. This workflow was written in Node.js and is hosted on a serverless cloud function on Google Cloud Platform. An inference call to DialogFlow is then made from each of these workflows to score the user's response. The numeric score output by the BERT model is then routed to the Node.js handler, which outputs a success code 200 response to the Google Cloud Function, which in turn triggers the next question to be displayed to the user via the frontend API and finally back to the client. Kommunicate, a tool for automating conversations with a chatbot [36], was used for the frontend implementation of Marcus, as it allowed interfacing with all the technologies used and enabled deployment on multiple platforms. The original dataset of phrases with corresponding PHQ-9 scores comes from Perla (translated from Spanish), which is also a BERT-modeled chatbot version of PHQ-9 [12]. Additional phrases were scored and added to the dataset through multiple iterations of piloting the chatbot with undergraduate university students, including the researchers.

Marcus was developed for iOS and as a web application. iOS was chosen due to the ease of development, large support system, large number of APIs available, and the large prevalence of iOS devices amongst college students [37]. iOS was also chosen as the primary user platform for its consistent user interface across devices and overall ease of use for the user. The web application serves as an alternative for participants who do not have access to an iOS device. Marcus is embedded in the iOS application through the Kommunicate API using native Swift coding and providing the chatbot's visual interface (Figure 2). We slightly revised the wording of subsequent questions after the first one to make the conversation appear more natural, since the questionnaire reads differently in a multiple-choice format (e.g., all questions were preceded with a phrase like "How often over the past two weeks…"). We also considered inserting extra prompts and phrases between questions to increase the naturalness of the conversation, but after consulting with a psychometrician from the university's counselling and psychological services, we were advised against this practice, as it would potentially compromise the validity of the instrument.

Figure 2. Screenshot of typical Marcus conversation on an iPhone.

IV. Methods

The research study was approved by the Institutional Review Board of the University of Virginia with protocol IRB-SBS#4005/2022-01-20. The period of data collection was between March and June of 2022, during a semester when the university was transitioning to removing protections and the use of masks in classrooms.

A. Participants

Participants were recruited mainly through email listservs at the University of Virginia and consisted of mostly Engineering and Psychology undergraduate students. LinkedIn and additional social media were also used but college students were prioritized to address the research questions regarding depression screening in college aged populations. A total of 187 people started the survey, but 57 participants did not consent or dropped before being shown either the PHQ-9 or Marcus and are excluded from analysis. Out of the remaining 130 people, 72 participants reported demographic information, including age, gender, and education level. The majority of participants identified as female (N = 46, 63.89%) and male (N = 23, 31.94%), but there were also three participants who identified as neither (N = 3, 4.17%). The largest age group was participants who reported being 18-24 years old (N = 65, 90.28%), which falls within the demographic under investigation. Most participants reported that their highest level of education received was an undergraduate college degree. Nine extra participants, for a total of 81, completed both assessments but had incomplete demographic information. For the 72 participants who fully completed the survey, the demographic information results are shown in Table I.

TABLE I. DEMOGRAPHIC BREAKDOWN OF PARTICIPANT DATA

Demo-graphic	N (%)	Marcus Mean	Marcus SD	PHQ-9 Mean	PHQ-9 SD
Gender					
Female	46 (63.89)	11.61	7.18	12.02	6.73
Male	23 (31.94)	6.74	4.85	7.26	4.44
Other	2 (2.78)	13.50	14.85	12.00	14.14
Decline[a]	1 (1.39)	13.00	0.00	9.00	0.00
Age					
18	5 (6.94)	14.60	7.06	13.00	8.34
19	14 (19.44)	11.57	6.65	13.36	6.31
20	20 (27.78)	10.35	7.24	10.65	6.03
21	22 (30.56)	7.55	6.04	8.05	6.40
22	2 (2.78)	6.50	9.19	5.00	5.66
23-29[b]	3 (4.17)	9.00	9.00	7.00	4.36
30 and over[b]	6 (8.33)	13.50	7.71	13.33	6.15
Highest Education Received					
High School	5 (6.94)	15.60	6.02	14.60	8.44
Undergrad	61 (84.72)	9.62	6.74	10.13	6.32
Graduate	6 (8.33)	10.67	9.16	10.33	7.15

a. Due to the limited sample size, N = 3, "Decline" was grouped with "Other" during our analysis.

b. Based on the limited sample size for some age groups, these ages are reported as intervals.

B. Procedure

Participants were introduced to the research study through a Qualtrics survey, with the first page acting as an opt-in informed consent. Each participant was asked to take the PHQ-9 online embedded in the Qualtrics survey as well as the chatbot version of the screening, in a randomized order handled by the survey tool. Participants were given the option to experience Marcus either on an iOS device (provided with the link to download the app from the App Store) or through the web application (provided with a link to the web interface on Kommunicate). The multiple-choice PHQ-9 score was recorded automatically from the participants' responses on Qualtrics, while they had to manually enter the score outputted by Marcus to Qualtrics for the chatbot version. Participants were also asked demographic questions at the end of the survey, such as their age, gender, education level, location, and employment status. The participants' preference of screening method was also recorded, both regarding the perceived comfort, honesty and accuracy of interaction with the tools (including a neutral/no preference option), as well as an open-ended text to justify the reasons for their preference.

V. RESULTS

The results presented in this section aim at both addressing our key research questions and uncovering any extra insights that will inform our iteration of the chatbot. A variety of statistical tools were used to conduct analysis on the results, such as descriptive statistics, T-tests, analysis of variance (ANOVA), and correlation coefficients. Whenever normality is not reported, the distribution was found to be normal based on a histogram analysis. We started by checking the internal consistency of the online PHQ-9 responses, *Cronbach's a* = 0.904; we had no question-level records from Marcus, as the tool simply output the total score.

A. Accuracy of Chatbot for Measuring Depression

A two-tailed paired samples T-test was conducted on data from the 81 participants who completed screenings through both Marcus and the PHQ-9. The results, $t(80) = -0.971$, $p = 0.355$, found that there is no significant difference between the two screening scores, with Marcus average score ($M = 10.05$, $SD = 7.17$) being very similar compared to the online PHQ-9 average score ($M = 10.44$, $SD = 6.74$). The paired samples correlations indicated a highly significant correlation between the tools ($r = 0.863$, $p < 0.001$). The number of depression cases marked by Marcus and the PHQ-9 based on score classification varied slightly. According to Marcus, 11.11% (N = 9) of participants were identified as having a severe risk of suffering from a depression-related disorder, while data from the PHQ-9 questionnaire indicated that 12.35% (N = 10) of participants were at a severe risk. Marcus additionally found that 34.57% (N = 28) of participants classified as having moderate or moderately severe risk of depression compared to 38.27% (N = 31) for the PHQ-9. Complete score classification results between the screening tools for participants reporting their gender (N = 72) is shown in Figure 3.

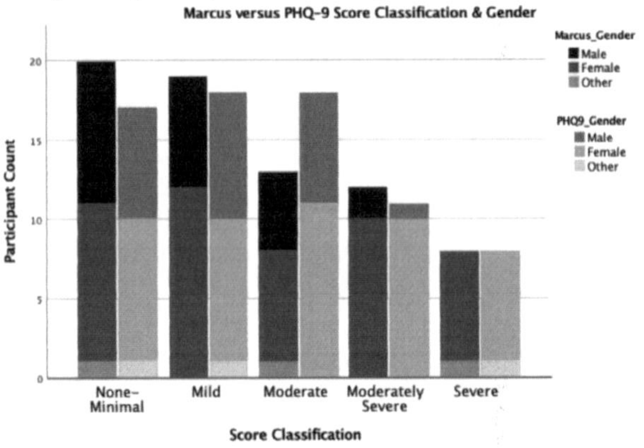

Figure 3. Marcus vs online PHQ-9 score classification by gender (N = 72).

Descriptive statistics were calculated for male and female participants that successfully completed the Marcus screening and the PHQ-9 assessment (see Table I). The average score across the two tools indicated a large discrepancy between the screening score of male ($M = 7.00$) and female ($M = 11.82$) participants. Investigating the significance of this relationship we ran a one-way ANOVA with bootstrapping (resampling the dataset across 1000 simulated samples with a 95% confidence intervals) due to violating the assumption of homogeneity of variance as shown by a Levene's test $F(1,67) = 5.696$, $p = 0.020$. Participants who reported their gender as "Other" or declined to respond were excluded due to the very small sample size (N = 3). Because of no significant difference found between Marcus and PHQ-9 scores based on the t-Test, the average of the two scores for each participant was used as the dependent variable in the ANOVA. We found a statistically significant difference between the depression screening scores, $F(1,67) = 9.904$, $p = 0.002$, with male participants having a significantly lower score as compared to females; the effect size was fairly large *Hedges' g* = 0.72 (preferred over Cohen's d due to unequal variance).

TABLE II. TOOL ORDER, INTIATION, COMPLETIION, AND PLATFORM

Tool order	N (%)	Initiated[a] (%)	Completed (%)	iOS Application (%)	Kommunicate (%)
Presented First					
Marcus	71 (54.62)	71 (100.00)	49 (69.01)	31 (63.27)	18 (36.73)
PHQ-9	59 (45.38)	59 (100.00)	49 (83.05)		
Set to Appear Second					
Marcus	59 (45.38)	49[b] (83.05)	32 (65.31)	22 (68.75)	10 (31.25)
PHQ-9	71 (54.62)	49[c] (69.01)	49 (100)		
Overall					
Marcus	130 (100.00)	120[b] (92.31)	81 (67.50)	53 (65.43)	28 (34.57)
PHQ-9	130 (100.00)	108[c] (83.08)	98 (90.74)		

a. The times a participant reached the survey page to download the app or follow the website link.

b. Ten (10) participants never reached the Marcus access screen and therefore were not counted.

c. Twenty-two (22) participants never reached the PHQ-9 questions and therefore were not counted.

Even though the study had a wide range of participants' age, the majority of them were between 18 and 21 years old (since undergraduates were mainly recruited). Once more, after averaging the scores across the two tools, we noticed a large variance between the screening score of younger undgraduates of ages 18 ($M = 13.80$) and 19 ($M = 12.46$) compared to older undergraduate students of ages 20 ($M = 10.50$) and 21 ($M = 7.80$). Examining further the significance of this relationship, we ran a one-way ANOVA with four levels, one for every one of the typical ages for U.S. college students; a Levene's test $F(3,57) = 0.199, p = 0.897$, showed that the homogeneity of variance assumption was met. A non-statistically significant difference between depression scores among the four college-age groups was discovered, $F(3,57) = 2.257$, $p = 0.092$; the above mean differences constituted a small effect size $\eta^2 = 0.106$.

B. *Effectiveness of Chatbot Compared to Online PHQ-9*

We defined effectiveness based on the initiation and completion rates of the screening sessions per tool. Initiation was originally defined as reaching the survey page with the link to download the mobile app or visit the screening tool website. Completion was based on recording a PHQ-9 score (calculated by Qualtrics) or a chatbot score (entered by the participant). The achieved response rate enabled obtaining complete screening data from 62.31% (81/130) of the overall sample. An additional 17 participants did only the PHQ-9 assessment and not the chatbot screening, while 32 participants completed neither. In addition, the order of tool presentation was also taken into account to investigate the effect of the randomized approach—regarding which tool was presented first—on completion rate. The majority of participants were presented with Marcus first ($N = 71$, 54.62%), while only 59 participants started with the online PHQ-9 (45.38%). The full data on completion rate, initiation rate, order of tool presentation, and chatbot platform are presented in Table II.

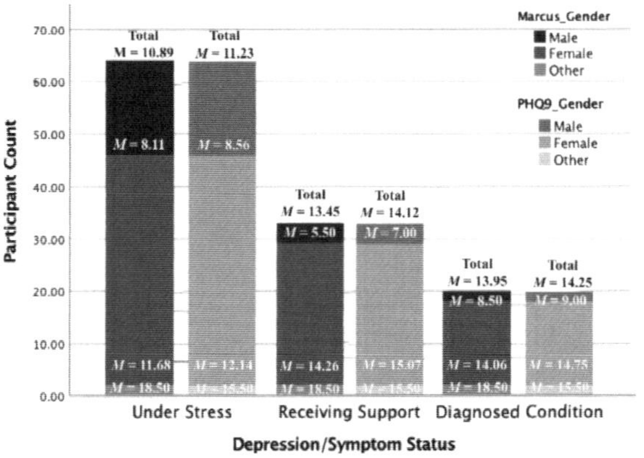

Figure 4. Marcus vs online PHQ-9 score by gender and stress factors; "Under Stress" includes only participants who somewhat/strongly agreed in that question; participant count does not add to the total of $N = 72$.

Tool effectiveness additionally considered a mean score comparison between Marcus and the PHQ-9 for the 72 participants who provided a response regarding if they were under considerable stress, had received recent mental health support, or were diagnosed with a mental or psychological condition over the last year. A majority replied that they "Strongly" or "Somewhat" agreed to being under considerable stress ($N = 64$, 88.89%); almost half reported having received mental health support ($N = 33$, 45.83%); while the majority were not diagnosed with a mental health condition ($N = 50$, 69.44%). Mean comparisons based on tool and gender for the self-reported stress assessment and their associated PHQ-9 scores are shown in Figure 4.

C. *Perceived Preference of Screening Tool*

A total of 72 participants reported an overall preferred tool for screening. A majority preferred the online PHQ-9 ($N = 44$, 61.11%) with the remainder of participants being either neutral ($N = 15$, 20.83%) or preferring Marcus ($N = 13$, 18.06%).

In addition to submitting their holistic tool preference, participants were also requested to report their screening tool preferences in terms of comfort, honesty, and accuracy. The results from the 70 participants who rated Marcus and the PHQ-9 on these three factors are shown in Figure 5.

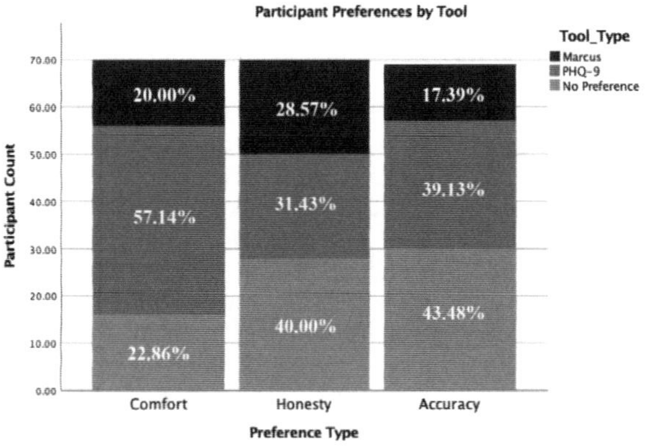

Figure 5. User preference between Marcus vs online PHQ-9 across three factors for $N = 70$ ("Accuracy" was completed by one less participant).

Participant comments regarding overall tool preference resulted in various common sentiments across individuals who partook in the study. Those who preferred the PHQ-9 assessment made note of the questionnaire being a much faster screening method with the multiple-choice option allowing for straightforward responses, which participants felt were being correctly correlated to a numeric score. Participants who preferred the Marcus screening noted their preference for the open-ended response system and that the chatbot "felt more natural." Concerns with Marcus included a lack of clarity on acceptable responses and the accuracy of the scoring methodology from the chatbot, while some also stated that the tool lacked realism and diversity. Many indicated a neutral stance that the tools were similar.

Regarding user comfort, results were generally mixed with some participants reporting that Marcus felt "more personable" and made them feel "more comfortable because it was like talking to a human." However, others who found the PHQ-9 to be a more comfortable tool noted its easier process and not feeling comfortable talking to a person, which Marcus simulates. Regarding the ability to provide honest answers, Marcus was stated to have "more flexibility" regarding responses and provided the ability to convey more information. Users additionally noted the positives in the flexibility for answers to be more vague or specific with the chatbot, as opposed to the preset responses with the PHQ-9.

VI. Discussion

Here we discuss our findings for addressing our research questions, also comparing with results from similar studies and presenting opportunities for improving our chatbot.

A. *Psychometric Properties [RQ1]*

Marcus' output score correlated significantly with the output score by the control PHQ-9, as indicated by the paired samples T-test. Additionally, the overall classification rates of the two screening methods were correlated, even though Marcus had the tendency to underscore participant responses (see Figure 3). The correlation between mean scores and classification rates between Marcus and the PHQ-9 control survey indicates that Marcus is a relatively accurate method for depression screening for a college population, performing comparably to similar chatbots [12][13]. Marcus' overall lower classification scores and slightly higher standard deviation indicates that Marcus' BERT model was not 100% accurate in translating user responses to entity scores. However, literature on PHQ-9 indicates that the instrument appears to expectedly have increased specificity and declining sensitivity in the middle part of the scale—between mild and moderate depression [38]—the classification levels where Marcus seemed to be mostly misaligned with the online PHQ-9.

Furthermore, gender seemed to be a predictor of depression screening score for both Marcus and the online PHQ-9, with female participants scoring higher, i.e., classified as having "severe" or "moderately severe" depression (Figure 3), compared to male participants—a significant finding based on an ANOVA. Our findings are in line with prior research, which has shown that females are more susceptible to depression than males [39], especially in a college setting [23]. Moreover, our score differences based on age, even if non-significant, indicate a tendency of younger adolescents to express higher stress and depression symptoms, as found by other studies [25]. It is possible that a larger sample might have been able to statistically confirm this inclination.

B. *Completion Rate and Preference [RQ2]*

Our measure of effectiveness compared the initiation and completion rates of using the chatbot versus the online PHQ-9 (Table II). The analysis of survey data showed that Marcus had an overall higher initiation rate (92.31%) than PHQ-9 (83.08%), but much lower completion rate (67.50% vs 90.74%). Considering participants had to follow an external link to either visit the online Kommunicate interface or download the iOS app to interact with Marcus, we speculated that the recorded rates—based on participants simply reaching the survey page with the link—were not accurate. A follow-up analysis of the Kommunicate logs allowed us to identify 38 participants who had no timestamped interactions with the chatbot within a 3-hour window following the survey initiation. This means that they either did not open the web-based chatbot link or did not download the app, depending on their selected platform. Only one participant was identified with a matching conversation but dropped halfway through the conversation. Based on this added analysis, the corrected initiation rate was found to be lower at 63.08% (82/130), but the corrected completion rate was much higher at 98.76% (81/82). The corrected rates are similar to findings by other studies [12]–[14], while the drop-out rate can be explained by the overhead needed to visit an external page, which some participants probably found detrimental to their participation.

Examining the correlation of participants' self-reported level of stress or having received support or even having been diagnosed with depression, with their PHQ-9 scores from both tools (Figure 4), we can clearly see that both tools were excellent in their assessment of depression-like symptoms. This is very similar to the association of depression references in social media with high scores of assessed depression using the PHQ-9 found by [22]. In terms of user preference, our findings were mixed despite most participants expressing a preference for the online PHQ-9 in most factors (Figure 5). We note that the online PHQ-9 was perceived as more comfortable and accurate due to the ease of use and speed of operation of completing a multiple-choice assessment, as opposed to Marcus, which was perceived equally honest, probably due to its anthropomorphism [32].

Nonetheless, it is also interesting to note that a couple of participants felt uncomfortable with the human representation of Marcus; one expressed a general discomfort with virtual chatbots, while another one felt unease due to Marcus represented as a white male. We recognize a tradeoff between the potential increased social presence and emotional affinity versus discomfort afforded by a human-like chatbot. Some comments confirmed findings from other studies about the increased freedom offered by a chatbot as a screening tool [12] [14], while a few participants complained about the chatbot not understanding their free-text responses. Similar challenges have been reported by other researchers [33][40], with better training data needed for optimizing chatbot performance.

C. Limitations

Despite comparing our chatbot with the online PHQ-9, we do not claim that either of the two tools were able to accurately detect depression; therefore, by "accuracy" we actually examined how close our tool came to the PHQ-9 as the standard in clinical practice. A higher sample size would have potentially increased the power of our findings, especially in terms of examining the differences in depression scores between college year of study. Similarly, a more diverse demographic in terms of geographic location, gender, race, and ethnicity would have allowed us to draw more generalizable results. Further analysis in terms of the number of questions presented to participants and natural language prompts recognized by the chatbot, could also serve to better identify the factors affecting completion rate and user preference; however, due to IRB restrictions we could not assign a unique ID to each participant to match survey data with chatbot interactions. Finally, the chatbot's limited training dataset can partly explain why multiple prompts by users could not be interpreted to intents by the BERT model, compromising accuracy (misclassification of some responses) and comfort (not understanding some answers). Some users reported the latter was a significant negative factor in their experience using Marcus.

VII. Conclusions and Future Work

The present work includes findings from a study with 130 participants in the U.S., comparing accuracy and effectiveness of two ways of administering the PHQ-9 depression screening instrument. Our chatbot, Marcus, was found comparable to the online PHQ-9 in terms of scores but the slight tendency to underscore participant responses produced a lower classification in some cases as compared to the traditional instrument. User comments and rating of the two tools indicated a preference for the online PHQ-9 in all factors but honesty, where Marcus was equally preferred. This leaves room for improving Marcus in terms of comfort, which is an important aspect of any health assessment interaction for the results to be accurate [41]. Overall, Marcus was found to be an effective first step for accessible depression screening, especially during the challenging times of a pandemic when college students were affected the most and were struggling to access emotional support.

Future work is focused towards three directions: a) improving classification accuracy of Marcus, b) accessing a wider, more diverse demographic of college students, and c) customizing the chatbot to be more inclusive for different populations. Regarding the first goal, additional supervised learning should be performed on the Marcus' BERT model along with more refined configuration values (e.g., entity scores based on identified intents). A more diverse population will allow us to run a between-subjects experiment—a better approach for such a sensitive health practice as depression screening—and gain insights about the use and perception of the chatbot based on factors like socioeconomic status, education, race, gender, etc. In line with this goal, we plan to test how customization of Marcus' representation (name, image) might affect accessibility by different demographics and increase comfort level, similar to how a research-based mobile app like Healthy Minds includes different meditation guides to accommodate multiple user preferences [42]. We anticipate such a follow-up study will provide insights to health and HCI researchers working in the domain of creating inclusive technologies for medical applications.

Acknowledgments

We would like to thank Nicole Ruzek, director of the university's Counseling & Psychological Services, and Bethany Teachman, professor at the department of Psychology and director of the Program for Anxiety, Cognition and Treatment (PACT) Lab, for their guidance and advice in the experimental design of this work. We also want to acknowledge the significant support by Raul Arrabales for providing the data from the Perla chatbot implementation.

References

[1] Institute of Health Metrics and Evaluation, "Global Health Data Exchange (GHDx)." http://ghdx.healthdata.org/gbd-results-tool?params=gbd-api-2019-permalink/d780dffbe8a381b25e1416884959e88b (accessed Mar. 18, 2023).

[2] V. Lorant, D. Deliège, W. Eaton, A. Robert, P. Philippot, and M. Ansseau, "Socioeconomic inequalities in depression: A meta-analysis," *Am J Epidemiol*, vol. 157, no. 2, 2003, doi: 10.1093/aje/kwf182.

[3] R. Shao *et al.*, "Prevalence of depression and anxiety and correlations between depression, anxiety, family functioning, social support and coping styles among Chinese medical students," *BMC Psychol*, vol. 8, no. 1, pp. 1–19, Dec. 2020, doi: 10.1186/s40359-020-00402-8.

[4] E. Sheldon *et al.*, "Prevalence and risk factors for mental health problems in university undergraduate students: A systematic review with meta-analysis," *J Affect Disord*, vol. 287, pp. 282–292, 2021, doi: 10.1016/j.jad.2021.03.054.

[5] J. P. Lépine and M. Briley, "The increasing burden of depression," *Neuropsychiatr Dis Treat*, vol. 7, no. Suppl. 1, pp. 3–7, May 2011, doi: 10.2147/NDT.S19617.

[6] K. O. Conner *et al.*, "Mental health treatment seeking among older adults with Depression: The impact of stigma and race," *American Journal of Geriatric Psychiatry*, vol. 18, no. 6, pp. 531–543, 2010, doi: 10.1097/JGP.0b013e3181cc0366.

[7] L. H. Andrade *et al.*, "Barriers to mental health treatment: Results from the WHO World Mental Health surveys," *Psychol Med*, vol. 44, no. 6, pp. 1303–1317, 2014, doi: 10.1017/S0033291713001943.

[8] M. Neathery, E. J. Taylor, and Z. He, "Perceived barriers to providing spiritual care among psychiatric mental health nurses," *Arch Psychiatr Nurs*, vol. 34, no. 6, pp. 572–579, 2020, doi: 10.1016/j.apnu.2020.10.004.

[9] K. Daley, I. Hungerbuehler, K. Cavanagh, H. G. Claro, P. A. Swinton, and M. Kapps, "Preliminary Evaluation of the Engagement and Effectiveness of a Mental Health Chatbot," *Front Digit Health*, vol. 2, pp. 1–7, Nov. 2020, doi: 10.3389/fdgth.2020.576361.

[10] R. Crasto, L. Dias, D. Miranda, and D. Kayande, "CareBot: A mental health chatbot," in *2nd International Conference for Emerging Technology (INCET 2021)*, 2021, pp. 1–5. doi: 10.1109/INCET51464.2021.9456326.

[11] B. Arroll *et al.*, "Validation of PHQ-2 and PHQ-9 to Screen for Major Depression in the Primary Care Population," *The Annals of Family Medicine*, vol. 8, no. 4, pp. 348–353, Jul. 2010, doi: 10.1370/afm.1139.

[12] R. Arrabales, "Perla: A Conversational Agent for Depression Screening in Digital Ecosystems. Design, Implementation and Validation," *arXiv preprint*, Aug. 2020, [Online]. Available: https://arxiv.org/abs/2008.12875 (accessed Mar. 23, 2023).

[13] G. Dosovitsky, E. Kim, and E. L. Bunge, "Psychometric Properties of a Chatbot Version of the PHQ-9 With Adults and Older Adults," *Front Digit Health*, vol. 3, pp. 1–8, Apr. 2021, doi: 10.3389/fdgth.2021.645805.

[14] I. Hungerbuehler, K. Daley, K. Cavanagh, H. G. Claro, and M. Kapps, "Chatbot-based assessment of employees' mental health: Design process and pilot implementation," *JMIR Form Res*, vol. 5, no. 4, pp. 1–11, Apr. 2021, doi: 10.2196/21678.

[15] M. C. Klos, M. Escoredo, A. Joerin, V. N. Lemos, M. Rauws, and E. L. Bunge, "Artificial intelligence⇓based chatbot for anxiety and depression in university students: Pilot randomized controlled trial," *JMIR Form Res*, vol. 5, no. 8, pp. 1–9, Aug. 2021, doi: 10.2196/20678.

[16] S. Suharwardy *et al.*, "116: Effect of an automated conversational agent on postpartum mental health: A randomized, controlled trial," *Am J Obstet Gynecol*, vol. 222, no. 1, p. S91, 2020, doi: 10.1016/j.ajog.2019.11.132.

[17] J. Wosik *et al.*, "Telehealth transformation: COVID-19 and the rise of virtual care," *Journal of the American Medical Informatics Association*, vol. 27, no. 6, pp. 957–962, 2020, doi: 10.1093/jamia/ocaa067.

[18] A. R. Dennis, A. Kim, M. Rahimi, and S. Ayabakan, "User reactions to COVID-19 screening chatbots from reputable providers," *Journal of the American Medical Informatics Association*, vol. 27, no. 11, pp. 1727–1731, 2020, doi: 10.1093/jamia/ocaa167.

[19] K. Kroenke and R. L. Spitzer, "The PHQ-9: A new depression diagnostic and severity measure," *Psychiatr Ann*, vol. 32, no. 9, pp. 509–515, 2002, doi: 10.3928/0048-5713-20020901-06.

[20] M. Ghazisaeedi, H. Mahmoodi, I. Arpaci, S. Mehrdar, and S. Barzegari, "Validity, Reliability, and Optimal Cut-off Scores of the WHO-5, PHQ-9, and PHQ-2 to Screen Depression Among University Students in Iran," *Int J Ment Health Addict*, vol. 20, no. 3, pp. 1824–1833, 2022, doi: 10.1007/s11469-021-00483-5.

[21] N. Fanaj and S. Mustafa, "Depression measured by PHQ-9 in Kosovo during the COVID-19 outbreak: an online survey," *Psychiatr Danub*, vol. 33, no. 1, pp. 95–100, Apr. 2021, doi: 10.24869/psyd.2021.95.

[22] M. A. Moreno *et al.*, "A Pilot Evaluation of Associations Between Displayed Depression References on Facebook and Self-reported Depression Using a Clinical Scale," *J Behav Health Serv Res*, vol. 39, no. 3, pp. 295–304, Jul. 2012, doi: 10.1007/s11414-011-9258-7.

[23] A. K. Boggiano and M. Barrett, "Gender differences in depression in college students," *Sex Roles*, vol. 25, no. 11–12, pp. 595–605, Dec. 1991, doi: 10.1007/BF00289566/METRICS.

[24] L. Zhao *et al.*, "Gender Differences in Depression: Evidence From Genetics," *Frontiers in Genetics*, vol. 11. Frontiers Media S.A., Oct. 15, 2020. doi: 10.3389/fgene.2020.562316.

[25] K. M. Kiely, B. Brady, and J. Byles, "Gender, mental health and ageing," *Maturitas*, vol. 129, pp. 76–84, Nov. 2019, doi: 10.1016/j.maturitas.2019.09.004.

[26] M. Altemus, N. Sarvaiya, and C. Neill Epperson, "Sex differences in anxiety and depression clinical perspectives," *Front Neuroendocrinol*, vol. 35, no. 3, pp. 320–330, Aug. 2014, doi: 10.1016/j.yfrne.2014.05.004.

[27] K. Kosyluk *et al.*, "Mental Distress, Label Avoidance, and Use of a Mental Health Chatbot: Results from a U.S. Survey," Nov. 2022. doi: 10.31124/ADVANCE.21431079.V1.

[28] V. Venkatesh, "Determinants of Perceived Ease of Use: Integrating Control, Intrinsic Motivation, and Emotion into the Technology Acceptance Model," *Information Systems Research*, vol. 11, no. 4, pp. 342–365, 2000, doi: 10.1287/isre.11.4.342.11872.

[29] H. Liu, H. Peng, X. Song, C. Xu, and M. Zhang, "Using AI chatbots to provide self-help depression interventions for university students: A randomized trial of effectiveness," *Internet Interv*, vol. 27, p. 100495, Mar. 2022, doi: 10.1016/j.invent.2022.100495.

[30] O. Romanovskyi, N. Pidbutska, and A. Knysh, "Elomia chatbot: The effectiveness of artificial intelligence in the fight for mental health," in *CEUR Workshop Proceedings of the 5th International Conference on Computational Linguistics and Intelligent Systems*, 2021, pp. 1–10.

[31] G. Giunti, M. Isomursu, E. Gabarron, and Y. Solad, "Designing Depression Screening Chatbots," in *Studies in Health Technology and Informatics*, vol. 284, pp. 259–263, Dec. 2021. doi: 10.3233/SHTI210719.

[32] D.-C. Toader *et al.*, "The Effect of Social Presence and Chatbot Errors on Trust," *Sustainability*, vol. 12, no. 1, p. 256, Dec. 2019, doi: 10.3390/su12010256.

[33] V. Dogra *et al.*, "A Complete Process of Text Classification System Using State-of-the-Art NLP Models," *Comput Intell Neurosci*, vol. 2022, pp. 1–26, Jun. 2022, doi: 10.1155/2022/1883698.

[34] J. Devlin, M.-W. Chang, K. Lee, and K. Toutanova, "BERT: Pre-training of Deep Bidirectional Transformers for Language Understanding," *arXiv preprint*, Oct. 2018, [Online]. Available: http://arxiv.org/abs/1810.04805 (accessed Mar. 24, 2023).

[35] Google Cloud Documentation, "DialogFlow ES." https://cloud.google.com/dialogflow/es/docs/training (accessed Feb. 24, 2023).

[36] "Kommunicate." https://www.kommunicate.io/ (accessed Mar. 09, 2023).

[37] Piper Sandler, "Taking Stock With Teens," 2021. [Online]. Available: https://www.pipersandler.com/teens (accessed: Feb. 28, 2023).

[38] K. Kroenke, R. L. Spitzer, and J. B. W. Williams, "The PHQ-9," *J Gen Intern Med*, vol. 16, no. 9, pp. 606–613, Sep. 2001, doi: 10.1046/j.1525-1497.2001.016009606.x.

[39] L. Zhao *et al.*, "Gender Differences in Depression: Evidence From Genetics," *Front Genet*, vol. 11, pp. 1–15, Oct. 2020, doi: 10.3389/fgene.2020.562316.

[40] C. R. Zgraggen, S. B. Kunz, and K. Denecke, "Crowdsourcing for creating a dataset for training a medication chatbot," in *Public Health and Informatics: Proceedings of MIE 2021*, IOS Press, 2021, pp. 1102–1103. doi: 10.3233/SHTI210364.

[41] C. Wensley, M. Botti, A. McKillop, and A. F. Merry, "Maximising comfort: how do patients describe the care that matters? A two-stage qualitative descriptive study to develop a quality improvement framework for comfort-related care in inpatient settings," *BMJ Open*, vol. 10, no. 5, p. e033336, May 2020, doi: 10.1136/bmjopen-2019-033336.

[42] S. B. Goldberg *et al.*, "Testing the Efficacy of a Multicomponent, Self-Guided, Smartphone-Based Meditation App: Three-Armed Randomized Controlled Trial," *JMIR Ment Health*, vol. 7, no. 11, p. e23825, Nov. 2020, doi: 10.2196/23825.

Effects of Saliency of an Agent's Input Information on Estimation of Mental States toward the Agent

Yuki Ninomiya
Institute of Innovation for Future Society
Nagoya University
Aichi, Japan
0000-0002-6032-8003

Asaya Shimojo
KONICA MINOLTA,Inc.
Tokyo, Japan
email:asaya.shimojo
@konicaminolta.com

Shota Matsubayashi
Institute of Innovation for Future Society
Nagoya University
Aichi, Japan
email:matsubayashi.shota.v0
@f.mail.nagoya-u.ac.jp

Hitoshi Terai
Faculty of Humanity-Oriented Science and Engineering
KINDAI University
Fukuoka, Japan
email:teraihitoshi@gmail.com

Kazuhisa Miwa
Graduate School of Informatics
Nagoya University
Aichi, Japan
email:miwa@is.nagoya-u.ac.jp

***Abstract*—Humans predict the behaviors of an autonomous agent by estimating its mental state via anthropomorphization of the agent. This paper examines the effect of the saliency of input information used by an agent on user estimation of the agent's mental state. The results demonstrate that observers can correctly estimate the mental states of agents whose input information has both high and low saliency. However, we found that observers face difficulties when asked to report their estimations verbally. This suggests that a discrepancy exists between the estimation of the agent's mental state and the user's verbal reporting.**

Keywords; agent, goal inference, theory of mind.

I. INTRODUCTION

In recent years, a variety of different autonomous agents have been developed and used in practical applications. In such situations, users are required to predict and understand the behavior of autonomous agents. Here, humans may attempt to identify the cause of behavior by anthropomorphizing the object and estimating its mental state by, for example, wondering what the vacuum cleaner is having trouble with [1]. If there is something observable, e.g., an obstacle, the cause can be identified easily. However, if the cause is difficult to recognize to just at first glance, e.g., a slippery floor, it is impossible to estimate what the agent is struggling with. In this paper, we examine the estimation of an agent's mental state to predict and understand an agent's behaviors.

Projecting a mental state onto an agent is useful relative to predicting and understanding the agent's behavior [1]. Reference [1] explained that knowledge about the general human being serves as an easily accessible base for estimating the mental states and characteristics of an unknown agent. In other words, humans predict the behavior of an unknown non-human agent by projecting common human mental states, e.g., beliefs and desires, onto the non-human agent.

Many studies have demonstrated the effectiveness of estimating the mental states of robots and machines. For example, it has been shown that placing robotic eyes on automated vehicles facilitates communication between automated vehicles and pedestrians [2].

However, inaccurately estimating the mental state of such agents can lead to serious accidents [2] [3]. Thus, to allow humans to identify an agent's mental state, it is necessary to clarify how humans correctly estimate agent's mental states.

To correctly estimate the mental state of a target, e.g., its goals or intentions, it is necessary to accurately recognize two types of information, environment as a situational constraint and behavior [4] [5]. In terms of estimating the mental state of an autonomous agent, the environment corresponds to the input information used by the agent, and behavior corresponds to the agent's output. In other words, it is important to correctly recognize what the agent is using as input information and accurately estimate the mental state from the agent's output. For example, consider a situation where an agent moves away from an enemy, as illustrated in Figure 1. Here, the behavior corresponds to agent's movement to the lower left, and the environment corresponds to the presence of the enemy to the agent's upper right. In such a case, the observer estimates that the agent's purpose for moving to the lower left is to escape the enemy.

In this study, we focused on saliency as a factor affecting the accuracy of estimating the mental state of agents. Saliency is a property of how attention-grabbing a stimulus is compared to its surroundings, and salient stimuli or events cause bias of attention [6]. Humans do not perceive all given information equally but distinguish between figure and ground and recognize figure information preferentially [7]. Visual perception studies have demonstrated that more salient features are more likely to be recognized as figure [8]. In addition, high saliency is sometimes taken as an indicator of the ease of recognition as a figure. Although the concepts of figure and ground are related to perception, these concepts are also discussed in

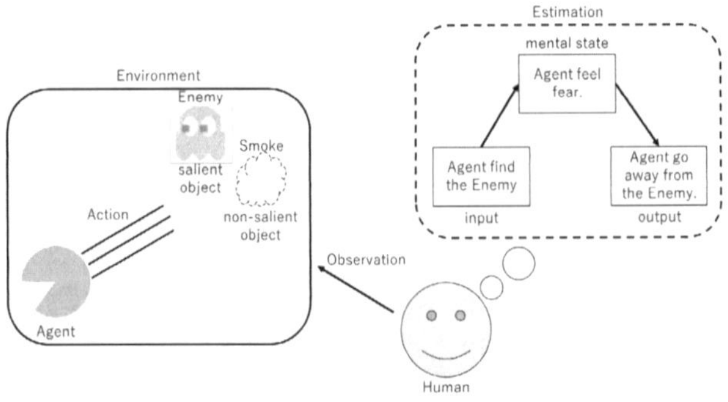

Figure 1. Estimating an agent's mental state.

higher cognitive domains, e.g., reasoning and problem-solving [9].

Thus, the saliency of information may contribute to the ease of recognizing that information when humans estimate the mental state of an agent. In other words, if the saliency of the input information is low, correct estimation of the mental state is likely to be disturbed. Consider the example shown in Figure 1. Here, the agent may not be escaping from the enemy, which is highly salient for the observer, the agent may actually want to escape from the smoke, which is considerably less salient for the observer. If the observer is unaware of the less salient information and only the smoke is present in the environment, it will fail to estimate the agent's mental state or predict its behavior accurately.

This paper examines the effect of the saliency of an agent's input information on the accuracy of the estimation of its mental state. If the saliency of the agent's input information is high, the observer will be more likely to pay attention to that information; thus, the agent's mental state will be estimated correctly. In contrast, if the saliency of the agent's input information is low, observers will be less likely to pay attention to that information; thus, the agent's mental state will be estimated incorrectly. In addition, we examine a case in which the agent uses both high- and low-saliency information as inputs concurrently. In this case, the presence of the high-saliency information can cause the low-saliency information to be neglected by focusing of the high-saliency information. To support this, a previous study found that directing attention to salient information inhibits problem solving that can be achieved by directing attention to less salient information [10]. Thus, we consider the following Research Question (RQ).

RQ1: Can participants (i.e., observers) correctly estimate an agent's mental state even when the agent utilizes less salient information?

We also investigate whether observers can verbally report the information on which they focus to estimate the agent's mental state. Previous research has shown that verbalizing thoughts promotes further focus on information that is easy to pay attention to, and as a result, other information is more likely to be ignored [10] [11]. This finding suggests that verbal reporting may lead to a focus on highly salient information and to ignoring less salient information. In other words, even if the observers can estimate mental states by focusing on the correct information, it may be difficult for them to report less salient information. Thus, we also consider RQ2.

RQ2: Is there a discrepancy between the results of the estimation of mental state and verbal reports?

II. METHOD

In this section, we describe the experiments to validate the two RQs.

A. Participants

The participants were 108 Japanese university students (N_{female} = 19, N_{male} = 91, M_{age} = 20.23, SD_{age} = 0.88).

B. Procedure

The experiment was conducted using an online environment. The experiment program was created using jspsych [12]. The experimental task comprised three phases, i.e., an observation phase, an estimation phase, and a verbal reporting phase.

In the observation phase, the participants observed a video of an agent moving through a maze (Figure 2(a)). While moving through the maze, the agent changed its speed and color in four steps according to the surrounding environment (Figure2(c)). Here, the number of enemies (zero, one, two, three or more) and the number of escape routes (four or more, three, two, or one) were used as the input information to determine the output (i.e., the speed and color). The color is as shown in Figure2(c), and the speed was quickened in four steps depending on the degree of fear. Enemies are placed as objects in the maze and exist as figures, while the routes require attention to the background information, i.e., the ground information. Thus, information regarding the number of enemies is considered to have higher saliency than the number of escape routes.

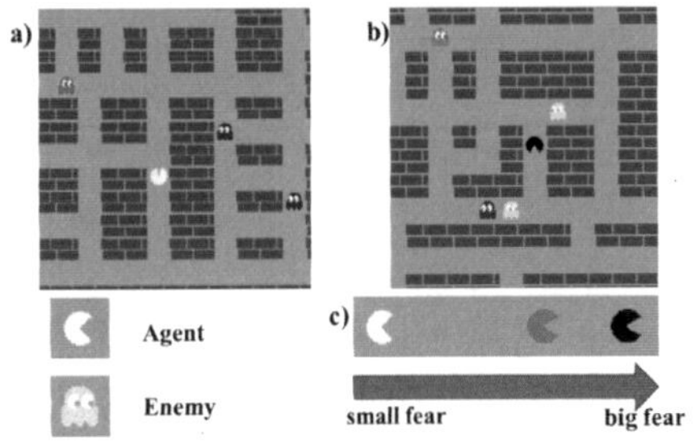

Figure 2. (a) Example screenshot of the observation phase and (b) an evaluation image in the estimation phase. (c) The output (i.e., the color) changes in response to the surrounding environment.

The agents and enemies were created based on PAC-MAN (BANDAI NAMCO Entertainment Inc., 1980), which is a common Japanese video game. The similarity of motion and morphology to humans is a factor that facilitates anthropomorphizing agents [1]. PAC-MAN has a mouth, an organ morphologically similar to that of humans, that opens and closes in a motion that is similar to that of humans; thus, PAC-MAN is easily anthropomorphizable. As a result, this character is a natural target for the estimation of mental states.

Prior to performing the observation phase, the participants were told that the agent was functionally capable of feeling fear and changing its behavior in response to the environment. The participants were then told, "After the observation, you will be asked to answer in which situations the agent felt fear." The video observed by the participants showed the agent moving through a maze with an enemy from the start to the goal. To experience the full combination of the number of enemies, this set of videos presented 16 patterns, i.e., the number of enemies (four patterns) and the number of escape routes (four patterns).

In the subsequent estimation phase, a screenshot of the experimental video (Figure 2(b)) was displayed to the participants. Then, the participants answered the following question using a seek bar to rate their level of fear on a scale from 0–100: "How scared the agent feels in this situation?". For each of the 16 patterns, the evaluation stimuli consisted of the number of enemies (four) times the number of escape routes (four) presented four times, i.e., 64 patterns in total.

After the estimation phase, we examined whether the participants could verbally report their estimation of the mental state. Here, the participants responded to which situation the agent felt fear by completing the following if-then sentence: "If ____, the agent would feel fear." Here, the participants were able to describe as many rules as they could think of.

C. Experimental design

To examine the effect of the saliency of the input information on the estimation of the mental state, we prepared an enemy condition and a route condition. In the enemy condition, the agent changed its output (i.e., its speed and color) using the number of enemies as input, which is highly salient information. For the route condition, the agent changed its output by taking the number of escape routes, which is less salient information, as input. We also set the enemy-path condition, where the agent uses both the low- and high-saliency information as inputs. This condition was designed so that the same weight was used between the number of enemies and the number of paths when determining the output. As a control condition, we added a condition that returns a random output for the input information. We predicted that if the participants could estimate the agent's mental state correctly, then their mental state estimation was more likely to rely on the information that was used as input the agent in the other conditions than in the control condition.

III. Results

To examine RQ1, we analyzed the participants' responses in the estimation phase to determine whether they estimated the agent's mental state by focusing on the correct information. First, the following multiple regression equation (1) was calculated for each participant using the environmental information (number of enemies and routes) in the evaluation images as explanatory variables and the participant's fear rating as the explained variable. Here, the partial regression coefficients for the number of enemies and escape routes were estimated using the maximum likelihood estimation method.

$$Fear = \beta_{enemy} * number_of_enemies + \beta_{escaperoute} * number_of_routes + e \quad (1)$$

We used β as a measure of how much attention the participants paid to each type of information when estimating the agent's mental state. To examine whether the participants were estimating the correct mental state under each condition, we compared the β value for each condition to that of the control condition. This analysis demonstrated that for all conditions, the β values for the only input information used by the agents were higher than those in the control condition (Figure 3). Note that no significant differences were found for input information not used by the agent. Specifically, there was an interaction in the enemy and route conditions(enemy: $F(1,53) = 68.11, p < .001$, route: $F(1,53) = 8.92, p < .01$), but not in the enemy route condition($F(1,52) = 1.42, p > .10$). Because of the interaction, in Figure 3, we shown the results of the simple main effect for the enemy condition(βenemy: $F(1,53) = 76.26, p < .001$, βroute: $F(1,53) = 1.87, p = ns.$) and route condition(βenemy: $F(1,53) = 2.44, p < ns.$, βroute: $F(1,53) = 12.17, p < .001$). In addition, because of no interaction, we shown the main effect for the enemy-route condition(conditions: $F(1,52) = 10.87, p < .01$; variable:$F(1,52) = 47.46, p < .001$).

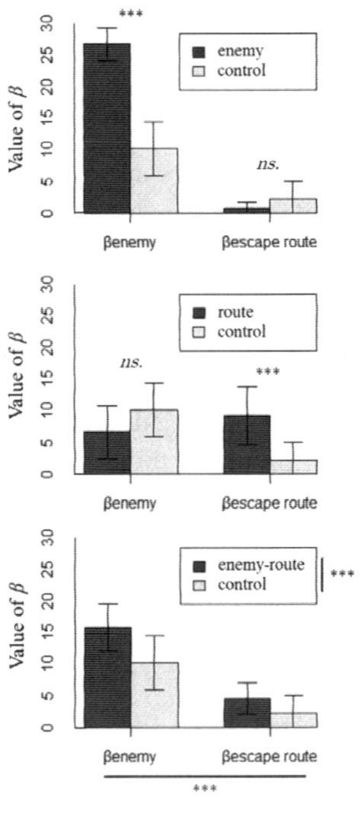

Figure 3. Comparison of β for each condition. ***: $p < .001, ns. : p > .10$

We then coded the participants according to whether they provided verbal reports about the number of enemies (e.g., “there are many ghosts around”) or escape routes (e.g., “there is only one way to go”). We created a crosstabulation table of the verbal reports with the presence of the description (2) × experimental condition (4) (TABLE I). χ^2 tests revealed significant differences between the descriptions of both the enemies ($\chi^2(3)$ = 34.10, $p < .01$) and escape routes ($\chi^2(3)$ = 26.26, $p < .01$). A residual analysis demonstrated that the ratio of descriptions of enemies was higher for the enemy and enemy-route conditions, and lower for the route condition. In contrast, the ratio of descriptions of routes was low for the enemy condition and high for the route condition; however, there was no difference for the enemy-route condition.

TABLE I
FREQUENCY AND RESIDUALS FOR THE NUMBER OF VERBAL REPORTS

A. Number of participants who described the enemy

	enemy	route	enemy-route	control
R	24(3.46)↑	10(−5.26)↓	24(2.34)↑	20(−0.51)
NR	0(−3.46)↓	17(5.26)↑	2(−2.34)↓	8(−0.51)

B. Number of participants who described the route

	enemy	route	enemy-route	control
R	1(−4.82)↑	19(3.25)↓	13(0.77)	14(−0.80)
NR	26(4.82)↓	8(−3.25)↑	13(−0.77)	14(−0.80)

[a]Direction of difference is noted for items with $p < .05$.
[b]R means Reported. NR means not Reported.

IV. Discussion and Conclusion

The analysis of the mental state estimation (Figure 3) demonstrated that even for the route condition, where the agent's input represented low-saliency information, the participants were able to focus on that information and estimate the agent's mental state. Similar results were obtained for the enemy-route condition, where the agent's input information comprised both high- and low-saliency information. These results suggest that the participants could estimate agent's mental states by correctly focusing on the low-saliency information regardless of the presence of high-saliency information, thereby providing an answer to RQ1.

The analysis of verbal reporting (TABLE.IB) demonstrated that low-saliency information, i.e., the route information, is less likely to be described for the enemy-route condition. This means that when agents use both high- and low-saliency information, the participants could provide a correct estimation but could not give a verbal report, thereby answering RQ2.

This study provides the following two contributions. First, we have demonstrated that estimation of the agent's mental state can be conducted by focusing on the correct information regardless of the saliency of the input information or the combination of information. This means that participants can estimate mental states by focusing on less salient information in a simple situation where only two pieces of information are used by the agent. However, in real-world situations, users must update their estimation of the agent's mental state according to the changing situation, e.g., during version upgrades. In addition, many practical systems use more input information. Examining the influence of the saliency of input information in such diverse situations would make it possible to elaborate on the discussion of the influence of saliency on correct estimation of mental states.

Second, we have demonstrated that the participants could estimate mental states correctly but faced difficulty reporting them verbally. This finding has implications for methods to investigate users' evaluations and understanding of autonomous agents. Specifically, if verbal methods are utilized to survey users' understanding, the evaluator may underestimate their understanding of autonomous agents. Thus, the impact of such verbalization when examining methods for surveying users' understanding of autonomous agents must be considered.

Acknowkedgment

Support for this work was given by JSPS KAKENHI Grant Number 22H03912, 22H00211 and Toyota Motor Corporation (TMC). However, note that this article solely reflects the opinions and conclusions of its authors and not TMC or any other Toyota entity.

References

[1] N. Epley, A. Waytz, and J. T. Cacioppo, “On seeing human: A three-factor theory of anthropomorphism.” *Psychological Review*, vol. 114, pp. 864–886, 2007, doi:10.1037/0033-295X.114.4.864.
[2] C. M. Chang, K. Toda, X. Gui, S. H. Seo, and T. Igarashi, “Can eyes on a car reduce traffic accidents?” ACM, 9 2022, pp. 349–359, doi:10.1145/3543174.3546841.
[3] S. Matsubayashi, H. Terai, and K. Miwa, “Development of a driving model that understands other drivers' characteristics.” Springer International Publishing, 2020, pp. 29–39, doi:10.1007/978-3-030-50537-0_3.
[4] C. L. Baker, R. Saxe, and J. B. Tenenbaum, “Action understanding as inverse planning,” *Cognition*, vol. 113, pp. 329–349, 12 2009, doi:10.1016/j.cognition.2009.07.005.
[5] G. Gergely and G. Csibra, “Teleological reasoning in infancy: the naive theory of rational action,” *Trends in Cognitive Sciences*, vol. 7, pp. 287–292, 7 2003, 10.1016/S1364-6613(03)00128-1.
[6] L. Itti and C. Koch, “Computational modelling of visual attention,” *Nature Reviews Neuroscience*, vol. 2, pp. 194–203, 3 2001, doi:10.1038/35058500.
[7] N. Rubin, “Figure and ground in the brain,” *Nature Neuroscience*, vol. 4, pp. 857–858, 9 2001, doi:10.1038/nn0901-857.
[8] D. D. Hoffman and M. Singh, “Salience of visual parts,” *Cognition*, vol. 63, pp. 29–78, 4 1997, doi:10.1016/S0010-0277(96)00791-3.
[9] T. C. Kershaw and S. Ohlsson, “Multiple causes of difficulty in insight: The case of the nine-dot problem.” *Journal of Experimental Psychology: Learning, Memory, and Cognition*, vol. 30, pp. 3–13, 2004, doi:10.1037/0278-7393.30.1.3.
[10] L. J. Ball, J. E. Marsh, D. Litchfield, R. L. Cook, and N. Booth, “When distraction helps: Evidence that concurrent articulation and irrelevant speech can facilitate insight problem solving,” *Thinking & Reasoning*, vol. 21, pp. 76–96, 1 2015, doi:10.1080/13546783.2014.934399.
[11] J. W. Schooler, S. Ohlsson, and K. Brooks, “Thoughts beyond words: When language overshadows insight.” *Journal of Experimental Psychology: General*, vol. 122, pp. 166–183, 6 1993, doi:10.1037/0096-3445.122.2.166.
[12] J. R. de Leeuw, “jspsych: A javascript library for creating behavioral experiments in a web browser,” *Behavior Research Methods*, vol. 47, pp. 1–12, 3 2015, doi:10.3758/s13428-014-0458-y.

Distinct Characteristics between "Anshin" and Feeling of Safety Evaluations

Shota Matsubayashi
Institutes of Innovation for Future Society (InFuS)
Nagoya University
Aichi, Japan
e-mail: matsubayashi.shota.v0@f.mail.nagoya-u.ac.jp

Kazuhisa Miwa
Graduate School of Informatics
Nagoya University
Aichi, Japan
e-mail: miwa@is.nagoya-u.ac.jp

Hitoshi Terai
Faculty of Humanity-Oriented Science and Engineering
Kindai University
Fukuoka, Japan
e-mail: terai@fuk.kindai.ac.jp

Yuki Ninomiya
Institutes of Innovation for Future Society (InFuS)
Nagoya University
Aichi, Japan
e-mail: ninomiya.yuki.t1@f.mail.nagoya-u.ac.jp

***Abstract*—In Japan, there is a well-known idiomatic expression called "anshin anzen." Generally, "anshin" is defined as "subjective peace" and "anzen" as "objective safety." However, previous studies have shown that objective safety, which is determined by physical measurements, does not always match the subjective feeling of safety. How does the feeling of safety differ from "anshin," which is inherently subjective? In this study, participants were asked to evaluate "anshin" or feeling of safety for automobile features, and the two evaluations were compared. The results showed that both evaluations decreased in response to high malfunction rates, but the feeling of safety evaluations did not decrease for the high criticality features. Additionally, both evaluations increased for moderate or low malfunction rates, but the feeling of safety evaluations did not increase for low criticality features. These findings indicate that the feeling of safety is sensitive to feature criticality and information.**

Keywords-component; anshin; anzen; subjective evaluation.

I. Introduction

A. Concept of "Anshin and Anzen"

In the Japanese language, there is a well-known idiomatic expression called "anshin anzen." "Anshin" is translated as "peace of mind and freedom from care [anxiety]" and "anzen" as "safety, security, and freedom from danger" [1]. Although these two are often used together, there are subtle differences in their meanings. "Anshin" has unique nuances that cannot be translated into English accurately [2]. Hereafter, "anshin" is used as it is although "anzen" is replaced with "safety".

Actually, the terms "anshin" and "anzen" are used differently. For example, "koutsu anzen (traffic [road] safety)", "anzen unten (safe driving)", and "anzen kijun (safety standards)" are listed in the Japanese dictionary; however, "koutsu anshin (traffic [road] peace)", "anshin unten (peaceful driving)", or "anshin kijun (peace standards)" are not listed [1].

According to the Japanese definitions, "anshin" is subjective and safety is objective. "Anshin" is a subjective feeling based on psychological factors. There are no definite steps to evoke "anshin," whereas safety can be ensured with technology [3]; "anshin" varies significantly from person to person and is strongly dependent on trust whereas safety evaluation requires an objective and quantitative approach [4]. "Anshin" is the belief that the situation is not very different from what one expects and that one can accept a sudden unexpected mishap. In contrast, safety is objectively defined as the absence of damage to individuals and communities [5].

B. "Anzen-kan" (Feeling of Safety)

In recent years in traffic studies, subjective evaluations from drivers or pedestrians have become important. Studies have focused on aspects, such as risk perception [6]–[8], comfort/discomfort [9]–[12], and fear [11].

Objective safety, which is determined based on physical measurements such as speed and gap between two vehicles, does not always match subjective evaluations [13]. For example, passengers in an automated vehicle perceive risk even when the vehicle maintains an objectively safe speed and gap [8]. A model was built to estimate risk perception of pedestrians based on physical measurements [13].

Thus, it is important to verify how people perceive objective safety subjectively. The feeling of safety is apparently the same as the subjective "anshin", but with some subtle differences. The term "safety" is mostly used in the context of nuclear power and disasters while "anshin" is mainly used for life and economy; thus, the two terms are clearly used differently in Japan. It is predicted that feeling of safety evaluation will be lower than "anshin" evaluation for machinery posing a high risk to human life because the objective criteria would be stringent. Therefore, the first goal of this study is to verify the differences between "anshin" and feeling of safety evaluations for automobile features with different levels of criticality.

Subjective evaluations of automobile features are affected by information about their performance, that is, how they function. Drivers' subjective evaluations change in response to information regarding Adaptive Cruise Control (ACC); these evaluations change further when they practically use of ACC [14]. Thus, information indicating functional instability may affect "anshin" and feeling of safety evaluations, especially when the feature is critical. Therefore, the second goal of this study is to verify how "anshin" and feeling of safety evaluations change before and after the provision of information regarding the unstable performance of automobile features having varying levels of safety criticality.

Section 2 describes the experimental method and Section 3 describes the results of the experiment. In Section 4, we discuss the differences between "anshin" and feeling of safety evaluations.

II. Method

A. Experimental Design

The following four factors were manipulated in the experiment: Evaluation ("Anshin"/Feeling of Safety; between-participant factor); Malfunction (MHigh/MMid/MLow; between-participant factor); Criticality (CHigh/CMid/CLow; within-participant factor); and Phase (Pre-evaluation/Post-evaluation; within-participant factor). The Evaluation factor is set as a between-participant factor to prevent confusion between "anshin" and safety. The Malfunction factor was also set as a between-participant factor to prevent direct effects of values of malfunction rates.

B. Participant

We recruited 270 participants using a crowdsourcing service and randomly assigned each participant to one of six conditions. Due to incomplete questionnaires, 29 participants were excluded. Thus, 241 participants were included in the analysis (Table I; $M_{age} = 40.96, SD_{age} = 8.77$).

TABLE I
DISTRIBUTION OF PARTICIPANTS

	MHigh[1]	MMid[1]	MLow[1]
"Anshin" Evaluation	37	37	42
Feeling of Safety Evalulation	40	43	42

[1] MHigh = Malfunction High, MMid = Malfunction Mid, MLow = Malfunction Low.

C. Procedure

All the procedures were conducted on a browser, and informed consent was obtained in advance. First, participants were asked to respond freely to the question: "What do you think about 'anshin'?" in the "anshin" conditions or "What do you think about safety?" in the feeling of safety conditions to improve the validity of the subsequent evaluations. Next, the automobile feature to be evaluated was presented. For example, a question in the anshin-CHigh condition was as follows: "In recent years, the automatic driving feature has become popular. This feature allows a vehicle to sense its surroundings and automatically drive to the destination. Although this feature is effective in reducing drivers' efforts, malfunctions can still occur. What do you feel about its 'anshin'?" Participants were asked to respond using a 7-point scale (Pre-evaluation).

Subsequently, as a report, a total of six malfunction rates measured for three regions by two companies were presented. The six malfunction rates were approximately 2% in the MHigh conditions, 0.02% in the MMid conditions, and 0.0002% in the MLow conditions on average. Participants responded to the same question as in the pre-evaluation considering the malfunction rates (Post-evaluation).

Similarly, participants responded to questions about the automobile features in CMid and CLow conditions, which were automatic parking and automatic wipers, respectively. The order of three safety criticality conditions was counterbalanced among participants.

III. Results

A. Pre-Evaluations

In order to verify the differences between "anshin" and feeling of safety evaluations of automobile features varying in safety criticality, Evaluation × Criticality ANOVA was conducted in the pre-evaluation (Figure 1). The results showed that the main effect of Evaluation was significant ($F(1,239) = 23.78,\ p < .001,\ \eta_p = .09$), and feeling of safety evaluation was higher than the "anshin" evaluation. The main effect of Criticality was also significant ($F(2,478) = 165.66,\ p < .001,\ \eta_p = .40$), and further analysis showed that the evaluations were higher for CHigh, CMid, and CLow in that order ($ts > 7.43,\ ps < .001$). However, the interaction was not significant ($F(2,478) = 0.30,\ p < .001,\ \eta_p = .09$). Thus, although the feeling of safety evaluation was higher than the "anshin" evaluation in pre-evaluation, there was no difference between "anshin" and feeling of safety with respect to the safety criticality of the automobile features.

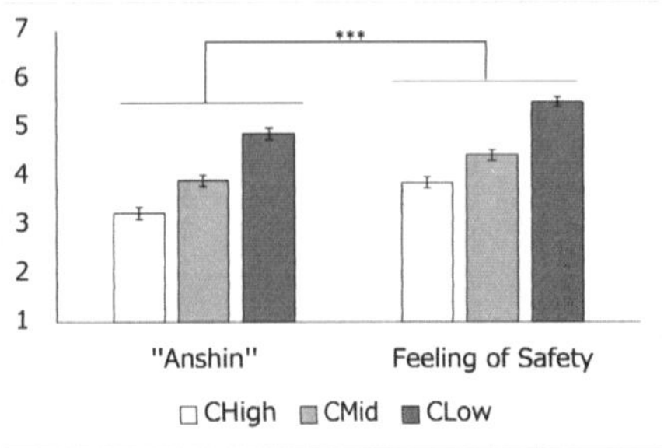

Figure 1. Pre-evaluation. Error bars represent standard errors. CHigh = Criticality High, CMid = Criticality Mid, CLow = Criticality Low. $***p < .001$.

B. Changes due to Information

To verify the differences in changes in "anshin" and feeling of safety evaluations before and after the provision of information regarding the unstable performance of features varying in safety criticality, Malfunction × Criticality × Phase ANOVAs were conducted in the two evaluations (Figure 2). The common and distinct characteristics are separately reported below.

1) Common Characteristics: The main effects of Criticality were significant in both "anshin" and feeling of safety evaluations and further analysis showed that the evaluations were higher for CLow, CMid, and CHigh in that order ("anshin": $ts > 5.54,\ ps < .001$; feeling of safety: $ts > 5.54,\ ps < .001$). Malfunction × Phase interactions were significant, and the simple main effects were significant in MHigh, MMid, and

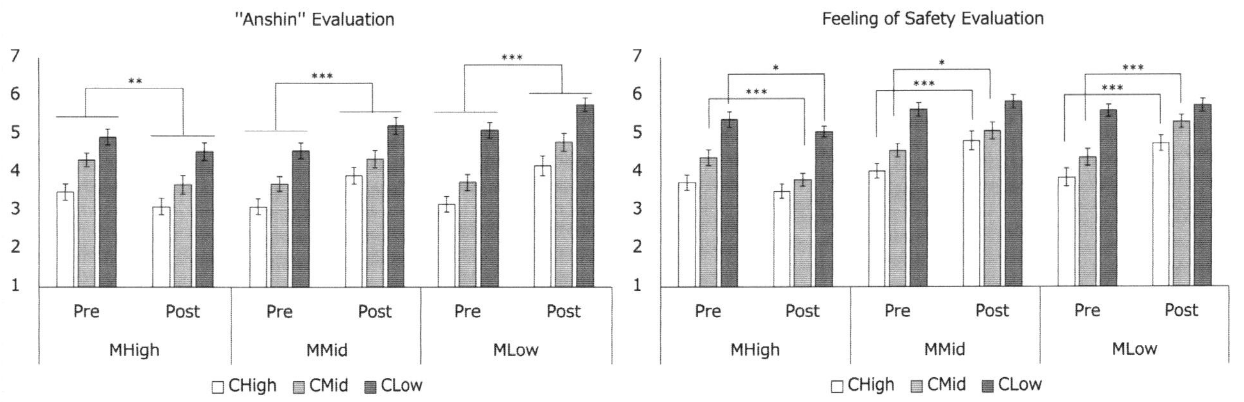

Figure 2. Evaluations in "anshin" and feeling of safety conditions. Error bars represent standard errors. MHigh = Malfunction High, MMid = Malfunction Mid, MLow = Malfunction Low, CHigh = Criticality High, CMid = Criticality Mid, CLow = Criticality Low. *$p < .05$, **$p < .01$, ***$p < .001$.

TABLE II
RESULTS OF ANOVAS IN "ANSHIN" AND FEELING OF SAFETY CONDITIONS

	"Anshin"					Feeling of Safety				
	df	F	p		η_p	df	F	p		η_p
Malfunction	2, 113	2.23	.111	***	.03	2, 122	6.79	.001	**	.10
Criticality	2, 226	82.97	< .001	***	.42	2, 244	114.97	< .001	***	.48
Phase	1, 113	19.54	< .001	***	.14	1, 122	9.47	.002	**	.07
Malfunction × Criticality	4, 226	0.82	.510		.01	4, 244	0.62	.641		.01
Malfunction × Phase	2, 113	23.63	< .001	***	.30	2, 122	14.09	< .001	***	.18
Criticality × Phase	2, 226	0.05	.350		.00	2, 244	9.95	< .001	***	.07
Malfunction × Criticality × Phase	4, 226	1.28	.275		.02	4, 244	4.07	.003	**	.06

**$p < .01$, ***$p < .001$.

MLow conditions ("anshin": Fs > 8.57, ps $< .006$, η_ps $> .19$; feeling of safety: Fs > 9.56, ps $< .004$, η_ps $> .19$). Specifically, the pre-evaluations were higher in the MHigh condition and the post-evaluations were higher in the MMid and MLow conditions. Thus, both of "anshin" and feeling of safety evaluations decreased with high malfunction rates, but increased with moderate or low malfunction rates.

2) *Distinct Characteristics:* Because the second-order interaction of Malfunction × Criticality × Phase was significant only in the feeling of safety condition, further analysis was conducted (Table III). The results showed that the decreases due to high malfunction rates were not found in the CHigh condition. On the other hand, the increases due to moderate or low malfunction rates were not found in the CLow condition. In sum, the following two differences were found. First, with high malfunction rates, the "anshin" evaluations decreased uniformly, but the feeling of safety evaluations did not decrease for the high criticality features (i.e., automatic driving). Second, with moderate or low malfunction rates, the "anshin" evaluations increased uniformly, but the feeling of safety evaluations did not increase for the low criticality features (i.e., automatic wipers).

IV. CONCLUSION AND FUTURE WORK

The first goal of this study was to verify the differences between "anshin" and feeling of safety evaluations of automobile features having varying levels of safety criticality. The results revealed that the feeling of safety evaluations was higher than the "anshin" evaluations. Additionally, the higher the criticality, the higher both evaluations, but no difference was found between the two evaluations. The safety evaluations had been expected to be lower than the "anshin" evaluations for high criticality features, but they were higher overall. This indicates that "anshin" is more stringent than feeling of safety. This difference needs to be verified in future research.

The second goal was to verify the differences in changes in "anshin" and feeling of safety evaluations before and after the provision of information about the unstable performance of features having varying levels of criticality. The results revealed that both evaluations decreased in response to high malfunction rates, but the feeling of safety evaluations did not decrease for the high criticality features. Additionally, both evaluations increased for moderate or low malfunction rates, but the feeling of safety evaluations did not increase for the low criticality features.

It has been shown that drivers' trust in ACC decreases immediately after some problems of ACC are presented [14]. Assuming that ACC is a high criticality feature and that the information indicates instability, the finding is similar to this previous study that the information about a malfunctioning critical feature decreases "anshin" evaluations.

It is notable, however, that such a decrease was not ob-

TABLE III
RESULTS OF FURTHER ANALYSIS OF MALFUNCTION × CRITICALITY × PHASE IN FEELING OF SAFETY EVALUATIONS

			df	*F*	*p*		η_p
CHigh[1]	Malfunction × Phase		2,122	8.43	< .001	***	.12
	Phase	at MHigh[2]	1,39	1.61	.211		.03
		at MMid[2]	1,42	13.58	< .001	***	.24
		at MLow[2]	1,41	14.78	< .001	***	.26
CMid[1]	Malfunction × Phase		2,122	18.58	< .001	***	.23
	Phase	at MHigh[2]	1,39	12.96	< .001	***	.24
		at MMid[2]	1,42	6.49	.014	*	.13
		at MLow[2]	1,41	30.43	< .001	***	.42
CLow[1]	Malfunction × Phase		2,122	3.67	.028	*	.05
	Phase	at MHigh[2]	1,39	6.15	.017	*	.13
		at MMid[2]	1,42	1.61	.211		.03
		at MLow[2]	1,41	0.89	.348		.02

[1] CHigh = Criticality High, CMid = Criticality Mid, CLow = Criticality Low.
[2] MHigh = Malfunction High, MMid = Malfunction Mid, MLow = Malfunction Low.
$*p < .05$, $***p < .001$.

served in the feeling of safety evaluations. That may be because feeling of safety evaluations involves a deep process with respect to the significance of the unstable-performance-related information of a critical feature. Although unstable performance is inherently problematic, it may be favorably interpreted as an indication of the technical complexity of a critical feature, preventing a decrease in feeling of safety evaluation. Similarly, feeling of safety evaluations did not improve when non-critical features were described as stable. The reason may be that the stable performance of low-critical features is objectively interpreted as non-relevant to safety. Further verification is needed on this point.

These findings that the feeling of safety is sensitive to feature criticality of function and information about unstable performance suggests the possibility that the feeling of safety is based on objective physical measurements. In this sense, "anshin" may be relatively insensitive and more subjective. Although it has been suggested that "anshin" includes processes of prediction and trust [4], whether the feeling of safety includes these processes must be carefully verified.

ACKNOWLEDGMENT

Support for this work was given by JSPS KAKENHI Grant Number 22H03912 and 22H00211, and by Toyota Motor Corporation (TMC). However, note that this article solely reflects the opinions and conclusions of its authors and not TMC or any other Toyota entity.

REFERENCES

[1] T. Watanabe, E. R. Skrzypczak, and P. Snowden, *Kenkyusha's New Japanese-English Dictionary*. Tokyo, Japan: Kenkyusha Co., Ltd., 2003.

[2] M. Mukaidono, *Nyuumon Tekisuto: Anzengaku (Introductory Text: Safety Science)*. Tokyo, Japan: KENSEISHA Co., Ltd., 2016.

[3] T. Kikkawa, S. Shirato, S. Fujii, and K. Takemura, "The pursuit of informed reassurance ('an-shin' in society) and technological safety ('an-zen')," *Sociotechnica*, vol. 1, pp. 1–8, 2003, doi:10.3392/sociotechnica.1.1.

[4] M. Mukaidono, M. Kitano, M. Kikuchi, A. Komatsubara, T. Yamamoto, and T. Matsubara, *Anzengaku Nyuumon (Introductory Safety Science)*. Tokyo, Japan: Toyo Keizai Inc., 2009.

[5] Ministry of Education, Culture, Sports, Science and Technology (MEXT), "Anzen anshin na shakai no kouchiku ni kansuru kagaku gijutsu seisaku ni kansuru kondankai houkokusho (Report of the advisory committee on science and technology policy contributing to the construction of safe and secure society)," 2014, [Online]. Available from: https://www.mext.go.jp/a_menu/kagaku/anzen/houkoku/04042302.htm 2023.03.23.

[6] C. Castanier, F. Paran, and P. Delhomme, "Risk of crashing with a tram: Perceptions of pedestrians, cyclists, and motorists," *Transportation Research Part F: Traffic Psychology and Behaviour*, vol. 15, no. 4, pp. 387–394, 2012, doi:10.1016/j.trf.2012.03.001.

[7] E. Lehtonen, V. Havia, A. Kovanen, M. Leminen, and E. Saure, "Evaluating bicyclists' risk perception using video clips: Comparison of frequent and infrequent city cyclists," *Transportation Research Part F: Traffic Psychology and Behaviour*, vol. 41, pp. 195–203, 2016, doi: 10.1016/j.trf.2015.04.006.

[8] J. Petit, C. Charron, and F. Mars, "A pilot study on the dynamics of online risk assessment by the passenger of a self-driving car among pedestrians," in *HCI in Mobility, Transport, and Automotive Systems. Automated Driving and In-Vehicle Experience Design*, H. Krömker, Ed. Cham: Springer International Publishing, 2020, pp. 101–113, ISBN:978-3-030-50523-3.

[9] H. Bellem, B. Thiel, M. Schrauf, and J. F. Krems, "Comfort in automated driving: An analysis of preferences for different automated driving styles and their dependence on personality traits," *Transportation Research Part F: Traffic Psychology and Behaviour*, vol. 55, pp. 90–100, 2018, doi:10.1016/j.trf.2018.02.036.

[10] I. Kaparias, M. G. Bell, A. Miri, C. Chan, and B. Mount, "Analysing the perceptions of pedestrians and drivers to shared space," *Transportation Research Part F: Traffic Psychology and Behaviour*, vol. 15, no. 3, pp. 297–310, 2012, doi:10.1016/j.trf.2012.02.001.

[11] T. Q. Pham, C. Nakagawa, A. Shintani, and T. Ito, "Evaluation of the Effects of a Personal Mobility Vehicle on Multiple Pedestrians Using Personal Space," *IEEE Transactions on Intelligent Transportation Systems*, vol. 16, no. 4, pp. 2028–2037, 2015, doi:10.1109/TITS.2014.2388219.

[12] A. Telpaz, M. Baltaxe, R. M. Hecht, G. Cohen-Lazry, A. Degani, and G. Kamhi, "An Approach for Measurement of Passenger Comfort: Real-Time Classification based on In-Cabin and Exterior Data," *2018 21st International Conference on Intelligent Transportation Systems (ITSC)*, pp. 223–229, 2018, doi:10.1109/ITSC.2018.8569653.

[13] Y. Hasegawa, C. Dias, M. Iryo-Asano, and H. Nishiuchi, "Modeling pedestrians' subjective danger perception toward personal mobility vehicles," *Transportation Research Part F: Traffic Psychology and Behaviour*, vol. 56, pp. 256–267, 2018, doi:10.1016/j.trf.2018.04.016.

[14] M. Beggiato and J. F. Krems, "The evolution of mental model, trust and acceptance of adaptive cruise control in relation to initial information," *Transportation Research Part F: Traffic Psychology and Behaviour*, vol. 18, pp. 47–57, 2013, doi:10.1016/j.trf.2012.12.006.

e^2Logos: A Novel Software for Evaluating Online Student Project Reports

Results from a comparative usability study with undergraduate teaching assistants

Panagiotis Apostolellis
Department of Computer Science
University of Virginia
Charlottesville, VA, USA
panaga@virginia.edu

Philip Hart
Department of Computer Science
University of Virginia
Charlottesville, VA, USA
ph9aa@virginia.edu

Ketian Tu
Department of Computer Science
University of Virginia
Charlottesville, VA, USA
kt9sh@virginia.edu

***Abstract*—Most assignments in engineering design courses include open-ended, real-word projects, where groups of students work together and produce a collection of deliverables, which need to be reported and evaluated by the instructor so that the students can act upon the feedback. The complexity of the work often demands that project artifacts be reported online, but there is no software designed to assess and grade web-based technical reports. This paper introduces e^2Logos, a novel custom grading/feedback tool designed for evaluating online reports and presents results from a comparative usability study with Gradescope, a popular grading tool for PDF submissions. Findings from grading two project phases in two semesters for a computer science Human-Computer Interaction (HCI) course, revealed that e^2Logos was perceived as more efficient, motivating, dependable, and attractive than Gradescope, by using the User Experience Questionnaire (UEQ) and our own usability goals. However, it was not shown to improve grading consistency among graders. Implications for designing similar software are presented as design requirements, along with our plans to evaluate e^2Logos for its effectiveness in improving learning outcomes in Project-Based Learning (PBL) courses.**

Keywords—usability test; grading software; web annotation tools; project-based learning; student feedback.

I. INTRODUCTION

Within the field of engineering, managing and contributing to complex projects are essential parts of the learning process [1]. A common method to achieve this in many upper-level engineering courses is to use open-ended, client-driven, team-based problems, most commonly known as Model-Eliciting Activities (MEAs) [2]. MEAs are a form of PBL that have been applied increasingly to engineering courses over the past decade, offering a form of assignment intended to emulate the design process of a derived solution for real-world problems within a limited time [3]. Throughout these activities, students are encouraged to integrate and apply knowledge from past and current courses toward producing a cohesive solution for an open-ended problem.

Tackling a complex, open-ended design problem can be challenging for engineering students, particularly with a lack of experience in multi-disciplinary skills like self-reliance, collaboration, and time management [4]. Furthermore, there is often an inconsistency between the instructor's and students' learning objectives within the context of semester-long, real-world projects [5]. Thus, engaging students with MEAs is difficult due to the requirements for consistent and accessible feedback throughout project development. To apply MEAs to a large class, the grading and feedback process must be expedited yet remain simplistic for graders [4].

Many methodologies are used to grade MEAs and other project-based deliverables, including self-assessment, peer assessment, co-assessment, and performance assessment, all of which involve a way of evaluating work whether it be from the students themselves, their peers, or staff [6]. Another method is specifications grading, which introduces a pass/fail system toward assignments, focusing more on certain learning objectives being met to earn a certain grade [7]. Adaptive rubrics have also been used and even integrated within modern grading software. This approach has been shown to help graders focus on deeply understanding student work before deciding on point deductions through tailoring the rubric based on student submissions [8].

Many tools are available for the grading of online assignments, such as various Learning Management Systems (LMS) or dedicated grading tools like Gradescope. Gradescope is geared toward the grading of handwritten work and quiz style questions [9], while LMSs may provide administration of course content, scheduling, announcements, assignments, quizzes, and other functionalities in addition to grading student work [10]. These systems are well equipped to grade work that can be uploaded, such as images or PDFs [9], but not for student submissions in an online (website) format. Moreover, student work often entails different problem-solving patterns when tackling open-ended design problems [3], meaning outcomes may vary. Thus, grading needs to be specific and tailored to the project. To our knowledge, there is no grading tool that provides customized grade deductions, collaborative grading, and support for within-context commenting of web-based technical reports, a widely used format in PBL courses.

The novel tool e^2Logos, evaluating electronic logos (from the Greek work *λόγος*, for speech), aims to address challenges faced in courses where online technical and reflective reports are a significant part of the evaluation process. e^2Logos combines assessment, annotation, feedback, and dialogue features and is built on the open-source Hypothes.is platform [11]. The primary focus of this grading tool is to provide timely and consistent feedback to students and assess PBL outcomes. The tool has a client-side interface for instructors and graders to grade students' work, and for students to access their grades and individual feedback. There is also a backend management portal for instructors to review and release grades for projects. e[2]Logos has been deployed and tested in an undergraduate engineering course at a large public U.S. university during fall 2022, collecting 1444 comments from 6 graders in the class.

This paper aims to provide context for the design of e[2]Logos and examine its usability to respond to the question: *How does e[2]Logos compare to an established grading software (Gradescope), in terms of efficiency and ease of use for grading students' online project work?*

The paper begins with a review of relevant grading and annotation tools (Section II), then presents the design of e[2]Logos (Section III), continues with the description of the usability studies (Section IV) and the results of our analysis (Section V), finishing with a discussion of main findings (Section VI), and the conclusions and future work (Section VII).

II. BACKGROUND

A. Importance of feedback in PBL student work

While engaging with PBL work, students must synthesize past knowledge with new skills learned from their current course. However, design courses in higher education require multidisciplinary skills and not all students will perform similarly, especially when first introduced to PBL, but they can improve in the proper learning environment [12]. Feedback should aim to reduce the gap between current understanding and the desired goal [13], hopefully, setting a personalized measure of current collective achievement and indicating how to improve upon that achievement.

Good feedback should be timely and efficient [13], and using grading tools streamlines the grading process. However, the challenge for instructors is in being accurate and consistent in grading open-ended projects that have more than one correct solution [14]. There are currently many software tools that support grading but may not be best suited for grading while providing feedback essential to guiding PBL work.

B. Computer-based assessment tools for PBL work

There are many educational technologies used by higher education institutions to evaluate student learning; some are more suited for only grading, while others offer a way to display a grader's feedback. In this review, we will mainly focus on computer-based tools for grading and evaluating digital student submissions.

Grading/Feedback Tools. Gradescope is a platform that allows instructors to assess handwritten assignments and exams online, with such features as automated grading, peer review, and customizable grading rubrics [9]. It has been shown to save instructors time and improve the consistency and fairness of grading. In a study of two undergraduate mechanical engineering courses, Gradescope reduced the instructor's grading time by approximately 2.5 hours, while both the rubric structure and the ease of switching between submissions helped ensure that grades were consistent for all students [15]. It has also been used to gather real-time feedback from students, as demonstrated in an introductory data science class where instructors used Gradescope's tagging system to track student learning objectives and adjust their curriculum based on the feedback received [16].

A LMS is a type of software that helps educators administer, document, track, report, automate, and deliver educational courses [10]. LMSs have become increasingly popular, especially due to the transition to online learning during the COVID-19 pandemic [17]. In a recent study, the use of Moodle [18], a popular LMS, was evaluated as an e-learning platform in a project-based undergraduate course [19]. Students worked in groups of 3 to 5 on an open-ended project throughout the semester. A survey administered at the end of the semester revealed that 10% of students cited the feedback mechanism as their favorite aspect of using Moodle, while 15% reported that the tool made it difficult to locate work and had too many confusing links on the page. Overall, the use of Moodle as a LMS in a PBL course was seen as a useful tool for instructors to provide feedback to students, but there were challenges in terms of navigation and organization. The evaluation of another popular LMS, Blackboard [20], in terms of its usefulness in an undergraduate computer literacy course, revealed that immediate feedback on online quizzes was the most helpful aspect of Blackboard, while collaborative work and communication with peers and instructors were rated as the least effective aspects [21].

iRubric is a web-based rubric development, assessment, and sharing software, commonly integrated with LMS platforms to facilitate matrix-style grading [22]. During evaluation of student work, a grader must select a pre-defined rubric criterion and then write specific feedback in a table format. A study evaluating iRubric found that it streamlined the grading process by promoting a consistent grading element throughout the university-wide adoption of the tool, as a replacement of the previously used paper rubrics [23]. Most contemporary LMSs provide embedded grading functionality using rubrics, where instructors can define grading criteria and associate them with specific learning outcomes. Canvas, as an example, has been shown to be very effective for assessing student learning using its rubric tool by gauging the students' level of achievement in some disciplinary area [24]. Such tools are limited for assessing online work as grading is disassociated from the work and graders must switch multiple times between web submission and the rubric hosted on the LMS, plus the assigned criteria are fixed to evaluating broader outcomes/expectations. Others have worked on developing rubrics for STEM courses to facilitate goal setting and self-evaluation [25], but such tools have not made it into an interactive software, nor have they been tested for their usability.

Annotation Tools. Hypothes.is is an open-source software platform that allows users to annotate web pages and PDF files with highlights and comments [11]. In a study conducted in an undergraduate engineering course, students who used Hypothes.is to annotate and discuss articles in a group performed better than those who did not in the final exam. While there was no quantitative data available on the instructor's perspective, the researcher noted that Hypothes.is promotes communication and peer review, which are essential factors for effective PBL [26]. In another study, the use of Hypothes.is in combination with a Google Doc was found to be effective for annotating articles and summarizing points made by groups of students [27]. Hypothes.is can also be integrated with a LMS to provide added grading functionality. However, this integration only allows students to annotate an instructor-selected online resource and provide a single score based on the quality of student annotations.

Diigo is a social bookmarking tool that allows users to add digital sticky notes to web pages [28]. It is frequently used in educational settings due to its ability to annotate and organize data. A case study conducted in a technology course introduced Diigo to pre-service teachers through multiple lectures and gathered feedback from both students and instructors. The majority of students had a favorable impression of the tool, and instructors reported that students engaged more deeply with course concepts through searching and annotating course content. However, some participants expressed concerns that Diigo offered too many features for a bookmarking tool [29]. Another tool for sharing digital content, Digication [30], allows students to submit a snapshot of their website reports through LMS integration, but commenting can only happen on the live website and lacks grading functionality.

An empirical study of EDUCOSM, a set of tools for asynchronous collaborative knowledge construction, in a statistics course determined that digital systems equipped with annotation technology improved a student's affinity for learning on a collaborative document through student markings [31]. A more recent study examined the efficacy of digital annotations for feedback in comparison to other modes of delivering feedback to students, and found that a single mode of feedback, electronic annotations or digital recordings, were better for offering detailed and personalized feedback [32]. Another study evaluating a custom web-based tool for providing corrective feedback to English essays via annotations, showed that the gap between high-level and low-level student performance was eliminated through the application of corrective feedback [33]. Overall, examining annotation technologies has shown to benefit a grader when generating feedback for students [34]. However, such technologies are largely focused on providing students with feedback while analyzing digital submissions and are deprived of any grading functionality.

A focus of this review has been to examine the current functionalities and usability of grading and feedback tools in order to determine what types of tools are most efficient for evaluating online student work. However, none of the tools reviewed have been directly evaluated for their usability or compared with each other. In 2021, Gradescope introduced (as a beta version) a new format for grading essay-type assignments that provided combined grading and annotation functionality for digital submissions. However, submissions were restricted to a PDF format and the lack of a collaborative grading made it difficult to resolve grading inconsistencies between graders. Overall, the tools available for providing effective, personalized, and collaborative feedback, such as annotation software, lack course management and grading functionalities. Conversely, tools that enable course management and grading lack a way of providing personalized and specifically marked feedback in a collaborative manner. A tool that automates collaborative grading, while allowing a grader's in-context feedback to be as specific as possible is hypothesized to expedite and offer consistency to the grading process for online, open-ended, group design projects.

III. E²LOGOS DESIGN

A. *Extracting requirements for good feedback of PBL work*

In order to reach the point of developing e²Logos, the lead author tested combinations of different tools for assessing the design work of student groups in two HCI courses. Over multiple semesters, different tools included the use of Google Spreadsheets for grading and feedback as notes (exported and released to students as PDF files); a combination of Diigo or Hypothes.is (used for within-context feedback) with Google Spreadsheets (for grading); and Gradescope's *Essay* assignment format (released as beta for the 2021-22 academic year only). None of these approaches proved effective in accommodating the unique demands of leaving good graded feedback within the context of rich online technical reports that students generated while reporting their project work.

The outcome of these iterations was a compiled list of design requirements that could satisfy the identified demands. This list was derived from personal experience, conversations with colleagues teaching similar courses, and feedback from teaching assistants who helped grade project design work.

1) Within-context feedback and grading: A crucial learning factor for PBL work is for students to review and understand the provided feedback within the context of their own work. Prior approaches combining tools, such as [27] and our own experimentation, decoupled feedback and grading from the students' own work, making it hard for them to understand how and where their work could be improved.

2) Personalized adjustment of score and feedback: A unique aspect of assessing project work is that fixed rubrics fail to capture adequately the element of quality. Thus, it is imperative that a grader has the flexibility to adjust the score and adapt the feedback provided to specific submissions for the same identified rubric item. In comparison, attempting to do so in Gradescope will change the score and associated comment to all submissions the item has been applied to.

3) Collaborative grading: Due to the open-ended nature of design projects it is rather challenging to achieve inter-grader consistency. Communication between graders is, therefore, necessary, allowing the instructor and more experienced staff to provide guidance to all graders and decrease grading inconsistencies among student submissions.

4) General feedback and regrade requests: Considering the difficulty of evaluating design work objectively, it is necessary to provide overall guidance to students after all grading is done. Additionally, student groups should be able to dispute the way their work has been assessed by requesting a regrade and providing their rationale.

The list of design requirements included above guided the design and implementation of e²Logos, which is described briefly in the next section. Some of these requirements were also tested during the usability studies and findings in support of them are presented under the Discussion section.

B. *Technical Design of e²Logos*

Before discussing the technical aspects of e²Logos, it is crucial to note that the tool is built using the open-source Hypothes.is software [11], which allows users to annotate and converse on websites across the internet. We repurposed Hypothes.is to include a grading component but maintained all functionality for providing feedback on an online project report, including highlighting text within the page, adding and replying to comments, navigating to highlighted text when selecting a comment, all while storing this type of information in a PostgreSQL database. e²Logos, similar to Hypothes.is, is mainly a web-based client administered as a Chrome extension that communicates with a backend server through API calls. The server application is developed using various Pylons Project packages, such as the pyramid web framework, colander, and deform, as well as Elasticsearch for annotation lookup. The client (Chrome extension) is based on React for user interface and logic, and Redux for session management.

The backend website handles all administrative work and allows instructors to create courses, groups, and assignments. Assignments have an associated rubric, which is currently uploaded as a json file, but in future versions would be created using a dedicated rubric creation tool similar to Gradescope. Through the website, an instructor can assign students to groups, assign teaching assistants as graders (including a lead grader role with elevated privileges), and release grades to students. Graded comments are listed in buckets according to what assignment and group those annotations belong to, including the total score for each group. Searching by group name, grader username, or assignment name filters these buckets to only show the relevant comments. Since the backend website has not been included in the usability test, we will not elaborate further on its functionality.

The main operation of e²Logos is accomplished through the extension, where graders can evaluate a project report on the online submission itself (website or PDF). After navigating to the report's URL and selecting the desired assignment to be graded from the drop-down menu of the Rubric tab (Figure 1a), graders follow this workflow: a) they highlight the relevant text on the page and select "Grade" from a popup menu, b) they select the appropriate rubric item from the list and the corresponding pre-defined comment appears in the Comments tab (Figure 1b), which c) they can then edit in terms of text and/or score to fit the submission's quality, and d) they click "Post" to submit the item to the backend. This simple workflow satisfies the two first design requirements listed above. As a safety measure, graders cannot apply/deduct more points for an item beyond the thresholds defined by the instructor. Graders also have the option to only comment or highlight text without applying a rubric item, to simply provide feedback to students.

Graders can navigate between group websites by selecting the group's name from the drop-down menu at the top. If the website has been graded already, comments are fetched from the backend and displayed through highlights on relevant text within the page and text-based feedback in the Comments tab. Commenting includes a rich-text editor that can be used to emphasize specific parts or even embed an image.

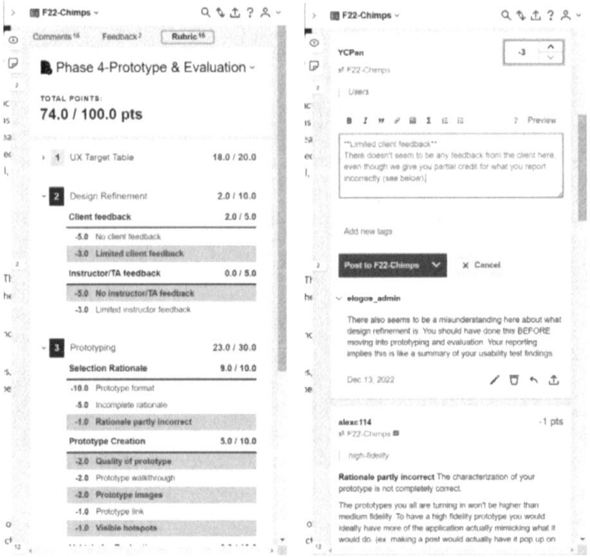

Figure 1. The Rubric tab (a-left) for grading online reports, along with the augmented Comments tab (b-right) for editing/adjusting graded comments.

To augment the grading and feedback process even further, lead graders and instructors can either edit existing comments and scores or add further explanations to justify an applied rubric item (as is the case with the added comment by *elogos_admin* in Figure 1b). To facilitate design requirement #3, we included a "Graders only" option for replying to existing comments, which allows inter-grader communication about project assessment hidden from student view (see Figure 2). This feature, in addition to having multiple graders work on the same project report—the tool recognizes changes and allows a grader to update the highlights, comments, and rubric deductions with any changes made by someone else—makes e²Logos a much more collaborative grading tool than other currently available software.

Finally, the tool allows graders to leave general feedback through the Feedback tab, which may include comments on the overall quality of the submission or advice for future work. The same tab can be used for student regrade requests, where students can question some parts of the assessment or provide extra rationale for their design choices that the grader(s) might have missed, contributing to a more equitable grading process. This is similar to functionality offered by Gradescope and satisfies our last design requirement from the list above. Future versions of e²Logos will allow an instructor to choose if students could reply to existing comments for regrade purposes, offering their rationale on a comment-by-comment basis.

It is also worth mentioning that in an effort to increase grading consistency, a common challenge for evaluating PBL and especially design work, e²Logos allows for multiple grader-groups to evaluate the same sample submission. In this scenario, every grader has their own group which they use to assess a sample project report. The instructor is able, then, to switch between grader-groups reviewing the applied rubric items (gray items in Figure 1a), commenting and providing extra guidance to graders during a grading practice session.

IV. METHODS

A. Usability Study Context

In order to test the efficacy of the tool from the graders' perspective, we conducted a usability test of e[2]Logos in fall 2022 (F22). Since we have been using Gradescope's Essay submission feature for the 2021-2022 academic year, we also tested the usability of Gradescope for grading technical reports in spring 2022 (S22). Gradescope discontinued the use of this type of submission since summer 2022, so we were unable to collect data beyond that point. Both grading tools were tested on an upper-level engineering course on HCI, usually taken by third- and fourth-year undergraduate students at a large public U.S. university. The course employed a PBL approach, where student work is broken down into four project phases throughout the whole semester and is submitted as a technical report on a website. The reports typically include a variety of static text and dynamic content, like image carousels, embedded Google slide presentations, or links to external applications (e.g., YouTube videos and Figma prototypes).

Since Gradescope's Essay assignment type required uploading of student work as a PDF file, student groups in S22 were instructed to export their website to a PDF file. The grading rubric was created by the instructor of the course in Gradescope's dedicated tool or a json file for each one of the semesters, respectively. The rubrics were broken down in categories (e.g., *Prototyping*) and sub-categories (e.g., *Rationale*), even though Gradescope did not support the extra level like e[2]Logos did (see Figure 1). The teaching assistants (TAs) of the course were then tasked to use each grading software to grade the last two phases of the project in each semester. Grading of the first two phases was used as practice, so TAs could familiarize themselves with the tools' features and their application. The grading process involves three passes (TAs, project lead TA, instructor), where each user grades and leaves feedback on student work, as well as suggestions for improvement. When grading is completed—usually within a week—submissions are returned and scores/feedback are reviewed by students, either on Gradescope (S22) or the website itself with the associated e[2]Logos Chrome extension installed (F22). Since the tool was under development during the same time, graders were asked to install (unpack) the extension on their browser instead of downloading it from the Chrome store. As part of this usability test, we did not evaluate the effectiveness of the feedback provided with the tools, in terms of student learning.

The usability study was approved by the Institutional Review Board of the University of Virginia with protocol IRB-SBS#5515/2022.

B. Measuring Instruments

Assessing the efficacy of the two grading tools involved a two-prong strategy. The TAs and instructor first created a UX target table, inspired by a typical usability engineering process [35], to measure specific UX goals related to the project report assessment (Table I). Our decision about goals was led by the two key outcomes included in our research question: efficiency and ease of use.

TABLE I. UX TARGET TABLE FOR EVALUATING THE GRADING TOOLS

Goal	Measure	Instrument	Metric
Efficiency	User performance	BT1: Finish project grading	Avg. time on task
Efficiency	Critical incidents (limitations)	BT1: Finish project grading	Avg. # of instances impeding grading
Efficiency	User performance	BT2[a]: Apply a predefined deduction	Avg. time on task
Accuracy	Experienced usage error	BT2[a]: Apply a predefined deduction	Avg. # of errors
Ease of use	Experienced usage error	BT3: Leave a comment to a deduction	Avg. # of errors
Ease of use	Experienced usage error	BT4: Remove rubric deduction	Avg. # of errors
Efficiency	User performance	BT5: Write general feedback	Avg. time on task
Ease of use	User performance (communication)	BT6: Communicate grading issues/questions	Avg. # of times a comment was left for lead TA or instructor
Efficiency	User performance (consistency)	BT7[b]: Reviewing an existing graded project	Avg. time on task
Effectiveness	User performance (consistency)	BT7[b]: Reviewing an existing graded project	Avg. # of changes to existing grading
Effectiveness	User performance (consistency)	BT7[b]: Reviewing an existing graded project	Avg. # of critical incidents

a. This measurement involved selecting a rubric item from the lower sections, like a Bonus.

b. Data for BT7 were measured both during the lead TA's and the instructor's grading review.

Benchmark tasks (BTs) 1-6 referred to TAs as graders, while BT7 referred to the lead TA and instructor as grader-reviewers. We then used a questionnaire for measuring the perceived user experience (UX) by the TAs. We chose the User Experience Questionnaire (UEQ) [36] over the System Usability Scale (SUS) [37] or similar instruments, because the former covers a broader range of subjective measures related to using interactive software. More specifically, the UEQ gathers insights about an application's perceived usability in terms of six factors: *attractiveness*, *perspicuity* (commonly known as learnability), *efficiency*, *dependability* (also known as user control and freedom), *stimulation*, and *novelty*.

C. Participants

Nine undergraduate college students were recruited for the usability studies over the two semesters. In each semester, the five students that served as TAs for the HCI in Software Development course, part of the Computer Science department curriculum, were the grader-participants that helped evaluate the two grading applications. Only one of them was a returning TA in F22, who also served as the lead TA in that semester. No demographic data was recorded about the participants, as they were deemed irrelevant to the outcomes of the study. Since participants were mainly conducting their regular TA duties, no compensation was given for their participation. The instructor of the course remained the same in both terms.

D. Procedure

The procedure followed during each one of the semesters was exactly the same, with the grading tool being the only difference. The TAs would start grading the project submissions either on Gradescope (S22) or the website itself with the e²Logos extension (F22), using the same pre-defined rubric. Since grading of the earlier phases was not recorded for testing purposes, TAs had the opportunity to learn using the software. While conducting the student project report grading for phases 3-4, TA participants were asked to log the different data requested in the UX target table (see *Metric* in TABLE I.). This was done on a separate spreadsheet created specifically for this case in each semester. When all grading was done, the lead TA would take over to review submitted grades and TA feedback/comments. During this process, the lead TA would often need to coordinate with the graders to resolve any concerns with grading. While e²Logos provided the option to collaborate through replies to graded comments hidden from students (Figure 2), grading review on Gradescope was done offline through platforms and tools like email, GroupMe, or Discord. After the second pass, the instructor reviewed the graded submissions and made any final adjustments to grading/feedback. Similarly, communication with TA-graders was done either outside the tool (S22) or within the tool (F22), for resolving grading inconsistencies. Both the lead TA and the instructor logged their data (i.e., BT7 in TABLE I.), before recording their updated project submission score.

Right after the last project phase was graded at the end of the semester, the TAs would complete the UEQ—created and administered on Qualtrics—to capture their overall experience using each software. No discussion would precede this evaluation to avoid influencing the participants' opinion. Two open-ended fields were added to the UEQ to record the positive aspects and points of improvement for each software.

Figure 2. Within-tool communication between TA grader (*kate*), lead TA (*alex*), and instructor (*elogos_admin*), which is hidden from students (the lock icon indicates "Graders only" replies).

V. Results

A. Analysis of UX Goals

The analyzed e²Logos data derived from a total of 506 rubric items and comments applied/left by the five TAs for the two graded project phases included in the study (86 items/ comments deleted), and 111 items/comments left by the instructor (6 of them deleted). For Gradescope, there were 419 final comments left by the five TAs and the instructor (there is no grader designation stored during grading and no record of deleted items/comments in that software). Per our initial UX evaluation plan (Table I), we consolidated all data from both semesters in a spreadsheet, identifying any missing data points and outliers. The only outliers removed—more than two standard deviations from the mean—were two extreme times recorded by one TA for BT5 in S22-Phase 3. Table II summarizes the final values for each benchmark task per semester and project phase, as well as the total average values. Even though we broke down BT7 data (logged during grading review) to comments and rubric items edited/added/removed, we decided to aggregate them in one value (#changes) per our original BT7 metric. Gradescope was used to assess/grade a total of 38 student reports in PDF format (19 project groups in S22), while e²Logos was used to assess/grade 20 online student reports (10 project groups in F22). Statistical analysis included the comparison of the Total calculated values (bold).

TABLE II. LOGGED UX GOAL DATA FOR GRADED PROJECT PHASES

		e²Logos [N=20 [a]]			Gradescope [N=38 [a]]		
	Metric	*Ph-3*	*Ph-4*	*Total*	*Ph-3*	*Ph-4*	*Total*
BT1	mins	62.00	61.20	**61.60**	60.53	71.32	**65.92**
BT1	#incidents	0.30	0.10	**0.20**	2.32	**1.95	**2.13**
BT1 [b]	*#items*	*10.70*	*10.10*	***10.40***	*8.68*	**6.32*	*7.50*
BT1 [b]	*#comment*	*5.40*	*4.67*	***5.03***	*6.16*	*5.26*	***5.71***
BT2	secs	3.50	1.70	**2.60**	8.58	**6.16	**7.37**
BT2	#errors	0.00	0.00	**0.00**	0.37	*0.37	**0.37**
BT3	#errors	0.00	0.00	**0.00**	0.68	**0.58	**0.63**
BT4	#errors	0.90	0.00	**0.45**	1.11	0.37	**0.74**
BT5	secs	135.00	175.40	**157.44**	194.00	155.47	**170.88**
BT6	#contacts	0.70	0.70	**0.70**	0.37	0.53	**0.45**
BT7 [c]	mins	35.88	23.38	**29.63**	28.14	[e]	**28.14**
BT7 [c]	#changes	5.25	6.25	**5.75**	4.45	[e]	**4.45**
BT7 [c]	#incidents	0.00	0.50	**0.25**	0.44	[e]	**0.44**
$BT7_i$ [c]	mins	28.30	20.60	**24.45**	27.11	14.71	**20.91**
$BT7_i$ [c]	#changes	6.70	3.50	**5.10**	6.21	3.26	**4.74**
$BT7_i$ [c]	#incidents	0.10	0.00	**0.05**	1.26	**0.47	**0.87**
BT7 [b]	$\Delta1_{score}$ [d]	*3.00*	*4.40*	***3.70***	*4.05*	*3.11*	***3.58***
BT7 [b]	$\Delta2_{score}$ [d]	*4.50*	*3.13*	***3.81***	*4.42*	[e]	***4.42***

a. Sample size denotes the number of total observations; some metrics had missing data.

b. Data in italics were not included in the original UX goals but were analyzed for context.

c. The first BT7 metrics are from the lead TA's review and the last from the instructor's (i) review.

d. Difference between instructor and TAs (Δ1), and instructor and lead TA (Δ2) project scores.

e. The lead TA did not complete their review for project phase 4, therefore no values are included.

* Gray BTs were significant at the <0.05 level (*) or highly significant at the <0.001 level (**).

We used an independent-samples (unequal variance assumed), two-tailed Student's t-test to examine any statistical difference between the measured UX targets for the two grading tools. The null hypothesis was that there will be no difference between the two grading tools in terms of measured outcomes and sample data drawn from the observations were partly normally distributed. For non-normally distributed data, a non-parametric test's results are reported, using Mann-Whitney U test [38]. Missing values were handled by excluding cases on an analysis-by-analysis basis and only significant findings are reported below (indicated with gray in Table II).

Our analysis found that using e²Logos presented TA graders with a statistically significantly lower number of critical incidents (*U = 112, n = 58, p < 0.001*) as compared to Gradescope, while they applied a higher number of rubric items for the two project phases (*t = -6.36, n = 58, p = 0.041*). While applying an item lower in the rubric, TA graders were significantly slower (*U = 45.50, n=58, p < 001*) and did more errors (*U = 280, n = 58, p = 0.013*) than when completing the same task with e²Logos. TAs also did a significantly higher number of errors when completing the most common task of leaving a comment using the rubric in Gradescope than using e²Logos (*U = 240, n = 58, p = 0.002*). Finally, during the instructor's review of the graded submissions, the instructor reported significantly more critical incidents when using Gradescope than when using e²Logos (*U = 204.50, n = 58, p = 0.001*). No other UX target was found to reject the null hypothesis.

B. UEQ Comparison Analysis

We used an independent-samples (equal variance), two-tailed Student's t-test to examine if the two grading tools performed equally well in terms of the six UX factors recorded by the UEQ. The results of the t-tests with significance values are summarized in Table III and depicted in Figure 3. Results indicate that e²Logos outperformed Gradescope—rejecting the null hypothesis—in *attractiveness (d = 2.44), efficiency (d = 2.20), dependability (d = 2.32)*, and *stimulation (d = 1.68)*, while there was no statistical difference in *perspicuity (d = 1.29)* and *novelty (d = 1.84)*. A Cronbach's alpha test indicated that all six scales were reliable above a threshold of $\alpha = 0.711$ for both samples (tools), with average $\alpha = 0.789$. For assessing e²Logos the average was $\alpha = 0.7287$, while Gradescope's assessment using the UEQ yielded an $\alpha = 0.662$. All results indicate an acceptable to good internal consistency considering the small sample of the study [39].

TABLE III. T-TEST COMPARISON STATISTICS FOR UEQ SCALES

	e²Logos		Gradescope		Statistics	
Scale	*Mean*	*STD*	*Mean*	*STD*	*t stat*	*p value*
Attractiveness	1.30	0.88	-0.83	0.87	3.852	0.005*
Perspicuity	1.35	0.84	0.20	0.89	2.100	0.069
Efficiency	1.55	0.74	-1.05	1.18	4.183	0.003*
Dependability	0.65	0.86	-0.80	1.10	2.329	0.048*
Stimulation	1.00	0.64	-0.35	0.80	2.946	0.019*
Novelty	0.85	1.04	-0.35	0.65	2.186	0.060

* Indicates statistical significance at the 0.05 level (95% confidence intervals).

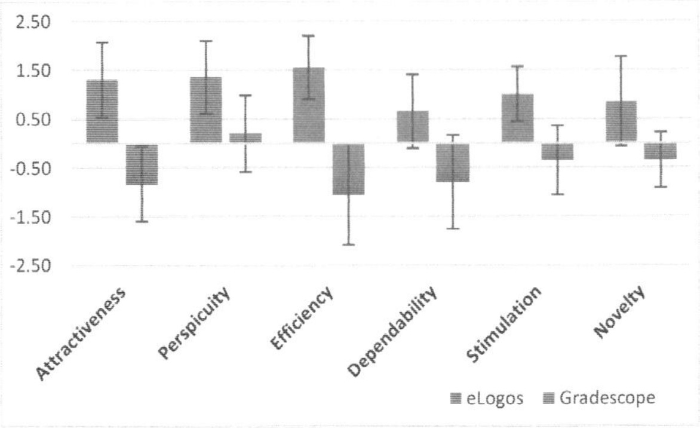

Figure 3. UEQ comparison between e²Logos and Gradescope.

C. Qualitative Findings

Analysis of participant input through the UEQ open-ended questions involved reviewing and grouping responses in relevant themes. We considered using thematic analysis, but the pool of responses was too limited for this technique to yield any significant benefit. Overall, e²Logos was perceived very positively by the TAs, mostly commenting about the constant availability of a rubric for easy reference, being able to highlight and indicate within the web page exactly what an item (deduction) refers to, and the flexibility offered by being able to adjust points and comments, customizing the score and feedback to each project. On the downside, there were a couple of complaints about the screen space that the sidebar occupied, obstructing part of the text while reading/grading. Another complaint was about a URL identifier (authuser) that was added to the websites by Chrome based on the active Google account and as a result comments/highlights were not displayed. This demanded manually deleting the identifier text from the browser's address bar. Finally, the issue of having to download and install the extension manually due to it not being an official extension in the Chrome store, was commented by one TA.

For Gradescope, positive feedback included the ease of reviewing the rubric using the sidebar (very similar to e²Logos), while also being able to search for a rubric item using the search box embedded in a drop-down menu that appeared after highlighting text. The workflow was found to be fairly intuitive, while TAs who have been involved with the course in prior semesters commended the significant improvement over using a grading spreadsheet. Downsides mainly had to do with the restrictions imposed by the non-searchable PDF format, which often included non-selectable text (depending on the website export process used by the students submitting the report). The PDF format made loading each submission rather slow (reports were often more than 30 pages) and prevented inclusion of dynamic content, demanding graders to visit the actual website to check and evaluate that material. The long drop-down menu with all deductions was found cumbersome to navigate, while not being able to adjust grading based on each submission's quality was noted multiple times as restrictive. Finally, the lack of collaboration while grading—comments left by another grader would not update automatically—was commented by two of the participants.

VI. Discussion

Overall, the findings from our analysis comparing the newly developed tool with an established grading software for evaluating digital online reports was very positive. However, the lack of similar usability studies on grading and annotation software does not allow us to compare our findings with prior work. Therefore, we will focus on discussing our comparison results as an effort to extract design implications for developing similar interactive grading software, also acknowledging the limitations of the current work.

A. UX Outcomes and Design Implications

Correlating the results from the UEQ and our own UX targets (Table I), it is obvious that e[2]Logos satisfied the most significant goal of efficiency as compared to Gradescope's Essay assignment type. The most critical task for grading software of applying a predefined deduction from the rubric (BT2) took significantly less time on average, $M_{elogos} = 2.60s$ *vs* $M_{Gradescope} = 7.37s$, with no errors reported across the two project phases for our own tool, including both grading and commenting (BT3). Additionally, there were statistically fewer critical incidents reported for e[2]Logos both during TA grading (BT1), $M_{elogos} = 0.20$ *vs* $M_{Gradescope} = 2.13$, and instructor review (BT7), $M_{elogos} = 0.05$ *vs* $M_{Gradescope} = 0.87$, an important indicator of improved efficiency, as well. Even though grading time on average was not decreased significantly using our tool, it is important to note that TAs left significantly more comments on average using e[2]Logos, $M_{elogos} = 10.40$ *vs* $M_{Gradescope} = 7.50$.

The new tool was also found to be more dependable, even if marginally, than Gradescope's Essay assignment type. We believe this stems from the flexibility that e[2]Logos offers to graders, as well as the fact that it is very responsive and robust compared to Gradescope, which frequently crashed or took a long time to load large PDF files. Regarding inter-grader communication, despite e[2]Logos offering a within-tool mechanism for collaboration and resolution of grading concerns, logged comments by TAs revealed that they perceived using outside tools like Discord or Groupme as "easy" and "unproblematic". Also, even though our tool was found more motivating to use, there was no significant difference in terms of clarity and ease of use (perspicuity for the UEQ). We attribute that to the multiple issues and unfinished features that TAs had to tolerate due to using the software being under development. Some features, such as the lead TA's access to edit/delete comments, were added at a later iteration of development, undoubtedly affecting the grading experience.

Qualitative feedback from the participants is fully supportive and explanatory of these findings. e[2]Logos proved to be more dependable than Gradescope in providing graders with the flexibility of adjusting the applied score and associated comment to fit the quality of assessed project work (satisfying our 2nd design requirement). Collaborative grading was only attempted in the early phases because it would interfere with accurate logging of individual grading in the final two phases that were used in our study; therefore, we have no solid findings about our 3rd requirement besides the ease of communicating through replies on graded comments. Such communication, however, did not yield more consistent grading results with e[2]Logos, as is shown by the calculated average project score difference between instructor and TAs, $\Delta 1_{elogos} = 3.70$ *vs* $\Delta 1_{Gradescope} = 3.58$, as well as instructor and lead TA, $\Delta 2_{elogos} = 3.81$ *vs* $\Delta 2_{Gradescope} = 4.42$. We attribute this to the limitations discussed below and the level of subjectivity that is involved in grading design work, a necessary evil of HCI projects.

B. Limitations

We need to acknowledge that the usability test had a rather limited sample of just nine participants, which does not allow us to draw statistically robust conclusions. The unbalanced number of projects between semesters might have affected the quality of grading done by the TAs (i.e., graders in S22 being more rushed to finish grading), but more importantly, the quality of the project submissions themselves was probably a confounding factor for the logged grading data between the two semesters (i.e., some submissions being harder to grade). We need also recognize that the process of logging data in the spreadsheet had a negative impact both on grading accuracy (distraction) but also on the measured completion time (overhead caused from switching between application and logfile). Finally, testing of e[2]Logos happened while the tool was being developed with different features added and refined between graded project phases. This had the unintended side-effect of influencing the measured user experience (e.g., negative comment about needing to manually update the extension).

VII. Conclusions and Future Work

This paper reports the results of a first-of-its-kind usability study comparing the efficiency and learnability of a newly developed grading tool, e[2]Logos, against Gradescope's Essay assignment type, for grading open-ended design projects. The findings were encouraging, revealing that the new tool was perceived as superior to its competitor in terms of efficiency, dependability, stimulation, and attractiveness based on the UEQ. Logged data while grading two phases of a design project in an HCI class, as well as open-ended comments by the participants (TAs in the course), justified the perceived higher efficiency and dependability (user control and freedom) of e[2]Logos. Finally, our contribution includes a list of design requirements we argue any similar software should satisfy.

Our immediate plans involve finishing development of the e[2]Logos Chrome extension, making it available and testing it in more courses at the university. This will allow collecting data from a much larger sample and assessing more accurately the usability of the tool, this time comparing it with the benchmark data set of typical interactive products offered by the UEQ researchers [40]. Even more importantly, we plan to evaluate the learning efficacy of the type and quality of feedback that can be provided by the tool. This will entail collecting data from students in courses that employ e[2]Logos, but it demands that reviewing and acting on the provided feedback is part of the learning objectives of the course. Such an approach might involve techniques like feedforward [41], with students' academic performance being compared between the ones who access the feedback on e[2]Logos and the students who do not review (or respond to) their graded comments on the platform. Overall, we hope our findings and design requirements tested can provide guidance for future design and development of assessment tools of online student PBL work.

ACKNOWLEDGMENTS

We would like to thank all teaching assistants who dedicated extra time to learn the new tool and log their grading data during the two semesters this study was conducted.

REFERENCES

[1] B. Pérez and Á. L. Rubio, "A Project-Based Learning Approach for Enhancing Learning Skills and Motivation in Software Engineering," in *Proceedings of the 51st ACM Technical Symposium on Computer Science Education*, Feb. 2020, pp. 309–315. doi: 10.1145/3328778.3366891.

[2] J. Zawojewski, H. Diefes-Dux, and K. Bowman, *Models and modeling in engineering education: Designing experiences for all students*. Rotterdam, the Netherlands: Sense Publishers, 2008.

[3] T. Pinar Yildirim, L. Shuma, and M. Besterfield Sacre, "Model-eliciting activities: assessing engineering student problem solving and skill integration processes," *Int J Eng Educ*, vol. 26, no. 4, pp. 831–845, 2010.

[4] Y. Kharitonova, Y. Luo, and J. Park, "Redesigning a software development course as a preparation for a capstone: An experience report," in *SIGCSE 2019 - Proceedings of the 50th ACM Technical Symposium on Computer Science Education*, Feb. 2019, pp. 153–159. doi: 10.1145/3287324.3287498.

[5] J. J. Olarte, C. Dominguez, A. Jaime, and F. J. Garcia-Izquierdo, "Student and Staff Perceptions of Key Aspects of Computer Science Engineering Capstone Projects," *IEEE Transactions on Education*, vol. 59, no. 1, pp. 45–51, Feb. 2016, doi: 10.1109/TE.2015.2427118.

[6] V. Van den Bergh, D. Mortelmans, P. Spooren, P. Van Petegem, D. Gijbels, and G. Vanthournout, "New assessment modes within project-based education - the stakeholders," *Studies in Educational Evaluation*, vol. 32, no. 4, pp. 345–368, Jan. 2006, doi: 10.1016/J.STUEDUC.2006.10.005.

[7] L. B. Nilson and C. J. Stanny, *Specifications Grading : Restoring Rigor, Motivating Students, and Saving Faculty Time*. Stylus Publishing, 2014.

[8] M. Carmosino and M. Minnes, "Adaptive Rubrics," in *Proceedings of the 51st ACM Technical Symposium on Computer Science Education*, Feb. 2020, vol. 7, no. 20, pp. 549–555. doi: 10.1145/3328778.3366946.

[9] A. Singh, S. Karayev, K. Gutowski, and P. Abbeel, "Gradescope: A fast, flexible, and fair system for scalable assessment of handwritten work," in *L@S 2017 - Proceedings of the 4th (2017) ACM Conference on Learning at Scale*, Apr. 2017, pp. 81–88. doi: 10.1145/3051457.3051466.

[10] R. K. Ellis, "Field Guide to Learning Management Systems." ASTD Learning Circuits, 2009. Accessed: Mar. 11, 2023. [Online]. Available: http://www.astd.org/NR/rdonlyres/12ECDB99-3B91-403E-9B15-7E597444645D/23395/LMS_fieldguide_20091.pdf

[11] Hypothes.is. https://web.hypothes.is/ (accessed Feb. 25, 2023).

[12] M. C. Kitsantas, "Supporting Student Self-Regulated Learning in Problem-and Project-Based Learning," *Interdisciplinary Journal of Problem-Based Learning*, vol. 7, no. 2, pp. 9–14, 2013, doi: 10.7771/1541-5015.1339.

[13] J. Hattie and H. Timperley, "The Power of Feedback," *Rev Educ Res*, vol. 77, no. 1, pp. 81–112, Nov. 2007, doi: 10.3102/003465430298487.

[14] M. E. Cardella, H. A. Diefes-Dux, M. Verleger, A. Fry, and M. T. Carnes, "Work in progress - Using multiple methods to investigate the role of feedback in open-ended activities," *Proceedings - Frontiers in Education Conference, FIE*, 2011, doi: 10.1109/FIE.2011.6143106.

[15] S. Atwood and A. Singh, "Improved Pedagogy Enabled by Assessment Using Gradescope," in *2018 ASEE Annual Conference & Exposition Proceedings*, Jun. 2018. doi: 10.18260/1-2--30627.

[16] A. W. Stevens, "Assessing Student Learning Using a Digital Grading Platform," *Applied Economics Teaching Resources (AETR)*, vol. 1, no. 1, pp. 18–24, 2019, doi: 10.22004/AG.ECON.294011.

[17] S. A. Raza, W. Qazi, K. A. Khan, and J. Salam, "Social Isolation and Acceptance of the Learning Management System (LMS) in the time of COVID-19 Pandemic: An Expansion of the UTAUT Model," *Journal of Educational Computing Research*, vol. 59, no. 2, pp. 183–208, Apr. 2021, doi: 10.1177/0735633120960421.

[18] Moodle | Open-source learning platform. https://moodle.org/ (accessed Feb. 25, 2023).

[19] Y. A. Hussain and M. Jaeger, "LMS-supported PBL assessment in an undergraduate engineering program-Case study," *Computer Applications in Engineering Education*, vol. 26, no. 5, pp. 1915–1929, Sep. 2018, doi: 10.1002/cae.22037.

[20] Blackboard | Educational Technology Services. https://www.blackboard.com/ (accessed Mar. 12, 2023).

[21] F. Martin, "Blackboard as the Learning Management System of a Computer Literacy Course," *MERLOT Journal of Online Learning and Teaching*, vol. 4, no. 2, pp. 138–145, 2008.

[22] RCampus, "iRubric: Home of free rubric tools." https://www.rcampus.com/indexrubric.cfm (accessed Mar. 02, 2023).

[23] D. Myers, A. Peterson, A. Matthews, and M. Sanchez, "One Team's Journey with iRubrics," *Curr Issues Emerg Elearn*, vol. 4, no. 1, pp. 248–261, Jul. 2018.

[24] F. Burrack and D. J. M. Thompson, "Canvas (LMS) as a means for effective student learning assessment across an institution of higher education," *Journal of Assessment in Higher Education*, vol. 2, no. 1, pp. 1–19, Jan. 2021, doi: 10.32473/JAHE.V2I1.125129.

[25] B. Huang and M. S. Y. Jong, "Developing a Generic Rubric for Evaluating Students' Work in STEM Education," in *Proceedings - 2020 International Symposium on Educational Technology, ISET 2020*, Aug. 2020, pp. 210–213. doi: 10.1109/ISET49818.2020.00053.

[26] D. Grossu, "Using the Hypothesis Tool in a Synchronous Learning Environment," 2021. Accessed: Feb. 25, 2023. [Online]. Available: https://www.merlot.org/merlot/viewMaterial.htm?id=773409069

[27] C. C. Goller, M. Vandegrift, W. Cross, and D. S. Smyth, "Sharing Notes Is Encouraged: Annotating and Cocreating with Hypothes.is and Google Docs †," *J Microbiol Biol Educ*, vol. 22, no. 1, pp. 1–4, Apr. 2021, doi: 10.1128/jmbe.v22i1.2135.

[28] Diigo. https://www.diigo.com/ (accessed Feb. 26, 2023).

[29] V. P. Dennen, M. L. Cates, and L. M. Bagdy, "Using Diigo to Engage Learners in Course Readings: Activity Design and Formative Evaluation," *International Journal for Educational Media and Technology*, vol. 11, no. 2, pp. 3–15, 2017.

[30] DIGI[cation] | Make Learning Visible. https://www.digication.com/ (accessed Mar. 09, 2023).

[31] P. Nokelainen, J. Kurhila, M. Miettinen, P. Floreen, and H. Tirri, "Evaluating the role of a shared document-based annotation tool in learner-centered collaborative learning," in *Proceedings - 3rd IEEE International Conference on Advanced Learning Technologies, ICALT 2003*, 2003, pp. 200–203. doi: 10.1109/ICALT.2003.1215056.

[32] T. Ryan, M. Henderson, and M. Phillips, "Feedback modes matter: Comparing student perceptions of digital and non-digital feedback modes in higher education," *British Journal of*

Educational Technology, vol. 50, no. 3, pp. 1507–1523, May 2019, doi: 10.1111/bjet.12749.

[33] S.-W. Yeh and J.-J. Lo, "Using online annotations to support error correction and corrective feedback," *Comput Educ*, vol. 52, no. 4, pp. 882–892, May 2009, doi: 10.1016/j.compedu.2008.12.014.

[34] J. Wolfe, "Annotation technologies: A software and research review," *Comput Compos*, vol. 19, no. 4, pp. 471–497, Dec. 2002, doi: 10.1016/S8755-4615(02)00144-5.

[35] R. Hartson and Pardha. S. Pyla, *The UX Book: Process and Guidelines for Ensuring a Quality User Experience*. Elsevier, 2012.

[36] B. Laugwitz, T. Held, and M. Schrepp, "Construction and Evaluation of a User Experience Questionnaire," in *HCI and Usability for Education and Work (SAUB 2008) Lecture Notes in Computer Science*, vol. 5298, A. Hlzinger, Ed. Berlin, Heidelberg: Springer Verlag, 2008, pp. 63–76. doi: 10.1007/978-3-540-89350-9_6.

[37] J. Kirakowski and M. Corbett, "Measuring User Satisfaction," in *Proceedings of the Fourth Conference of the British Computer Society on People and computers IV*, 1988, pp. 329–338.

[38] K. L. Sainani, "Dealing With Non-normal Data," *PM&R*, vol. 4, no. 12, pp. 1001–1005, Dec. 2012, doi: 10.1016/J.PMRJ.2012.10.013.

[39] K. S. Taber, "The Use of Cronbach's Alpha When Developing and Reporting Research Instruments in Science Education," *Res Sci Educ*, vol. 48, no. 6, pp. 1273–1296, Dec. 2018, doi: 10.1007/S11165-016-9602-2/TABLES/1.

[40] M. Schrepp, A. Hinderks, and J. Thomaschewski, "Construction of a Benchmark for the User Experience Questionnaire (UEQ)," *International Journal of Interactive Multimedia and Artificial Intelligence*, vol. 4, no. 4, p. 40, 2017, doi: 10.9781/IJIMAI.2017.445.

[41] N. Duncan, "'Feed-forward': improving students' use of tutors' comments," *Assess Eval High Educ*, vol. 32, no. 3, pp. 271–283, 2007, doi: 10.1080/02602930600896498.

Reassessing the Effect of Videoconferencing Features on Trust in Triadic Negotiations

Siavash Kazemian
Dept. of Computer Science
University of Toronto
Toronto, Canada
kazemian@cs.toronto.edu

Cosmin Munteanu
Dept. of Systems Design Engineering
University of Waterloo
Waterloo, Canada
cosmin@taglab.ca

Gerald Penn
Dept. of Computer Science
University of Toronto
Toronto, Canada
gpenn@cs.toronto.edu

***Abstract*—Globalization, lingering threats of pandemics and ever-increasing travel costs have made videoconferencing a necessary tool in many environments, ranging from corporate meetings with potential clients who may not have met previously, to mediated negotiations between antagonists who must necessarily remain at a safe distance. This raises several questions about how videoconferencing affects the efficiency, fairness and trust that is desired of negotiations. Significant research has been conducted on the effectiveness of video-based collaborative environments, and more recently, on how one specific aspect of trust called credibility develops in videoconference-mediated, collaborative, one-on-one social dilemmas. Much less is known, however, about how typical videoconferencing features affect the full spectrum of trust-connoting attributes that are known within the social science literature, or outside the idealized confines of two-party social dilemmas. We report here the results of a broader experimental investigation that has exhibited significance across other dimensions of trust (dependency and expectancy), both objectively and subjectively, in the presence of more videoconferencing features than just video (chat and screen sharing), and in a realistic three-way negotiation. We make recommendations for designers, administrators, and corporate decision makers with regard to appropriately using these features in videoconferencing systems.**

***Index Terms*—videoconferencing; trust; technology-mediated negotiation; chat systems; shared displays.**

I. Introduction

Videoconferencing is often used in settings where participants do not know each other well, and yet need to engage in sensitive transactions. These transactions invariably require some degree of trust, often involve negotiations as part or all of the transaction, and at times also involve the sharing of documents and presentations, or the collaborative editing of a document, such as a license agreement.

Often such meetings are asymmetrical, for example two participants from a large company, each of them being situated in a different location, engage by videoconference with a third potential client who is located in yet another place. Many videoconferencing systems support text-chat functionality that can allow for back-channel private communications in these cases. But there must still be at least some degree of trust. It has been argued that trust is more difficult to establish through computer-mediated communication (CMC) than through face-to-face communication when it lacks body language and other cues that are used to build trust [1]–[4]. It is widely assumed that streaming live video of the participants will mitigate this problem to some extent. Does it? What about in relation to other features, such as display-sharing or chatting?

The answer turns out to depend on what we mean by "trust" and which CMC features we intend to use. The two studies presented here evaluate three features of videoconferencing systems — all by now staples of that industry — in terms of their effect on several dimensions of trust. They do so, furthermore, in a more realistic setting than a two-party social dilemma — by now, the staple of HCI studies of trust. *Social dilemmas*, such as the well-known prisoner's dilemma problem, pit two or more players against each other in a task in which the pursuit of rational self-interest by every player leads to an outcome that is worse than if they pursue some other coordinated strategy that contradicts their self-interests. By contrast, our studies involve a realistic, three-party business negotiation, in which participants had competing interests, the outcomes of the negotiation were not a zero-sum game, and the negotiated settlements (or "deals") were not necessarily symmetrical. Triadic and higher-order interaction effects have been argued [6] to be essential to understanding the dynamics and formation of social networks. Trust has been shown to be a key potential factor in keeping certain triadic, collaborative problem-solving activities on track in the face of lapses in mutual understanding [7]. This paper attempts to revisit earlier experimentation on trust in CMC in view of these more recent developments.

This paper demonstrates that there are significant differences that emerge in risk tolerance and in other dimensions of trust through variations to affordances that are independent of the presence of video. These other dimensions are significantly impaired by the addition of private chatting functionality and significantly enhanced by screen-sharing functionality. Earlier work on video-enhanced versus audio-only interfaces has found the provable benefits of adding high-quality video or viewrange-expanded video to be less straightforward to quantify. Ours is also among the very few studies to date to have observed significance in an objective measure of trust (specifically, risk tolerance) other than efficiency. These results were observable because of a controlled experimental design that eschews social dilemmas and embraces a fuller conception of trust that is already pervasive within the social sciences.

II. RELATED WORK ON THE CHOSEN AFFORDANCES

Video itself has already received a fair amount of attention.[1] The two most closely related studies to what we undertake here are those of Bos et al. [8] and Teoh et al. [9], both of which we shall consider in detail presently. The former concerned videoconferencing relative to three alternatives; the latter compared two different videoconferencing views.

In qualitative studies [10], video has been argued to "build trust and relationship," and even to discourage deception [11]. Where measured, the frame rate of the video seems almost totally irrelevant, on the other hand; even showing the other parties' faces occasionally in a series of still images is enough to achieve the same effect [12].[2] Another study [14] used a social dilemma game to investigate potentially trust-improving warm-up activities, such as casual introductory interactions by email, visual identification through photos and reading dossiers of personal information. Of these, visual identification was found to be the most significant by far.

As for related work on chatting and screen-sharing, there have been other studies of chat systems apart from Bos et al.'s [8], e.g., [15], but they likewise consider chat in the absence of video and audio, or, in one exceptional case, speech synthesized from text chats [16]. This is mainly a reflection of their age; we consider video and audio now to be a minimum baseline that any software for negotiation would incorporate. In other studies, chat, where it is present at all, often augments at least one of video or audio. One study [17] compared face-to-face communication with text chat in both low-interdependence tasks like brainstorming and high-interdependence tasks like negotiation, and found openness and trust to be beneficial to the highly interdependent task. They also found that a wide "temporal scope" in the relationships of participants (i.e., how long they had known each other) mitigates the difference between face-to-face and text-chat communications. Another [18] conversely observed higher levels of trust emerging from both video-mediated and chat-mediated brainstorming tasks than from similarly mediated negotiation tasks. Studies of shared workspaces (called "shared displays" in the literature, although this does not refer to streaming video broadcasts) are comparatively rare. One study [19] observes that shared displays may create a false sense of shared data validity in certain collaborative work environments.

III. RELATED WORK ON TRUST

In one respect, our present study continues a thread of HCI research that is perhaps epitomized by Bos et al. [8], who studied differences in trust as outcomes of a two-person social dilemma resolved through videoconferencing, a three-way phone call or text chatting software, relative to a face-to-face topline. Their subjective, Likert-scaled measures of trust are based on Butler [20], together with correlations of those subjective measures to ultimate aggregated payoff. Statistically significant correlations, as a function of the communication modality, were calculated to group payoff (0.53), self-ratings of trustworthiness (0.69) and self-ratings of consistency (0.61). The trust responses were found to have the same profile of pairwise differences as group payoff. There are important differences in baseline selection relative to our study; the alternatives used by [8] were either a phone call or text chatting, but not even audio with chatting. Even today, audio with chatting is still a very common CMC setup for low-bandwidth communication. Otherwise, this was a very thorough study, but a study based upon only one dimension of trust.

A. *What is Trust?*

Our own five-dimensional view of trust is based upon the instrument that Alston [21] selected in a study of trust in technology-driven organizations, called the Organizational Trust Index [22], although for clarity we will use less domain-specific terms for the dimensions: expectancy trust, dependency trust (which, following [23], we take to be synonymous with risk tolerance[3]), credibility trust, empathy and competence.[4]

Butler's [20] account of trust, upon which the measures of trust in [8] are based, is by contrast entirely affective. This kind of trust might better be called trustworthiness, i.e., a partly emotive, entirely human-centred account of what makes people trustworthy, such as, for example, their status as authority figures in a society. This is not atypical of treatments of trust found in the behavioural sciences literature (e.g., [25]). When studying features of communication-mediating technology, however, the design of the experimental scenario should reflect instead on the trust requirements of the situation or context in which the communication takes place.[5] In addition, as Wierzbicki [23] argues, the technology should, to the extent possible, be rooted in an entirely rational or what he terms "cognitive" view of trust in order to be computationally realizable. CMC technology should not strive to be inert, in other words, but rather to be an intelligent component of the communication channel. But in these negotiations, the communications technology is not cast in the role of a would-be human participant. It silently enables and mediates.

Our own multi-dimensional view has allowed us to calculate similar correlation scores to those of Bos et al. [8], but further-

[1]An earlier body of research had attempted to disabuse technologists of the proposition that videoconferencing can ever be a direct replacement for face-to-face meetings [5]. Those studies did not vary the interaction mode settings of a videoconferencing system, however. Instead they looked to shortcomings in both needs assessment methods and the argumentation surrounding promised reductions in business-related travel to draw their conclusions, taking the technology of videoconferencing itself to be a *fait accompli*.

[2]From the standpoint of security and deception prevention, on the other hand, photos of models have been found to impair participants' abilities to identify trustworthy e-commerce sites [13].

[3]This view of risk considers tolerance to be a contextually variant resultant state, which is conditioned over time by experience dealing with other actors. An alternative view is adopted by [24] in which certain individuals are inherently more risk-*prone* than others. They find this alternative to correlate positively with an individual's construal of self as being defined by his or her relationships.

[4]The OTI's terms are openness/honesty, identification, reliability, concern for employees, and competence, respectively.

[5]See, as an example, Riegelsberger et al.'s [4] taxonomy.

more to do so for each dimension of trust independently. Very few previous CMC studies take trust to be multi-dimensional (versus being a desirable primitive alongside other positive attributes of communication, such as fairness, openness, etc.). Although it would certainly be an overstatement to claim that there is universal agreement in the social sciences literature on what "trust" means, there has been a growing awareness within management science since Butler's [20] early work on the subject that trust is in fact multi-dimensional. Alston [21] (p. 30) went so far as to include the ability to measure multiple dimensions of trust as one of four selectional criteria for her survey instrument, alongside validity and ease of completion within less than 10 minutes. One finds this sentiment outside of management science as well. Mitchell and Zigurs alone have found 10 unequivocally distinct definitions of trust in other literature [26]. See also Uslaner [27] on the multidimensional nature of trust resulting from factor analysis of trust surveys. Any CMC research that has claimed to measure primitive "trust" according to any single definition, no matter which definition they select, has in some sense failed to capture what trust really is.

B. Social Dilemmas

Teoh et al. [9] is a rare exception of a CMC study that does recognize trust as multi-dimensional, but it is still based upon a two-personal social dilemma. They were interested in removing the experiential bias that earlier comparisons to face-to-face communication had not satisfactorily addressed, as well as in evaluating the effect of varying amounts of visual information through a combined video/audio/chat interface across two different types of tasks, creative and negotiating. There found a generally greater amount of trust using a wider camera angle,[6] but which type of task exhibited greater trust depended on the specific dimension of trust measured.

Social dilemma games, which have been used by numerous CHI/CSCW papers on the topic of trust over the last 25 years, e.g., [14]–[16], [29], [31]–[34], have been widely criticized in the social sciences literature as inadequate for the study of trust because, *inter alia*, the only cause for distrust in a classical social dilemma game is the fear of defection. This fear can be equated with the negation of *commitment trust*.

Social dilemma games are convenient because they are abstract, zero-sum games, in which it is comparatively easy to conduct controlled experiments. Nevertheless, they are not representative of a great many real negotiations. In the case of Teoh et al. [9], the choice of a dyadic social dilemma tragically prevented them from measuring objective risk tolerance. The ecological setting of the negotiations we use in our study is very similar to theirs, and among our several objective measures of trust are their measures of time to completion and fairness of payout. As will be seen below, the only one in which we found significance was risk tolerance. Fairness of payout has elsewhere been observed to improve in videoconferencing negotiations when the tasks are more difficult or have more competing trade-offs, and when less information is exchanged per conversational turn [34].

Indeed, most previous work with social dilemmas has focussed on dyadic (two-person or two-group) social dilemmas,[7] in which there is generally no opportunity to measure any kind of trust apart from *credibility trust* because blame is so readily assignable to the other party.

IV. Research Questions and Hypotheses

The main goal of our research was answering the question of whether videoconferencing features, such as chat and screen sharing, influence the (by definition, measurable) attributes of deal-making and the outcomes of multi-party negotiations. In particular, we are interested in the following attributes and their outcomes: participants' trust in each other, their tolerance for risk, the perceived and real (i.e., time-elapsed or turn-counted) efficiency of the negotiation, participants' sense of equity (we shall call it; more precisely, it is distributive fairness [23]:p.16) and transparency. All of these attributes pertain to the aforementioned five dimensions of trust from the OTI [21].

To answer these research questions, we formulated several inter-related hypothesis schemata **H(Y)**, where Y is a variable ranging over (e)fficiency, (r)isk tolerance, (c)redibility trust and e(x)pectancy trust. In addition, we formulated hypothesis subschemata relating to the chat function **Hc(Y)** and the screen sharing function, **Hs(Y)**:

H_(e): Participants' **efficiency** is affected by the videoconferencing features available for use. Public and private chat leads to decreased perceived and real efficiency of the meeting negotiation (Hc(e)). Screen sharing (Hs(e)) leads to increased perceived and real efficiency.

H_(r): Participants' **tolerance for risk** is affected by the videoconferencing features available for use, with public and private chat leading to decreased risk tolerance (Hc(r)) and screen sharing (Hs(r)) leading to increased tolerance.

H_(c): Other participants' perceived **credibility** is affected by the videoconferencing features available for use, with public and private chat leading to decreased perceived transparency (Hc(c)) and screen sharing (Hs(c)) leading to increased transparency.

H_(x): Perceived **expectancy trust** among participants during negotiations is affected by the videoconferencing features available for use, with public and private chat leading to decreased perceived equity (Hc(x)) and screen sharing (Hs(x)) leading to increased equity.

Our hypothesized positive sentiment towards screen sharing followed from [19] and our expectation that screen sharing would likewise create a sense of transparency during negotiations.

[6]Other papers have studied the use of multiple cameras and camera angles [29], and the relative merits of listener-controlled versus speaker-controlled video cameras [30].

[7]See, however, [15] for a pioneering exception, in which a non-anonymized electronic mailing list was evaluated against a face-to-face baseline in six-person social dilemmas. [35] also observes the effects of group formation on trust in three-person groups.

As for the presence of text chat, Birnholtz et al. [36] proposed that it can provide a sufficient situational awareness for completing collaborative problem-solving tasks without necessarily ensuring a complete understanding of the situation. Lee and Tatar [7] showed that, in those same activities, trust could be a key factor in keeping the task on track in the face of lapses in mutual understanding. [7] also showed that dyadic orientations can emerge within a triad that lead to different criteria of understanding among different pairs of participants. Turning instead to triadic negotiation activities, we hypothesized that dyadic sub-orientations would still exist (although we have not tested this hypothesis directly), and therefore that the availability of text chat in the interface would likely lead to a situational awareness of being excluded from one of those dyads that would be sufficient only to causing a breakdown in trust. Because the situations that we constructed are not zero-sum games, this would not be a foregone conclusion; it would say something very contingent about the dynamics of group orientations, negotiation tasks and trust.

V. Experimental Design

In order to test our hypotheses, we designed a within-subjects study in which participants were exposed to differing subsets of interaction modes, in an official, group-meeting scenario. Three student participants and one mediator negotiate over the inclusion of various facilities into a new recreation centre that will be built on our university's campus.

A. Participants

The study was conducted using 72 students (32 female and 40 male), grouped into 24 meeting groups. All participants were undergraduate and graduate students from various disciplines at the same university. While the maximum age was 45, the median age was 25, with 80% of the participants being between the ages of 18 and 27.

B. Independent Variable

Video Only (VO) — a baseline setting available to all modern videoconferencing systems, consisting of two-way voice and video interaction.

Video+Chat (VC) — the Video-Only setting augmented with a chat interface for exchanging text messages (and no screen sharing). Text messages can be "broadcast" to all participants or sent privately to a single party. There is no defined limit to the lengths of the text messages, although the 33-character width for the chat column would make it awkward for transmissions of more than a paragraph in length. Figure 1 shows the videoconferencing system with these features enabled.

Video+Screen (VS) — the Video-Only setting augmented with H.239 dual-stream screen-sharing (and no text chatting[8]). The screen-sharing feature is capable of annotating content and highlighting text on the screen to bring the attention of other participants to it, and also features a "content-slider" that allows viewers to slide back and forth in past time, independently of the presenter's current state of presentation. Figure 2 illustrates the screen-sharing feature of the videoconferencing application.

[8]A single setting in which all three were available was not investigated in order to avoid confounds from participant preferences and selection of non-audio/video affordances, due to more than one being available.

Fig. 1. The videoconferencing system, displaying participants video feeds, the list of participants, and the chat panels (private and public). For privacy considerations, participants' faces have been blurred.

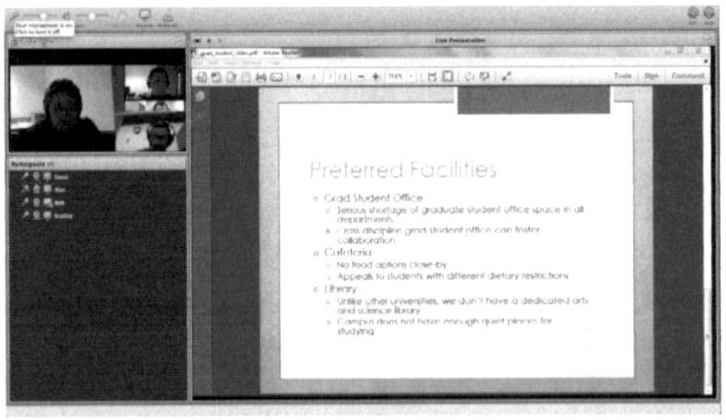

Fig. 2. The videoconferencing system, displaying participants video feeds, the list of participants, and the screen sharing feature. Private and public chat were not functional for this condition.

All three conditions were rendered using a popular commercial videoconferencing system that runs an IETF Session Initiation Protocol stack (SIP) on a remote server, and broadcasts streaming, high-definition (720p at 30 frames per second) H.264 video, G.722.1 ("Polycom") audio and other content between browser-based Java clients that each run on their own Windows desktop computer. The overall system requires 1 Gbps channel capacity.

C. Task

In both studies, each participant in the experimental trials plays the role of a student representative for one of the large extracurricular societies on campus, who negotiates on behalf of their society for the facilities of a new recreational centre that will be built at the university. Depending on the facilities chosen, there is also the risk of a tuition increase, which subjects must balance against the desirability of the facilities. Given that our subjects are students, this task is ecologically valid because of its direct pertinence to their lives on campus.

D. Allocation of Roles and Experimental Conditions

These experiments call for a repeated-measures (within-subjects) design in order to account for the natural variance that exists in human-subject interaction styles and negotiating abilities. Each experimental session or trial consists of a meeting with four participants. The governing council student representative, an interactor who ran the experiment, was the same in every trial and served as a moderator. The other three participants, the human subjects, participated in their roles as student representatives. The moderator was trained to not intervene in negotiations, and was only active in the initial phase of each trial (describing the task and outlining the scenario, namely the facilities to be discussed and the student groups whose interests were at stake), and as a voting facilitator.

Each group of three human subjects participated in three negotiating sessions with each other (and the moderator), one for each setting of the interaction mode. Every human subject negotiated with the same two other human subjects in his/her three trials, with no other participants added or removed.

A Latin square design of size three was chosen to randomize the order in which participant groups were exposed to the three settings of the independent variable [37]. 8 squares were used in both studies, but not the same squares. The two studies were run independently in order to avoid the exponential increase in time and expense that would have resulted from a single, size-five grid, but the two size-three grids do at least share one common variable setting (VO). The squares were designed so that: (1) each setting of an independent variable was matched with one of three negotiation scenarios an equal number of times, and (2) each of the three scenarios appeared in some position in the sequence given to each group of three participants.

The three scenarios are defined by the three societies represented in their negotiations:

1) athletic society, graduate students' society, MBA students' society
2) arts society, athletic society, undergraduate students' society
3) Christian students' society, health-and-fitness society, undergraduate students' society.

The two societies that appear in more than one scenario (athletic and undergraduates) appear in either instance with different rankings and different tuition-increase judgements.

E. Measures and Instruments

For the purpose of comparing the effect of each interaction mode setting, we followed [23] in eliciting a range of both subjective *user perception* judgements and objective *performance* measures that instantiated and integrated our multiple dimensional scales of trust.

These two types of data were collected and measured for each[9] experimental condition in both studies. We used a metric conjoint analysis [38] on a triadic variant of the actor-partner interdependence model [39], in which each actor evaluates both other partners together. This relies on no individual appearing in more than one group.

1) User perception data: We asked participants upon completion of each of the three meeting tasks (one for each experimental condition) to indicate their agreement to statements related to their perception of trust, and the degree of transparency, efficiency, and equity in the meetings. Agreements were represented on a 5-point Likert scale, from 1 for strongly disagree to 5 for strongly agree. The statements included:

1) "I could trust the other participants,"
2) "The other participants were exchanging important information that I could not see,"
3) "The other participants were withholding information from me,"
4) "The other participants disclosed all relevant information during the meeting,"
5) "I feel that I completed the task in its entirety,"
6) "The other participants were effective negotiators,"
7) "I had the tools necessary to complete the task efficiently,"
8) "I had to work under pressure,"
9) "It was difficult to understand the voices of the other participants,"
10) "The settlement that we reached was fair to all parties,"
11) "I was able to participate actively in the meeting,"
12) "The other participants dealt with me fairly,"

as well as a general question related to the interface: "I found the interface intuitive and easy to use." Each statement was rephrased to a statement of the opposite polarity independently with 50% probability to control for bias in the wording.[10] Statements were also presented in a randomly selected order.

2) Objective performance data: Our research focus was on measuring participants' attitudes and perceptions with respect to various trust-like attributes. As such, most of the data collected were subjective in nature. However, participants' willingness to engage in transactions that are riskier with respect to the potential for a fairer payout for them is often cited as an indicator of trust [23]. Since, during negotiations, our participants had to advance proposals based on preferences and risks that were assigned to them for each of the facilities (illustrated in Table I), we collected their aggregated tolerance for lower- or higher-risk facility selections. The process for selecting facilities and factoring in the risks is outlined in Section V-F. The value for the **aggregate risk tolerance** of a given session was calculated as the total number of times any

[9]To maintain ecological validity, the scenarios were not altered in order to "force" participants to use the features that were enabled/disabled for each conditions. As such, participants were free to make use of all features available for each condition: the chat feature was extensively used by all three participants in only 10 of the undiscarded 22 meetings of the video study, while the screen sharing feature was used by all participants in 13.

[10]The exception is statement (7), in which the modals "necessary" and "efficiently" were combined in a single statement so that the topic would not be overrepresented in the questionnaire. From among this statement and two rephrasals:

- "I was unable to find all of the information I needed on the interface," and
- "The task required a great deal of effort."

one was independently selected with 33.3% probability.

TABLE I
AN EXAMPLE RANKED LIST OF FACILITIES, TOGETHER WITH ASSESSMENTS OF WHETHER THEY WOULD RISK A TUITION HIKE.

Facility	Rank	Risk of Tuition Hike
Weight Room	1	No
Swimming Pool	2	No
Physiotherapy Centre	3	No
Grad Student office	4	Yes
Cafeteria	5	No
Library	6	Yes
Rentable Office Space	7	Yes
Meeting Rooms	8	No
Virtual Stock Market	9	No

of the four facilities chosen by consensus appeared at risk of a tuition hike in any participant's facilities table.

In addition to risk tolerance, we instrumented the experiment to collect objective data on the **disparity in the preference rankings** of the facilities ultimately agreed upon by the negotiations, a measure of fairness or equity. Performance-related efficiency measures, such as **time to reach a settlement** and **number of voting rounds** needed to agree on a settlement, were intrinsically available and thus also incorporated into our analysis.

F. Balance Conditions

The tables of ranks and risks that were provided to subjects were balanced so that, in a single session: (1) the ranks of each facility were all different on the three tables, (2) the sum of the ranks of any facility was constant, depending on its classification as high importance (sum = 18), medium importance (sum = 15) or low importance (sum = 12; the importance of the facilities was not disclosed to subjects), (3) every society's top-ranked facility was assigned no risk of a tuition hike in its own table, but a risk of a tuition hike in the tables of the other two subjects in the same scenario, (4) every society's third-ranked facility was assigned no risk of a tuition hike in its own table, and in the table of one other subject in the same scenario, but a risk of a tuition hike in the table of the third subject, and (5) every society's second-ranked facility was assigned no risk of a tuition hike in the tables of all three subjects in the same scenario. These balance conditions ensure that some negotiation is required, but that a best solution (consisting of the three second-ranked facilities plus one other) and several near-best alternatives are always available, without resorting to a zero-sum game (as in [9], [10]). Unlike [9], in particular, these balance conditions do not entail that the sum of ranks is always the same, which would preclude our computation of risk tolerance (see below), as the removal of any facility would result in a constant reduction in payout.

This aspect of our design is also important because our coordinated use of facility rank and risk (in our sense of a tuition-hike) actually decouples our framing of risk (in the sense of the dependency trust dimension of Wierzbicki's scales [23]) into the threat of a realized loss (in the form of a tuition increase) plus the possibility of an unrealized gain (of desirable facilities being incorporated into the recreational centre), thus addressing, and possibly neutralizing, the bias that either could exert by itself on human risk assessment [40]. It furthermore does so without the use of exogenous auxiliary hypotheses (as in [14]) that may inadvertently convey the impression to participants that their decisions are less consequential or less precise in their effects.

G. Rounds of Voting

Successive rounds of voting were conducted until the participants converged on a choice of 4 facilities (each receiving 3 votes), or until 30 minutes had elapsed for the session. Of the 24 groups (=72 sessions) that we convened, 22 reached consensus in all three of their sessions. The data for the 2 meetings without consensus were discarded.

The potential for multiple rounds of voting in the experimental design is also important, as it fundamentally differentiates the structural incentives inherent to this task from those inherent to social dilemmas, which are generally one-shot, highly symmetrical contests, in which both parties must simultaneously act as both potential trustors and potential trustees. The multiple proposals that can be advanced during negotiation, together with potentially multiple rounds of voting makes trust more amenable to analysis as a signalling problem [4]. Ongoing discussions between rounds of voting also create ample opportunities for constructive verbalization about trust and distrust. This has been recommended (again by [4]) as a means of addressing their third dimension, sources of vulnerability. The only vulnerability that players face in social dilemmas is the possibility of defection, which is oversimplistic.

It must be conceded, however, that the potential for multiple rounds of voting was largely underutilized. Of the sessions that ever reached a certain conclusion, 64% terminated after one vote, and 35% terminated after 2, leaving only 1% with more than 2 rounds of voting. On the other hand, there was a substantial amount of verbalization. Of the 129 sessions in the 43 groups across both studies that always reach consensus, 29 (14 from the video study) included pejorative comments relating to trust (mainly complaints of being left out of the discussion, accusations of defection and statements of incredulity), and 36 (24 in the video study) included positive comments relating to trust (mainly affirmations that a recent proposal is fair to everyone, approving statements about the outcomes of previous agreements, and comparative arguments that a participant should agree to a current proposal because they had agreed to a similar one earlier).

H. Procedures

Subjects were first screened to confirm their student status and that they were unacquainted with the other two subjects in their group. The two studies were run in non-overlapping sequence (video study first) and no student participated in both studies.

Prior to the commencement of the first session, subjects were indoctrinated into the setting in which all of the fictitious negotiations took place. Each participant was informed that they would play a different character in each of the three sessions. Each character has a name, and the participants were required to address each other in each session by their character's name in that session. Participants were also informed that the university would act upon the consensus that they established, and that their re-election as student society representatives would depend crucially on the outcomes of the negotiation. This creates realistic (but fictional) social risks on top of those that pertain to the negotiation's direct outcomes.

Participants were seated in separate offices on the same floor of an academic building, each of which was equipped with office furniture and a desktop computer running the videoconferencing system. Between sessions, participants took on the roles of new characters from new student societies, but did not switch office spaces.

In each session, the moderator allowed discussion to take place for about 10 minutes, provided the other participants with some positive reinforcement for their efforts and suggested that they vote after another 5 minutes of discussion. After each round of voting, the results of the voting were announced, and, in case the votes were overdispersed, the moderator would select the 5 or more facility choices that received the highest numbers of votes, and encourage more discussion about these, excluding the other facilities from consideration. The moderator never cast a ballot. Note that while the top-ranking facilities were announced, the ballots of individual participants were not, and there were always three voting participants. Again, without the use of exogenous hypotheses, the presence of a third voter allows us to avoid certain attribution of loss in almost every case. Certainly attributable loss is another common shortcoming cited of two-player social dilemma games, as this is often not the case in real negotiations either. At the same time, the presence of a third participant allows pairs of participants to "gang up" in settings where private chatting is available.

At the conclusion of the final ballot in each session, a written post-meeting questionnaire was distributed for each participant to answer by themselves. At the conclusion of the third session's post-meeting questionnaire, an additional post-experimental questionnaire was distributed to gather additional comparative user perception data and demographic information, followed by an experimental debriefing.

I. Data Analysis

In order to test our hypotheses, the most suitable statistical test for this within-subjects design is a repeated-measures multilinear model (MLM), a generalization of ANOVA [41] common to quantitative research on the actor-partner independence model of trust [39], that includes an explicit variable for group-level effects, as there almost certainly will be interactions between individual subjects in the same negotiations.[11]

[11]Because no two groups shared an individual, we also speculatively calculated an ANOVA by modelling each group as an individual with subjective preference scores equal to the average of its three individuals' scores. The results of that analysis were not substantially different from the MLM analysis presented here.

The exception is the objective performance data, which can only be calculated at the group level. For these, we used a simple repeated-measures ANOVA as implemented by the PAST system [42]. F-tests in the MLM were approximated with the Kenward-Roger method using the *pbkrtest* library in the R programming language [43]. All tests were evaluated assuming a size of $\alpha = 0.05$ for the null hypothesis's rejection region, and all post-hoc Tukey tests were calculated using a Bonferroni correction quotient. No other transformations were applied to the data. We tested the data for homoscedasticity, but also computed a non-parametric test, Wilcoxon's signed-rank test, and χ^2 scores in order to confirm the validity of the F-scores obtained. We also calculated simple descriptive statistics for each setting of the independent variables.

VI. RESULTS

Synopsis: Most of the hypotheses **Hc**(Y) and **Hs**(Y) are confirmed by the experimental results. The analysis of both the objective and subjective data collected from the experiment suggests that chat, particularly private chat, does not facilitate a positive environment for conducting negotiations in an equitable, transparent, and risk-free manner (hypotheses Hc(Y)). However, some of these negative effects are reversed when participants use screen sharing as their main collaborative features. Screen sharing also contributes a somewhat positive boost to the efficiency of the negotiations (hypotheses Hs(Y)).

All the subjective data were collected as participant agreement or disagreement with various statements on each post-treatment questionnaire as previously detailed in Section V-E. Our goal was to analyze how each experimental treatment condition (that is, chat or screen sharing) influenced the deal-making attributes of the whole meeting vs. the baseline treatment (video only), yet the subjective data was collected individually for each participant.

A. Efficiency

Several post-experiment questions elicited participants' impressions of how efficiently the negotiations proceeded. The MLM on some of the efficiency-related statements shows a significant relation between the videoconferencing features and participants' perceptions of efficiency ($F(2,130)=3.77$, $p=0.03$, and averages illustrated in Figure 3(a) for the "I was able to find all of the information I needed on the interface" statement), confirming hypothesis H(e). Post-hoc Tukey tests showed significant differences both between the screen sharing condition (VS) and the video only treatment (VO; $p=0.01$) and between the chat condition (VC) and VO ($p=0.03$), thus confirming both sub-schemata Hs(e) and Hc(e). The assessment, "I had the tools necessary to complete the task efficiently," was marginally significant across treatments ($F(2,130)=2.56$, $p=0.08$) but the other subjective assessments of efficiency ("I feel that I completed the task in its entirety," "The other participants were effective negotiators") did not show significant differences. Similarly, objective measurements of efficiency, such as meeting duration (viz. time to completion), did not exhibit statistical significance across treatments.

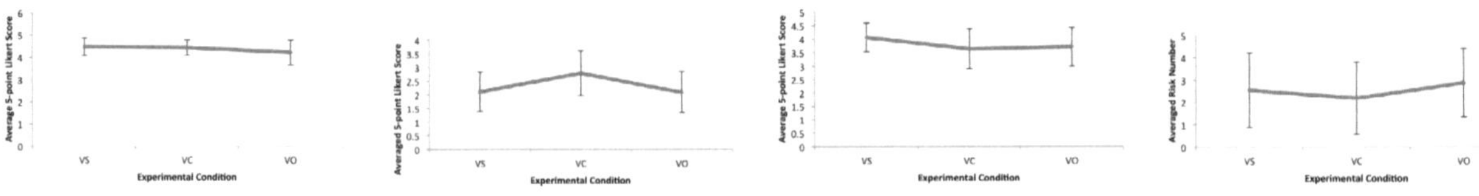

(a) (b) (c) (d)

Fig. 3. Responses to the statements: (a) "I was able to find all of the information I needed on the interface," (b) "The other participants were exchanging important information that I could not see," and (c) "I felt that the settlement we reached was fair to all parties," averaged for each of the three experimental conditions: VS (Video+Screen sharing), VC (Video+Chat), and the baseline VO (Video only), along with (d) the risk tolerance value. The variance of the risk tolerance is large, but correct. The effect size was calculated as small (0.030), but significant above Cohen's threshold of 0.01.

B. Risk Tolerance

A main objective measure used in the study was the participants' tolerance for risk. Each participant negotiated under a certain set of preferences for facilities that were to be selected, and a set of tuition fee increases. These increases were presented as yes/no "rumours" of increases to avoid a temptation to simply perform addition on precise tuition increments when determining the overall merit of a proposal. To quantify the risk taken by participants during negotiations, we have tallied for each session the number of times any of the four facilities chosen by consensus appeared at risk of a tuition hike in any participant's facilities table. As indicated in Section V-D, these tables were not identical across participants, both in the preferred rank of facilities and in the rumoured tuition fee increase. Participants were prohibited from divulging their preferred ranks, but they were allowed to reveal the rumoured tuition increase if needed to move the negotiations along. There were several permutations possible in which participants could have settled for facilities that were favourably-ranked (in the top third of their tables), yet these permutations carried different tuition increase risks. As such, the aggregated risk number was an objective measure of participants' willingness to opt for a riskier selection of preferred facilities in exchange for a settlement that was somewhat optimal for all participants.

The MLM on the aggregated risk numbers indicates a statistically-significant relation between videoconferencing features and participants' tolerance for risk ($F(2,42)=3.271$, $p=0.048$, and averages illustrated in Figure 3(d)[12]), thus confirming hypothesis H(r). The sub-schema Hc(r) was also confirmed — a Tukey post-hoc test shows that using chat led to participants being less willing to take risks than when using only the video ($p=0.01$). Screen sharing did not exhibit any influence on participants' risk tolerance as compared to the baseline feature.

C. Credibility Trust

Several statements on the post-treatment questionnaires were related to transparency or obscurity of the negotiations. Of these, the analysis for the answers to the most salient one ("The other participants were exchanging important information that I could not see") indicate a statistically-significant strong influence of the videoconferencing features on participants' perceived transparency of negotiations ($F(2,130)=9.73$, $p < 0.01$, averages in Figure 3(b)), thus confirming H(c). Pairwise Tukey post-hoc tests reveal that chat had a negative influence on transparency compared to both screen sharing and basic features ($p < 0.01$ for both).

The statement "The other participants were withholding information from me" also exhibited a significant influence by the chat condition on participants' perceptions of transparency ($F(2,130)=4.06$, $p=0.02$), strengthening the confirmation of Hc(c). The statement, "The other participants negotiated with me honestly," was marginally significant over the different treatments ($F(2,130)=2.54$, $p=0.08$) but other statements that were less-obviously connected to transparency (e.g., "I was able to understand the motivations of the other participants") did not exhibit any statistically significant variations.

D. Expectancy Trust

An important aspect of any negotiation is to have all participants engaged equitably and fairly in discussions, and to reach a mutually beneficial compromise. It relates to trust for the same reason that fairness does (see above). In our study we asked participants if they felt that "the settlement that we reached was fair to all parties." The MLM analysis on the agreement/disagreement answers shows that these were significantly affected by the videoconferencing features, thus confirming hypothesis H(x) ($F(2,130)=3.43$, $p=0.04$, averages in Figure 3(c)). Tukey pairwise comparisons show a significant differences ($p=0.046$) between the effect of screen sharing (VS) and that of both chat (VC) and video only (VO). While the separate hypothesis sub-schema Hc(x) was not confirmed independently, the confirmation of H(x) together with the situation of average responses for VO between VS and VC suggests that chat may have a negative effect on the equity of the negotiation while screen sharing may provide the opposite.

The other equity-related statements (such as "I was able to participate actively in the meeting" or "The other participants dealt with me fairly") did not exhibit any significant results, perhaps attributable to the overall civilized environment and respectful behaviour of all participants (which may not be always reflected in real-life negotiations).

We also measured equity objectively through a max-min difference, computed by summing the ranks (in the given

[12]The substantially greater variance in this figure is due to the group-level calculation of objective scores, because of which there is a smaller sample size.

preference tables) of the facilities chosen by each participant, and then subtracting the smallest of these sums from the largest. It was also not found to have been influenced by the videoconferencing features.

E. Empathy and Competence Trust

No subjective elicitations in the dimensions of empathy or competence trust showed statistically significance.

F. Stated Trust

We also directly elicited a subjective judgment on trust itself ("I could trust the other participants"), upon which influence by the videoconferencing features was found to be marginally significant ($F(2,130)=2.73$, $p=0.069$), with a post-hoc Tukey comparison pointing to video plus chat (VC) as the outlier ($p=0.02$). Following Bos [8], we calculated correlations using Kendall's tau between this judgement and the others, finding values ranging between -0.43 and +0.58, with the highest correlates all indicating expectancy trust, and the lowest (anti-)correlations all belonging to the negative indicators of credibility.

VII. Discussion and Implications for Design

The analysis of post-condition questionnaire answers indicates that in several cases the hypothesis schemata Hc(Y) hold true. This suggests that, in general, chat is a feature that leads to an observed decrease in risk tolerance for participants, as well as to a decrease in credibility trust, expectation trust and stated trust. This is most likely attributed to the possibility for private chatting since negotiations could be conducted simultaneously between ad-hoc pairs of participants with private chat. We can thus state that **private chat in videoconferencing systems can be detrimental to participants' risk tolerance, credibility trust, stated trust and their perception of fairness.** This prompts us to recommend that:

> Designers and administrators of videoconferencing systems disable private chat by default for participants engaged in negotiations.

An interesting future direction is the investigation of appropriate ways to enable or disable private chat, and establishing who has control over such decisions.

As outlined in Section VI, the addition of screen sharing led to a relative increase in perceived efficiency, but not to a significant decrease in actual time to completion. It also led to a relative increase in expectancy trust over the video-only baseline, but not to a significant increase in the objective equity of the outcome. While we did not test screen-sharing in the absence of a mug-shot video interface in either study, it is worth underscoring that the observed benefits did accrue on top of whatever might have been conferred by videos of the other participants. We can thus state that **screen sharing improves the subjective experience of efficiency and fairness**. Therefore, we recommend that:

> Designers and administrators of videoconferencing systems consider enabling access to screen sharing features for participants in negotiations.

Where does this leave video? Earlier studies that used two-person social dilemmas generally had no opportunity to measure any kind of trust apart from credibility trust. This is in stark contrast to the addition of screen sharing, for which benefits accrued on top of whatever video may have added, and to the elimination of chat functionality, which the presence of video and audio alone was incapable of ameliorating in any of the several affected categories of trust. Video almost certainly does provide other, marginal, non-trust-related advantages, such as improved vocal intelligibility due to modal enhancement, as well as perceived efficiency due to increased engagement. But it is due to the broader conception of trust in our studies' design that we have been able to observe a wider range of significant benefits and detriments from screen-sharing and chat functionality. The presence of video, it appears, is by no means the end of the conversation about videoconferencing.

VIII. Conclusion and Future Work

Many real-life situations involve multi-party negotiations that cannot be reduced to a zero-sum situation or a social dilemma; instead, the range of outcomes can vary from convergence on one of several possible compromises to an outcome that is very favourable for some participants at the expense of others. Increasingly, such negotiations are carried out by videoconference. To this extent, our experimental setup replicated this real-life situation and thus provided ecological validity to our analysis, as the experimental task was designed to be relevant and familiar to our pool of participants (students, discussing tuition fee hikes and facilities). On the other hand, participants were aware of the role-playing aspect of the experiment, and while most were engaged and passionate about selecting facilities, the lack of real-life stakes may have toned down some of the results, such as equity and how participants treated each other fairly.

This paper evaluated the effect that two ubiquitous features of videoconferencing systems (chat and screen sharing) have on trust, relative to video. They were conducted in a business-like setting in which three participants had competing interests in a negotiation, with possible outcomes ranging from significant disparity between participants' share of the final settlement to a relatively fair, albeit slightly sub-optimal, deal for all participants. This setting is more realistic than the typical two-party social dilemma that is so often used as a setting for studying trust in videoconferencing systems.

At the same time, our findings provide a very relevant insight into triadic group activities, where the research emphasis has generally been on collaborative problem-solving. Future work should include conversational analysis of realistic group negotiation tasks such as the one pursued here, in order to explore the potential links between interface affordances and group dynamics, such as the dyadic sub-orientations found by [7], more thoroughly. A potential limitation of the present study was the presence of the moderator; triadic negotiations in the absence of a moderator may respond differently to changes in the affordances of the conferencing interface.

The analysis of our experimental results uncovered evidence of significantly negative and positive effects that chat and screen sharing have on various aspects of trust that distinguish them from the presence of video alone. These findings provide useful information for designers, administrators, and decision makers about the appropriate setting for the use of videoconferencing features. Future work should extend this analysis to other settings, such as remote, mobile or home-based participation in meetings. This is of great interest to designers of mobile and tablet-based conferencing systems, where it is understood that one or more participants do not have access to a full-featured application.

ACKNOWLEDGEMENTS

This research was supported by the Canadian Network Centre of Excellence in Graphics, Animation and New Media (GRAND) and Avaya.

REFERENCES

[1] S. Whittaker and B. O'Conaill, "The role of vision in face-to-face and mediated communication," in *Videomediated Communication*, 1997.

[2] N. Döring, *Sozialpsychologie des Internet: Die Bedeutung des Internet für Kommunikationsprozesse, Identitäten, soziale Beziehungen und Gruppen*. Hogrefe, Verlag für Psychologie, 1999.

[3] A. Mitra, "Trust, authenticity, and discursive power in cyberspace," *Comm. ACM*, vol. 45, no. 3, pp. 27–29, 2002.

[4] J. Riegelsberger, M. A. Sasse, and J. D. McCarthy, "The researcher's dilemma: evaluating trust in computer-mediated communication," *Intl. J. Human-Computer Studies*, vol. 58, no. 6, pp. 759–781, 2003.

[5] C. Egido, "Videoconferencing as a technology to support group work: a review of its failure," in *Proc. CSCW*, pp. 13–24, ACM, 1988.

[6] Z. Fang and J. Tang, "Uncovering the formation of triadic closure in social networks," in *Proc. IJCAI*, pp. 2062–2068, 2015.

[7] J.-S. Lee and D. Tatar, "Sounds of silence: Exploring contributions to conversations, non-responses and the impact of mediating technologies in triple space," in *Proc. CSCW*, pp. 1561–1572, ACM, 2014.

[8] N. Bos, J. Olson, D. Gergle, G. Olson, and Z. Wright, "Effects of four computer-mediated communications channels on trust development," in *Proc. CHI*, pp. 135–140, ACM, 2002.

[9] C. Teoh, H. Regenbrecht, and D. O'Hare, "Investigating factors influencing trust in video-mediated communication," in *Proc. OZCHI*, pp. 312–319, 2010.

[10] W. Standaert, S. Muylle, and A. Basu, "Assessing the effectiveness of telepresence for business meetings," in *Proc. 46th Hawaii Intl. Conf. on System Sciences (HICSS)*, pp. 549–558, IEEE, 2013.

[11] J. T. Hancock, J. Thom-Santelli, and T. Ritchie, "Deception and design: The impact of communication technology on lying behavior," in *Proc. CHI*, pp. 129–134, ACM, 2004.

[12] T. Mvumbi, F. Kundaeli, Z. Manzi, K. Williams, and H. Suleman, "An online meeting tool for low bandwidth environments," in *Proc. Annu. Conf. South African Institute for Computer Scientists and Information Technologists*, pp. 226–235, 2012.

[13] J. Riegelsberger, M. A. Sasse, and J. D. McCarthy, "Shiny happy people building trust?: Photos on e-commerce websites and consumer trust," in *Proc. CHI*, pp. 121–128, ACM, 2003.

[14] J. Zheng, E. Veinott, N. Bos, J. S. Olson, and G. M. Olson, "Trust without touch: jumpstarting long-distance trust with initial social activities," in *Proc. CHI*, pp. 141–146, ACM, 2002.

[15] E. Rocco, "Trust breaks down in electronic contexts but can be repaired by some initial face-to-face contact," in *Proc. CHI*, pp. 496–502, ACM, 1998.

[16] C. Jensen, S. D. Farnham, S. M. Drucker, and P. Kollock, "The effect of communication modality on cooperation in online environments," in *Proc. CHI*, pp. 470–477, ACM, 2000.

[17] B. J. Alge, C. Wiethoff, and H. J. Klein, "When does the medium matter? Knowledge-building experiences and opportunities in decision-making teams," *Organizational Behavior and Human Decision Processes*, vol. 91, no. 1, pp. 26–37, 2003.

[18] X. Sun, Q. Zhang, S. Wiedenbeck, and T. Chintakovid, "Gender differences in trust perception when using IM and video," in *CHI Extended Abstracts*, pp. 1373–1378, ACM, 2006.

[19] B. T. Kane, P. J. Toussaint, and S. Luz, "Shared decision making needs a communication record," in *Proc. CSCW*, pp. 79–90, ACM, 2013.

[20] J. K. Butler Jr, "Toward understanding and measuring conditions of trust: Evolution of a conditions of trust inventory," *J. Management*, vol. 17, no. 3, pp. 643–663, 1991.

[21] F. Alston, *Culture and Trust in Technology-Driven Organizations*. CRC Press, 2013.

[22] P. Shockley-Zalabak, K. Ellis, and R. Cesaria, "Measuring organizational trust: trust and distrust across cultures.," in *The Organizational Trust Index*, IABC Research Foundation, 1999.

[23] A. Wierzbicki, *Trust and Fairness in Open, Distributed Systems*. Springer, 2010.

[24] M. K. Lee, N. Fruchter, and L. Dabbish, "Making decisions from a distance: The impact of technological mediation on riskiness and dehumanization," in *Proc. CSCW*, pp. 1576–1589, ACM, 2015.

[25] J. K. Burgoon and J. L. Hale, "Validation and measurement of the fundamental themes of relational communication," *Communication Monographs*, vol. 54, pp. 19–41, Mar. 1987.

[26] A. Mitchell and I. Zigurs, "Trust in virtual teams: Solved or still a mystery?," *ACM SIGMIS Database: the Data Base for Advances in Information Systems*, vol. 40, no. 3, pp. 61–83, 2009.

[27] E. M. Uslaner, "Measuring Generalized Trust: In Defense of the 'Standard' Question," in [28], pp. 72–82.

[28] F. Lyon, G. Mollering, and M. Saunders, eds., *Handbook of Research Methods on Trust*. Edward Elgar Publishing, 2011.

[29] D. T. Nguyen and J. Canny, "Multiview: improving trust in group video conferencing through spatial faithfulness," in *Proc. CHI*, pp. 1465–1474, ACM, 2007.

[30] J. MacCormick, "Video chat with multiple cameras," in *Proc. CSCW*, pp. 195–198, ACM, 2013.

[31] E. Bradner and G. Mark, "Why distance matters: effects on cooperation, persuasion and deception," in *Proc. CSCW*, pp. 226–235, ACM, 2002.

[32] J. P. Davis, S. Farnham, and C. Jensen, "Decreasing online 'bad' behavior," in *CHI Extended Abstracts*, pp. 718–719, ACM, 2002.

[33] L. E. Scissors, A. J. Gill, K. Geraghty, and D. Gergle, "In CMC we trust: The role of similarity," in *Proc. CHI*, pp. 527–536, ACM, 2009.

[34] W. Dong and W.-T. Fu, "One piece at a time: why video-based communication is better for negotiation and conflict resolution," in *Proc. CSCW*, pp. 167–176, ACM, 2012.

[35] P. Slovák, P. Novák, P. Troubil, P. Holub, and E. C. Hofer, "Exploring trust in group-to-group video-conferencing," in *CHI Extended Abstracts*, pp. 1459–1464, ACM, 2011.

[36] J. P. Birnholtz, T. A. Finholt, D. B. Horn, and S. J. Bae, "Grounding needs: Achieving common ground via lightweight chat in large, distributed, ad-hoc groups," in *Proc. CHI*, pp. 21–30, 2005.

[37] R. E. Kirk, *Experimental Design: Procedures for the Behavioral Sciences*. Brooks Publishing, USA, 1995.

[38] R. Priem and A. Weibel, "Measuring the decision to trust using metric conjoint analysis," in [28], pp. 212–225.

[39] D. L. Ferrin, M. C. Bligh, and J. C. Kohles, "The actor–partner interdependence model: a method for studying trust in dyadic relationships," in [28], pp. 189–198.

[40] D. Kahneman, P. Slovic, and A. Tversky, *Judgments under Uncertainty: Heuristics and Biases*. Cambridge University Press, 1982.

[41] D. C. Howell, *Fundamental Statistics for the Behavioral Sciences*. Nelson Education, 2016.

[42] O. Hammer, D. Harper, and P. Ryan, "Past: Paleontological statistics software package for education and data analysis," *Palaeontologia Electronica*, vol. 4, pp. 1–9, 2001.

[43] U. Halekoh and S. Højsgaard, "A Kenward-Roger approximation and parametric bootstrap methods for tests in linear mixed models–the R package pbkrtest," *J. Statistical Software*, vol. 59, no. 9, pp. 1–30, 2014.

A User-centred Design and Feasibility Analysis of the WiGlove - A Home-based Rehabilitation Device for Hand and Wrist Therapy after Stroke

Vignesh Velmurugan
Robotics Research Group
University of Hertfordshire
Hatfield, United Kingdom
email: v.velmurugan2@herts.ac.uk

Luke Jai Wood
Robotics Research Group
University of Hertfordshire
Hatfield, United Kingdom
email: l.wood@herts.ac.uk

Farshid Amirabdollahian
Robotics Research Group
University of Hertfordshire
Hatfield, United Kingdom
email: f.amirabdollahian2@herts.ac.uk

***Abstract*—Stroke survivors often experience deficits in their hand's motor function, which can greatly impact their ability to perform activities of daily life. Home-based rehabilitation with robotic devices has been shown to improve the recovery of hand functions. The WiGlove is a home-based robotic orthosis that has been developed using a user-centred approach to offset the hyperflexion in the hand and wrist of hemiparetic stroke survivors. It facilitates training the distal joints of the upper limb at home while performing activities of daily life or playing therapeutic games on a tablet. In a formative evaluation, stroke therapists positively rated the WiGlove's usability and provided feedback which assisted in improving its design. Additionally, the preliminary results of a feasibility analysis at a stroke survivor's home showed evidence of the WiGlove's usability and acceptance with a noticeable impact on reducing the tone in the impaired hand.**

***Keywords*—Stroke rehabilitation; Robot-aided rehabilitation; Home-based therapy; Hand-wrist orthosis; Feasibility.**

I. INTRODUCTION

Stroke often results in hemiparesis, where the survivors experience motor function deficits on one side of their body. Hemiparetic stroke survivors often experience weakness and abnormal synergies such as excessive involuntary flexion (hyperflexion) in their hand which severely affects their ability to independently perform Activities of Daily Life (ADL) [1]. While rehabilitation is prescribed to regain the hand's functions, the traditional approach of one-to-one physical therapy limits the amount of training due to factors such as the availability of therapists' appointments. Robot-aided rehabilitation techniques have shown the potential to act as a valuable companion to therapists, offering the ability to provide high repetitions and objective measures of assessments without requiring their presence [2].

Robotic devices that allow stroke survivors to independently perform exercises at home at a flexible schedule can lead to an overall increase in training intensity and associated recovery [3]. Home-based rehabilitation devices enable therapists to remotely monitor the progress and use their expertise to help more stroke survivors which is invaluable in times like the COVID-19 pandemic. While a variety of robotic devices have been proposed for the neurorehabilitation of the hand [4][5][6][7], the majority focus only on training either the wrist or the fingers but not both [8], neglecting the synergy between them. Most of them are only suitable for use in a clinical environment, resulting in limited training durations. Only SCRIPT Passive Orthosis (SPO) [1] was found to be suitable for training independently at home.

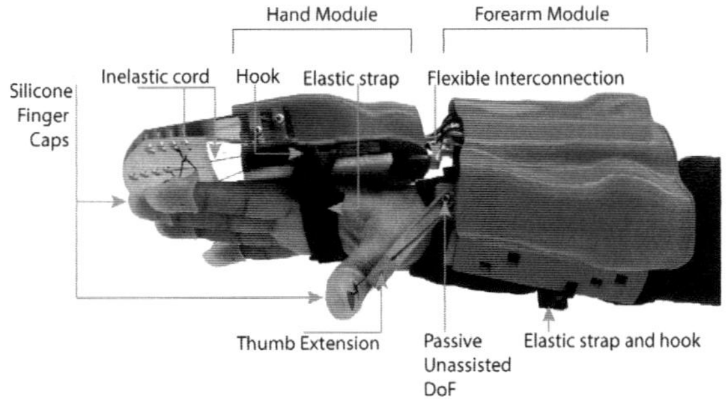

Figure 1. WiGlove.

SPO is a passive orthosis that allows stroke survivors to perform hand and wrist exercises. Developed in a European Framework 7 project, it is a part of the SCRIPT system that includes interactive games and a back-end system for clinical monitoring. While a study involving 23 stroke survivors validated SPO's feasibility, it also identified several functional and usability shortcomings [1][9]. Usability is one of the significant user requirements that affect the acceptance of such devices [10].

Hence, the overarching aim of the research presented in this paper aims to design and develop a home-based rehabilitation device for the hand and wrist that addresses the limitations of SPO through a user-centred design approach (UCD). Beginning with the features of the WiGlove in Section II, this paper focuses on discussing the methods (Section III) and findings (Section IV) of its formative usability evaluation with stroke therapists and presents preliminary results from the feasibility study conducted at a stroke survivor's home.

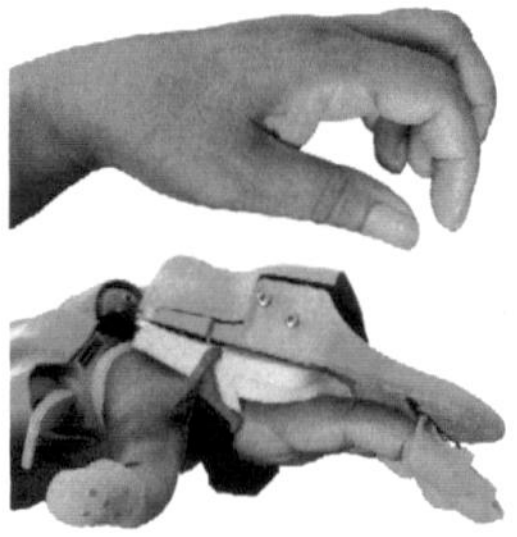

Figure 2. Image showing a stroke survivor's hand with hyper-flexion in the fingers being offset by WiGlove.

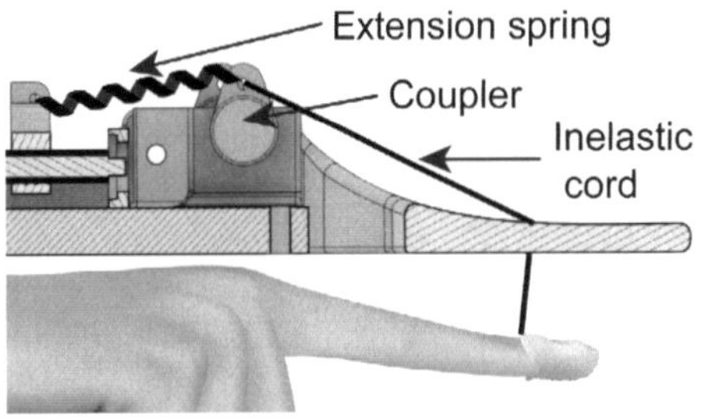

Figure 3. Extension assistance mechanism.

II. WiGlove

In a user-centred design process, an extensive review of the state of the art including task analysis and user studies by the SCRIPT consortium was used to compile a comprehensive set of user requirements for such a device [10]. Building on the knowledge from SPO, the WiGlove was designed to satisfy these requirements. The WiGlove is a passive dynamic orthosis that assists hemiparetic stroke survivors in performing flexion/extension exercises with their fingers and wrist while performing ADL or playing therapeutic games on a tablet. In addition to providing support, a dynamic orthosis also helps to articulate the joint. The WiGlove consists of a forearm and a hand module coupled using a flexible interconnection to allow for ab/adduction of the wrist reducing the risk of hypertonia from non-use. It uses elastic straps with hooks for easy don/doffing of the device with the unimpaired hand. Furthermore, all the surfaces of the device that come in contact with the body while wearing are lined with thermoplastic polyethene foam to ensure comfortable soft interaction. Since the modules are 3D printed, it allows the user to customise their appearance which could enhance its acceptance.

A. *Extension assistance*

The WiGlove uses extension springs as passive actuators to assist with the extension of the wrist and fingers to a more neutral position from a fully flexed position (Figure 2). This allows the stroke survivors to voluntarily perform flexion against the resistive force of the springs. This mechanism where the device remains passive during training is adopted due to its reduced safety concerns compared to its active counterparts.

The wrist's assistance mechanism is located on the forearm module from which the spring force is transmitted to the joints using an inelastic cord that is attached to the hand module. Similarly, each finger is individually assisted, where the cord is attached to the distal segment of the finger in a base-to-distal configuration that eliminates the concerns of misalignment between the centres of rotation of the fingers and the device. This also ensures that the ab/adduction of the fingers is unrestricted. The cords are guided through an extension structure and are attached to the fingers using a silicone digit cap that allows for tactile feedback while grasping objects (Figure 3). The extension structure is transparent to permit visual feedback while training. The thumb's mechanism is attached to the forearm module to reduce the weight acting on the hand. Additionally, it has a passive joint to facilitate the thumb's ab/adduction, which is essential for its opposing action while grasping.

B. *Feedback sensors*

The spring in each assistance module is attached to the respective inelastic cord through a coupler that rotates about the shaft of a rotary potentiometer. When a finger or the wrist is flexed, the inelastic cord exerts a torque on the coupler which rotates the potentiometer's shaft. This generates an analogue output voltage that is interpreted by the microcontroller to measure the flexion/extension angle of the wrist and individual fingers. Furthermore, the microcontroller used to interpret the joint angles contains a built-in 9-axis Inertial Measurement Unit (IMU) which is used to estimate the arm's posture.

C. *Tension adjustment*

Based on the degree of hyperflexion experienced by the user, springs of appropriate stiffness can be used. However, the amount of assistance required could change during training with recovery. Therefore, the WiGlove has a motorised tension adjustment system that increases or decreases the free length of a given spring. This allows the user and the therapists to modulate the assistance so that the user is adequately challenged during training using a slider interface on a touchscreen tablet.

D. *Wireless connectivity and tablet interface*

Unlike SPO which is tethered, the WiGlove is a wireless device and as such does not require the user to be at a specific location. This allows the user to train in different places in their home. The microcontroller transmits all the data to a touchscreen tablet through Bluetooth 4.0. This allows both therapists and users to monitor the performance including the range of motion (RoM), number of repetitions, training duration, etc. It also allows the user to interact with therapeutic games on the tablet while training with the WiGlove to enhance motivation. It can be charged using a micro-USB cable.

III. Methods

In a previous study, a comparative evaluation of the WiGlove and SPO in a counterbalanced, within-subject experiment involving 20 healthy participants, showed statistically

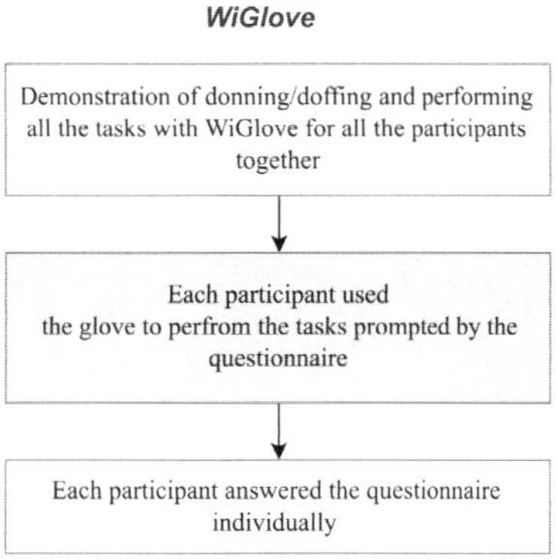

Figure 4. Experiment flow.

significant evidence of the WiGlove improvements over the SPO in the following usability aspects: ease of donning and doffing, ease of adjusting the assistance, unrestricted natural DoF, suitability for ADL and perception of aesthetics, wireless operation and safety [11]. Building on this preliminary validation, further usability evaluation was conducted in two stages with stroke therapists and stroke survivors as follows.

A. *Formative evaluation - Stroke therapists*

The objective of this phase was to leverage the expertise of therapists with experience in post-stroke rehabilitation to improve the WiGlove's usability and safety before introducing it to stroke survivors. This study was approved by the University's Ethics Committee (Ethics protocol number: aSPECS/ PGR/ UH/ 04896(1)).

1) Study protocol: In this in-person heuristic evaluation process, stroke therapists ($N = 6$) from the Luton and Dunstable hospital, UK used the WiGlove and assessed its usability. Firstly, a demonstration of using the WiGlove was provided to all the participants (Figure 4). Following this, each of them used the device and performed a set of tasks designed to help evaluate the above-mentioned aspects of usability, similar to [11].

They involved don/doffing the different modules of the device in a specific sequence, performing ab/adduction of the wrist to ensure that the device does not block this degree of freedom which could lead to hypertonia, and adjusting the amount of extension assistance, etc. To assess the WiGlove's suitability for performing ADL while wearing it, three different grasping tasks, namely palmar pinch (key), cylindrical grasp (bottle) and a spherical grasp(ball) were included (Figure 5). These precision (palmar pinch) and power (spherical and cylindrical) grasps are significant to perform ADL [12].

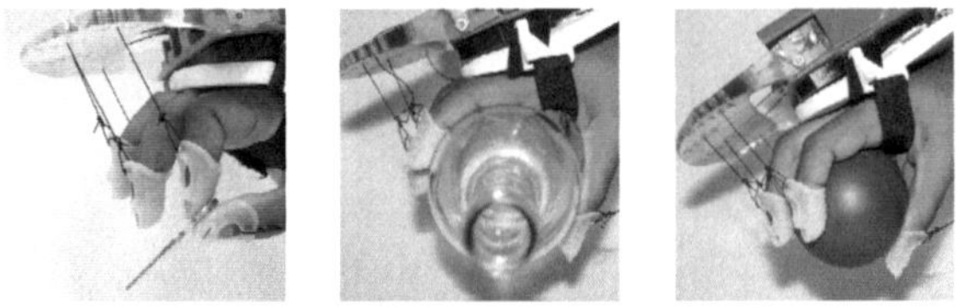

(a) Palmar Pinch (Key). (b) Cylindrical grasp (bottle). (c) Spherical grasp (bottle).

Figure 5. Grasping Tasks

2) Data Acquisition: Upon completing the tasks, the therapists individually gave feedback using a 7-point Likert scale questionnaire. Each question related to the individual tasks that they performed. For example, the following is one of the questions that requested the participant to rate the ease with which they could perform the cylindrical grasp.

How easy was it to grasp the bottle while wearing the device ?

	1	2	3	4	5	6	7	
Very Difficult	○	○	○	○	○	○	○	Very Easy

This approach was adopted since traditional usability scales such as System Usability Scale (SUS) are tailored for end users (stroke survivors in our case) and hence was rendered unsuitable for this study. Additionally, open-ended questions were also used to record their thoughts in a more detailed and descriptive manner on the WiGlove's suitability of ADL, don/doffing and safety. Each participant took approximately 15 minutes to answer the questionnaire. This approach provided invaluable context to their Likert scale scores and helped to better address their concerns in improving the WiGlove's design.

B. *Feasibility Study - Stroke Survivors*

Having incorporated the therapists' feedback, the revised WiGlove is undergoing a 6-week evaluation at a hemiparetic stroke survivor's home. The participant uses the WiGlove to perform flexion/extension exercises without the supervision of a therapist. This study was approved by the University's Ethics Committee (Ethics protocol number: aSPECS/ PGR/ UH/ 05084(1)).

1) Study Protocol: The participant was recruited using flyers placed in the stroke unit of the Luton and Dunstable Hospital. He is a 78-year-old male, who experienced strokes twice 15 months ago, resulting in left-sided hemiparesis. It is evidenced by the excessive tone in the hand that resulted in a clenched fist (as seen in Figure 2) which prevented the participant from grasping any boxes or pegs in Box and Block(BnB) and Nine Hole Peg Test (NHPT) [13]. These tests were administered to establish a baseline similar to a recent study investigating the feasibility of a hand exoskeleton [5].

Firstly, in the fitting stage, measurements were taken so that the device was customised to the participant's hand dimensions. After this, the WiGlove and its tablet interface were

(a) Wrist exercise game

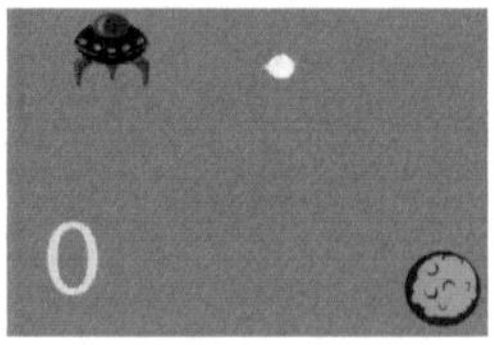

(b) Fingers exercise game

Figure 6. Games for training

delivered to the participant's home. During the first week, the participant was encouraged to get familiar with the device by performing flexion/extension exercises and simple activities of daily life like drinking from a bottle and eating with a spoon. Following this familiarisation phase, apart from performing ADL, the participant was introduced to two therapeutic games designed to enhance engagement and motivation for training. These games entailed the user controlling the position of a character and triggering specific actions (e.g., hitting a moving target) by performing flexion/extension of their wrist and fingers (Figure 6).

2) Data Acquisition: During the home-based training period, the tablet logs training data such as joint angle information, number of repetitions, training duration and time, which are later retrieved to analyse and monitor the participant's performance. The participant was also encouraged to complete an online questionnaire about their experience with the device once a week. Furthermore, an in-person semi-structured interview after the first three weeks and at the end of 6-weeks is used to gather his feedback on training with the device. The audio of the responses is recorded, transcribed and analysed. Additionally, similar to [5], The Quebec User Evaluation of Satisfaction with Assistive Technology (QUEST 2.0) questionnaire was used to record his level of satisfaction with the WiGlove on a 5-point Likert scale [14]. During this first half of the study, the participant was visited twice to collect the data.

IV. RESULTS

This section presents the results from the formative study with the stroke therapists and the feasibility analysis involving one stroke survivor.

A. *Formative evaluation - Stroke therapists*

The statistical results of the therapists' feedback are presented in Table I. Overall the participants gave a median score above 4 for most categories while performing a cylindrical task with the WiGlove was judged to be the easiest with a median score of 6.5. Furthermore, the participants unanimously gave high scores for the WiGlove's aesthetic appeal and safety as evidenced by their corresponding interquartile ranges. Among the different grasps, performing the palmar pinch received the lowest median score of 4 indicating a neutral opinion. The following remark by a participant provides insight into the probable cause for this low score.

TABLE I. RESULTS OF THERAPISTS' FEEDBACK (1 - VERY DIFFICULT, 7 - VERY EASY)

	Median	**Inter Quartile Range**
Ease of donning the forearm module	4.5	1
Ease of donning the hand module	5	0.75
Ease of donning the fingercaps	5	1.5
Ease of doffing the forearm module	5	1.5
Ease of doffing the hand module	5	0.75
Ease of doffing the fingercaps	5	0.75
Ease of performing the ab/adduction of the wrist	4.5	2.5
Ease of performing the ab/adduction of the fingers	3.5	1
Perception of the weight	4.5	2
Ease of performing a palmar pinch (key grasp)	4	1.5
Ease of performing a cylindrical grasp(bottle)	6.5	1.75
Ease of performing a spherical grasp(ball)	5.5	1.75
Suitability for ADL	4	2
Aesthetic appeal	5	0.75
Perception of user safety	5	0.75
Perception of safety for the family	5	0

Therapist 2 - *"I found that the nuts of the glove were resisting my normal movement."*

1) Design Revisions:

- The palmar pinch requires the thumb and the index finger to flex more than the other grasps. The presence of nuts on the device above the metacarpophalangeal (MCP) joints of the fingers (knuckle) could have restricted their flexion and ab/adduction reflected by its corresponding median score of 3.5. Although. Plastazote foams were used to provide padding from such nuts, the above comment shows that this did not provide adequate isolation. Hence in the revised design, a custom-made foam found in SaeboFlex was used in the WiGlove to provide isolation and ensure comfortable interaction. This foam was used in SPO where no such issues were reported in user trials. This revision was implemented in the WiGlove before the next phase of evaluations.
- Similarly, another participant raised a concern about a pressure point near the wrist due to impingement from the thumb's mechanism. In the revised design, the thumb's passive joint was moved such that it is located proximal to the line of the wrist to ensure that it does not create a pressure point for people with larger hand sizes. Although, given that this was raised by only one participant, this could be due to a mismatch in the glove's size where the thumb's passive mechanism impinges on a participant with a larger wrist. Unlike this study, the device's dimensions will be customised to the stroke survivor's hand in the succeeding stages.

B. *Feasibility Study - Stroke Survivors*

This manuscript reports the results from the first half of a 6-week home-based training study with the first participant. The participant, using his dominant (unimpaired) hand, was able to move 34 blocks in 60 seconds during the BnB test and complete the NHPT test in 35 seconds. However, when using their impaired (left) hand, the participant was unable to

TABLE II. USER EXPERIENCE FEEDBACK

Usability Aspects	**Comments**
Ease of donning/doffing	Due to substantial tone in the elbow and shoulder, the participant was unable to independently don the device and required the caregiver's help. On the other hand, he was able to doff the finger caps and forearm module without help.
Safety	The participant did not find or experience any safety concerns.
Suitability for the home environment	Due to its small size the participant found it easy to store away from the reach of kids. The wireless operation allowed them to train in different rooms including while lying in their bed. It was deemed very suitable for the home environment.
Learnability	Operating the device was perceived to be straightforward and easy to learn.
Battery	No concerns of battery life were raised. It was charged for 30 minutes every day.
Games	The participant found the games very interesting and was very satisfied with the WiGlove's sensitivity for playing them. "**Felt very happy even when I hit just twice**". He suggested that games involving musical triggers and multiplayer games where other members of the family like the grand kids also can be involved would be even more stimulating. "**The grand kids, yeah, they always want to win, yeah that motivating factor** "
Comfort	It was perceived to be very comfortable
Weight	The participant felt that the device could be lighter. "**It's not heavy, but it could be lighter**"
Feedback on WiGlove's effectiveness	The participant reported observable improvements in his hand with a noticeable reduction in the finger's stiffness. "**It was not supple enough, but over the last two weeks, the mornings, it is very relaxed and soft**", "**How long will, I need, I don't know, but, Definitely, the glove makes a difference**".

grasp any blocks or pegs due to a hyperflexion-induced closed fist. While wearing the WiGlove did enable the participant to grasp boxes they were still unable to complete the test as a result of excessive muscle tone in the shoulder and elbow, impeding gross movements in the arm. Therefore, the baseline for the hand alone was established through an examination of the number of items that the participant was able to grasp, which was 2 blocks in 60 seconds. The participant lacked the necessary range of motion to grasp a peg for the NHPT test. After 3-weeks of training, while wearing the WiGlove, the participant was able to actively pick and drop 9 blocks in 60 seconds compared to the 2 at the beginning of the study. The participant had not yet gained enough RoM to perform NHPT. Both tests will be performed again at the end of the study to evaluate the impact of the intervention.

Based on the data logged in the tablet, the participant performed hand exercises without the therapist's supervision for an average of 50 ($\pm$42) minutes/day with the WiGlove. It also showed that he often split his daily training into multiple sessions with a maximum of 3 sessions on a specific day leading to a total training duration of 175 minutes. Furthermore, the participant's comments during the 25-minute semi-structured interview are summarised in Table II. Based on his experience of using the WiGlove for three weeks, he gave it a rating of 3.75 on the QUEST 2.0 satisfaction scale.

V. DISCUSSION

Overall, the therapists positively rated the ease of donning/doffing the WiGlove independently. Evident in their comments shown below, the therapists believed that hemiparetic stroke survivors would be able to don/doff the WiGlove easily and would only be limited by their cognitive ability. They pointed out the need for written instructions to guide the users during the familiarisation stage.

Therapist 1 - "*Appears suitable for patients to do. However, would be limited to those cognitively able to do so*"

Therapist 3 - "*Would need a good level of cognitive ability. Can be a bit fiddly the first few times*"

With regard to the WiGlove's weight, although the therapists' scores indicate a neutral opinion, this is similar to the median score (4.5) given by healthy participants in the previous study who tried the WiGlove first before trying [11]. In the previous study, the participants who rated the WiGlove after trying SPO overwhelmingly rated the WiGlove to be lighter. Since the therapists only tried the WiGlove, the neutral score could be attributed to a lack of reference for comparison. This will be verified in the study with stroke survivors. This and the ease of performing a palmar pinch could explain the neutral score for the WiGlove's suitability for performing ADL. Given the changes implemented, we anticipate that stroke survivors will not face the above issue faced by therapists and find it easy to perform activities of daily life while wearing the WiGlove.

Unfortunately, due to the excessive weakness in the proximal joints of the first participant (stroke survivor) who is discussed in this study, he was unable to perform any ADL, precluding the evaluation of the effects of these design upgrades at this stage. However, the participant was still able to use the WiGlove to regularly train for long durations by performing flexion/extension exercises.

Prior to his involvement in this study, his rehabilitation involved 6 weeks of in-patient therapy to the lower limb immediately after the stroke. Since then, the participant has had three one-hour sessions of therapy(one-to-one with a therapist) every week of which only five minutes were dedicated to hand exercises. On the contrary in the first 20 days of the study, the participant performed hand exercises for an average of 50 ($\pm$42) minutes/day with the WiGlove without the therapist's supervision by splitting his training session. The participant's improved performance in the BnB test after 3 weeks could be ascribed to him regaining some active RoM due to this increased training intensity and familiarisation with the device. This serves as promising preliminary evidence for the WiGlove's effectiveness.

The participant's adherence to training could be attributed to the usability of the WiGlove based on their feedback in the semi-structured interview. Overall, the responses indicate a positive experience and acceptance of the device as evidenced by their QUEST 2.0 score of 3.75 which is classified as "more or less satisfied to quite satisfied". Although the games were introduced to him 10 days after the study began, he did not interact with them more than twice, due to unrelated secondary health complications which reduced his overall daily training durations and the use of the WiGlove. This precludes analysis of the effects of the games on the training duration in the first half of the study. This will be studied upon completion of the 6-week study period. However, his feedback based on the initial interaction with the games shows a positive impression and attitude towards training with the games.

VI. Conclusion

The WiGlove is a passive robotic orthosis designed to facilitate home-based rehabilitation of the hand and wrist in stroke survivors. This manuscript highlights the different aspects of the device and reports on its evaluation by six stroke therapists and early evidence from a feasibility trial that has begun with one stroke survivor. The objectives of these evaluations were to assess the WiGlove's usability and its feasibility as a home-based rehabilitation device. Stroke therapists positively rated the usability of the WiGlove and their feedback was used to improve its design. The preliminary results of the study with the one stroke survivor serve as evidence supporting the feasibility of the WiGlove for home-based therapy and reaffirm its usability. Due to the supportive results, a second stroke survivor is now being enrolled with an expectation to recruit up to 4 patients for this feasibility trial.

Future work will involve the continuation of this study with stroke survivors experiencing varying levels of motor function deficits in the hand to validate its feasibility further and evaluate its effectiveness in helping hemiparetic stroke survivors regain their ability to perform activities of daily life.

Acknowledgement

The authors express their gratitude to the stroke clinicians at Luton and Dunstable Hospital in the UK and the stroke survivor who participated in this research by dedicating their time and providing valuable feedback at various stages of this research.

References

[1] F. Amirabdollahian, *et al.*, "Design, development and deployment of a hand/wrist exoskeleton for home-based rehabilitation after stroke-script project," *Robotica*, vol. 32, no. 8, pp. 1331–1346, 2014.

[2] S. Straudi, *et al.*, "Effectiveness of robot-assisted arm therapy in stroke rehabilitation: An overview of systematic reviews," *NeuroRehabilitation*, no. Preprint, pp. 1–15, 2022.

[3] S. C. Cramer, *et al.*, "Efficacy of home-based telerehabilitation vs in-clinic therapy for adults after stroke: A randomized clinical trial," *JAMA neurology*, vol. 76, no. 9, pp. 1079–1087, 2019.

[4] A. Borboni, M. Mor, and R. Faglia, "Gloreha—hand robotic rehabilitation: Design, mechanical model, and experiments," *Journal of Dynamic Systems, Measurement, and Control*, vol. 138, no. 11, 2016.

[5] A. Yurkewich, S. Ortega, J. Sanchez, R. H. Wang, and E. Burdet, "Integrating hand exoskeletons into goal-oriented clinic and home stroke and spinal cord injury rehabilitation," *Journal of Rehabilitation and Assistive Technologies Engineering*, vol. 9, p. 20556683221130970, 2022.

[6] T. Bützer, O. Lambercy, J. Arata, and R. Gassert, "Fully wearable actuated soft exoskeleton for grasping assistance in everyday activities," *Soft robotics*, vol. 8, no. 2, pp. 128–143, 2021.

[7] H. Al-Fahaam, S. Davis, S. Nefti-Meziani, and T. Theodoridis, "Novel soft bending actuator-based power augmentation hand exoskeleton controlled by human intention," *Intelligent Service Robotics*, vol. 11, no. 3, pp. 247–268, 2018.

[8] B. Noronha and D. Accoto, "Exoskeletal devices for hand assistance and rehabilitation: A comprehensive analysis of state-of-the-art technologies," *IEEE Transactions on Medical Robotics and Bionics*, vol. 3, no. 2, pp. 525–538, 2021.

[9] S. Ates, *et al.*, "Technical evaluation of and clinical experiences with the script passive wrist and hand orthosis," in *2014 7th International Conference on Human System Interactions (HSI)*. IEEE, 2014, pp. 188–193.

[10] V. Velmurugan, L. Wood, and F. Amirabdollahian, "Requirements for a home-based rehabilitation device for hand and wrist therapy after stroke," in *UKRAS21: The 4th UK Robotics and Autonomous Systems Conference*, jul 2021, p. 23.

[11] V. Velmurugan, L. J. Wood, and F. Amirabdollahian, "Formative usability evaluation of wiglove-a home-based rehabilitation device for hand and wrist therapy after stroke," in *Companion of the 2023 ACM/IEEE International Conference on Human-Robot Interaction*, 2023, pp. 272–276.

[12] B. Leon, *et al.*, "Grasps recognition and evaluation of stroke patients for supporting rehabilitation therapy," *BioMed Research International*, vol. 2014, 2014.

[13] L. Haverkate, G. Smit, and D. H. Plettenburg, "Assessment of body-powered upper limb prostheses by able-bodied subjects, using the box and blocks test and the nine-hole peg test," *Prosthetics and orthotics international*, vol. 40, no. 1, pp. 109–116, 2016.

[14] L. Demers, R. Weiss-Lambrou, and B. Ska, "The quebec user evaluation of satisfaction with assistive technology (quest 2.0): an overview and recent progress," *Technology and Disability*, vol. 14, no. 3, pp. 101–105, 2002.

Involving Users in the Development of AI-Supported CAM Systems by Co-Creation Methods

Nina Rußkamp, Lorena Niebuhr, and Eva-Maria Jakobs
Human-Computer Interaction Center / Text Linguistics and Technical Communication
RWTH Aachen University
Aachen, Germany
email: {n.russkamp, l.niebuhr, e.m.jakobs}@tk.rwth-aachen.de

Abstract—**In many German key industries, the process planning for manufacturing workpieces is carried out with Computer-Aided Manufacturing (CAM) systems. Shorter innovation cycles and greater product customization in the industry 4.0 era are rapidly increasing the complexity of products and CAM systems, making it even for experienced CAM planners challenging to carry out their work on time. This is also because CAM systems are still difficult to use and learn. The research and development project CAM2030 aims to partially automate parameter optimization in the CAM-planning process with the help of artificial intelligence, cloud computing, and evolutionary algorithms. The aim is to save time, get closer to the perfect process planning, and relieve the user. An interdisciplinary team of experts from industry and academia is developing approaches for a new generation of CAM systems. This paper focuses on how co-creation facilitates the involvement of software users in developing new software generations that integrate new technologies, such as artificial intelligence. A methodological co-creation framework was developed to continuously incorporate the actors involved in the innovation process. The framework was applied to the project case study to investigate (i) the potential of the co-creation framework for eliciting user expectations relevant to acceptance and usability, and (ii) what retraining needs the integration of artificial intelligence requires and how users could be supported when switching to the new system. The co-creation approach shows a high potential to integrate the user's (CAM planner's) perspective in interdisciplinary innovation processes. It facilitated the identification of general and selective relearning needs induced by redesigning CAM-planning processes, the system (interface), and the integration of novel technologies. Applying this knowledge to the design and implementation of new software generations benefits the users and companies; it makes the system introduction easier, faster, and less prone to disruptions. Future research should provide guidance for introducing new generations of CAM software and accompanying the transformation process.**

Keywords- user perspective; co-creation; computer-aided-manufacturing; artificial intelligence; software training.

I. INTRODUCTION

In the manufacturing industry, transformation towards shorter innovation cycles and greater product customization increases the complexity of Computer-Aided Manufacturing (CAM) tasks and systems. CAM planners face the challenge of meeting rising quality requirements under time pressure. CAM planners usually achieve a process planning quality close to the optimum within a few hours (80 % solution). Most of their working time is spent on parameter adjustments to identify and eliminate minor but technically relevant errors. A basic assumption is that enriching software systems with novel technologies, especially Artificial Intelligence (AI), can reduce the users' workload [1].

In the research and development project CAM2030, an interdisciplinary team of experts from industry and academia is developing approaches for a new generation of CAM systems that integrate technologies, such as artificial intelligence, cloud computing, and evolutionary algorithms. The innovation process focuses on partially automating CAM-planning processes, especially CAM parameterization. The automation requires a modification of the parameterization process which will also lead to changes in the working processes of CAM planners. Thus, AI integration raises the challenges of finding out where CAM planners need to rethink and relearn working routines, which solutions are acceptable and comprehensible to users, and what support they need to adapt to changing workflows as efficiently as possible.

An essential prerequisite for achieving the project goal is to bring actor-specific perspectives together, close knowledge gaps, and integrate user perspectives [1]. This paper focuses on the involvement of CAM users in the innovation process. Therefore, a methodological co-creation framework was developed that systematically incorporates the actors involved in the innovation process [2][3]. The co-creation framework is intended to support the development process in and across different innovation stages. Selected co-creation methods were adapted and combined for collaboration in online workshops under remote conditions. The approach was tested and evaluated guided by the following research questions (RQ):

RQ1: Does the co-creation approach provide early indications of acceptance-relevant user expectations and requirements for the new system generation (criterion: acceptance and usability)?

RQ2: Does the co-creation approach enable early indications of potential support needs and suitable measures to cover them? Where do users need support and explanations when switching to the new system (e.g., in the interface design or by training)? How should new routines, interfaces, and knowledge requirements be introduced? How high is the retraining requirement?

Section II presents related work on developing AI-supported systems for the manufacturing industry. The methodological approach of this study, developing and implementing the co-creation framework, is described in Section III. The results of the study are presented in Section IV. Section V concludes the findings and provides an outlook for future research. Finally, the limitations of the study are outlined in Section VI.

II. Related Work

In this section, the state of the art is shortly summarized with respect to two foci: requirements for AI-supported systems and their use in the manufacturing industry (Subsection A) and co-creation approaches for product and process innovation (Subsection B).

A. *Requirements for AI-Supported Systems and Their Use in the Manufacturing Industry*

When AI technologies are introduced in the context of the manufacturing industry, they face a unique set of challenges compared to their general use [4]. Introducing technologies into production environments involves considering existing facilities, IT systems, and the employees who run that production. Therefore, requirements for integrating AI technologies can be derived from general requirements but must be adapted to the area of application [4]. Few publications address requirements for AI technologies in a production environment [4][5].

Hoffmann et al. [4] introduce 16 requirements divided into five categories: Adaptation, Engineering, Embedding, Security, and Trust, that need to be considered when introducing AI technologies in a production environment.

Adaption: When introducing AI technologies, they should be adapted to the existing production environment. The introduction should be gradual, firstly keeping the human employee in control of all decisions, serving as a decision support system. In addition, the availability of the data needed by the AI has to be considered, and potential conflicts in terms of legal, cultural, technical, and security issues have to be clarified.

Engineering: Keeping the AI system as simple as possible is a primary goal when designing the AI system. The complexity of the system should be hidden. The user of the AI-based system most likely doesn't have a background in computer science. The simplicity of the design contributes to the robustness of the system. The AI system should be able to physically and virtually learn and incrementally adapt to the production environment [4].

Embedding: When embedding AI technologies, a trust space and boundary need to be defined, such as a checkpoint for the human employee to prove the plausibility of the AI's decisions. AI knowledge should be distributed to other AIs via higher-level systems or communication networks. However, the AI should not base its conclusions on data created by another AI [4].

Safety: The safety and security of AI technologies are a very broad area for research and requirements engineering. It is important to ensure that production systems are safe in accordance with applicable laws and regulations and do not pose a risk to human employees, even in the case of self-improvement. The risk for failure should be transparent. Industrial AI must be robust against random and deliberate adversary input [4].

Trust: Trust contributes to security and performance; it is an important factor for acceptance [5]. To support trust, the AI system's decisions should be as transparent and understandable as possible. The system should be able to explain its decision, e.g., through visualizations [6]. Any errors in the AI's assumptions should be detectable and correctable. Levels of trust or levels of quality should be used to express the probability of failure [4]. The AI's capabilities should be provable in a test run or a virtual environment. AI systems in the manufacturing industry need to be free of bias in treating all vendors' equipment equally. A measure of confidence should be made when giving action recommendations. AI systems are expected to have a 100 % solution rate, which cannot be achieved by a technical system [4]. The level of uncertainty should therefore be communicated to the user [5].

Both the system and the user require an effective learning process. While the system needs time to learn the user's behavioral patterns, intentions, and operational status, users need adequate training with the system [5].

A critical challenge is establishing a skilled workforce for the future manufacturing industry [7]. However, it is rarely discussed how to cover CAM users' relearning needs resulting from the integration of AI-based features. Jiao et al. [7] postulate to meet digitalization-related challenges by fostering nontechnical skills, such as continuous learning, communication, critical thinking, and making decisions using incomplete knowledge. To our knowledge, guidelines for the design of AI-sensitive training formats are still missing.

B. *User Integration: Co-Creation Approaches for Product and Process Innovation*

To date, software engineering methods tailored to developing AI-based systems are scarce [8]. Existing approaches focus more on identifying system-immanent challenges than user needs [2]. One approach to actively involve users throughout the whole innovation process is co-creation. Despite its high potential, the use of co-creation methods for the user-centered innovation of complex software systems for the manufacturing industry is hardly discussed (but, e.g., [7][8]).

The key element of co-creation is the collaboration between software production- and application-related actors as part of "an active, creative and social process" [11]. The process facilitates reducing uncertainties by providing access to two types of information: customer and market needs, e.g., users' motives and preferences for new products and services *(need information)* and possibilities for their (technological) implementation *(solution information)*. The co-creation typology proposed by [11] classifies co-creation methods based on three dimensions:

The stage in the innovation process: It refers to the point in time when the method is applied to the innovation process. *Front-end* co-creation at the early stages of the innovation process mainly focuses on conceptual tasks, i.e., idea generation and selection. In contrast, *back-end* co-creation deals with the design and testing of a product at later innovation stages.

The degree of collaboration: It is determined by the number of collaborating partners and the company-to-customer ratio (developer-to-user ratio), e.g., 1:n or n:m.

The degrees of freedom: They determine the customer's autonomy in the innovation process resulting from the type of task (open vs. predefined task).

Due to the Covid-19 pandemic, research on virtual co-creation methods has increased (e.g., [12]).

III. METHODOLOGY

The methodology comprises three subsections: a description of the innovation process segmented into five innovation stages the co-creation framework is based on (Subsection A), development of the framework and the methodological design of the single stages in general (Subsection B), and detailed insights into the procedure of selected stages (Subsection C).

A. *Overview of the Co-Creation-Based Framework*

The co-creation-based framework was abstracted from the innovation process in the project CAM2030 between 2020 and 2023. It covers five innovation stages, from eliciting the as-is condition of the CAM-planning process to introducing next-generation CAM systems (see Fig. 1).

Stage i aimed at creating a shared understanding of the status quo and, based on this, at deriving requirements for its partial automation. The first step was to elicit, model, and visualize the CAM-planning process and its embedment in the higher-level production process as currently conducted in the manufacturing industry. In the second step, the resulting process models were used to identify weak points and automation potential of CAM-planning processes and their implications for the design of

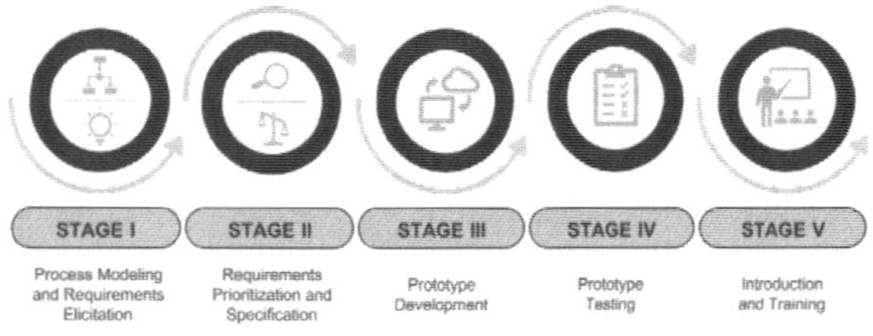

Figure 1. Innovation stages for developing AI-supported CAM systems using co-creation.

next-generation CAM systems. The results comprised improved and enriched process models [13], a ranked list of role-related, topically clustered no-go measurements, and, inverted and complemented, a structured catalog of requirements for the design of CAM systems.

Based on stage i, stage ii served the prioritization, specification, and complement of requirements, mainly focusing on the user interface redesign for optimizing CAM parameter settings. The outcome was a prioritized and categorized list of requirements for CAM systems in general and the user interface in particular.

Stage iii marked the transition from conceptualization to implementation. The focus was on consolidating knowledge about system design requirements and developing a typical user path, a mockup for the future CAM-planning process, and an interactive prototype for the user interface.

Stage iv was iteratively conducted with prototypes of different maturity levels. The prototypes were evaluated with regard to weaknesses and potential for optimization. In addition to guidelines for improving the prototype, user feedback regarding integrated help functions and training was gathered.

Stage v (not yet fully implemented) is supposed to yield a requirements profile for introducing next-generation CAM systems and further training of CAM planners. The profile should consider different categories, such as the content and format of training and the planner's expertise.

B. *Stage-Wise Development of the Framework*

For each stage, a methodological approach was developed, implemented, and evaluated, inter alia [14]. The approaches were mainly based on co-creation, partly complemented by other formats, e.g., online surveys. Co-creation was applied in online workshops involving developers, CAM users, human-centered work design experts, and technical communication experts. The workshops were moderated by a team of workshop leaders who accompanied the participants to work together on system development tasks. The CAM planners were asked to provide input and/or evaluate possible solutions in all innovation stages. Each workshop ended with an evaluation of the methods used in the workshop. The co-creation workshop tasks varied in several aspects:

- the group size (single-work tasks vs. group tasks in separated teams or the plenum)
- the group composition (role-related teams vs. interdisciplinary teams),
- the methods used (front-end vs. back-end co-creation, integration of co-creation and process modeling based on the C3 notation [15] [16])
- the tools used (selection of Zoom, Google Docs, Google Forms, Mural, Figma, and Microsoft Office). Google Docs was also used, among other things, to share organizational information, such as the workshop agenda and the list of participants. It served as a guide for the workshop procedure.

- the synchrony of user involvement (preparatory tasks prior to the workshop vs. collaboration tasks during the workshop vs. inter-workshop tasks vs. evaluation tasks after the workshop).

The workshops were digitally recorded. The recording included video and audio data as well as written documents and visualizations created during the workshop, e.g., notes in shared text documents and online whiteboards. The audio was transcribed. The transcripts were supplemented with notes and evaluated qualitatively (content analysis). Surveys were analyzed qualitatively and quantitatively (descriptive statistics). The results were made available to all project partners. They were a prerequisite and input for the next innovation step.

C. *Methodological Design of Stages i, ii, and iv*

As this paper mainly refers to results yielded from stages i, ii, and iv, the methodological approaches of these stages are described in more detail:

The key design element of *stage i* was the combination of co-creation and process modeling methods [14]. The purpose of integrating process modeling was tripartite: (i) to equalize differences in knowledge about the CAM-planning process, (ii) to identify and merge role-specific perspectives (e.g., general mechanical engineering vs. aircraft manufacturing), and (iii) to facilitate getting in the requirements elicitation. The elicitation, modeling, and visualization of CAM-related processes, as they are typically conducted in the manufacturing industry, took place before the co-creation workshop pictured in Fig. 2.

The workshop applied front-end co-creation (e.g., warm-up challenge as an idea generation task with high degrees of freedom). Group sizes and compositions were varied task-by-task while a shared text document was accessible for all participants throughout the workshop serving as results log.

For the co-creation workshop in *stage ii*, the digital whiteboard tool Mural was used to enable the workshop participants to capture all workshop results – topically clustered requirements and their prioritization – at once. Dot voting was used to prioritize requirements and identify the need for requirements specification (see Fig. 3).

Stage iv was divided into three parts: (i) a preliminary survey with CAM users, (ii) a co-creation test workshop, and (iii) a complementary prototype evaluation (see Fig.

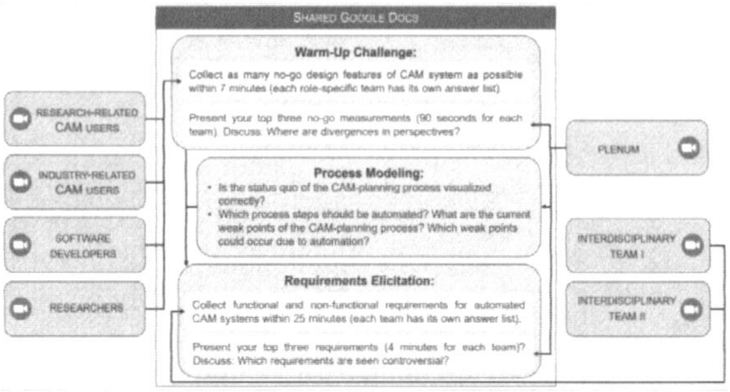

Figure 2. Co-creation workshop (stage i).

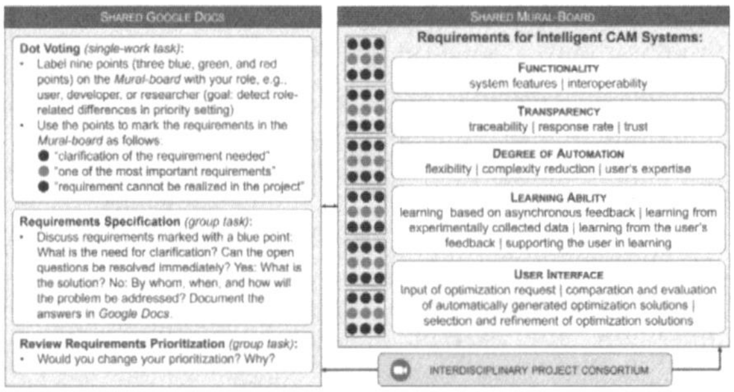

Figure 3. Co-creation workshop (stage ii).

4). To get multiple feedback, especially from CAM planners, the approach alternates synchronous (part ii) and asynchronous (parts i and iii) formats. This enabled the discussion of the pre-survey results during the workshop and the prototype evaluation to take place either during or after the workshop. Different tools, e.g., Figma and Google Forms, were combined for the prototype evaluation. Figma allowed self-experience with the interactive prototype; the questionnaire was created in Google Forms.

IV. Results and Discussion

The approach shows a high potential to support all stakeholders in creating a shared understanding of the innovation process and the resulting CAM system. The co-creation workshops helped to identify and reconcile diverging perspectives (Subsection A). The user input was very productive: It provided the need for the redesign of the overall system and the user interface and, as a result, the need for relearning working routines (Subsection B). Additionally, it gave valuable hints for the design of integrated help functions and software training (Subsection C).

A. *Role-Specific Perspectives on AI Integration*

From the perspective of manufacturing companies, one risk is that workers will perceive automation as unnecessary, arguing that it is too complex and offers too little benefit compared to the current process. High training requirements and costs associated with the lack of intuitive operation of partially automated CAM systems are rejected. AI-based CAM systems must be practical and

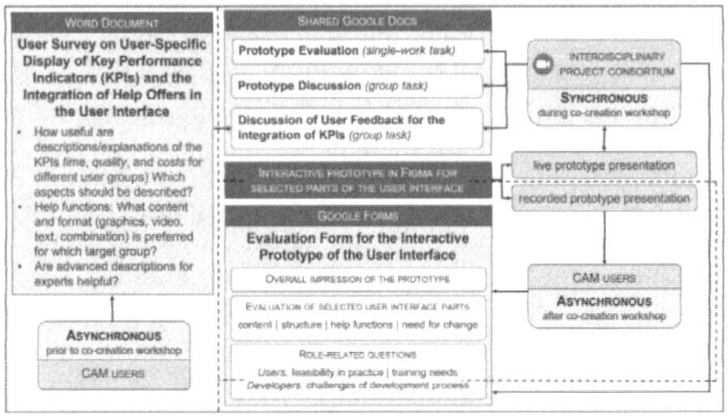

Figure 4. Structure of the prototype testing (stage iv).

appropriate for the application domain.

Developers, especially artificial intelligence experts, consider intransparency, i.e., lacking traceability of automated decisions made, as one of the three most significant inhibitors to the acceptance by CAM planners (see also [4]). A related issue is the unpredictability of the system's runtime for automated tasks and the automatically generated results' quality. The developers believe that making the system more transparent and giving the user continuous feedback on the system's current state will increase acceptance among CAM planners (see also [5]). Another barrier to acceptance, which can be exacerbated by the factors mentioned above, is the disenfranchisement of the CAM planner.

CAM planners see the risk that automation will reduce their freedom of action. They emphasize the need to balance simplifying the CAM-planning process against limiting the user's flexibility. This is coupled with the requirement for the system to adapt to the user's expertise. In addition, the lack of trustworthiness of the CAM system is considered a no-go characteristic.

Overall, the workshop participants' perspectives on tipping points for the acceptability and comprehensibility of automated CAM features gradually differ. The participants agree that the decision-making authority of the user is a prerequisite for acceptance. They emphasize the need for automation on demand.

B. *Redesign and Relearning Needs*

Stage iv has shown that automating the CAM parameterization has multiple consequences. It affects the workflow, the significance of Key Performance Indicators (KPIs) for the workflow, the system interface design, and the requirements for the user. The new workflow comprises three steps: (i) configuration of the CAM parameterization request (user task), (ii) execution of the optimization resulting in a set of high-quality parameter settings (automatically generated by the system), and (iii) evaluation, selection, and refinement of parameter settings (user task). The interface must be adapted to the new sequence of actions, e.g., by extending the interface to include input screens for selecting optimization preferences. Changes in the workflow and the interface force CAM planners working with present CAM systems to partly rethink and acquire specific knowledge. Setting evaluation and target values during step (i) requires knowledge of KPIs concerning production time, quality, and costs. The CAM planners need to develop an understanding of which KPIs are important and what effects they have. Partly, AI is seen as a black box that users cannot fully understand. To accept the system, users should have access to AI-specific knowledge so that they can trust the system, interpret AI-generated results, and customize AI-enhanced CAM features.

C. *Implications for the Design of Integrated Help Functions, Introduction, and Training*

In the workshops, the CAM planners gave valuable hints for the design of user support, which information users want to access in the CAM system (explanations and help functions as part of the user interface), and what should be taught in introductory and advanced training. A critical issue is introducing and representing KPIs for the automated CAM parameter optimization. The training should provide a basic understanding of the KPIs and CAM parameters, while the CAM system should provide help functions for further information.

The training should give users a basic understanding of the CAM system and its AI-enhanced features. CAM planners need to be sensitized to CAM-planning steps that require new knowledge or rethinking previous user paths and actions. A demonstration of the new optimization workflow and user interface should be part of the training. The introductory training should also explain how the CAM system technically processes an optimization request to increase the user's understanding of what data the system needs to be able to carry out an optimization task. The introduction of KPIs and CAM parameters should be restricted to explaining which target values can be optimized and how they relate to the KPIs time, quality, and costs. CAM parameters should be introduced as threshold values that limit the solution space of the AI-based optimization.

Regarding integrated help functions, there is a high demand for KPI descriptions explaining the KPIs time, quality, and costs. For each KPI, providing explanations in the user interface was rated as "very useful," "useful," or "rather useful" across all user groups (see Fig. 5).

Descriptions of the KPI *costs* are perceived as most important independently of the user's expertise. The KPI time should be explained for all user groups, particularly novices. The KPI *quality* is useful for all user groups; experts are particularly predestined to handle quality-related information.

There is a broad consensus on how to integrate KPI descriptions into the user interface. Depending on the type of the KPI, the preferred format varies: Time- and cost-related information should be displayed as graphics. For quality, the combination of video and graphics is most suitable. Occasionally, texts (for time) or a combination of text and graphics (for quality and costs) are requested.

Integrated help functions should give the CAM planners indications of what effect the single KPIs have:

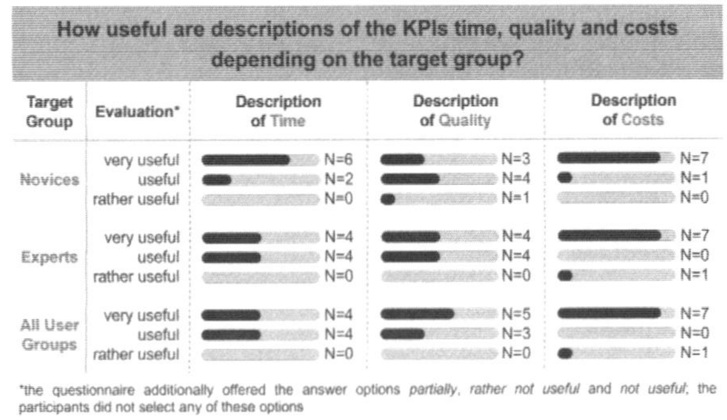

Figure 5. Ratings of the usefulness of KPI descriptions in the user interface.

Time: CAM planners should be able to calculate the processing time of their CAM plans and identify and take advantage of the potential for time reduction.

Quality: CAM planners must be able to evaluate in advance if the requested component quality can be ensured during production. Thus, they need quality estimations of, e.g., the CAM path and tools.

Costs: CAM planners need an overview of the different types of costs, e.g., machining costs, tooling costs, and personnel costs. It should be clear how changes in CAM planning affect expenses and how much the execution of the final CAM process planning costs the company.

V. Conclusion and Future Work

The user's role in developing innovative software systems is often underestimated. Co-creation-based approaches are suitable means to integrate the user's perspective in interdisciplinary innovation processes. Users' involvement allows for identifying general and selective relearning needs induced by the redesign of working processes and the system. Applying this knowledge to the design and implementation of new software generations benefits the users and companies; it makes the system introduction easier, faster, and less prone to disruptions. Future research should further investigate how to introduce new generations of CAM software and accompany the transformation process.

VI. Limitations

Limitations arise from the end users' reluctance to advance research at the expense of the daily business. Other limiting factors concern the restriction of automation to one selected CAM-planning step (the CAM parameterization) in one specific CAM system and the application context (well-educated CAM planners in German SMEs).

Acknowledgment

This research and development project is funded by the German Federal Ministry of Education and Research (BMBF) within the "Innovations for Tomorrow's Production, Services, and Work" Program (funding number: 02J19B081) and implemented by the Project Management Agency Karlsruhe (PTKA). The authors are responsible for the content of this publication.

References

[1] A. Csiszar, P. Hein, M. Wächter, A. Verl, and A. Bullinger, "Towards a user-centered development process of machine learning applications for manufacturing domain experts," Third International Conference on Artificial Intelligence for Industries (AI4I), Irvine, CA, USA, 2020, pp. 36-39, doi: 10.1109/AI4I49448.2020.00015.

[2] N. Rußkamp, C. Digmayer, and E.-M. Jakobs, "Co-creation-based Framework for the agile Development of AI-supported CAM Systems," 14th International Conference on Applied Human Factors and Ergonomics (AHFE 2023), unpublished.

[3] H. Belani, M. Vuković, and Ž. Car, "Requirements Engineering Challenges in Building AI-Based Complex Systems," 2019 IEEE 27th International Requirements Engineering Conference Workshops (REW), 2019, pp. 252-255, doi: 10.1109/REW.2019.00051.

[4] M. Hoffmann, R. Drath, and C. Ganz "Proposal for requirements on industrial AI solutions," in Machine Learning for Cyber Physical Systems: Selected papers from the International Conference ML4CPS 2020, J. Beyerer, A. Maier, and O. Niggemann, Eds. Berlin: Springer Vieweg, pp. 63-72, 2021, doi: 10.1007/978-3-662-62746-4.

[5] S. Pütz et al., "An Interdisciplinary View on Humane Interfaces for Digital Shadows in the Internet of Production," 15th International Conference on Human System Interaction (HSI), 2022, pp. 1-8, doi: 10.1109/HSI55341.2022.9869467.

[6] L. Tonejca, G. Mauthner, T. Trautner, V. König, and W. Liemberger, "AI-Based Surface Roughness Prediction Model for Automated CAM-Planning Optimization," 2022 IEEE 27th International Conference on Emerging Technologies and Factory Automation (ETFA), 2022, pp. 1-4, doi: 10.1109/ETFA52439.2022.9921281.

[7] R. Jiao et al., "Design Engineering in the Age of Industry 4.0," Journal of Mechanical Design, vol. 143, 070801, July 2021, doi: 10.1115/1.4051041.

[8] S. Martínez-Fernández et al., "Software Engineering for AI-Based Systems: A Survey," ACM Transactions on Software Engineering and Methodology, vol. 31, pp. 1-59, 2022, doi:10.1145/3487043.

[9] M. Tandi and E.-M. Jakobs "Two Heads are Better than One: Co-Creation as a Resource for User Interface Design of CAx Systems," 2019 IEEE International Professional Communication Conference (ProComm), 2019, pp. 71-78, doi: 10.1109/ProComm.2019.00019.

[10] M. Oliveira, A. Bettoni, E. Coscia, and H. Torvatn "Applying Co-creation Principles to Requirement Elicitation in Manufacturing," in: HCI International 2019 – Late Breaking Papers, HCII 2019, Lecture Notes in Computer Science, vol 11786, C. Stephanidis, Ed. Cham: Springer, pp. 54-61, 2019, doi: 10.1007/978-3-030-30033-3_5.

[11] F. T. Piller, C. Ihl, and A. Vossen, "A typology of customer co-creation in the innovation process," SSRN Electronic Journal, vol. 4, Dec. 2010, doi: 10.2139/ssrn.1732127.

[12] T. Benson et al. "Virtual Co-Creation: A Guide to Conducting Online Co-Creation Workshops," International Journal of Qualitative Methods, vol. 20, 2021, doi: 10.1177/16094069211053097.

[13] F. Burgert, M. Schirmer, M. Harlacher, V. Nitsch, and S. Mütze-Niewöhner, Participative elicitation and modeling of a CAM planning process for the manufacturing of complex components using the K3 notation. Aachen: Institute of Industrial Engineering and Ergonomics, 2022, doi:10.18154/RWTH-2022-01188.

[14] N. Rußkamp et al., "New ways to design next-generation CAM systems. An integrated approach of co-creation and process modeling," in: Human Aspects of Advanced Manufacturing. AHFE (2022) International Conference. AHFE Open Access, vol 66, W. Karwowski and S. Trzcielinski, Eds. USA: AHFE International, 2022, pp. 1-12, doi: 10.54941/ahfe1002682.

[15] S. Killich et al., "Task modeling for cooperative work," Behaviour & Information Technology, vol. 18, pp. 325-338, 1999, doi: 10.1080/014492999118913.

[16] A. Nielen, Systematik für die leistungs- und zuverlässigkeitsorientierte Modellierung von Arbeitsprozessen mit kontrollflussorientierten Notationssystemen. Aachen: Shaker, 2014.

Using Language Model for Implementation of Emotional Text-To-Speech

Mingguang Cao, Jie Zhu
Department of Electronic Engineering, Shanghai Jiaotong University, 800 Dongchuan Road, Shanghai 200240, China
Email:{mg_cao, zhujie}@sjtu.edu.cn

***Abstract*—With the development of neural network, Text-To-Speech (TTS) technology is booming unprecedentedly. The speech generated by modern text-to-speech systems almost sound as natural as human audio. However, the style control of synthetic speech usually limits to discrete emotion type and the emotion embedding which controls emotion transfer contains redundant transcript information. In this paper, we apply pre-trained language model Bidirectional Encoder Representations from Transformer (BERT) to our TTS system to achieve style control and transfer. Using BERT makes our proposed model study the relationship between text representations and acoustic emotion embedding. The experimental results show that our proposed model outperforms baseline Global Style Token (GST)-Tacotron2 model in both parallel and non-parallel style transfer.**

Keywords*—*emotional text-to-speech; style transfer; pre-trained language model

I. INTRODUCTION

Text-to-speech (TTS), also knowed as speech synthesis, is the technology which aims to synthesize intelligible and natural speech from raw text. Early speech synthesis techniques mainly include waveform concatenation [1][2] and statistical parametric speech synthesis [3]–[6]. A classic Statistical Parametric Speech Synthesis (SPSS) system usually includes three components which contain a front-end model (convert text symbols to linguistic features), an acoustic model (map linguistic features to acoustic features) and a vocoder (generate speech from acoustic features). In the past decades, this method was widely used in industrial production due to the advantages of robustness and efficiency. However, the generated speech of this method has lower naturalness and intelligibility because of artifacts such as muffled and noisy audio. The voice quality has been largely improved on neural network approaches [5][6] instead of Hidden Markov models (HMM) [4]. Deep Voice [7] still follows the three components in statistical parametric synthesis, but upgrades them with the corresponding neural network models. Furthermore, WaveNet [8], proposed to directly generate waveform from linguistic features, is regarded as the first modern neural TTS model.

Recent end-to-end speech synthesis models surpass traditional parametric systems in many ways, including the use of an encoder to replace linguistic features, a neural vocoder to replace the traditional vocoder, and an attention mechanism for the purpose of end-to-end training. Tacotron [9] is a sequence-to-sequence model which simplifies the traditional speech synthesis pipeline by replacing the production of magnitude spectrograms from text with a single neural network trained from data alone. Like many modern TTS systems, it learns an average prosody of the training data. Afterwards, Tacotron2 [10] gains a great success through refining Tacotron model structure and cascading with a modified WaveNet vocoder. Tacotron and Tacotron2 first generate mel spectrograms from text directly, then synthesize audio samples produced by a vocoder, such as Griffin Lim algorithm or WaveNet. Using an end-to-end network, the quality of synthesized audio is greatly improved and even comparable to human recordings on some datasets. The end-to-end TTS model contains two components, an encoder and a decoder. The encoder maps sequence of text into semantic space and generates a sequence of encoder hidden states, and the decoder, taking these hidden states as context information with an attention mechanism, constructs every mel spectrogram symbol per step. However, these generated models adopt recurrent neural network which limits the parallel processing capability both in training and inference stage. To deal with this problem, some models [11]–[13] leverage Transformer [14] network to replace recurrent neural network in TTS system. Among these models, FastSpeech 1/2 [12][13] use self-attention mechanism in order to deal with long distance dependency problem on the last previous hidden state and improve parallelization capability. The generated audio of these models is more robust than that of sequence-to-sequence models. However, because the audio generated by these models only contains neutral prosody is limited in many scenarios like AI voice assistants and navigation systems, there has been an increasing interest in emotional TTS and the method to control the generated speech style.

In expressive TTS, the speaking style is modeled in supervised or unsupervised manner. Lee et al. [15] proposed an emotional end-to-end speech neural speech synthesizer, controlling speech emotion with discrete label. Luong et al. [16] introduces a DNN-based text-to-speech system which takes speaker, gender and age codes as inputs in order to modify synthetic speech characteristics based on the input codes. Lorenzo-Trueba et al. [17] evaluates a large-scale corpus of emotional speech from a professional voice actress for the purpose of investigating different representation for modeling and controlling multiple emotions in DNN-based speech synthesis. However, the control of speech emotion is only limited to the emotion category which, we have predefined and synthetic speech cannot convey a variety of emotion. With the rapid progress of sequence-to-sequence architecture, especially Tacotron family, reference-based style transfer has emerged as another solution with great potential to solve this problem. The reference-based model learns a latent style embedding from the reference audio and generate speech which matches the prosody of the reference speech even if their speakers are different from each other. To model reference speech as style input, there has evolved a plenty of work, such as Global Style Token (GST) [18][19], Variational Autoencoder (VAE) [20][21] and their variants. Global Style Token (GST) [19] introduces a reference encoder that extracts style embedding from the acoustic signal and encodes various speaking styles into a fixed number of tokens. Variational Autoencoder (VAE) [21] infers style representation through the recognition of VAE, then feeds it into TTS network to guide the style in synthesizing speech.

The remaining part of this paper proceeds as follows. Section II introduces related work. The overview and each component of the proposed model are described in Section III. Experiments and results are reported in Section IV. Lastly, the conclusion and future work are covered in Section V.

II. Related Work

In this section, we first introduce reference-based TTS model, followed by a brief description about language model in TTS.

A. Reference-based TTS model

The reference-based TTS model aims to synthesize speech whose style is transferred from reference audio. The most straightforward way is to obtain style embedding from reference speech and use it as condition control to guide speech synthesizing. Skerry-Ryan et al. [18] proposes the concept of prosody embedding and merges prosody encoder into Tacotron architecture for computing low-dimension information of reference speech. The embedding captures audio features independent of speech information and specific speaker features such as accent, intonation, and speech rate. At the inference stage, we can use this embedding to perform prosody transfer and produce speech from a completely different speaker's voice. The embedding can also transfer temporally aligned precise prosody from one phrase to a slightly different one, even though the reference and target phrases are similar in length and structure. On the basis of previous work [18], global style token (GST) [19] is an updated method to learn the style representation by encoding various speaking style into a fixed number of tokens. By adding an additional attention mechanism to Tacotron, it enables it to express the prosody embedding of any speech segment as a linear combination of a fixed set of base embedding. The attention weights represent the contribution of each style token, and style embedding is made up of the weighted sum of all style tokens. In the training stage, each token is randomly initialized in an unsupervised manner. During the inference step, we can use a different audio signal or specify the attention weights of style tokens to achieve style transferring and controlling. Um et al. [22] introduces an inter-to-intra emotional distance ratio algorithm to the embedding vectors which can balance the distance between the target emotion category and the other categories. Li et al. [23] is also a GST-based method for expressive TTS, where the authors insert two classifiers into GST-Tacotron2 [19] model for improving emotion discrimination ability of emotion and deliver emotional speech with preferred strength.

B. Language model in TTS

Language model (LM) is often used in many natural language processing applications, such as speech recognition, machine translation, syntactic analysis, handwriting recognition and information retrieval. With the development of neural network, language model becomes increasingly powerful and is exploited in TTS system to improve the quality of synthetic speech. Jia et al. [24] introduce a new encoder model which takes both phoneme and grapheme representations of text as input and is trained in a self-supervised manner. Fang et al. [25] uses BERT [26] in TTS system to know when to stop decoding and help faster converge during training. Zhang et al. [27] employs BERT in a unified front-end model for the purpose of improving polyphone disambiguation accuracy. In [28], style tag makes synthetic audio more interpretable and natural compared with style index of reference speech. Shin et al. [29] proposes a style encoder which models the relationship between the text embedding and speech embedding with a pre-trained language model.

III. Proposed Model

Our proposed model architecture is shown in Figure 1. The proposed model is based on Tacotron2 with an emotion recognition network, an additional network and a semantic network.

A. Encoder

The encoder is made up of a character embedding layer, 3 convolutional layer and a single bi-directional LSTM [30].

Because a character is represented as a 512-dimensional one-hot vector, the input character sequence which contains n characters is converted to a n $\times$ 512-dimensional character embedding through character embedding layer. In order to capture a longer range of contextual information and obtain features of character sequence, the character embedding is then passed through 3 convolutional layers and each layer has 512 filters where each cover 5 characters, followed by batch normalization and ReLU activation. The output of the last convolutional layer is sent to a bi-directional LSTM layer which contains 512 units to generate encoded features. After the above operations, the encoder finally encodes the input character sequence into a 512-dimensional hidden feature vector.

B. Decoder

As we all konw, the decoder is an autoregressive recurrent neural network trained from the input sequence of the encoder to predict the output mel spectrogram. The mel spectrogram at the previous moment is first passed into a pre-net which is comprised of two fully connected layer with 256 hidden ReLU activations. It is important for the pre-net to learn attention alignment mechanism. The output of pre-net and the anttention vector are connected with each other and sent to two one-way LSTM layers with 1024 units. The output vector of LSTM is concatenated with the attention context vector output by the encoder, and then passed to a linear projection

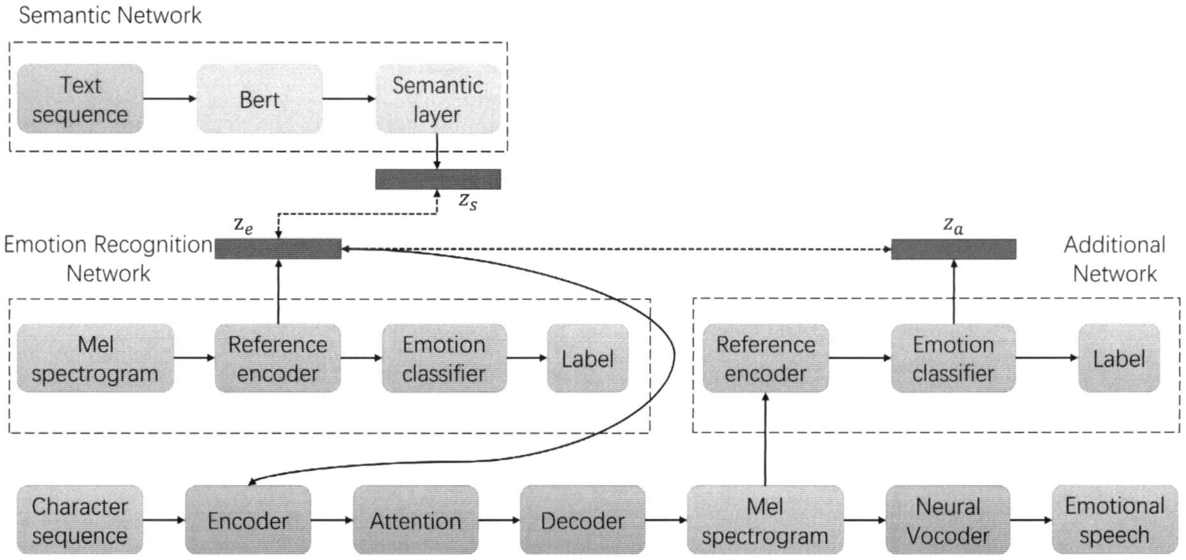

Figure. 1. Model Architecture

layer to predict the current mel spectrogram frame. Finally, the post-net containing 512 filters with shape 5×1 with batch normalization takes the predicted mel spectrogram as input to add the residual to previous mel spectrogram for improving reconstruction ability.

C. Emotion Recognition Network

From the top left of Figure 1, the emotion recognition network contains a reference encoder and an emotion classifier.

1) Reference encoder: The reference encoder we adopted in our model is the same in [18]. It is composed of six 2D convolutional network where each layer equipped with batch normalization has 3×3 filters with 2×2 stride. The output of convolutional network is then passed through a GRU [31] layer, and we use a fully connected layer followed by a tanh activation in order to map the final GRU state to our desired 128-dimensional embedding.

2) Emotion classifier: We use emotion classifier followed by reference encoder to facilitate the discrimination ability of emotion types. The classifier consists 5 fully connected layers with tanh activation. In the classifier, the size of first layer is 128-unit and that of the remaining layers is 256-unit. For the downstream emotion classifier task, a softmax layer is applied to produce the probability of each emotion category, such as neutral, happy and angry. The output of third layer and the hidden feature vector from the encoder are concatenated for teach-forcing speech waveform generation.

D. Additional Network

The additional network shares the same structure with the emotion recognition network, as is shown in the top right of Figure 1. In detail, we plug an additional network to the decoder , which enables the predicted mel spectrogram to identify emotion category. The output of third layer from additional network acts as an emotion embedding of the generated speech and is compared with the emotion representation of input audio for better training and optimizing.

E. Semantic Network

The semantic network is composed of a pre-trained BERT model and semantic layer. We use this network to map text sequence to semantic representations, which aims to remove text-related information from acoustic features and leverage transcript dataset to assist TTS training.

1) BERT: BERT is of great significance to a large amount of NLP tasks. It consist a stack of Transformer [14] blocks and is trained with Mandarin text data. The input text sequence is made up of many characters where each is transformed to a linguistic feature, and is encoded to capture contextual information from Mandarin text by BERT. BERT can be trained in two unsupervised manners, one is mask language modeling where we randomly replace the token in each training sequence with a [MASK] token and then predict the original word at the [MASK] position, and the other is next sentence prediction where the model has the ability to understand the relationship between two sentence in many downstream tasks.

2) Semantic layer: To adapt to downstream task, we design the semantic layer that is connected with BERT in order to modeling the input text sequence. Similar to Emotion classifier, the semantic layer is built with 3 fully connected layer followed by tanh activation. The output of semantic layer is used to reduce impact on acoustic representations and focus on emotion dimension of the synthetic speech.

F. Training and inference

During training, we use five loss terms summed as a total loss in our model. The loss function of the basic acoustic model, referred as L_{tac} which is followed with Tacotron2 [10], is the Mean Square Error (MSE) between the input ground-truth mel spectrogram and the predicted mel spectrogram. To make the reference encoder only extract emotion features, we adopt L_{emo_sem} that calculates the loss between the emotion vector z_e extracted from the emotion recognition network and the semantic embedding z_s extracted from semantic network.

$$L_{emo\_sem} = \sum_{i=1}^{N}(z_{ei} - z_{si})^2 \tag{1}$$

To improve the distinguish capability of the generating speech, the loss function, L_{emo_add}, is determined by MSE between emotion embedding z_e fetched from the emotion recognition network and addition embedding z_a fetched from the additional network as follows.

$$L_{emo\_add} = \sum_{i=1}^{N}(z_{ei} - z_{ai})^2 \tag{2}$$

Besides, L_{cls_src} and L_{cls_pre} denote the cross entropy loss for the source audio classifier in emotion recognition network and the predicted audio classifier in additional network, respectively. The total loss of the proposed model is:

$$L = L_{tac} + L_{emo\_sem} + L_{emo\_add} + L_{cls\_src} + L_{cls\_pre} \tag{3}$$

In the inference stage, we use reference speech or emotional vector to achieve style control and transfer. For the emotional vector method, emotional vector v_e is determined by averaging the samples of the corresponding emotion category as follows:

$$v_e = \frac{1}{N_e}\sum_{x_i \subset X_e} x_i \tag{4}$$

where X_e represents all the weight vectors of the emotional category and N_e and x_i donate the number of weight vectors and weight vector belonging to the emotional category, respectively.

IV. Experiments and Results

In this section, we evaluate the performance of our proposed model in parallel style transfer and non-parallel style transfer through subjective evaluations and objective evaluations.

A. Dataset and settings

In our experiments, we use a high-quality emotional speech corpus which is recorded by a Chinese female professional speaker and contains <text, audio, emotion label> tuples. The emotions of all the speeches are classified by 2 categories (neutral and happy). The corpus consists of 12000 utterances (12 hours), among which 10000 (10 hours) belong to the neutral emotion and the happy emotion has the remanent 2000 utterances (2 hours). We down-sample all the recordings from 48kHz to 22.05 kHz for model training. 80-dimensional mel spectrogram is extracted from the dataset as acoustic features. The frame length and frame shift are set to 50ms and 12.5ms, respectively.

The experimental environment configuration is shown in the Table I.

TABLE I
EXPERIMENTAL ENVIRONMENT PARAMETERS

Operating System	Ubuntu18.04
Graphics Card	NVIDIA GeForce RTX 3090
Memory	24G
Python	3.7.6
PyTorch	1.8.1
CUDA	11.1

We train our model for 500 epochs with a batch size of 32 because using BERT makes our model size larger. We use the Adam [32] optimizer with a learning rate of 1e-5 to learn the parameters in a single GeForce GTX 3090 GPU. In the reference encode, the number of GRU hidden units is set to 128. As for speech generation, we build a WaveRNN [33] as the vocoder trained by ground-truth mel spectrogram.

B. Text preprocessing

In our acoustic model, we use traditional Chinese representation as the input sequence for speech generation. Figure 2 shows the process of translating traditional Chinese characters into phonemes. We first represent Chinese characters with Chinese phonetic alphabet, then convert Chinese phonetic alphabet to combination of initials and finals instead of English alphabet.

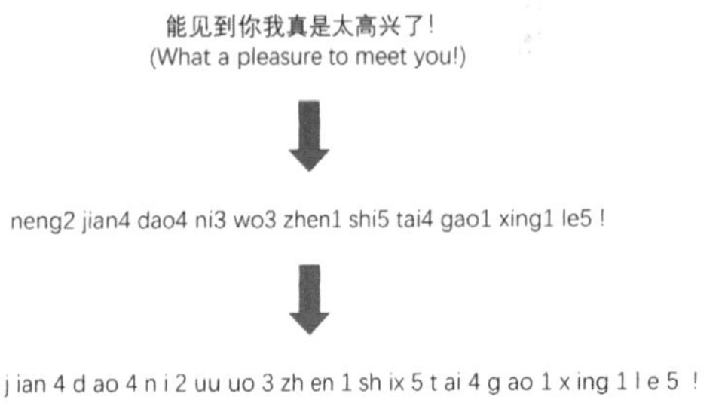

Figure. 2. Example of translating traditional Chinese characters into phonemes

C. Subjective evaluations

To subjectively evaluate the performance of our model, we compare our proposed model with baseline model on the Mean Opinion Score (MOS) and ABX preference subjective tests. Some samples can be found from https://light-cao.github.io/.

We evaluate the naturalness of the generated speech utterances by using the Mean Opinion Score (MOS) test. Ten native Mandarin speakers are asked to stay in a quiet room and listen recordings with noise canceling headphones, and then make their judgements of the performance with five-point scale (1: Bad, 2: Poor, 3: Fair, 4: Good, 5: Excellent). We randomly select 10 sentences from each emotion category for both parallel style transfer and non-parallel style transfer experiments with our proposed model and baseline model. Parallel style transfer means the transcript of the synthetic speech matches that of the reference audio. Non-parallel style transfer refers to synthesizing the audio with arbitrary text in the prosodic style of the reference signal.

The MOS test results in Table II confirm that our proposed model performs better than the baseline model both in parallel style transfer and non-parallel style transfer. Parallel style transfer outperforms non-parallel style transfer in speech quality because the transcript seen during training is beneficial to better modeling the synthetic audio.

TABLE II
MEAN OPINION SCORE(MOS) WITH 95% CONFIDENCE INTERVALS ON PARALLEL AND NON-PARALLEL STYLE TRANSFER

	parallel transfer	non-parallel transfer
Ground truth	4.25 ± 0.15	-
GST-Tacotron2	3.90 ± 0.16	3.57 ± 0.19
Proposed	4.07 ± 0.16	3.79 ± 0.18

To demonstrate that our model can control style transfer, we conduct a ABX preference test with the baseline GST-Tacotron2 and our proposed model. In this test, the participants are provided a fair number of samples from baseline and the proposed model and rated which sample is as expressive as the reference speech. If there is no obvious difference between the two samples, they can choose no preference. The results in Figure 3 show that our proposed model outperform the baseline model in both neutral and happy emotion category.

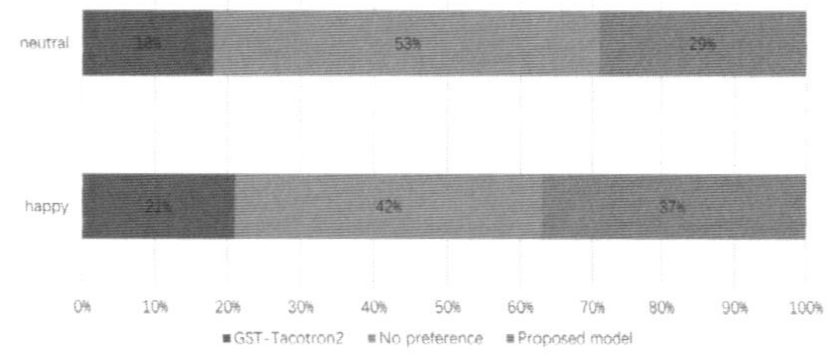

Figure. 3. ABX preference test results on two emotion categories between baseline model and the proposed model

D. Objective evaluations

We visualize the attention alignment of the decoder in Figure 4 and check if the attention mechanism learns how to align between the text sequence and the reference audio. In Figure 4, the attention alignment of our proposed model is slightly brighter than that of the baseline GST-Tacotron2 in many places, which indicates the proposed model surpass

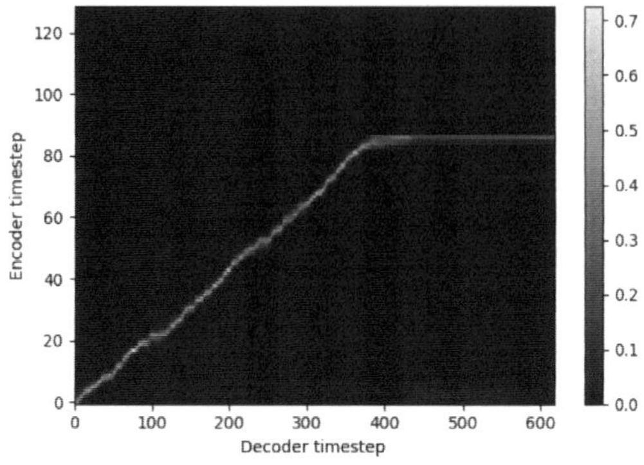

(a)

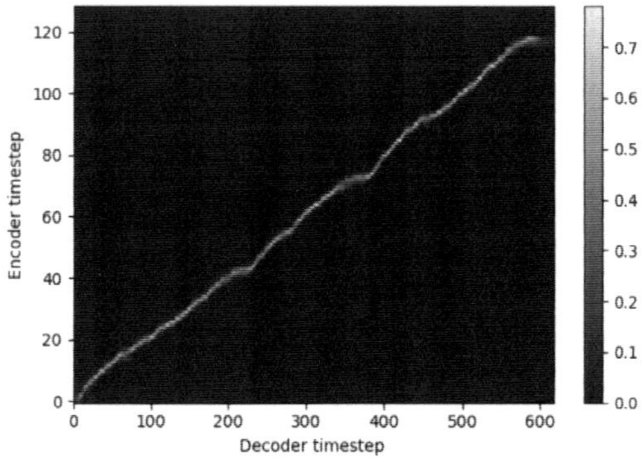

(b)

Figure. 4. Comparison on attention alignment between text and speech. (a) From the baseline GST-Tacotron2. (b) From our proposed model

the baseline model. From the analogous shape of the proposed attention, we can see that our proposed model could align the reference speech to the text well.

V. CONCLUSION AND FUTURE WORK

In our work, we utilized semantic network in our model to control and transfer style. In order to deliver the emotion more accurate, we inserted two classifiers after the reference encoder to enhance the emotion discriminative ability of the emotion embedding and the predicted mel spectrogram. Compared with the baseline model, the proposed model improved the quality of synthetic speech and achieves excellent performance on parallel and non-parallel style transfer. Besides, our proposed model could align the reference speech to the text better than the baseline model. In the future work, we want to improve the model for excluding the transcript information in acoustic features more precisely and experiment on more emotion categories.

REFERENCES

[1] A. J. Hunt and A. W. Black, "Unit selection in a concatenative speech synthesis system using a large speech database," in *1996 IEEE International Conference on Acoustics, Speech, and Signal Processing Conference Proceedings*, vol. 1. IEEE, 1996, pp. 373–376.

[2] A. BLACK, "Automatically clustering similar units for unit selection in speech synthesis," *Proc. EUROSPEECH, Sep 1997*, 1997.

[3] H. Zen, K. Tokuda, and A. W. Black, "Statistical parametric speech synthesis," *speech communication*, vol. 51, no. 11, pp. 1039–1064, 2009.

[4] K. Tokuda, T. Yoshimura, T. Masuko, T. Kobayashi, and T. Kitamura, "Speech parameter generation algorithms for hmm-based speech synthesis," in *2000 IEEE international conference on acoustics, speech, and signal processing. Proceedings (Cat. No. 00CH37100)*, vol. 3. IEEE, 2000, pp. 1315–1318.

[5] H. Ze, A. Senior, and M. Schuster, "Statistical parametric speech synthesis using deep neural networks," in *2013 ieee international conference on acoustics, speech and signal processing*. IEEE, 2013, pp. 7962–7966.

[6] Y. Qian, Y. Fan, W. Hu, and F. K. Soong, "On the training aspects of deep neural network (dnn) for parametric tts synthesis," in *2014 IEEE International Conference on Acoustics, Speech and Signal Processing (ICASSP)*. IEEE, 2014, pp. 3829–3833.

[7] S. Ö. Arık, M. Chrzanowski, A. Coates, G. Diamos, A. Gibiansky, Y. Kang, X. Li, J. Miller, A. Ng, J. Raiman *et al.*, "Deep voice: Real-time neural text-to-speech," in *International conference on machine learning*. PMLR, 2017, pp. 195–204.

[8] A. v. d. Oord, S. Dieleman, H. Zen, K. Simonyan, O. Vinyals, A. Graves, N. Kalchbrenner, A. Senior, and K. Kavukcuoglu, "Wavenet: A generative model for raw audio," *arXiv preprint arXiv:1609.03499*, 2016.

[9] Y. Wang, R. Skerry-Ryan, D. Stanton, Y. Wu, R. J. Weiss, N. Jaitly, Z. Yang, Y. Xiao, Z. Chen, S. Bengio *et al.*, "Tacotron: Towards end-to-end speech synthesis," *arXiv preprint arXiv:1703.10135*, 2017.

[10] J. Shen, R. Pang, R. J. Weiss, M. Schuster, N. Jaitly, Z. Yang, Z. Chen, Y. Zhang, Y. Wang, R. Skerrv-Ryan *et al.*, "Natural tts synthesis by conditioning wavenet on mel spectrogram predictions," in *2018 IEEE international conference on acoustics, speech and signal processing (ICASSP)*. IEEE, 2018, pp. 4779–4783.

[11] N. Li, S. Liu, Y. Liu, S. Zhao, and M. Liu, "Neural speech synthesis with transformer network," in *Proceedings of the AAAI conference on artificial intelligence*, vol. 33, no. 01, 2019, pp. 6706–6713.

[12] Y. Ren, Y. Ruan, X. Tan, T. Qin, S. Zhao, Z. Zhao, and T.-Y. Liu, "Fastspeech: Fast, robust and controllable text to speech," *Advances in neural information processing systems*, vol. 32, 2019.

[13] Y. Ren, C. Hu, X. Tan, T. Qin, S. Zhao, Z. Zhao, and T.-Y. Liu, "Fastspeech 2: Fast and high-quality end-to-end text to speech," *arXiv preprint arXiv:2006.04558*, 2020.

[14] A. Vaswani, N. Shazeer, N. Parmar, J. Uszkoreit, L. Jones, A. N. Gomez, Ł. Kaiser, and I. Polosukhin, "Attention is all you need," *Advances in neural information processing systems*, vol. 30, 2017.

[15] Y. Lee, A. Rabiee, and S.-Y. Lee, "Emotional end-to-end neural speech synthesizer," *arXiv preprint arXiv:1711.05447*, 2017.

[16] H.-T. Luong, S. Takaki, G. E. Henter, and J. Yamagishi, "Adapting and controlling dnn-based speech synthesis using input codes," in *2017 IEEE International Conference on Acoustics, Speech and Signal Processing (ICASSP)*. IEEE, 2017, pp. 4905–4909.

[17] J. Lorenzo-Trueba, G. E. Henter, S. Takaki, J. Yamagishi, Y. Morino, and Y. Ochiai, "Investigating different representations for modeling and controlling multiple emotions in dnn-based speech synthesis," *Speech Communication*, vol. 99, pp. 135–143, 2018.

[18] R. Skerry-Ryan, E. Battenberg, Y. Xiao, Y. Wang, D. Stanton, J. Shor, R. Weiss, R. Clark, and R. A. Saurous, "Towards end-to-end prosody transfer for expressive speech synthesis with tacotron," in *international conference on machine learning*. PMLR, 2018, pp. 4693–4702.

[19] Y. Wang, D. Stanton, Y. Zhang, R.-S. Ryan, E. Battenberg, J. Shor, Y. Xiao, Y. Jia, F. Ren, and R. A. Saurous, "Style tokens: Unsupervised style modeling, control and transfer in end-to-end speech synthesis," in *International Conference on Machine Learning*. PMLR, 2018, pp. 5180–5189.

[20] D. P. Kingma and M. Welling, "Auto-encoding variational bayes," *arXiv preprint arXiv:1312.6114*, 2013.

[21] Y.-J. Zhang, S. Pan, L. He, and Z.-H. Ling, "Learning latent representations for style control and transfer in end-to-end speech synthesis," in *ICASSP 2019-2019 IEEE International Conference on Acoustics, Speech and Signal Processing (ICASSP)*. IEEE, 2019, pp. 6945–6949.

[22] S.-Y. Um, S. Oh, K. Byun, I. Jang, C. Ahn, and H.-G. Kang, "Emotional speech synthesis with rich and granularized control," in *ICASSP 2020-2020 IEEE International Conference on Acoustics, Speech and Signal Processing (ICASSP)*. IEEE, 2020, pp. 7254–7258.

[23] T. Li, S. Yang, L. Xue, and L. Xie, "Controllable emotion transfer for end-to-end speech synthesis," in *2021 12th International Symposium on Chinese Spoken Language Processing (ISCSLP)*. IEEE, 2021, pp. 1–5.

[24] Y. Jia, H. Zen, J. Shen, Y. Zhang, and Y. Wu, "Png bert: Augmented bert on phonemes and graphemes for neural tts," *arXiv preprint arXiv:2103.15060*, 2021.

[25] W. Fang, Y.-A. Chung, and J. Glass, "Towards transfer learning for end-to-end speech synthesis from deep pre-trained language models," *arXiv preprint arXiv:1906.07307*, 2019.

[26] J. Devlin, M.-W. Chang, K. Lee, and K. Toutanova, "Bert: Pre-training of deep bidirectional transformers for language understanding," *arXiv preprint arXiv:1810.04805*, 2018.

[27] Y. Zhang, L. Deng, and Y. Wang, "Unified mandarin tts front-end based on distilled bert model," *arXiv preprint arXiv:2012.15404*, 2020.

[28] M. Kim, S. J. Cheon, B. J. Choi, J. J. Kim, and N. S. Kim, "Expressive text-to-speech using style tag," *arXiv preprint arXiv:2104.00436*, 2021.

[29] Y. Shin, Y. Lee, S. Jo, Y. Hwang, and T. Kim, "Text-driven emotional style control and cross-speaker style transfer in neural tts," *arXiv preprint arXiv:2207.06000*, 2022.

[30] A. Graves and A. Graves, "Long short-term memory," *Supervised sequence labelling with recurrent neural networks*, pp. 37–45, 2012.

[31] K. Cho, B. Van Merriënboer, C. Gulcehre, D. Bahdanau, F. Bougares, H. Schwenk, and Y. Bengio, "Learning phrase representations using rnn encoder-decoder for statistical machine translation," *arXiv preprint arXiv:1406.1078*, 2014.

[32] D. P. Kingma and J. Ba, "Adam: A method for stochastic optimization," *arXiv preprint arXiv:1412.6980*, 2014.

[33] N. Kalchbrenner, E. Elsen, K. Simonyan, S. Noury, N. Casagrande, E. Lockhart, F. Stimberg, A. Oord, S. Dieleman, and K. Kavukcuoglu, "Efficient neural audio synthesis," in *International Conference on Machine Learning*. PMLR, 2018, pp. 2410–2419.

Introduction and Evaluation of an Alternative Training Approach as Indicator of Performance Improvement in Martial Arts with the Help of Kinematic Motion Analysis Using Motion Capture

Leonie Laskowitz
Technical University Würzburg-Schweinfurt
Leonie.Laskowitz@thws.de
Würzburg, Germany

Nicholas Müller
Technical University Würzburg-Schweinfurt
Nicholas.Müller@thws.de
Würzburg, Germany

***Abstract*— There are numerous areas in which we can optimize ourselves and our lives in a wide variety of ways. One area is sports, where coaches, athletes and sports scientists are working on their training methods and still researching innovative methods that will bring lasting success. This study focuses on kinematic motion analysis using motion capture (MoCap), a technology for implementing human motion in a virtual environment. The goal is to introduce a training approach in the combat sport of Muay Thai that will promote performance improvement in athletes. The study deals with three different training approaches and two different assessment methods. For this, 15 participants took part in the study and trained three Muay Thai techniques: straight punch, front kick and roundhouse kick. The study shows that a training approach should be individualized to enhance athlete performance. In any case, technologies help generate high-quality data sets that provide detailed insight into nuances in the incorrectness of a movement. In addition to fairness and objectivity, visual feedback promotes internalization and contributes to self-based observational learning. Especially for highly complex movements, motion capture supports athletes' performance growth.**

Keywords – Technique improvements; performance enhancement; training approach; kinematic motion analysis.

I. INTRODUCTION

The original need for motion capture arose in the animation and film industry, where human walking was to be realistically imitated. Today, motion capture systems are used in biomechanics to perform various gait analyses for medical purposes. Not only medicine but also sports are interested in this deeper understanding of diverse movements. Injury prevention, performance enhancement, technique improvement, and objective assessments are driving numerous coaches, judges, and athletes to embrace this new way of motion capture. Future scenarios range from new training approaches to risk reduction during and after rehabilitation, to virtual reality implementations for remote analysis. Reliable analytics, provided by different vendors in various forms, are indispensable. Too few feedback methods yet use cutting-edge technologies, though these can lead to greater effectiveness and efficiency. It is a matter of adopting and establishing new practices in the training environment. To help learners improve and alert them to errors, constant feedback is crucial. Current methods used by coaches to evaluate athletes' performance are neither efficient nor adapted to technological advances in certain sports. For the most part, videos of each team member or student must be analyzed individually to provide feedback [1]. Especially in martial arts, precision, speed, and coordination are crucial. As Muay-Thai is a part of martial art, there are many difficulties by analyzing the movement of the students compared to other sports, as described in the following: With the naked eye of a coach, the fast, dynamic movement sequences can hardly be reliably and accurately detected, tracked, and measured. In addition, most of the time a grandmaster has to control several students at the same time. It is a great challenge to give each student the same attention and thus to improve their performance rapidly and sustainably. The aim of this study is to find out how the intervention of an alternative training approach using motion capture affects the performance improvement of young beginners in martial arts in order to draw conclusions about the most predestined methodology with the highest learning effect.

The paper is divided into five sections, beginning with a short introduction to the topic. Thereupon, the research question is pursued, which results from the problem definition of the initial situation. While first the hardware used and then the associated motion capture software are explained in more detail, the thesis then focuses on the theoretical construct. In the third section, the methodology of the study is discussed in chronological order according to its development. The results are summarized in the fourth section. Finally, the fifth section demonstrates how the research question is answered and the potential of motion capture technology in the field of sports science in the future.

II. RELATED WORK & THEORETICAL FOUNDATIONS

In the following section, the theoretical foundations of the study are described in more detail. In addition to a theoretical construct, similar reference studies are mentioned.

A. *Theoretical construct*

The final model relied upon in the study is shown in Figure 1. The arrows illustrate the dependent relationships. The submodels from past research are marked with numbers and can thus be assigned to authors and related studies. Component 5 has been newly added as it serves as a basis for future research. In the following, the theoretical sub-models are explained in more detail and the boundaries of previous studies in future science are concretized.

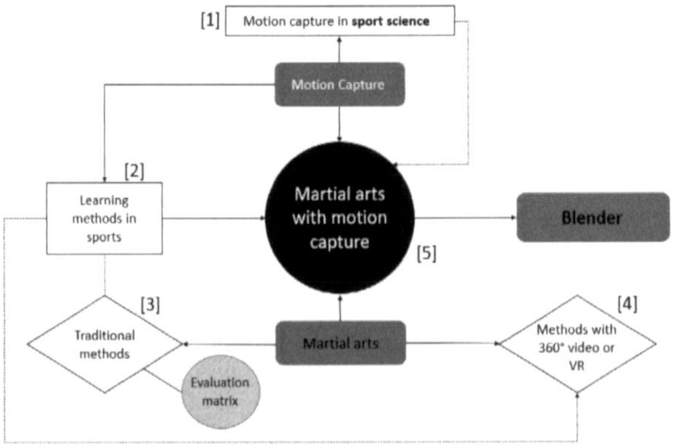

Figure 1. Theoretical construct: [1] = (Grontman et al., 2020), [2] = (Anderson & Campbell, 2015), [3] = (Čoh & Milovan, 2004), (Vít et al., 2016) [4] =(Chan et al., 2011), (Le Naour et al., 2019)

Motion capture in sports counteracts the subjective evaluation in the judging panel and still inaccurate measurement methods. Therefore, an algorithm was developed by a research group to analyze the patterns of correct intersection of the recorded MoCap data by comparing Euclidean distances and the recorded trajectories of the amateurs with the baseline model of the professional athlete Model 1. For this purpose, the techniques of sword fencing, a historically European martial art, were examined. The study analyzed only a few marker positions and neglected execution speeds. Furthermore, closely spaced markers were still omitted [2].

Providing feedback when learning new motor skills is essential in sports. Different methods can be used to address different senses, such as auditory, olfactory, gustatory, visual, and tactile perception. The results of a more recent study suggest that the combination of simultaneous self-observation and real-time expert modeling has a positive effect on accelerating learning. The acceleration of skill acquisition in rowing was investigated. Self-observation was implemented through live video transmission, while expert movement was previously recorded and transmitted in real time. The rowers saw themselves in real time and a slightly delayed image of their execution as soon as it differed from the expert modeling [3] [4].

Studies show that performance is dependent on the learning method. It is assumed that optimized learning conditions can lead to a faster increase in performance, but this does not apply to situations that are different from the learning situation. The methods must be chosen depending on the biological age, the level of knowledge about the techniques and the motor experience of the athletes. It is recommended to focus first on the causes of the wrong movements rather than on the consequences. Faulty conception of technique execution, insufficient motor skills, and close morphological constitution of athletes' bodies are the causes of incorrect movement execution in most cases [5] [6].

Specifically in martial arts training, there are set teaching methods. After the instructor demonstrates the techniques and the student observes, the movements are imitated and repeated. This is followed by verbal extrinsic feedback by the instructor. One study examined the difference between extrinsic feedback in the form of a video and verbal feedback. The researchers concluded that learners are more critical of their own technique execution when they see it on a video [7].

Meanwhile, different technologies can support feedback to improve motor skills. Researchers are investigating training systems based on motion capture and virtual reality. They developed a prototype that implements a student's imitation of a virtual expert's movements. Results showed that the simulation was a successful training methodology because the student's movements, animated in VR, were captured and analyzed in real time while the virtual instructor could point out errors to them [4] [8].

Another study compared the benefits of diverse types of visual feedback to improve movement execution in gymnastics. Additionally, subjective (compared to quantitative) measurement methods were used. The subjective assessment was in the form of a battle court, while the quantitative measurement method consisted of time series analyses. Four different 3D visualizations were contrasted. Learners made the best progress using the 3D feedback, which compared the expert's execution with the learners. Finally, correlational analyses confirmed that subjective judgments by the referee cannot be predicted or justified by objective measurements [9].

III. Methods

The study references diverse approaches from past research and combines diverse measurement methods with different training approaches to identify the most predestined learning methodology in the martial art of Muay Thai. In the theoretical construct, this is placed in the middle [5] of the reference studies (Figure 1).

A. Setup

The study used the OptiTrack system from NaturalPoint, which is one of the world's largest suppliers in the motion capture field. The experiments took place in a motion capture lab equipped with 28 OptiTrack PrimeX 13s to capture the movements of the trainer and students in real time. At the same time, a virtual figure representing the trainer or the students was animated on a 2.04 m x 3.63 m monitor. The study was conducted in the MoCap laboratory at the Technical University in Würzburg (THWS). The real-time analysis and recording software Motive:Body was used in conjunction with the OptiTrack motion system. Together with the Blender software, the movements could be recorded, measured and analyzed.

The software as well as the high-speed tracking cameras are used in the fields of film, gaming, sports and biomechanics. An optical motion capture system based on infrared markers uses multiple cameras equipped with infrared diodes (IR LEDs) whose infrared light is reflected by the markers. Using multiple 2D images, the 3D position of the markers can be calculated and determined within the space. The OptiTrack systems have a measurement or position error of less than 0.2 mm. In small measuring ranges even only 0.1 mm or less. During tracking, rotation errors of less than 0.5° also occur. The accuracy is maintained by regular self-calibrations throughout the entire service life.

Primex 13 cameras are also particularly suitable for motion capture applications characterized by higher speeds, accelerations or jerky movements, as they have a higher frame rate and therefore higher resolution, lower latencies and a longer focal length.

The resolution affects the minimum distance between markers and the minimum size of markers defined at a certain distance from the cameras. Each actor wears the Motion Capture Suit during motion tracking, which is antimicrobial, stretchy and breathable, so they are comfortable enough to wear even during longer shoots. The suit can be worn over everyday clothing and fits snugly to the body when worn. Components included shoes, a full body suit, gloves and a hat. Attached to the entire suit are X-base markers from OptiTrack. They are embedded in a Velcro base and have a spherical structure with an outer diameter of 14 mm.

B. Participants

- 15 healthy participants took part in the study. The fifteen subjects were divided into 5 females and 10 males with an age range of 20-31. The average height of the subjects was 1.77 m (1.50-1.95 m) with an average weight of 75 kg (50-115 kg). In each group, there was one participant who had previous martial arts experience (<5 y), whereas in group 2 there were two experienced participants, one of whom had even done martial arts for over 5 years. Nearly all subjects reported regular exercise, no known mobility impairments, or other health problems that could affect their mobility. They were familiarized with the study objectives and mode of implementation before the experiment and signed written informed consent to participate in the study. The groups were randomly selected, with the first two groups performing the techniques in the laboratory twice at four-month intervals and the third group performing the techniques five times at four-week intervals.
- They were instructed and evaluated by a multiple world (WKA) and European (MTBD) champion in Muay Thai and kickboxing. As a black belt holder who himself has been training the Far Eastern martial arts daily since the age of 3, he teaches many students in all disciplines in his own fighting schools. Together with the trainer, the three Muay Thai techniques were selected and the most important sub-steps of a single execution were discussed, which were later analyzed in more detail. Prior to the study, he was recorded in the MoCap laboratory, first 2D via video and then 3D via motion capture during the technique execution. Before the 15 students were divided into three groups of five, they received a joint training session with the sensei, during which an initial introduction of the three Muay Thai techniques was given. The professional Muay Thai trainer supervised the subjects during the first sessions of the three groups to be available to answer questions about technique and technique execution. In addition, the sensei evaluated the participants individually via evaluation matrix. For this purpose, a video of the participants at the beginning and at the end of the study was sent to him. The aim of this measurement method is to be able to draw a comparison between the observation of a professional athlete and trainer with the quantitative analysis (angle measurement).
- No subject was motor impaired and all were able to perform the techniques. The focus is on the correct execution of the techniques, performance progress, and knowledge transfer under different training conditions.

C. Measurements

The first group trained with a demonstration video showing the three techniques Straight Punch, Front Kick and Roundhouse Kick, demonstrated by the sensei (shown in Figure 2).

Figure 2. Demonstration video of the sensei

After importing the trainer data from the motion capture recordings into Blender, the second group used this software to track the techniques in 3D. The amateurs were thus provided with a virtual training environment that simulates a real trainer but works even when no real sensei can be present. The third group trained at home with the 2D video and every four weeks in the lab. After each session, the subjects' movements were analyzed in detail. For this purpose, the angles of the joints were evaluated for each partial technique, and then the angles between the bones were measured. After the evaluation, the subject's data was compared with the trainer's data to identify incorrect executions. The Blender software was ideal for showing the students their errors as well as demonstrating the differences between the trainer and the individual performance.
Figure 3 demonstrates the deviation of the angles between the trainer and the amateur in Blender.

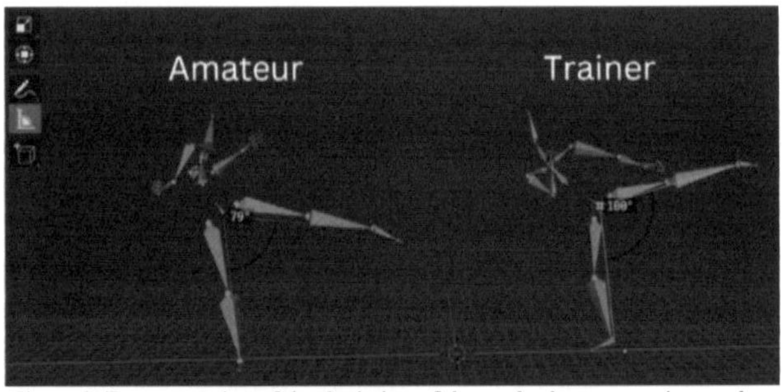

Figure 3. Demonstration of the deviation of the angles between trainer and amateur

It was also possible to show the path of the movement of the sensei to compare to the students as shown in Figure 4.

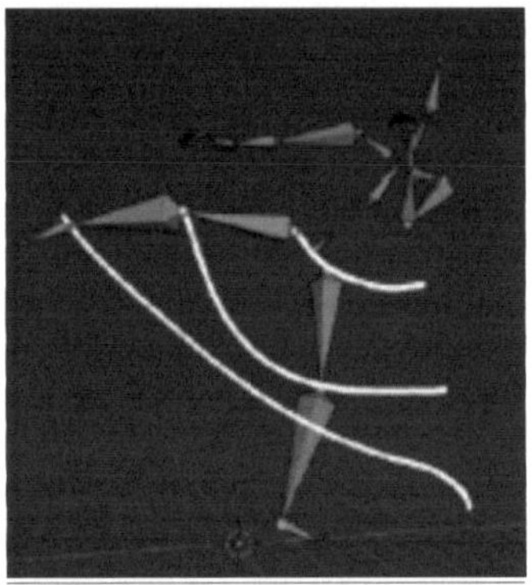

Figure 4. Path of the movement shown in Blender

Overall, two different evaluation methods were used to analyze the angles, but both are based on the consideration of the deviation of the angles between student and trainer. Thus, both evaluation approaches follow the same approach.

In the first evaluation method, the ideal of the coach is determined via rotation angles and compared with the athletes. In the second evaluation method, a simplified model is used for validation. This is based on the 2D angles between individual bones and limbs as shown in Figure 3 (thigh, lower leg, shoulder, etc).

In the following section "Results" we will talk about improvements and deteriorations of the individual groups and athletes. The improvements are always evaluated relative to the ideal in both evaluation methods. The ideal always describes the execution of the coach and its angle between individual body parts or change of angles during a movement. An improvement of 10 %, for example, means that the athlete has come 10 % closer to the ideal execution of the sensei.

IV. RESULTS

The first evaluation methodology shows that one subject from each group improved in straight punch from the first to the last training session. One subject from group 2 has the greatest improvement in performance. Most of the students have deteriorated after the training, some to a lesser extent and some to a slightly greater extent. This can be caused by two reasons. First, it is very challenging to communicate which joint needs to be adjusted and how to achieve the ideal, even though the feedback was supported by visual images in Blender. However, once understanding was present in the student, another hurdle arose. The technical implementation is very complex for martial arts amateurs in this short training period. The Straight Punch represents the most straightforward technique of all three Muay Thai techniques, so the subjects were already extremely confident in their intuitive execution. This is another assumption why performance on this movement could not be significantly increased by any training methodology. One outlier, who already had experience from another martial art, could be enticed to perform the technique in the way he knew.

Just under half of the subjects (approximately 46.67%) improved their execution of the front kick over the training period. In Group 1 and 2, three amateurs each improved, whereas in Group 3 only one did and one student showed almost no change. The training methods used with group 1 and 2 showed successful results and a strong tendency to improve. Especially group 1, who trained with a video of the trainer, showed improvements up to 40% while deteriorations were in the range below 10%. Similarly to group 2, which in addition to the video could view the execution of the trainer in 360°, improvements up to almost 50% and deteriorations below 15% were measured in this group.

Results that differed greatly from the previous techniques were found for the last and most challenging technique. The roundhouse kick, which was an unknown technique for all amateurs, is the most complicated of all three Muay Thai techniques due to its 360° rotation. Nevertheless, almost all students from group 3 improved, whereas the first two groups did not improve significantly. In fact, these two groups showed the greatest drop in performance on the roundhouse kick. This indicates that the novel training method that was used regularly by group 3 produced the greatest success with complex techniques. The regular training at home with video combined with the training in the lab resulted in 80% of Group 3 improving. Using Blender, which visually placed the students next to the trainers and vividly communicated the nature of the rotational deficits, increased performance throughout the training period despite the challenging implementation. Students from Group 3 were intrinsically motivated to excel, especially with this difficult technique.

The results of the second evaluation methodology for the Straight Punch show that 13 out of 15 participants improved while the other two students deteriorated by approximately 2% and 5%. The subjects from Group 3 show the largest increases in performance.

The demonstration, which memorably visualized the deviation between student and trainer, was used regularly with group 3 and resulted in all students from group 3 achieving a deviation below 10% after training. The subjects from group 1 and 2 who improved achieved a low deviation of no more than 10%. Group 3, on the other hand, achieved improvements above 16%, while two other participants increased their performance by approximately 10%.

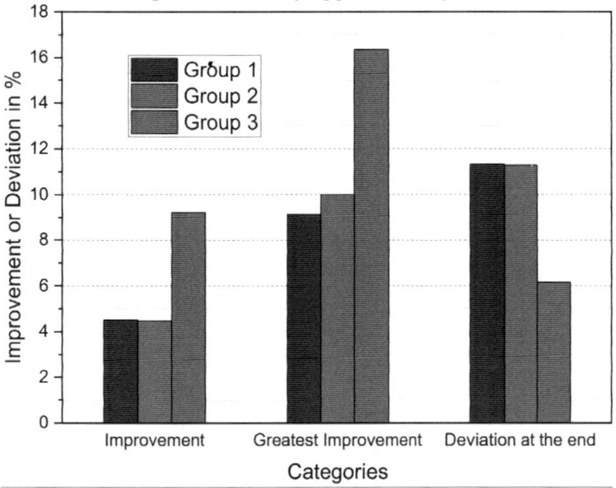

Figure 5. Statistic for the Straight Punch in three different categories

Figure 5 shows exemplarily for the Straight-Punch three different categories, namely the average improvement of the 5 participants, the highest improvement in one group and the average deviation from the ideal at the end of the training sessions. It can be clearly seen that group 3 achieves the best results. The average improvement is more than double that of group 1 and group 2. The absolute best improvement is also highest in group 3. Lastly, it should be noted that the final result (average deviation at the end) for group 3 is also almost half of the other two groups. Thus, group 3 is significantly closer to the ideal at the end than the other two groups - at least in this case shown for the Straight Punch.

Fewer students improved on front kicks than on straight punches. 10 out of 15 athletes were able to improve their performance, of which most from Group 1, three participants from Group 2 and also three students from Group 3 improved. The three subjects from group 3 showed the smallest deviations of max. 6% after the training. Analogous to the straight punches, the front kicks are shown divided into the three categories in Figure 6. It can be seen that group 1 has improved slightly more on average, while in the other two categories group 3 achieves the best results.

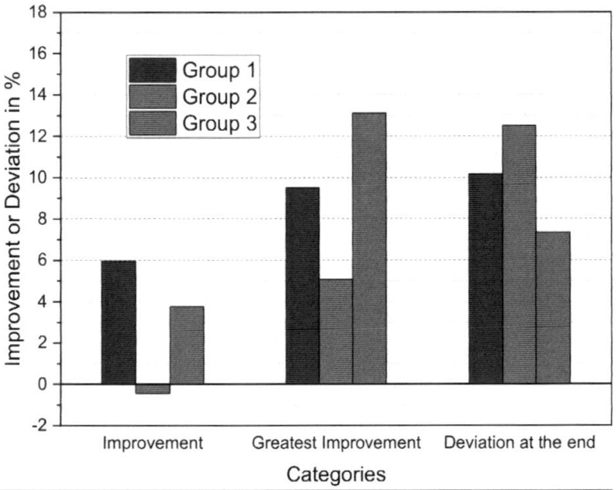

Figure 6. Statistic for the Front Kick in three different categories

When comparing their own execution with the trainer, the simple 2D video may have helped more than the 360° view of the trainer, which is why more students from the first group improved than from the second group. There is less improvement in front kicks than straight punches in group 2.

In the Roundhouse Kick, 10 out of 15 students improved, of which 50% overall came from the first two groups. 50% of the performance increases come from group 3. It can be seen that group 3 was able to improve particularly strongly, which can be seen from the relative deviations before and after training. These are just under 7% for as many as four students. In Group 1, 40% increased their performance, but slightly. The technique contains complex movement sequences and is characterized by its expressive dynamics. The video that Group 1 received for training could not be played in slow motion. The trainer's technique could not be inspected as explicitly as by group 2, which received additional support in the form of the 360° view of the trainer. This may have resulted in more participants from Group 2 improving than from group 1, although both groups showed small improvements on average. For group 1 it was a maximum of 3.9% and for group 2 even only a maximum of 3.27%.

The results of the Roundhouse-Kick are shown in Figure 7. Group 3 got the best results in every single category. Especially in the average improvement, where Group 1 and Group 2 have almost no deviation while Group 3 reached more than 10 %.

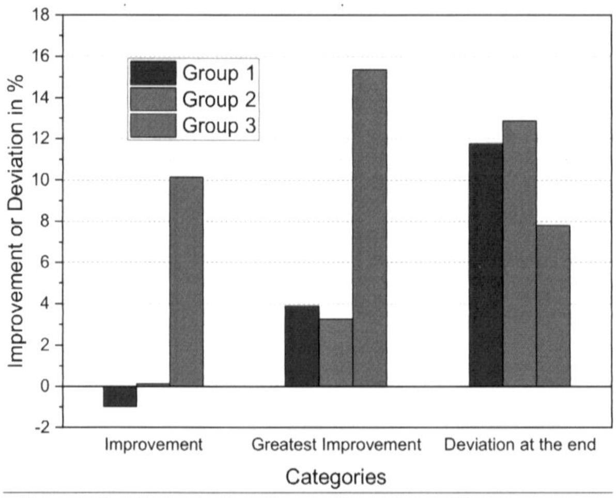

Figure 7. Statistic for the Roundhouse-Kick in three different categories

As with the first evaluation methodology, the second evaluation methodology also confirms that the training method using motion capture and Blender helps to increase the performance of amateurs, especially in complex motion sequences. The results showed that the trainer's assessment was mostly consistent with the assessment that emerged from the two measurement methods.

V. Conclusion, Limitations and Future Research

The aim of the study was to find out how the intervention of an alternative training approach using motion capture affects the performance improvement of young beginners in martial arts in order to draw conclusions about the most predestined methodology with the highest learning effect.

This objective was achieved by analyzing three different training methods and evaluating them in two different ways. These implied the first training method, in which the participants of group 1 trained with a video demonstration of the trainer. The second training method of group 2 used in addition to the video the software Blender, which demonstrated the technique execution of the trainer in a 360° view. The third and final training method used by group 3 used the motion capture system and Blender software. Various measurement tools were used to provide feedback to the students in different ways. Both evaluation methods in combination were relevant to ensure appropriate analysis. The evaluation was first done qualitatively by the instructor, who assessed each technique using relevant criteria. This assessment was compared with the quantitative results. For the simplest technique, the Straight Punch, only 20% were able to improve, which was due to the complicated implementation and challenging teaching of the joint adjustments. The results of the evaluations of the Front Kick, on the other hand, showed that it was the training methods of the first two groups that produced positive changes in performance and that they were particularly well suited for this Muay Thai technique. The more demanding a technique was, the more likely the newly introduced training methodology applied to the third group produced the greatest success. The qualitative assessment by the trainer and the quantitative analyses show three crucial changes in performance:

(1) All three groups significantly worsened in straight punches during the first evaluation methodology but significantly improved in straight punches during the second evaluation methodology.

(2) In front kicks, the training methods applied to group 1 and 2 showed successful results and a strong tendency to improve, shown by evaluation methodology 1.

(3) Both evaluation methods confirmed that group 3 achieved the strongest improvements in the roundhouse kick.

This leads to the conclusion that a training approach supported by motion capture and blender leads to a successful increase in performance, especially in dynamic and complex movement sequences.

The Motion Capture method achieved the highest learning effect with the most demanding martial arts techniques and is considered the most predestined methodology for these.

In order to promote sustainable performance increases, individualized training supported by technology is a prerequisite. This allows reliable, accurate data to be determined and communicated to athletes in a comprehensible manner. In addition, this type of kinematic motion analysis promotes fairness and objectivity of evaluation in a competition. This is not intended to replace professional evaluation by a coach, but to complement it.

In the future, this training setup can be extended with virtual reality to ensure location-independent training. Furthermore, this allows the implementation of diverse training environments and scenarios that can provide different frameworks at low cost and low effort, depending on the use case. This also exceeds the limitations of a traditional training room today. Furthermore, the use of AI can enable even more precise (early) detection of details in (faulty) execution, thus promoting and expanding injury prevention and performance enhancement. These methods can be transferred or directly applied to other sports in future research.

ACKNOWLEDGMENT

A special thanks goes to the THWS for providing the mocap room and the experimental setup. Furthermore to the trainer P. Ulsamer for teaching the students. Finally, a great thanks goes to the participants who regularly participated in this study and were willing to learn and improve a new martial art.

REFERENCES

[1] P. Cunha, V. Carvalho, F. Soares, "Real-Time Data Movements Acquisition of Taekwondo Athletes: First Insights. Springer International Publishing.", 2019.

[2] A. Grontman, M. Śmiertka, M. Trybała, Ł. Horyza, K. Koczan, M. Marzec, "Analysis of sword fencing training evaluation possibilities using Motion Capture techniques.", IEEE 15th International Conference of System of Systems Engineering (SoSE), 325-330, 2020.

[3] R. Anderson and M. J. Campbell, "Accelerating skill acquisition in rowing using self-based observational learning and expert modelling during performance, International Journal of Sports Science & Coaching, 10, 425-37., 2015.

[4] A. Lamošová and O. Kyselovičová, "The Effect of Different Types of Feedback on Learning of Aerobic Gymnastics Elements", Applied Sciences, 12:8066, 2022.

[5] M. Čoh and B. Milovan, "Motor learning in sport", Facta Univ Phys Educ Sport, 2, 2004.

[6] T. Bompa, "Periodization, Theory and Methodology of Training", Champaign IL: Human Kinetics, P.O. Box 5076, 1999.

[7] M. Vít, Z. Reguli, J. Cihounkova, "Extrinsic feedback in martial arts training", Revista de Artes Marciales Asiáticas, 11(2s), 82, 2016.

[8] J. C. P. Chan, H. Leung, J. K. T. Tang, T.Komura, "A Virtual Reality Dance Training System Using Motion Capture Technology", IEEE Transactions on Learning Technologies, 4(2), 187–195, 2011.

[9] T. Le Naour, C. Ré, J.-P. Bresciani, "Application to the roundoff movement in gymnastics", Human Movement Science, 66, 564–577, 2019.

RHM: Robot House Multi-view Human Activity Recognition Dataset

Mohammad Hossein Bamorovat Abadi, Mohamad Reza Shahabian Alashti,
Patrick Holthaus, Catherine Menon and Farshid Amirabdollahian
Robotics Research Group, School of Engineering and Computer Science
University of Hertfordshire, Hatfield, United Kingdom
Email: {m.bamorovat, m.r.shahabian, p.holthaus, c.menon, f.amirabdollahian2}@herts.ac.uk

***Abstract*—With the recent increased development of deep neural networks and dataset capabilities, the Human Action Recognition (HAR) domain is growing rapidly in terms of both the available datasets and deep models. Despite this, there are some lacks of datasets specifically covering the Robotics field and Human-Robot interaction. We prepare and introduce a new multi-view dataset to address this. The Robot House Multi-View (RHM) dataset contains four views: Front, Back, Ceiling (Omni), and robot-views. There are 14 classes with 6701 video clips for each view, making a total of 26804 video clips for the four views. The lengths of the video clips are between 1 to 5 seconds. The videos with the same number and the same classes are synchronized in different views. In the second part of this paper, we consider how single streams afford activity recognition using established state-of-the-art models. We then assess the affordance for each view based on information theoretic modelling and mutual information concept. Furthermore, we benchmark the performance of different views, thus establishing the strengths and weaknesses of each view relevant to their information content and performance of the benchmark. Our results lead us to conclude that multi-view and multi-stream activity recognition has the added potential to improve activity recognition results. The RHM dataset is available at Robot House.**

***Keywords*—Human Action Recognition; Human-Robot Interaction.**

I. INTRODUCTION

With the growing prevalence of robots and autonomous systems in our daily lives, the domain of Human-Robot Interaction (HRI) is rapidly developing. An essential aspect of HRI recognizes human behaviour and actions [1]. This has resulted in the emergence of the Human Action Recognition (HAR) domain, as well as the creation of numerous HAR datasets relevant to different environments. However, finding a suitable HAR dataset, which contains a robot-viewpoint has historically been challenging [1].

Human activity recognition using top-view cameras or using a dynamic robot-view has been less accurate compared to the front or back-view observation of the activity. We inquire whether combining viewpoints can improve the top-view and robot-view detection accuracy. To explore this, we have created a new multi-view HAR dataset, known as Robot House Multi-view (RHM) dataset, that contains a robot-viewpoint, a top-view fish-eye camera labelled here as the omni-view, as well as two wall-mounted camera views positioned to observe front and back. These views capture the same task consisting of 14 different activities of daily living performed in front of the cameras.

To compare and contrast results between different viewpoints and their combination, we developed a comparison framework that allowed us to record changes in neural network models used and their resulting recognition accuracy and other performance parameters. Our methodology involved performing comparative analysis using different machine learning models, as well as Information Theoretic Analysis to identify and further characterise the relationship between multiple camera viewpoints.

Section II presents a comprehensive overview of the existing HAR datasets. In Section III, we introduce the RHM dataset and analyse it based on Mutual Information [2] in Section IV-A, and benchmark models in Section IV-B, and conclude in Section V.

II. RELATED WORKS

This section reviews the most known RGB/D HAR datasets with a comprehensive comparison between them.

Investigating existing HAR datasets reveals that these datasets are categorised according to multiple features, including the activity's theme, camera properties, environment, subject, situation, or the activity's scenario. For example, an activity theme could be a daily, sport, industrial or surveillance activity performed by an individual or a group in an indoor or outdoor environment, controlled or uncontrolled, or in the wild. Additionally, the camera types could be RGB or RGB-D with static or dynamic positions and single or synchronized multiple views.

KTH [3] is the first RGB HAR dataset presented in 2004 with six activity classes and 599 videos.*Weizmann* [4], in 2005, has 10 classes containing 90 videos. These two datasets were prepared in an outdoor controlled environment with a static background. Daniel Weinland et al. in [5] published the first Multi-View RGB HAR dataset with five views. *INRIA XMAS* contains 390 videos with 13 activities in a controlled indoor environment. *MuHAVi* dataset [6] is published by Sanchit Singh et al. with 238 videos in 17 classes and 8 Third Person fixed Views (TPV) in an indoor controlled environment. H. Kuehne et al. in 2011 published a dataset with 51 classes and 6849 videos [7] termed as *MHDB51*, which is a collection of static images collected mainly from movies, YouTube and Google Videos.

UCF HAR datasets are a group of datasets with different varieties of the number of classes, action types, modalities, and even views. For example, *UCF11* [8] with 11 classes and 1,160 videos, and *UCF50* [9] with 50 classes and 6,676 videos are the early versions of *UCF101* [10] with 101 classes and 13,000 videos, which is one of the most famous datasets for HAR. All of them are RGB videos prepared from YouTube clips in a diverse environment and uncontrolled situation with static and dynamic scenes. *UCF Sport* is created from sports actions in 10 classes with 150 videos [11]. *UCF-ARG* is a Multi-View dataset with ten actions and 480 videos in each view [12]. The views are Aerial camera, Rooftop camera, and Ground camera. These views are fixed, and the actions are recorded in an outdoor controlled environment. *ACT4* is a Multi-View dataset with four views, 14 actions, and 6,844 videos [13]. ACT4 is recorded in a controlled indoor environment. *ASLAN* is another HAR dataset with 432 classes and 10,000 videos [14]. It is trimmed from YouTube videos in an uncontrolled and diverse environment.

More recently, larger volumes of data have been needed due to the use of neural networks and deep learning models. This has resulted in the production of some comparatively large HAR datasets, such as *Sport-1M*, the first large dataset with more than 1,000,000 videos and 487 action classes. It is Annotated on YouTube clips only with a focus on sports [15]. Also, *YouTube-8M* is another large dataset with more than 8,000,000 annotated clips in 4,800 classes with diverse environment videos [16]. **NTU** HAR datasets are two Multi-View RGB+D datasets, which have been created in a controlled indoor environment with daily activities. The first version is *NTU RGB+D* with 1,000,000 annotated samples in 60 classes [17]. The second version is *NTU RGB+D 120* with 8,000,000 annotated videos in 120 classes [18].

Kinetics HAR dataset is another well-known and more usable dataset for action recognition. *Kinetics 400* was presented by Will Kay et al. in 2017 with 400 action classes, and 300,000 annotated videos from YouTube clips [19]. *Kinetics 600* was published in 2018 with 600 classes, and 496,000 annotated videos [20]. *Kinetics 700* was presented by Joao Carreira et al. in 2019 with 650,000 videos in 700 action classes [21]. *Ava Kinetics* is a localized human action, which was created from kinetics 700 with ava kinetics annotation protocol [22]. It consists of 230,000 annotated clips with 80 classes. *Kinetic_700_2020* is a 2020 edition of kinetics 700 with at least 700 videos in each class [23].

Some of the HAR datasets present another view of human actions, which are primarily helpful for human-object interaction. This view is from the human view, which is called Ego or First Person (FP) View. *20BN-Something-Something* is presented with FP view of actions [24]. Raghav Goyal et al. have prepared 100,000 videos in 174 action classes. *20BN-Something-Something-V2* is published with the same view (FP) and same classes (174) but with 220,000 videos in [25]. *Charades-Ego* is another dataset, which presented an FP or Ego view [26]. It provides a Multi-View HAR dataset with FP and third-person (TP) views. It contains 8,000 videos and 68,500 annotated frames in 157 classes.

LEMMA is another Multi-View dataset, which contains one FP and two TP views [27]. Baoxiong Jia et al. prepared LEMMA with 1,093 videos clip and 900,000 annotated frames in 641 classes. *HOMAGE* is the next Multi-View HAR dataset consisting of FP view [28]. HOMAGE presented one FP and at least one TP view for each action. Nishant Rai et al. prepared HOMAGE with 12 different sensors such as RGB, IR, microphone, acceleration, magnet, and so on. The RGB modality contains 5,700 annotated videos in 75 classes. *EPIC-KITCHENS-100* is the next Ego view HAR dataset presented in kitchen actions [29]. EPIC-KITCHENS-100 is the second version of *EPIC-KITCHENS* with 149 classes [30]. Dima Damen et al., in EPIC-KITCHENS-100, presented an EGo view (FP) dataset with 4053 classes in 700 videos and about 90,000 instances.

A few of the HAR datasets use a robot to provide the dynamic view for Human Action Recognition. The first dataset with a moving robot is *LIRIS* [31]. *LIRIS* is a Multi-View HAR dataset with one robot-view and one depth TP view. It contains ten classes in 828 videos. Another dataset, which uses robots is *InHARD* [32]. Although *InHARD* used a robot for the dataset, all three (Top, Left, and Right) views are static. Since This dataset has a robot in interaction with a human, this dataset is suitable for Human-Robot interaction works.

In Table I, we list 42 HAR datasets with comprehensive details of each. Assessing the existing HAR datasets as described above identifies the following omissions:

- Dynamic Perspective (Robot View): There is only *LIRIS* [31] with robot-view and motion. In the human-robot interaction domain, recognising human actions through the robot-view is crucial, and the most apparent feature of a robot-view is the motion frames. We note that though some of the existing datasets that can be seen in the motion part of the Table I as dynamic include motions in some videos, they are not in a separate part as a motion camera dataset.
- Top View (Fish eye view): For caring scenarios, using fish eye or ceiling views is common. However, we could not find a HAR dataset with ceiling views.
- Redundancy: To find the redundancy, we have to check the multi-view datasets. Most of them have a different static camera at different degrees from the sides, and some with ego view. There are only *LIRIS* [31], and *InHARD* [32] with robot-view and motion.

Based on these conclusions, we prepared the RHM HAR dataset to cover the HAR dataset's shortcomings.

III. ROBOT HOUSE MULTI-VIEW HAR DATASET

The Robot House Multi-View (RHM) is a new Multi-View RGB benchmark for Human activity recognition that includes four viewpoints. It focuses on human-robot interaction in the home caring domain. This dataset fully addresses the omissions identified at the end of the section II.

TABLE I: OVERVIEW OF POPULAR HAR AND THEIR PROPERTIES, PRESENTED IN DESCENDING ORDER OF YEAR STARTING FROM 2022 AND ENDING WITH 2010.

Dataset Name	Year	Video	An	Act	FV	En	Si	Mot	PoV	Modality	B	MV	AT	L	So	U	T	Acc
BON [33]	2022	2.6K	2.6K	18	_	Di	UC	Dy	FP	RGB	Dy	No	No	No	C	Home	Tr	No
EPIC-KITCHENS-100 [29]	2021	700	90K	4053	_	I	UC	Di	FP	RGB	Dy	No	No	No	C	Kitchen	A	Link
HOMAGE [28]	2021	5.7K	5.7K	75	2	I	UC	Di	FP/TP	12 Sensors	Dy	Yes	Yes	No	C	Home	A	Link
HA500 [34]	2021	10K	591K	500	_	Di	UC	St	TP	RGB	Dy	No	Yes	No	W	Diversity	A	Link
M-MiT [35]	2021	1M	2M	292	_	Di	UC	St	TP	RGB	Dy	No	No	Yes	W	Diversity	A	Link
MovieNet [36]	2020	1.1K	65K	80	_	Di	UC	St	TP	RGB	Dy	No	No	No	M	Diversity	A	Link
Multi-ViewPointOutdoor [37]	2020	2.3K	503K	20	3	O	UC	Di	TP	RGB	Dy	Yes	No	No	YT	Sport	A	No
HVU [38]	2020	572K	9M	3457	_	Di	UC	St	TP	RGB	Dy	No	No	No	YT	Diversity	A	Link
AViD [39]	2020	80k	80K	887	_	Di	C	St	TP	RGB	St	No	No	No	W	Diversity	A	Link
LEMMA [27]	2020	1.1K	0.9M	641	3	I	C	Di	FP/TP	RGB,D	Dy	Yes	Yes	No	C	Home	A	Link
InHARD [32]	2020	4.8K	2M	14	3	I	C	S	TP	RGB,D	Dy	Yes	No	No	C	Industrial	A	Link
FineGym [40]	2020	503	32.5K	15	_	I	UC	Di	TP	RGB	Dy	No	Yes	No	M	Sport	A	Link
Ava_Kinetic [22]	2020	500	230K	80	_	Di	UC	St	TP	RGB	Dy	No	No	Yes	YT	Diversity	A	Link
Kinetic_700_2020 [23]	2020	648K	648K	700	_	Di	UC	St	TP	RGB	Dy	No	No	No	YT	Diversity	A	Link
Jester [41]	2019	148K	5.3M	27	_	I	C	St	TP	RGB	Dy	No	Yes	No	C	Gesture	Tr	No
HACS [42]	2019	504K	1.5M	200	_	Di	UC	St	TP	RGB	Dy	No	No	Yes	YT	Diversity	A	Link
Kinetic_700 [21]	2019	650K	650K	700	_	Di	UC	St	TP	RGB	Dy	No	No	No	YT	Diversity	A	Link
NTU RGB+D 120 [18]	2019	114K	8M	120	155	I	C	St	TP	RGB,D	Dy	Yes	Yes	No	C	Daily	A	Link
MiT [43]	2019	1M	1M	339	_	Di	UC	Di	TP	RGB	Dy	No	No	No	W	Diversity	Tr	Link
20BN-sth_sth-V2 [25]	2018	220K	220K	174	_	I	UC	Di	FP	RGB	Dy	No	No	No	W	Diversity	A	No
Kinetic_600 [20]	2018	496K	496	600	_	Di	UC	Di	TP	RGB	Dy	No	No	No	YT	Diversity	A	Link
Charades-Ego [26]	2018	8K	68.5K	157	2	I	C	Di	FP/TP	RGB	Dy	Yes	Yes	Yes	C	Daily	A	Link
AVA [44]	2017	430	197K	80	_	Di	UC	St	TP	RGB	Dy	No	Yes	Yes	M	Diversity	A	Link
SLAC [45]	2017	520K	1.17M	200	_	Di	UC	Di	TP	RGB	Dy	No	No	Yes	YT	Diversity	A	No
MultiTHUMOS [46]	2017	38.6K	38.6K	65	_	Di	UC	Di	TP	RGB	Dy	No	No	No	W	Diversity	A	Link
20BN-Sth_Sth [24]	2017	100K	100K	174	_	I	UC	Dy	FP	RGB	Dy	No	Yes	No	W	Diversity	Tr	No
Kinetic_400 [19]	2017	300K	300K	400	_	Di	UC	St	TP	RGB	Dy	No	Yes	No	YT	Diversity	A	Link
M2I [47]	2017	1784	1784	22	2	I	C	St	TP	RGB,D	Dy	Yes	Yes	No	C	Diversity	Tr	No
DALY [48]	2016	8133	8133	10	_	Di	UC	St	TP	RGB	Dy	No	Yes	Yes	YT	Diversity	A	Link
YouTube-8M [16]	2016	8.2M	8.2M	4800	_	Di	UC	Di	TP	RGB	Dy	No	No	No	YT	Diversity	A	Link
NTU RGB+D [17]	2016	56K	56K	60	3	I	C	St	TP	RGB,D	Dy	Yes	Yes	No	C	Daily	Tr	Link
Charades [49]	2016	10K	10K	157	2	I	UC	St	TP	RGB	Dy	No	No	Yes	YT	Daily	Tr	Link
UTD-MHAD [50]	2015	861	861	27	5	I	C	St	TP	RGB,D	St	Yes	Yes	No	C	Daily	Tr	Link
ActivityNet [51]	2015	23K	23K	203	_	Di	UC	St	TP	RGB	Dy	No	No	No	W	Diversity	A	Link
Sport-1M [15]	2014	1M	1M	487	_	Di	UC	Di	TP	RGB	Dy	No	No	No	YT	Sport	A	Link
Berkeley MHAD [52]	2013	660	660	11	12	I	C	St	TP	RGB,D	St	Yes	Yes	No	C	Diversity	Tr	Link
Multi-View 3D Events [53]	2013	3.8K	383K	11	3	I	C	St	TP	RGB,D	Dy	Yes	Yes	No	C	Diversity	Tr	No
ASLAN [14]	2012	10K	10K	432	_	Di	UC	St	TP	RGB	Dy	No	No	No	YT	Diversity	Tr	Link
UCF101 [10]	2012	13K	13K	101	_	Di	UC	Di	TP	RGB	Dy	No	Yes	No	YT	Diversity	Tr	Link
LIRIS [31]	2012	828	828	10	2	I	C	Di	TP	RGB,D	Dy	Yes	Yes	Yes	C	Daily	Tr	Link
HMDB51 [7]	2011	6.8K	6.8K	51	_	Di	UC	Di	TP	RGB	Dy	No	No	No	YT	Daily	Tr	Link
UCF_ARG [12]	2010	480*3	480*3	10	3	O	C	St	TP	RGB	Dy	Yes	Yes	Yes	C	Daily	Tr	Link

The details of the Table I are, An: Number of Annotation, Act: Number of classes, FV: Number of Fixed Views, En: Environment Type (I: Indoor, O: Outdoor, Di: Diverse), Si: Situation (C: Controlled, UC: UnControlled), Mot: Camera motion capability (Dy: Dynamic, St: Static, Di: Diverse), PoV: Point of View (FP: First Person, TP: Third Person), B: Background (Dy: Dynamic, St: Static), Mu: Multi-View, At: Atomic, L: Localization, So: Source (C: Created, W: Web, M: Movie, YT: YouTube, U: Usage, T: data preparation type (Tr: Trimm, A: Annotation), Acc: Accessibility)

A frame of each class and viewpoint is shown in Figure 4.

A. Camera Types and Viewpoints

RMH uses Fetch Robot for the robot-view camera. The second unique view is a top view using a fish-eye camera, termed OmniView. There are additionally two wall-mounted cameras providing a static and side view for all actions to provide a better comparison between the views. The back-view and front-view cameras are paced in front of each other. Table II contains more details of the cameras and viewpoints in RMH.

B. Subject

As a result of COVID-19, populating this dataset with different participants was not possible, and only one person, therefore, performed the actions.

C. Content

RHM activity classes are selected from Bedaf et al. work in [54], which features essential daily activities for persons living independently. The work highlights that companion robots and ambient-assistive systems could provide a value proposition should they be able to detect these activities. The list of activities is: Walking, Sitting Down, Standing Up, Lifting Objects, Carrying Objects, Drinking, Stairs Climbing Up, Stairs Climbing Down, Stretching, Putting Objects Down, Reaching, Opening Can, Closing Can, and Cleaning.

D. Training-Validation-Testing

The RHM dataset has 14 classes in each view, and the number of videos in each class and each view is between 407 to 700. The total number of videos in each view is 6,701 and for all 4 views is 26,804. The data is split into training (65%), testing (20%), and validation(15%) for each view. Table III shows the number of videos for the training, testing, and validation in each view, and for all views. Clip length varies between 1 to 5 seconds.

TABLE II: RHM VIEWOINTS DETAILS (FR: Frame Rate)

View Name	Motion	Position	Resolution	FR
FrontView	Static	Wall	640 * 480	30
BackView	Static	Wall	640 * 480	30
RobotView	Dynamic	Robot	640 * 480	30
OmniView	Static	Ceiling	512 * 486	30

TABLE III: NUMBER OF VIDEOS IN EACH VIEW/SPLIT

	Train	Validation	Test
Each View	4278	1076	1347
All Views	17112	4304	5388

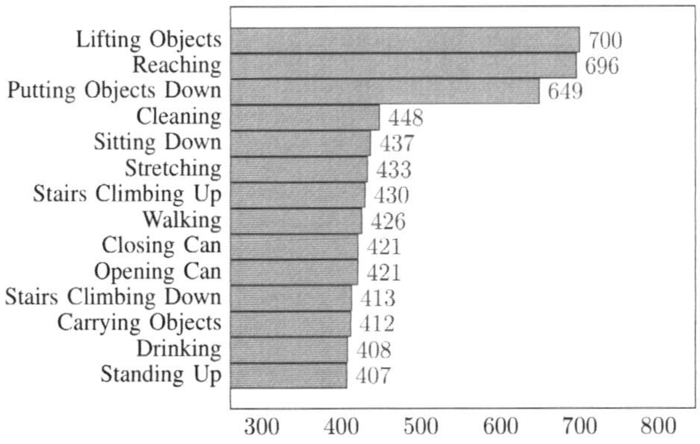

Figure. 1: Number of videos in each class

E. Naming Protocol

RHM contains four folders; each folder's name corresponds with the view name. Each splits into training, testing, and validation folders. The split folder comprises 14 folders, which are class names. The clips are inside the class folders with the ordered numbering. The naming protocol is like below:

ClassName_ViewName_clipNumber.avi

For example, Drinking_RobotView_103.avi refers to clip 103 of the action class 'drinking' from the robot-viewpoint.

F. Time Synchronising

All the clips with the same class name and number with various view names are synchronised. For instance, Clip 320, in reaching action, is time-synchronised with the remaining views.

G. RHM Skeleton dataset and Analysis

Also, we propose the human skeleton extraction in another paper in [58]. On the other hand, we propose a lightweight activity recognition pipeline that utilizes skeleton data from multiple perspectives to combine the advantages of both approaches and thereby enhance an assistive robot's perception of human activity in [59].

IV. RHM DATASET ANALYSIS

As we embark on exploring fusion for multiple views, it is crucial to consider mutual information, as well as single-view performance based on benchmark models comparing different views, before two-stream fusion.

TABLE IV: BENCHMARK MODEL ON RHM DATASET

	Robot View		Front View		Back View		Omni View		Kinetic 400	
Model	Top1	Top5	Top1	Top5	Top1	Top5	Top1	Top5	Top1	Top5
C3D [55]	55.53	93.83	70.3	**97.85**	69.48	97.84	67.48	97.69	71.4	NA
R3D [56]	61.98	94.28	69.04	**97.55**	69.33	97.4	69.71	97.25	74.4	91
R2+1D(RGB) [56]	55.6	91.9	65.79	95.91	66.96	**96.58**	64.73	95.99	72	90
Slow-Fast(8*8-R50) [57]	55.15	91.61	62.28	**97.25**	63.62	96.43	60.65	96.51	77	92.6
Slow-Fast(8*8-R101) [57]	58.57	92.79	59.39	**96.51**	60.43	95.61	61.76	96.36	77.9	93.2

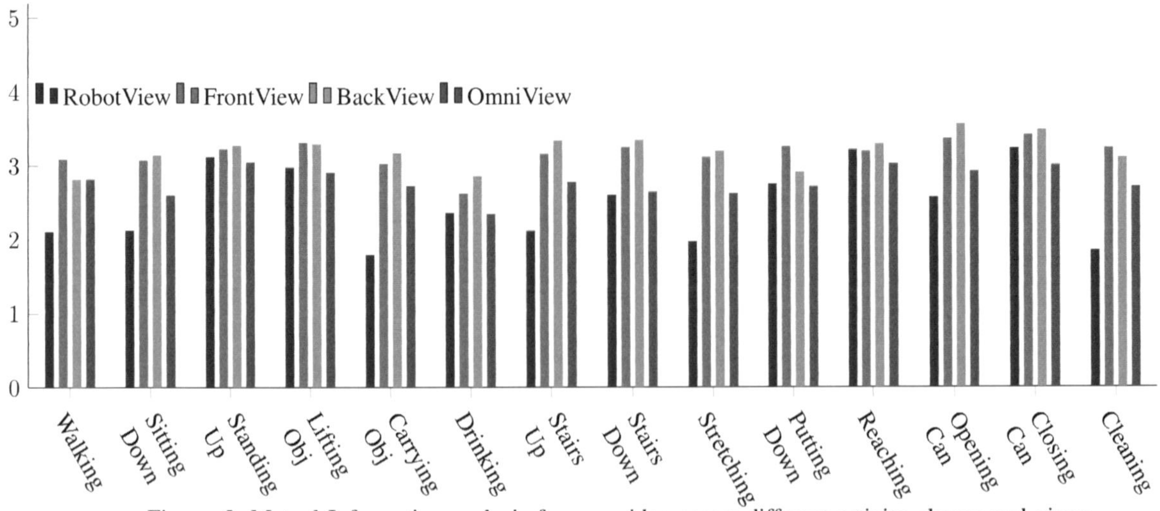

Figure. 2: Mutual Information analysis for one video across different activity classes and views

A. *Mutual Information*

We calculate Mutual information (MI) [2] analysis for a video in each class and view to determine the difference between the viewpoints.

$I(X;Y)$ is a Mutual Information of two variables X and Y with joint probability distribution $P(X,Y)$ [2]:

$$I(X;Y) = \sum_{x,y} P(x,y) \log \frac{P(x,y)}{P(x)P(y)} \quad (1)$$

We adopt MI [2] for a video with m frames as below:

$$MI(f_i, f_m) = \sum_{i=1}^{m} P(f_i, f_{i+1}) \log \frac{P(f_i, f_{i+1})}{P(f_i)P(f_{i+1})} \quad (2)$$

Which $MI(f_i, f_m)$ is the sum of all MI of two adjacent frames in a video and f_i is the first frame, and f_m is the last frame.

Since the $MI(f_i, f_m)$ adds all MI for every two adjacent frames together, so we divided the calculated MI by $m-1$ to reach the average result:

$$Ave_{mi} = \frac{1}{m-1} MI(f_i, f_m) \quad (3)$$

Which Ave_{mi} is the average of all MI of two adjacent frames in a video, m is the number of frames, and f_i is the first frame, and f_m is the last frame.

The video is selected randomly in each class. We extract the video frames, calculate the mutual information between two simultaneous frames, and continue this method until the last two frames. We then perform the same method for the same video in another view. For instance, the video is 100 for all four views for walking. The results of performing our method to realise the difference between the same video in all views are in Figure 2. High mutual information means high redundancy, and low mutual information means low redundancy between frames in a video.

As it is clear, robot-viewpoint has the lowest mutual information in all actions except reaching, especially in the actions that involve a significant movement component, e.g. walking. This result could be estimated since the camera has motion and the frames have different information. The fish-eye (Omni) view has the second lowest MI. Front and back-views have more mutual information since they are fixed on the wall and have a fixed viewpoint.

B. *Deep models Analysis*

Another method for comparing the viewpoints is performing some benchmark models. We have performed C3D [55], R2+1D [56], R3D [56], and Slow-Fast [57] models.

Table IV shows the results of performing the benchmark models on the RHM dataset. We have additionally added kinetic_400 results to have better information to compare. Red data are the best of Top1 and the blue ones are related to the best of Top5. The underlined values indicate the highest accuracy for the Top 1 and Top 5 metrics.

One notable outcome of the results relates to the robot's viewpoint. The Top1 and Top5 accuracy is the lowest for all

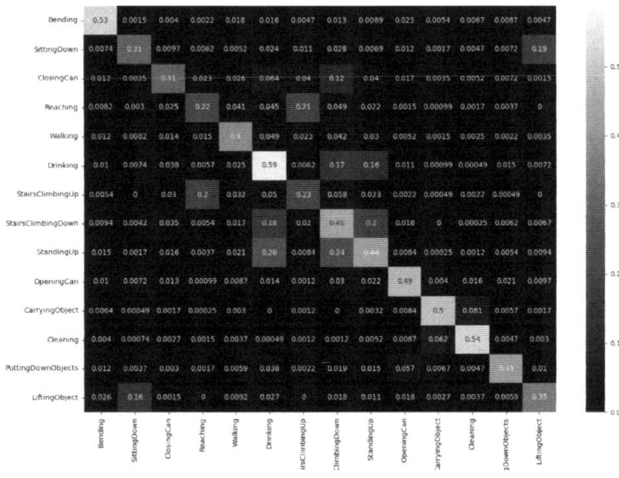

(a) Front View

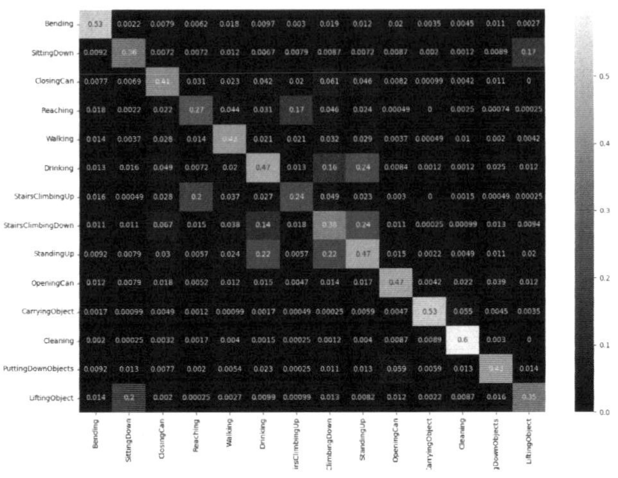

(b) Back View

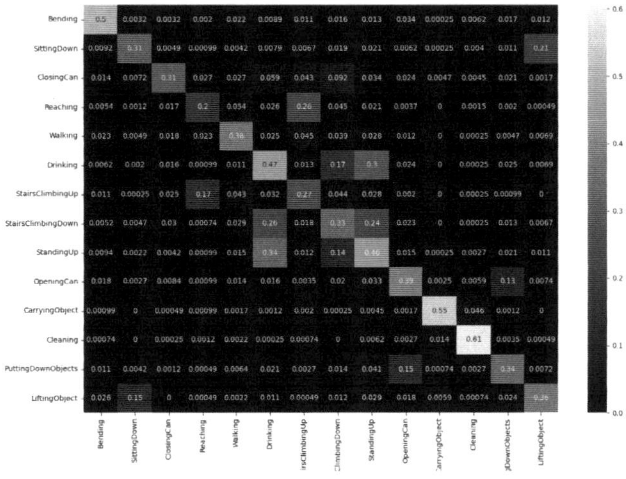

(c) Omni View

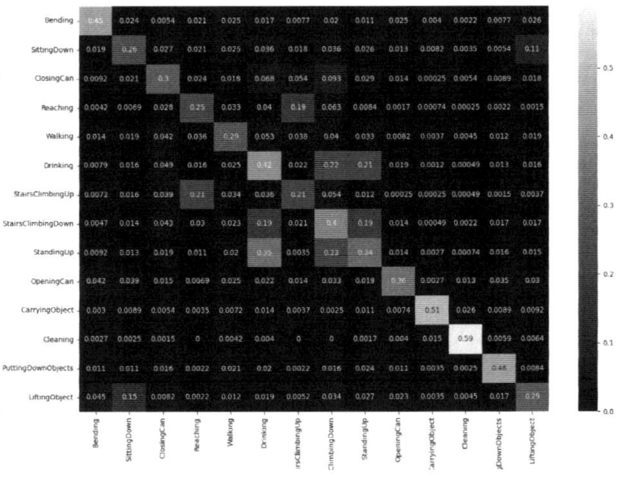

(d) Robot View

Figure. 3: RHM Confusion Matrix for all views with C3D Model

models for robot-view. Having motion in the robot-view is the main reason for these results. Another interesting result relates to the Omni (ceiling) view, which achieves two of the best Top 1 accuracy results. This is because of having a good and comprehensive viewpoint from the top for all activities. We also note that the front-view attains all the Top 5 best accuracy results except the R2+1D model. In terms of the top1 and top5, the wall fixed views (Front and back-views) are the best, which is understandable because they do not have a motion, and also they have an excellent viewpoint to cover all the action areas. In general, the front-view in the C3D model provides the highest overall accuracy results.

Figure 3 shows the confusion matrices from the C3D model for each view, separately. In all of the confusion matrices, almost the same classes have confusion with each other. It means that the confusion is not related to the viewpoint. There is confusion in Sitting down & Lifting objects, Reaching & Stairs up, Drinking & Standing Up and Stairs Down, and Opening Cans & Putting down objects classes in all views.

V. Conclusion

We introduced the Robot House Multi-View HAR (RHM) Dataset, with Front (static), Back (static), Ceiling (fish-eye), and Robot (dynamic) views. RHM contains 6,701 videos in 14 classes for each view separately. The total number of clips for all views is 26,804 videos. The videos with the same number and the same classes are time-synchronised in different views. We analysed the RHM with mutual information and various benchmark models. The robot-view has the lowest level of mutual information compared to other views. Also, the C3D model and front-view had the best results in the benchmark analysis. Our future work will focus on the dynamic choice of complementary channels based on the affordance of views supporting an activity guided by mutual information. We aim to explore channel combination and multi-stream activity recognition, aiming to improve activity recognition for more complex cases.

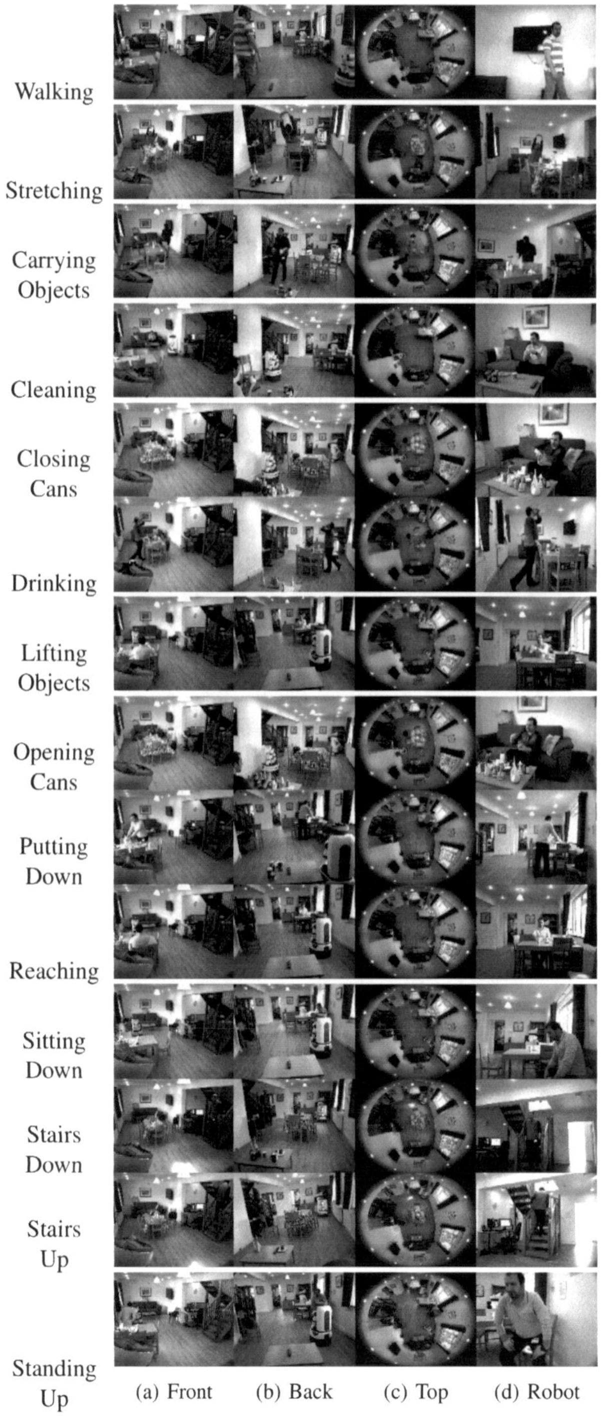

Figure. 4: Example activities of the dataset from all perspectives.

REFERENCES

[1] M. H. B. Abadi, M. R. S. Alashti, P. Holthaus, C. Menon, and F. Amirabdollahian, "Robot house human activity recognition dataset," *UKRAS21*, 2021. 1

[2] T. M. Cover, *Elements of information theory*. John Wiley & Sons, 1999. 1, 5

[3] C. Schuldt, I. Laptev, and B. Caputo, "Recognizing human actions: a local svm approach," in *Proceedings of the 17th International Conference on Pattern Recognition, 2004. ICPR 2004.*, vol. 3. IEEE, 2004, pp. 32–36. 1

[4] L. Gorelick, M. Blank, E. Shechtman, M. Irani, and R. Basri, "Actions as space-time shapes," *IEEE transactions on pattern analysis and machine intelligence*, vol. 29, no. 12, pp. 2247–2253, 2007. 1

[5] D. Weinland, R. Ronfard, and E. Boyer, "Free viewpoint action recognition using motion history volumes," *Computer vision and image understanding*, vol. 104, no. 2-3, pp. 249–257, 2006. 1

[6] S. Singh, S. A. Velastin, and H. Ragheb, "Muhavi: A multicamera human action video dataset for the evaluation of action recognition methods," in *2010 7th IEEE International Conference on Advanced Video and Signal Based Surveillance*. IEEE, 2010, pp. 48–55. 1

[7] H. Kuehne, H. Jhuang, E. Garrote, T. Poggio, and T. Serre, "Hmdb: a large video database for human motion recognition," in *2011 International conference on computer vision*. IEEE, 2011, pp. 2556–2563. 1, 3

[8] J. Liu, J. Luo, and M. Shah, "Recognizing realistic actions from videos "in the wild"," in *2009 IEEE Conference on Computer Vision and Pattern Recognition*. IEEE, 2009, pp. 1996–2003. 2

[9] K. K. Reddy and M. Shah, "Recognizing 50 human action categories of web videos," *Machine vision and applications*, vol. 24, no. 5, pp. 971–981, 2013. 2

[10] K. Soomro, A. R. Zamir, and M. Shah, "Ucf101: A dataset of 101 human actions classes from videos in the wild," *arXiv preprint arXiv:1212.0402*, 2012. 2, 3

[11] K. Soomro and A. R. Zamir, "Action recognition in realistic sports videos," in *Computer vision in sports*. Springer, 2014, pp. 181–208. 2

[12] A. Nagendran, D. Harper, and M. Shah, "New system performs persistent wide-area aerial surveillance," *SPIE Newsroom*, vol. 5, pp. 20–28, 2010. 2, 3

[13] Z. Cheng, L. Qin, Y. Ye, Q. Huang, and Q. Tian, "Human daily action analysis with multi-view and color-depth data," in *European Conference on Computer Vision*. Springer, 2012, pp. 52–61. 2

[14] O. Kliper-Gross, T. Hassner, and L. Wolf, "The action similarity labeling challenge," *IEEE Transactions on Pattern Analysis and Machine Intelligence*, vol. 34, no. 3, pp. 615–621, 2011. 2, 3

[15] A. Karpathy, G. Toderici, S. Shetty, T. Leung, R. Sukthankar, and L. Fei-Fei, "Large-scale video classification with convolutional neural networks," in *Proceedings of the IEEE conference on Computer Vision and Pattern Recognition*, 2014, pp. 1725–1732. 2, 3

[16] S. Abu-El-Haija, N. Kothari, J. Lee, P. Natsev, G. Toderici, B. Varadarajan, and S. Vijayanarasimhan, "Youtube-8m: A large-scale video classification benchmark," *arXiv preprint arXiv:1609.08675*, 2016. 2, 3

[17] A. Shahroudy, J. Liu, T.-T. Ng, and G. Wang, "Ntu rgb+ d: A large scale dataset for 3d human activity analysis," in *Proceedings of the IEEE conference on computer vision and pattern recognition*, 2016, pp. 1010–1019. 2, 3

[18] J. Liu, A. Shahroudy, M. Perez, G. Wang, L.-Y. Duan, and A. C. Kot, "Ntu rgb+ d 120: A large-scale benchmark for 3d human activity understanding," *IEEE transactions on pattern analysis and machine intelligence*, vol. 42, no. 10, pp. 2684–2701, 2019. 2, 3

[19] W. Kay, J. Carreira, K. Simonyan, B. Zhang, C. Hillier, S. Vijayanarasimhan, F. Viola, T. Green, T. Back, P. Natsev *et al.*, "The kinetics human action video dataset," *arXiv preprint arXiv:1705.06950*, 2017. 2, 3

[20] J. Carreira, E. Noland, A. Banki-Horvath, C. Hillier, and A. Zisserman, "A short note about kinetics-600," *arXiv preprint arXiv:1808.01340*, 2018. 2, 3

[21] J. Carreira, E. Noland, C. Hillier, and A. Zisserman, "A short note on the kinetics-700 human action dataset," *arXiv preprint arXiv:1907.06987*, 2019. 2, 3

[22] A. Li, M. Thotakuri, D. A. Ross, J. Carreira, A. Vostrikov, and A. Zisserman, "The ava-kinetics localized human actions video dataset," *arXiv preprint arXiv:2005.00214*, 2020. 2, 3

[23] L. Smaira, J. Carreira, E. Noland, E. Clancy, A. Wu, and A. Zisserman, "A short note on the kinetics-700-2020 human action dataset," *arXiv preprint arXiv:2010.10864*, 2020. 2, 3
[24] R. Goyal, S. Ebrahimi Kahou, V. Michalski, J. Materzynska, S. Westphal, H. Kim, V. Haenel, I. Fruend, P. Yianilos, M. Mueller-Freitag *et al.*, "The" something something" video database for learning and evaluating visual common sense," in *Proceedings of the IEEE international conference on computer vision*, 2017, pp. 5842–5850. 2, 3
[25] F. Mahdisoltani, G. Berger, W. Gharbieh, D. Fleet, and R. Memisevic, "On the effectiveness of task granularity for transfer learning," *arXiv preprint arXiv:1804.09235*, 2018. 2, 3
[26] G. A. Sigurdsson, A. Gupta, C. Schmid, A. Farhadi, and K. Alahari, "Actor and observer: Joint modeling of first and third-person videos," in *Proceedings of the IEEE Conference on Computer Vision and Pattern Recognition*, 2018, pp. 7396–7404. 2, 3
[27] B. Jia, Y. Chen, S. Huang, Y. Zhu, and S.-c. Zhu, "Lemma: A multi-view dataset for learning multi-agent multi-task activities," in *European Conference on Computer Vision*. Springer, 2020, pp. 767–786. 2, 3
[28] N. Rai, H. Chen, J. Ji, R. Desai, K. Kozuka, S. Ishizaka, E. Adeli, and J. C. Niebles, "Home action genome: Cooperative compositional action understanding," in *Proceedings of the IEEE/CVF Conference on Computer Vision and Pattern Recognition*, 2021, pp. 11 184–11 193. 2, 3
[29] D. Damen, H. Doughty, G. M. Farinella, A. Furnari, E. Kazakos, J. Ma, D. Moltisanti, J. Munro, T. Perrett, W. Price *et al.*, "Rescaling egocentric vision: collection, pipeline and challenges for epic-kitchens-100," *International Journal of Computer Vision*, vol. 130, no. 1, pp. 33–55, 2022. 2, 3
[30] D. Damen, H. Doughty, G. M. Farinella, S. Fidler, A. Furnari, E. Kazakos, D. Moltisanti, J. Munro, T. Perrett, W. Price *et al.*, "Scaling egocentric vision: The epic-kitchens dataset," in *Proceedings of the European Conference on Computer Vision (ECCV)*, 2018, pp. 720–736. 2
[31] C. Wolf, J. Mille, E. Lombardi, O. Celiktutan, M. Jiu, M. Baccouche, E. Dellandréa, C.-E. Bichot, C. Garcia, and B. Sankur, "The liris human activities dataset and the icpr 2012 human activities recognition and localization competition," *LIRIS Umr*, vol. 5205, 2012. 2, 3
[32] M. Dallel, V. Havard, D. Baudry, and X. Savatier, "Inhard-industrial human action recognition dataset in the context of industrial collaborative robotics," in *2020 IEEE International Conference on Human-Machine Systems (ICHMS)*. IEEE, 2020, pp. 1–6. 2, 3
[33] G. Abebe Tadesse, O. Bent, K. Weldemariam, M. A. Istiak, T. Hasan, and A. Cavallaro, "Bon: An extended public domain dataset for human activity recognition," *arXiv e-prints*, pp. arXiv–2209, 2022. 3
[34] J. Chung, C.-h. Wuu, H.-r. Yang, Y.-W. Tai, and C.-K. Tang, "Haa500: Human-centric atomic action dataset with curated videos," in *Proceedings of the IEEE/CVF International Conference on Computer Vision*, 2021, pp. 13 465–13 474. 3
[35] M. Monfort, B. Pan, K. Ramakrishnan, A. Andonian, B. A. McNamara, A. Lascelles, Q. Fan, D. Gutfreund, R. Feris, and A. Oliva, "Multi-moments in time: Learning and interpreting models for multi-action video understanding," *IEEE Transactions on Pattern Analysis and Machine Intelligence*, 2021. 3
[36] Q. Huang, Y. Xiong, A. Rao, J. Wang, and D. Lin, "Movienet: A holistic dataset for movie understanding," in *European Conference on Computer Vision*. Springer, 2020, pp. 709–727. 3
[37] A. G. Perera, Y. W. Law, T. T. Ogunwa, and J. Chahl, "A multiviewpoint outdoor dataset for human action recognition," *IEEE Transactions on Human-Machine Systems*, vol. 50, no. 5, pp. 405–413, 2020. 3
[38] A. Diba, M. Fayyaz, V. Sharma, M. Paluri, J. Gall, R. Stiefelhagen, and L. V. Gool, "Large scale holistic video understanding," in *European Conference on Computer Vision*. Springer, 2020, pp. 593–610. 3
[39] A. Piergiovanni and M. Ryoo, "Avid dataset: Anonymized videos from diverse countries," *Advances in Neural Information Processing Systems*, vol. 33, pp. 16 711–16 721, 2020. 3
[40] D. Shao, Y. Zhao, B. Dai, and D. Lin, "Finegym: A hierarchical video dataset for fine-grained action understanding," in *Proceedings of the IEEE/CVF conference on computer vision and pattern recognition*, 2020, pp. 2616–2625. 3
[41] J. Materzynska, G. Berger, I. Bax, and R. Memisevic, "The jester dataset: A large-scale video dataset of human gestures," in *Proceedings of the IEEE/CVF International Conference on Computer Vision Workshops*, 2019, pp. 0–0. 3
[42] H. Zhao, A. Torralba, L. Torresani, and Z. Yan, "Hacs: Human action clips and segments dataset for recognition and temporal localization," in *Proceedings of the IEEE/CVF International Conference on Computer Vision*, 2019, pp. 8668–8678. 3
[43] M. Monfort, A. Andonian, B. Zhou, K. Ramakrishnan, S. A. Bargal, T. Yan, L. Brown, Q. Fan, D. Gutfreund, C. Vondrick *et al.*, "Moments in time dataset: one million videos for event understanding," *IEEE transactions on pattern analysis and machine intelligence*, vol. 42, no. 2, pp. 502–508, 2019. 3
[44] C. Gu, C. Sun, D. A. Ross, C. Vondrick, C. Pantofaru, Y. Li, S. Vijayanarasimhan, G. Toderici, S. Ricco, R. Sukthankar *et al.*, "Ava: A video dataset of spatio-temporally localized atomic visual actions," in *Proceedings of the IEEE Conference on Computer Vision and Pattern Recognition*, 2018, pp. 6047–6056. 3
[45] H. Zhao, Z. Yan, H. Wang, L. Torresani, and A. Torralba, "Slac: A sparsely labeled dataset for action classification and localization," *arXiv preprint arXiv:1712.09374*, vol. 2, 2017. 3
[46] S. Yeung, O. Russakovsky, N. Jin, M. Andriluka, G. Mori, and L. Fei-Fei, "Every moment counts: Dense detailed labeling of actions in complex videos," *International Journal of Computer Vision*, vol. 126, no. 2, pp. 375–389, 2018. 3
[47] A.-A. Liu, N. Xu, W.-Z. Nie, Y.-T. Su, Y. Wong, and M. Kankanhalli, "Benchmarking a multimodal and multiview and interactive dataset for human action recognition," *IEEE Transactions on cybernetics*, vol. 47, no. 7, pp. 1781–1794, 2016. 3
[48] P. Weinzaepfel, X. Martin, and C. Schmid, "Human action localization with sparse spatial supervision," *arXiv preprint arXiv:1605.05197*, 2016. 3
[49] G. A. Sigurdsson, G. Varol, X. Wang, A. Farhadi, I. Laptev, and A. Gupta, "Hollywood in homes: Crowdsourcing data collection for activity understanding," in *European Conference on Computer Vision*. Springer, 2016, pp. 510–526. 3
[50] C. Chen, R. Jafari, and N. Kehtarnavaz, "Utd-mhad: A multimodal dataset for human action recognition utilizing a depth camera and a wearable inertial sensor," in *2015 IEEE International conference on image processing (ICIP)*. IEEE, 2015, pp. 168–172. 3
[51] F. Caba Heilbron, V. Escorcia, B. Ghanem, and J. Carlos Niebles, "Activitynet: A large-scale video benchmark for human activity understanding," in *Proceedings of the ieee conference on computer vision and pattern recognition*, 2015, pp. 961–970. 3
[52] F. Ofli, R. Chaudhry, G. Kurillo, R. Vidal, and R. Bajcsy, "Berkeley mhad: A comprehensive multimodal human action database," in *2013 IEEE workshop on applications of computer vision (WACV)*. IEEE, 2013, pp. 53–60. 3
[53] P. Wei, Y. Zhao, N. Zheng, and S.-C. Zhu, "Modeling 4d human-object interactions for event and object recognition," in *Proceedings of the IEEE International Conference on Computer Vision*, 2013, pp. 3272–3279. 3
[54] S. Bedaf, G. J. Gelderblom, D. S. Syrdal, H. Lehmann, H. Michel, D. Hewson, F. Amirabdollahian, K. Dautenhahn, and L. De Witte, "Which activities threaten independent living of elderly when becoming problematic: inspiration for meaningful service robot functionality," *Disability and Rehabilitation: Assistive Technology*, vol. 9, no. 6, pp. 445–452, 2014. 4
[55] D. Tran, L. Bourdev, R. Fergus, L. Torresani, and M. Paluri, "Learning spatiotemporal features with 3d convolutional networks," in *Proceedings of the IEEE international conference on computer vision*, 2015, pp. 4489–4497. 5
[56] D. Tran, H. Wang, L. Torresani, J. Ray, Y. LeCun, and M. Paluri, "A closer look at spatiotemporal convolutions for action recognition," in *Proceedings of the IEEE conference on Computer Vision and Pattern Recognition*, 2018, pp. 6450–6459. 5
[57] C. Feichtenhofer, H. Fan, J. Malik, and K. He, "Slowfast networks for video recognition," in *Proceedings of the IEEE/CVF international conference on computer vision*, 2019, pp. 6202–6211. 5
[58] M. Shahabian Alashti, M. Bamorovat Abadi, P. Holthaus, C. Menon, and F. Amirabdollahian, "Rhm-har-sk: A multi-view dataset with skeleton data for ambient assisted living research," in *ACHI 2023: The Sixteenth International Conference on Advances in Computer-Human Interactions*. IARIA, 2023. 4
[59] ——, "Lightweight human activity recognition for ambient assisted living," in *ACHI 2023: The Sixteenth International Conference on Advances in Computer-Human Interactions*. IARIA, 2023. 4

Analysis of EEG Microstates During Execution of a Nine Hole Peg Test

Shadiya Alingal Meethal
Robotic Research Group
University of Hertfordshire
Hatfield, United Kingdom
email: s.alingal-meethal@herts.ac.uk

Volker Steuber
Biocomputation Research Group
University of Hertfordshire
Hatfield, United Kingdom
email: v.steuber@herts.ac.uk

Farshid Amirabdollahian
Robotic Research Group
University of Hertfordshire
Hatfield, United Kingdom
email: f.amirabdollahian2@herts.ac.uk

***Abstract*—Electroencephalogram(EEG) microstates are brief periods of time during which the brain's electrical activity remains stable. The analysis of EEG microstates can help to identify the background neuronal activity at the millisecond level. The utilization of haptic and robotic technologies can help in evaluating human motor skills. A haptic device Geomagic Touch is used in this study to recreate Nine Hole Peg Test (NHPT) in an embedded reality setup. A preliminary study is conducted to explore changes in neural assemblies related to resting state and fine motor state EEG when fatigue sets in. Five healthy participants are recruited to perform a haptic NHPT under different physical conditions. Three distinct microstates are observed during the resting state and a separate set of 3 states are observed during the NHPT. Changes are assessed by utilising microstate parameters such as occurrence, coverage, duration, and global explained variance. It is found that the coverage of microstate C for resting states decreases for all the participants after the dumbbell exercise. During the fine-motor task, the coverage of microstate MS3 decreases for all participants except one. These results support the involvement of different neural assemblies, but also highlight the potential that physical fatigue can be observed and identified by assessing changes in microstate features, in this case, a parameter such as coverage.**

***Index Terms*—EEG; microstates; NHPT; Geomagic Touch.**

I. INTRODUCTION

Human movements are controlled by the Central Nervous System. Stroke is a condition where the blood supply to the brain is disrupted, resulting in oxygen starvation, brain damage and loss of function. One in six people worldwide will have a stroke in their lifetime [1]. Over three-quarters of stroke survivors report arm weakness, which makes their daily living activities difficult [2]. Understanding the neural mechanisms related to hand movements will help in effective therapy designs for stroke patients. Therapy often benefits from assessment to inform progress. The Nine Hole Peg Test (NHPT) is one of the easiest and widely used tests for measuring dexterity. A reliable outcome measure of NHPT is the time taken to complete placing nine pegs into nine holes [3]. Haptic devices have the potential to provide further performance metrics to inform on the quality of the fine motor task. We have designed haptic instruments for simulating the NHPT as detailed in earlier work [4] [5]. These studies indicated that the addition of haptic and virtual reality may introduce new cognitive demands while providing more extensive performance metrics. To explore this further, we decided to utilise the brain's microstate recording before, during, and after NHPT. Separately, we have also explored the electromyographical impact of fatigue on gross motor muscles [6] that highlighted needs to further explore neural correlates at the brain level, to understand the complete chain of events leading to mental and physical fatigue.

Human-computer interaction can induce fatigue. The state of mental and physical fatigue can be attributed to the reduced activity of the central nervous system, which is characterized by prolonged cognitive processing time and decreased attention levels [7]. When people start to feel fatigued in human-computer interaction, they tend to use the peripherals in significantly different ways. Studies suggest methods to classify levels of fatigue by taking interaction patterns as input [8].

The concept of EEG microstates was developed by Dietrich Lehmann and his team in the late 1970s to quantify the spatio-temporal dynamics of the brain [9]. They suggested that the multichannel EEG recorded over the brain follows a stable map configuration for a short period of time. EEG microstates were called atoms of thought since they were thought to reflect individual high-level aspects of cognition and information processing [10]. Changes in the scalp electric field configuration imply changes in the distribution of underlying neural generators. This means that different microstate topographies at any time reflect the neural network activity predominating at that time [11]. The effect of fatigue on microstate intensity has been investigated and it was found that the amplitude of microstates increases when going from alert to the fatigued state [12]. Not many studies have investigated changes in EEG microstates during physical fatigue, however, changes in microstate parameters during mental fatigue are described in [13]. Most of the studies of EEG microstates deal with resting state microstates. Here, an attempt is made to perform the analysis of microstates for EEG data acquired from a person while performing the NHPT, before and after a fatiguing condition that is induced using a wrist dumbbell exercise.

The rest of this paper is organised as follows. Section II explains the materials and methods used in the study. In Section III, the results of the study are explained and further discussion on the results is done in Section IV. Finally, Section V concludes the study.

II. Materials and Methods

This section details the experimental setup and protocol used in the study. Additionally, methodologies for finding EEG microstates are also briefed here.

A. Experiment Set up

The experiment setup includes an EEG signal acquisition device (g.USBamp), g.GAMMAcap, the haptic device Geomagic Touch, which recreated the NHPT in a virtual environment and a physical rig for NHPT.

EEG signals from each participant are collected with the help of biosignal amplifier g.USBamp at a sampling rate of 1200Hz. EEG signals are recorded from electrodes FP1, FP2, F3, Fz, F4, FC3, FCz, FC4, C5, C3, C1, Cz, C2, C4, C6, and CP3 by means of g.GAMMAcap. Virtual and physical NHPT rig are localised in a way to provide an embedded reality task setup. A C++ code running on a Windows 10 (64-bit) machine using Visual Studio 2017 is used to configure the virtual reality environment and the Geomagic Touch. NHPT is performed using the stylus of the Touch device. The physical rig is kept in front of the participant and mapped onto a virtual rig on the LCD screen. There are nine pegs and a peg board on the screen. A peg is attached to the end of the stylus with the help of a rubber end cap. In each trial of NHPT, the participant has to pick the pegs on the screen one by one and insert them into one of the holes. The haptic feedback helps the participants to feel the virtual pegs. The time at which each peg is picked and released is recorded as peg status. At the beginning of the experiment, participants are allowed a practice run to get familiarised with the haptic device. Fig.1 shows a participant performing the experiment.

B. Experiment Protocol

Five healthy right-handed participants with no previous injuries to the upper limb or brain are recruited for the study. Table I has details about participants' physical characteristics. The total duration of the experiment, including setup time, for one participant, was 45-60 minutes. The ethics approval was obtained from the University of Hertfordshire under approval reference: ECS/PGR/UH/04035.

TABLE I
Physical characteristics of participants.

Subject	Gender	Age	BMI
1	Male	25	22
2	Female	36	21
3	Male	36	28
4	Male	34	36
5	Male	28	25

Two 4-minute-long EEG recordings are taken with eyes closed and eyes open at the beginning and end of the experiment. The participants are instructed to stay focused and try to minimise eye blinks, swallowing or any other motions that alter EEG recordings. Subsequently, they are asked to do two trials of NHPT followed by a fatiguing exercise for the forearm. Once the participants report fatigue, they are asked to do the next two trials of NHPT. There was no break given between the end of the dumbbell exercise and the start of trial 3, however, 20 - 30 seconds elapsed between them during the experiment. The experiment flow is given in Fig.2. The experiment is designed in a way that each participant can be their own control. Data is gathered during pre and post-fatigue to allow comparing neural correlates of these phases.

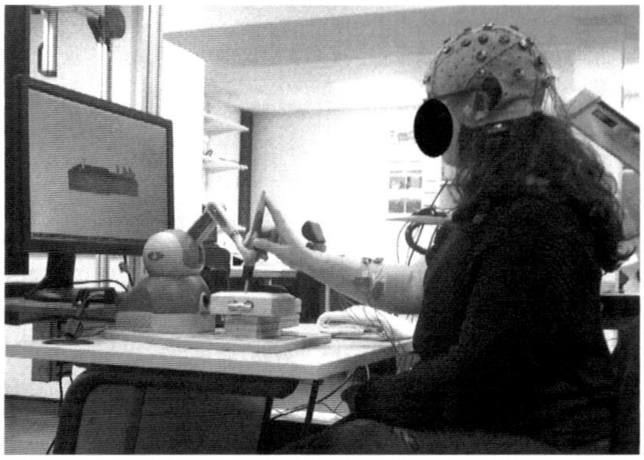

Figure. 1. A participant performing the NHPT experiment.

The fatigue exercise involves flexion and extension of the wrist using a dumbbell. Participants are asked to select one dumbbell from the set of weights provided and they are asked to perform 3 sets of 12, 10, and 8 repetitions with a 30 seconds rest in between the sets. All participants reported fatigue after the 3 sets.

A questionnaire is provided as part of the experiment in order to assess their fatigue status. Participants are asked to fill out parts of the questionnaire at the beginning of the experiment and requested to update their fatigue status before NHPT Trial1, after NHPT Trial2, before NHPT Trial3 and after NHPT Trial4.

C. Methodology

MATLAB R2019A is used to develop the EEG processing algorithms. The recorded EEG signals are segmented to extract data corresponding to each phase of the experiment and each NHPT trial. To remove high-frequency noise and low-frequency drift all signals are filtered in the frequency band 0.5-60 Hz using an FIR filter. Independent Component Analysis (ICA) is used for removing EEG artefacts [14].

Microstates are found for the resting state data at the beginning and the end. Also, microstates are found for pre-fatigue and post-fatigue NHPT trials. The EEG microstate analysis is performed with the help of the microstate EEGLAB toolbox in MATLAB 2019a [15]. The main part of the microstate analysis involved segmenting the EEG recordings into quasi-stable states using a clustering method. Modified K means clustering is used in this project to find the microstates. A two-step clustering is used to find microstate maps. The first

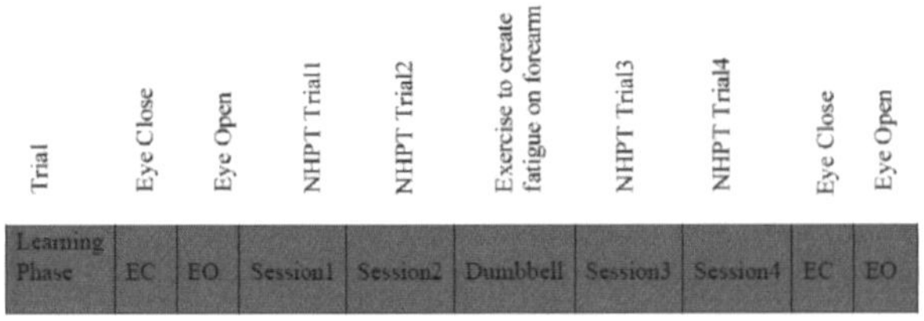

Figure. 2. Experiment Flow and different phases.

clustering is performed on individual participants and in the next level, the clustering is done across the subjects [16].

Eye close data at the beginning and end are used for finding resting state microstates. Each of the recordings is segmented into 20 sets of 2s data segments. The data is divided into 2s epochs. For the analysis of microstates, topographies at maximal potential field strength are considered. The strength of the scalp potential can be quantified using global field power (GFP), calculated as

$$GFP(t) = \sqrt{\frac{\sum_i^k \left(V_i(t) - V_{mean}(t)\right)^2}{k}} \tag{1}$$

where $V_i(t)$ is the voltage at electrode i at time t, $V_{mean}(t)$ is the mean voltage across all electrodes at time t and k is the number of electrodes [17].

The optimal signal to noise ratio and stable topography are obtained at the local maximum of GFP [18]. In the first step, the GFP of all aggregated data sets is generated. EEG maps that correspond to GFP peaks are submitted to modified K-means clustering for generating microstate prototypes. During the clustering, the polarity of the maps is ignored. Microstate prototypes are sorted by decreasing global explained variance.

Most of the literature predefined the number of microstates as four which previously has been reported as able to explain more than 70% of the total topographic variance [17]. In contrast, in this project, the number of microstates are selected based on the evaluation of prototype topographies and measures of fitness. The microstate clusters obtained at the individual level are then again clustered to obtain the global microstate maps [19]. Three microstates are observed for both the resting state and NHPT trials EEG. To find the microstate parameters, these global microstate maps are backfitted to the original EEG data [16]. After backfitting, microstate labels are smoothed temporally to remove small segments of unstable topography. For each microstate class, different microstate parameters are calculated.

The microstate parameters found here are the duration, occurrence, coverage, and global explained variance. The duration of a microstate is the average time for which a given microstate remains stable whenever it appears. The coverage of a microstate is the fraction of the total recording time when the given microstate is dominant. The occurrence is the average number of times per second a microstate is dominant [20].

III. RESULTS

Initially, microstates are found for resting state data at the beginning and end of the experiment. Furthermore, microstates are found for the first peg transfer in trial 1 and trial 3. Both of these sets of microstates are shown in Fig.3.

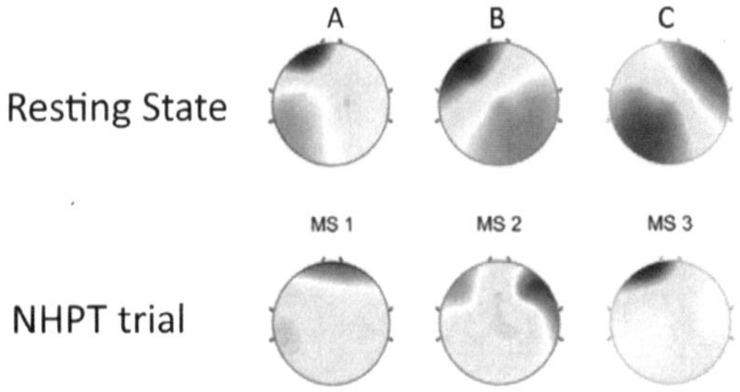

Figure. 3. Microstates during resting state and an NHPT trial. These microstate maps are found by clustering EEG topographies at the local GFP maxima of all the participants. Red colour shows positive and blue colour shows negative potential areas.

A. Microstate analysis for resting state data

The participants are asked to keep their eyes closed for two minutes at the beginning and end of the experiment. Microstate analysis is performed on this EEG data to find any changes in microstate parameters while a person undergoes a fatiguing exercise. Three microstates A, B and C are found for the resting state data. The microstate parameters derived from the resting state data are shown in Table II. It can be seen that the occurrence of microstate A increases for all subjects except subject 4. For microstates B and C, the occurrence increases for three subjects and decreases for two subjects. At the same time, the duration of microstate A increases for all subjects except subject 4. The duration of microstate B increases for three subjects and decreases for one subject. The duration of microstate C decreases for all subjects.

The Coverage of microstate A increases for all subjects except subject 4. The coverage of microstate B increases for three subjects and decreases for two subjects. The coverage of microstate C decreases for all the subjects. Changes in coverage for resting state microstates are shown in Fig.4. The global explained variance of microstate A increases for all subjects except subject 4. GEV of microstate B increases for three subjects and decreases for two subjects. GEV of microstate C decreases for four subjects and remains the same for one subject.

B. Microstate analysis for NHPT trial data

The microstates are found when a person performs the first peg transfer in trial 1 and trial 3. Other trials were excluded because this study is comparing neurological changes

TABLE II
RESTING STATE MICROSTATE PARAMETERS.

Subject	Microstates	Occurrence			Duration(ms)			Coverage(%)			GEV		
		Pre	Post	Change	Pre	Post	Change	Pre	Post	Change	Pre	Post	Change
1	A	4.32	4.57	↑	78.34	150.32	↑	34	64	↑	0.17	0.36	↑
	B	4.12	3.10	↓	77.74	57.16	↓	32	18	↓	0.15	0.07	↓
	C	4.35	2.85	↓	80.18	61.47	↓	35	18	↓	0.19	0.08	↓
2	A	2.00	2.42	↑	49.68	54.79	↑	10	13	↑	0.03	0.03	
	B	4.72	4.45	↓	101.05	140.23	↑	47	60	↑	0.18	0.21	↑
	C	4.77	3.55	↓	92.85	76.75	↓	43	27	↓	0.17	0.07	↓
3	A	0.57	1.30	↑	40.00	44.26	↑	3	6	↑	0.00	0.01	↑
	B	4.20	4.60	↑	123.88	106.72	↓	48	46	↓	0.17	0.13	↓
	C	4.25	4.47	↑	119.89	119.71	↓	49	48	↓	0.18	0.15	↓
4	A	1.15	0.62	↓	72.49	30.90	↓	11	3	↓	0.02	0.01	↓
	B	2.37	3.57	↑	116.21	116.41	↑	27	41	↑	0.07	0.14	↑
	C	2.45	3.67	↑	402.22	165.44	↓	62	55	↓	0.25	0.25	
5	A	0.95	2.30	↑	47.18	64.40	↑	6	15	↑	0.01	0.03	↑
	B	2.75	3.75	↑	60.34	74.45	↑	17	28	↑	0.03	0.08	↑
	C	3.62	4.30	↑	233.95	145.44	↓	77	56	↓	0.32	0.26	↓

↑ and ↓ indicates increase and decrease of microstate parameters respectively

happening to a person while performing NHPT when fatigue sets in. Trial 1 is the first trial when the participant is not fatigued yet. Trial 3 is the trial just after the fatiguing exercise and can therefore be called the post-fatigue trial. Three microstates are observed in the task EEG and named MS1, MS2 and MS3 in order to distinguish them from the resting state microstates. Just like for the resting state microstates here also the microstate parameters, occurrence, coverage, duration and GEV are calculated and tabulated. Table III shows the pre-fatigue and post-fatigue values of the microstate parameters.

For MS1, the occurrence increases with fatigue for two participants and decreases with fatigue for three participants. The duration of MS1 increases with fatigue for three subjects and decreases for the other two. The coverage of MS1 increases for all subjects except one. The global explained variance of MS1 increases with fatigue for all subjects.

For MS2 all the parameters increase with fatigue for three subjects and decrease with fatigue for two subjects. No MS3 is present for subject 2. In the other four subjects, duration, coverage and GEV decrease with fatigue for MS3. The changes in coverage for trial microstates are shown in Fig.5. The Occurrence of MS3 increases for one subject and decreases for three subjects.

C. Assessment of performance time during NHPT task for different trials

Table IV shows the time taken for each trial which is recorded with the help of Geomagic Touch API. A paired sample t-test is done between trial 1 and trial 3 and it is found that the time taken for post fatigue trial is not statistically different from the time taken for pre-fatigue trial(p-value .608). However, given the small number of samples, looking at the individual values for trial 1 versus trial 3, two participants (Subject 1 and Subject 2) show an increase in completion time while the remaining participants show an improvement in the peg-placement and task completion.

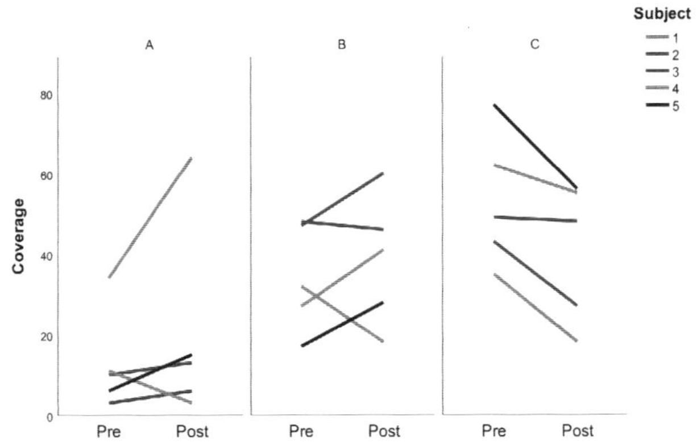

Figure. 4. Changes in coverage with fatigue for resting state microstates A, B and C.

D. Questionnaire assessment of fatigue during experiment progression

The forearm fatigue status of each participant is recorded during the experiment. Participants are asked to update their fatigue status on a scale of 1 indicating not fatigued, to 10 indicating extremely fatigued, before trial 1, after trial 2, before trial 3 and after trial 4. The fatigue score of each participant is shown in Table V. This table indicates that all participants report fatigue after the Dumbbell exercise, but the reduction of scores from before trial 3, to after trial 4, for participants 1, 3 and 5 could indicate an adjustment to the task complexity.

IV. DISCUSSIONS

The present study investigates the changes in EEG microstates when performing an embedded reality NHPT, pre and post fatigue. To the best of our knowledge, this is the

TABLE III
TASK MICROSTATE PARAMETERS.

Subject	Microstates	Occurrence			Duration(ms)			Coverage(%)			GEV		
		Pre	Post	Change	Pre	Post	Change	Pre	Post	Change	Pre	Post	Change
1	MS1	0.81	1.52	↑	78.89	65.56	↓	6.40	10.00	↑	0.0023	0.02	↑
	MS2	1.08	1.28	↑	48.96	61.98	↑	5.30	8.82	↑	0.0035	0.01	↑
	MS3	2.16	3.31	↑	409.69	266.01	↓	88.30	81.19	↓	0.63	0.38	↓
2	MS1	0.29	0.67	↑	3.46*	1.76*	↓	100	98.29	↓	0.69	0.81	↑
	MS2	0	0.33	↑	0	25.69	↑	0	1.72	↑	0	0.0011	↑
	MS3	0	0		0	0		0	0		0	0	
3	MS1	1.86	1.00	↓	492.02	975.00	↑	91.68	97.79	↑	0.81	0.87	↑
	MS2	0.53	0.50	↓	75.42	44.17	↓	4.02	2.21	↓	0.0023	0.0015	↓
	MS3	1.06	0	↓	40.42	0	↓	4.30	0	↓	0.0054	0	↓
4	MS1	2.67	2.62	↓	154.72	399.78	↑	42.45	73.67	↑	0.30	0.61	↑
	MS2	2.67	2.24	↓	258.64	102.69	↓	49.31	24.67	↓	0.33	0.07	↓
	MS3	1.00	0.25	↓	69.21	33.13	↓	8.23	1.66	↓	0.02	0.0007	↓
5	MS1	3.92	1.31	↓	189.08	703.75	↑	74.13	92.45	↑	0.41	0.75	↑
	MS2	1.18	1.31	↑	39.72	57.50	↑	4.67	7.55	↑	0.01	0.01	↑
	MS3	3.92	0	↓	54.08	0	↓	21.20	0	↓	0.05	0	↓

↑ and ↓ indicates increase and decrease of microstate parameters respectively
*Duration of MS1 for subject 2 is in seconds

first study to identify microstates during the performance of a NHPT, and to reflect on changes to these microstates after a fatiguing exercise.

A. *Resting state microstates*

Several studies in the field of microstates found that microstate maps generally fall into four categories. However, in our study, we used the polarity invariant measures of fit global explained variance and cross validation to determine the optimum number of microstates and found three microstates for resting state data. Microstates B and C found in our study resembled resting state microstates B and A in the literature. It was interesting to investigate how microstate parameters like occurrence, coverage, duration and GEV changed when a person became fatigued physically and mentally. The dumbbell exercise in this experiment contributed to physical fatigue for the participants whereas performing NHPT using the haptic device Geomagic Touch provided a cognitive load for the participants. It was found that with fatigue all the parameters of microstate A increased for all subjects except one. The coverage of microstate C decreased for all subjects, which implies that fatigue made microstate C less dominant and increased the occurrence of other microstates. It could be seen that less coverage of microstate C was compensated by the increase in the occurrence of microstate B.

B. *NHPT trial microstates*

Three microstates were observed in the EEG while performing NHPT trials. The microstate parameters were determined for transferring the first peg in pre-fatigue and post-fatigue trials (trial 1 and trial 3). MS3 was not present for one subject and, for all the other subjects, the coverage of microstate 3 decreased. This implies that new neural correlates were introduced with fatigue which reduced the coverage of microstate 3. While the coverage of MS3 decreased, the coverage of MS1

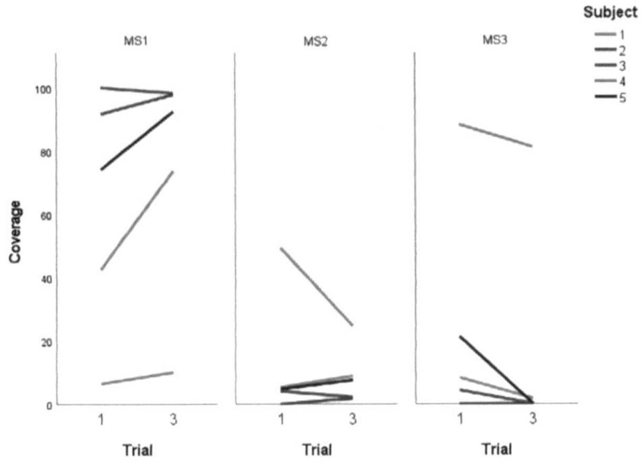

Figure. 5. Changes in coverage with fatigue for trial microstates MS1, MS2 and MS3.

TABLE IV
TIME TAKEN FOR EACH TRIAL OF NHPT IN SECONDS.

Subject	Trial 1	Trial 2	Trial 3	Trial 4
1	67	58	78	67
2	90	118	127	102
3	53	49	46	37
4	114	86	79	69
5	96	62	47	55
Mean (SD)	84 (21.59)	74.6 (27.85)	75.4 (32.99)	66 (23.81)

TABLE V
SELF-REPORTED FATIGUE STATUS.

Subject	Before Trial1	After Trial2	Before Trial3	After Trial 4
1	1	2	8	7
2	1	1	8	8
3	1	1	8	6
4	1	4	9	9
5	1	2	8	7

increased, which means that the fatigue caused changes in brain signals which created more MS1. A similar trend could also be seen in the GEV values. For MS1, GEV increased which was compensated by a decrease in GEV of MS3. The duration of MS1 was very high compared to the other microstates and it could be seen that its duration sometimes reached seconds. For subject 2 the duration of MS1 was in the order of seconds because only that particular microstate was present in the pre-fatigue trial, and in the post-fatigue trial, MS2 was present for a very short duration.

C. Performance time and fatigue status

Subject-score for fatigue for participants 1, 3 and 5 were reduced after trial 4, also there is an improvement in NHPT performance from trial 3 to trial 4. From Table V it can be seen that NHPT alone induces fatigue for subjects 1,4 and 5 after trial 2. But looking at the trial time there was a reduction in trial time for these subjects which indicates NHPT performance improvement. This could indicate that while participants worked harder, and perceived to work harder, they actually improved their performance score as indicated by the reduction in peg placement time.

When comparing the time between trial 1 and trial 3, it can be seen that participants 1 and 2 took more time to complete NHPT when fatigued. Participants 3, 4 and 5 completed NHPT trial 3 in less time compared to trial 1, while all reported fatigue after the dumbbell exercise. These observations can indicate that physical fatigue alone is not impacting NHPT performance. This could be because these participants did not find the NHPT task challenging and haptic/visual assistance given to these tasks provided a good medium for reducing their completion time despite fatigue in their wrist. It could be also possible that the NHPT task involves a different neural assembly compared to the assemblies needed for the wrist exercise. Furthermore, it is possible that participants' fitness level could impact their recovery from fatigue. Participant 4 who had a higher BMI increased his fatigue level by doing NHPT alone compared to others. Comparing Table I and Table V it can be seen that participants with better BMI recovered soon from fatigue except for participant 2. No MS3 is present for participant 2 while NHPT trial time is more for each trial compared to others. Also, this participant struggled a lot to place the pegs in the hole during the experiment. This suggests that cognitive fatigue might also have an impact on MS3. Research on human-computer interaction supports the notion that performing mental tasks using a video display terminal can lead to cognitive fatigue [21]. Coverage of MS3 for all other participants decreased after fatiguing exercise which shows the impact of physical fatigue on microstates.

V. CONCLUSION

This is a preliminary study which investigated the changes in EEG microstates while a person performed a widely used manual dexterity test, the Nine Hole Peg Test, before and after fatigue conditions. The main goal of the study was to observe differences in resting state and task performance microstates and to observe the changes due to a physically fatiguing dumbbell exercise. We observed these differences, as highlighted by the topological maps, but also observed changes in the microstate parameters. With resting state microstates it was found that two of the microstates observed resembled the microstates already established in the literature [22]. It was also found that the coverage of some microstates decreased with fatigue for both resting state and trial data which was also backed up by a reduction in global explained variance. This suggests that assessing the microstate parameter coverage can help to identify physical fatigue. All participants reported fatigue on the forearm after the dumbbell exercise. We found that physical fatigue did not affect the NHPT performance as some participants reporting physical fatigue improved performance during the NHPT trials. However, alterations in microstate parameters were observed after the physical fatigue. We intend to further explore this by comparing the microstates during NHPT trials, with microstates observed during the dumbbell exercise. This can convey further information regarding the similarity or dissimilarity of the neural assemblies present during motor tasks performed in this experiment. Furthermore, expanding the number of participants will enhance the likelihood of conducting a statistically sound analysis of the results.

REFERENCES

[1] "Learn about stroke," March. 15, 2023. [Online]. Available: https://www.world-stroke.org/component/content/article/16-forpatients/84-facts-and-figures-about-stroke

[2] E. S. Lawrence *et al.*, "Estimates of the prevalence of acute stroke impairments and disability in a multiethnic population," *Stroke*, vol. 32, no. 6, pp. 1279–1284, 2001.

[3] D. T. Wade, "Measurement in neurological rehabilitation," *Current Opinion in Neurology*, vol. 5, no. 5, pp. 682–686, 1992.

[4] M. E. Bowler, "Interactive haptics for remote and on-site assessment of arm function following a stroke," Ph.D. dissertation, University of Hertfordshire, 2019.

[5] F. Amirabdollahian and G. Johnson, "Analysis of the results from use of haptic peg-in-hole task for assessment in neurorehabilitation," *Applied Bionics and Biomechanics*, vol. 8, no. 1, pp. 1–11, 2011.

[6] A. Thacham Poyil, V. Steuber, and F. Amirabdollahian, "Adaptive robot mediated upper limb training using electromyogram-based muscle fatigue indicators," *Plos one*, vol. 15, no. 5, p. e0233545, 2020.

[7] A. Murata and A. Uetake, "Evaluation of mental fatigue in human-computer interaction-analysis using feature parameters extracted from event-related potential," in *Proceedings 10th IEEE International Workshop on Robot and Human Interactive Communication. ROMAN 2001 (Cat. No. 01TH8591)*. IEEE, 2001, pp. 630–635.

[8] A. Pimenta, D. Carneiro, J. Neves, and P. Novais, "A neural network to classify fatigue from human–computer interaction," *Neurocomputing*, vol. 172, pp. 413–426, 2016.

[9] T. Koenig, M. I. Tomescu, T. A. Rihs, and M. Koukkou, "Eeg indices of cortical network formation and their relevance for studying variance in subjective experience and behavior," *In Vivo Neuropharmacology and Neurophysiology*, pp. 17–35, 2017.

[10] D. Lehmann, "Brain electric microstates and cognition: the atoms of thought," in *Machinery of the Mind*. Springer, 1990, pp. 209–224.

[11] A. P. Zanesco, B. G. King, A. C. Skwara, and C. D. Saron, "Within and between-person correlates of the temporal dynamics of resting eeg microstates," *Neuroimage*, vol. 211, p. 116631, 2020.

[12] R. A. Thuraisingham, Y. Tran, A. Craig, N. Wijesuriya, and H. Nguyen, "Using microstate intensity for the analysis of spontaneous eeg: Tracking changes from alert to the fatigue state," in *2009 Annual International Conference of the IEEE Engineering in Medicine and Biology Society*. IEEE, 2009, pp. 4982–4985.

[13] W. Li, S. Cheng, H. Wang, and Y. Chang, "Eeg microstate changes according to mental fatigue induced by aircraft piloting simulation: An exploratory study," *Behavioural Brain Research*, vol. 438, p. 114203, 2023.
[14] T.-P. Jung *et al.*, "Removing electroencephalographic artifacts by blind source separation," *Psychophysiology*, vol. 37, no. 2, pp. 163–178, 2000.
[15] A. T. Poulsen, A. Pedroni, N. Langer, and L. K. Hansen, "Microstate eeglab toolbox: An introductory guide," *BioRxiv*, p. 289850, 2018.
[16] D. F. D'Croz-Baron, M. Baker, C. M. Michel, and T. Karp, "Eeg microstates analysis in young adults with autism spectrum disorder during resting-state," *Frontiers in human neuroscience*, vol. 13, p. 173, 2019.
[17] A. Khanna, A. Pascual-Leone, and F. Farzan, "Reliability of resting-state microstate features in electroencephalography," *PLoS ONE*, vol. 9, no. 12, pp. 1–21, 2014.
[18] K. Zhang *et al.*, "Reliability of eeg microstate analysis at different electrode densities during propofol-induced transitions of brain states," *NeuroImage*, vol. 231, p. 117861, 2021.
[19] M. Baradits, I. Bitter, and P. Czobor, "Multivariate patterns of eeg microstate parameters and their role in the discrimination of patients with schizophrenia from healthy controls," *Psychiatry Research*, vol. 288, p. 112938, 2020.
[20] A. Khanna, A. Pascual-Leone, C. M. Michel, and F. Farzan, "Microstates in resting-state eeg: current status and future directions," *Neuroscience & Biobehavioral Reviews*, vol. 49, pp. 105–113, 2015.
[21] M. J. Smith, F. T. Conway, and B.-T. Karsh, "Occupational stress in human computer interaction," *Industrial health*, vol. 37, no. 2, pp. 157–173, 1999.
[22] C. M. Michel and T. Koenig, "Eeg microstates as a tool for studying the temporal dynamics of whole-brain neuronal networks: a review," *Neuroimage*, vol. 180, pp. 577–593, 2018.

Usability of An Immersive Authoring Tool: An Experimental Study for the Scenarization of Interactive Panoramic Videos

Daniel Xuan Hien Mai, Guillaume Loup, Jean-Yves Didier
IBISC Lab
Univ Evry, Université Paris Saclay
Evry, France
e-mail: danielxuanhien.mai@univ-evry.fr, guillaume.loup@univ-evry.fr, jeanyves.didier@univ-evry.fr

***Abstract*— The need for remote education and reduced learning costs has led to rapid development of virtual immersive learning environments. However, creating these environments using authoring tools still requires trainers to have a range of technical skills. Recently, a new approach has been developed that allows trainers to construct educational scenarios using panoramic video-based immersive authoring tools. This approach demands fewer technical skills compared to the modeling of 3D environments. To evaluate the usability of the Human-Computer Interaction (HCI) of this approach between two different types of interfaces, our experimental study was conducted. This study compared a Virtual Reality (VR) interface, which consists of a Head-Mounted Display (HMD) and its controllers, to a traditional Windows, Icons, Menus, Pointer (WIMP) interface in creating interactive scenarios. Both quantitative and qualitative measures were collected and later quantified to evaluate effectiveness, efficiency, user satisfaction, and motivation towards the interfaces. The results of the study showed that: (1) there was a better correlation between the trajectories of 3D objects positioned by the user (in this study, the trainer) and the entities targeted in the panoramic video using an immersive interface; (2) there was a significant difference in task execution time between the VR interface and the traditional WIMP interface; (3) trainers had greater satisfaction and motivation towards the VR interface compared to the traditional WIMP interface, despite symptoms of cybersickness.**

Keywords- panoramic videos; authoring tools; virtual reality; WIMP interface; immersive environments; interaction techniques.

I. INTRODUCTION

Investment by major technology companies in recent years, and growing demand for immersive environments in the domains of entertainment, communication, and education have created a strong impetus for the development of Virtual Reality (VR). Additionally, new technological breakthroughs have made VR hardware devices, such as VR headsets and omnidirectional cameras more accessible to the public. However, the development of VR applications in general and immersive environments for human learning in particular still presents many challenges, both in terms of processes and production tools, requiring the participation of a multidisciplinary team ranging from designers, artists, programmers and so forth [1]. These tools often require trainers to have certain expert knowledge for effective use to achieve the desired results.

Depending on the interaction needs, immersive environments will be designed differently, where each interaction scenario is a sequence of user interactions with the environment [2]. Therefore, interaction design methods and different forms of information representation will impact user experience as well as interaction outcome. Immersive environments based on panoramic videos are thus the proposed solution that simulates interactive scenarios close to the real environment, and enhances users' sense of presence when they use Head-Mounted Display (HMD) [3]. The panoramic video can be enriched by adding interactive elements such as text information, sounds, 2D/3D objects, as well as questions, in order to not only improve the user experience [4], but also integrate narrative and educational elements into the interactive scenarios. These additional elements require a particular structure tailored to the spatial and temporal dimensions of the panoramic video [5]. While 2D video editing tools primarily focus on the temporal dimension, creating interactive panoramic videos requires a more comprehensive set of tools that handle both spatial and temporal dimensions.

A suitable authoring tool will actively aid trainers in constructing the learning content [6]. New requirements for authoring tools for interactive scenarios based on panoramic videos have led to the concept of an exclusively immersive tool. Thanks to this approach, trainers, instead of using the traditional Windows, Icons, Menus, Pointer (WIMP) interface, can now use the VR interface to create and modify the content of the interactive scenario. This immersive environment will allow trainers to have learner-like access to quickly obtain a set of information and to self-assess the results of their work throughout the design process [7].

However, it remains to be determined whether the new interactive VR interface differs in terms of usability and user motivation compared to the traditional WIMP interface. To answer this question, our experiment was carried out to evaluate and compare the effectiveness and efficiency of trainer interactions with an authoring tool, based on a defined scenario, using both the traditional WIMP interface and the VR interface. The satisfaction and motivation of trainers towards the tool were assessed through questionnaires collected after the experiment.

It is worth noting that conducting experiments on usability and motivation are important for evaluating the effectiveness of the tool and identifying any potential issues that may arise when using the tool in real-world scenarios.

In Section II, we present a discussion of related work. Section III presents our research hypotheses. Section IV details the method, then Section V presents the results of the experiment. Our conclusions and future work are presented in sections VI and VII. The references close the article.

II. Background And Related Work

A. *Authoring tools and interactions with panoramic videos*

The interactive design that complements panoramic videos presents not only technical challenges (with respect to video asset management, video environment fidelity, and natural navigation) but also design challenges [8]. These issues include designing non-intrusive and non-distracting user interfaces, creating effective navigation and orientation mechanisms, and incorporating engaging elements into the design.

In addition, the feeling of immersion can affect the difference in visual navigation effectiveness between the traditional WIMP and VR interfaces [9]. One of the main tasks of the designers is to overlay a 3D object upon the panoramic video. To ensure consistency between these two entities, a predetermined trajectory based on the timeline of the panoramic video [5] must be defined. This requires capturing the spatiotemporal motion of the designers, which allows them to specify the movements of the 3D object.

For user interaction studies, in the absence of a specific classifier, the object of research is usually the end user or, in this context, the learner. Research work in the context of panoramic videos is most often devoted to the effect of motion parallax [10][11] the perception of content, as well as different methods of rendering and displaying panoramic videos and incorporating 3D entities to improve user experience [12].

Recently, several studies have been dedicated to designing panoramic video tools in VR, where users act as trainers. T. Adão et al. performed an experiment to evaluate the usability of a rapid prototyping tool [13] through tasks such as adding and removing 3D objects in space and time. Another experiment was carried out to evaluate the continuity of integrating video animations, 3D objects as well as 3D sounds [14] by utilizing non-complex interaction techniques.

Pakkanen et al. proposed a comparison of three models of interaction techniques (remote control, pointing with head orientation, and hand gestures) in VR for controlling panoramic video playback [15]. The results of this study showed that the participants experienced a reduction in nausea on their second attempt. This suggests that cybersickness survey results may be influenced by participants' previous experience (working time) in the VR environment. Regarding the usability of the three types of interactions, the remote control was found to be more accurate and users liked it more than the other two types of interactions.

The Fonseca & Kraus experiment [16] evaluated learners' attitudes and behaviors after watching panoramic videos in both VR and mobile platforms, making it one of the few studies that cover multiple platforms. The conclusion of this research mentioned a more positive emotional impact on the user when they viewed panoramic videos in a virtual reality environment compared to an equivalent environment on a tablet. The experiment did not assess participants' interactive behaviors, but only focused on behavioral analysis of perception after receiving narrative information.

As a case study of panoramic video authoring tools, the research by Coelho & Melo [7] is remarkable when it comes to evaluating the usability of three different types of interfaces: WIMP, VR, and tangible. Results showed that participants' gender had no effect on dependent factors. Regarding the usability, the VR and tangible interfaces had a higher level of satisfaction than the WIMP interface. However, the WIMP interface had the lowest task execution time and the authors concluded that this was due to participants' greater familiarity with the keyboard and mouse. The effectiveness was not determined conclusively as the experimental procedure only took into account the number of performed errors, which was not statistically significant.

These experiments have shown that running the same interaction technique on different types of environments or interfaces will have different usability results. The requirement for spatiotemporal coherence in interaction is a critical element of panoramic video-based immersive environments. It is thus necessary to compare the interaction technique specific to authoring tools on panoramic videos, between the traditional WIMP interface and the VR interface, through a new experimental study.

B. *The immersive authoring tool Wixar[17]*

To accurately compare the usability of two types of interfaces, the analysis and evaluation of interaction techniques must be performed on the same authoring tool to balance the workload between the two types of interfaces and ensure uniformity of statistical data.

Most authoring tools support the WIMP interface, but a limited number support the VR interface [6]. In order to limit differences in statistical data of two different interfaces, we chose the Wixar authoring tool for our experiment. Wixar is a multi-platform authoring tool already on the market, offering a range of options for creating scripted content for interactive panoramic videos. It aims to empower trainers without programming skills to design immersive learning environments using panoramic videos.

The selected interaction techniques for this experiment, including visual perception (head movement or camera rotation with keyboard buttons), navigation (joystick or mouse movement), and selection and manipulation, are commonly used in panoramic video contexts.

Wixar offers both a PC version and a VR version with the same user interface (UI). The PC version uses a mouse for navigation instead of a joystick and keyboard buttons for rotation instead of head movement, making it a suitable comparison to the VR version. These standard human-computer interfaces do not negatively affect the outcome of the experiment. The selected user interfaces (Figure 2) will not negatively impact the results of the experiment.

Hence, Wixar is a suitable authoring tool for evaluating the usability of WIMP and VR interactive interfaces, as it satisfies the requirements and purpose of this experiment.

III. RECHEARCH HYPOTHESIS

Our first hypothesis (H1) is that the difference in navigation (viewpoint changing) and selection and manipulation (trajectory recording) actions during task execution between the VR and WIMP interfaces will lead to a difference in usability between them. In the context of this experiment, operations requiring spatiotemporal coordination of panoramic videos are supposed to have better accuracy and execution time in VR compared to WIMP.

Our second hypothesis (H2) is that the use of a VR headset for the authoring tool will not significantly increase mental load or symptoms of cybersickness compared to a traditional WIMP interface.

Our third hypothesis (H3) is that participants using the VR interface will exhibit higher motivation than those using the WIMP interface in this experiment.

IV. METHOD

A. *Participants*

The participants in the experiment ranged in age from 20 to 50 years old, with an average age of 30.7 years. Both groups, VR and WIMP, had 15 participants each and were evenly distributed in age. All participants had a good command of French, enabling them to comprehend information presented in the language and engage in conversations throughout the experiment. The informed consent form, which included details on withdrawal rights, confidentiality rights, benefits, and potential risks of the study, was understood by all participants.

This study was approved by the Paris-Saclay research ethics committee and participants signed the consent form after being fully informed of the progress of the experiment.

B. *Wixar Authoring Tool*

We utilized Wixar version 1.4, which was released in July 2021, that offers both WIMP and VR interfaces. The main steps of using Wixar are outlined in Figure 1. The trainer's process of designing an application was divided into three phases: 1) Adding media resources, such as panoramic videos, audios, and 360 images, 2) Integrating and configuring the interaction techniques offered by Wixar, and 3) Releasing a new immersive educational environment.

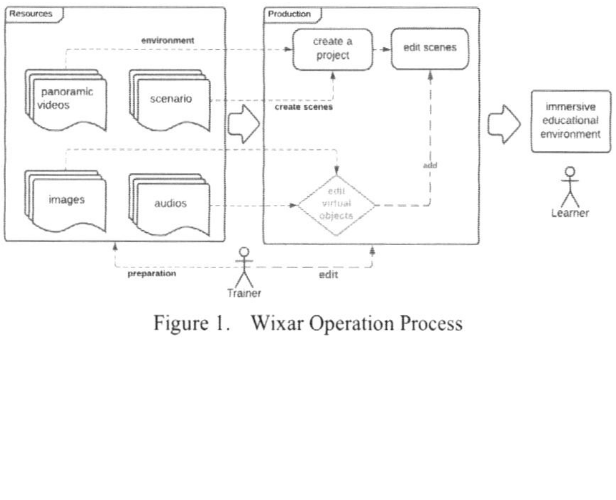

Figure 1. Wixar Operation Process

In this experiment, different panoramic video scenes were provided and a preview of the scenario to be enacted was presented to the participant beforehand.

C. *Material*

Devices used in this experiment included: a laptop computer equipped with the Wixar 1.4 PC authoring tool; an Oculus Quest 2 headset equipped with the Wixar 1.4 VR authoring tool. To ensure hygiene, the equipment was thoroughly cleaned before each participant's session and participants were instructed to sanitize their hands and wear a respiratory protection mask throughout the entire procedure.

D. *Measurements*

Our team had developed an algorithm which was then integrated into Wixar 1.4 to gather quantitative data on user behavior during task performance.

Questionnaires were used to collect demographic information (identified only by participant number) and data on cybersickness (SSQ [18], NASA-TLX [19]), satisfaction (SUS) [20], and motivation (SIMS) [21].

The obtained data was then analyzed to evaluate the usability of two different types of interfaces during participant interactions. Usability, as defined by ISO 9241-11 [22], is "the extent to which a system, product or service can be used by specified users to achieve specified goals with effectiveness, efficiency and satisfaction in a specified context of use". This definition highlights three criteria that must be considered during the construction of the experiment so that the results obtained can be analyzed with precision afterwards: (1) Effectiveness: accuracy and completeness with which users achieve specified goals (2) Efficiency: relationship between the results and the resources used to achieve them. (3) Satisfaction: comfort and subjective evaluation of user interaction.

Specifically in this experiment, effectiveness was linked to the precision of the participant's manipulation, efficiency was measured by the time it took to perform tasks and finally, satisfaction was assessed through questionnaires.

E. *Scenarios & Procedure*

The participants were divided into two groups, each corresponding to a different interface (WIMP and VR). Participants were asked to position themselves in front of a PC or to wear an Oculus Quest 2 headset. After starting the Wixar 1.4 application, the participant faced 5 task sequences. The main tasks involved positioning and configuring a virtual object on a fish in a panoramic video by superimposing a virtual marker on the fish. The fish had different, increasingly complex trajectories step by step, such as linear movement, slight wave, underfoot, around space variable acceleration, and vertical movement (Figure 2).

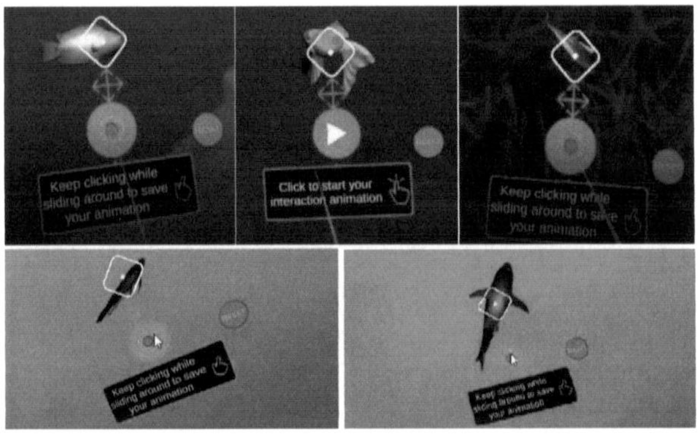

Figure 2. Fish with different trajectories

Following the 5 sequences, the participant was invited to complete the questionnaires. The total duration of each experiment was approximately 45 minutes.

F. Quantitative data

During the experiment, participant behavior data was automatically collected, including head movements, joystick or mouse movements, the operations concerning the creation, deletion and movement of objects, and the recording of movement of the virtual marker tracking the fish.

These data were subsequently analyzed to compare the effectiveness and efficiency between the two interface types.

G. Questionnaires (qualitative data)

1) Before their activity

The experiment used the NASA-TLX scale, translated into French by Ganier, F., Hoareau, C., & Devillers in 2013 [23], to assess the workload involved.

In virtual reality immersion research, cybersickness is frequently evaluated. The French questionnaire used in this study was proposed by Kennedy, R.S. et al. in 1993[18].

2) After their activity

The F-SUS scale is the French version of the SUS (System Usability Scale) proposed by Gronier, G., & Baudet, A. in 2021 [24]. This scale is widely used to measure the usability of interactive systems.

And finally, this experiment also assessed the participants' motivation through the SIMS situational motivation scale (French version suggested by Lambert-Le Mener, M. (2012) [25]).

H. Analysis method

The space of a virtual reality application that uses panoramic videos is usually designed using polar coordinates [5]. Thus, all the spatial parameters of the added virtual objects are saved as polar coordinates (quaternion rotation).

During the experiment, the movement of the virtual marker while tracking a fish in the video was recorded for each frame, and then resampled to a fixed frame rate of 50 FPS for ease of analysis.

At time t in the video, marker m had position p_m and fish f had position p_f. The distance d_t (p_m, p_f) represented the distance between the marker and the fish at time t.

The participants were instructed to place the marker on the fish, but we realized that the targeted part of the fish (e.g., head, body, tail) varied among participants. Consequently, we did not use the d_t index directly for the analysis. Instead, we used the relative distance between two consecutive periods $t+1$ and t, i.e. $\Delta_{t+1,\,t} = |\, d_{t+1} - d_t \,|$ with the goal of making the Δ as small as possible. Our objective was to measure and compare the variations and the stability of the recorded trajectories considering the targeted trajectory.

V. RESULTS

The collected quantitative and qualitative data were normalized to select appropriate parameters and then analyzed with SPSS (version 25, IBM Corp).

A Student Test was performed for the bivariate correlation test if the sample met the covariance criteria. Conversely, if the sample did not meet the criteria, a Mann-Whitney non-parametric test was used.

Data were collected on two experimental groups, each with 15 participants, corresponding to two types of WIMP and VR interactive interfaces.

A. Effect of interactive interface on effectiveness

The average difference (Δ) used for the effectiveness tests on the 5 tasks (corresponding to 5 different trajectories in 5 scenes from s1 to s5). Effectiveness is inversely proportional to the Δ coefficient, so as seen in Figure 3, the VR group recorded more stable trajectories than the WIMP group. The results were consistent across all 5 trajectory types.

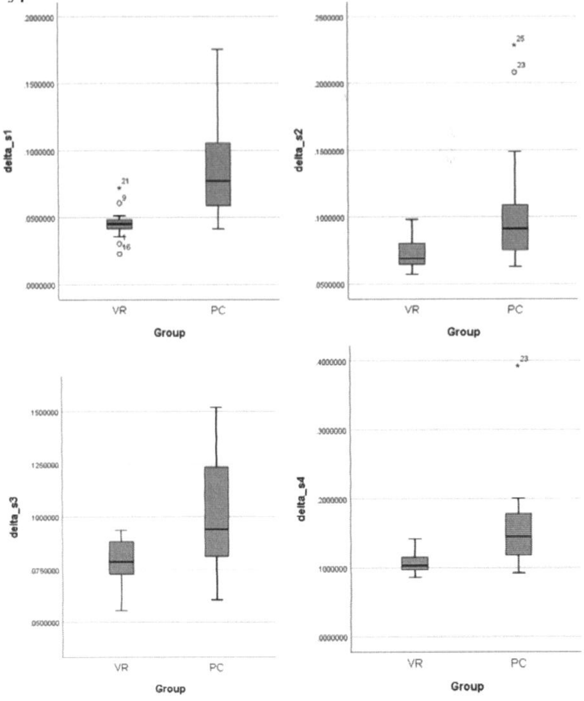

Figure 3. Distribution of Mean Trajectory Differences for VR and WIMP Groups per Sequence

The Mann-Whitney U tests revealed significant differences between the WIMP and VR groups in the average Δ in 4 trajectories s1, s2, s4 and s5. A similar result was found in the Student Test on Δs3 (Table I) with a significant Levene's Test result of 0.001687. The hypothesis that there is a difference in variance between the two groups (WIMP and RV) was accepted, indicating a significant difference in the mean of the two groups (significant T-Test result of 0.01585).

TABLE I. STATISTICAL SIGNIFICANCE TESTS BETWEEN VR AND WIMP GROUPS FOR MEAN DIFFERENCE IN TRAJECTORY ACROSS 5 MISSIONS

	Group	Shapiro-Wilk	Mann-Whitney U	Levene Test	T-Test
Δs1	VR	0.379511	0.000841	--	--
	WIMP	0.037481			
Δs2	VR	0.181733	0.004494	--	--
	WIMP	0.001477			
Δs3	VR	0.527049	--	0.001687	0.01585
	WIMP	0.245281			
Δs4	VR	0.338854	0.000622	--	--
	WIMP	0.000542			
Δs5	VR	0.700370	0.005114	--	--
	WIMP	0.000039			

B. *Effect of interactive interface on efficiency*

Regarding execution efficiency, the group using VR completed tasks faster than the group using WIMP interface (Figure 4).

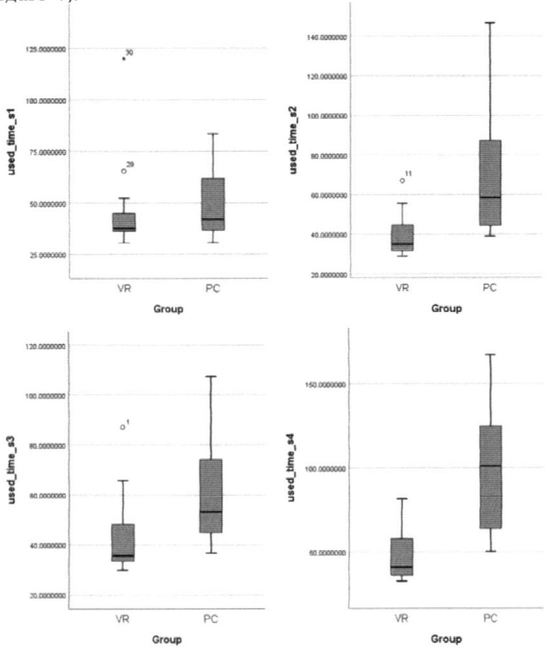

Figure 4. Distribution of Execution Time Differences for VR and WIMP Groups by Sequence

The Mann-Whitney U Tests (Table II) indicated significant differences between the WIMP and VR groups in terms of execution time for s2, s3, s4, and s5. The tests showed no significant difference for s1 (Sig.=0.351).

TABLE II. STATISTICAL SIGNIFICANCE TESTS BETWEEN VR AND WIMP GROUPS FOR MEAN DIFFERENCE IN TRAJECTORY ACROSS 5 MISSIONS

	Group	Sig. Shapiro-Wilk	Sig. Mann-Whitney U
Δs1	VR	0.000030	0.350688
	WIMP	0.023687	
Δs2	VR	0.021897	0.001130
	WIMP	0.020213	
Δs3	VR	0.001141	0.005114
	WIMP	0.043944	
Δs4	VR	0.010367	0.000125
	WIMP	0.169789	
Δs5	VR	0.000014	0.000205
	WIMP	0.574785	

However, when comparing data for scene s1 to other scenes, we observed that the VR group completed the task in a relatively shorter amount of time.

C. *Satisfaction*

Results of the F-SUS questionnaire to assess satisfaction rate showed no significant difference between the VR group (M=79.6, S.D.=11.7) and the WIMP group (M=76.8, SD=15.4). Despite the high diversity of opinions shown by the significant values of the standard deviations, the averages of the SUS [26] indicated that both systems resulted in an acceptable level of user satisfaction.

D. *Cybersickness*

The outcome of the Cybersickness Questionnaire (SSQ), which measured symptoms of nausea and oculomotor disorders, showed a significant difference between the VR and WIMP groups. The Shapiro-Wilk normality test led to a Mann-Whitney U evaluation, revealing that participants using the low-cost VR headset experienced significant cybersickness. These results were further confirmed by the questions regarding oculomotor disorders, where a Levene's Test and T-test established a greater feeling of oculomotor disorders among the VR group than the WIMP group (as shown in Table III).

TABLE III. EVALUATION OF CYBERSICKNESS SYMPTOMS

	Group	Shapiro-Wilk	Mann-Whitney U	Levene Test	T-Test
Nausea	VR	0.009	0.001	--	--
	WIMP	--			
Oculomotor	VR	0.150	--	0.447	0.023
	WIMP	--			

E. Motivation

Results of the SIMS questionnaire made it possible to identify the type of user motivation using the Situational Motivation Scale. Regarding intrinsic motivation, there was a significant difference between the VR group (M=23.8 and SD=2.9) and the WIMP group (M=19.7 and SD=5.4). A second significant difference was discovered between the VR group (M=8.9 and SD=4.6) and the WIMP group (M=13.9 and SD=7.1) for external regulation. These two differences highlighted a greater sense of autonomy for the VR group compared to the WIMP group (Table IV).

TABLE IV. STATISTICAL SIGNIFICANCE TESTS BETWEEN VR AND WIMP GROUPS FOR MEAN DIFFERENCE IN TRAJECTORY ACROSS 5 MISSIONS

	Group	N	Medium	S.D	T-Test
Intrinsic Motivation	VR	15	23.80	2.883	0.017
	WIMP	15	19.73	5.496	
Identified regulation	VR	15	20.73	5.663	0.121
	WIMP	15	17.53	5.276	
External regulation	VR	15	8.93	4.559	0.031
	WIMP	15	13.87	7.080	
Amotivation	VR	15	9.33	4.065	0.225
	WIMP	15	11.93	7.015	

Although differences in identified regulation and amotivation were not significant, the values remained consistent with the results for the other motivations.

VI. DISCUSSION

Our first hypothesis has been supported by the results of the study, which showed that the VR interface was more effective, efficient, and satisfactory than the WIMP interface in performing various tasks. This conclusion contradicted the findings of Coelho and Melo [7], who evaluated the usability of three different interfaces (WIMP, VR, and tangible). The difference between the two studies can be attributed to the nature of the interaction being tested. Indeed, our work focused on a particular interaction, the trajectory of objects and the spatiotemporal relationship in a panoramic video-based immersive environment. We collected quantified data, namely the trajectory and the duration of the missions. Conversely, whereas Coelho and Melo only counted the number of errors during task execution, which showed no statistically significant differences.

The analysis demonstrated that the marker-to-fish tracking using VR was more stable than the one using WIMP, resulting in higher effectiveness of VR interaction. This was due to better coordination of viewpoint change (navigation) and trajectory recording (selection and manipulation) in both spatial and temporal dimensions of the panoramic video. The VR interface allowed for better spatial perception and object movement speed compared to WIMP.

For object motion tracking, findings of our study also revealed that if coordination of spatial and temporal motion was not maintained at all times (which happened on the WIMP interface when the fish moved out of the viewing area), an interrupt action was necessary. This affected not only the recorded trajectory results but also the execution time of the experiment tasks. Spatial navigation (change of viewpoint) when combined with simultaneous and uninterrupted trajectory recording, resulted in better performance of the VR interface in terms of time and accuracy.

The assumption which can be made at this stage is that the mouse sensitivity (Dots Per Inch - DPI) on the WIMP interface was not adjusted to match participants' usage habits, which led to poor accuracy results. Indeed, feedback from left-handed participants and from the participants who were accustomed to using touchpads supported this assumption. Regardless, if true, it still highlighted the VR interface's advantage in better adapting to the user's natural movements.

According to the cybersickness analysis, levels of nausea and oculomotor disorder were more pronounced on the VR interface than on the WIMP interface. The experimentation process for the 5 tasks was long, so we did not detail this aspect as deeply as the study conducted by Pakkanen et al. [15] where participants repeated the tasks to assess their adaptation to the immersive environment over time.

The Situational Motivation Scale questionnaires showed a significant difference in intrinsic motivation and external regulation between the VR and WIMP groups, with the VR group exhibiting higher results. This indicated a higher sense of autonomy and better motivation to complete tasks in the VR group.

VII. CONCLUSION

The goal of our experiment was to evaluate and compare the usability of the VR interface of an HMD and its controllers to that of the classic WIMP interface by conducting the same set of tasks for designing interactive scenarios for panoramic videos. So as to fulfill this aim, evaluations of the effectiveness, efficiency and user satisfaction for each of the interfaces were carried out.

The experiment findings showed better results in terms of motion tracking as well as interaction execution time on the VR interface than on the WIMP interface. The level of satisfaction was comparable between the two groups and fell within acceptable range, with no significant difference observed. In terms of usability, the VR interface, thanks to its superior spatiotemporal coordination of interactions, seemed better suited than the WIMP interface.

Although the VR interface had its issues with cybersickness, trainers still reported a higher level of satisfaction and motivation while performing tasks in VR as compared to the traditional WIMP interface.

The immersive environment based on interactive panoramic videos not only includes space-time interactive objects, but also other objects, such as text and sound. Therefore, the creation of these objects using an authoring tool requires further evaluation of cross-platform usability.

In the future, we will examine and evaluate the system's adaptability to various scenarios, with the aim of developing a model for a scripting assistant to aid trainers in the process of building an immersive learning environment.

REFERENCES

[1] Sundström, Y. (2013). Game design and production: frequent problems in game development.

[2] J. L. Rubio-Tamayo, M. Gertrudix Barrio, and F. García García, "Immersive Environments and Virtual Reality: Systematic Review and Advances in Communication, Interaction and Simulation," *Multimodal Technologies and Interaction*, vol. 1, no. 4, Art. no. 4, Dec. 2017, doi: 10.3390/mti1040021.

[3] M. G. Violante, E. Vezzetti, and P. Piazzolla, "Interactive virtual technologies in engineering education: Why not 360° videos?," *Int J Interact Des Manuf*, vol. 13, no. 2, pp. 729–742, Jun. 2019, doi: 10.1007/s12008-019-00553-y.

[4] T. Chambel, M. N. Chhaganlal, and L. A. R. Neng, "Towards immersive interactive video through 360° hypervideo," in *Proceedings of the 8th International Conference on Advances in Computer Entertainment Technology*, New York, NY, USA, Tháng Mười Một 2011, pp. 1–2. doi: 10.1145/2071423.2071518.

[5] P. R. C. Mendes, Á. L. V. Guedes, D. de S. Moraes, R. G. A. Azevedo, and S. Colcher, "An Authoring Model for Interactive 360 Videos," in *2020 IEEE International Conference on Multimedia & Expo Workshops (ICMEW)*, Jul. 2020, pp. 1–6. doi: 10.1109/ICMEW46912.2020.9105958.

[6] M. Khademi, M. Haghshenas, and H. Kabir, "A Review On Authoring Tools," presented at the Proceedings of the 5th International Conference on Distance Learning and Education, IPCSIT, Sep. 2011, vol. 12, pp. 40–44.

[7] Coelho, Hugo, et al. "Authoring tools for creating 360 multisensory videos—Evaluation of different interfaces," *Expert Systems*, vol. 38, no. 5, p. e12418, 2021, doi: 10.1111/exsy.12418.

[8] L. Argyriou, D. Economou, V. Bouki, and I. Doumanis, "Engaging Immersive Video Consumers: Challenges Regarding 360-Degree Gamified Video Applications," in *2016 15th International Conference on Ubiquitous Computing and Communications and 2016 International Symposium on Cyberspace and Security (IUCC-CSS)*, Oct. 2016, pp. 145–152. doi: 10.1109/IUCC-CSS.2016.028.

[9] G. Robertson, M. Czerwinski, and M. van Dantzich, "Immersion in desktop virtual reality," in *Proceedings of the 10th annual ACM symposium on User interface software and technology - UIST '97*, Banff, Alberta, Canada, 1997, pp. 11–19. doi: 10.1145/263407.263409.

[10] A. Serrano *et al.*, "Motion parallax for 360° RGBD video," *IEEE Transactions on Visualization and Computer Graphics*, vol. 25, no. 5, pp. 1817–1827, May 2019, doi: 10.1109/TVCG.2019.2898757.

[11] B. Luo, F. Xu, C. Richardt, and J.-H. Yong, "Parallax360: Stereoscopic 360° Scene Representation for Head-Motion Parallax," *IEEE Transactions on Visualization and Computer Graphics*, vol. 24, no. 4, pp. 1545–1553, Apr. 2018, doi: 10.1109/TVCG.2018.2794071.

[12] T. Rhee, L. Petikam, B. Allen, and A. Chalmers, "MR360: Mixed Reality Rendering for 360° Panoramic Videos," *IEEE Transactions on Visualization and Computer Graphics*, vol. 23, no. 4, pp. 1379–1388, Apr. 2017, doi: 10.1109/TVCG.2017.2657178.

[13] T. Adão *et al.*, "A rapid prototyping tool to produce 360° video-based immersive experiences enhanced with virtual/multimedia elements," *Procedia Computer Science*, vol. 138, pp. 441–453, 2018, doi: 10.1016/j.procs.2018.10.062.

[14] K. Choi, Y.-J. Yoon, O.-Y. Song, and S.-M. Choi, "Interactive and Immersive Learning Using 360° Virtual Reality Contents on Mobile Platforms," *Mobile Information Systems*, vol. 2018, p. e2306031, Oct. 2018, doi: 10.1155/2018/2306031.

[15] T. Pakkanen *et al.*, "Interaction with WebVR 360° video player: Comparing three interaction paradigms," in *2017 IEEE Virtual Reality (VR)*, Mar. 2017, pp. 279–280. doi: 10.1109/VR.2017.7892285.

[16] D. Fonseca and M. Kraus, "A comparison of head-mounted and hand-held displays for 360° videos with focus on attitude and behavior change," in *Proceedings of the 20th International Academic Mindtrek Conference*, New York, NY, USA, Oct. 2016, pp. 287–296. doi: 10.1145/2994310.2994334.

[17] "Wixar - Your Human Resources Metaverse." https://www.wixar.io/ (accessed Mar. 13, 2023).

[18] R. S. Kennedy, N. E. Lane, K. S. Berbaum, and M. G. Lilienthal, "Simulator Sickness Questionnaire: An Enhanced Method for Quantifying Simulator Sickness," *The International Journal of Aviation Psychology*, vol. 3, no. 3, pp. 203–220, Jul. 1993, doi: 10.1207/s15327108ijap0303_3.

[19] S. G. Hart and L. E. Staveland, "Development of NASA-TLX (Task Load Index): Results of Empirical and Theoretical Research," in *Advances in Psychology*, vol. 52, P. A. Hancock and N. Meshkati, Eds. North-Holland, 1988, pp. 139–183. doi: 10.1016/S0166-4115(08)62386-9.

[20] J. Brooke, *SUS: A "Quick and Dirty" Usability Scale*. CRC Press, 1996, pp. 207–212. doi: 10.1201/9781498710411-35.

[21] F. Guay, R. J. Vallerand, and C. Blanchard, "On the Assessment of Situational Intrinsic and Extrinsic Motivation: The Situational Motivation Scale (SIMS)," *Motivation and Emotion*, vol. 24, no. 3, pp. 175–213, Sep. 2000, doi: 10.1023/A:1005614228250.

[22] I. ISO, "9241-11: 2018 Ergonomics of Human-System Interaction—Part 11: Usability: Definitions and Concepts," *International Organization for Standardization. https://www. iso. org/obp/ui/\# iso: std: iso*, vol. 9241, no. 11, 2018.

[23] F. Ganier, C. Hoareau, and F. Devillers, "Évaluation des performances et de la charge de travail induits par l'apprentissage de procédures de maintenance en environnement virtuel," *Le travail humain*, vol. 76, no. 4, pp. 335–363, 2013, doi: 10.3917/th.764.0335.

[24] G. Gronier and A. Baudet, "Psychometric Evaluation of the F-SUS: Creation and Validation of the French Version of the System Usability Scale," *International Journal of Human–Computer Interaction*, vol. 37, no. 16, pp. 1571–1582, Oct. 2021, doi: 10.1080/10447318.2021.1898828.

[25] M. L. L.-L. Mener, "The academic performance of university students in their first-year : influence of cognitive abilities and motivation," phdthesis, Université de Bourgogne, 2012. Accessed: Mar. 13, 2023. [Online]. Available: https://theses.hal.science/tel-00780578

[26] A. Bangor, "Determining What Individual SUS Scores Mean: Adding an Adjective Rating Scale," vol. 4, no. 3, 2009.

RHM-HAR-SK: A Multiview Dataset with Skeleton Data for Ambient Assisted Living Research

Mohamad Reza Shahabian Alashti, Mohammad Hossein Bamorovat Abadi,
Patrick Holthaus, Catherine Menon and Farshid Amirabdollahian
Robotics Research Group, School of Engineering and Computer Science
University of Hertfordshire, Hatfield, United Kingdom
Email: {m.r.shahabian , m.bamorovat, p.holthaus, c.menon, f.amirabdollahian2}@herts.ac.uk

***Abstract*—Human and activity detection has always been a vital task in Human-Robot Interaction (HRI) scenarios, such as those involving assistive robots. In particular, skeleton-based Human Activity Recognition (HAR) offers a robust and effective detection method based on human biomechanics. Recent advancements in human pose estimation have made it possible to extract skeleton positioning data accurately and quickly using affordable cameras. In interaction with a human, robots can therefore capture detailed information from a close distance and flexible perspective. However, recognition accuracy is susceptible to robot movements, where the robot often fails to capture the entire scene. To address this we propose the adoption of external cameras to improve the accuracy of activity recognition on a mobile robot. In support of this proposal, we present the dataset *RHM-HAR-SK* that combines multiple camera perspectives augmented with human skeleton extraction obtained by the *HRNet* pose estimation. We apply qualitative and quantitative analysis to the extracted skeleton and its joints to evaluate the coverage of extracted poses per camera perspective and activity. Results indicate that the recognition accuracy for the skeleton varies between camera perspectives and also joints, depending on the type of activity. The RHM-HAR-SK dataset is available at Robot House.**

***Keywords*—Assistive Robot, Non-generative, Multi-view dataset, Skeleton-based, Activity Recognition**

I. Introduction

Assistive robots are predominantly being developed to support older people who may have difficulty with daily living [1], [2]. To be able to offer effective assistance, such robots have to monitor people's activities, for example, to help with their medication. Skeleton-based Activity Recognition (SAR) algorithms present a viable option in such scenarios since they can capture fine-grained details of human motion, providing accurate and nuanced information about the actions performed by an individual [3]. Moreover, the mobility of assistive robots allows them to move the camera in order to gather a high-resolution view of the human's posture and movements from a close-up perspective.

Detection accuracy is imperative in assistive robotics, since such robots often support vulnerable people and mistakes might have a serious outcome [4], [5]. However, robot cameras often suffer from a restricted field of view and can also be influenced negatively by robot and camera movements, for example, when they are mounted on the robot's head, which might be required to be moved away from the human for communicational purposes.

Combining the robot's view with external cameras allows us to capture the scene from additional perspectives, thereby increasing the overall robustness of activity recognition. Moreover, such an approach can take advantage of its situatedness, allowing recognition results from certain camera perspectives to be weighted depending on the current interaction with the human.

With this paper, we present two main contributions to human activity detection in ambient assisted living scenarios. Firstly, we present the novel dataset RHM-HAR-SK comprised of human skeleton data on top of an existing video dataset [6]. The dataset contains extracted skeletons of human activities from four different perspectives and aims to provide a rich information source to train and test the performance of human activity recognition approaches in indoor scenarios. Moreover, the dataset allows for detection algorithms to rely on low-dimensional skeleton data instead of videos and therefore reduces computing resources and networking requirements, which are otherwise computationally expensive considering the multiple parallel video streams. Secondly, we demonstrate how using additional camera perspectives enhances an assistive robot's activity recognition pipeline. For that, we measured the information contained in the different views by analysing the number of missed frames and missed poses.

Results show that certain camera views provide more valuable activity recognition data than others. For example the robot's mobility helps to follow humans and capture more details of some actions. Moreover, a wider view from environment could be a complimentary. This suggests that using additional external camera views can significantly improve reliability of activity detection to allow an assistive robot to maximise its functionality and thereby increase the users' safety, comfort, and quality of life.

To present our approach, we discuss related works that apply HAR to support assistive robots in providing their functionality and introduce methods that our recognition pipeline relies upon in Sec. II. We present the new dataset and how we augmented it with additional information to enhance its versatility within the application domain in Sec. III. We evaluate the quality of each camera view in terms of missed frames and poses in Sec. IV and discuss implications for assistive robotics in Sec. V before concluding the paper in Sec. VI.

II. Related Work

In this section, a brief review of the various technologies utilized for HAR is presented, with emphasis on the significance of the development of corresponding datasets. Subsequently, an overview of pose estimation techniques is provided, and finally, a discussion of the two distinct categories of multi-view datasets and related skeleton-based works is highlighted.

A. Human activity recognition methods

Vision-based HAR methods [7], [8], [9] rely on 2-dimensional (RGB), or 3-dimensional (RGB-D) video data acquired by a wide range of devices, e.g. stereo cameras, webcams, smartphones, etc. Video material is often sourced from video streaming platforms like YouTube or social media. *Sensor-based* recognition instead, relies on additional sensors, including global positioning systems (GPS), gyroscopes, accelerometers, or magnetometers [10], [11]. Some attempts (e.g. Bharti et al. [12]) combine both approaches and fuse recognition results from multiple sensors and cameras. Our approach allows fusing recognition results using multiple cameras without relying on external sensory technology.

Vision-based activity recognition methods can operate directly on the video input (RGB or RGB-D) or on derived data, such as *skeleton* information that is generated using pose extraction methods on the raw data. Methods operating on raw camera data extract features directly from image frames in the video stream and typically perform at high accuracy [8]. By contrast, our approach relies on derived data using a pose extraction method [13] to generate skeleton-based representations of human activities in a domestic environment. Such an approach has shown to be more robust than operating on raw data (RGB) against environmental clutter and varying light circumstances and could concentrate on the activity being conducted [14].

B. Human activity recognition in assistive robotics

Human activity recognition enables robots to understand and respond to human users' needs and activities. However, few studies specifically focus on the Ambient Assisted Living (AAL). Additionally, referring to comprehensive review works of assisted living technology [15] and HAR [16], [9], there is a lack of skeleton-based and multi-view HAR datasets in this field. Therefore, developing a new dataset focusing on assistive robotics will open a new horizon in this field.

C. Pose Extraction for activity recognition

Since the pose extraction method is applied at an early-stage task in the HAR pipeline, it plays a vital role in skeleton-based HAR [17]. Low or high accuracy in this section directly affects the rest of the procedure. Thus, a reliable HAR method is dependent on a high-accuracy pose extraction method. Pose extraction typically relies on either 2-dimensional (RGB) or 3-dimensional (RGB-D) input data [18], [19]. While depth data in 3-dimensional approaches allows for better recognition results, they require special sensors that are sometimes costly or unsuitable for the environment. Moreover, the storage size of such datasets increases drastically compared to RGB-based ones. Hence, publicly available datasets often provide 2-dimensional data only. To allow for later comparison to other datasets and approaches, our work relies on 2-dimensional data. Moreover, the simplicity, affordability and accessibility of RGB cameras allow us to apply a high-performance pose extraction method independent of specific hardware on a robot.

There are two general methods in two-dimensional pose estimators, *BottomUp* [19] and *TopDown* [20], [21]. The difference between the two is the sequence of finding poses and humans. The TopDown method first finds the Region of Interest (ROI), which is the human body, and then finds the poses. The provided dataset in this work also used the TopDown method. On the other hand, in the BottomUp approach, we need to find the poses, and then by grouping them, the human skeleton data will be created.

D. Generative and non-generative datasets

When it comes to data preparation techniques, generative and non-generative view invariant HAR methods are the two primary dataset groups. As implied by the name, generative approaches produce their input data from one or more actual views [22], whereas non-generative approaches acquire their data from genuine input devices like sensors and cameras. For instance, [23] is a SOTA prospective shifting approach that transforms an action into many views and is based on the angle representation in skeletons data. Their method proved reliable when dealing with incomplete data. Moreover, Generative Adversarial Networks (GAN) [24] and encoder-decoder CNN networks are popular for RGB-based approaches [25], [26]. However, there currently exist no non-generative skeleton-based HAR dataset including a robot view, and this work address this gap. Additionally, the presented dataset can provide sufficient data to create generative datasets in the future and can be adopted for the future development of assistive scenarios.

III. RHM-HAR-SK Dataset

This section provides information about the *RHM-HAR-SK* dataset that we created on top of the extended version of RHM [6] RGB data, a multi-view human activity dataset. It includes a *single person, trimmed video* from *four* independent cameras, two wall-mounted cameras (Front-view and Back-view), one mobile robot camera (Robot-view), and one ceiling fish-eye camera (Omni-view). Cameras were used to cover the whole area resembling an ordinary living room, and we note that the videos from different views overlap. This dataset captures fourteen daily indoor activities *[walking, bending, sitting down, standing up, cleaning, reaching, drinking, opening can, closing can, carrying object, lifting object, putting down object, stairs climbing up, stairs climbing down]* in a typical living room of a British home. The conspicuous feature is a *mobile robot* camera synchronized with three other cameras. It

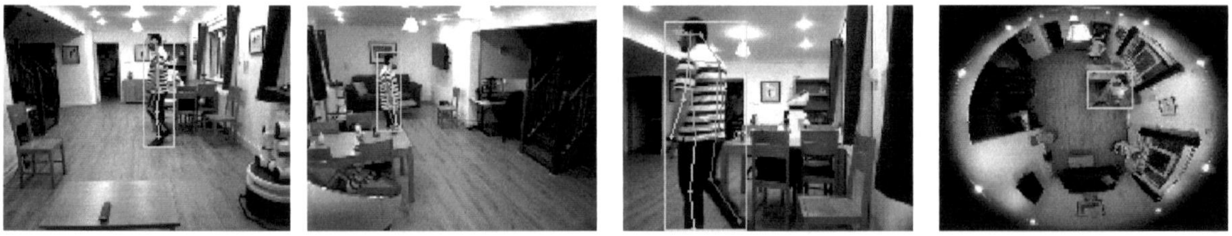

(a) Walking Back-view. (b) Walking Front-view (c) Walking Robot-view. (d) Walking Omni-view.

Figure 1. Synchronized skeleton output from different views of the "walking" action.

enables us to explore the added value of mobile observations in HRI in the context of social and assistive robotics.

In all video clips, the frame size is 640×480. As shown in Figure 1 the bounding box size varies in different frames. The variation is based on the distance of the detected human to the camera, the camera type and position, the subject's body dimension, and the number of detected poses. The *HRNet* [13] has been used to extract poses from videos. This model has been trained over the *COCO* keypoint detection dataset [27], and the *MPII* Human Pose dataset [28].

One body skeleton with 17 poses has been extracted from each frame, and the total number of video frames varies and is not fixed in each video stream and activity. Total number of synchronized videos from each camera view in all actions is 6700. Each pose includes *X* and *Y* positions in the 2D scene. In the first step, we store the extracted poses in a *JSON* file. The JSON file was transformed to the *Tensor* file to feed the ML Training mode.

All actions from different views are combined in a single five-dimensional tensor: $T = \{n, c, f, p, s\}$, where $n \in \{\mathbb{N}_0 | n < 6700\}$ denotes the *sample number*. Note: videos are synchronized, meaning each sample across the four videos from a different camera. Some of the videos are filled with zero (0) values. These refer to a video clip with missing poses; $c \in \{\mathbb{N}_0 | c < 4\}$ identifies one of the four *camera views*; $f \in \{\mathbb{N}_0 | f < 34\}$ refers to the frame number. Because the nature of the matrix does not support different dimensions, to unify it, 34 frames randomly selected and sorted as the original sequence. $p \in \{\mathbb{N}_0 | p < 17\}$ denotes the *number of extracted poses* up to a maximum of 17 identifiable poses (c.f. TABLE . I); $s \in \{\mathbb{R} | s < 3\}$ combines the relative x and y position plus the *score* of this pose are in this section. The confidence score depicts the reliability level of the extracted pose. $l \in \{\mathbb{N} | l < 14\}$ is an individual tensor L with the same dimension of sample number, which shows the class labels for the actions.

A. The Input Data Size and Sampling

One of the most challenging parts of the HAR task is the video frame sampling. Every video is labelled as a single activity, and the video length is different based on action type and situation. Then, for the ML models, this variation means having a dynamic input size. Consequently, all parameters in the model should modify based on the input size. Designing this dynamic model is a significant structural challenge in AI modelling, which is still an open area for improvement. Similarly, the skeleton-based methods need to use fix size input data. However, sampling or other reduction-based methods could lose valuable data from a video stream. In this work, *ordered random sampling* method has been used, which a fix the number of frames like 34, 64 and 128, have been selected randomly from entire frames.

A 2D image (Figure 2) visualizes the spatial-temporal data. It shows the results of transforming 20 videos stream of skeleton data from walking action in robot view to 2D images. The spatial information which is extracted from each video frame is transformed into a single row, one dimension vector with 17 elements. Each element of this row can show the relevant body pose information. They could be X, Y, or the results of a specific function like the Mean square. The X value of all 17 positions is shown in Figure 2. We have depicted the information of these experiments with a grayscale image to give a better understanding.

Figure 3 displays a real frame capturing a human engaged in stair climbing down action, along with the extracted body poses and skeleton, as depicted in Figure 3a. Additionally, Figure 3b showcases the individual human skeleton data devoid of RGB data. Each pose is represented by a unique index number, as demonstrated in Figure 3c, with corresponding nomenclature provided in TABLE I.

TABLE I. TABLE OF KEYPOINTS INDEX

Index	Keypoint	Index	Keypoint
0	Nose		
1	Left eye	2	Right eye
3	Left ear	4	Right ear
5	Left shoulder	6	Right shoulder
7	Left elbow	8	Right elbow
9	Left wrist	10	Right wrist
11	Left hip	12	Right hip
13	Left knee	14	Right knee
15	Left ankle	16	Right ankle

IV. QUANTITATIVE AND QUALITATIVE ANALYSIS

This section focuses on the *quantity* and *quality* of the extracted skeleton and its poses from the RHM-HAR-SK dataset. Two general terms are considered to describe the quality of extracted skeleton from RGB images, the number of *missed frames* and the number of *missed poses*. The primary objective of the analysis is to provide an improved comprehension of

Figure 2. The two dimension representation of x position from 20 videos with different length in Robot-view from walking action.

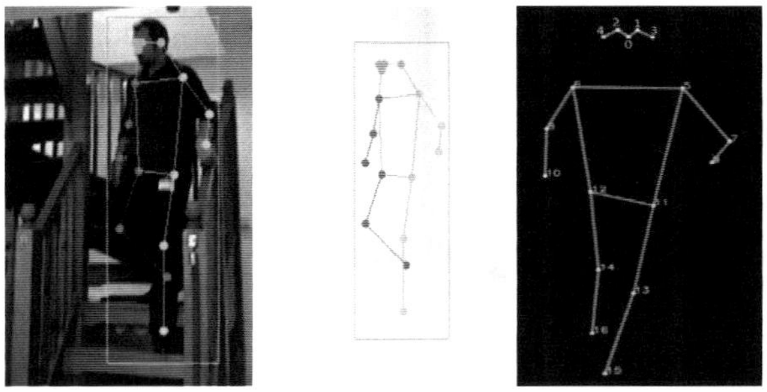

(a) (b) (c)

Figure 3. 3a shows a subject performing the "stair climbing down" action with skeleton overlay. 3b shows only the skeleton of the same action, and 3c another skeleton with index.

the effectiveness of different camera views in human detection and pose extraction quality.

A. Missed Frames

The RGB frames on which the pose extraction methods could not find any human skeleton is considered a *missed frame*. In the RHM-HAR-SK dataset, 14 actions have been captured from four synchronized camera views. The number of frames in all views is the same, but it's different from action to action. Figure 4 depicts the total number of missed frames in four views and 14 actions separately. The balck bars show the total frame number distribution in the dataset and each activity individually. The orange bar shows the statistics of Omni-view's camera missed frames, which illustrates that the majority of actions missed the frames, higher than 45%. Meanwhile, the *walking* and *carrying object* actions by 29.6% and 36.5% have the lower missed frames in the Omni-view, respectively. At the same time, these actions have higher frames error in the Robot-view with 0.9% for walking and 1.3% for carrying objects, which is negligible.

Excluding the Omni-view, the highest missed frames belong to the Front-view in *stairs climbing up/down* with 13.3% and 9.4%. Following that, the Back-view has the same pattern in stairs climbing actions by 10.2% and 4.7%.

B. Missed Poses

There are three parameters for each pose, X and Y values in 2D space and the *confidence* score. The confidence value refers to how much the extracted position is accurate. This value is between *0 to 1*, and we considered the values less than *0.5* as *missed poses*. Figure 5 illustrates the total number of all actions' missed poses from three views, and 17 poses separately. The total number of each pose in all activities is almost the same and hovers around 500000. The red, green, and blue bars show the robot, back, and front view cameras' missed poses. The percentage of missed poses is also shown on top of each bar.

Overall, in the Figure 5 the Back-view has the lowest confidence (highest number of missed poses) in all poses, and the Front-view and Robot-view have the highest confidence, which changes in different joints. For the Robot-view, the highest number of missed poses belong to the lower body, with more than 50% in ankle joints and around 31% in knee joints. Except stairs climbing up and down actions all other action has the similar pattern, for instance, Figure 6 illustrates the walking action statistics, on the other hand, the statistics in stairs climbing up (Figure 7) and down are slightly different from all other actions. Robot camera-view shows superior results in these actions with very low missed poses. The left and right shoulders have fewer missed poses in almost all actions among all body joints. The relevant total frame numbers of each individual action is shown on top of balck bar in Figure 4.

V. Discussion

The missed frames statistics show that an omnidirectional camera is an unreliable source for body pose extraction. However, we note that it delivers good information in actions with long-range movements like walking and carrying objects. Meanwhile, there is still significant room for developing this view further, such as improving the accuracy of pose estimation by incorporating details of other views or distortion factors.

These statistics also reveal that the number of missed frames is correlated with the action type. Actions like *stair climbing up and down*, *bending*, *sitting down*, and *cleaning* that need more vertical and horizontal courses have more missed value in two fixed wall mount cameras compared to the Robot-view. This is because the robot head follows the human, whereas the wall-mounted cameras do not. At the same time, the robot view has moderately more missed frames due to being too close to the human or being within a cluttered environment. These manifest mainly in actions *carrying objects*, *walking*. Considering the results of both missed frames and missed poses in Robot-view, we deduce that being close to the human when they are moving around quickly or for long distances can

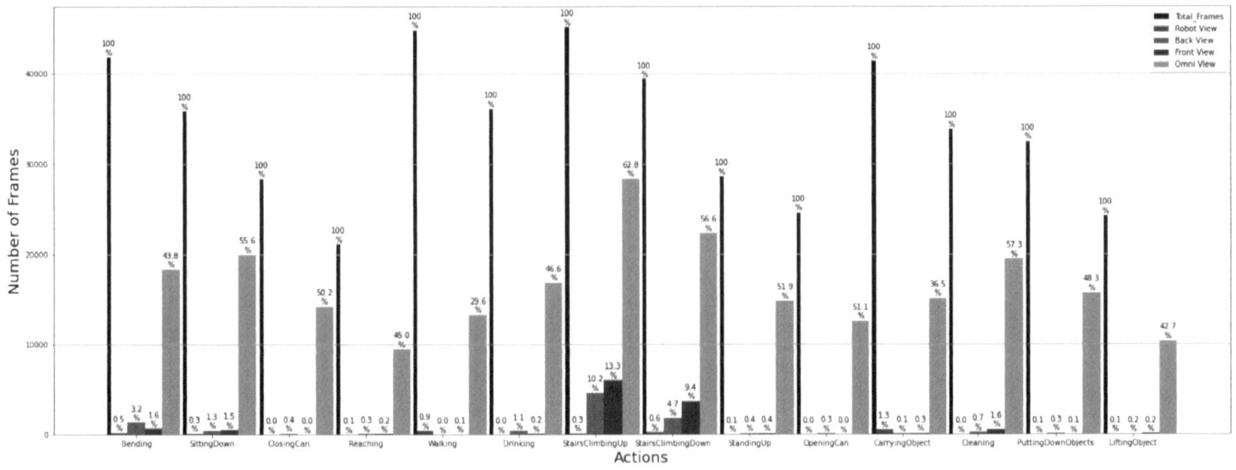

Figure 4. Missed frames Across all actions grouped by view

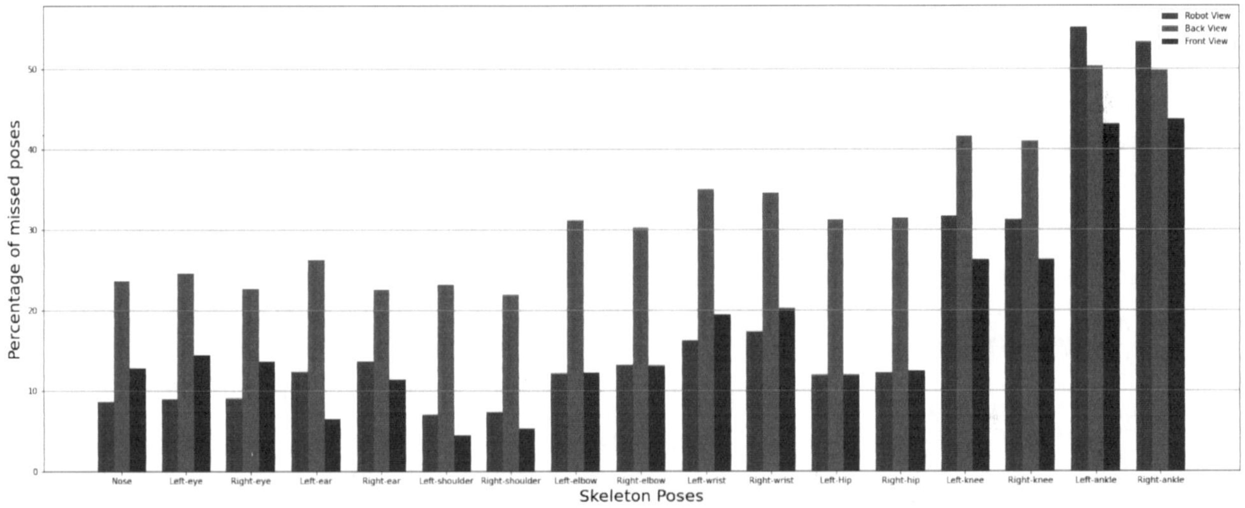

Figure 5. Percentage of frames with missed skeleton poses across all actions grouped by view.

decrease recognition quality due to partially observable or not observable joints. The reason is that this view has a closer view of the human and the scene, causing missing the lower body joints.

The previous discourse might led to the proposition that utilizing a wide-angle camera in robot could potentially facilitate the research; nevertheless, comparable cameras were employed in order to circumvent any further technical examination, which may be explored in a subsequent investigation.

The statistics in stairs climbing actions prove that the robot's camera movement and ability to follow the human results in fewer errors. The human has vertical movement in this action, which can be followed by a robot camera that other cameras might miss. For example, the front-view, which has the fewest missed poses on all actions on average, has the higher number of missed poses in stairs climbing up (Figure 7) and down actions.

Comparing two wall-mounted cameras with the same technical feature emphasizes the effectiveness of the viewpoint. The missed pose statistics index in Figure 5 shows that the Front-view has better results regarding pose extraction quality. On the other hand, the Back-view, which is also a wall-mount camera with the same technical features, results in the most missed poses in almost all actions. The only difference between these two wall-mount cameras is the altitude and view side. Reviewing the videos from these camera views in different activities suggests that the higher attitude and broader view in wall-mounted cameras can decrease the missed poses.

It is important to note that our dataset has a high level of accuracy, as demonstrated by the quantitative and qualitative results that differentiate between the various conditions. The variations in camera type and viewing angle have a discernible impact on the performance of pose extraction, and our dataset is of a sufficient quality to capture these differences. This high-

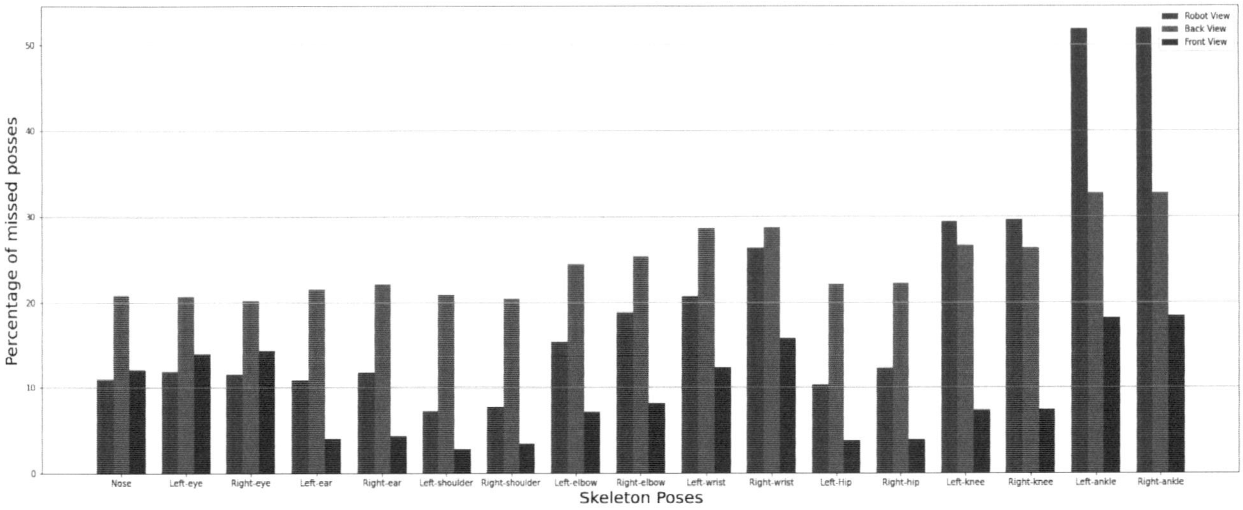

Figure 6. Percentage of frames with missed skeleton poses of "walking actions" grouped by view.

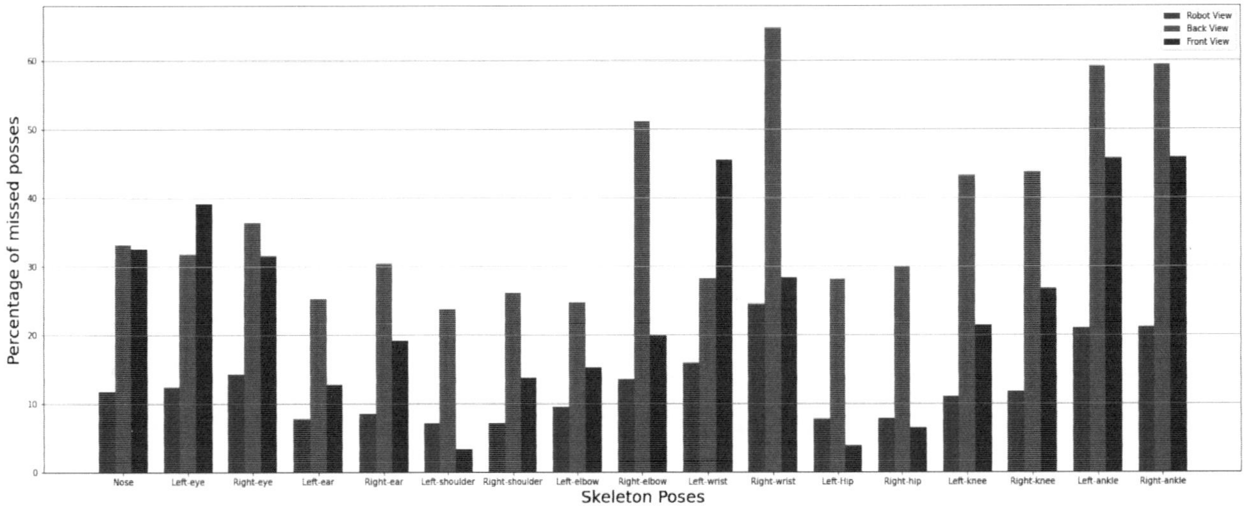

Figure 7. Percentage of frames with missed skeleton poses of the "stairs climbing up" actions grouped by view.

lights the importance of carefully selecting data acquisition techniques to ensure accurate and reliable results.

Overall, the results show that the camera position, view, activity type, and joints are highly significant in the quality of pose extraction. Theoretically, combining a Robot-view camera and two other cameras can enhance skeleton extraction. The integration of an extra camera may incur substantial expenses both in terms of computational resources and monetary cost, yet this concern has been subject to further discussion in a parallel work which we utilise this dataset to train a light-weight MV-HAR model, and our results indicate that adding other views has a good impact on the robot's HAR accuracy [29].

VI. Conclusion

In this paper, we have presented the novel dataset RHM-HAR-SK that provides human skeleton data from multiple perspectives to facilitate human activity in ambient assisted living scenarios. Our findings reveal that the accuracy of skeleton recognition varies depending on both the camera perspective and the specific joint being analyzed, with variations being particularly pronounced for different types of activities. In particular, we have shown that a broader view and higher installation height positively impact the extracted skeleton quality. In addition, results in an accompanying paper have shown that combining the robot camera with an external camera can increase HAR accuracy. Grafting all information into a single HRI scenario, we conclude that the proposed dataset can practically help to develop a high-level robot perception in assistive technology. Our future work will consider application of generative views from existing synchronised data in order to achieve close to real-time detection in AAL scenarios.

REFERENCES

[1] F. Amirabdollahian, R. op den Akker, S. Bedaf, R. Bormann, H. Draper, V. Evers, J. G. Pérez, G. J. Gelderblom, C. G. Ruiz, D. Hewson *et al.*, "Assistive technology design and development for acceptable robotics companions for ageing years," *Paladyn, Journal of Behavioral Robotics*, vol. 4, no. 2, pp. 94–112, 2013. 1

[2] M. Ghafurian, J. Muñoz, J. Boger, J. Hoey, and K. Dautenhahn, "Socially interactive agents for supporting aging," in *The Handbook on Socially Interactive Agents: 20 years of Research on Embodied Conversational Agents, Intelligent Virtual Agents, and Social Robotics Volume 2: Interactivity, Platforms, Application*, 2022, pp. 367–402. 1

[3] R. Planinc, A. Chaaraoui, M. Kampel, and F. Florez-Revuelta, "Computer vision for active and assisted living," 2016. 1

[4] M. J. Matarić and B. Scassellati, "Socially assistive robotics," *Springer handbook of robotics*, pp. 1973–1994, 2016. 1

[5] D. Feil-Seifer, K. Skinner, and M. J. Matarić, "Benchmarks for evaluating socially assistive robotics," *Interaction Studies*, vol. 8, no. 3, pp. 423–439, 2007. 1

[6] M. Bamorovat Abadi, M. Shahabian Alashti, P. Holthaus, C. Menon, and F. Amirabdollahian, "Rhm: Robot house multi-view human activity recognition dataset." IARIA, Mar. 2023, aCHI 2023: The Sixteenth International Conference on Advances in Computer-Human Interactions, ACHI 2023 ; Conference date: 24-04-2023 Through 28-04-2023. [Online]. Available: https://www.iaria.org/conferences2023/ACHI23.html 1, 2

[7] D. R. Beddiar, B. Nini, M. Sabokrou, and A. Hadid, "Vision-based human activity recognition: a survey," *Multimedia Tools and Applications*, vol. 79, no. 41, pp. 30 509–30 555, 2020. 2

[8] C. Feichtenhofer, H. Fan, J. Malik, and K. He, "Slowfast networks for video recognition," in *Proceedings of the IEEE/CVF international conference on computer vision*, 2019, pp. 6202–6211. 2

[9] M. H. Arshad, M. Bilal, and A. Gani, "Human activity recognition: Review, taxonomy and open challenges," *Sensors*, vol. 22, no. 17, p. 6463, 2022. 2

[10] H. Yan, Y. Zhang, Y. Wang, and K. Xu, "Wiact: A passive wifi-based human activity recognition system," *IEEE Sensors Journal*, vol. 20, no. 1, pp. 296–305, 2019. 2

[11] K. Xia, J. Huang, and H. Wang, "Lstm-cnn architecture for human activity recognition," *IEEE Access*, vol. 8, pp. 56 855–56 866, 2020. 2

[12] P. Bharti, D. De, S. Chellappan, and S. K. Das, "Human: Complex activity recognition with multi-modal multi-positional body sensing," *IEEE Transactions on Mobile Computing*, vol. 18, no. 4, pp. 857–870, 2018. 2

[13] K. Sun, B. Xiao, D. Liu, and J. Wang, "Deep high-resolution representation learning for human pose estimation," in *Proceedings of the IEEE/CVF conference on computer vision and pattern recognition*, 2019, pp. 5693–5703. 2, 3

[14] W. Zheng, L. Li, Z. Zhang, Y. Huang, and L. Wang, "Relational network for skeleton-based action recognition," in *2019 IEEE International Conference on Multimedia and Expo (ICME)*. IEEE, 2019, pp. 826–831. 2

[15] S. Aleksic, M. Atanasov, J. C. Agius, K. Camilleri, A. Cartolovni, P. Climent-Peerez, S. Colantonio, S. Cristina, V. Despotovic, H. K. Ekenel *et al.*, "State of the art of audio-and video-based solutions for aal," *arXiv preprint arXiv:2207.01487*, 2022. 2

[16] M. M. Islam, S. Nooruddin, F. Karray, and G. Muhammad, "Human activity recognition using tools of convolutional neural networks: A state of the art review, data sets, challenges, and future prospects," *Computers in Biology and Medicine*, p. 106060, 2022. 2

[17] L. Song, G. Yu, J. Yuan, and Z. Liu, "Human pose estimation and its application to action recognition: A survey," *Journal of Visual Communication and Image Representation*, vol. 76, p. 103055, 2021. 2

[18] B. Cheng, B. Xiao, J. Wang, H. Shi, T. S. Huang, and L. Zhang, "Higherhrnet: Scale-aware representation learning for bottom-up human pose estimation," in *Proceedings of the IEEE/CVF conference on computer vision and pattern recognition*, 2020, pp. 5386–5395. 2

[19] Z. Cao, T. Simon, S.-E. Wei, and Y. Sheikh, "Realtime multi-person 2d pose estimation using part affinity fields," in *Proceedings of the IEEE conference on computer vision and pattern recognition*, 2017, pp. 7291–7299. 2

[20] Y. Chen, Z. Wang, Y. Peng, Z. Zhang, G. Yu, and J. Sun, "Cascaded pyramid network for multi-person pose estimation," in *Proceedings of the IEEE conference on computer vision and pattern recognition*, 2018, pp. 7103–7112. 2

[21] G. Papandreou, T. Zhu, N. Kanazawa, A. Toshev, J. Tompson, C. Bregler, and K. Murphy, "Towards accurate multi-person pose estimation in the wild," in *Proceedings of the IEEE conference on computer vision and pattern recognition*, 2017, pp. 4903–4911. 2

[22] L. Wang, Z. Ding, Z. Tao, Y. Liu, and Y. Fu, "Generative multi-view human action recognition," in *Proceedings of the IEEE/CVF International Conference on Computer Vision*, 2019, pp. 6212–6221. 2

[23] R. Hou, Y. Li, N. Zhang, Y. Zhou, X. Yang, and Z. Wang, "Shifting perspective to see difference: A novel multi-view method for skeleton based action recognition," in *Proceedings of the 30th ACM International Conference on Multimedia*, 2022, pp. 4987–4995. 2

[24] J. Cui, S. Li, Q. Xia, A. Hao, and H. Qin, "Learning multi-view manifold for single image based modeling," *Computers & Graphics*, vol. 82, pp. 275–285, 2019. 2

[25] T. Zhou, S. Tulsiani, W. Sun, J. Malik, and A. A. Efros, "View synthesis by appearance flow," in *European conference on computer vision*. Springer, 2016, pp. 286–301. 2

[26] G. E. Hinton, A. Krizhevsky, and S. D. Wang, "Transforming auto-encoders," in *International conference on artificial neural networks*. Springer, 2011, pp. 44–51. 2

[27] S. Jin, L. Xu, J. Xu, C. Wang, W. Liu, C. Qian, W. Ouyang, and P. Luo, "Whole-body human pose estimation in the wild," in *Proceedings of the European Conference on Computer Vision (ECCV)*, 2020. 3

[28] D. C. Luvizon, D. Picard, and H. Tabia, "2d/3d pose estimation and action recognition using multitask deep learning," in *Proceedings of the IEEE conference on computer vision and pattern recognition*, 2018, pp. 5137–5146. 3

[29] M. Shahabian Alashti, M. Bamorovat Abadi, P. Holthaus, C. Menon, and F. Amirabdollahian, "Lightweight human activity recognition for ambient assisted living." IARIA, Mar. 2023, aCHI 2023: The Sixteenth International Conference on Advances in Computer-Human Interactions, ACHI 2023 ; Conference date: 24-04-2023 Through 28-04-2023. [Online]. Available: https://www.iaria.org/conferences2023/ACHI23.html 6

Lightweight Human Activity Recognition for Ambient Assisted Living

Mohamad Reza Shahabian Alashti, Mohammad Hossein Bamorovat Abadi,
Patrick Holthaus, Catherine Menon and Farshid Amirabdollahian
Robotics Research Group, School of Engineering and Computer Science
University of Hertfordshire, Hatfield, United Kingdom
Email: {m.r.shahabian , m.bamorovat, p.holthaus, c.menon, f.amirabdollahian2}@herts.ac.uk

***Abstract*—Ambient Assisted Living (AAL) systems aim to improve the safety, comfort, and quality of life for the populations with specific attention given to prolonging personal independence during later stages of life. Human Activity Recognition (HAR) plays a crucial role in enabling AAL systems to recognise and understand human actions. Multi-view human activity recognition (MV-HAR) techniques are particularly useful for AAL systems as they can use information from multiple sensors to capture different perspectives of human activities and can help to improve the robustness and accuracy of activity recognition. In this work, we propose a lightweight activity recognition pipeline that utilizes skeleton data from multiple perspectives with the objective of enhancing an assistive robot's perception of human activity. The pipeline includes data sampling, spatial temporal data transformation, and representation and classification methods. This work contrasts a modified classic LeNet classification model (M-LeNet) versus a Vision Transformer (ViT) in detecting and classifying human activities. Both methods are evaluated using a multi-perspective dataset of human activities in the home (RHM-HAR-SK). Our results indicate that combining camera views can improve recognition accuracy. Furthermore, our pipeline provides an efficient and scalable solution in the AAL context, where bandwidth and computing resources are often limited.**

***Keywords*—classification, Multi-view, Skeleton-based, Activity Recognition Pipeline, Assistive Robot**

I. Introduction

Multi-View Human Activity Recognition (MV-HAR) is an extension of traditional HAR in which multiple views or perspectives of activity are used to improve recognition performance. This is thought to be beneficial due to ability to provide a clear and undisturbed view of a dynamic activity. In indoor environments, this can be achieved by using multiple cameras or sensors to capture different views of the same activity and then fusing the information provided by different views to achieve a more robust and accurate recognition.

The process of MV-HAR typically involves capturing video or sensor data, pre-processing the data to extract features, and then using machine learning algorithms to classify the activities. A lightweight pipeline is important for real-time and resource-constrained applications, such as those on mobile devices like robots, where computational efficiency and low power consumption are key requirements. Additionally, lightweight pipelines can enable more widespread deployment of activity recognition technology, such as in smart homes or smart cities, where large numbers of cameras or sensors need to be integrated.

For assistive living systems, using a lightweight MV-HAR pipeline can provide a complete and accurate understanding of the activities performed by residents, including older adults or people with disabilities. This can enable the development of more effective and personalized support services, such as fall detection and home security, and also supports principles of prevention and pro-active care.

In this work, we modify a classic LeNet [1] classification model, termed as M-LeNet for the HAR task. To contrast, we also use the Vision Transformer [2] (ViT) for the classification task, and compare the results between both models. The rationale behind selecting the LeNet and Vision Transformer (ViT) classifiers for the Human Activity Recognition (HAR) task stems from their distinctive characteristics in terms of architecture and design. Specifically, LeNet is a widely used and relatively simplistic Convolutional Neural Network (CNN) in image classification tasks, whereas ViT is a more advanced transformer-based model that has gained popularity in recent years owing to its ability to process images without relying on traditional convolutional layers. Both classifiers were chosen due to their comparable number of training parameters, thus allowing for a fair comparison between the two models. Besides, several parts of the HAR pipeline like input spatial temporal data transformation, data sampling, and representation and classification methods have been modified.

With this work, we therefore present:

- **Development of a lightweight HAR pipeline:** Data sampling, input data type, and representation and classification.
- **Comparison of camera views:** model execution in support of an experiment to find the performance of individual views and their combination for M-LeNet and ViT.

To provide context for our approach, we first review related works in Sec. II that have been applied to three popular HAR datasets, and discuss the importance of multi-view datasets for assistive robots scenarios. In Sec. III, we present a new lightweight multi-view pipeline and provide a detailed explanation of its structure. In Sec. IV, we evaluate the performance of different camera views in terms of accuracy and number of parameters of two different classifier models. Finally, we conclude our paper in Sec. V.

II. RELATED WORK

A. Skeleton-based Methods

Based on the spatial and temporal nature of human activity, different methods have emerged. *Sequence models* like Recurrent Neural Network (RNN) [3] or Long Short Term Memory (LSTM) influence the sequentially of extracted human skeleton data as time series. *Convolutional Neural Network* (CNN) based models [4] have great potential in spatial information compared to RNN models. The other successful methods are *Graph Neural network* based (GNN) [5], [6] which represent spatial and temporal information by the human skeleton's natural topological graph structure. Spatio-Temporal Graph Convolutional Network (ST-GCN) [5] is the first model in this category that notices harmony in spatial and temporal data that allows for combining spatial structures with time-series while still benefiting from a convolutional neural network.

Besides, *transformer* models have been engaged in HAR tasks to gain competitive outcomes. They can be used to capture long-range dependencies between regions of an image, allowing the model to better express understand the relationships between objects and their context [2]. Some of them rely on modified GCN models [7], [8] and others [9] are purely transformer based.

B. Skeleton-based HAR Leader board analysis

The investigation of skeleton-based action recognition reveals that NTU-RGB+D [10], NTU-RGB+D 120 [11], and Kinetics-skeleton [12] datasets are trending nowadays. Table I illustrates these datasets' top-ranked skeletal model performances. The rank number, model's accuracy, and year of publication have been provided to show the diversity of ML models and their sometimes varying behavior in different datasets.

The *PoseC3D* [13] method has the highest accuracy in two datasets (Kinetics-Skeleton and NTU-RGB+D) and stands at rank nine in one other. In addition, a different variation of PoseC3D, RGB + Pose, has ranked five in kinetics skeleton and first and second rank in two others.

Considering the available number of Skeleton-based HAR models, NTU RGB+D has the highest with 85, followed by NTU RGB+D 120 with 38, and then Kinetics-skeleton with 18. In Table I, the top ten models in terms of accuracy in almost all datasets have been considered. Kinetics-skeleton is the base dataset for sorting the models ranks. Given that not all models are applied in all three datasets, comparable results are not always available. The total number of models is 21.

The range of accuracy is not the same in all datasets. The highest performance in Kinetics-Skeleton dataset belongs to PoseC3D (w.HRNet 2D skeleton) with 47.7%, following that by almost 9% difference, the 2s-AGCN+TEM [14] model accuracy is 38.36%. Ironically, the rest of the models' accuracy was distributed in 1%, from 38.4% for DualHead-Net [15], the 3rd rank, to 37.4% for ST-TR-agcn [7] , the 10th rank. However, the total accuracy range of ranks in two other datasets is like a uniform distribution. Low difference, 0.7% for NTU RGB+D and 3%, for NTU RGB+D 120. However, based on this evidence, it is unreliable to say that a method is superior by considering its rank in just one dataset. For example, EfficientGCN-B4 [16] model stands in the third stage on the leader board for NTU RGB+D 120 dataset, but its rank in NTU RGB+D is 22. Likewise, PoseC3D (w. HRNet 2D skeleton), which has outstanding results in the Kinetics-skeleton dataset, and the highest accuracy in NTU RGB+D, stands in stage nine in the leader board for NTU RGB+D 120 dataset. However, another variant of PoseC3D (RGB + Pose) has conspicuous accuracy in NTU RGB+D 120 (95.3%) dataset and high accuracy in two others.

TABLE I. RESULTS OF SKELETON-BASED HAR LEADER BOARD IN THREE DATASETS

Model	Kinetics-Skeleton	NTU-RGB+D	NTU-RGB+D120
PoseC3D(Pose)	1 , 47.7% , 2021	1, 97.1%, 2021	9, 86.9%, 2021
PoseC3D(P+RGB)	5 , 38% , 2021	2, 97.0%, 2021	1, 95.3%, 2021
CTR-GCN	NA	3, 96.8%, 2021	2, 89.9%, 2021
EfficientGCN-B4	NA	22, 95.7%, 2021	3, 88.3%, 2021
Skeletal GNN	NA	4, 96.7%, 2021	7, 87.5%, 2021
PA-ResGCN-B19	NA	17, 96%, 2021	8, 87.3%, 2020
Ensemble-top5	NA	NA	9, 87.22%, 2020
2s-AGCN+TEM	2 , 38.6%, 2020	NA	NA
4s Shift-GCN	NA	6, 96.5%, 2020	13, 85.9%, 2020
DualHead-Net	3, 38.4%, 2021	5, 96.6%, 2021	4, 88.2%, 2021
AngNet-JA	NA	7, 96.4%,2021	6, 88.2%, 2021
DSTA-Net	NA	8, 96.4% 2020	11, 86.6%, 2020
Sym-GNN	NA	9, 96.4%, 2019	NA
MS-G3D	4, 38%, 2020	NA	NA
Dynamic GCN	6, 37.9%, 2020	13, 96%, 2020	NA
MS-AAGCN	7, 37.8%, 2019	11, 96.2%, 2019	NA
CGCN	8, 37.5%, 2020	10, 96.4%, 2020	NA
JB-AAGCN	9, 37.4%, 2019	15, 96%, 2019	NA
ST-TR-agcn	10, 37.4, 2020	12, 96.1%, 2020	17, 82.7%, 2020

Three values in datasets' row define the *Rank* , *Accuracy*, and *Year* of publication respectively.

On the other hand, models like CTR-GCN [17], Skeletal GNN [18], 2s-AGCN+TEM [14], DualHead-Net, AngNet-JA + BA + JBA + VJBA [19], MS-G3D [6], CGCN [20], has reasonable accuracy because they stand in top rank in two or all datasets, respectively.

To summarise, although the number of skeleton-based human activity recognition methods and their variation is increasing, there is still room for improvements for models to be applied in challenging datasets like Kinetics-Skeleton. The comparison reveals that dataset details have a direct effect on the ML model accuracy. For example, kinetic-skeleton data is collected from Youtube videos and includes uncontrolled environment, and the NTU RGB+D videos were captured in a controlled environment. Top accuracy for the kinetic is almost 50% fewer than others. Besides, this review illustrates that the same model may not perform as well in a different dataset.

On the other hand, developing a comprehensive and real-world activity recognition is demanding, particularly given the nature of some *Deep-Learning* (DL) approaches, which require extensive data and significant processing power e.g.

CPU and GPU nodes. This results in a lack of comprehensive benchmarks [21] for evaluating the performance of activity recognition algorithms. One approach to solve this problem is dataset specialization, in which elements such as theme, activity, task, and subject adhere to a specific idea. In this work, we aim to apply HAR in the AAL context using a skeleton-based and multi-view dataset.

C. Multi-view HAR

Recent research in MV-HAR with skeleton models in indoor environments has focused on developing methods that can effectively utilize the temporal and spatial information provided by skeleton data. Methods such as deep neural networks [22], convolutional neural networks [10], recurrent neural networks, and attention-based models [23] have been proposed to improve the robustness and accuracy of the recognition system.

In MV-HAR systems, a lightweight machine learning approach is essential for providing real-time and resource-constrained applications like robots. A low computational cost, fewer training parameters, and an efficient algorithm enable the system to be more practical for long-term deployment in assistive living scenarios. However, focusing on the number of training parameters of the existing skeleton-based models shows that many methods are not computationally effective. For example, considering some single-view high-accuracy models in the Table I, *PoseC3D* [13] in different variation has 2m to 8m parameters and 2s-AGCN+TEM [14] has 6.94m parameters. Expanding the comparison to the multi-view, this could indicate models with significantly more parameters.

III. Lightweight MV-HAR Pipeline

The process of recognizing human activity via a skeleton-based multi-view approach typically encompasses the acquisition or loading of video data, the extraction of joint information, and the generation of skeleton data. Subsequently, a machine learning algorithm is employed to classify the recorded actions. The utilization of a lightweight pipeline in this context allows for the integration of cameras in robotic and AAL systems, enabling their effective operation in a variety of scenarios. As depicted in Figure 1, our proposed methodology for Multi-View Human Activity Recognition (MV-HAR) emphasizes the central concept of leveraging multiple camera viewpoints to enhance the recognition of activities via a lightweight pipeline. The pipeline started with data collection from different views, followed by pose extraction and preprocessing. Then, the prepared tensor file feeds the training model.

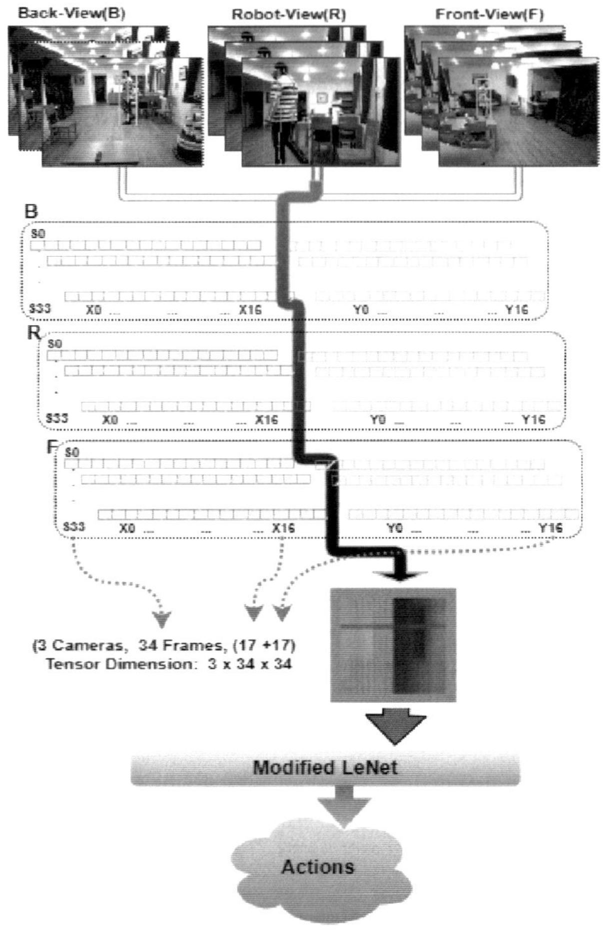

Figure 1. The MV-HAR pipeline, as described in detail in section III begins with capturing video from multiple views (III-A) and the extraction of skeletons from multiple viewpoints (III-B, followed by the conversion of each viewpoint into a spatial-temporal matrix (III-C). These matrices are subsequently combined into a single tensor file, which is finally classified by the modified LeNet model (III-D).

A. Input Data

In a parallel work, we have developed the RHM-HAR-SK [24] dataset on the top of a RGB dataset (RHM) [25]. This non-generative multi-view skeleton-based human activity recognition dataset includes fourteen daily actions *[walking, bending, sitting down, standing up, cleaning, reaching, drinking, opening can, closing can, carrying object, lifting object, putting down object, stairs climbing up, stairs climbing down]* captured in an indoor typical British house. A robot-view camera, two wall-mounted cameras (Front-view and Back-view), and an omnidirectional view (Omni-view) camera capture the activities synchronously. However, analysis of that dataset reveals that the Omni-view data has low accuracy in the skeleton-based method, and it has consequently been omitted.

B. Pose extraction

The utilization of RGB cameras is due to their simplicity, affordability, and accessibility in conjunction with a high-performance pose extraction method applied to RGB data, results in improved human body skeleton extraction. In RHM-HAR-SK dataset, a pretrained HRNet model as described in [26] is utilized to extract poses from videos. This model has

TABLE II. MODIFIED LENET NETWORK ARCHITECHTURE

Layer Type	I/O Chanel	Kernel Size	Stride	Out Shape
Conv2D	3/10	(3×3)	(1×1)	(34×34)
ReLU	-	-	-	-
MaxPool2D	-	(2×2)	(2×2)	(34×34)
Dropout	-	-	-	-
Conv2D	10/20	(3×3)	(1×1)	(17×17)
ReLU	-	-	-	-
MaxPool2D	-	(2×2)	(2×2)	(34×34)
Dropout	-	-	-	-
FC Linear	In:	980	Out:	500
ReLU	-	-	-	-
FC Linear	In:	500	Out:	250
ReLU	-	-	-	-
FC Linear	In:	250	Out:	14
LogSoftmax	-	-	-	-

been trained on the COCO keypoint detection dataset [27] and the MPII Human Pose dataset [28].

C. Preprocessing

Following the extraction of the skeleton data, the spatial and temporal input data was transformed into a $3 \times 34 \times 34$ tensor. In Figure 1 the process of finding a single person from three cameras to make the tensor file is shown. The first digit (3) refers to three cameras, and the 34×34 dimension refers to 34 frames of skeleton data, and two 17 columns. The first 17 columns belong to the X value and the second half to the Y value. Random sampling has been used to choose 34 frames for each video stream. The three-channel matrix is illustrated as an RGB image in Figure 1, with each camera view being mapped to the red, green, and blue channels.

Figure 2 illustrates three samples of two types input data, the RGB in 2b and grayscale in 2a. The former refers to three channels, each indicating a camera view and the latter a single-view camera. Each 2D image depicts skeletons data frames in an action. Subsequent to the extraction of skeletons from the video stream and preparing the 2D image, two general machine learning models were applied as outlined below.

D. The Modified LeNet model

The base model that has been used in this experiment for CNN-based machine learning model is LeNet [1]. This is a simple convolution model for image representation that we have modified as follows to use as the skeleton-based action classification. Table II illustrates the structure of the Modified CNN model. Two convolution layers are applied in this model, which we test by two different configurations, 10 and 20 channels for the low parameter and 20 and 40 channels for the high parameter configuration. The difference between the original LeNet and this modified version is the number of convolution layers (reduced from 3 to 2) and the kernel size (reduced from 5 to 3). Two dropout layers have also been added to avoid over-fitting. One more fully connected layer was also added to increase the learning parameters.

E. Vision Transformers (ViT) Architecture

The other classification model used is the ViT [2]. In the ViT architecture each input picture is divided into patches of sub-images. Then by applying the positional encoding, the model is trained. Each patch is considered a word and projected to the feature space. In Figure 3 a random input data with its patches and the ViT classification architecture is shown. The process of preparing the input data for the ViT and M-LeNet is the same.

F. Decentralised structure

Implementing multiple cameras with separate processors in human-robot interactions offers numerous advantages. Extracting and transmitting only the crucial skeleton information reduces the robot's computational load, making it more efficient and responsive in providing assistance. Figure 4 illustrates the proposed concept of decentralized structure of the multi-view camera with robotic agent. Two individual cameras refer the front-view and back-view in our experiment. The mobile robot with a camera is following the human to recognise its activities.

The use of multiple cameras can enhance the accuracy of the interaction, as the robot can take inputs from different angles into account. This leads to a more human-like interaction, which is crucial in assistive settings where the goal is to create a seamless and intuitive experience, making the assistive robot even more efficient in providing aid. Overall, this approach significantly enhances the capabilities of assistive robots and provides a better experience for those in need of assistance.

IV. RESULTS

This section compares the results of the *M-LeNet* and *ViT* classification models in different conditions. Table III shows the comparison results of parameters like *accuracy*, number of total *trainable parameters*, different *camera views*, number of skeleton *positions*, and *classes*.

These two models are applied to the RHM-HAR-SK dataset, including a synchronized three-view video stream. Table III show the results of the models trained on full views, for all 14 classes, and all poses in the upper section and the lower section show the same comparison with excluded ankle poses (marked with 0-15 on poses column). The results show that the overall accuracy is between 69 and 77 percent for all views and 57 to 78 percent for single and double views. Among them, the comparison of models with all poses and removed ankles shows that for the ViT model, the accuracy moderately increased by 3% in all views and remains the same in a single view. In contrast, the M-LeNet model decreased by about 2% in both high and low parameters models. The difference between these M-LeNet classifiers is the number of parameters in linear layers, which one is double compared to the other. The high parameter M-LeNet has higher accuracy.

In the last part of the lower and upper section, the details of *single view* training models are shown. Interestingly, the ViT model results follow the missed poses statistics in the RHM-HAR-SK dataset [24], in which the front and robot views have fewer missed poses, and the highest accuracy among all views, and the back view is less accurate with more missed poses. Moreover, the front-view accuracy is 78% in

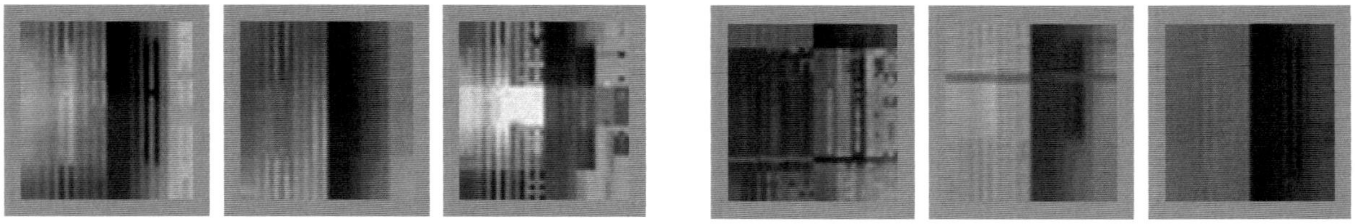

(a) Three samples of Single view of bending action.

(b) Three samples of combined three views as a RGB image of bending action

Figure 2. Synchronized skeleton output from different views of bending action.

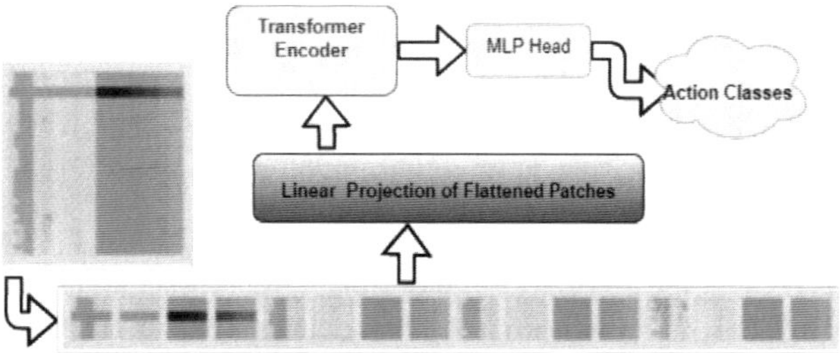

Figure 3. The ViT classification Architecture Applied on one of the RHM-HAR-SK dataset's sample [2]

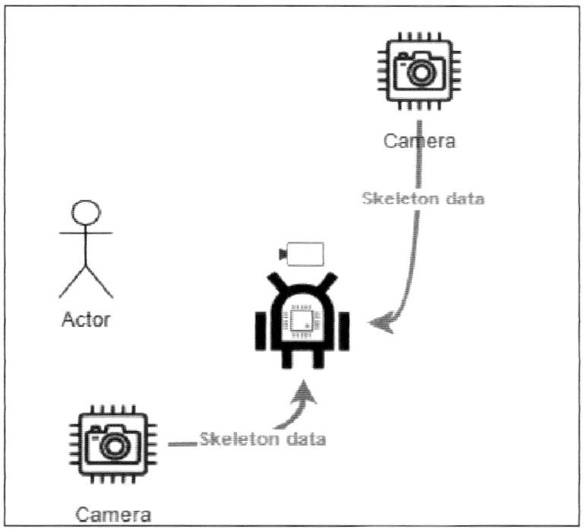

Figure 4. The decentralised structure of MV-HAR with Low computational cost in the robot

ViT model, and robot-view accuracy is 70% in M-LeNet. The double-view combination results are shown in the second part of the upper section. Combinations of Front (F), Back (B) and Robot (R) views are considered for assessing their impact on accuracy. The average accuracy of the double-view in the ViT models is higher than the lowest accuracy in the relevant single-view and less than the higher one, which means that the accuracy of the view with a lower value increased. For instance, the individual robot-view accuracy increased from 72% to 75% in combination with front-view and back-view increased from 61% to 69% when fused with front-view. For M-LeNet models, all single-view accuracy increased in the

TABLE III. RESULTS OF VIT AND M-LENET CLASSIFICATION METHODS ON RHM-HAR SKELETON DATASET IN DIFFERENT CONDITIONS.

Model	Accuracy	Params	Views	Poses	Classes
M-Lenet	70%	0.6M	ALL	ALL	14
M-Lenet	**77%**	1M	ALL	ALL	14
ViT	71%	2.2M	ALL	ALL	14
M-Lenet	71%	0.6M	R+B	ALL	14
M-Lenet	70%	0.6M	R+F	ALL	14
M-Lenet	70%	0.6M	B+F	ALL	14
ViT	**75%**	2.1M	R+F	ALL	14
ViT	69%	2.1M	B+F	ALL	14
ViT	68%	2.1M	R+B	ALL	14
M-Lenet	70%	0.6M	Robot	ALL	14
M-Lenet	57%	0.6M	Back	ALL	14
M-Lenet	66%	0.6M	Front	ALL	14
ViT	72%	2.1M	Robot	ALL	14
ViT	61%	2.1M	Back	ALL	14
ViT	**78%**	2.1M	Front	ALL	14
M-Lenet	69%	**0.32M**	ALL	0-15	14
M-Lenet	**75%**	1.2M	ALL	0-15	14
ViT	74%	2.1M	ALL	0-15	14
M-Lenet	69%	**0.32M**	Robot	0-15	14
M-Lenet	58%	**0.32M**	Back	0-15	14
M-Lenet	69%	**0.32M**	Front	0-15	14
ViT	73%	2.1M	Robot	0-15	14
ViT	61%	2.1M	Back	0-15	14
ViT	**77%**	2.1M	Front	0-15	14

combination of double-views. The comparison of the upper section and lower one proves that removing low confidence joints like the ankle joints does not affect negatively even in ViT all-views model accuracy increased by 3%. For M-LeNet and all single views, the accuracy fluctuated about 1%. An examination of the number of parameters in Table III illustrates that the M-LeNet model exhibits a significantly lower number of parameters in comparison to the ViT model. Furthermore, the results of removing poses with lower accuracy further contribute to the reduction in the model's parameters.

V. CONCLUSION

In this paper, we proposed a lightweight multi-view skeleton-based human activity recognition (HAR) method for enhancing ambient assisted living scenarios. The suggested pipeline combines the advantages of both multi-view and skeleton-based activity recognition by fusing information from multiple RGB cameras to enhance the activity perception of the AAL system. A modified LeNet classification model and Vision Transformer were utilized for the classification task. A performance assessment of the two models and their variations on a publicly available dataset found that combining camera views can improve recognition accuracy. Furthermore, the proposed pipeline presents a more efficient and scalable solution for ambient assisted living systems, thus providing a potential for improving the safety, comfort and quality of life for AAL users. Our findings indicate that multiple recognition models, for example, *M-LeNet* and *ViT* could potentially be selected automatically based on information found in the scene, utilising the richness of captured data and information-theoretic modelling, which we plan to develop this further in our future work.

REFERENCES

[1] Y. LeCun, L. Bottou, Y. Bengio, and P. Haffner, "Gradient-based learning applied to document recognition," *Proceedings of the IEEE*, vol. 86, no. 11, pp. 2278–2324, 1998. 1, 4

[2] A. Dosovitskiy, L. Beyer, A. Kolesnikov, D. Weissenborn, X. Zhai, T. Unterthiner, M. Dehghani, M. Minderer, G. Heigold, S. Gelly *et al.*, "An image is worth 16x16 words: Transformers for image recognition at scale," *arXiv preprint arXiv:2010.11929*, 2020. 1, 2, 4, 5

[3] G. Lev, G. Sadeh, B. Klein, and L. Wolf, "Rnn fisher vectors for action recognition and image annotation," in *European Conference on Computer Vision*. Springer, 2016, pp. 833–850. 2

[4] M. Liu, H. Liu, and C. Chen, "Enhanced skeleton visualization for view invariant human action recognition," *Pattern Recognition*, vol. 68, pp. 346–362, 2017. 2

[5] S. Yan, Y. Xiong, and D. Lin, "Spatial temporal graph convolutional networks for skeleton-based action recognition," in *Thirty-second AAAI conference on artificial intelligence*, 2018. 2

[6] Z. Liu, H. Zhang, Z. Chen, Z. Wang, and W. Ouyang, "Disentangling and unifying graph convolutions for skeleton-based action recognition," in *Proceedings of the IEEE/CVF conference on computer vision and pattern recognition*, 2020, pp. 143–152. 2

[7] C. Plizzari, M. Cannici, and M. Matteucci, "Skeleton-based action recognition via spatial and temporal transformer networks," *Computer Vision and Image Understanding*, vol. 208, p. 103219, 2021. 2

[8] D. Yang, Y. Wang, A. Dantcheva, L. Garattoni, G. Francesca, and F. Bremond, "Unik: A unified framework for real-world skeleton-based action recognition," *arXiv preprint arXiv:2107.08580*, 2021. 2

[9] F. Shi, C. Lee, L. Qiu, Y. Zhao, T. Shen, S. Muralidhar, T. Han, S.-C. Zhu, and V. Narayanan, "Star: Sparse transformer-based action recognition," *arXiv preprint arXiv:2107.07089*, 2021. 2

[10] Y. Xiao, J. Chen, Y. Wang, Z. Cao, J. T. Zhou, and X. Bai, "Action recognition for depth video using multi-view dynamic images," *Information Sciences*, vol. 480, pp. 287–304, 2019. 2, 3

[11] J. Liu, A. Shahroudy, M. Perez, G. Wang, L.-Y. Duan, and A. C. Kot, "Ntu rgb+ d 120: A large-scale benchmark for 3d human activity understanding," *IEEE transactions on pattern analysis and machine intelligence*, vol. 42, no. 10, pp. 2684–2701, 2019. 2

[12] W. Kay, J. Carreira, K. Simonyan, B. Zhang, C. Hillier, S. Vijayanarasimhan, F. Viola, T. Green, T. Back, P. Natsev *et al.*, "The kinetics human action video dataset," *arXiv preprint arXiv:1705.06950*, 2017. 2

[13] H. Duan, Y. Zhao, K. Chen, D. Lin, and B. Dai, "Revisiting skeleton-based action recognition," in *Proceedings of the IEEE/CVF Conference on Computer Vision and Pattern Recognition*, 2022, pp. 2969–2978. 2, 3

[14] Y. Obinata and T. Yamamoto, "Temporal extension module for skeleton-based action recognition," in *2020 25th International Conference on Pattern Recognition (ICPR)*. IEEE, 2021, pp. 534–540. 2, 3

[15] T. Chen, D. Zhou, J. Wang, S. Wang, Y. Guan, X. He, and E. Ding, "Learning multi-granular spatio-temporal graph network for skeleton-based action recognition," in *Proceedings of the 29th ACM International Conference on Multimedia*, 2021, pp. 4334–4342. 2

[16] Y.-F. Song, Z. Zhang, C. Shan, and L. Wang, "Constructing stronger and faster baselines for skeleton-based action recognition," *IEEE Transactions on Pattern Analysis and Machine Intelligence*, 2022. 2

[17] Y. Chen, Z. Zhang, C. Yuan, B. Li, Y. Deng, and W. Hu, "Channel-wise topology refinement graph convolution for skeleton-based action recognition," in *Proceedings of the IEEE/CVF International Conference on Computer Vision*, 2021, pp. 13 359–13 368. 2

[18] A. Zeng, X. Sun, L. Yang, N. Zhao, M. Liu, and Q. Xu, "Learning skeletal graph neural networks for hard 3d pose estimation," in *Proceedings of the IEEE/CVF International Conference on Computer Vision*, 2021, pp. 11 436–11 445. 2

[19] Z. Qin, Y. Liu, P. Ji, D. Kim, L. Wang, B. McKay, S. Anwar, and T. Gedeon, "Fusing higher-order features in graph neural networks for skeleton-based action recognition," *arXiv preprint arXiv:2105.01563*, 2021. 2

[20] D. Yang, M. M. Li, H. Fu, J. Fan, and H. Leung, "Centrality graph convolutional networks for skeleton-based action recognition," *arXiv preprint arXiv:2003.03007*, 2020. 2

[21] M. R. S. Alashti, M. H. B. Abadi, P. Holthaus, C. Menon, and F. Amirabdollahian, "Human activity recognition in robocup@ home: Inspiration from online benchmarks," *UKRAS21*, 2021. 3

[22] X. Chang, "Deep multi-view learning for visual understanding," Ph.D. dissertation, Queen Mary University of London, 2019. 3

[23] Y. Bai, Z. Tao, L. Wang, S. Li, Y. Yin, and Y. Fu, "Collaborative attention mechanism for multi-view action recognition," *arXiv preprint arXiv:2009.06599*, 2020. 3

[24] M. Shahabian Alashti, M. Bamorovat Abadi, P. Holthaus, C. Menon, and F. Amirabdollahian, "Rhm-har-sk: A multi-view dataset with skeleton data for ambient assisted living research." IARIA, Mar. 2023, aCHI 2023: The Sixteenth International Conference on Advances in Computer-Human Interactions, ACHI 2023 ; Conference date: 24-04-2023 Through 28-04-2023. [Online]. Available: https://www.iaria.org/conferences2023/ACHI23.html 3, 4

[25] M. Bamorovat Abadi, M. Shahabian Alashti, P. Holthaus, C. Menon, and F. Amirabdollahian, "Rhm: Robot house multi-view human activity recognition dataset." IARIA, Mar. 2023, aCHI 2023: The Sixteenth International Conference on Advances in Computer-Human Interactions, ACHI 2023 ; Conference date: 24-04-2023 Through 28-04-2023. [Online]. Available: https://www.iaria.org/conferences2023/ACHI23.html 3

[26] K. Sun, B. Xiao, D. Liu, and J. Wang, "Deep high-resolution representation learning for human pose estimation," in *Proceedings of the IEEE/CVF conference on computer vision and pattern recognition*, 2019, pp. 5693–5703. 3

[27] S. Jin, L. Xu, J. Xu, C. Wang, W. Liu, C. Qian, W. Ouyang, and P. Luo, "Whole-body human pose estimation in the wild," in *Proceedings of the European Conference on Computer Vision (ECCV)*, 2020. 4

[28] D. C. Luvizon, D. Picard, and H. Tabia, "2d/3d pose estimation and action recognition using multitask deep learning," in *Proceedings of the IEEE conference on computer vision and pattern recognition*, 2018, pp. 5137–5146. 4

User Perceptions and Attitudes in the Data Economy and their Contradictions

Uwe V. Riss, Edith Maier
Institute for Information and Process Management
Eastern Switzerland University of Applied Sciences
St.Gallen, Switzerland
email: {uwe.riss, edith.maier}@ost.ch

Michael Doerk
Institute of Social Pedagogy and Education
Lucerne University of Applied Sciences and Arts
Lucerne, Switzerland
email: michael.doerk@hslu.ch

Ute Klotz
School of Computer Science and Information Technology
Lucerne University of Applied Sciences and Arts
Lucerne, Switzerland
email: ute.klotz@hslu.ch

***Abstract*—The data collection through digital applications in the evolving data economy is becoming an increasing risk for the users in terms of possible manipulation and misuse. Although users have obtained more rights (e.g, EU General Data Protection Regulation GDPR), there are doubts that users can actually exercise them. In parallel, the service providers' data collection becomes more ubiquitous and the tools for data analytics more powerful, which exacerbates the problem. The paper aims at identifying design targets for digital systems to better support users in this respect. The suggestions are based on the analysis of videos that three groups of workshop participants produced in a design fiction approach. The participants' goal was to anticipate the challenges of the data economy in 2037 and how they might be addressed. The aim of the study was to learn more about the perceptions and attitudes of the participants that they expressed in their videos. To this end, we analysed contradictions in the videos. These contradictions illustrate problems which the participants could not resolve. The analysis of the contradiction identifies targets for design of digital applications to better support users in the face of the challenges of the digital economy.**

***Index Terms*—privacy; data protection; contradictions; data economy.**

I. INTRODUCTION

The economy becomes increasingly data-driven and affects how users interact with digital applications. Devices become personalised and more interactive. To achieve this, companies continuously and pervasively gather and analyse high volumes of personal data. In the VA-PEPR project [1], a multidisciplinary team of experts in design, human-computer interaction, digital service economy, and computer science investigates how the private use of voice assistants or smart home devices affects people's lives, routines and attitudes [2]. These omnipresent systems are typical examples of how data-collecting devices penetrate people's lives today.

Big tech companies, such as Google, Amazon, Facebook, Apple, Baidu, Alibaba, and Tencent, which provide these systems, gain control of an increasing amount of person-related data. In this way, they expand their influence, which unsettles users, who do not fully understand the underlying data flows; users only guess the possibilities behind data collection and analytics [4]. They have mixed feelings about the aggregation [2] and distrust the data-aggregating companies [3]. Although they regard the collection of personal data as a significant risk for their privacy, they rely on digital applications every day while they try to keep pace with the digital evolution. This results in a dilemma because people are forced to choose between the use of digital applications for their convenience and the protection of their privacy [5]. Moreover, in the course of the progressive exploitation of data for commercial and other purposes, users feel increasingly manipulated by Internet content and social media [6]. This increases their discomfort even more.

All this leads to a wide range of concerns in terms of ethics, economics, politics and other areas [7]. Likewise, it leads to phenomena, such as the so-called privacy paradox: people continuously use massively data-processing applications although they are concerned about the consequences—they just have no alternative [5]. In a previous study we conducted empirical investigations to examine the feelings and observations of people using digital applications, such as voice assistants in their homes [2]. The present study uses an indirect approach to users' perceptions and attitudes in the data economy. It rather resembles the image analysis with respect to people's understanding of privacy in [8]. However, we have used videos instead of images. Videos allow people to express their views in a creative way and express their attitudes and feelings, even those that are rather subliminal.

To this end, we held a Summer School, in which we asked the participating students to create videos on the challenge "Data protection and privacy in the use of virtual assistants in 2037" with regard to the individual, organisational/economic and legislative/societal levels, respectively. Each level was handled by a group of 6 students in separate workshops. The videos were then analysed for hidden contradictions. The aim was to identify issues for which the participants had not found a unambiguous solution. We see these issues in relation to design targets for digital systems that better respect users' privacy.

The paper is organised as follows. Section II describes related work (on topics like data economy, data-based manipulation, users' perceived vulnerability, privacy by design). In Section III, we explain the methodology that we have applied in setting up the workshops and analysing the results. In Section IV, we present the results. We conclude the paper with a discussion of the findings in Section V and derive recommendations.

II. Related Work

There are several studies that have investigated the impact of the digital economy on users. They discuss and illustrate how users perceive the influence on their lives. This includes users' fear of losing control and manipulation.

Data economy: Allen states that the massive collection of data by big tech companies, such as Google, Amazon, Facebook, Apple, Baidu, Alibaba, and Tencent, presents major challenges to the users of digital applications in terms of control over personal information [9]. While initially the digitalisation was expected to bring empowerment and better lives to people, we can now observe a downside of digitalisation that challenges individual privacy and autonomy. Zuboff refers to the business model related to this as surveilance capitalism [4]. Users of digital applications do not really understand the privacy-related terms of service they agree to when they use digital applications [10]. The new world is not as bright as expected bringing forward issues in quality and reliability of data, ethics, privacy and other areas [11]. Investigations have shown that users are even willing to pay a fee to avoid the collection and commercial use of their data [12].

Data-based manipulation: After it became known that Cambridge Analytica used social networks, such as Facebook, to manipulate users by using their personal data for microtargeting [13], many users became aware of the threats related to such procedures. However, many see the danger more in the security of sensitive information (e.g., credit card numbers) than in the insidious collection of data and the building of user profiles that allow manipulation [14]. Users do not always realise that the transition between friendly persuasion and unfriendly manipulation is continuous [15].

Perceived vulnerability of users in the data economy: Users' vulnerability in the data economy has been identified as a sociotechnical problem that determines how people use systems and which choices they make [16]. It is the task of system designers to resolve users' concerns and give them more control [17]. Although the use of personal data is very common today, users and their needs are not sufficiently reflected in research and practices as studies have shown [18]. It has been argued that it is important to include users in the discourse about the evolution of the data economy [19] but this requires that we understand their situation and know what is at stake for them.

Privacy by design: The attempt to integrate privacy-preservation in the design and development of applications is known as *privacy by design* [20]. Although the principles of *privacy by design* are generally accepted, there are no clear guidelines on how to implement them [21]. It is the complexity of privacy, which causes problems for methods that realise *privacy by design* [22]. For this reason, the principles have mainly theoretical relevance [23].

III. Methodology

After we had already obtained a picture of users' perception and attitudes regarding privacy from our home studies [2], this study investigated how users imagined alternatives to the current situation in terms of privacy. Since this required a more elaborate approach, we conducted this study with a smaller group of appropriately prepared students in a Summer School that took place at the end of August 2022. The participants consisted of 18 students of the University of Applied Sciences and Arts, Lucerne, who had different backgrounds and major subjects—see Table I. As preparation for the Summer School, the students had a preceding kick-off meeting with two instructors in May 2022, where they gained a first overview of the Summer School programme on "Creativity and Future Studies". It also included pointers to the overall challenge described "Data Capitalism, Data Colonialism and Possible Future Scenarios". The students were provided with the online toolbox *becreate*, which included the web-based training "create – Free thinking, creative stimulation and ground-breaking solutions" with an introduction to the topics *creativity*, *innovation management* and instruction for *(inter)connected media learning and projects* [24]. A guideline with detailed quality criteria and indicators was offered as additional orientation. This was to ensure that each group used a comparable approach. At the end of the kick-off meeting, three tasks were assigned to the students:

1) They were asked to research four publications relevant to the given challenge and upload the sources to an online platform. In addition, they were asked to explain why they regarded the publications to be relevant.
2) They were asked to study the web-based training.
3) They were asked to produce a short video, in which they talked about their competences in the areas of creativity, innovation management and media competence and about their motivation.

Finally, the instructors assembled the teams for the different workshops in a way that ensured the best possible interdisciplinary mix and the participation of at least one person with strong media skills in each team.

The instructors also used the kick-off meeting to obtain the students' verbal consent for the use of videos, collected literature (including explanations) and other results in the VA-PEPR project. The Summer School was not compulsory for the students and their participation was voluntary. To make the results available to the project, they were stored on a research platform and password-protected. The students were informed that the results of the analysis would be anonymised and then used in the research project; the provision of data to the project was voluntary. Shortly before the start of Summer School, the students were asked again whether the videos and other work results could be used for research purposes; the access to the work results on the Internet or other generally accessible media was excluded.

The provision of the workshop results was not remunerated, however, as a special appreciation, the students were invited to an optional networking event at the end of the Summer School, where they had the opportunity to exchange experiences among each other and with the instructors as well as the accompanying researchers of the VA-PEPR project.

TABLE I. DATA PROTECTION AND PRIVACY—INDIVIDUAL LEVEL.

Group	Major Subject	Gender
1	real estate	male
1	socio-cultural studies	female
1	value network management	female
1	mechanical engineering	male
1	social pedagogy	female
1	spatial design	female
2	real estate	female
2	communication	female
2	management and law	female
2	architecture	male
2	market and consumer psychology	male
2	social work	female
3	real estate	male
3	real estate	male
3	socio-cultural studies	female
3	architecture	male
3	finance and banking	male
3	marketing	female

During the week of the Summer School students were asked to explore and answer the following questions related to the future of the data economy:

- What opportunities as well as dangers or problems will the data economy in 2037 be associated with?
- How can the challenges related to privacy and data protection in 2037 be addressed?

The latter question was split into three levels (individual, organisational/economic, legislative/societal) and assigned to one group each.

At the end of the week, each group should have produced a video as a result of the creative and discursive process as well as the documentation of the process that led to this result. The documentation should also include possible side paths or discussion threads that they had decided not to pursue.

The **video analysis** was conducted for each of the three videos in an iterative approach [25]. One researcher (R1 in Table II) described the individual scenes of each video one by one. The results were tabulated (timestamp, description) and can be found in Tables III-V. The interpretation team (R2-R4 in Table II) elaborated the core message in each scene and identified contradictions in these messages. According to [26], whole-media (audio and video) analysis results in higher accuracy, a denser description and reveals more informative reports than analysing the transcripts only. According to [27], the researchers of the interpretation team looked at core images of the scene, interpreting the content from their personal background and experience. Each researcher in the interpretation team looked for contradictions, which were then discussed and interpreted in the team. Only those contradictions that the team agreed on were included. Due to the small number of videos and the clear recognizability of the contradictions, intercoder reliability was not applied [28].

TABLE II. RESEARCHERS IN THE INTERPRETATION TEAM.

No.	Research Focus	Gender	Education
R1	Future of Work, Information Technology	female	Political Economics Information Science
R2	Digital Business Knowledge Management	male	Mathematics Computer Science
R3	Digital Health	female	Anthropology
R4	Social Work Digital health	male	Psychology

In analysing the videos, we adopted an approach in which we considered the respective future scenarios as narratives in the sense of **design fiction** [29]. This was in line with the briefing, where participants were instructed to identify a problem in the specified areas and create a video with a fictitious content that described an approach to solve current and future data protection problems [30]. Each video can be understood as a narrative of how the participants envisioned the future protection of data and privacy. Narratives reflect people's perceptions and attitudes. Moreover, they can serve as boundary objects between people with different knowledge and backgrounds [31], a factor that was relevant beacuse of the interdisciplinary teams. According to [32], narratives are most valuable if they reveal gaps and contradictions. Such contradictions point to issues that the storyteller obviously cannot easily resolve. The advantage of a narrative is that it is cognitively processed in a different way than non-fiction. Thus, the producers and consumers of narratives are more open to accept multiple meanings and possibilities, ambiguity and contradictions [33]. Similarly, the workshop participants built their contradictions (unconsciously) into their videos, as there was no obvious solution for them. Studies of contradictions have a longstanding tradition in human-computer interaction, mainly related to activity theory [34]. They have been considered a suitable tool to carve out problematic user situations [35] and serve as a source of inspiration for the development of new ideas [36].

In a final step, we conducted an **analysis of contradictions** in the videos—as indicators for antagonistic forces that are inherent in the setting and cannot be easily resolved. We looked for deeper-seated challenges that could explain why the contradictions could not be resolved. In addition, we expanded the scope of these challenges and found several dimensions that helped us to structure the results systematically.

IV. RESULTS

In the following, we present short descriptions of the three videos and the results of the subsequent analysis.

Video 1 - Individual Level (length 9 min.): The 2037 scenario assumes that all personal data, such as health or financial data, will be deposited in a personal data wallet of a newly created Federal Department of Property. The fundamental problem identified in the video's future scenario is that every data repository can be hacked, today and in the future. This is in line with the conventional wisdom in the field of IT security that attacks happen wherever a security gap opens up. The proposed solution in the scenario is simple and complex at the same time: an avatar—a digital twin of the real person—is supposed to anticipate threats to personal data and defend the user against them. It is based on artificial intelligence, which makes the avatar powerful enough to protect the user's data wallet, while also making it intelligent enough to understand the users' requirements. Cf. to Table III for scene descriptions.

TABLE III. DATA PROTECTION AND PRIVACY—INDIVIDUAL LEVEL.

Scenes of Group 1's Video
Time Stamp 00.50-01.05 In the future scenario, data ownership is handled the same way online and offline.
Time Stemp 01.12-01.42 A persona logs into the personal wallet using Face ID or biometric data. Personal data (e.g., health, insurance, financial data) are stored in a wallet at the Federal Department.
Time Stamp 01.43-01.59 The account is hacked: It is explained that even in 2037 not everything works without problems.
Time Stamp 03.10-03.33 The personal problems related to data are mentioned: Addiction and social media, plus the unresolved legal situation and capitalism.
Time Stamp 04.30-05.13 For the future scenario "ownership and property", an IT expert is interviewed: he sees the same problems as today also in 2037, i.e., passwords are revealed or databases are hacked.
Time Stamp 05.18-05.40 An IT expert: Security measures must be further developed, especially encryption procedures. Quantum computers bring new uncertainty.In addition, users should always remain up to date with the latest technology due to the constant development of the digital world.
Time Stamp 06.16-06.43 A well-known scientist is quoted warning against quantum computers. However, such computers do not yet exist.
Time Stamp 06.46-07.30 Blockchain technology plays a crucial role in protection, which is constantly being further developed by researchers.
Time Stamp 08.04-08.44 Two solutions to close security gaps in the future are proposed: (1) use of multi-factor authentication and (2) more education, T&Cs should become more user-friendly.
Time Stamp 08.46-09.15 An avatar (AI) is introduced (as clone of the real person) that prevents the hacking of the user's data.

In the video of Group 1 (Table III), we find the following contradictions: (1) "Central repository, data must be controlled by the state" (Time Stamp 01.12-01.42) *vs.* "Distributed repositories, data must not be controlled by a single institution" (blockchain) (Time Stamp 06.46-07.30), (2) "Technology is a threat to the user" (quantum computing) (Time Stamp 06.16-06.43) *vs.* "Technology is a friend of the user" (avatars) (Time Stamp 08.46-09.15). If we look at these contradictions in more detail, we find in (1) the problem of protecting data, which is not a question of where the repository is located; a state-owned repository can be hacked in the same way as a private one. The critical point behind the contradiction is the confidence in the security and transparency of the storage. In the case of the state-owned repository users simply transfer their security problem to an authority. In the case of blockchain, it is the dispersion of data that ensures security because the data are everywhere and nowhere. The points that are important for users are that they **know that their data are secure and protected by an institution that is more powerful than themselves**. This is also closely related to contradiction (2), which reflects the users' attitude towards technology. On the one hand, users are aware that digital technology is required to protect data. On the other hand, they see new technology as a threat to the security of their data. It is not about *good* and *bad* technology but the *same* technology can be used in both ways. The insight is that **we need technology to cope with the dangers of technology**. However, users need support to keep up in the race for safety excellence.

Video 2 - Organisational Level (length 12.5 min.): The future scenario in this video starts with a job interview, in which the recruiter has access to personal information about the female applicant gleaned from social media during the interview (e.g. her wish to have children or her political opinion). On the basis of the provided data, she is rejected. Discrimination against the applicant is the central theme of the video. It seems that the students identify themselves with the female victim: they declare the issue of discrimination to be a major future problem, which is also associated with the digital divide in society. Although an explicit expression of trust or distrust in data capitalism or technology is not mentioned, people realise that they have to deal with it in some way. The proposed solution is a virtual assistant that suggests with whom to share data or which personal data should be deleted. It remains unclear who runs the data platform, the state or private companies. Further scenes show how the virtual assistant makes recommendations. For example, the woman should not eat chocolate because she is pregnant, she should not smoke because that might make her health insurance premiums rise, she should not drink beer because that might deteriorate her social ranking. It looks like she accepts the advice unconditionally and uncritically. The conclusion is that the individual must decide to be *socially* compliant or non-compliant. Cf. to Table IV for scene descriptions.

In the video of Group 2 (Table IV), we see the following contradictions: (1) "Use of personal data is in users' interest" (Time Stamp 03.09-03.24) *vs.* "Use of personal data is in the interest of companies" (health insurance) (Time Stamp 02.48-02.58), (2) "Users can control data-based discrimination" (deleting personal data) (Time Stamp Time Stamp 12.25-12.38) *vs.* "Users become victims of data-based discrimination" (training bias in data that are not their own) (Time Stamp 04.06-05.14). The contradiction (1) is related to the purposes for which person-related data are used. Intelligent assistants can either recommend suitable solutions to users' problems based on their available profiles or they serve other parties' interests to the harm of the users. In connection with the problem of trust in intelligent assistants, there is the additional

TABLE IV. DATA PROTECTION AND PRIVACY—ORGANISATIONAL LEVEL.

Scenes of Group 2's Video
Time Stamp 01.50-02.04 The future scenario starts with a job interview in which the interviewer uses personal background information about the applicant (e.g. desire to have children, political orientation), which leads to a rejection.
Time Stamp 02.34-02.48 The same person wants to buy chocolate and asks her voice assistant for the nearest kiosk. The voice assistant answers that the protagonist should not eat chocolate because she is pregnant.
Time Stamp 02.48-02.58 The question whether one should rather smoke instead of chocolate is answered in the negative. The reason given is health and possible increases in health insurance premiums.
Time Stamp 02.59-03.08 When asking for a beer, the assistant points out the negative effects in the social ranking.
Time Stamp 03.09-03.24 The request for a holiday with the order to book a flight to Hawaii is refused because the account balance is too low.
Time Stamp 03.24-03.35 It is noted that this is an aspect of discrimination.
Time Stamp 03.36-04.05 In further analysis, further future scenarios are developed with the result that discrimination will be a major problem in 2023.
Time Stamp 04.06-05.14 Examples of discrimination through digitalisation are listed. This affects women in application processes, as the algorithm tries to match the company and the applicant, while the training data contain a bias.
Time Stamp 07.00-09.47 In three interviews, the interviewees are asked about the dangers and opportunities of data mining by large companies.
Time Stamp 09.48-11.52 Possible solutions for 2037: a label to guarantee privacy, people themselves determining the algorithms, educational offers in terms of prevention, research projects in the field of data protection, customers who can control access to their data at any time.
Time Stamp 11.59-12.23 Discrimination in the job interview can be prevented by avoided by a deliberate decision which data are shared.
Time Stamp 12.25-12.38 A personal intelligent voice assistent gets the order to delete certain personal data.

question of the extent to which users should bow to the supposedly *optimal* advice of intelligent assistants. Users may feel they have to bow to the applications, mostly overlooking the limitations of such technologies. This raises the question of **privacy in relation to intelligent applications**. It raises the question to which extent we transfer responsibilities to technical applications. The contradiction (2) reflects the desire to influence the impact of data use, while at the same time it is clear that such data use must be transparent to be controllable—users can hardly control a bias in training data. The central theme behind this contradiction is the wish to **understand and control the use of data in digital applications**. Such control requires transparency and explainability, which has already been identified as a key research topic in artificial intelligence research [37].

Video 3 - Societal Level (length 15 min.): The future scenario describes a social principle of "digital first" or "digital only", i.e., you must be online or you are excluded from society. The question is raised whether social life can or should only take place online. Social media play a central role in society, but they are organised in a decentralised way in the sense of communities (not in the sense of big tech). It is also difficult to distinguish between true and untrue information. Various solutions for dealing with misinformation are proposed. One is that users categorise posts as fact, opinion or scientifically verified statement. Other solutions include a traffic light system based on a central assessment and a point system which involves sanctions for misbehaviour by spreading misinformation. Two people from two opposing political parties are asked about the problem: one person wants a solution controlled by the state, while the other person wants as little state influence as possible and insists on freedom of expression. Finally, the importance of this issue for democracy is highlighted. Cf. to Table V for scene descriptions.

In the video of Group 3 (Table V), we see the following contradictions: (1) "Credibility criteria for information are objective" (Time Stamp 08.30-10.00) *vs.* "Credibility criteria for information are subjective" (Time Stamp 08.30-10.00), (2) "Information shared in social media is democratic" (liberal view) (Time Stamp 03.52-05.16) *vs.* "Information shared in social media in manipulative" (Time Stamp 06.40-08.10). Regarding contradiction (1), the solution to the problem of fake news proposed by the students primarily suggests that there is a clear distinction between objective *truths* and subjective *opinions*. At the same time, this categorization is conducted by individual users and is therefore subjective, which raises the question of clear criteria for such a categorization. More likely, it is a social issue rather than one that can be based on technical means or individual opinion. Thus, we need **social processes to ensure the trustworthiness of content**. We must learn how to establish such processes. Contradiction (2), on the one hand, refers to the fact that anyone can contribute to social media, while, on the other hand, it is becoming increasingly apparent that such possibilities open the doors for various kinds of manipulation (example: filter bubble). The problem is similar to the one in contradiction (1), but its focus is rather on the mechanisms in social media than on the assessment of content quality. Some social media groups are more like conspiracy circles than fora for public discourse. This raises the question whether such groups increase or weaken users' autonomy as responsible members of the society. It must be ensured that there are mechanisms that **enhance users' autonomy**, for example, by resolving information fragmentation and support open exchange since openness appears to be an essential precondition for better user control.

V. DISCUSSION

The videos describe issues that the students perceive as most urgent today or expect to become critical challenges in 2037. The students have dealt extensively with the subject matter in their preparation, so that we do not assume that the occurring contradictions were merely inaccuracies. Instead, we assume more fundamental issues behind these contradictions. That this assumption is not unfounded is illustrated by the so-called privacy paradox; it describes that people express concerns about the violation of their privacy by big digital

TABLE V. DATA PROTECTION AND PRIVACY—SOCIETAL LEVEL.

Scenes of Group 3's Video
Time Stamp 0.08-01.06 Scenario in the year 2037: A reporter wants to interview randomly selected people on the above topic. The person interviewed (a group member) answers reluctantly. The person expresses that he or she distrusts the truthfulness of the news and has difficulties understanding topics, that classic media (e.g. books) are no longer used.
Time Stamp 01.12-01.33 Description of a utopian vision of the future in which life takes place only in digital space.
Time Stamp 01.51-02.14 The task and, in part, the methodological procedure are explained.
Time Stamp 02.30-02.50 Five thematic areas are defined: (1) Addiction/Internet, (2) Invasion of privacy/sensitive data, (3) Misinformation/Consumption, (4) Influence/economy (advertising), (5) Misinformation/State/Politics, from which the topic misinformation is selected.
Time Stamp 02.51-02.58 Question: How can society curb misinformation on social media?
Time Stamp 03.25-03.50 Future scenario in 2037: reality and the internet are merging more and more, you can't escape it. You can no longer be offline. Social media are increasingly dominated by communities, it is no longer clear what is true or false.
Time Stamp 03.52-05.16 Interview with two male politicians on the subject of misinformation in 2037: (1) older politician: the state must bear responsibility. (for what remains unclear); (2) younger politician: liberal thoughts are important. Filters mean a bit of censorship. Providers should set as few filters as possible.
Time Stamp 05.30-06.20 Future scenario 2037: The blending of internet and reality leads to social division; certain interest groups turn away from others; money is replaced by collected data; data in social media feeds rating system; social media become more and more personalised.
Time Stamp 06.40-08.10 Five main problems in future scenarios: (1) Power shift to social media and loss of control over the distribution of information; (2) Dependence on social media and more and more time spent using social media and electronic devices (danger of filter bubbles); (3) Societal change through digitalisation depends on more and more population groups; (4) Division of society through digitalisation; (5) Misinformation that can no longer be controlled. Misinformation is seen as the biggest problem.
Time Stamp 08.30-10.00 Approaches to the issue of social media and misinformation: (1) Self-tagging of social media posts: This distinguishes fact, opinion and scientifically verified statement; (2) Traffic light system distinguishes the truth content of posts; (3) Point system after repeated publication of fake news blocks the responsible persons; (4) The state punishes misinformation more severely (deterrence).
Time Stamp 10.02-10.55 Interviews on possible solution: very time-consuming (time, staff); traffic light system is a good idea, clearly visible.
Time Stamp 11.02-13.00 Conclusion: Relation to democracy is important Main finding: Flexibility/adaptability is required, new inventions, one has to be open as a human being so that society can move forward. Cooperation between organisations is important.
Time Stamp 13.00-14.00 Retrospective: View to 2027 is limited, we have to look further ahead.
Time Stamp 14.00-14.53 Supplementary information.

service providers but don't show a corresponding reaction in their behaviour [38]. Group 1's contradiction (2) is related to it. In the analysis of the paradox, Solove explained that users practically have no other choice than to surrender to circumstances that are perceived as a threat to their privacy [5]. This is one example of how contradictions can point to broader problems.

In order to check the generalisability of the results we compared them to results of previous studies that we had conducted with another group of users, who were more diverse (e.g., between the ages of 17 and over 70, lower as well as higher affinity to technology)—for more details refer to [2]. In this study, we identified the following connections (The numbering of contradictions follows Table VI):

C1.1: Ambivalence towards data retention and the role of the state corresponds to recent studies that found that the Swiss population tends to trust their government (due to their effort in the COVID-19 crisis) [39]. On the other hand, there is a fundamental distrust in general particularly in terms of surveillance [40]. Both views were also reflected in our studies of attitudes towards voice assistants.

C1.2: The ambiguous attitudes towards the dangers of digital technology as friend or foe correspond to our previous studies of voice assistants. Some people had developed an almost personal relationship to their voice assistant whereas others remained suspicious of them—some even stopped using them at all. Since users did not consider these voice assistants as essential for their daily life stopping the use was easy. This does not apply to more important digital applications, where the conflict persists.

C2.2: The conflict regarding control also appeared in the use of voice assistants, where some users switched them off if they wanted to make sure that their utterances remain private. Some participants completely banned voice assistants from certain rooms, e.g., bedroom or bathroom. Apart from switching off the device they were never completely sure what happened to their conversations, that is, they did not have the feeling to control the use of their data.

TABLE VI. CONTRADICTIONS IN THE VIDEOS.

C1.1: "Central storage, data must be controlled by the state" *vs.* "Distributed storage, data must not be controlled by a single institution" **C1.2:** "Technology is a threat to the user (quantum computing)" *vs.* "Technology is a friend of the user"
C2.1: "Use of personal data is in users' interest" *vs.* "Use of personal data in in the interest of companies" **C2.2:** "Users can control data-based discrimination" *vs.* "Users become victims of data-based discrimination "
C3.1: "Credibility criteria for information are objective" *vs.* "Credibility criteria for information are subjective" **C3.2:** "Information sharing in social media is democratic" *vs.* "Information sharing in social media in manipulative"

Connections to other contradictions were less obvious, which was generally due to the limited intelligence and performance of current voice assistants. For example, participants did not think that the assistants would harm their autonomy due to manipulation, although they recorded enough data to produce a very detailed personal profile. Equal access to information was no problem either since most information sources on voice assistants were free. Similarly, the content was not regarded as a problem since a considerable part of the information provided came from Wikipedia or other well-known sources. However, we can imagine these three aspects might become problematic once voice assistants are misused by parties with a polarising agenda and content of unclear origin or if users only get high-value information if they pay for it.

The value of contradictions for design is that they provide insights into users' attitudes towards data-related issues. The contradictions in the proposed solutions reveal deeper-seated problems. It is important for the design of effective solutions that these are taken into account.

To provide better insight in the design targets that might tackle the problems we have derived general challenges from the contradictions und categorized them in various dimensions. One dimension refers to the different manifestations of information (as thing, as knowledge, as process) according to Buckland [41]—according to [42], we regard the knowledge dimension to be related to the application of information. The second dimension refers to the distinction between primarily individual or social concern. The results are compiled in Table VII. Moreover, we have included examples of design targets that address the challenges in the design of applications that use personal data.

TABLE VII. CATEGORISATION OF CHALLENGES

	Information-as-thing	
	Individual	***Social***
Challenge	data ownership	equal access to technology
Design Target	user sovereignty over their data	infrastructure supporting technology updates
	Information-as-knowledge	
	Individual	***Social***
Challenge	control over data use	avoidance of discrimination
Design Targett	transparency regarding data use	evidence of unbiased data
	Information-as-process	
	Individual	***Social***
Challenge	information reliability	information autonomy
Design Target	systematic reliability checks	control of ethical information usage

Finally, we regard the suggested design targets in more detail to illustrate how the challenges might be addressed:

- **"User sovereignty over their data"**: Currently, the business models of most digital service providers take user data in exchange for their digital services. Thess business models are increasingly being distrusted due to privacy concerns [43]. The measures that have been suggested so far put the burden on the users, who on the whole cannot cope with it, e.g., GDPR [44]. The only effective measure seems to be that users retain full control over their data. For example, data trustee solutions have been suggested to supported users in protecting their data [45]. System designers should take the role of data trustees in digital applications into account.
- **"Infrastructure supporting technology security updates"**: Users cannot keep pace with the developments in cyber security, which appears to be a technological race between defenders and attackers of cyber security. Therefore, users need a system infrastructure that automatically installs all relevant system updates. Partially, systems already provide automatic updates but automatic technology updates should become mandatory and part of the infrastructure.
- **"Transparency regarding data use"**: Use of person-related data is necessary to individualise digital services, e.g., for recommendations. Users have to understand what this individualisation means and what their data are used for. System designers should take care of such transparency.
- **"Evidence of unbiased data"**: Bias in data-trained machine learning applications is well known, e.g., [47]. Measures have been suggested to avoid bias [48]. Data used to train algorithms should be checked for known biases and certified accordingly if necessary.
- **"Systematic reliability checks"**: To which degree information is trustworthy is often difficult to decide because even correct and validated information can be misleading if it is used in the wrong context. Designers must provide each user the opportunity to contribute to such checks and make the sources of information transparent. Systematic checking means that a procedure must be set in operation that ensures a high probability of detecting content of low quality.
- **"Control of ethical informational usage"**: Subliminal manipulation of users by data-based applications depends on the depth of available user profiles and the quality of algorithms. Protecting user data is already a decisive step for preventing manipulation but cannot prevent manipulation completely [14]. Protection also requires checks of the purposes, for which algorithms were trained. System designers should support users in conducting such checks. The purpose of data use should be made as transparent as possible.

The contradictions that we have identified reflect the participants' perceptions and attitudes with respect to their data and privacy protection requirements. The respective narratives helped them to express their views in a less restrictive way that show the tensions they experience. Thus, we were able to expand the insights we had gained in the earlier in-home studies. Nevertheless, further investigations of the multifaceted challenges are required. It is obvious that individual users cannot deal with these challenges on their own but need qualified institutions and suitable infrastructures that support them. The current study only had the aim to point at a first set of the existing issues of data-based applications. They are likely to represent a small spectrum of possible issues resulting from other scenarios. However, they already give an impression of the effort that is required to reconcile users' privacy interests and economic demands in the future.

ACKNOWLEDGMENT

This study was funded by the Swiss National Science Foundation (SNF) project VA-PEPR, ref. no. CRSII5_189955.

REFERENCES

[1] "VA-PEPR - How do we live in the omnipresence of voice assistants?" https://sites.hslu.ch/va-pepr/en/ [retrieved: March, 2023]

[2] E. Maier, M. Doerk, M. Muri, U. Reimer, and U. V. Riss, "What does privacy mean to users of voice assistants in their homes?" Proceedings of the ETHICOMP, pp. 300–314, 2022.

[3] B. Dembrow, "Investing in human futures: How big tech and social media giants abuse privacy and manipulate consumerism," University of Miami Business Law, vol. 30, no. 3, pp. 324–349, 2021.

[4] S. Zuboff, The age of surveillance capitalism. London, UK: Profile books Ltd, 2019.

[5] D. J. Solove, "The myth of the privacy paradox," George Washington Law Review, vol. 89, no.1, pp. 1—51, 2021.

[6] N. Andalibi and J. Buss, "The human in emotion recognition on social media," Proceedings of the CHI Conference on Human Factors in Computing Systems, pp. 1–16, 2020.

[7] F. Lauf et al., "Linking data sovereignty and data economy," Wirtschaftsinformatik 2022 Proceedings, 19, 2022.

[8] M. Oates, Y. Ahmadullah, A. Marsh, C. Swoopes, S. Zhang, R. Balebako, and L. F. Cranor, "Turtles, locks, and bathrooms: Understanding mental models of privacy through illustration," Proceedings on Privacy Enhancing Technologies, pp. 5–32, 2018.

[9] A. L. Allen, "Protecting one's own privacy in a big data economy," Harvard Law Review Forum, vol. 130, pp. 71–78, 2016.

[10] C. L. White and Boatwright, "Social media ethics in the data economy," Public Relations Review, vol. 46, no. 5, Article 101980, 2020.

[11] K. Löfgren and C. W. R. Webster, "The value of big data in government," Big Data & Society, vol. 7, no. 1, 2020.

[12] S. A. Elvy, "Paying for privacy and the personal data economy," Columbia Law Review, vol. 117, no. 6, pp. 1369–1459, 2017.

[13] K. Ward, "Social networks, the 2016 US presidential election, and Kantian ethics," Journal of media ethics, vol. 33, no. 3, pp.133–148, 2018.

[14] U. V. Riss, E. Maier, and M. Doerk, "Perceived risks of the data economy," Proceedings of the ETHICOMP, pp. 413–427, 2022.

[15] K. Vold and J. Whittlestone, "Privacy, autonomy, and personalised targeting," in Report on Data, Privacy, and the Individual in the Digital Age, by IE University's Center for the Governance of Change, Madrid, Spain: IE University, 2019.

[16] M. W. Skirpan, T. Yeh, and C. Fiesler, "What's at stake: Characterizing risk perceptions of emerging technologies," Proceedings of the CHI Conference on Human Factors in Computing Systems, pp. 1–12, 2018.

[17] A. Adams and M. Angela Sasse, "Privacy in multimedia communications," in People and computers XV—Interaction without frontiers. London, UK: Springer, pp. 49–64, 2001.

[18] M. M. Rantanen and J. Koskinen, "Humans of the European data economy ecosystem-what do they demand from a fair data economy?" Proceedings of IFIP International Conference on Human Choice and Computers. Springer, Cham, pp. 327–339, 2022.

[19] S. Knaapi-Junnila, M. M. Rantanen and J. Koskinen, "Are you talking to me?" Information Technology & People, vol. 35, no. 8, pp. 292–310, 2022.

[20] A. Cavoukian and J. Jonas, "Privacy by design in the age of big data," 2012. https://www.iab.org/wp-content/IAB-uploads/2011/03/fred_carter.pdf [retrieved: March, 2023]

[21] M. Colesky, J. H. Hoepman, and C. Hillen, "A critical analysis of privacy design strategies," Proceedings of IEEE security and privacy workshops (SPW), pp. 33–40, 2016.

[22] M. Alshammari and A. Simpson, "Towards a principled approach for engineering privacy by design," Privacy Technologies and Policy: 5th Annual Privacy Forum, APF 2017, Revised Selected Paper, pp. 161–177, 2017.

[23] S. Barth, D. Ionita, and P. Harte, "Understanding Online Privacy—A Systematic Review of Privacy Visualizations and Privacy by Design Guidelines," ACM Computing Surveys (CSUR), vol. 55, no. 3, pp. 1–37, 2022.

[24] M. Doerk and W. Zenker, "(Inter)connected media-learning," in Problembasiertes Lernen, Projektorientierung, forschendes Lernen & beyond, J. Weißenböck, W. Gruber, C. F. Freisleben-Teutscher and J. Haag, Eds., pp. 127–139, 2018.

[25] H. Knoblauch, R. Tuma, and B. Schnettler, "Video analysis and videography," in The Sage Handbook of Qualitative Data Analysis, U. Flick, Ed., pp. 2—24, 2018.

[26] D. T. Markle, R. E. West, and P. J. Rich, " Beyond transcription: Technology, change, and refinement of method," in Qualitative Social Research, Vol. 12, No. 3, Article 21, 2011.

[27] G. Rose, Visual methodologies: An introduction to researching with visual materials. London, UK: SAGE.

[28] A. Nili, M. Tate, and A. Barros, "A Critical Analysis of Inter-Coder Reliability Methods in Information Systems Research," Proceedings of ACIS, no. 99, 2017.

[29] B. Sterling, "Cover story design fiction," interactions, vol. 16, no. 3, pp. 20–24, 2009.

[30] P. Coulton and J. G. Lindley, "More-than human centred design: Considering other things," The Design Journal, vol. 22, no.4, pp. 463–481, 2019.

[31] R. J. Boland Jr and R. V. Tenkasi, "Perspective making and perspective taking in communities of knowing," Organization Science, vol. 6, no.4, pp. 350–372, 1995.

[32] C. Booth, M. Rowlinson, P. Clark, A. Delahaye, and S. Procte, "Scenarios and counterfactuals as modal narratives," Futures, vol. 41, no. 2, pp. 87–95, 2009.

[33] G. Lively, "Narrative: Telling social futures," Routledge Handbook of Social Futures, London, UK: Routledge, pp. 224-232, 2021.

[34] Y. Engeström, Learning by expanding. Cambridge, UK: Cambridge University Press.

[35] S. Bødker and C. N. Klokmose, "The human–artifact model: An activity theoretical approach to artifact ecologies," Human–Computer Interaction, vol. 26, no. 4, pp. 315–371, 2011.

[36] P. Mogensen, "Towards a provotyping approach in systems development," Journal of Information Systems, vol. 4, no. 1, pp. 31–53, 1992.

[37] W. Brunotte, A. Specht, L. Chazette, and K. Schneider, "Privacy explanations–a means to end-user trust," Journal of Systems and Software, vol. 195, Article 111545, 2023.

[38] P. A. Norberg, D. R. Horne, and D. A. Horne, "The privacy paradox: Personal information disclosure intentions versus behaviors," Journal of consumer affairs, vol. 41, no. 1, pp. 100–126, 2007.

[39] Y. Willi, G. Nischik, D. Braunschweiger, and M. Pütz, "Responding to the COVID-19 crisis," Tijdschrift voor economische en sociale geografie, vol. 111, no. 3, pp. 302–317, 2020.

[40] L. A. Viola and P. Laidler. Trust and Transparency in an Age of Surveillance. London, UK and New York, NY: Routledge, 2021.

[41] M. A. Buckland, "Information as thing," Journal of the American Society for Information Science, vol. 42, no. 5, pp. 351–360, 1991.

[42] D. J. Saab and U. V. Riss, "Information as ontologization," Journal of the American Society for Information Science and Technology, vol. 62, no. 11, pp. 2236–2246, 2011.

[43] N. Couldry and U. A. Mejias. "Data colonialism: Rethinking big data's relation to the contemporary subject," Television & New Media, vol. 20, no. 4, pp. 336–349, 2019.

[44] I. van Ooijen and H. U. Vrabec, "Does the GDPR enhance consumers' control over personal data? An analysis from a behavioural perspective," Journal of consumer policy, vol. 42, pp. 91–107, 2019.

[45] W. Kerber. " From (horizontal and sectoral) data access solutions towards data governance systems," SSRN Electronic Journal, 2020.

[46] R. Buch, D. Ganda, P. Kalola, and N. Borad, "World of cyber security and cybercrime," Recent Trends in Programming Languages, vol. 4, no. 2, pp. 18-–23, 2017.

[47] N. Mehrabi, F. Morstatter, N. Saxena, K. Lerman, and A. Galstyan, "A survey on bias and fairness in machine learning," ACM Computing Surveys (CSUR), vol. 54, no. 6, pp. 1–35, 2012.

[48] C. DeBrusk, "The risk of machine-learning bias (and how to prevent it)," MIT Sloan Management Review, 2018. https://sloanreview.mit.edu/article/the-risk-of-machine-learning-bias-and-how-to-prevent-it [retrieved: March, 2023]

Comparing the Effect of Different Styles of Voice on Children's Engagement with a Virtual Robot: A Preliminary Study

Romain Vallée
Enchanted Tools & LIG - CNRS
Paris, France
email: romain@enchanted.tools

Lucas Prégaldiny
Enchanted Tools
Paris, France
email: lucas@enchanted.tools

Véronique Aubergé
LIG - CNRS
Grenoble, France
email: veronique.auberge@univ-grenoble-alpes.fr

Émilie Cénac
Sème!
Rennes, France
email: emilie.cenac0@gmail.com

Serge Tisseron
IERHR
Paris, France
email: serge.tisseron@gmail.com

Olivier Aycard
LIG - CNRS
Grenoble, France
email: aycardol@univ-grenoble-alpes.fr

***Abstract*—This paper aims at understanding the influence of prosody during a child-virtual robot interaction. We provide and analyze an experiment including 30 children aged 6 to 10, who interact with several virtual robots in a video game. This preliminary study highlights the impact of voice on children, as they tend to prefer an expressive voice using non-lexical vocal elements rather than an acted voice simulating stereotypical synthetic voices.**

***Index Terms*—human-virtual robot interaction, human-agent interaction, socio-affective prosody, trust with children, non-verbal speech.**

I. Introduction

Prosody (the sum of phonic elements such as intonation, pitch, rhythm, vocal timbre etc.) is a key element of human interaction, and thus a major issue in human interaction with a physical or virtual communicating machine [1]. Prior studies have shown that the "breathy voice" prosodic factor, characterized by a lax vocal tract and a very relaxed control of the glottis, is an intrinsic marker of relational proximity [2]–[4]. It has been shown that the prosody of speech — generated by the gestures of the vocal tract — and holistically the prosody of gestures of the communicative body elements orients and feeds the nature of the relationship between humans — and thus between prosody-emitting machines and humans [5]. The prosodic artifacts of speech synthesis systems, without any analysis of the markers and relational effects of these artifacts [4], have gradually entered into everyday life until the massive diffusion of these synthetic voices in GPS systems and in voice assistants embodied by "smart speakers", such as Amazon Echo or Google Home. These voices, whose characteristics are more and more often in the "breathy" stereotype [6], seem to be becoming cultural references for the voices of virtual or robotic agents, especially among adults. The prosody of these Alexa-like voices (i.e., breathy, intimate, etc.) is distinct from prosodies of vernacular situations such as play, especially in adult-child situations. The type of relationship these Alexa-like voices build with humans has not been extensively studied and is poorly understood, even though these voices have demonstrated their enduring appeal. Researchers such as Tisseron [7] and Sparrow [8] warn about the ethically toxic effects of voices that trigger an illusion of intimacy and trust invariable to any situation, without any other expressive mark.

Yet, as Vinciarelli et al. [9] or Hofstetter and Keevallik [10] have shown, non-lexical speech primitives (i.e., not containing words) convey relational roles, attitudes, intentions, mental states, emotions, moods and other socio-affects, and build a relationship by guiding its value (e.g., the altruistic relationship without dominance [11], [12]). Some speech synthesis systems offer voices which include non-lexical elements, and some robots implement them (such as Paro or Spoony), but without relying on a fine understanding of these vocal elements and their effects on the engagement and relational nature evoked, in consistency with the lexicalized prosody.

This paper proposes to the Human-Computer Interaction community a reflection on the still under-researched importance of speech posody in virtual agents and robots. In Section II, we introduce the research question and motivation behind the study. In Section III, we present the experimental design and methodology. In Section IV, we report the results of the study and discuss our indicators and potential biases. Finally, in Section V, we draw provisional conclusions and outline directions for future research.

II. Objectives

The long-term goal of our research is to understand how strong and how is established (with what nature - in particular, trust) the engagement in the interaction between a human and a robot, through the strong and weak prosodic signals conveyed within an overall relationship by all elements of the body, including the vocal tract. The adjective *prosodic* is assumed here in its extension to all body signals, not restricted to the speech prosody. In this very first step presented here, we focus only on the voice (no variation of other body gestures), and only on the invariable *breathy voice* stereotype (Alexa type), in comparison to a non-breathy but overly expressive voice (to oppose it very clearly to the always "breathy" and confident voice, friendly but unresponsive to interactional changes) with or without non-lexical vocal elements. In order for this caricature to be ecologically relevant, and also because the "breathy" stereotype is essentially intended for adults, we proposed this prosodic contrast on a virtual robot interacting with children during a playful task - a pretextual cooking game.

In this interaction protocol, we used three different vocal profiles, all acted by the same female comedian [13]:

- Voice A - Colloquial enunciation, aiming for a playful, dynamic style, exaggeratedly child-like cartoon voice: modal or tense voice (tensed), fast-paced, high pitched (mean fundamental frequency F0 = 320 Hz)
- Voice B - Same instructions and prosodic values as voice A, but including non-lexical socio-affective vocal primitives consistent with the global prosody (vocal bursts, grunts, onomatopoeia, etc.) (mean F0 = 320 Hz)
- Voice C - An acted voice simulating "stereotypical" synthetic voices (e.g., Alexa), i.e., globally breathy without attitude variations and without non-lexical vocal elements: systematically breathy voice, slow rhythm, lower pitch (mean F0=250 Hz)

Our research hypothesis is as follows: In a playful cooking task involving children interacting with virtual robots, a robot using an expressive voice and non-lexical speech elements will elicit more engagement, trust or interest than a robot using only lexical speech elements and a constant prosodic modality. An ethical issue of this work will be to measure the nature and strength of the installed relationship in order to make explicit in future commercial product, how the robot engages and bonds with the people it interacts with (note that as far as we know, none of the currently available conversational agents warn about the nature and the strength of the relationship created with their users). Thus, according to the specific uses (e.g., health or service) and the targeted audience (e.g., fragile, young or elderly), these warnings will be taken into account so that the ethical validity or invalidity of the implementation can be determined contextually.

III. MATERIALS AND METHOD

In this section, we describe the division of participants in three groups and the procedure used to gather data, involving a vocal interactive game.

A. Participants

The participants of our research were voluntary children visiting the Cité des Sciences et de l'Industrie in Paris. Thanks to the Laboratoire des Usages en Technologies d'Information Numériques (LUTIN), we recruited 30 children between the ages of 6 and 10. The gender distribution was 35% girls / 65% boys, with an average age of 7.8 years (± 1.7 SD). We set up 3 groups of 10 children. The A/B group interacted only with voice profiles A & B, the B/C group with the profiles B & C , and the A/C group with the profiles A & C. Presenting only 2 voice profiles per child seemed necessary to limit the child's cognitive load. All interactions occurred in French, and were translated to English for this article.

B. Method

a) Description of the procedure for a participant The research protocol described below was submitted to the multi-disciplinary ethics committee of the Grenoble Alpes University (CERGA), which analyzed and evaluated it positively. Two experimenters intervene in the experimentation room: one in charge of guiding the child through the task, and another in charge of the "Wizard of Oz" procedure, giving the child the impression that the virtual robots were understanding the child's requests. The child sits on a chair in front of a screen where the game is projected. Shown in Fig. 1, the game consists of making a virtual cooking recipe with the help of two virtual robots who bring to the player the 6 ingredients needed to make a chocolate cake.

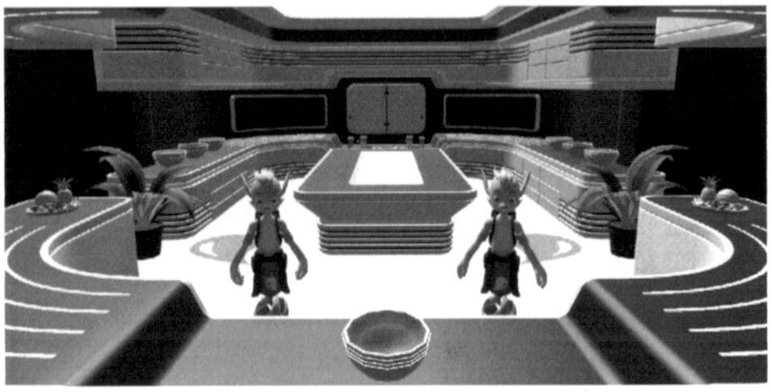

Fig. 1. Screenshot of the game, with the two virtual characters.

The experimenter first asks the child a few open-ended questions before starting the game (about their background with video games, cooking, robots) and then at the end about their experience of the game. It is made clear to the child that there are no right or wrong answers and that they must answer according to what they have seen or felt in the game. When the game starts, both virtual robots welcome the child at the same time. The experimenter then asks the child to pick (using a counting-out rhyme) the robot which will start the task and fetch the first ingredient. The robots then interact successively with the child to fetch ingredients. The game unfolds at the child's own pace, through their vocal statements, on which the "Wizard of Oz" experimenter bases the triggering of the different sequences of the game. At the end of the game, both robots say goodbye to the child at the same time. Note that when the two robots speak at the same time (only at the beginning and end of the game), a slight delay (about 100 ms) between the 2 voices is used, to make the voices more distinguishable. The average duration of the game is about 4 minutes. The progress of the task is recorded by a webcam (audio and video) located under the projection screen. Finally, two boxes physically present in the experimentation room are placed under each virtual robot projected on the screen, each box containing stickers representing the character under which it is located (the characters differ only by the direction of the symbol which decorates their apron). At the end of the experiment, the experimenter asks the child to take a sticker of the virtual robot they prefer from one of the two boxes, to keep a souvenir of the game. This forces the child to make a choice between the two virtual robots presented (contrary to the preliminary questions asked to the child where the answers can be multiple without requiring a final choice). In this choice between two stickers, we also wish to mobilize the body and to see the choice which results from this request which is not only addressed to the mind (as it was the case in the previous questions where the body was not solicited). We believe that the reasons that lead a child to choose one of the virtual robots over the other may not be easily conscientizable and that the conscious representations that the child has of the robot do not necessarily induce a given behavior towards the robot.

b) Avoiding potential biases Apart from the differences in speech profiles between the two virtual robots, we made sure that the robots' animations and the elements of the game's virtual kitchen decor were as symmetrical as possible. Moreover, different potential biases (related to the child's age, gender or laterality, their number of interactions with each robot. . .) have been identified. We will be vigilant to neutralize at best these biases in future analyses.

IV. RESULTS AND DISCUSSIONS

All the children said they enjoyed the game, 95% said they appreciated the help they got from the robots and 75% appreciated the help provided by the first experimenter. These responses support a real involvement of the children in this research protocol.

A. Perceived differences in voices

85% of the children noticed that the two virtual robots did not speak in the same way. When the first experimenter asked what is different for the children who perceive a difference, the answers were mostly about pitch differences between the voices, as shown in Tab. I. As a reminder, the actual fundamental frequency (F0) of C is lower than the one of A and B. Some of the children who noticed a difference in pitch assumed that the robot with a higher pitched voice was a female, and that the other one was a male. Other less salient factors are reported by the children, for instance the laughter included in some utterances of voice B, and an "alien" characterization of voice C. Although some qualifiers (e.g., *enthusiastic* (A), *laughing* (B), *cheerful* (B), *softer* (B), *nicer* (B), *better* (B)) have a more positive valence than others (*shouting* (B), *unpleasant* (B), *alien* (C)), it is difficult to identify children's preferences from the data we collected.

TABLE I
QUALIFIERS FOR EACH VOICE BY NUMBER OF OCCURRENCES (NB)

Voice A		Voice B		Voice C	
qualifier	**nb**	**qualifier**	**nb**	**qualifier**	**nb**
higher than C	3	higher than C	3	lower than B	3
lower than B	2	higher than A	2	lower than A	2
higher than B	2	softer than C	1	male	2
female	2	nicer than C	1	bigger than B	1
high	1	smaller than C	1	slow	1
fast	1	better than C	1	alien	1
enthusiastic	1	lower than A	1	not too fast nor too slow	1
		laughing	1		
		shouting	1		
		unpleasant	1		
		cheerful	1		
		female	1		

reading hint: voice A is reported as higher than voice C by 3 children

B. Potential indicators of trust

We wished to pay particular attention to the relationship of trust in which the social signals of the robot (virtual in this game and physical in the future) could engage children. To begin the evaluation of this potential trust, we did not explicitly ask questions using the notion of trust, in order to avoid any bias, especially with children. We addressed it indirectly; when asked, "Would you lend a precious object or a toy to one of the robots?" (Q5 in Tab. II), children responded positively, for one particular virtual robot or both, 70% of the time. When a child's response was positive for only one virtual robot, that virtual robot was also chosen by the child 75% of the time when making the final sticker choice. When asked "Would you let one of the robots enter your bedroom?" (Q6), children responded positively for one or both virtual robots in 70% of cases. When a child's answer was positive for only one virtual robot, that virtual robot was also chosen by the child 75% of the time in the final choice of a sticker. If we compare the results of questions 5 and 6 in group B/C, more children are willing to let robot B into their room than to lend it their toys. This trend is reversed for robot C. It would therefore be interesting to distinguish more carefully in a future research two axes of trust; one axis of *centrifugal* trust in lending an object to the other, and a second axis of *centripetal* trust in letting the other into the home.

C. Preference between voices

We will now look specifically at the data collected in each group A/B, A/C and B/C. Among all the questions asked to each child, 6 questions allow determining whether or not the child expresses or not a preference towards a virtual robot. The final choice of the sticker also gives information about the child's preference. All these answers and choices are summarized in Tab. II to evaluate the engagement, trust or interest that a child has toward virtual robots.

D. Calculation of the total score for each robot

In a first simplifying approach to evaluate the engagement, trust or interest that a child has towards a virtual robot, we assign an identical weight to the positive answers for the 6 questions above and to the final choice of the sticker. If a robot is chosen or preferred by X% for a question or for the choice

TABLE II
ANSWERS FOR ENGAGEMENT & TRUST-RELATED QUESTIONS

group	answer	Q1	Q2	Q3	Q4	Q5	Q6	sticker	score
A/B	none	90%	70%	90%	70%	10%	30%		
	both					40%	30%		
	A	10%	30%	10%	10%	40%	30%	**60%**	**26**
	B				20%	10%	10%	40%	15
A/C	none	80%	80%	80%	90%	40%	30%		
	both					40%	60%		
	A	10%	20%	20%		10%	10%	**70%**	**24**
	C	10%			10%	10%		30%	16
B/C	none	50%	30%	50%	40%	40%	30%		
	both								
	B	30%	20%	40%	20%	20%	50%	**80%**	**26**
	C	20%	50%	10%	40%	40%	20%	20%	20

Q1 Is there a robot who helped you more?
Q2 Is there a robot you liked more?
Q3 Is there a robot you understood better?
Q4 Is there a robot you preferred to talk to?
Q5 Would you lend a precious object or a toy to one of the robots?
Q6 Would you let one of the robots enter your bedroom?

of the sticker, we assign it X/10 points. Each group containing 10 children, this is equivalent to assigning one point to a robot each time it is chosen by a child. For example, the score for voice A in group A/C is 24 points, obtained as follows: 1 point (Q1 : 10% for only A) + 2 points (Q2 : 20% for only A) + 2 points (Q3 : 20% for only A) + 4 points (Q5 : 40% for both A and C) + 1 point (Q5 : 10% for only A) + 1 point (Q6 : 10% for only A) + 6 points (Q6 : 60% for both A and C) + 7 points (Sticker : 70% for A).

These data show an overall tendency for children to express a preference for vocal profile A (whether it is opposed to B or C), and to prefer profiles A and B when they are opposed to profile C. This is confirmed by grouping the results of groups A/C and B/C, which allows us to compare the so-called "expressive" voices (A and B) with the stereotypical voice C. If we aggregate the scores of A and B in groups A/C and B/C, and compare this score with the aggregate score for voice C in these two groups, we obtain a score of 50 for expressive voices versus 36 for the stereotypical voice, again showing a tendency for children to prefer expressive voices. These tendencies will naturally have to be confronted to a larger sample of participants. We also plan to study different kinds of embodiment and situations to get a better insight of the robustness and generalization of these tendencies.

E. Effect of non-lexical primitives

The comparison of the results obtained between groups A/C and B/C is revealing of the effect of non-lexical primitives since this is the only element of the game that changes between these two groups. The frequency of negative answers ("none") to questions 1, 2, 3 and 4 change substantially, with the average of these frequencies dropping by 40% when the non-lexical primitives are introduced (cf Tab. II). Even if the direct contrast in the A/B group did not induce a preference for the B voice, this drop in frequency seems to indirectly show a positive cleavage effect of the non-lexical primitives on the children that would be useful to study further with a larger number of children. This is consistent with the results of previous studies for adults [14], [15].

F. Relevance of holistic gestural behavior

In the protocol of the experiment, it is also important to notice the interest that the expression of the preference of a child towards a virtual robot is not only verbalized but more generally gesturalized: the final choice of the sticker of the preferred robot implies the physical displacement of the child and its gripping. This interest seems to be quite visible for the B/C group. Indeed, the answers to the 6 questions highlighted in Tab. II do not show a clear preference between the voices B and C, with a score of 20 for the virtual robot B and 18 for the virtual robot C (if we exclude the final choice of the sticker). Yet, a clear preference appears for the virtual robot B which is chosen at 80% by the sticker.

G. Potential biases

Further research will be needed to estimate the impact of potential biases in this study such as the robot design and its kinematics, the laterality of the child or the order of the questions.

V. CONCLUSIONS AND FUTURE WORK

This first experiment with a limited number of children allows us to draw several provisional conclusions, showing the interest of continuing this research:

- As expected, the voice seems to have a significant impact in a video game context intended for children, where many other parameters intervene (the visual aspect of the game, its playability, its novelty, the presence of an adult at the child's side...), which could have strongly limited this impact. The voice being one of the elements of the relational construction in the physical robot, we will have to work on the voice in coherence with the other modalities of expressivity of the robot to come.
- The factors of voices A and B do not place the child in the intimacy of voice C (which they sometimes describe as "polite", "friendly"), but in an expressiveness (e.g., "enthusiastic"), which attract their preference (remember that voice C imitates voice assistants like Alexa).
- Non-lexical speech primitives seem to have a determining role in the child's perception, installing a relational space different from the one installed by strictly lexical elements. This will guide further research devoted to analyzing more precisely the relational effects pointed by the inconsistency when comparing directly voice A and B.

These first results reinforce the importance of the choice of the voice prosody that can be given to a robot. The seductive power of stereotypical voice C, which creates the illusion of intimacy, gentleness, politeness, seems complex to analyze in its effects. In any case, even if children assign positive qualifiers to it, it does not attract their overall preference. More generally, the prosodies of all gestural modalities (gaze, head, arms, navigation...) will be studied in order to establish an ethically justified choice.

These initial findings will lead to future experiments involving other virtual robots as well as physical robots currently under development at Enchanted Tools.

ACKNOWLEDGMENTS

We would like to thank all the people who participated in this experiment, the members of the Ethics Committee of the Grenoble-Alpes University (CERGA) and the Laboratoire des Usages en Technologies d'Information Numériques (LUTIN).

Thanks also to Enchanted Tools who funded this research.

REFERENCES

[1] N. Ward, "Prosody Research and Applications: The State of the Art, Keynote", Interspeech Conference, 2019

[2] C. Wightman and R. C. Rose, "Evaluation of an efficient prosody labeling system for spontaneous speech utterances", Proceedings of the Automatic Speech Recognition and Understanding Workshop, pp. 1837-1840, 1999

[3] N. Campbell and P. Mokhtari, "Voice quality: the 4th prosodic dimension", 15th ICPhS, pp. 2417-2420, August 2003

[4] V. Aubergé, "Gestual-facial-vocal prosody as the main tool of the socio-affective 'glue': interaction is a dynamic system", International workshop on audio-visual affective prosody in social interaction, Bordeaux, France, 2015

[5] V. Aubergé, "The Socio-Affective Robot: Aimed to Understand Human Links?", AVEC'2019: Proceedings of the 9th International on Audio/Visual Emotion Challenge and Workshop, p.1, 2019

[6] M. Cohn and G. Zellou, "Prosodic differences in human-and Alexa-directed speech, but similar local intelligibility adjustments", Frontiers in Communication, vol. 6, no. 675704, 2021

[7] S. Tisseron, "Le Jour où mon robot m'aimera. Vers l'empathie artificielle", Albin Michel, Paris, 2015

[8] R. Sparrow, "Why machines cannot be moral", AI & SOCIETY, 36(3), pp. 685-693, 2021

[9] A. Vinciarelli, M. Pantic, and H. Bourlard, "Social signal processing: Survey of an emerging domain", Image and vision computing, vol. 27, no. 12, pp. 1743-1759, 2009

[10] E. Hofstetter and L. Keevallik, "'More than meets the eye': Accessing senses in social interaction", Video Based Studies of Human Sociality, vol. 4, no. 3, 2021

[11] Y. Sasa and V. Aubergé, "Socio-affective interactions between a companion robot and elderly in a Smart Home context: prosody as the main vector of the 'socio-affective glue'", SpeechProsody, pp.86-90, 2014

[12] G. De Biasi., V. Aubergé, L. Granjon, and A. Vanpé, "Perception of social affects from non lexical sounds", In Proceedings of VII GSCP International Conference: Speech and Corpora, Brazil, 2012

[13] The audio files used in the experiment are available at https://lpy-et.github.io/ACHI2023/

[14] N. Campbell, "Specifying affect and emotion for expressive speech synthesis", International Conference on Intelligent Text Processing and Computational Linguistics, pp. 395-406, Springer, Berlin, Heidelberg, 2004

[15] Y. Sasa and V. Aubergé, "Caractéristiques prosodiques de la 'glu socio-affective' de l'interaction face à face: un robot-compagnon médiateur d'un habitat intelligent pour personnes âgées", 3rd SWIP-Swiss Workshop on Prosody, pp. 185-196, 2014

Validating Usability Heuristics for Augmented Reality Applications for Elderly Users

Anna Nishchyk, Norun Christine Sanderson, Weiqin Chen
Department of Computer Science
Faculty of Technology, Art and Design, Oslo Metropolitan University
Oslo, Norway
e-mail: anna.nishchyk@oslomet.no, norun-christine.sanderson@oslomet.no, weiqin.chen@oslomet.no

Abstract— **Literature has shown that Augmented Reality (AR) technologies can positively influence older people's quality of life. However, to achieve its potential, we need to ensure the usability of AR for elderly users. One of the most common usability evaluation methods is testing a product towards heuristics. Usability heuristics are also used to guide the interface design to improve usability. Unfortunately, the well-known general usability heuristics do not consider aspects specific to AR technologies as well as elderly users' needs. Therefore, there is a need to develop and validate heuristics specifically tailored for AR for elderly users. In our previous study, we developed a set of usability heuristics for elderly users and validated it by collecting feedback from usability experts. In this study, we have further validated the heuristics by asking designers/developers to use them for creating an AR application prototype. The results show that the heuristics are useful in the design phase of creating usable AR applications for elderly users. According to the participants, it can also be used in other phases of the application development cycle.**

Keywords-augmented reality; elderly; usability; heuristics.

I. INTRODUCTION

Augmented Reality (AR) technologies can help the elderly to increase their quality of life, enhance their care and autonomy, develop social interactions, and improve their overall wellbeing [1]. However, to achieve these potential benefits, we need to ensure the usability of AR applications for elderly users [2][3]. Usability is overall an important aspect in designing technologies for older people [4]. Due to age-related difficulties, most elderly experience challenges using Information and Communication Technologies (ICT) [5]. Thus, this group of users has specific usability needs and requires special attention [6]. For instance, modern game interfaces often use sounds, lights, and colors that are pleasant for younger users but often cause an adverse reaction from older users [7].

Heuristic evaluation is a common recognized method for testing the usability of ICT systems [8][9]. In addition, using heuristics as a guide for interface design to improve usability is a commonly adopted practice [10]. Unfortunately, well-known generic sets, such as Nielsen's heuristics [11], do not address characteristics specific to some types of ICT [9]. For instance, AR has certain hardware features, safety and privacy issues, and high importance in the surrounding environment [8]. That is why there is a need for new sets of heuristics that cover features specific to particular technologies [12]. All of the above-mentioned AR characteristics, as well as the specific needs of elderly users [6], need to be considered by new usability heuristics [8][13].

In our previous paper, we developed a set of usability heuristics for AR systems for elderly users [14]. However, it should not be the end of the process once heuristics for a specific domain are proposed, further validation needs to be conducted [12]. According to the systematic review by Nurgalieva et al. [15], only 11.5% of the selected papers reported validating the developed guidelines and heuristics. At the same time, the rest of the studies did not include the validation stage. That is why we have validated the developed heuristics through the expert judgment method [16] (interviews with AR experts with industrial and academic backgrounds). However, it should be further validated to ensure the quality of the set of heuristics and its applicability for creating usable AR.

Usability heuristics are commonly used for evaluating the usability of products, with most studies validating their effectiveness for this purpose. Despite this, designers also widely use usability heuristics to guide their design decisions. That is why, in this research, we have further validated the developed set of heuristics by using it to design an AR application interface and gathering feedback from the designers and front-end developers about the usefulness of the heuristics.

This paper has the following structure. Section 1 introduces the importance of usability heuristics specifically tailored for AR and elderly users. Section 2 reviews related work on AR usability and methodologies for new heuristics development. Section 3 describes the methods used for the validation of previously developed heuristics. Section 4 presents the study's results, including the prototype design created by the participants and their feedback on the set of heuristics. Section 5 discusses the results and implications of our findings and compares them with the reviewed literature. This paper's main contribution is presented in section 6, and it states that the developed set of usability heuristics can help to create usable AR applications for elderly users.

II. RELATED WORK

The following section presents a review of the related work on usability heuristics for AR and older users, along with the methodologies for developing and validating new heuristics.

A. *Usability Heuristics*

Usability evaluation of AR applications needs to address certain technological aspects specific to AR, such as hardware, its features, and potential limitations; privacy, safety issues, and related concerns that might appear due to using of cameras and video in users' environment; the importance of users' surroundings as a part of application interface; ease and comfort of use [8].

Several studies have focused on AR usability and presented new developed sets of heuristics or usability checklists tailored or adapted to AR specifics, including some aspects listed in the paragraph above. Franklin et al. [17] presented heuristics adopted for collaborative distributed AR systems and validated with a case study method. Another study focused on mobile AR usability and mapped and adapted Nielsen's heuristics to the specific features of AR home design applications [18]. Derby and Chaparro [13] created and validated a usability heuristics checklist for AR and Mixed Reality applications. Guimaraes and Martins [19] adapted the ISO 9241-11 [20] and Nielsen's heuristics and presented a checklist for AR usability evaluation. Yet, none of the studies mentioned above have focused on elderly users' usability needs. To our knowledge, only a few studies investigated AR usability in elderly users' context. Liang [2] developed general AR design principles for elderly users, however, they focus only on mobile AR [21].

In our previous study [14], we developed a set of usability heuristics that focuses on elderly users and considers aspects specific to AR applications. The developed set can be used as guidelines for creating AR systems for older people and heuristics for performing usability evaluation of existing AR applications.

B. *Validation methodologies*

When we discuss establishing new usability heuristics for a specific domain, two recommended methodologies are commonly used in the studies: [22] and [16]. Quiñones et al. [16] also mentioned other proposed methodologies for the heuristics development [12][23][24][25][26]. However, they do not provide a defined approach for validating the developed heuristics [16]. They also lack a comprehensive description of the formal steps involved in the development process [16].

Both Quiñones et al. [16] and Rusu et al. [22] recommended methods for validating the new developed heuristics. Rusu et al. [22] recommended evaluating the set of heuristics against Nielsen's heuristics in specific case studies. The authors recommended evaluating the same system with one group of experts using the new set of heuristics and a second group using Nielsen's heuristics and comparing the results. Quiñones et al. [16] recommended three methods of heuristics validation. First, using heuristics evaluation to compare the new heuristics with a control set of traditional heuristics. The second method is to involve experts and ask for their feedback on the developed set. And a third one is to compare the results of the heuristic evaluation with the developed set with the results of user testing. However, in both cases, the authors perceived the heuristics as a tool only for usability evaluation and proposed the methods of heuristics' validation for this purpose only.

Nurgalieva et al. [15] mentioned two other methods of heuristics validation that have also been used in research: first, designers using the proposed guidelines to design applications and giving feedback, and second, end-user testing of the applications developed following the guidelines.

III. METHOD

The process of heuristics development [14] was inspired by the eight-step methodology [16] and included a systematic literature review and interviews with usability experts. The developed set contains 55 heuristics divided into six categories: User involvement, Cognitive and physical load, Usability and accessibility, Privacy, Hardware, and Gamification. Eighteen heuristics have supplementary information added as a note to clarify the meaning of the heuristic.

We propose further validating the developed set of heuristics by using it to design and develop an AR application and then gathering feedback from the designers/developers about the set's usefulness. We have involved three experts (P1-P3) that work with frontend design and development and have usability and elderly users' needs knowledge and experience with AR. The participants were recruited by contacting IT companies by email. More detailed information about the participants' work experience is presented in Table 1.

TABLE I. INFORMATION ABOUT THE PARTICIPANTS.

Information	**Participants**		
	P1	***P2***	***P3***
Type of work	Front-end developer and UX designer	Front-end developer, has experience with design tasks	UX designer specializing in user research
Years of experience	4.5	9.5	4
Experience with AR	Yes, as a user	Yes, as a developer	Yes, as a designer
Usability knowledge	Yes	Yes	Yes
Experience designing for and/or testing with elderly	No experience, but has knowledge of elderly users' needs	No experience, but has knowledge of elderly users' needs	Included elderly in user testing

First, the participants received the task instructions that specified: the user group of the project (elderly people), the product that needs to be produced (augmented reality application for performing physical exercises), the exercise that needs to be included in the game (move the hands over the head during 30 seconds), game scenario (the users need to imagine that there are flying over a canyon) and the task that the participants need to complete (create a prototype of an AR application with 3-5 interface sketches using the set of heuristics). The participants did not get instructions on how to proceed with the task since we wanted to make the task closer to a real design/development project. We also wanted to see how the participants would approach the heuristics and how they would work with them.

The participants were supposed to choose a hardware technology for the project. They had three options: a smartphone (mobile AR), a combination of Microsoft Kinect and TV, and a head-mounted device. The participants were also asked to make notes throughout the process and mark heuristics that were especially helpful or/and influenced their prototypes and overall results.

Within a week after the task instructions were sent, the interview sessions with the participants were arranged. The interviews were semi-structured, and their purpose was to discuss participants' experiences with the task and collect their feedback on the set of heuristics. Each interview session lasted approximately one hour. The interviews were audio-recorded, and notes were taken during the process. In addition, during the sessions, the interviewer went through the notes of the participants together with them and asked clarifying questions. The recorded interviews were transcribed and analyzed by creating inductive semantic codes and categories using the conventional approach to content analysis [27].

IV. RESULTS

We interviewed three participants, each focusing on a different hardware device (P1 – Microsoft Kinect and TV, P2 – smartphone (mobile AR), P3 – head-mounted device). All the participants independently chose the following way to proceed with the task: first, quickly looked through the list of heuristics; then made initial prototypes; after that, went through the list again more carefully, paying attention to the details, checking if the prototypes were compliant with the heuristics and, if not, made corresponding changes in the process.

The interview sessions demonstrated that the participants found the task interesting and engaging. All of them expressed a positive attitude toward the set of heuristics.

The remaining section is organized based on the categories established through the content analysis.

A. *The design of the prototype made by the participants*

The participants made several changes to their initial prototypes to make them compliant with the heuristics. For instance, in accordance with the heuristic number 31, "Use representative figures and icons that the user can distinguish and differentiate. Note: Elderly people may not be familiar with many standard Internet icons, so, when possible, to use short text, use it instead of an icon" P1 added a text to a button "Back" in the interface sketches to make the purpose of the button clearer for the users (Figure 1).

Based on the heuristic number 15, "Use large fonts and virtual objects," P1 reduced the number of elements on the screen in each sketch and made them and the text even bigger than in the initial sketches. To make the prototype compliant with the heuristic number 39, "Ensure the transparency of information regarding content privacy, data collection, and its purposes," P1 added a section "About" and later decided to include it in the package of the product since it could be difficult to read a lot of text from the screen. P1 has also decided to make the base version of the app available without an internet connection, based on the heuristic number 5 "Consider the greater care needs of the residents and the institutional infrastructure (e.g., internet accessibility)."

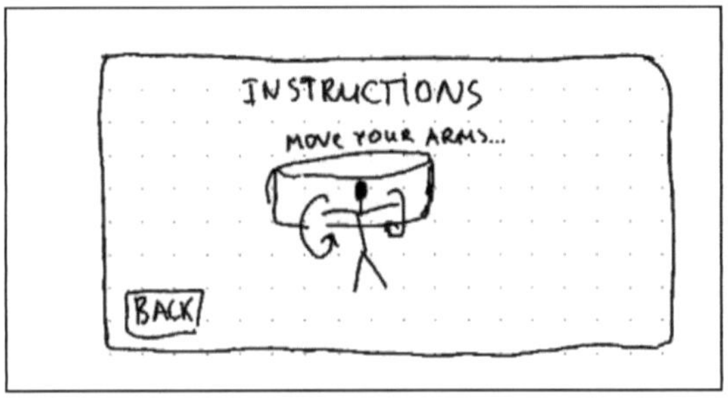

Figure 1. A sketch of Participant 1 with the added text "Back" to the button.

P2 added a navigation bar with text instead of buttons with icons to make the sketches more consistent following heuristic number 29, "The system and its response and user interface should be consistent in appearance and behavior, predictable, clear, and transparent," and heuristic number 31, "Use representative figures and icons that the user can distinguish and differentiate. Note: Elderly people may not be familiar with many standard Internet icons, so, when possible, to use short text, use it instead of an icon". Based on section 2 of the heuristics' set "Cognitive and physical load" and the heuristic number 9 "Design the interface to enable the user to focus on the actual task and reduce the cognitive overhead needed to interact with the application", P2 added a possibility to play the game without a login. P2 made the text on the sketches bigger, based on the heuristic 15, "Use large fonts and virtual objects." P2 decided to add video instructions instead of pictures to make it easier to understand the instructions and added a possibility to repeat the video (Figure 2), based on the heuristic 8 "Consider older adults' individual needs and skill levels" and heuristic number 28 "When relevant, provide guidance (including visual instructions) in a step-by-step manner."

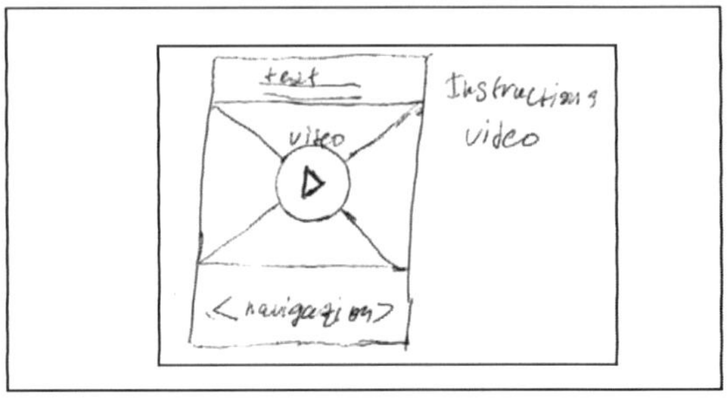

Figure 2. A sketch of Participant 2 with the video instructions. It has a text field on the top of the screen, followed by a video content and navigation bar at the bottom.

P3 decided to reduce the number of elements on the screen in each sketch and made the design more minimalistic, based on the heuristic number 9 "Design the interface to enable the user to focus on the actual task and reduce the cognitive overhead needed to interact with the application" and heuristic number 13 "Consider that virtual elements hide real content." P3 also added a two-players mode to support the social aspect of the game and increase users' motivation to exercise (Figure 3), based on the heuristic number 51 "Consider adding an optional multi-player mode, since playing together with family or friends can motivate elderly users to start and continue playing." During the interview, P3 mentioned that they also should add "Back" buttons to each screen.

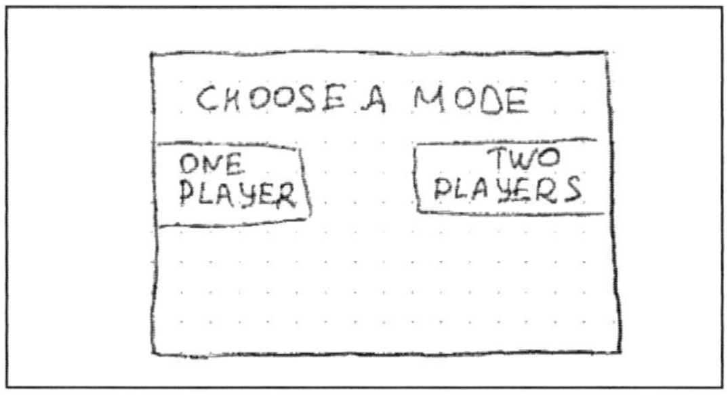

Figure 3. A sketch of Participant 3 with different game modes.

B. *Applicability*

All participants agreed that some heuristics should be used before sketching the interface, and some will be used later in the development process. Participants 1 and 2 also discussed that heuristics cover tasks typically related to the work of different roles in the team, such as UX researcher, UX designer, front-end developer, hardware developer, and product manager.

P2 stated that the set overall is very good for the refinement stage and can be a good checklist, while P3 noted that the set is a good start for the research and design process and usability testing at the end of the project.

C. *Understandability*

Overall, all the participants stated they had no issues understanding the heuristics. P3 said that the set is well structured, mostly understandable, and turned out to be useful for creating a usable AR application for the elderly. The majority of the heuristics were also understandable. They did not cause any confusion and were easy to use and apply. All the participants agreed that the additional notes for some of the heuristics were highly helpful and explained some details that needed to be clarified with the notes. The only heuristic that raised some questions and was unclear to 2 out of 3 participants (P1 and P2) is heuristic number 7: "Involve and stimulate older adults' social networks." Both participants perceived it as a recommendation to incorporate multiple players mode, however, the intended meaning was to incorporate the social networks of older adults into the research and design process. Participants suggested that adding an additional note clarifying this heuristic could prevent misunderstanding and improve understandability.

P2 claimed that all the heuristics are well decoupled, even though some of them are overlapping, for instance: heuristic number 11, "Users should be able to accomplish a task with minimal interaction steps; avoid "unnecessary" interventions by the user" and heuristic number 24 "Menu navigation and general navigation within the application should be logical, with clear and minimal steps." However, the participant stated that it is not a disadvantage of the list: "The heuristics are talking about the same issue, but they cover it from different angles."

D. *Familiarity and novelty*

P2 stated that some of the heuristics were common knowledge for an experienced UX designer, but still, having them in the set as a reminder and a part of a checklist that needs to be completed is good. P1 agreed that some heuristics were evident for a designer, such as those that concern the interface's simplicity, logical navigation, screen brightness, and big text (the participant mentioned that it mainly concerns category 3. Usability and Accessibility). However, P1 also highlighted that this set of heuristics is a good checklist and "nothing needs to be cut." P3 mentioned that some of the heuristics are familiar from more general usability heuristics and guidelines, however, it also contains heuristics more specific for elderly people that are not mentioned in other lists.

There were also things the participants hadn't considered relevant for the prototype before reading the heuristics. For instance, P1 claimed that they would not think about the higher importance of outdated technology consideration for the elderly (heuristic number 33); the greater care needs of the elderly residents and the institutional infrastructure (heuristic number 5); older adults' privacy needs and concerns (heuristic number 38) and most privacy heuristics overall (category 4 – Privacy); also, a need to consider specific conditions of older adults living environments (heuristic number 3). Overall, P1 highlighted that the heuristics that are specific for elderly users were the most useful ones. P2 mentioned that they wouldn't think about the support the user's procedural and semantic memory to enhance the learnability and usability of the interface (heuristic number 25).

E. *Context and hardware*

P1 also commented on the heuristics that concern hardware. They mentioned that it is not always possible to develop hardware in the project, or even sometimes choose it, so designers and developers do not always have an influence on the hardware.

There was also a heuristic that got different feedback from the participants. P2 and P3 found the heuristic number 13, "Consider that virtual elements hide real content." very useful since they designed for hardware that "projects" the computer-generated elements on the real content. While for P1, who was covering the Microsoft Kinect and TV hardware, this heuristic was not useful at all.

Overall, the participants provided useful feedback demonstrating the usefulness of the developed set of heuristics for creating usable AR applications for elderly people. The set includes general information about usability in the form of a well-structured checklist with decoupled and understandable heuristics, and, according to the participants, is important to have. Moreover, it also includes heuristics specific to AR technologies and elderly users, which the participants found the most useful. Based on participants' feedback, the set of heuristics is useful for the starting point of the research and design process, as well as for the refinement stage of the project and usability testing at the end.

V. DISCUSSION

Previous studies demonstrated that well-known general heuristics do not cover all the aspects specific to AR applications [8], and there is a need to create a set of heuristics that consider AR specifics [12], such as hardware, surrounding environment, privacy, security and comfort of use [8]. All these aspects were considered, and recommendations towards them were included in the developed set of usability heuristics [14]. The set has a separate section covering potential privacy issues and proposed solutions. The study participants expressed that heuristics concerning privacy were valuable and important to consider. P1 stated that a designer might not be aware of the older adults' special privacy needs and concerns. Regarding the surrounding environment, most participants highlighted the importance of the heuristic number 13, "Consider that virtual elements hide real content," which covers an issue specific to AR that combines a real environment with computer-generated elements [1].

The developed set of heuristics considers AR hardware. It has a dedicated section covering guidelines that can help to overcome potential issues related to AR hardware, for instance, comfort and safety of use, consider the weight of the wearable devices and time of use, consideration of existing elderly aids, and different input and output devices. However, the participants' feedback did not include much information about their opinions and attitude toward this category of heuristics. P1 commented that a project often predetermines hardware, and designers and front-end developers mostly do not have an influence on the hardware decisions. That is why P1 did not find this section of heuristics particularly useful for the design of AR applications. The other participants did not have many comments about the heuristics from this section. This might be due to the fact that none of the participants had experience working on a project in which hardware was developed as an in-house solution.

The developed set of heuristics is trying to cover recommendations for all types of AR hardware devices, even though they can have some differences [1]. The interview with participants demonstrated that some heuristics are only relevant for some types of AR but not others. The heuristic number 13, "Consider that virtual elements hide real content," was very useful for mobile AR and AR with a head-mounted display since these types of AR "project" virtual elements on the users' surroundings. While P1, who focused on the Microsoft Kinect and TV hardware, did not find this heuristic relevant.

Research has also shown that elderly users have specific usability needs [6], so the developed heuristics included recommendations for this user group. The results of the study demonstrated that the heuristics that were explicitly focused on elderly users were found the most useful by the participants and helped them to adjust the created prototypes to elderly users' needs. Examples of these heuristics include consideration of elderly users' environment, particular privacy concerns, and a higher focus on outdated technologies.

A. *Limitations*

One of the study's limitations is the small number of participants. However, they performed an extensive task, developing and adjusting prototypes of an AR application interface using the heuristics and providing thorough feedback about the process and the set of heuristics. Their design has also covered all types of hardware devices.

Another limitation is that the task that participants received was covering only the initial design phase of a project. Therefore, they provided us with low-fidelity prototypes, while the heuristics covered more stages, including user research, hardware decisions, and some parts of front-end and back-end development. However, during the interview sessions, we gathered participants' feedback on all heuristics considering the AR prototype, including those that did not apply to the initial design phase.

In addition, not all participants had experience designing for and testing with elderly users, which may have limited the findings of the study.

VI. CONCLUSION AND FUTURE WORK

In this study, we aimed to validate the set of usability heuristics for AR for elderly users by creating an AR prototype by design and front-end development experts. The participants were asked to prototype an AR application interface using the set of heuristics. After they had completed the prototypes, interview sessions were arranged to collect participants' feedback on their experiences using the set of heuristics. Overall, the participants expressed a positive attitude towards the heuristics and stated its usefulness, ease of use, and understandability. The set of heuristics was found to be a good checklist that can be used at different stages of the AR design and development process.

In the future, it is important to validate the heuristics for the whole AR development process. In addition, the effectiveness and usefulness of the heuristics should be evaluated with a user study to investigate how designers/developers following the heuristics can influence the usability of an AR application.

REFERENCES

[1] L. N. Lee, M. J. Kim, and W. J. Hwang, "Potential of augmented reality and virtual reality technologies to promote wellbeing in older adults," Applied sciences, 9(17), pp. 3556, 2019, doi:10.3390/app9173556.

[2] S. Liang, "Establishing Design Principles for Augmented Reality for Older Adults," 2018, Sheffield Hallam University (United Kingdom), 2018.

[3] T. C. Endsley et al., "Augmented reality design heuristics: Designing for dynamic interactions," Proceedings of the Human Factors and Ergonomics Society 2017 Annual Meeting, 2017, Sage Publications Sage CA: Los Angeles, CA, pp. 2100-2104, doi:10.1177/1541931213602007.

[4] A. d. Lima Salgado, L. Agostini do Amaral, R. P. d. Mattos Fortes, M. Hortes Nisihara Chagas, and G. Joyce, "Addressing mobile usability and elderly users: Validating contextualized heuristics," International Conference of Design, User Experience, and Usability, 2017, Springer, pp. 379-394, doi:10.1007/978-3-319-58634-2_28.

[5] D. E. Chisnell, J. C. G. Redish, and A. Lee, "New heuristics for understanding older adults as web users," Technical Communication, 53(1), pp. 39-59, 2006,

[6] M. S. Al-Razgan, H. S. Al-Khalifa, and M. D. Al-Shahrani, "Heuristics for evaluating the usability of mobile launchers for elderly people," International Conference of Design, User Experience, and Usability (DUXU 2014), 2014, Springer, pp. 415-424, doi:10.1007/978-3-319-07668-3_40.

[7] J. Marin, E. Lawrence, K. F. Navarro, and C. Sax, "Heuristic evaluation for interactive games within elderly users," Proceedings of the 3rd International Conference on eHealth, Telemedicine, and Social Medicine (eTELEMED'11), 2011, pp. 130-133,

[8] J. L. Derby and B. S. Chaparro, "The Challenges of Evaluating the Usability of Augmented Reality (AR)," Proceedings of the Human Factors and Ergonomics Society Annual Meeting, 2021, SAGE Publications Sage CA: Los Angeles, CA, pp. 994-998, doi:10.1177/1071181321651315.

[9] D. Quiñones and C. Rusu, "How to develop usability heuristics: A systematic literature review," Computer standards & interfaces, 53, pp. 89-122, 2017, doi:10.1016/j.csi.2017.03.009.

[10] R. Langevin et al., "Heuristic evaluation of conversational agents," Proceedings of the 2021 CHI Conference on Human Factors in Computing Systems, 2021, pp. 1-15, doi:10.1145/3411764.3445312.

[11] C. Jiménez, C. Rusu, S. Roncagliolo, R. Inostroza, and V. Rusu, "Evaluating a methodology to establish usability heuristics," 2012 31st International Conference of the Chilean Computer Science Society, 2012, IEEE, pp. 51-59, doi:10.1109/SCCC.2012.14.

[12] S. Hermawati and G. Lawson, "Establishing usability heuristics for heuristics evaluation in a specific domain: Is there a consensus?," Applied ergonomics, 56, pp. 34-51, 2016,

[13] J. L. Derby and B. S. Chaparro, "The Development and Validation of an Augmented and Mixed Reality Usability Heuristic Checklist," International Conference on Human-Computer Interaction, 2022, Springer, pp. 165-182, doi:10.1007/978-3-031-05939-1_11.

[14] A. Nishchyk, N. C. Sanderson, and W. Chen, "Elderly-centered usability heuristics for Augmented reality design and development," Universal Access in the Information Society, unpublished,

[15] L. Nurgalieva, J. J. J. Laconich, M. Baez, F. Casati, and M. Marchese, "A systematic literature review of research-derived touchscreen design guidelines for older adults," IEEE Access, 7, pp. 22035-22058, 2019, doi:10.1109/ACCESS.2019.2898467.

[16] D. Quiñones, C. Rusu, and V. Rusu, "A methodology to develop usability/user experience heuristics," Computer standards & interfaces, 59, pp. 109-129, 2018, doi:10.1016/j.csi.2018.03.002.

[17] F. Franklin, F. Breyer, and J. Kelner, "Usability heuristics for collaborative augmented reality remote systems," 2014 XVI Symposium on Virtual and Augmented Reality, 2014, IEEE, pp. 53-62, doi:10.1109/SVR.2014.31.

[18] A. Labrie and J. Cheng, "Adapting usability heuristics to the context of mobile augmented reality," Adjunct Publication of the 33rd Annual ACM Symposium on User Interface Software and Technology, 2020, pp. 4-6, doi:10.1145/3379350.3416167.

[19] M. D. P. Guimaraes and V. F. Martins, "A checklist to evaluate augmented reality applications," 2014 XVI Symposium on Virtual and Augmented Reality, 2014, IEEE, pp. 45-52, doi:10.1109/SVR.2014.17.

[20] I. O. f. Standardization, ISO standard: Ergonomics of human-system interaction — Part 11: Usability: Definitions and concepts., [cited 2023 February 28], Available from: https://www.iso.org/obp/ui/#iso:std:iso:9241:-11:ed-2:v1:en.

[21] J. L. Derby and B. S. Chaparro, "Use of Augmented Reality by Older Adults," International Conference on Human-Computer Interaction, 2020, Springer, pp. 125-134, doi:10.1007/978-3-030-50252-2_10.

[22] C. Rusu, S. Roncagliolo, V. Rusu, and C. Collazos, A Methodology to establish usability heuristics, in ACHI 2011 : The Fourth International Conference on Advances in Computer-Human Interactions. 2011.

[23] A. Yeratziotis, D. Pottas, and D. Van Greunen, "A three-phase process to develop heuristics," 13th Annual Conference on World Wide Web Applications, 2011, pp. 14-16,

[24] M. Hub and V. Čapková, "Heuristic evaluation of usability of public administration portal," The International Conference on Applied Computer Science, 2010, pp. 234-239,

[25] F. F. Franklin, Usability Heuristics for Collaborative Augmented Reality Remote Systems. Heurísticas de usabilidade para sistemas colaborativos remotos de realidade aumentada. 2014, Universidade Federal de Pernambuco.

[26] B. Lechner, A. Fruhling, S. Petter, and H. Siy, The chicken and the pig: User involvement in developing usability heuristics, in Nineteenth Americas Conference on Information Systems. 2013: Chicago, Illinois. p. 3263-3270.

[27] H.-F. Hsieh and S. E. Shannon, "Three approaches to qualitative content analysis," Qualitative health research, 15(9), pp. 1277-1288, 2005, doi:10.1177/1049732305276687.

The Role of a Human Host Onboard of Urban Autonomous Passenger Ferries

Leander Pantelatos, Mina Saghafian, Ole A. Alsos
dept. of Design
Norwegian University of Science and Technology
Trondheim, Norway
e-mail: leander.s.pantelatos@ntnu.no
e-mail: mina.saghafian@ntnu.no
e-mail: oleanda@ntnu.no

Asun Lera St.Clair
Group Technology and Research
DNV
Oslo, Norway
e-mail: asun.lera.st.clair@dnv.com

Øyvind Smogeli
Zeabuz AS
Trondheim, Norway
e-mail: oyvind.smogeli@zeabuz.com

Abstract— **Zero-emission Urban Autonomous passenger Ferries (UAFs) is a promising concept to serve as flexible, cost effective and sustainable public transport utilizing urban waterways. The perception of users and their attitudes plays a vital role in acceptance and use of autonomous technologies. For UAFs to be accepted, there are more factors to consider beyond having a robust and mature technology. The public should perceive it as safe, trustworthy, and convenient to use. In the future, from a technical perspective, abandoning a human host onboard is possible when reaching a higher level of autonomy. To understand the consequences or implications of human host removal in the future, we need to understand the current influence of the human host onboard. This research aims to shed light on the role of the human host onboard in acceptance and use of the UAF, and the implications it has for implementing remote supervision of such a ferry. We address this through the analysis of a set of citizen engagement activities performed as part of an ongoing R&I project exploring trust in zero emission UAFs. The citizen engagement consisted of table discussions, VR mixed reality simulations, and in-situ trips in the fully functional autonomous ferry prototype milliAmpere2. The findings outline six sub-themes to define the significance of a human host onboard an UAF. The qualitative results show that the perceived importance of the presence of a human host onboard is decreasing throughout the sessions. This is in a non-linear fashion, and especially after the immersive sessions. The context of where and how the ferry trials were conducted, meaning short distance within enclosed waters and the use of a small UAF, allows for alternatives to the full-time onboard presence of a safety host to be discussed.**

Keywords-urban autonomous ferries; citizen engagement; safety; trust; acceptance; convenience; level of autonomy; remote supervision.

I. INTRODUCTION

Autonomous technologies including unmanned ships in the maritime sector are gaining popularity due to their potential benefits, namely cost efficient, environmentally sustainable, and safe maritime transportation [1]. Currently, around 90% of the urban areas, including several of the largest cities in the world, are coastal [2]. With urban sprawl across the globe, urban population is expected to increase, thus requiring better integrated, sustainable, and more efficient modes of transport ensure the quality of mobility and life in urban spaces [3]. Battery powered zero-emission Urban Autonomous passenger Ferries (hereafter UAFs) can be a solution for future public transport in cityscapes. This solution has been partly explored as in for example the modular system Roboat in Amsterdam [4], the passenger service Captn Vaiaro in Kiel [5], and the AutoFerry project in Trondheim resulting in the prototypes milliAmpere1 (mA1) and milliAmpere2 (mA2) [6]. Autonomous systems can be characterized by their Level Of Autonomy (LOA). Smogeli [7] has defined five levels of autonomy for UAFs specifically, ranging from manual operation (level 0) to full autonomy with remote support (level 5). Level five would imply the UAF to monitor itself and the passengers, make decisions and determine actions by itself, and asking for assistance when needed. The operation of the ferry within a fleet of several, is monitored by operators at a remote support centre, similar to an air traffic control centre in its structure. Local emergency response would handle any emergency situations occurring [7]. The prototype mA2 is currently operated at level 2 (onboard supervised autonomy) but aiming towards operating at level 4. Beside the technological development required to reach higher levels of autonomy, investigating user perceptions is important to understand various risks associated to UAFs. Goerlandt [8] rightfully highlights the importance of understanding publics risks and safety perceptions and risk communication. In the work of N. P. Reddy [9], societal communication is emphasised to establish trust related to the operation of autonomous systems. However, there is a gap in perceived benefits, concerns, and safety perception of autonomous solutions and specifically urban autonomous ferries, which motivated Goerlandt [3] to fill the gap by investigating user perceptions towards UAFs amongst the senior urban population in Halifax, Canada. A key finding there, was that increased levels of autonomy was supported, with the condition that an onboard operator would be present [3]. Both in the perspective of safety (personal and vessel related) and security (especially physical), an onboard

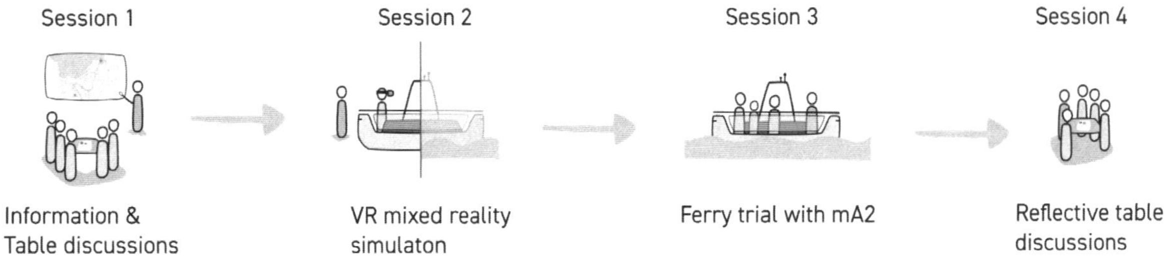

Figure 1: The four sessions of the citizen engagement.

operator would alleviate those concerns [3]. As such, the onboard operator is the doorkeeper to introduce fully unmanned UAFs towards the higher levels 3-4 defined in [7].

This paper seeks to explore the role of a human host onboard UAFs, and to discuss possible measures needed for a trustworthy operation of fully unmanned UAFs. The study is conducted through citizen engagement, where the participants would experience the fully functioning UAF prototype mA2. The use of an immersive VR mixed reality simulation, as well as the functioning prototype to explore and evaluate the user perceptions is, to the knowledge of the authors, a novelty in the given context.

This paper is part of the TRUSST project – Assuring Trustworthy, Safe and Sustainable Transport for All. The primary objective of TRUSST is to innovate an integrated assurance framework, stemming from an interdisciplinary and socio-technical perspective. This project is a collaboration between DNV, as risk management assurance provider, Norwegian University of Science and Technology (NTNU) and Zeabuz, a spin-off company from NTNU seeking to introduce autonomous cost-cutting waterborne mobility solutions.

As part of the citizen engagement objective, we have used a multimodal data collection method which will be described in section II. Quantitative and qualitative results are presented in section III. A discussion and presentation of future research concludes in section IV.

II. Methodology

This research was conducted through an exploratory approach due to the context novelty. The overall aim was to gain a deeper understanding of the public perception of UAFs. In this paper we will focus on the data regarding the significance of the human host onboard and the implications of removing the human host when progressing towards level 4 (remote supervised autonomy), that was collected over the length of four sessions. The overview of the sessions design and the detail about the participants is presented next and can be seen in detail in appendix 1.

A. The sessions

Altogether 4 sessions (Figure 1) were conducted consisting of:

1. Information and table discussions
2. An immersive virtual mixed reality simulation of the ferry trial between Ravnkloa and Vestre Kanalkai (Figure 2, right)
3. Real ferry trials with the autonomous prototype milliAmpere2 within the real context (Figure 2, left and middle)
4. Reflective table discussions

The sessions focused on the topics of safety, sustainability, and societal impact. The study was designed this way to both capture initial perceptions, but also to see how this would change after more knowledge and immersion with the overall concept. The arrangement of several workshops with some time in between was done to capture both immediate feedback and reflected answers. The citizen engagement activities were designed under the guidance of Missions Publiques [10], a professional citizen engagement consultancy.

1) Table discussions: Before the first session a briefing was provided to the participants with basic information and some pictures of the UAF concept by Zeabuz. As soon as the participants arrived at the first session the first questionnaire (WS1-A) was handed out to capture the initial perceptions of the participants. This was followed by informative presentations on future possibilities for urban spaces, the technology, and a visualized user journey. Afterwards, four groups were formed for a table discussion. The table discussion was guided by large worksheets which contained a set of questions which are listed in the appendix 1. For each question the participants were asked to reflect on their own and note their thoughts on post-its. Then the post-its were posted on the big sheet and presented to the group, whereby a discussion arose naturally. A plenary presentation of the discussion concluded each question. During these plenary presentations the participants also had the chance to ask questions to the different stakeholders present. Each group was accompanied by a facilitator taking notes and keeping time. At the end of the session a second questionnaire (WS1-B) was handed out to capture changes in participant perceptions after the interactive session.

2) VR Mixed Reality Simulation: In the second session the participants were offered to try a VR mixed reality simulation of mA2 in the canal. This was conducted with the use of two full-size mock ups of mA2 and thereby making it a tangible VR lab as described in [6]. Three different scenarios were simulated as described in appendix 1. A facilitator was following the participant during the whole simulation and taking notes on behaviour, actions, and thoughts of the participant. After the simulations a questionnaire (VR) was handed out to capture the participants immediate thoughts. A focus group moderated by a facilitator concluded the session. An interview guide for the facilitator was prepared. The session was conducted in smaller groups (5-7 participants) spread over three different dates, where the participants could choose a preferred date.

3) Ferry Trial: Following the same structure, the third session offered a real ferry trial with the prototype mA2 (Figure 2), spread across three dates in smaller groups. The trials were divided in two parts, where the ferry crossed the canal without interventions in the first part, whereas in the second a leisure boat simulated traffic crossing the route and provoked mA2 to act. Two engineers onboard monitored the autonomous system during all the trails and answered questions the participants would have. Two facilitators noted behaviour, actions, and thoughts of the participants. It should be noted that the personnel on mA2 during the ferry trials would only partly play the role of a human host [3], or in the case of autonomous buses [12]. There was not a designated human host aboard. As in the VR session, a questionnaire (FERRY) was handed out and a focus group concluded the session.

4) Reflective Table Discussion: Lastly, a reflective session with a similar structure as in the first session was conducted (appendix 1). Divided into smaller groups, a set of open-ended question were asked in order for the participants to reflect on and build recommendations for the further development of the UAF concept. The table discussions, conducted in the same manner as in session 1, were followed by plenary presentation of the recommendations discussed in the groups. At the end a final questionnaire (WS2) was handed out.

B. Questionnaires

Through the sessions five different questionnaires were handed out. The questionnaires consisted of both a quantitative and qualitative part. Some of the questions were repeated through several and even all the questionnaires. This allowed investigating how the different sessions would influence the participants. As the context was new, the questions were developed through brainstorming within the research team and inspired from earlier studies within the field of autonomous transportation such as [3], and a local study with an autonomous bus service in Trondheim conducted by the public transport company AtB in 2020 [13]. The quantitative part consisted of 5-point Likert scale questions about safety, society and sustainability. The qualitative part consisted of open-ended questions where the participants were asked about thoughts, needs, expectations related to UAFs, in the light of the recent workshop. Appendix 1 gives an overview of the questionnaires and questions asked and analysed in this paper.

C. Participants

Due to the resource intensive nature of the study, the citizen engagement was designed for a maximum of 20 participants. Altogether, 15 participants completed all four sessions who consisted of 47% women and 53% men. The age stretched from 19 to 64 years, with an average of 42 years. An age-limit was set to 18 years. Emphasis was put on recruiting an adequate representation of the inhabitants of Trondheim already using public transport in the city centre. The recruitment was done through the recruitment office Nordic Viewpoint, based on a recruitment profile that was produced by the research team to ensure an adequate representation of the inhabitants. The recruitment profile included postal codes, use of public transport, gender, age, disabilities, education, and ethnicity. Additionally, a slight overrepresentation of young adults was granted due to the large student population in the city. The selection and transference of contact details of the participants was GDPR compliant. All participants were informed about the purpose of the study, and how data will be collected, processed, and stored, that participation would be voluntary, and that

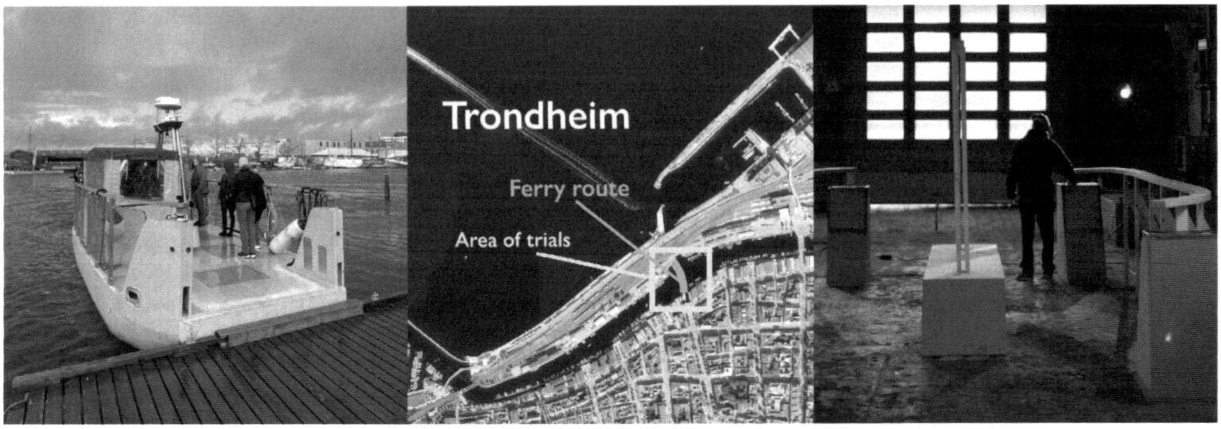

Figure 2: Prototype mA2 (left) (Photo: Ole Andreas Alsos), area of trials in Trondheim (middle) adapted from [11], VR mixed reality simulation (right) (Photo: Nicholas Lund).

confidentiality is ensured. The informed consent form, and data management has been approved by the Norwegian centre for research data (NSD) under project number 37623.

III. RESULTS

This section presents the results from both the quantitative and qualitative data obtained regarding a human host onboard an UAF. The quantitative results reflect on the trends observed and the qualitative section explains the themes observed in the dataset.

A. *Quantitative Results*

1) Commuting routines, previous experience, and perceptions of the participants: Most of the participants used the bus as a daily mode of transport for commuting with an average commuting time of 15 min. Initially, the interest for using new means of transport was generally high with an average of 4,67 within a five-point liker scale. Some of the participants had previous experience with an autonomous vessel/vehicle before (21%) which could relate to the trial of an autonomous bus in the city centre a year before (Øya Project) [13]. The participants had great initial interest in the topic of "self-driving transport" where 80% answered to be "very interested". After the ferry trial almost all the participants answered "agree" to "very agree" to the question if they would like to travel with an autonomous ferry again. Only one participant did not answer the question.

2) Perceived importance of a human host onboard: Before the first session the human host was perceived to be "important" to "very important" by 40% of the participants, and 20% being "neutral" to the question (Figure 3). This changed in a non-linear fashion through the sessions and at the end only 20% found the host to be at least "important" to have onboard (WS2). A larger share of the participants was uncertain (33%). Notably, the lowest importance for a human host was perceived after the VR session where only 13% answered "important" contrasting 67% finding the

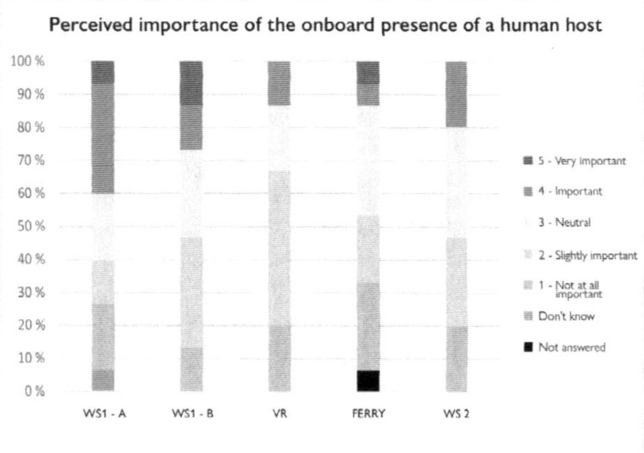

Figure 3: Percieved importance of a human host onboard

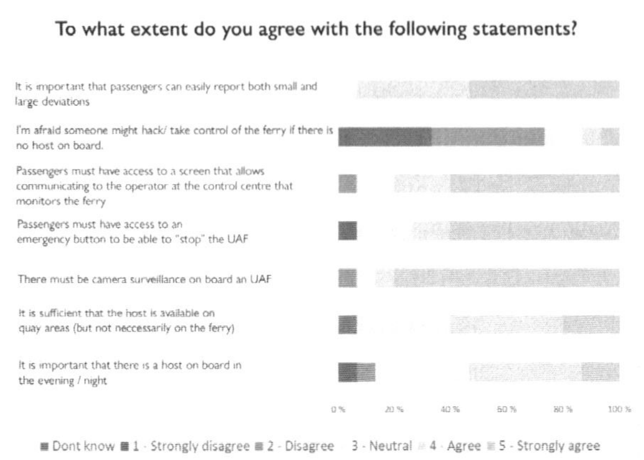

Figure 4: Percieved importance of other safety related questions.

matter to be "not so important" to "not important at all".

3) Perceived importance of other safety related measures: Further questions related to the human host and other safety related measures, obtained from the questionnaire after the last session (WS2), are presented in Figure 4. Regarding certain time frames, 53% did at least "agree" that it is important that a human host is onboard in the evening and at night. The possibility to report deviations and problems, communication to the monitoring shore control centre, and camera surveillance onboard found great resonance by the participants. Interestingly, 60% did at least agree that it would be sufficient that a human host would be available on quay areas. Furthermore, most participants did not believe that the onboard presence of a human host would hinder any cyber threats towards the UAF. Here 73,3% answered "do not agree" to "do not agree at all".

B. *Qualitative Analysis*

All the notes collected during the workshops and all the responses were converted into text in one document. We applied thematic analysis [14] to the text to find the most important themes and subthemes regarding the human host onboard the autonomous ferry. The role of a human onboard a UAF was not explicitly defined to the participants through the sessions. A notable amount of the data collected, contains information regarding a human host aboard.

The overarching theme in the data was the importance of the general perceptions of safety. The general perception of safety is an important antecedent to acceptance and use of the autonomous ferry in the long term. The decision to use the ferry depends on feeling safe as can be seen from this quote by one of the passengers: "my perceived safety must be taken care of!" This theme in turn consisted of several subthemes. These subthemes are various dimensions that together form the perception of safety, and they include the following:

1) Contextual and the environmental factors onboard and around the ferry and the need for resilience: The perceived safety of the autonomous ferry depends on safety onboard and around the ferry. One of the key notions was mentioned to be "safety for all" when using the ferry. The importance of a human host onboard is to ensure that the ferry trip goes smoothly and that the people on and around the ferry are safe. The context of a ferry is one of a floating platform on water, a closed space where one cannot run away if something happens, despite being in the open space of sea or canal. It was mentioned that the external environment of the ferry can also pose a threat if somebody decides to challenge the ferry and expose the ferry to danger. As such it was mentioned that we need a resilient system that will function despite any attempt to challenge it. Since the context of a ferry is one that is open to external threats while being an enclosed space – it is a context where people cannot escape – it is important that surveillance is in place. However, it was also mentioned that one might feel safer on board a ferry that has video surveillance rather than walking alone at night in the streets. The perceived safety of the passengers was mentioned to need further work. Interestingly the perception of the context changed throughout the workshops as one participant mentioned after the ferry trial that it was "safe because of the short distance, and it is possible to see both the start and the end". This subtheme focused on external factors, but the most salient subtheme was about an internal challenge: the need to create social order and prevent unsafe behaviour of the passengers as presented next.

2) The importance of human host onboard to create social order in certain time windows: This subtheme is the most prevalent one across the dataset and the focal point when it came to the importance of having a human host onboard. There were several references made to the need for a host to ensure social order and safety as an authority figure onboard. The participants believed that a human host is needed in the case of robbery, abuse, violence, for keeping peace onboard and ensure safety for everyone by preventing unsafe behaviour. Participants were mainly concerned that people will not respect order if there is no authority onboard. The threat posed by drunk people to themselves and to other passengers was a salient concern. They believed that drunk people and children need to be supervised onboard by a human host. The participants referred to a time-window where the human host would be even more important. Repeated references were made to not wanting to be alone at night, or after big festivals or football matches. For example, it was mentioned that "social safety is important to prevent unsafe behaviour and it is situation-based, for example after a football match" and that "a human host is needed to control who will get onboard and who should not board the ferry. If that is not the case, then the ferry should provide an overview of the other passengers". However, it was also mentioned that abusive conduct also happens in manned vehicles such as taxi and in a subway where the driver is also present but not able to respond fast. The data showed that people need video surveillance and quick spotting of potential criminal activity by land-based operators. One of the participants mentioned that "so long that there is video surveillance from a land-based station, it is not needed to have a human host onboard", while another participant believed that "one should be able to get help immediately and even with the possibility of pushing a button to get help, it is not clear how fast and how well you will be helped". Another participant added that "it maybe even safer to travel with a ferry that has video surveillance than to walk alone at night". After the ferry trial, having immersed with the concept, a participant stated that "regarding strangers, it is possible to choose not to board the ferry if there are passengers acting out. The distance is also short". An interesting question that was raised was "whether the presence of human host could actually create a false feeling of safety" since what the human host could do in the face of danger and with respect to vigilance over everything, is limited.

Although the most salient subtheme was the importance of a human host for intervening in the socially induced danger, and at specific times in the day/night, another important role of the human host was to intervene with other unexpected incidents and accidents.

3) The role of human host in emergency situations, rescue, and evacuation: In cases of emergency, such as a passenger suddenly getting a heart attack, a human host can immediately intervene. The human host is the annotated responsible person when the unexpected happens. The participants expressed the need for a human host onboard if somebody falls overboard, if a life-threatening situation happened that would demand a short response time, and if an evacuation order should be placed and performed. However, it was also mentioned that "accidents also happen onboard of manned ships" and that the important thing here is that "people should get help very fast when in need". According to the participants "a very good system would be needed onboard of the autonomous ferries to put out fire". In addition to intervention in unexpected situations, the human host was important in offering ad-hoc services for an improved passenger experience.

4) The importance of technical and ad-hoc services offered by human host: Human hosts can offer services that improve the passenger experience onboard the ferry. For example, they can make sure that onboarding and offboarding go well and control the number of passengers. Another point that was mentioned, was that the human host could offer services to the elderly passengers if needed. In addition to that, a human host could resolve technical issues should the ferry's technical system fail. This can also improve the ferry trip experience for the passengers. This was mentioned to be "especially important for long term trips" and especially for the first trips, but not necessary after a few trips. A safety host is important to keep an overview of what is happening and intervene if needed, which was aligned with the notion of general perception of safety and dealing with the unexpected. It was mentioned that "the human aspect must be in balance with the technical aspect" meaning that the perceived safety is still key despite having technical safety. It is expected that one should be able to trust that all the prerequisites for the trip are taken care of, and if so, then there is no need for human host as long as the ferry is remotely watched and operated. Furthermore, it was mentioned that it is difficult for a human host to always keep focus. Nevertheless, in times of higher traffic or higher risk, such as during the high season for tourism, it is better to have a human host onboard to ensure a better ferry trip experience.

5) The need for gradual transition towards unmanned ferries: The participants emphasized the importance of a gradual transition from having a human host onboard towards an unmanned ferry. They mentioned that "the ferry should have the possibility to be steered manually by a human host" since a slow shift "will be more reassuring". The data showed that at the start phase, the presence of a human host can help passengers to trust the ferry, and this was a necessity at the start up phases of having an operational autonomous, unmanned ferry. Also, when there is high traffic, it can be helpful to have a human host onboard. Passengers need to trust that the ferry have had time to build resilience towards various scenarios as can be seen from this quote: "the learning process for autonomous ferry is a long process for dangerous situations, and in the meantime, one wants to feel safe with a host onboard".

6) The importance of information and transparency in transition towards unmanned ferries: The participants expressed the need to understand and to see that the technology is safe. Since there will be no person steering the ferry, it will be essential to have good and clear information. Passengers need to be made aware of what the ferry is doing and why, as can be seen from this quote: "having sufficient information from people who have designed and made the system is very reassuring to know what is going on. This was specifically mentioned in retrospect to a ferry trial when the ferry's sensors captured waves by its own thrusters as obstacles and stopped in its track. The participants mentioned that the engineers aboard informing about what was happening felt reassuring. In addition to that, people need to have information about onboarding and offboarding. Generally, the participants also mentioned in retrospect that the information obtained through the workshops increased their level of trust towards urban autonomous passenger ferries. Here trust may be simply better understanding rather than reliability.

IV. Discussion and Conclusion

The aim of this paper was to understand the consequences or implications of a human host on an UAF, and in what way a human host would shape the passengers' perceived safety, trust, and convenience of UAFs. Furthermore, the aim was to understand the implications of a possible removal of a human host from an UAF. To achieve this objective, we examined the role of a human host onboard UAFs with data collected as part of a citizen engagement consisting of four sessions of both theoretical and immersive parts. The data collection was targeted towards the participants' perceptions of UAF in this context and followed them through the sessions. The data was subject to quantitative and qualitative analyses. The findings are discussed in the following.

A. Quantitative

Over time and throughout the session, the participants' emphasis on the presence of a human host decreases in a nonlinear manner. The decrease could be associated with the repeated exposure and immersion with the technology that creates familiarity and trust to a certain degree. Although trust may be simply better understanding rather a proven reliability and predictability of the technology in operation. Particularly after the tangible VR simulation (VR), the importance of a human host was rated as "not so important" to "not important at all" by the majority of the participants. A possible explanation for this could be the increased trust in the system as the simulation was partly hardcoded and, in that sense, "fail proof". Additionally, the VR simulation did not include other humans, and thereby social security aspects might not have been so evident. Furthermore, VR can be a novelty itself that can engage people in the mere experience rather than the operational implications of the concept.

This nonlinearity could be due to the group dynamics or the speculations and reflections as they are engaged in a novel situation and making sense of the technology itself and its implications for them and the society. Also, several participants claimed that they did not remember what they answered on earlier questionnaires, as several days where in between them. This in turn would make the participants answer on their current perceptions and experiences. The slight increase in the perceived importance of the human host during the ferry session (FERRY) can be explained by minor technical issues still present on the prototype. The presence of the personnel onboard, and the need for their interventions together with the information they provided to the participants, could have underlined the need of a human host in the transition towards fully unmanned UAFs.

Furthermore, the emphasis on the importance of a human host was highlighted during later pm hours, and it became limited to the quay areas. Therefore, it is becoming temporally and geographically more limited. This can be seen in relation to the context where the trial was conducted within closed waters, and where both ends of the crossing were always in sight. The short distance to land where a human host is overseeing from the quay areas could be seen as sufficient to feel safe.

The need for surveillance cameras onboard was highlighted, and even claiming that the ferry would be safer than the street at night. The accessibility to emergency response and the possibility to report any deviation to the responsible authority was highlighted at the end phase.

Communication in real time to an onshore control centre, knowing about, and being able to manually stop the boat with an emergency button, were also mentioned as essential. This could reflect on people already trying to find alternatives for a human host and shows a belief in digital technology to substitute a human host. Given that the study was conducted in Norway, this seems to be a plausible explanation as the general society has adopted many digital solutions in the everyday life. Furthermore, people started to see the shortcoming of a human host in the modern times with respect to new threats, such as cybersecurity breach.

However, this observed trend of how the participants think a human host could be restricted in its presence and replaced by features such as information screens, communication tools, remote monitoring, and surveillance, could be influenced by the workshop's discourse itself; the framing of the research may have directed the participants thinking and reflections.

B. Qualitative

The context played an important role which sets this paper apart from that of [3]. His operational context was concerning longer distances (across the Bedford basin in Halifax, Nova Scotia) framing the case around the current human operated ferries of 24 m in length and a maximum capacity of 390 passengers aboard. This is very much in contrast with the context of the current case where the crossing was short and the terminals were visible from both ends with the use of a small UAF, making it less risky in the minds of participants. Nevertheless, the unexpected contextual, technological and social incidents still asked for the intervention of a human host onboard that could explain the *what* and *why* of the situation. Thus, the human host still played a role as a resilience anchor and the agent to provide transparency and situational awareness. Given the operational context of the study, the results indicate that a level 3 [7] would be perceived as trustworthy by the participants. In the related field of autonomous vehicles, the willingness to use public autonomous vehicles is increasing with the level of supervision [15]. In the context of autonomous buses in Trondheim, a study described by [12], several participants emphasized the need of a human host aboard mainly for security reasons. Interestingly the participants were found to demand a bus host even more after the physical trial, which is discussed to be because of operational situations where the bus host had to intervene, described in [12]. Arguably there are differences in the context and between water-based and land-based transport. As this specific study was conducted during no traffic in the canal, the land-based real-life studies would be more prone to a higher traffic complexity. The vulnerability of other road users, higher differences in speed between different between the autonomous bus and other vehicles, and complexity in the interaction between road users would arguably have a role to play in the perceived importance of an onboard human safety host.

Technology acceptance extends to automation technology acceptance, and this requires that people trust the technology and suppliers. This process should happen over time and through a transitory period that allows people to evaluate if the technology is safe, reliable, and trustworthy. This is in line with [15] for instance, in the context of public autonomous buses, where transition from lower LOAs to higher LOAs must take place over time.

Although people started to speculate about less human host presence, they still mentioned the need to know what is going on (transparency) and to be able to intervene (emergency button and real-time communication with onshore) which emphasizes that the principle of designing for human-in-the-loop even for higher LOAs, whether that 'human' is the human host or the passenger, is still present. In the field of non-rail autonomous vehicles, [16] and [17] highlights that participants in their studies were interested in information and means to intervene. This reflects on a partial transition of responsibility from a human host to the passenger in the face of adversity. It is interesting to consider the legal and ethical implications thereof.

This paper highlights that although the trend of automation in maritime and urban transportation is moving towards higher levels of autonomy, this transition, and the end result, which is a service that will be continually used by real end-users, can benefit from such participatory workshops and a co-creative design perspective. This can balance the technology-centred and human-centred schools of thoughts into creating a product and a process that considers both aspects, people and technology.

C. Limitations and future research

As an early study within the context of UAFs the paper seeks to investigate the role of a human host onboard. It is acknowledged that the study has several limitations.

A first limitation is that the sample size of the population is very small (N=15). This was partly due to the resource intensive nature of four sessions with immersive components such as the VR experience and ferry ride only allowing for smaller groups. The sample is far too small to draw any significant conclusions, and the patterns observed should only be seen as preliminary insights which inspire more extensive future studies. A larger sample size would also allow for a closer investigation of how - age, gender and socio economical background would influence safety related perceptions. The second limitation is that the participants were only recruited from Trondheim, meaning that the findings might not be transferable to other locations However, given that this is a case study in a specific context some familiarity with the context is required. A further limitation is the recruitment, where the participants themselves signed up for the sessions in compliance with ethical standards. As seen in the results section, all the participants were "interested" to "very interested", which might induce that the population has generally more positive perceptions towards autonomous transportation.

Some limitations are also seen in the research design. To have a set of four different sessions with both informative and immersive parts are seen as an opportunity to investigate how the perceptions develop through immersion beyond the initial ones. It also allows for investigating how different events and topics would influence the perception of the population. On the other hand, social group dynamics did occur potentially biasing the population towards positive perceptions. Another factor was the aforementioned technological framing with comprehensive explanations and insights into technological possibilities for such a ferry system. The nature of having several events did make the topics in the later discussions somewhat repetitive and some of the participants felt they had nothing more to add. A reduction in the number of sessions, and a more streamlined undertaking would be preferable.

Beside mitigating the limitations above, future research should be expanded in both sample size and geographical context to confirm or challenge the findings of the current study. Furthermore, it would be of great interest to further explore the concerns of participants regarding safety and security onboard and specially safety at night, during festivals, and in emergency situations. This could be done through role play on the real ferry or VR simulations. An investigation of how age, gender and socio-economic status affects the demand for a human host aboard, would add further granularity to the research and this requires larger sample size to have valid and reliable findings. Within the context of enclosed water and small scale UAFs, a trial with no personnel aboard would be of interest. It is also recommended to angle further research into designing systems for the "passenger in the loop" in combination with a remotely located safety supervisor.

ACKNOWLEDGMENT

This work was sponsored by the Research Council of Norway (RCN), mainly through the project TRUSST (project number 313921), but also MAS (326676), MIDAS (331921) and SFI AutoShip (309230). The citizen engagement activities were designed by the project team in collaboration with NTNU Design Department and under the supervision of Mission Publiques (missionspubliques.org), a professional citizen engagement consultancy. The recruitment of the participants was done by Nordic Viewpoint (nordic-viewpoint.com/no/). The facilities at the NTNU Shore Control Lab were extensively used during the trials. The authors want to thank the reviewers for valuable comments and suggestions, and everyone contributing to the citizen engagement.

REFERENCES

[1] H.-C. Burmeister, W. Bruhn, Ø. J. Rødseth, and T. Porathe, "Autonomous Unmanned Merchant Vessel and its Contribution towards the e-Navigation Implementation: The MUNIN Perspective", Int. J. E-Navig. Marit. Econ., vol. 1, pp. 1–13, Dec. 2014, doi: 10.1016/j.enavi.2014.12.002.

[2] 'Climate Change | UN-Habitat'. https://unhabitat.org/topic/climate-change (accessed Feb. 02, 2023).

[3] F. Goerlandt and K. Pulsifer, "An exploratory investigation of public perceptions towards autonomous urban ferries", Saf. Sci., vol. 145, p. 105496, Jan. 2022, doi: 10.1016/j.ssci.2021.105496.

[4] 'Roboat project', https://roboat.org/. https://roboat.org/ (accessed Feb. 02, 2023).

[5] 'VAIARO – CAPTN'. https://captn.sh/en/vaiaro-englisch/ (accessed Feb. 02, 2023).

[6] O. A. Alsos et al., "NTNU Shore Control Lab: Designing shore control centres in the age of autonomous ships", J. Phys. Conf. Ser., vol. 2311, no. 1, p. 012030, Jul. 2022, doi: 10.1088/1742-6596/2311/1/012030.

[7] Ø. Smogeli, 'Autonomous Urban Passenger Ferries – A New Mobility Mode in Need of Appropriate Regulation?', in Autonomous Vessels in Maritime Affairs: Law and Governance Implications, UK: Palgrave Macmillan, In Press.

[8] F. Goerlandt, "Maritime Autonomous Surface Ships from a risk governance perspective: Interpretation and implications", Saf. Sci., vol. 128, p. 104758, Aug. 2020, doi: 10.1016/j.ssci.2020.104758.

[9] N. P. Reddy et al., "Zero-Emission Autonomous Ferries for Urban Water Transport: Cheaper, Cleaner Alternative to Bridges and Manned Vessels", IEEE Electrification Mag., vol. 7, no. 4, pp. 32–45, Dec. 2019, doi: 10.1109/MELE.2019.2943954.

[10] 'Missions Publiques', Missions Publiques. https://missionspubliques.org/ (accessed Feb. 02, 2023).

[11] 'Gule Sider® Kart'. https://kart.gulesider.no/?zoomfb=15&centerfb=10.393195,63.435975&maptypefb=aerial (accessed Feb. 02, 2023).

[12] T. Stålhane, T. Myklebust, and I. S. Haug, "Trust and Acceptance of Self-Driving Busses", in Proceedings of the 31st European Safety and Reliability Conference (ESREL 2021), 2021, pp. 2194–2201. doi: 10.3850/978-981-18-2016-8_147-cd.

[13] T. Myklebust, T. Stålhane, G. D. Jenssen, and I. S. Haug, "Trust Me, We Have a Safety Case for the Public", in Proceedings of the 31st European Safety and Reliability Conference (ESREL 2021), 2021, pp. 2180–2185. doi: 10.3850/978-981-18-2016-8_087-cd.

[14] V. Braun and V. Clarke, "Using thematic analysis in psychology", Qual. Res. Psychol., vol. 3, no. 2, pp. 77–101, Jan. 2006, doi: 10.1191/1478088706qp063oa.

[15] C. Goldbach, J. Sickmann, T. Pitz, and T. Zimasa, "Towards autonomous public transportation: Attitudes and intentions of the local population", Transp. Res. Interdiscip. Perspect., vol. 13, p. 100504, Mar. 2022, doi: 10.1016/j.trip.2021.100504.

[16] S. Nordhoff, J. de Winter, W. Payre, B. van Arem, and R. Happee, "What impressions do users have after a ride in an automated shuttle? An interview study", Transp. Res. Part F Traffic Psychol. Behav., vol. 63, pp. 252–269, May 2019, doi: 10.1016/j.trf.2019.04.009.

[17] P. Fröhlich et al., "What's the Robo-Driver up to?" Requirements for Screen-based Awareness and Intent Communication in Autonomous Buses', -Com, vol. 18, no. 2, pp. 151–165, Aug. 2019, doi: 10.1515/icom-2018-003.

Appendix 1: The agendas of the four sessions.

Session 1 Information and Discussion	**Session 2** VR Experience	**Session 3** Ferry trial	**Session 4:** Reflection & recommendations
Preread with information and visualization of the Urban autonomous ferry system before the session.	**Informative film** on the the use of simulations.	**Ferry trial:** between Ravnkloa and Vestre Kanalkai. Tour of the mA2.	**Informative presentation** Dag McGeorge (DNV): Building an assurance case
Questionnaire (WS1_A) at the very beginning of the session: *QB1* Age Sex Number of kids Have you read the preread? *QB2* How much time do you use to work/school? What mode of transportation do you use to work/school? What mode of transport do you use outside of work/school? How often do you use public transport? Have you tried an autonomous vehicle or vessel before? *QB3* How important is the following aspect to you (likert scale 1 (not important) - 5 Very important)): Human host aboard	**VR experience** With the use of mockups and three different scenarios: (1) Sunny day without traffic (2) Snow, wind and thunder without traffic (3) Rain and Traffic **Questionnaire** after the VR experience (VR). With the following questions, analysed in this paper: *QB6 Repeated* *QB3 Repeated* *QB7 Repeated* *QB8 Repeated* *QB9 Repeated*	**Questionnaire** after the ferry trial (FERRY), with the following questions analysed in this paper: *QB10: I would like to try a UAF again (Idk, not agree at all, not agree, neutral, agree, very agree)* *QB6 Repeated* *QB3 Repeated* *QB7 Repeated* *QB8 Repeated* *QB9 Repeated*	**Table discussions** on reflections and recommendations for further development: What is positive? What should be reconsidered? What should be dropped or changed? Universal Design – How can the urban autonomous ferry become a mean of transport for all?
Informative presentations: Hanna Maria van Zijp (Zeabuz): *Possibilities for Urban spaces through UAFs* Øyvind Smogeli (Zeabuz): *The Zeabuz history* Jon Arne Glomsrud (DNV): *Information about the TRUSST project* Leander Pantelatos (NTNU): *A user journey with the UAF.*		**Debrief session** after the ferry trial. The following questions were used as a guide to the facilitator How did you experience the ferry trial? Has your view on UAFs changed? – If so in what way? Was there anything that was uncomfortable? What are your thoughts on safety aboard the UAF? Did the experience influence your trust in the ability of the UAF to detect other traffic on the river? Do you have any thoughts on the design of the ferry?	**Questionnaire** after the session (WS2): *QB11* To what extent would you agree to the following statements? (likert scale 1 (do not agree at all) - 5 (Very agree)): Having a human host onboard an UAF is important to me. It is important that there is a human host onboard during the evening/night. It is sufficient that the host is available on Quay areas (but not onboard an UAF). There should be camera surveillance on board an UAF. Passengers must be able to access an emergency button to "stop" the UAF. Passengers must have access to a screen to be able to communicate with an operator at a shore control center who monitors the ferry. I am afraid that someone might hack/take control of the ferry if there is no human host onboard. It is important that passengers can easily both small and large deviations. *QB3 Repeated* *QB6 Repeated* *QB7 Repeated* *QB8 Repeated* *QB9 Repeated*
Table discussions on the topics of Safety, sustainability, and societal impact (only questions analysed in this paper are included here): What are your concerns regarding you as a passenger? How do you consider the importance of a human host aboard the UAF? What are your concerns regarding kayaks and other traffic on the canal?	**Debrief session** after the VR experience The following questions were used as a guide to the facilitator How did you experience the virtual reality simulation? As how real did you experience the virtual realty simulation? Was there anything you experienced as uncomfortable? In the simulation, you were alone on the UAF. What thoughts do you have about this, versus being more people onboard, concerning safety? Did the experience affect your confidence in the UAF perceiving what is happening around it, in any way? Do you have any thoughts on the design of the ferry?		
Questionnaire (WS1-B) after the session: *QB6* What are your three most important thoughts after this Session? *QB7* What are your most important expectations towards UAFs? *QB8* What are your most important concerns towards UAFs? *QB9* What are your most important needs towards UAFs? *QB3 Repeated*			

Deep Learning for Condition Detection in Chest Radiographs: A Performance Comparison of Different Radiograph Views and Handling of Uncertain Labels

Mubashir Ahmad
Department of Computer Science
University of Hertfordshire
Hatfield, UK
email: m.ahmad21@herts.ac.uk

Kheng Lee Koay
Department of Computer Science
University of Hertfordshire
Hatfield, UK
email: k.l.koay@herts.ac.uk

Yi Sun
Department of Computer Science
University of Hertfordshire
Hatfield, UK
email: y.2.sun@herts.ac.uk

Vijay Jayaram
Consultant Radiologist
The Princess Alexandra Hospital
Harlow, UK
email: vijay.jayaram@nhs.net

Ganesh Arunachalam
Consultant in Elderly Care
The Princess Alexandra Hospital
Harlow, UK
email: ganesh.arunachalam@nhs.net

Farshid Amirabdollahian
Department of Computer Science
University of Hertfordshire
Hatfield, UK
email: f.amirabdollahian2@herts.ac.uk

***Abstract*—Chest radiographs are the initial diagnostic modality for lung or chest-related conditions. It is believed that radiologist's availability is a bottleneck impacting patient's safety because of long waiting times. With the arrival of machine learning and especially deep learning, the race for finding Artificial Intelligence (AI) based approaches that allow for the highest accuracy in detecting abnormalities on chest radiographs is at its peak. Classification of radiographs as normal or abnormal is based on the training and expertise of the reporting radiologist. The increase in the number of chest radiographs over a period of time and the lack of sufficient radiologists in the UK and worldwide have had an impact on the number of chest radiographs assessed and reported in a given time frame. Substantial work is dedicated to machine learning for classifying normal and abnormal radiographs based on a single pathology. The success of deep learning techniques in binary radiograph classification urges the medical imaging community to apply it to multi-label radiographs. Deep learning techniques often require huge datasets to train its underlying model. Recently, the availability of large multi-label datasets has ignited new efforts to overcome this challenging task. This work presents Convolutional Neural Networks (CNNs) based models trained on publically available CheXpert multi-label data. Based on common pathologies seen on chest radiographs and their clinical significance, we have chosen pathologies such as Pulmonary oedema, Cardiomegaly, Atelectasis, Consolidation and Pleural effusion. We trained our models using different projections such as Anteroposterior (AP), Posteroanterior (PA), and lateral and compared the performance of our models for each projection. Our results demonstrate that the model for the AP projection outperforms the remaining models with an average AUC of 0.85. Furthermore, we use the samples with uncertain labels in CheXpert dataset and improve the model performance by removing the uncertainty using Gaussian Mixture Models (GMM). The results show improvement in all three views with AUCs ranging from 0.91 for AP, 0.75 for PA and 0.85 on the lateral view.**

Keywords– ***Chest radiograph; Deep learning; Multi-label classification; Uncertain labels***

I. INTRODUCTION

Respiratory diseases are one of the leading causes of death in the United Kingdom. According to a survey by Conor Stewart [1], prior to COVID-19, the mortality rate from respiratory diseases in the United Kingdom in 2020 was 130 per 100,000 male population and 89 per 100,000 female population. Chest radiographs are the most utilised diagnostic modality for lung or chest-related conditions. However, it requires an experienced radiologist to accurately analyse radiographs to detect chest-related conditions, such as Pulmonary oedema, Cardiomegaly, Atelectasis, Lung cancer, and Consolidation, besides other less common pathologies. A report in 2020 by the Royal College of radiologists [2] highlights the national shortage of radiologists resulting in reporting backlogs which can adversely impact patient care. A further predicted shortfall in radiologist numbers by 44% in 2025 will have a greater impact on reporting backlogs. Expenditure on outsourcing imaging examinations for reporting has increased by 58% in the last few years. In addition to the scarcity of radiologists, there is a problem with diagnostic errors in radiology reports. According to [3], worldwide, annually, at least 40 million out of 1 billion radiology reports contain errors. Chest radiographs are the most used diagnostic procedure for respiratory and cardiovascular diseases - errors in diagnosis and delays in reporting contribute to adverse outcomes for patients. In order to decrease the workload for existing and future radiologists, scientists have been working on automatic radiographic interpretation systems. Recently, Deep Learning especially Convolutional Neural Networks (CNNs) has boosted research in computer vision, especially in medical imaging and has demonstrated promising results in the detection of pathologies on chest radiographs. However, the interpretation of chest radiographs can be challenging. In order to provide good results, deep learning requires a large number of data samples for training. The presence of multiple conditions in one radiograph makes it difficult for the model to generalise as there can be an overlap in the imaging findings of two different chest pathologies, e.g., pulmonary oedema and infectious pathologies. Moreover, the presence of uncertain labels in a dataset further increases the difficulty. Samples with uncertain labels can cause difficulties in training the machine learning algorithm. Besides demonstrating the potential to improve diagnostic accuracy, deep learning models can also improve the reporting workflow by prioritising abnormal radiographs over normal ones. Training the model on different radiographic projections has the potential to improve the diagnostic accuracy of the model, particularly when dealing with a suboptimal radiograph in a critically ill patient.

This study trains a state-of-the-art CNN-based deep neural network DenseNet121 [4] on a large chest radiograph dataset, CheXpert [5][6]. Figure 1 shows a few radiographs from the CheXpert dataset. In addition, we trained separate models for different views Anteroposterior (AP), Posteroanterior (PA), and lateral and evaluated their performance. Furthermore, the study addresses uncertainty present in the data by relabelling uncertain samples using a Gaussian Mixture Model (GMM) [7] and including them in the training data. The performance is then compared before and after reducing the uncertainty. The following Section offers a review of the state of the art using deep learning for interpreting chest radiographs, identifying multiple conditions in a single radiograph, and addressing uncertain labels in data. Section III presents our approach, which involves utilizing various data and model-based methods, correcting uncertain labels, and addressing each radiographic view individually. In Section IV, we conduct comparative experiments on the CheXpert dataset and provide the results. Section V examines the main insights gained from the results. Lastly, in Section VI, we present the conclusion of the paper.

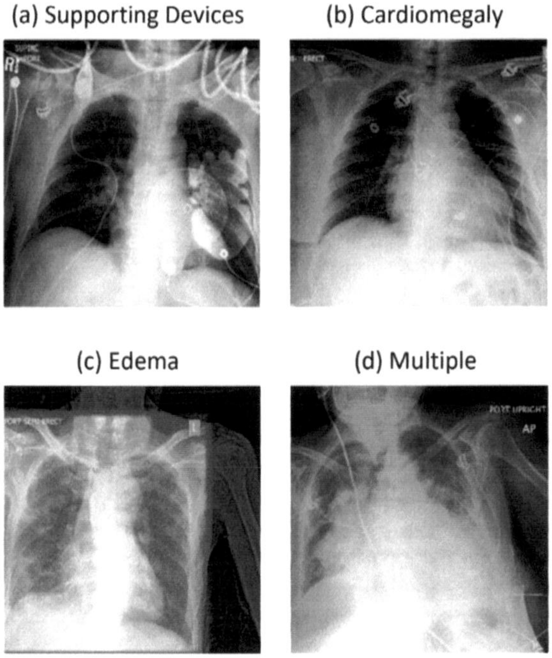

Figure 1: Images from CheXpert dataset. Each image has 14 labels corresponding to each condition. Mentioned conditions are positive labels for each of the four images.

II. Related Work

The availability of large labelled datasets [5][6][8] of chest radiographs has led many researchers to use deep learning for chest radiograph interpretation. Most recent work in this area has focused on CNN-based models and applied various techniques such as transfer learning, feature extraction, and region of interest analysis to improve the detection of abnormalities [9–12]. In one study, a 121-layered neural network trained on the CheXnet frontal view dataset, outperformed average radiologists in detecting pneumonia [9]. Additionally, data augmentation has been used to tackle the issue of insufficient data in new challenges such as COVID-19, as seen in [13] where a CNN model was trained to classify chest radiographs of COVID-19 patients. Many studies have focused on specific conditions such as pneumonia, COVID-19 and oedema [9][13][14]. In addition to the above, the power of deep learning allows for the detection of multiple conditions in a single radiograph [15][16]. Multiple-label detection on chest radiographs is much more challenging as compared to a single label. The overlapping and vanishing of features can hinder the model performance in a multi-label setting [17]. The hierarchical dependencies present between conditions are exploited in [15] by using a conditional training approach. This is achieved by training a deep neural network twice, first on data with only positive parent-level conditions, followed by training on the entire dataset. As CNN is very good at extracting prominent features, [18] suppresses the irrelevant features by assigning them smaller weights and enhancing the important features with higher weights to detect multiple conditions in chest radiographs. Different abnormal conditions appear on radiographs in different anatomical areas, such as a Pleural effusion, which can be identified by looking at the lower left and right corners of the lungs. Localising the correct anatomical region in [19] enables the model to learn the better relationship between different structures in the radiograph.

This paper examines the use of three different radiograph views (AP, PA, lateral) separately. In the first phase, we train a DenseNet121 model for each view, using techniques such as transfer learning, template matching, and augmentation to improve performance. We have repeated these experiments ten times to ensure generalisable results. In the second phase, we use a semi-supervised approach with GMM to label uncertain samples, which is an improvement over previous methods [5][15] that assigned positive labels to all uncertain samples or a random float between 0.55 to 0.85. We then include these relabelled uncertain samples in the training data and repeat all experiments. Our approach of individually analysing each view shows promising results and effectively reduces uncertainty in the data.

III. Methodology

In this section, we outline the method utilised to classify radiographs with multiple labels. We begin by introducing

DenseNet121 and CNN briefly along with the applied model training procedure in subsection A. Following that, we delve into explaining multi-scale template matching for data quality improvement and transfer learning techniques we employed to enhance the model's performance in subsection B. Furthermore, in subsection C, we expound upon the data augmentation methods we adopted to enhance data diversity and control model overfitting. Finally, we describe how we utilize GMM to eliminate uncertainty in the data in subsection D.

A. *DenseNet121 and Model Training*

In this paper, we chose DenseNet121 architecture as our base CNN model because of its popularity in computer vision, especially in medical imaging [15][20][21]. DenseNet121 utilizes convolutional neural networks (CNN) and comprises 121 layers. The layers in the network are connected in such a way that each layer receives inputs from all the previous layers; this helps the model retain important features recognized in the earlier layers [4]. CNN is a deep learning algorithm that performs a convolution operation on images to extract features. We also used pooling and dropout layers to prevent the model from overfitting. Finally, we trained the model using a batch size of 32, Adam optimizer, and used the Area under the Receiver Operating Characteristic Curve (AUC) as the evaluation metric, as in [15].

B. *Multi-scale Template Matching and Transfer Learning*

In order to improve the data quality, we employed a multi-scale template matching technique to eliminate unnecessary regions from both the training and testing images [15][22]. To achieve this, we picked a high-quality template image from each view, trimmed and scaled it to 224×224 pixels, and removed unnecessary areas such as the shoulders, neck, and pelvic sections. We then matched the template image at a scale range (empirically chosen) of (0.7 to 1.3) with the entire data and extracted the best-matched 224×224 section of the image, thus enabling the model to concentrate on the thoracic area and avoiding any confusion from other regions.

Furthermore, to help the model train fast and accurately we applied transfer learning. This is a powerful method to improve the accuracy of deep learning models. The idea is to leverage the knowledge gained by training on a generic data set, such as ImageNet [23], to gain knowledge of general image features (vertical and horizontal edges). The last layers of the model are then replaced and fine-tuned the model with data specific to the task at hand, such as CheXpert [5] in this instance. As the data in ImageNet is very different from the one in CheXpert, so instead of fine-tuning just the last layers of the model we fine-tuned all layers[24]. This makes all layers specialised to radiographs while getting help from general image features. Through experimentation, we have compared the performance of models with and without transfer learning. The detail is in section IV of this paper.

C. *Data Augmentation*

In the medical image classification domain, insufficient data has always been a problem. Chest radiograph data is no different. Although we have very large chest radiograph data sets available [5][6][8], these are still not enough for a deep-learning model to generalise ideally. This is because the same pathology can manifest differently on a radiograph depending on the patient's age, gender, lifestyle and stage of the disease, besides the radiographic projection and other technical factors. Multiple pathologies on a single radiograph make feature extraction more difficult. That is the reason, deep learning algorithms require a very large number of samples with the same pathology to capture sufficient important features. With data augmentation, we artificially enhance the size of the data set and add diversity to it. Various techniques can be used to modify the image, such as resizing and zooming. In order to improve feature extraction, we employed data augmentation on our data set which includes setting brightness randomly between 30% and 100%, randomly rotating the image by $7\pm$ degrees, applying a random shear range of $0.2\pm$, zooming the image by 0.2, adding random noise to the images, and finally flipping the images horizontally [25]. These six augmentation techniques were chosen empirically. We apply all six data augmentation techniques on all training images and send them to the model along with the original image for training. The results of the experiment reveal that applying image augmentation significantly improves performance.

D. *Relabelling Uncertain labels with GMM*

In the CheXpert dataset, almost 30% of the samples have uncertain labels, which means the condition may or may not be present in the radiograph. As this is a multi-label problem, the presence of one condition can impact the appearance of another coexisting condition on the radiograph. Instead of discarding the 30% of the data with uncertain samples in CheXpert, or assigning all positive/negative labels, we removed the uncertainty and relabelled the samples and include them in the training process. To do that, we chose GMM because of its ability to tackle a mixture of multiple data distributions. It is a probabilistic model that creates multiple clusters using an Expectation Maximization (EM) algorithm and updates the estimator parameters during the process [7]. We trained a GMM model for each of the five conditions separately using only certain samples. GMM operates by assigning each sample to the cluster with the distribution that is closest in terms of parameters. It created 100 clusters for Consolidation, 500 for Pleural Effusion, 200 for Cardiomegaly, 300 for Atelectasis and 350 for Edema. This results in many clusters, with multiple clusters of each class. Once the estimator was fully converged, we used it to get predictions for the uncertain samples. We conducted experiments excluding uncertain samples and then including them after relabelling in the model training. The results indicate that this approach leads to some performance improvement. Further detail is in section IV of this paper.

IV. Experimentation and Results

The dataset has 223,414 chest radiographs of 65,240 patients collected between October 2002 and July 2017. Each image has 14 labels corresponding to a medical condition. In this study, we chose five clinically important conditions Pulmonary oedema, Consolidation, Cardiomegaly, Atelectasis, and Pleural Effusion [5]. To make the performance comparison between different radiograph projections, we created a separate model for each projection. Also, to ensure fair performance comparison, we trained the models on an equal number of samples (29,421 images per view). We did not use the CheXpert validation set during training and instead used it to test the models after training. The experiments were conducted in two phases. In the first phase, we excluded samples with uncertainty from the model training process, further explained in subsection A. In the second phase of experiments, we incorporated 22,219 relabelled uncertain samples for each view in the training process. Through this method, we were able to observe the impact of eliminating data uncertainty on the performance of the models.

A. Experiments Excluding Uncertain Samples

In this paper, we used DenseNet121 as the main network and trained five different models for each radiograph view. These models include DenseNet121, DenseNet121 with multi-scale template-matched (TM) data, DenseNet121 with transfer learning (TL), DenseNet121 with data augmentation (AUG), and a combination of template matching, transfer learning, and augmentation. The AUC is used as the evaluation metric in all of the experiments done in this paper. Table I shows the results on the Anteroposterior view. We

TABLE I: AUC SCORES FOR VARIOUS DEEP LEARNING METHODS WITH DENSENET121 ON AP, WITHOUT UNCERTAIN SAMPLES. THE VALUES IN BOLD SHOW THE BEST RESULTS OF EACH MODEL.

	Anteroposterior				
Exp	**DN121**	**DN121_TM**	**DN121_TL**	**DN121_AUG**	**DN121_TM_TL_AUG**
1	**0.85**	0.79	0.76	**0.87**	0.84
2	0.79	0.74	0.81	0.76	0.85
3	0.76	0.75	0.86	0.79	0.82
4	0.78	0.81	0.8	0.8	0.83
5	0.76	**0.81**	0.84	0.84	0.83
6	0.76	0.72	**0.9**	0.86	0.83
7	0.8	0.79	0.67	0.8	0.88
8	0.82	0.63	0.8	0.84	0.85
9	0.81	0.79	0.82	0.82	0.86
10	0.74	0.78	0.81	0.8	**0.88**
Avg	0.79	0.76	0.81	0.82	0.85
Std	0.03	0.05	0.06	0.03	0.02

repeat each experiment ten times with different sample sets randomly chosen from CheXpert. We can see how different techniques applied with DenseNet121 performed better, especially transfer learning and data augmentation. The best-performing model is "$DN121\_TM\_TL\_AUG$" with statistical significance observed using Analysis of Variance (ANOVA) where $[F(4,45) = 5.504, p = 0.001]$. When repeating the same experiment for the other two views, PA and Lateral, a similar statistical significance is observed in favour of this combined model. The performance of this model, "$DN121\_TM\_TL\_AUG$", is then compared across the three views. Table II shows the results from this comparison. ANOVA results indicate statistically significant differences between the three views where $[F(2,27) = 64.677, p < 0.001]$. Summary statistics indicate that AP and Lateral views performed better than PA. AP performed more consistently with a standard deviation of 0.02 as compared to 0.04 for Lateral.

TABLE II: RESULTS OF EXPERIMENTS USING OUR BEST-PERFORMING MODEL ON AP, PA AND LATERAL VIEWS WITHOUT UNCERTAIN SAMPLES.

Exp	Anteroposterior(AP)	Posteroanterior(PA)	Lateral
1	0.84	0.69	0.79
2	0.85	0.73	**0.9**
3	0.82	0.74	0.84
4	0.83	0.74	0.78
5	0.83	**0.74**	0.87
6	0.83	0.73	0.82
7	0.88	0.73	0.84
8	0.85	0.69	0.86
9	0.86	0.7	0.82
10	**0.88**	0.72	0.81
Avg	0.85	0.72	0.83
Std	0.02	0.02	0.04

B. Experiments Including Uncertain Samples

In the second phase of experiments, we included the relabelled uncertain samples to the training data of the corresponding data set. We reran the whole series of experiments as in the first phase. Table III shows the results of the experiments for the best model of each view. ANOVA results indicate statistical significance for the difference between the three views where $[F(2,27) = 19.823, p < 0.001]$. Interestingly, on average AP is still ahead but if we look at the minimum and maximum AUC, it is 0.65 and 0.91, respectively, also represented by the larger standard deviation for AP.

TABLE III: RESULTS OF EXPERIMENTS USING OUR BEST-PERFORMING MODEL ON AP, PA AND LATERAL VIEWS WITH UNCERTAIN SAMPLES.

Exp	Anteroposterior(AP)	Posteroanterior(PA)	Lateral
1	0.87	0.72	0.78
2	0.65	0.73	**0.85**
3	0.87	0.73	0.84
4	0.89	0.75	0.82
5	**0.91**	0.73	0.77
6	0.9	**0.75**	0.82
7	0.85	0.72	0.83
8	0.88	0.72	0.81
9	0.89	0.73	0.83
10	0.88	0.73	0.83
Avg	0.86	0.73	0.82
Std	0.08	0.01	0.03

Figure 2 shows a better view of gradual improvement in the performance of AP models. The blue boxes indicate the performance of models before including uncertain samples and the orange boxes indicate the performance of models after including uncertain samples which were relabelled using GMM. Performing a Univariate Analysis of Variance for AP identified statistical significance at model level ($p < 0.001$) and also pre-post level ($p = 0.024$), but there was no significance for interaction effects for model and pre-post indicating that we can interpret and rely on significant differences observed at model and pre-post levels.

Overall, this indicates that our GMM approach to reduce uncertain labels contributes to betterment of the classification task.

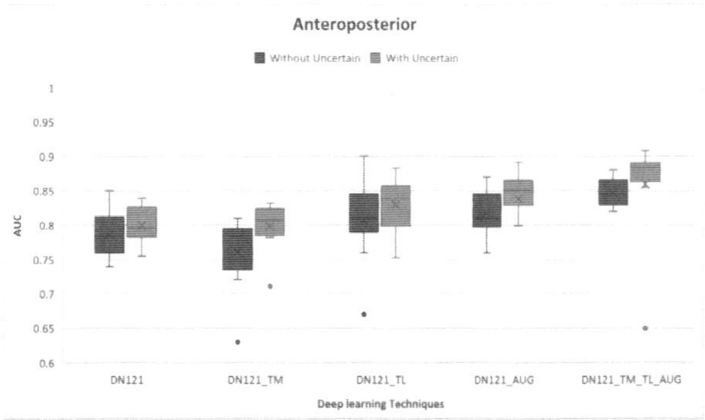

Figure 2: Performance comparison of AP models before and after including uncertain samples.

V. Discussion

By training a state-of-the-art deep learning algorithm on different views of chest radiographs, we identified that AP and Lateral views are comparably better than PA on DenseNet121 and its derivations using some of the state-of-the-art CNN backbone architectures. The process allowed us to identify a model with best performance for the AP and Lateral views. This is an interesting fact, keeping in view that PA radiographs are more commonly performed in the outpatient setting, while AP radiographs are performed in patients who are ill or unstable and therefore unable to cooperate for a PA view. Identifying a condition by a view-specialised model can be more reliable than a general model trained on all types of views. As the frontal and lateral views of the chest look different, important features of a frontal image can manifest differently on a lateral view resulting in uncertainty for interpretation both by the radiologist and the machine learning algorithm.

Machine learning techniques such as GMM can help resolve uncertain labels which can be utilised in the training process as shown in this work. Although the improvement after removing the uncertainty is not significant in terms of AUC increases, this approach shows the potential for further exploration and optimisation. This work has some limitations, for example the data set used contains radiographs from only one hospital. CNN is a data-hungry algorithm, more images are required for each projection to show significant improvements. A further point for investigation is to assess the model performance across different data sets, ideally obtained from different geographical areas.

In the presented work, we applied multiple techniques to improve the data quality and the model's ability. For transfer learning, we utilised a DenseNet121 model pre-trained on ImageNet data. Although the ImageNet dataset differs significantly from CheXpert, it does provide some assistance to the model, but this assistance does not result in any significant increase in AUC. A point for future investigation is to either fine-tuning the model with huge radiograph data or to pre-train the model on a different chest radiograph data and fine-tuning it on CheXpert, this will help the model to learn some basic radiograph features in the pre-training stage. Data augmentation has resulted in significantly improving the model performance. We believe that carefully engineered augmentation techniques can enhance the detection accuracy of radiographs. Counter-intuitively, the multiscale template matching approach did not provide significant benefits and sometimes even resulted in a decrease in performance. Further investigation is necessary to identify the cause of this observation.

The results of our experiments show the potential to improve diagnostic accuracy for chest radiographs and also classify radiographs in a reporting worklist as normal or abnormal thereby prioritising abnormal radiographs for more urgent reporting.

VI. Conclusion

This paper presented a performance comparison of five CNN-based deep learning models trained on different views of chest radiographs. Our results indicated the final derivation of the model utilising a combination of template matching, transfer learning, and augmentation provided the highest average AUC of 0.88. This observation led to choosing the final model as a tool to compare and contrast between different views. Our contrasting led to ordering AP, Lateral and PA views with a decreasing AUC from 0.85 to 0.83 and 0.72, respectively. Improving the model by labelling uncertain samples led to an increase in AUC, by a factor of 0.01, for each of these views. Our results indicated that it is possible to detect and label radiographs in multi-condition images, with anterio-posterior and lateral views outperforming the posterio-anterior view. We also highlighted that our approach to uncertainty reduction can have a positive impact on AUC improvement, indicating better detection accuracy. We now embark on evaluating if there are conditions where different views have a vested advantage in detection, using the above CNN model. We also plan co-design studies with radiologists in our partner hospital, to identify barriers to the acceptability of such models, but also ways to integrate such approaches into the clinical workflow.

References

[1] C. Stewart, "Respiratory disease in the united kingdom (uk) - statistics and facts." https://www.statista.com/topics/5908/respiratory-disease-in-the-uk/ [Retrieved: March, 2023].

[2] RCR, "Clinical radiology uk workforce census 2020 report." https://www.rcr.ac.uk/publication/clinical-radiology-uk-workforce-census-2020-report [Retrieved: March, 2023].

[3] M. A. Bruno, E. A. Walker, and H. H. Abujudeh, "Understanding and confronting our mistakes: the epidemiology of error in radiology and strategies for error reduction," *Radiographics*, vol. 35, no. 6, pp. 1668–1676, 2015.

[4] G. Huang, Z. Liu, L. Van Der Maaten, and K. Q. Weinberger, "Densely connected convolutional networks," in *Proceedings of the IEEE conference on computer vision and pattern recognition*, pp. 4700–4708, 2017.

[5] J. Irvin, P. Rajpurkar, M. Ko, Y. Yu, S. Ciurea-Ilcus, C. Chute, H. Marklund, B. Haghgoo, R. Ball, K. Shpanskaya, *et al.*, "Chexpert: A large chest radiograph dataset with uncertainty labels and expert comparison," in *Proceedings of the AAAI conference on artificial intelligence*, vol. 33, pp. 590–597, 2019.

[6] X. Wang, Y. Peng, L. Lu, Z. Lu, M. Bagheri, and R. M. Summers, "Chestx-ray8: Hospital-scale chest x-ray database and benchmarks on weakly-supervised classification and localization of common thorax diseases," in *Proceedings of the IEEE conference on computer vision and pattern recognition*, pp. 2097–2106, 2017.

[7] T. K. Moon, "The expectation-maximization algorithm," *IEEE Signal processing magazine*, vol. 13, no. 6, pp. 47–60, 1996.

[8] A. E. Johnson, T. J. Pollard, S. J. Berkowitz, N. R. Greenbaum, M. P. Lungren, C.-y. Deng, R. G. Mark, and S. Horng, "Mimic-cxr, a de-identified publicly available database of chest radiographs with free-text reports," *Scientific data*, vol. 6, no. 1, p. 317, 2019.

[9] P. Rajpurkar, J. Irvin, K. Zhu, B. Yang, H. Mehta, T. Duan, D. Ding, A. Bagul, C. Langlotz, K. Shpanskaya, *et al.*, "Chexnet: Radiologist-level pneumonia detection on chest x-rays with deep learning," *arXiv preprint arXiv:1711.05225*, 2017.

[10] H. Sharma, J. S. Jain, P. Bansal, and S. Gupta, "Feature extraction and classification of chest x-ray images using cnn to detect pneumonia," in *2020 10th International Conference on Cloud Computing, Data Science & Engineering (Confluence)*, pp. 227–231, IEEE, 2020.

[11] M. Heidari, S. Mirniaharikandehei, A. Z. Khuzani, G. Danala, Y. Qiu, and B. Zheng, "Improving the performance of cnn to predict the likelihood of covid-19 using chest x-ray images with preprocessing algorithms," *International journal of medical informatics*, vol. 144, p. 104284, 2020.

[12] T. Rahman, M. E. Chowdhury, A. Khandakar, K. R. Islam, K. F. Islam, Z. B. Mahbub, M. A. Kadir, and S. Kashem, "Transfer learning with deep convolutional neural network (cnn) for pneumonia detection using chest x-ray," *Applied Sciences*, vol. 10, no. 9, p. 3233, 2020.

[13] A. A. Reshi, F. Rustam, A. Mehmood, A. Alhossan, Z. Alrabiah, A. Ahmad, H. Alsuwailem, and G. S. Choi, "An efficient cnn model for covid-19 disease detection based on x-ray image classification," *Complexity*, vol. 2021, pp. 1–12, 2021.

[14] C. Hayat, "Densenet-cnn architectural model for detection of abnormality in acute pulmonary edema," *Khazanah Informatika: Jurnal Ilmu Komputer dan Informatika*, vol. 7, no. 2, pp. 73–79, 2021.

[15] H. H. Pham, T. T. Le, D. Q. Tran, D. T. Ngo, and H. Q. Nguyen, "Interpreting chest x-rays via cnns that exploit hierarchical disease dependencies and uncertainty labels," *Neurocomputing*, vol. 437, pp. 186–194, 2021.

[16] I. M. Baltruschat, H. Nickisch, M. Grass, T. Knopp, and A. Saalbach, "Comparison of deep learning approaches for multi-label chest x-ray classification," *Scientific reports*, vol. 9, no. 1, pp. 1–10, 2019.

[17] S. Albahli, H. T. Rauf, A. Algosaibi, and V. E. Balas, "Ai-driven deep cnn approach for multi-label pathology classification using chest x-rays," *PeerJ Computer Science*, vol. 7, p. e495, 2021.

[18] Q. Guan and Y. Huang, "Multi-label chest x-ray image classification via category-wise residual attention learning," *Pattern Recognition Letters*, vol. 130, pp. 259–266, 2020.

[19] N. N. Agu, J. T. Wu, H. Chao, I. Lourentzou, A. Sharma, M. Moradi, P. Yan, and J. Hendler, "Anaxnet: anatomy aware multi-label finding classification in chest x-ray," in *Medical Image Computing and Computer Assisted Intervention–MICCAI 2021: 24th International Conference, Strasbourg, France, September 27–October 1, 2021, Proceedings, Part V 24*, pp. 804–813, Springer, 2021.

[20] O. Gozes and H. Greenspan, "Deep feature learning from a hospital-scale chest x-ray dataset with application to tb detection on a small-scale dataset," in *2019 41st annual international conference of the ieee engineering in medicine and biology society (embc)*, pp. 4076–4079, IEEE, 2019.

[21] J. A. Dunnmon, D. Yi, C. P. Langlotz, C. Ré, D. L. Rubin, and M. P. Lungren, "Assessment of convolutional neural networks for automated classification of chest radiographs," *Radiology*, vol. 290, no. 2, pp. 537–544, 2019.

[22] R. Brunelli, *Template matching techniques in computer vision: theory and practice*. John Wiley & Sons, 2009.

[23] J. Deng, W. Dong, R. Socher, L.-J. Li, K. Li, and L. Fei-Fei, "Imagenet: A large-scale hierarchical image database," in *2009 IEEE conference on computer vision and pattern recognition*, pp. 248–255, Ieee, 2009.

[24] Z. Zhou, J. Shin, L. Zhang, S. Gurudu, M. Gotway, and J. Liang, "Fine-tuning convolutional neural networks for biomedical image analysis: actively and incrementally," in *Proceedings of the IEEE conference on computer vision and pattern recognition*, pp. 7340–7351, 2017.

[25] A. Krizhevsky, I. Sutskever, and G. E. Hinton, "Imagenet classification with deep convolutional neural networks," *Communications of the ACM*, vol. 60, no. 6, pp. 84–90, 2017.

Protecting User Privacy in Online Settings via Supervised Learning

Alexandru Rusescu, Brooke Lampe, and Weizhi Meng
SPTAGE Lab, Department of Applied Mathematics and Computer Science,
Technical University of Denmark, Denmark
Email: {blam, weme}@dtu.dk

***Abstract*—Companies that have an online presence—in particular, companies that are exclusively digital—often subscribe to this business model: collect data from the user base, then expose the data to advertisement agencies in order to turn a profit. Such companies routinely market a service as "free" while obfuscating the fact that they tend to "charge" users in the currency of personal information rather than money. However, online companies also gather user data for more principled purposes, such as improving the user experience and aggregating statistics. The problem is the sale of user data to third parties. In this work, we design an intelligent approach to online privacy protection that leverages supervised learning. By detecting and blocking data collection that might infringe on a user's privacy, we can then restore a degree of digital privacy to the user. In our evaluation, we collect a dataset of network requests and measure the performance of several classifiers that adhere to the supervised learning paradigm. The results of our evaluation demonstrate the feasibility and potential of our approach.**

***Index Terms*—User Privacy; Supervised Learning; Support Vector Machine; Logistic Regression; Decision Tree**

I. INTRODUCTION

Over the past few decades, the Internet has become a part of people's day-to-day lives. The activities facilitated by the modern Internet are varied and innumerable: browsing recipes, purchasing products, sharing videos, banking, billing, socializing, and many, many more. In the era of Internet-enabled expedience, users tend to overlook the slow decline of privacy in favor of staggeringly greater convenience. However, the discussion of Internet-related privacy infringement is becoming more relevant in the public eye. Some news agencies and governments have started to point out how these privacy-invading practices can affect people's lives—and even small businesses—without them realizing it [1]. International incidents have piqued the interest of news outlets and security specialists to look into this new "surveillance" business model, sparking comparisons between data collection and "Big Brother" from George Orwell's book "1984" [2], [3].

Privacy can be invaded by any number of means, and there is no clear distinction between that which is permissible and that which is strictly prohibited by law. It has been reported that a majority of Americans believe their online and offline activities are being tracked and monitored by both companies and the U.S. government with some regularity [6]. Invasions of privacy have become the norm, not the exception. In fact, privacy infringement is such a common condition of modern life that approximately 60% of U.S. adults say they do not think it is possible to go about daily life without having data collected by various companies or the U.S. government.

That said, some countries have made process and even forced companies to limit some of their practices; e.g., the European Union has implemented—and enforces—the General Data Protection Regulation (GDPR) [9]. Unfortunately, the GDPR is still not enough to defeat some external threats. For example, a malicious third party may exfiltrate data and documents that colleagues create, access, store, and share across an organization. When a third party gains access to an individual's private information, there is a risk of data loss, reputational damage, and regulatory fines.

Contributions. In the literature, we have seen many potential strategies (e.g., privacy-preserving techniques [25], [32]) to ensure data privacy in various environments, but safeguarding a user's privacy online is still an open challenge—especially with the rapid pace of digitization. In this work, we contribute to the defense of online privacy by introducing a tool that can be used to block HTTP requests that would gather users' data. Our main contributions are summarized below:

- We develop a tool which leverages supervised machine learning to detect malicious online requests and protect users' privacy. In addition, we detail the API implementation of our tool.
- In our evaluation, we collect a dataset of online requests and evaluate the performance of three supervised learning classifiers. The results demonstrate the feasibility and potential of our tool.

The remainder of this paper is organized as follows: Section II introduces related work on privacy protection. In Section III, we explain our proposed tool in detail, including the data collection process and the three supervised learning classifiers. In Section IV, we describe the API implementation of our tool and discuss experimental results. Section V concludes our work.

II. RELATED WORK

In this section, we highlight various privacy-enhancing schemes, each of which aims to ensure a user's privacy while he or she is online.

Rodrigo-Ginéss *et al.* [33] crafted a tool called "PrivacySearch" that contributes to the development of Privacy-Enhancing Technologies (PETs). This paper addresses the problem of personalized profiles based on Web Search Engines (WSEs). Such personalized profiles are created with the intent of selling information. The authors exploit the query-generalization principle: when a user types a query, the PrivacySearch tool replaces the text of the query with generic terms before submitting the generalized query to the WSE. The tool supports three different privacy levels: low, medium, and high. The three privacy levels refer to the degree of generalization provided by the tool; a higher privacy level will generate a more generic query (compared to the original query) than a lower privacy level.

Reiter *et al.* [34] proposed a system, dubbed "Crowds," to increase the privacy of web transactions. Crowds leverages the concept of a "crowd," in which one hides one's actions behind the actions of many, many others. Crowds—i.e., the "crowd" technique—works as follows:

1) A user gains access to the system called Crowds
2) The user's request to a web server is passed to a random member of the same system in an encrypted form
3) Upon receiving the request, the random member flips a biased coin to determine if he or she should submit the request or forward it to another randomly selected member (the request data is encrypted until the moment the request is submitted to the server)
4) The previous step repeats until the request is submitted
5) The web server's reply traverses the same path but in reverse

Their work provided a good strategy to anonymize web transactions, though the proposed Crowds strategy comes at the cost of additional overhead. This system also obfuscates the information that a local eavesdropping might use to learn about the identity of the receiver.

Mozilla offers a solution called "Facebook Container" [4] to set boundaries for Facebook and other Meta websites. Facebook Container is an extension that isolates Meta sites (e.g., Facebook, Instagram, and Messenger) from the remainder of the web to limit where the company can track its users. Meta's "like" and "share" contain Facebook trackers, and these buttons can be found in numerous websites, from news to shopping to blogs and more. Mozilla's Facebook Container alerts the user when trackers are discovered on a non-Meta site by adding an icon to the address bar and subsequently blocking the trackers. Users are given the option to disable Facebook Container on specific websites, allowing Facebook to see their activity there. Mozilla's tool constrains the volume of data that Meta is able to obtain, though other advertisers might still be able to correlate Facebook activity with a user's regular browsing.

Another solution, "Pi-Hole" [5], enhances digital privacy by blocking known advertising domains. Pi-Hole was conceived as an open-source alternative to Ad-Trap. A Raspberry Pi—a small, single-board computer—acts as a Domain Name System (DNS) server for a given private network. DNS servers are populated with the mappings of domain names to IP addresses. As such, Pi-Hole comes with a file of blacklisted hosts [7], which is properly maintained and up to date. Whenever queries

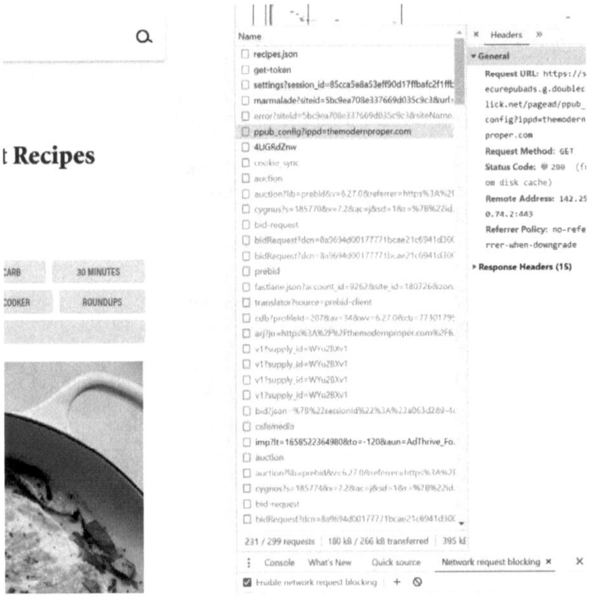

Fig. 1. A network request log from a cooking website.

are made to known advertising domains, a falsified IP address is given to the web server. Then, instead of an advertisement, the web server serves a tiny blank image file or web page. A user can surf the web freely and privately, knowing that an invasive request will be misdirected and will never reach its target IP address. Thus, users can avoid sharing private information (e.g., browsing habits) with unwanted sources.

III. Our Approach

Fig. 1 provides a snapshot of the network requests exchanged by a cooking website. A number of the requests are utterly irrelevant to the usability of the site, while a select few are necessary in order to supply the information that a user seeks. More than 80% of the network requests are involved in delivering information to third-party advertisers who can do what they please with the data.

Going a step further, we reviewed and analyzed the network requests of multiple websites. We inspected the network logs and verified that any suspicious requests were indeed transmitted to advertisement domains or other domains that had no relevance to the website in question.

A. Design Phase

A sequence diagram is depicted in Fig. 2, providing an abstract view of our design. To ensure that our proposed solution would be accessible, we decided to expose an endpoint. This endpoint would be responsible for receiving requests, pre-processing those requests, and invoking the tool. We implemented our endpoint as an application programming interface (API). This API receives an input, runs that input through our tool (a supervised machine learning model), and returns an output.

To build the tool itself, we needed to select a suitable machine learning model. The model would be expected to

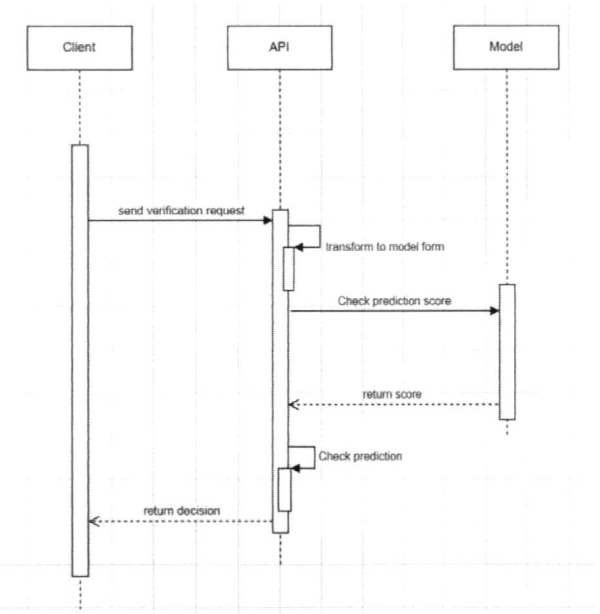

Fig. 2. A sequence diagram outlining our proposed approach.

differentiate between benign traffic and privacy-invading traffic. In this work, we considered three supervised learning classifiers due to their popularity and their reportedly good performance.

- **Logistic Regression (LR).** This is a type of statistical modeling often used for classification and for predictive analytics. [15]. Logistic regression falls under the umbrella of linear regression, but it is a special case: in logistic regression, the predicted outcomes are categorical. If there are two possible outcomes, it is referred to as binomial logistic regression, and if there are more than two possible outcomes, then it is called multinomial logistic regression [30]. During logistic regression, the model first computes the sum of the input features and then applies the logistic function. The output is guaranteed to be between 0 and 1. In our scenario, 0 would be "benign" and 1 would be "privacy-invading." The closer the value is to 1, the higher the probability that the current sample will be categorized as privacy-invading, and vice versa.
- **Decision Tree.** This is a supervised learning technique that operates on a tree-like structure: the nodes represent the features of the dataset, the branches represent the decision rules, and the leaf nodes represent the outcomes [11], [19]. To construct a decision tree, each feature in the dataset is mapped to a node. Starting at the root node, branches with decision rules are created to extend to the next nodes, each of which becomes a subtree. This process continues for each subtree that is created [36].
- **Support Vector Machine.** This supervised learning scheme uses data points plotted in an n-dimensional space, where n represents the number of features. Each feature corresponds to the value of a particular coordinate. During the training process, a hyperplane is constructed to subdivide all samples into one of two classes [20], [24]. The goals of SVMs can be summarized as follows [35]:
  1) Maximize the margin which separates the two classes
  2) Use relatively few training samples—or support vectors—to define the hyperplane which separates the two classes
  3) Classify data that is not linearly separable—with the help of a kernel

All of the classifiers were implemented in Python.

B. Data Collection

High-quality data is essential to machine learning. The quality of the training data can directly influence the model's performance.

As such, during the data collection process, we thoroughly investigated each of the logged network requests to determine which requests were required and which were not. It was crucial to properly validate the "required" requests (i.e., confirm that they were necessary), just as it was critical to ascertain that a supposed data-gathering request was purely gathering data and was *not* performing some sort of usability-related function. If data-gathering requests were mislabeled as benign requests, the model might produce false negatives; conversely, if benign requests were mislabeled as data-gathering requests, the model might produce false positives. If benign requests are mistakenly blocked, the user's browsing experience will be disrupted; if privacy-invading requests are mistakenly permitted, then the tool will fail to safeguard the user's privacy.

To attenuate such issues, we perform a particular two-stage test during our data gathering process. Given a request, we scrutinize the payload to determine what type of data will be transmitted to the server. Then, we check the domain name of the server: Is this domain name relevant to the website at hand? If the payload appears suspicious *and* the domain name of the server is unrelated to the current website, then the *curl* (Client URL) request will be copied to a separate backup file and the domain name will be blocked. Finally, we refresh the site in order to ensure that blocking the suspicious requests does not interfere with the usability of the current website.

If a request is deemed non-invasive (in terms of privacy), then the *curl* request will still be copied in order to provide the machine learning model with examples of both benign and privacy-invading requests.

Once we had collected a sufficient volume of data for training and evaluation, we transferred the data to a spreadsheet for easier accessibility when working with the model. During this process, we manually examined each request, including its URL, payload, and properties. The data was organized in the spreadsheet as follows:

- Request data that was *not* extracted from payload (e.g., properties)
  - `invasive` - a binary value that indicates whether or not a request was deemed privacy-invasive

- `url` - a string that specifies the domain name of the request's intended destination
- `req_type` - the type of request (e.g., GET, POST, PUT)
- `is_json` - the format of the payload—either JSON or non-JSON (at this time, for easier data collection, we limit our scope to JSON-formatted payloads)

- Request data that was extracted from the payload
  - `pl_isprebid`
  - `pl_appid`
  - `pl_domain`
  - `pl_imp`
  - etc.

For the initial implementation of our tool, we limit our scope to payloads that are formatted using the $JSON4$ clear text standard.

C. Data Processing

Data cleaning. The quality of a machine learning model is contingent on the quality of the data. As such, we applied several cleaning and pre-processing techniques to the data, as described below [37]:

Noise removal. "Noise" refers to (1) unwanted, meaningless data and (2) unwanted, meaningless perturbation. As a data pre-processing step, noise removal ensures that the data is free of interference, distortion, or uninformative values; that is, noise removal ensures that the data is clean.

In this step, we checked the dataset for duplicate entries. In addition, since the data was manually collected, we reviewed the dataset for human error.

Outlier filtering. "Outliers" are values which do not fall in the average range defined by existing data points. Outliers in datasets can often be attributed to measurement error during data collection, but they can also occur naturally; some data properties are innately prone to outliers.

Much of our data is one-hot encoded; that is, the variables have been converted to binary indicators. The one-hot encoding process implicitly completes the data filtering step.

Structural error correction & missing value correction. "Structural error" occurs mainly due to naming and spelling discrepancies. If naming conventions are not consistent across the dataset, then the machine learning model—which receives the data as input—might become muddled and inaccurate. Naming and spelling-related discrepancies can arise from typographical errors or from variations in the naming and spelling conventions used by different researchers. In our case, a sample will either be classified as "benign" or "privacy-invading." A simple spelling error could cause a benign sample to be labeled privacy-invading, or vice versa.

Missing values differ from structural error; a "missing value" occurs when no value is stored in a given attribute of a data object. If, during data collection, a request lacks a response, then one or more missing values might result.

We manually corrected for both structural error and missing values while collecting and populating the dataset. During the implementation phase, we decided to remove the `url` column from the dataset, as it is a categorical column with very few values that repeat themselves. In addition, we elected to one-hot encode the `req_type` column; we renamed the column `GET/POST` and converted the values to binary. Since our current dataset contains GET and POST requests, exclusively, the `req_type` column (now the `GET/POST` column) was an ideal candidate for the one-hot encoding tactic, reducing clutter in the dataset.

Data splitting. When it comes to training and testing data, the convention in the literature is the 70-30 split, meaning that 70% of the samples are used to train the model, while the remaining 30% are used to test the model.

Therefore, we separated the training column and the target column (which identifies a sample as "benign" or "privacy-invading"), creating four new variables:

- `x_train` - This variable contains 70% of the samples in the dataset, including all feature columns. These are the training samples.
- `x_test` - This variable contains 30% of the samples in the dataset, including all feature columns. These are the testing samples.
- `y_train` - This variable contains 70% of the target values in the dataset, which correspond to `x_train`. These are the training targets.
- `y_test` - This variable contains 30% of the target values in the dataset, which correspond to `x_test`. These are the testing targets.

IV. IMPLEMENTATION AND EVALUATION

In this section, we detail the API implementation of our tool and discuss the evaluation results.

A. API implementation

An application programming interface (API) is an intermediate piece of software that facilitates communication between two applications. This type of software interface is similar to a contract between two parties: There is an expected request structure, and the response adheres to a predetermined format. An API abstracts the particulars of an application and exposes only necessary services to other applications. As such, an API can easily share an application's functionality with external applications, clients, or services.

In this work, a web API was implemented. A web API is a service that runs on a machine and can be accessed by potential clients via HTTP requests. To use our tool, a potential client would send a data transfer object (DTO)—which carries data between processes—to the web API. The tool's response would contain either a "1" for invasive requests or a "0" for non-invasive requests.

To implement the web API, we leveraged the Python programming language. A contributing factor in our choice of programming language was Python's compatibility with other components of our tool. Our web API relies on a Python framework called Flask [8]. Flask provides tools and features that help its users to easily create and operate web applications.

A simple web server can be constructed with as little as five lines of code.

When the application executes, it will first load the previous model using the `pickle` module. The previously built model is then made available in the code. The application exposes two endpoints under the routes `/api/predict/lr` and `/api/predict/dt`. The former generates a prediction based on Logistic Regression, while the latter leverages a Decision Tree to determine if a given request is invasive ("1") or benign ("0"). Both endpoints expect a request with a specific $JSON$-formatted DTO.

The endpoints are strict; all variables are expected to be present in the payload. If the endpoints were not strict—i.e., if the endpoints generated predictions based on incomplete payloads—then the endpoints would be liable to output incorrect results. The required DTO should not be difficult to construct, as it consists of information that the client can extract from the original request.

B. Evaluation Results

To assess the performance of our design, we adopted a confusion matrix—i.e., a table that provides data regarding the performance of an algorithm. Confusion matrices contain the following four values:

- **True positives (TP).** The number of correctly predicted positive outcomes based on the predictive model.
- **True negatives (TN).** The number of correctly predicted negative outcomes based on the predictive model.
- **False positives (FP).** The number of incorrectly predicted positive outcomes based on the predictive model.
- **False negatives (FN).** The number of incorrectly predicted negative outcomes based on the predictive model.

These metrics are the building blocks for a number of popular performance measures:

- **Accuracy.** Accuracy measures how often the model correctly classifies a sample. It is one of the most commonly used metrics for evaluating models. That said, it is a biased measure and is not necessarily the best indicator of overall performance.
- **Precision.** Precision—or positive predictive value—is defined as the proportion of positive predictions that were actually correct. The formula for precision divides the number of true positives by the total number of positive predictions (true positives and false positives).
- **Recall.** Recall—or sensitivity—is defined as the proportion of actual positives that were predicted correctly. The formula for recall divides the number of true positives by the total number of positive samples in the dataset (true positives and false negatives).
- **Specificity.** Specificity is defined as the proportion of actual negatives that were predicted correctly. The formula for specificity divides the number of true negatives by the total number of negative samples in the dataset (true negatives and false positives). Specificity is similar to sensitivity, except that the perspective shifts from positive to negative.
- **F1-score.** F1-score is calculated as the "harmonic mean" of precision and recall. Both false positives and false negatives are factored into the F1-score; as such, it is a good metric for imbalanced datasets.

The dataset consists of 90 unique requests that were manually collected from various websites, and our supervised machine learning model was trained on 178 unique classes. It is important to note that a relatively small dataset can pose a problem to the predictive "power" of a machine learning algorithm, since a machine learning model's ability to recognize patterns is generally proportional to the size of the dataset. Smaller datasets correspond to less powerful and less accurate machine learning models [16].

We evaluated three supervised machine learning paradigms: logistic regression, decision tree, and support vector machine. All three models yielded a result in a very short amount of time. The model has been developed using the scikit-learn library [10]. The size of the training dataset was 60 samples, and the size of the testing dataset was 30 samples. Fig. 3 illustrates the confusion matrices that were generated by each of the three models. The results can be interpreted as follows:

- The confusion matrix for the support vector machine is depicted in Fig. 3(a). The model predicted `TRUE` for all samples, but it was wrong 30% of the time. The evaluation criteria, as well as the numerical evaluation results, are presented in Table I. The model demonstrated a precision of 0.7. The model achieved a perfect 1.0 score for recall, as it correctly identified all positive samples as invasive. Unfortunately, the model achieved this score by classifying all samples as positives, meaning that the model has a serious problem with false positives. These false positives are reflected in the model's specificity score, 0.0, which is the lowest possible score. The model achieved an F1-score of approximately 82%. We can see that the support vector machine has a severe bias toward privacy-invading predictions, which causes it to routinely misclassify benign samples as invasive.
- The confusion matrix for the decision tree is shown in Fig. 3(b). The model that was trained using the decision tree algorithm gave accurate predictions 56.(6)% of the time and inaccurate predictions 43.(3)% of the time. While $\approx$ 56% is better than 50-50 odds, it is not better by much. The precision of the model was 0.75—somewhat higher than the precision of the support vector machine. The recall, however, was 0.57, which is much lower than the 1.0 recall of the support vector machine. When it came to specificity, the model attained a modest 0.55(5), indicating that 55% of the non-invasive requests would be correctly whitelisted by the model. Note that the decision tree produced the fewest false positives of all the models; as such, it would be least likely to interfere with the usability of a given website. Unfortunately, the model's F1-score was 0.64, which is quite low for a machine learning model. The low F1-score can generally be attributed to the relatively high number of false negatives; the

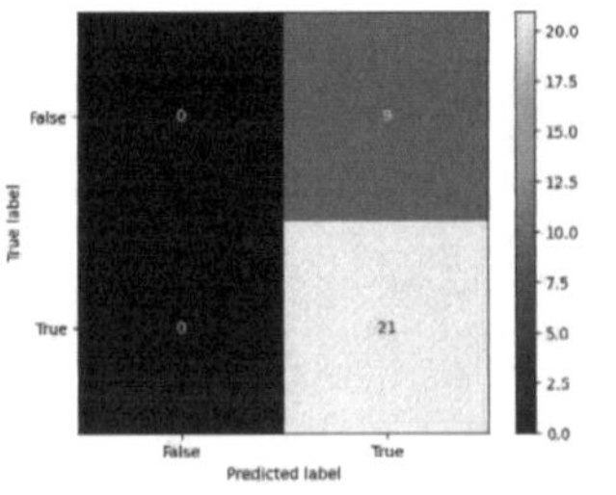

(a) SVM confusion matrix

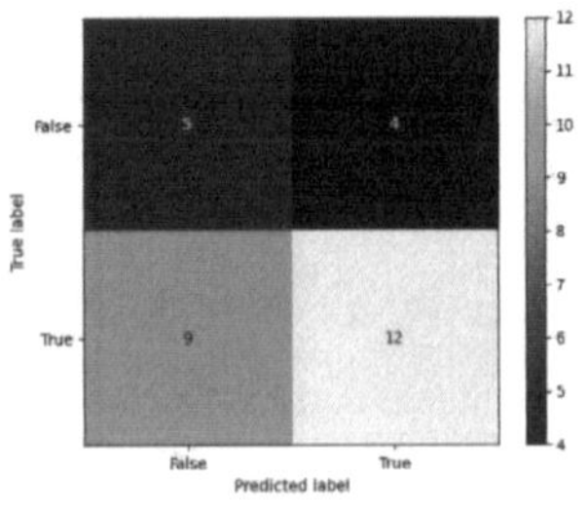

(b) Decision Tree confusion matrix

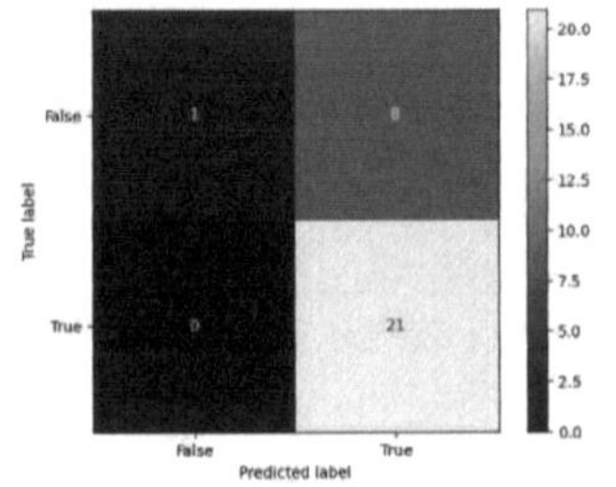

(c) Logistic Regression confusion matrix

Fig. 3. Confusion matrices for the support vector machine, decision tree, and logistic regression models.

TABLE I
EVALUATION RESULTS

	TP	TN	FP	FN	Accuracy	Precision	Recall	Specificity	F1-score
Support Vector Machine	0	21	9	0	0.7	0.7	1.0	0.0	0.82352
Decision Tree	5	12	4	9	0.56666	0.75	0.57142	0.55555	0.64864
Logistic Regression	1	21	8	0	0.73333	0.72413	1.0	0.11111	0.84

decision tree model misclassified nine invasive samples as benign. Neither the support vector machine nor the logistic regression model produced any false negatives.

- The confusion matrix for the logistic regression is illustrated in Fig. 3(c). The logistic regression-based model generated correct predictions for 73.(3)% of the samples and incorrect predictions for 26.(6)% of the samples. At a precision of 0.72, the logistic regression model sits between the support vector machine and the decision tree in terms of positive predictive value. The logistic regression model matched the support vector machine in terms of recall, achieving a perfect 1.0 score. Unfortunately, the logistic regression model has the same issue with false positives as the support vector machine—non-invasive requests are regularly misclassified as invasive. Fortunately, the logistic regression model achieved a somewhat better specificity score than the support vector machine—0.1(1) instead of 0.0. The logistic regression model achieved the highest F1-score of all the models: 84%.

C. *Limitation and Open Challenges*

As discussed earlier, each of the models—support vector machine, decision tree, logistic regression—comes with both advantages and disadvantages. In terms of recall (proportion of invasive requests that were correctly identified), the worst performing model was the decision tree with a score of 0.57. For the decision tree model, we can expect that approximately 43% of invasive requests might pass as non-invasive. 43% might seem quite high at first glance, but the current state of user privacy is much worse: for the average user, 100% of invasive requests will be allowed. Therefore, if we can block 57% of invasive requests, then we have made a significant step forward in terms of user privacy. The issue, then, is the false positives. If our tool blocks non-invasive requests that a website needs in order to function properly, then usability will be impacted. The specificity score of the decision tree was 0.55(5). As such, we anticipate that approximately 44% of non-invasive requests will be blocked, impeding a given website's ability to run.

The next model we need to address is the model trained using the support vector machine algorithm. On the surface, the model's accuracy, precision, and recall are all reasonable—0.7, 0.7, and 1.0, respectively. However, the SVM-based model would be impracticable in a real-world scenario due to its bias toward positive predictions. Under evaluation, the model incorrectly classified all the benign requests as invasive. If a user were surfing the web, the model would block all requests, both invasive and non-invasive, completely disrupting the user's day-to-day activities on the web.

Finally, we will review the logistic regression-based model. Similar to its support vector machine-based counterpart, it is exceedingly biased toward positive predictions. As such, it suffers similar limitations in a real-time scenario; it would disrupt a user's web-surfing experience by blocking most—if not all—non-invasive requests.

V. Conclusions and Future Work

The objective of Privacy-Enhancing Technologies (PETs) is to safeguard user data from misappropriation and mishandling. When a user's data is protected, the user's privacy should be protected as well. This work was built upon the following hypothesis: *It is possible to enhance the privacy of normal users without disrupting their day-to-day web surfing activities.* We set out to develop a proof-of-concept tool to confirm our hypothesis. We constructed a supervised machine learning model that classifies HTTP requests as invasive or non-invasive, and we evaluated three different machine learning paradigms as the foundation of the model. Our results demonstrate that our current solution has the potential to be used in real life—but at the cost of browsing convenience and usability.

Future work involves collecting a much larger dataset of online request and training new learning models to further improve the performance metrics. For example, some advanced learning algorithms can be explored to improve the results, such as deep learning [13], [17], semi-supervised learning [18], [21] and clustering methods [23], which can handle unlabeled data with various optimization approaches [12], [31]. Our tool can also be integrated with existing traffic sampling [22], [28] and traffic filtration methods [14], [27], [29].

Acknowledgment

This work was funded by the EU H2020 DataVaults project with GA Number 871755. The source code can be available at: https://sptage.compute.dtu.dk/.

References

[1] Australian Competition Consumer Commission. Accessed 15 Feb. 2023, published 28 April 2022. https://www.accc.gov.au/media-release/concerning-issues-for-consumers-and-sellerson-online-marketplaces

[2] P. Szoldra, Business Insider. Accessed 15 Feb.2023. https://www.businessinsider.com/snowden-leaks-timeline-2016-9?r=USIR=T

[3] The Harvard Gazette. Accessed 15 Jan. 2023. https://news.harvard.edu/gazette/story/2017/08/when-it-comes-to-internet-privacybe-very-afraid-analyst-suggests/

[4] Facebook Container by Mozilla Firefox. https://addons.mozilla.org/en-US/firefox/addon/facebook-container/

[5] Pi-hole: Network-wide protection. https://pi-hole.net/

[6] Americans and Privacy: Concerned, Confused and Feeling Lack of Control Over Their Personal Information. Accessed 15 Feb.2023. https://www.pewresearch.org/internet/2019/11/15/americans-and-privacy-concerned-confused-and-feeling-lack-of-control-over-their-personal-information/

[7] StevenBlack. Accessed 15 Feb. 2023. https://raw.githubusercontent.com/StevenBlack/hosts/master/hosts

[8] Flask. Accessed 15 Feb. 2023. https://flask.palletsprojects.com/en/2.2.x/

[9] General Data Protection Regulation (GDPR). Accessed 15 Feb. 2023. https://gdpr-info.eu/

[10] scikit-learn: Machine Learning in Python. Accessed 20 January 2023. https://scikit-learn.org/stable/

[11] A.C. Bahnsen, D. Aouada, and B.E. Ottersten, "Example-dependent cost-sensitive decision trees," *Expert Syst. Appl.* 42(19), pp. 6609-6619, 2015.

[12] A.N. Calugar, W. Meng, and H. Zhang, "Towards Artificial Neural Network Based Intrusion Detection with Enhanced Hyperparameter Tuning," *Proc. IEEE GLOBECOM*, pp. 2627-2632, 2022.

[13] M. Gong, J. Feng, and Y. Xie, "Privacy-enhanced multi-party deep learning," *Neural Networks* 121, pp. 484-496, 2020.

[14] Z. Jin, Z. Liang, Y. Wang, and W. Meng, "Mobile Network Traffic Pattern Classification with Incomplete a Priori Information," *Computer Communications* 166, pp. 262-270, 2021.

[15] M. Kim, "Two-stage logistic regression model," *Expert Syst. Appl.* 36(3), pp. 6727-6734, 2009.

[16] P. Kokol, M. Kokol, and S. Zagoranski, "Machine learning on small size samples: A synthetic knowledge synthesis," *Science Progress* 105(1), pp. 1-16, 2022.

[17] B. Lampe and W. Meng, "A Survey of Deep Learning-based Intrusion Detection in Automotive Applications," *Expert Syst. Appl.* 221, 119771, pp. 1-23, 2023.

[18] W. Li, W. Meng, Z. Tan, and Y. Xiang, "Towards Designing An Email Classification System Using Multi-View Based Semi-Supervised Learning," *Proc. TrustCom*, pp. 174-181, 2014.

[19] W. Li and W. Meng, "An Empirical Study on Email Classification Using Supervised Machine Learning in Real Environments," *Proc. ICC*, pp. 7438-7443, 2015.

[20] W. Li, W. Meng, and L.F. Kwok, "Evaluating Intrusion Sensitivity Allocation with Support Vector Machine for Collaborative Intrusion Detection," *Proc. ISPEC*, pp. 453-463, 2019.

[21] W. Li, W. Meng, and M.H. Au, "Enhancing Collaborative Intrusion Detection via Disagreement-based Semi-Supervised Learning in IoT environments," *Journal of Network and Computer Applications* 161, 102631, pp. 1-9, 2020.

[22] W. Li, W. Meng, and L. Yang, "Enhancing Trust-based Medical Smartphone Networks via Blockchain-based Traffic Sampling," *Proc. TrustCom*, pp. 122-129, 2021.

[23] Y.H. Lin and L. Chang, "An Unsupervised Noisy Sample Detection Method for Deep Learning-Based Health Status Prediction," *IEEE Trans. Instrum. Meas.* 71, pp. 1-11, 2022.

[24] L. Liu, J. Yang, and W. Meng, "Detecting Malicious Nodes via Gradient Descent and Support Vector Machine in Internet of Things," *Computers and Electrical Engineering* 77, pp. 339-353, 2019.

[25] Z. Liu, L. Wu, W. Meng, H. Wang, and W. Wang, "Accurate Range Query with Privacy Preservation for Outsourced Location-Based Service in IoT," *IEEE Internet of Things Journal* 8(18), pp. 14322-14337, 2021.

[26] Y. Meng, "The practice on using machine learning for network anomaly intrusion detection," *Proc. ICMLC*, pp. 576-581, 2011.

[27] W. Meng, W. Li, and L.F. Kwok, "EFM: Enhancing the Performance of Signature-based Network Intrusion Detection Systems Using Enhanced Filter Mechanism," *Computers & Security* 43, pp. 189-204, 2014.

[28] W. Meng, "Intrusion Detection in the Era of IoT: Building Trust via Traffic Filtering and Sampling," *IEEE Computer* 51(7), pp. 36-43, 2018.

[29] W. Meng, W. Li, and J. Zhou, "Enhancing the Security of Blockchain-based Software Defined Networking through Trust-based Traffic Fusion and Filtration," *Information Fusion* 70, pp. 60-71, 2021.

[30] O. Ouyed and M.S. Allili, "Group-of-features relevance in multinomial kernel logistic regression and application to human interaction recognition," *Expert Syst. Appl.* 148, 113247, 2020.

[31] S.V. Pingale and S.R. Sutar, "Remora whale optimization-based hybrid deep learning for network intrusion detection using CNN features," *Expert Syst. Appl.* 210, 118476, 2022.

[32] C. Qin, L. Wu, W. Meng, Z. Xu, S. Li, and H. Wang, "A Privacy-preserving Blockchain-based Tracing Model for Virus-infected People in Cloud," *Expert Syst. Appl.* 211, 118545, pp. 1-15, 2023.

[33] F.J. Rodrigo-Ginés, J. Parra-Arnau, W. Meng, and Y. Wang, "PrivacySearch: An End-User and Query Generalization Tool for Privacy Enhancement in Web Search," *Proc. NSS*, pp. 304-318, 2018.

[34] M.K. Reiter and A.D. Rubin, "Crowds: Anonymity for Web Transactions," *ACM Trans. Inf. Syst. Secur.* 1(1): 66-92 (1998)

[35] S. Tavara, "Parallel Computing of Support Vector Machines: A Survey," *ACM Comput. Surv.* 51(6), pp. 123:1-123:38, 2019.

[36] Y. Wang, W. Meng, W. Li, Z. Liu, Y. Liu, and H. Xue, "Adaptive machine learning-based alarm reduction via edge computing for distributed intrusion detection systems," *Concurr. Comput. Pract. Exp.* 31(19), pp. 1-12, 2019.

[37] X. Wang and C. Wang, "Time Series Data Cleaning: A Survey," *IEEE Access* 8, pp. 1866-1881, 2020.

How Should We Define Voice Naturalness

Sajad Shirali-Shahreza
Department of Computer Science, University of Toronto
Department of Computer Engineering, Amirkabir University
Email: shirali@aut.ac.ir

Abstract—**Naturalness is a commonly used criteria in Text-To-Speech (TTS) evaluations. The goal is to measure how close generated voice is to real human voice. This is measured through listening tests by human participants. However, no definition for naturalness is provided to participants. In this paper, we aimed to identify what definition participants used when they rank the naturalness. We conducted a user study similar to TTS evaluations and analyzed their responses. We noticed that users have different and sometimes contradictory definitions about it and a major dimension for them was how close it sounds to a real human. Our results show that we should explicitly define the naturalness for the participants. Furthermore, we should ask separate questions for different dimensions of naturalness such as clarity and having accent.**

Keywords-Text-to-Speech (TTS); Naturalness; Evaluation.

I. INTRODUCTION

Text-to-Speech (TTS) system evaluations usually have two parts: naturalness measurement via Mean-Opinion-Scores (MOS) and intelligibility measurement via transcription error rates of Semantically Uninterpretable Sentence (SUS). TTS systems are usually compared with each other and/or real human voices. As a result, naturalness is now regarded as an ordinal dimension of speech quality in its own right.

Recent advances in TTS systems results in deep-learning-inspired systems, such as Tactron [1] are almost indistinguishable from real-human voice. The way that such claims are presented is through MOS results that are almost 5. Mean opinion scores for TTS naturalness are generally calculated on a scale between 1 (worst) and 5 (best) as a subjective assessment by a human listener as to how *natural* a sample sounds, with no definition of what *natural* means, nor a provision of context within which the sample occurs, out of concern that it may prime the listeners [2]. Samples for this task are generally one sentence long.

What is interesting, however, is that up until about 1995, "*natural speech*" was the preferred technical term for describing human-generated speech. There was no discussion of an abstract *naturalness* that synthesizers could approximate on a scale from 1 to 5. There was a very detailed discussion, on the other hand, about the quality of synthesized speech, and indeed the earliest ITU-T P.85 standard [3] for evaluating speech synthesizers was equipped with three so-called Q-type scales that were designed to measure just that. The first mention of *naturalness* that we can find was actually in the speech coding literature [4], where it was used to describe degradations in subjective quality and speaker recognizability that did not also affect intelligibility.

The earliest Blizzard challenges [5] faithfully measured naturalness, along with another feature called *similarity*, in a context in which every synthesized prompt could be compared to a gold-standard recording of the same prompt by the same voice on which the synthesizer itself had been trained, and so every synthesized sample could be interpreted as an approximation of a human-generated sample. The connection to speech coding was very clear.

Our recent [6] comparison of the naturalness of TTS systems and ordinary human users shows that, by the empirical standards of the present-day TTS research community, TTS systems had reached statistical parity with human speech in its degree of naturalness at some point prior to 2013. This forces us to conclude that either the more recent quest for human-like speech quality by deep learning researchers is simply moot or that the concept of abstract naturalness is not well-founded.

One of the results of our previous study was that users rank accented speech as less natural. That was similar to an old study [7] that reported similarities between degradation due to synthesized speech and degradation due to foreign-accented speech. That was observed through a dimensionality reduction of more ecologically valid performance measures in the context of speech interfaces for pilot's cockpits by the United States Air Force [7].

In earlier Blizzard challenges (as per the recommendations for the ITU-Q scales), it was not uncommon to find considerably longer prompts, with very vertically directed instructions on how to establish one's impression:

"Overall impression: Please try to imagine what your reaction would be if this were an actual telephone message from a mail order house or a request for information from a travel agency."

"Acceptance: Please indicate whether or not you find that the voice you heard would be acceptable for such an automatic answering service by telephone."

However, these are not precisely defined instructions or definitions, as they require introspection on the part of the listener. This is in contrast to the transcription tasks for measuring intelligibility, in which the listener's accuracy is objectively measured.

In this paper, we try to see how users who participate in TTS evaluation implicitly define naturalness for themselves and then use it to perform the evaluation. We conducted a user study that mimics the usual evaluation of TTS systems and at the end, explicitly asked the participants to define the naturalness (Section II). Then, we coded the answers and extract concepts from them using grounded theory [8] (Section III). After that, we analyze our observations from coded data, identify some potential problematic area related to naturalness definition, and propose some potential solutions for them (Section IV).

II. Data Collection

As we mentioned earlier, it is common in TTS evaluation to measure the naturalness of generated speech. They ask the user to express how natural an example prompt is. For example, in the Blizzard challenge, they ask the user to:

"Now choose a score for how ***natural*** *or* ***unnatural*** *the sentence* ***sounded****. The scale is from* ***1 [Completely Unnatural]*** *to* ***5 [Completely Natural]****."*

The assumption is that the user already knows the definition of "natural". In our work, we designed a user study that closely mimics the usual TTS evaluations studies, such as the Blizzard challenge. Considering that we have both human and TTS-generated voices in our study, out ethics board did not allow us to tell the participants that they are evaluating TTS generated voices (which is common in TTS evaluations). Instead, they allowed us to use the phrase "evaluate computer-generated speech."

A. User Study Structure

Our user study had 5 main parts:

1) Consent

The first part is the welcome page that provides an overview of the study. The user is provided communication options, such as email address and phone number that they can use to obtain more information about the study before deciding whether they want to participate or not. If they decide to participate, they should indicate their acceptance of the rules which is used as the consent form.

2) Demographic questionnaire

After expressing the desire to participate in the research study, they will fill out a questionnaire that collects general information about the user. It includes items, such as their age range, whether they are native English speakers, how they would rate their English reading/listening/speaking/writing ability, etc. The information that collected is similar to what is collected in TTS evaluations, such as Blizzard challenge.

3) Individual prompt naturalness

We ask the user to perform two types of naturalness assessment. In the first type, they should assess the naturalness of a single prompt. This is how usually TTS evaluations, such as Blizzard ask the user to assess a TTS system. Considering that TTS evaluation tasks also ask the user to transcribe prompts (which is used to measure the intelligibility of the generated voices), we created a combined question for each prompt that first asks the user to transcribe the text, followed by a question that asks them to assess the naturalness. We tried to use question and prompt that closely resemble those that are used in previous Blizzard challenge and other TTS evaluations. Here is the instruction that we show to them for the naturalness assessment:

"Now rate how ***natural*** *or* ***unnatural*** *the sentence* ***sounded****"*

There were 5 options to select from:

1. Completely Unnatural
2. Mostly Unnatural
3. In Between Natural and Unnatural
4. Mostly Natural
5. Completely Natural

4) Pairwise Naturalness Comparison

We also added an extra section that asks the user to perform pairwise comparison of naturalness between prompts that are generated by different systems. TTS evaluations usually do not include this because they would need larger number of participants and longer study sessions inorder to have enough data to perform data analysis. However, it provides better evaluation between prompts because even if we assume that everyone have the same definition for naturalness, their expectations are not aligned. For example, one user may be more sensitive to small deficiencies and rank a prompt with a lower score, while another user gave them the same score.

For this part, the user could only listen to each prompt once, and they should also listen to prompt A first and after that prompt finished, they can listen to prompt B. After listening to both prompts, they should compare their naturalness. Here is the instruction that we gave them:

"Please listen to the following two voices and compare their naturalness. You should ignore the meanings of the sentences and instead concentrate on how natural or unnatural each one sounded. You can listen to each utterance by clicking on the play button beneath it. Note that you can only listen the utterance once, and you should listen to voice A at first."

We used almost identical wording to refer to the naturalness in this part. They should select one of the five options as the answer:

1. Voice A is significantly more natural than voice B
2. Voice A is slightly more natural than voice B
3. Their naturalnesses are similar
4. Voice B is slightly more natural than voice A
5. Voice B is significantly more natural than voice A

5) Naturalness Definition

After completing the naturalness assessment of different prompts from different speakers, we ask our main question as a single post-study questionnaire:

"Please define the naturalness definition that you used to rank the naturalness of voices in this user study:"

Our goal was to let the user complete the evaluation of the prompts as they would in other TTS evaluations and then ask them to define the naturalness that they used earlier.

B. Speaker Prompts

We included 25 different speakers in our study: 5 professional speakers (one from the original training data of Blizzard 2013 and 4 other professional speakers), 5 native Indian speakers, 5 native (but not professional) North American speakers, and 5 TTS systems from Blizzard 2013 (systems B, C, D, H, K). We selected our samples from the Blizzard 2013 challenge because it was the last year that they used English as their main task.

For each speaker, we selected to different sentences to mimic the different sentences that are used in TTS evaluations to eliminate the effect of text on the performance. The sentences were selected from the set of the sentences that were used for Blizzard 2013 challenge.

C. Participants

We wanted our user study to be similar to the Blizzard challenge. Therefore, it was designed as a web-based study that could be completed over the internet. We recruited participants from Amazon Mechanical Turk [9]. 175 participants completed the study. Amazon Mechanical Turk was used in various Blizzard challenges and also by different researchers for evaluation of TTS systems, which is why we used the same approach to participant recruitment.

III. Coding

We used the grounded theory and emergent coding approach that is presented in chapter 11 of [8] for coding.

A. Codes

We started with one pass of analyzing all definitions and extracting codewords from them. Each time we see a new keyword in an answer, we add it to the code list and consider it for the remaining answers. The output of this phase is 146 codewords, while each answer has in average 4.85 keywords.

Most of these codewords only appear in a few answers. For example, more than 85% of them appeared in less than 10 answers, two/third of them appeared in less than 5 answers, and more than one third of them only appeared in a single answer.

Then, we started to combine codewords that were closely related to each other or were used in the same context for the same meaning. For example, we grouped codewords *Tell* and *Express* together because both describes the same action. Another example is grouping of codewords *Human*, *People*, *Person*, *Mind*, *Everyone*, and *Someone* that were used to refer to a human user speaking. At the end of this pass, we reduced the number of codewords to 39 codes. Each answer has an average of 4.61 codes.

The reason that the average number of codes is reduced is because some answers were using related codewords that were combined during this process. For example, a user mentioned "reading from a paper" in their answer. In the first pass, we added both "reading" and "paper" as codewords. At the end, only 3 answers had codewords "reading" and no other answer had keyword "paper". Furthermore, both codewords were referring to the concept of a written text that is being read. So, we combined these two codewords (along with the codewords *Scripted* that was mentioned in another answer). This resulted in reduction of the codes that are assigned to this answer from 5 to 4.

B. Concepts

After finalizing the set of codes, we grouped similar and related codes into *concepts* [8]. We performed multiple iterations of grouping to finally come up with five concepts. The concepts and related code are presented in Table 1, along with the number of answers that have that code.

TABLE I. CONCEPTS AND CODES

Concept	Code	Answer Count
Speech Properties	Accent	20
	Clarity	30
	Emotion	4
	Flow	11
	Noise	5
	Pause	11
	Pitch	3
	Pronunciation	11
	Tone	14
	Smoothness	8
	Speed	3
	Understand	24
Classes	Computer	48
	Everyday	9
	Generated	24
	Human	64
	Mechanical	10
	Normal	22
	Reading	7
	Real	18
Adjective/ Adverbs	Adjective	18
	Adverb	13
Defining Process	I	53
	Feel	4
	How	15
	Comparison	18
	Like	45
	Mean	14
	Quality	5
	Rank	11
	Should	7
	Whether	14
Receiving Information	Hear	23
	Speak	26
	Speech	21
	Sounded	83
	Tell	4
	Understand	24
	Voice	66
	Word	21

1) Speech Properties

The first concept consists of codes that describe the properties of speech. Half of all answers (88) had at least one of these codes. This shows that for at least half of the users, the naturalness relates to speech properties.

In this concept, the main codes were Clarity (34%), Understand (27%), Accent (23%) and Tone (16%). This shows that users usually focus on the clarity of the voice and whether they can understand it. However, these two properties (especially the understand one) are more closely aligned with the intelligibility of the voice that is usually measured in TTS evaluations with transcription error.

Another important code here is *Accent*. 11% all answers have a word that express this code. Users used other words, such as *Native*, *American*, *Indian*, and *Foreign* to refer to this concept.

There was also a clear disagreement between users about whether they should or should not consider the accent as part of naturalness. While most users think that having an accent does not reduce the naturalness (such as saying "*Even if it were foreign, it could still sound natural*" or "*... not including accents which I did not use as a basis.*"), while another user says (such as a user that equate naturalness with speaking with American accent and says "*If the person had an American accent, I thought it was more natural than an Indian accent.*") However, this is in contrast to what our other study [6] shows: people rank speakers with Indian accent as less natural than speakers with North American accent.

2) Classes

The second concept was the classes that users use to define the naturalness. They usually consider two classes of speech such that one is natural and the other is not natural, and then use terms to describe them. Sometimes, they only refer to one of the classes and say that it is natural if it belongs to or not belongs to that group. Two-third of all answers use at least one code to describe these classes.

In general, these two groups are *Humans* (55%) and *Computers* (42%). In addition to using those nouns, they also used adjectives for speech to express this: *Generated* (21%) and *Mechanical* (9%) for computers and *Normal* (19%), *Real* (16%), *Everyday* (8%), and *Reading* (6%) for humans.

3) Receiving Information

The third concept consist of words that describe how they receive the information from the prompt. The majority of answers (85%) have at least one such code. Top codes in this concept are *Sounded* (56%), *Voice* (45%), *Speak* (18%), *Understand* (16%), and *Hear* (16%).

They can be grouped into two sub-concepts: those that related to how the speech is generated by the speaker (Speak, Speech, Tell, Voice, and Word) and how it is received by the listener (Hear, Sounded, and Understand).

4) Defining Process

The fourth concept is the group of words that describe how they define the naturalness. Two-third of answers have at least one such code. The most common one is *I* (46%) (that is a combined code for words such as I, my, me, we, etc.) which shows that users express how they would define naturalness. Only a few users' answers (6%) have code *Should* that represents what is the global definition of naturalness.

Other common codes in this concept are *Like* (39%), *Compare* (15%), and *Whether* (12%). They are used along class concept codes to express that users consider naturalness to be measurable by finding the class (human or computer) that it belongs to. In other words, users consider natural to be equivalent to human generated and unnatural with computer-generated. For example, one user says "*Naturalness to me means something that comes out of the person.*".

5) Adjective/Adverbs

The fifth concept was adjective and adverbs that they use to better express their idea. For example, they may say "*understand easily*". 17% of answers have such an adjective/adverb.

IV. Analysis

In the previous section , we provided the concepts and main codes that could be used to describe how users define naturalness. Now we provide a summary of what themes we observed from these codes and how they can help us to better define the naturalness.

A. *Is it necessary to define it?*

The first observation is that even for some users, the question of defining naturalness seems to be unnecessary, because they the consider the naturalness to be a primitive fact. Here is one example of a user's answer:

"*What? if it sounded more natural I voted it to sound more natural. what is this question asking?*"

Or another user says:

"*I'm not sure what you are asking, we were asked to rank which voices sounded more natural and less like computer-generated voices.*"

While this may signal that maybe everyone already knows what naturalness means, our results show that is not completely correct.

B. *Is there a universal definition?*

Our second observation was the use of codes from the defining process concept, such as *I* and *Mean* that shows that the users express how they define the naturalness and not how it is actually defined. This shows some sort of doubt and ambiguity about the universal definition of it. We could remove this ambiguity by providing a clear and concise definition of the naturalness.

Another result of this lack of universal definition is the difference between people in assigning numerical (or level-based) scores to prompts. Some users may be more precise and reduce score even for small errors and easily mark a prompt as somehow natural in that case, while other users are more lenient and still mark a prompt as completely natural even if it has small errors, such as s single mispronounced work. This can be referred to as the normalization problem.

One way of preventing this error is to ask the users to compare the naturalness of two prompts together (rather than asking them to individual rank them). This way, we will not have the need to normalize their rankings.

C. *Do people agree on specific factors?*

Third, we noticed that users may have contradictory opinions about how different properties of speech affects naturalness. One such aspect is the speaker's accent. Referring to the accent of the speaker was a common theme, although they used different terms to do it (such as accent, native, Indian, American, Foreign, etc.). And while most of the people who used such a term were trying to say that this factor is NOT affecting naturalness, we also has examples that users explicitly say that they consider foreign speakers who have an accent to be less natural.

Furthermore, our other research [6] revealed that even if most of the users think that they are ignoring accent, in practice they would rank speech samples with accent as less natural.

One possible solution is to explicitly pick a subset of criteria and ask the user to rank the samples base on that. For example, we can ask the user to rate the clarity of the voice, whether it had accent, how fluent it is (while also clearly define fluency to prevent mixing it with foreign speakers who have accent and are not considered fluent), how is the speakers pronunciation (which can include pronunciation errors that is present in a TTS system due to OOV words, or in real human speakers if the user do not know the correct pronunciation).

D. *Sounds like a human*

Our fourth observation was how people equate naturalness with being generated by a human. In other terms, people consider something to be natural if it is said by a human. Although users referred to aspects such as understandability (which is usually referred to as intelligibility by researchers) and clarity, their main criteria seems to be their belief of whether it is generated by a human or not. I.e., is it a real human speaking or is it created by a computer.

This is an important point to consider. If people equate naturalness with human-generated voice, then any computer-generated voice will not be completely natural. And it becomes unclear less useful to ask them to mark its naturalness if they do not consider it to be completely natural.

In other terms, if we tell the user that the speech sample is NOT said by a real human (e.g., by saying these are the output of different TTS systems), we already biased them to believe that it is not natural. Therefore, it would not be surprising that our results will show that our system is not completely natural (i.e., get a score of 5) and instead we would see a significant different between the naturalness score of our TTS systems and real human samples.

One potential wat to resolve this problem is to ask users to rate how close our system sounds like a real human (instead of asking them how natural it is). In that case, even if they know that it is not a real human and therefore not completely natural, they may still say that it sounds almost like a real human.

V. Conclusion and Future Work

In this paper, we visited the problem of what we mean by naturalness when are evaluating the TTS systems. We conducted a study that asked to users to perform similar TTS evaluations and at the end ask what naturalness definition they used. We coded the answers and groups them into concepts.

Our analysis revealed that even some users believe that it is not necessary to try to define the naturalness, yet most of them provide answers that show the definition that they provide is how they would define it (rather than a universal definition that they quote). Furthermore, their short definitions were contradicting each other about how should we consider properties such as accent.

Overall, our results show that not providing a precise definition for the naturalness caused confusion for the users and results in them using varying and conflicting definitions for the naturalness.

We provided some potential approaches to resolve these issues, which are primarily focused on how we can better define the naturalness for the participants. We plan to conduct a follow-up study to assess how these solutions may resolve the problems. For example, we can provide precise definition of different criteria such as clarity, understandability, fluency, and accent to the users and ask them to rank the samples base on them and then measure the correlation between them. This can be done by replacing a single naturalness question with multiple questions for each aspect of that. For example, one question just asks for the ranking of the prompts based on their clarity, while another one asks for the presence of the accent in the sample.

The main takeaway of our paper for TTS researchers is the need to clearly define the naturalness for the participants. Furthermore, considering different aspects of naturalness for human users, it is better to evaluate aspects such as clarity and accent individually rather than combine all of them as a single measurement of naturalness.

References

[1] J. Shen, et al.,"Natural TTS synthesis by conditioning wavenet on mel-sectrogram predictions," Proc. ICASSP 2018, 2018, pp. 4779-4783, doi: 10.1109/ICASSP.2018.8461368.

[2] M. Fraser and S. King, "The blizzard challenge 2007," in Proc. 3rd Blizzard Challenge, 6th ISCA Workshop on Speech Synthesis, 2007, paper 003, pp. 1-12.

[3] ITU-T, "Telephone transmission quality subjective opinion tests: A method for subjective performance assessment of the quality of speech voice output devices," ITU-T Recommendation P.85, 1994.

[4] W.B. Kleijn and K.K. Paliwal, "Principles of speech coding," in Speech Coding and Synthesis, Elsevier Science, 1995.

[5] Speech Synthesis Special Interest Group, Blizzard Challenge, https://www.synsig.org/index.php/Blizzard_Challenge, retrieved: April 2023.

[6] S. Shirali-Shahreza and G. Penn, "MOS Naturalness and the Quest for Human-Like Speech," 7th IEEE Workshop on Spoken Language Technology (SLT 2018), 2018, pp. 346-352, doi: 10.1109/SLT.2018.8639599.

[7] C.A. Sampson and T. Navarro, "Intelligibility of computer generated speech as a function of multiple factors," in Proc. National Aerospace and Electronics Conference, 1984, pp. 932–940.

[8] J. Lazar, J.H. Feng, and H. Hochheiser, "Research Methods in Human-Computer Interaction," 2nd Edition, Morgan Kaufmann, 2017

[9] Amazon, Amazon Mechanical Turk (MTurk), https://www.mturk.com, retrieved: April 2023.

International Academy, Research, and Industry Association (IARIA)
412 Derby Way
Wilmington, DE 19810

ISBN 978-1-7138-8059-2

CURRAN ASSOCIATES INC.
proceedings
.com

1st International Conference on Applied Computing and Smart Cities (ICACS21)

ITM Web of Conferences Volume 42 (2022)

Erbil, Iraq
22 – 23 January 2022

edp sciences